The Legal Issues of the Emerging Rights

Jianzong Yao
Editor

The Legal Issues of the Emerging Rights

中国人民大学出版社
CHINA RENMIN UNIVERSITY PRESS

Springer

Editor
Jianzong Yao
Haikou, China

Translated by
Kai Liu
Xuzhou, China

ISBN 978-981-97-0498-9 ISBN 978-981-97-0499-6 (eBook)
https://doi.org/10.1007/978-981-97-0499-6

Jointly published with China Renmin University Press
The print edition is not for sale in China (Mainland). Customers from China (Mainland) please order the print book from: China Renmin University Press.

This book's publication is subsidized by Chinese Fund for the Humanities and Social Sciences.

This Springer imprint is published by the registered company Springer Nature Singapore Pte Ltd.
The registered company address is: 152 Beach Road, #21-01/04 Gateway East, Singapore 189721, Singapore

Acknowledgement

This book represents the final outcome of the major research project "Research on Emerging Rights" (Project No. 05JJD82001) conducted by the Key Research Base of Humanities and Social Sciences of the Ministry of Education, which I led. The project has now been completed.

In this monograph, one of the authors, Song Yahui, is a doctoral student at the Law School of Nanjing University. Other authors include teachers from the Key Research Base of Humanities and Social Sciences of the Ministry of Education, Jilin University Theoretical Law Research Center, and Law School, as well as doctoral and master's students majoring in legal theory from various universities.

The Jilin University's legal theory discipline has implemented a postgraduate training method that involves master's and doctoral students in the scientific research work of their tutor group. This has been in place for several years. The research topic undertaken should be selected as the topic of one's own master's or doctoral dissertation.

The authors of each chapter of this book are as follows:

Chapter 1: Yao Jianzong (Professor of Law School, Doctor of Laws, Jilin University Theoretical Law Research Center)

Chapter 2: Song Yahui (Doctoral candidate of the Faculty of Law, Nanjing University)

Chapter 3: Zhang Long (Associate Professor of the Faculty of Law, Doctor of Law, Beijing Technology and Business University)

Chapter 4: Li Xiaohui (Associate Professor of Law School, Doctor of Law, Beijing Foreign Studies University)

Chapter 5: Liu Hongzhen (Associate Professor of Law School, Doctor of Law, Jilin University Theoretical Law Research Center)

Chapter 6: Li Yongjun (Associate Professor of Law School, Doctor of Laws, Jilin University Theoretical Law Research Center)

Chapter 7: Feng Hao (Doctoral student majoring in legal theory of Jilin University, currently a cadre of the President's Office of Jilin University, Master of Laws)

Chapter 8: Wen Jingfang (Professor of Dalian Radio and Television University, Doctor of Laws)

Chapter 9: Zheng Zhihang (Lecturer of Law School, Doctor of Laws, Shandong University)

Chapter 10: Zhang Hao (Master of Laws, cadre of Hebei Provincial Public Security Bureau)

Chapter 11: Zhang Yuxia (Master of Laws)

Chapter 12: Wu Ning (Lecturer, School of Law, Tongji University, Doctor of Laws)

After completing the first draft of this book, my doctoral students Yang Tiejun, Liu Tao, and Zheng Zhihang assisted me greatly in revising and reviewing the content to ensure academic quality. Their review and revision work were very careful and meticulous. I express my sincere gratitude to them for their invaluable help! I would also like to extend my appreciation to the authors mentioned above for their strong support and sincere cooperation.

June 2010
Jilin University Theoretical Law
Research Center

Jianzong Yao

Contents

Chapter 1
Introduction to the Emerging Rights

Jianzong Yao

1 Introduction

It is generally believed that not only the concept and consciousness of rights, but also the legal confirmation and guarantee system of rights in the Western world are comparatively the most developed from an overall point of view.[1] On the other hand, the oriental world, represented by China, has not only lacked the concept and consciousness of rights traditionally, but also lacked corresponding legal protection of the rights concerned at the national level. This situation did not substantially change until the first half of the twentieth century in terms of the legal rights protection system. Therefore, in the early 1990s, many countries had positively responded to the Universal Declaration of Human Rights, International Covenant on Civil and Political Rights, International Covenant on Economic, Social and Cultural Rights, and other human rights literatures, and had a high recognition of various human rights. Prof. Louis Henkin, a prolific scholar and teacher in the fields of constitutional and international law at Columbia University in the United States, proclaimed with pride that human rights are the concept of our time.[2]

Coincidentally, in the past more than four decades since the introduction of economic reforms, China has achieved extraordinary rapid development and great progress in terms of the economy, society, culture, and politics, which is reflected in China's socialist rule of law construction. That is to say, not only has Chinese society made significant progress in establishing the legal system to recognize and protect rights, but also the awareness of rights has been greatly strengthened. This can be vividly reflected in the large number of rights protection lawsuits filed each year. It is precisely because this situation is of great significance to contemporary

[1] Lucena [1].
[2] Henkin [2].

J. Yao (✉)
Law School of Jilin University, Haikou, China

J. Yao (ed.), *The Legal Issues of the Emerging Rights*,
https://doi.org/10.1007/978-981-97-0499-6_1

China that Professor Zhang Wenxian stated that our time is an era of rights,[3] an era where rights are paid attention to and respected, and an era in which the impact of rights is becoming more and more prominent. We are increasingly accustomed to understanding legal issues from the perspective of rights, as well as approaching the solutions of social problems from a legal perspective. Issues regarding rights in our world are arising at a geometric progression rate. In the context of the new era, classic rights have been confronted with newly emerging challenges. New types of rights are emerging almost every day, for example, animal rights and plant rights, while problems regarding the protection of rights have not been fundamentally solved. Consequently, we have not only refused to accept the concept of natural rights but are also confronting various emerging natural rights. What makes the situation even more complex is that legal rights are inextricably intertwined with other forms of rights, including moral rights and customary rights.[4]

It is arguable that, at least in contemporary China, rights have become a basic concept and a pattern of behavior for daily life. As new types of rights emerge, with complex natures that are continuously advocated and even legalized, they become part of the law. However, as the saying goes, every coin has two sides. On one hand, the publicity of rights in contemporary Chinese society, the expansion of claims for rights, the increasing number of types of rights, and the deepening practices of rights all demonstrate progress in building a socialist rule of law and promote the core values of modern society. On the other hand, the abuse of rights, the unscientific claims of rights, and the irrational promotion of rights practices endanger the very concept of rights by risking the vulgarization of rights.

As Mary Ann Glendon argues, this unique style of talk often works against our venerable rights tradition. It fits perfectly into the ten-second formats currently preferred by the news media, but severely limits opportunities for the ongoing dialogue on which a regime of ordered liberty ultimately depends. A rapidly expanding catalog of rights—extending to trees, animals, smokers, nonsmokers, consumers, and so on—not only multiplies the occasions for conflicts but also risks trivializing core democratic values..[5] This may be because, as various new rights are proclaimed or proposed, the list of individual liberties expands without much consideration of the ends to which they are oriented, their relationship to one another, corresponding responsibilities, or the general welfare.[6]

This objectively demonstrates that as contemporary China gradually embraces the socialist rule of law, rights are increasingly respected with sacred glory. Therefore, it is essential to take rights seriously both in theory and practice. To achieve this, we must delve into the various emerging rights in China through ideological and theoretical studies. This academic work should comprise two parts: firstly, to describe and categorize the various emerging rights that exist in our society from a macro perspective and explore their commonalities; secondly, to examine typical forms of

[3] Zhang [3].

[4] Zhang [4].

[5] Glendon [5].

[6] Glendon [6].

emerging rights to reveal the basic laws of their emergence and development from a microscopic perspective, outlining the conditions under which they are considered as rights.

2 Concept and Scope of the Emerging Rights

If we want to examine the progress of the legal system and the development of the rule of law driven by the comprehensive development of the whole society in the past 44 years since the introduction of reform and opening up in contemporary China, we must scrutinize the overall construction of the Chinese socialist legal system and the development of legal rights. Two issues deserve special attention: first, the consciousness and awareness of legal rights among Chinese citizens have rapidly developed in the past forty years, and they now dominate social concepts and ideas beyond ordinary discourse on rights; second, the number of legal rights in China has rapidly increased over the past three decades, and institutionalization has continued to progress.

In the context of the rapid increase in the number of legal rights in China and the continuous improvement in the level of institutionalization, we repeatedly encounter rights we have not seen before based on our life experiences. It takes some time to understand and become familiar with these new rights before they are put into practice. As we become accustomed to these legal rights, new unrecognized legal rights appear unnoticed. A more accurate description of this process is that the four decades since the introduction of the program of economic reforms termed 'socialism with Chinese characteristics' has witnessed the encounter, understanding, familiarization, and practice of new rights. New types of rights are constantly emerging, known and familiarized by people, and practiced in their lives so that they "hide" their "newness," and become 'old.' Therefore, the prosperity of the emerging rights is evident proof of the continuous unfolding of the historical picture of the construction of the socialist legal system in contemporary China.

The purpose of this research is not to describe and analyze in detail the process of the emergence, development, and maturity of the emerging rights that have emerged in our society in the past 40 years. Nor do we intend to analyze them in detail by means of in-depth exploration and accurate disclosure of the common basic laws contained in this process. Instead, the research focuses on formulating a general description and outline of the macro-pattern of the development of rights in the past 40 years of economic reforms. Therefore, we do not strictly define the emerging rights, but merely describe them in a generally unified form and locate their approximate boundaries by situating the scope of the emerging rights in terms of a catalog. The alleged emerging rights and their boundaries are actually determined by the following elements:

First, emerging rights refer to various new forms of rights that exist in Chinese society, and these so-called "new" forms of rights may have been found in other countries for a while and are therefore not new in those jurisdictions. For example, in most, if not all, developed countries, the issuance and trading of securities, as well as the trading of futures, have a history of hundreds of years. For that reason, the legal rights arising from the trading of securities and futures are not new. Nevertheless, in contemporary China, it was only after the reform and opening up that China gradually established various legal systems directly related to securities and futures trading. Therefore, the corresponding rights based on the purchase of stocks and futures in contemporary China are part of the emerging rights discussed in this book.

Second, emerging rights refer to various new forms of rights that have gradually appeared in Chinese society since 1978. For example, the property to private rights that our citizens are entitled to, the right to be informed in the administrative law setting (the right to know), the right to file an administrative lawsuit, and the right to obtain state compensation, among others.

Third, emerging rights refer to various "new" forms of rights after they have undergone changes leading to the expansion or limitation of rights in terms of subject, object, and content. For example, the right to credit as a result of the purchase of national debt should be recognized as part of the toolbox of rights accorded to any ordinary creditor. But as far as China is concerned, issuing national debts was not legalized before the economic reforms. On this point, a creditor's right on the basis of national debt purchasing is a relatively fresh new phenomenon and could be classified as an emerging right.

Fourth, emerging rights can be generally divided into three categories: (a) rights that have been legally recognized and have acquired legal meaning, that is, have been legislatively institutionalized or become part of the law, such as easement right, shareholders' right to know, shareholders' right to revoke resolutions of shareholders' general meetings, and shareholders' right to initiate derivative lawsuits; (b) social rights claims that have, for the time being, not yet been legislated or recognized through case law but have secured a certain degree of social recognition,[7] such as the right to euthanasia and the right to same-sex marriage,[8] among others.

Fifth, the scope of the emerging rights is relatively extensive, including not only the rights in a statutory setting but also rights in the form of freedom and even privilege. For example, the reproductive rights of unmarried women are seen as being part of the emerging rights in China. Reproductive rights are not enshrined in any Chinese law, and they can be understood as having the liberty to produce without constraint or undue interference by the state or any other party. In this context, the reproductive rights above are internally exchangeable with freedom and liberty.

In conclusion, it is argued that the emerging right is not actually a concept in the real legal sense, and what it refers to is actually a series of rights of different types and attributes. Therefore, it can be argued that the emerging rights represent a 'bundle' or a 'cluster' of rights. At the same time, it should be noted that the emerging rights are definitely not a legal positivism concept, meaning it is not a strict legal concept in the sense of positive law. On the contrary, it is largely a vague concept used to describe some specific claims and claims of rights that exist in China.

---

[7] Gorsuch [7].

[8] Shahid [8].

3 The Formal Standards of the Emerging Rights

From the aforementioned conceptual analysis of emerging rights, it is readily apparent that the specific connotations of emerging rights can be examined from two aspects: formal standards and substantive standards. As far as formal standards are concerned, emerging rights generally refer to new rights that meet the following standards:

First, with time as a benchmark, any rights that were not explicitly stipulated in Chinese legal texts in the past but are clearly stipulated or implied in recent laws or regulations, in the context of the established Chinese legal system, are emerging rights. This includes at least three types:

(a) New legal rights that the old legal texts did not have any stipulations over, but the laws now have very clearly stipulated over in the legal texts. Such legal rights can be described as emerging rights. For example, the Chinese Constitution did not expressly provide for the right to private property, but only that "the state protects citizens' lawful incomes, savings, ownerships of houses and other lawful properties" and "the state protects citizens' inheritance rights to private properties in accordance with the law" (Article 13 of the Constitution). The Constitutional Amendment adopted by the Second Session of the Tenth National People's Congress on March 14, 2004, namely the Fourth Amendment, brought forward changes to the provisions of Article 13 of the Constitution by providing that "citizens' lawful private properties are protected from being infringed", "the state protects citizens' private property rights and inheritance rights in accordance with the law", "the state may, in accordance with the law, expropriate or introduce requisition towards citizens' private properties for the sake of the public interests, but shall provide compensation". Because the Constitution has since clearly stipulated that the legitimate private property of citizens is free from being infringed, the private property right has become an emerging right in China. Another example is Article 17 of the Population and Family Planning Law, adopted at the 25th meeting of the Standing Committee of the Ninth National People's Congress on December 29, 2001, and implemented on September 1, 2002, which stipulates that "citizens have the right to reproductive choice". Nevertheless, this statute is relatively general by nature and did not take into account some special circumstances and requirements already in actual existence at that time. On September 27, 2002, the Jilin Province Population and Family Planning Regulations (hereafter the Jilin Regulations) were adopted at the 32nd meeting of the Standing Committee of the Ninth National People's Congress of Jilin Province and were approved on November 11, 2002. The Jilin Regulations stipulate that "women who have reached the legal age for marriage but decided not to be married and have no children may adopt legal medical-assisted reproductive technology to reproduce" (Paragraph 2, Article 30). After the promulgation of this regulation, it has aroused widespread concerns and fierce debates in China. As a local legislation, this regulation does not violate the Population and Family Planning Law as its superior law, while affirming and stipulating the rights and interests of "single women" among citizens, within the scope of its validity. That is to say, it introduced an emerging right as the right to reproductive choice. Likewise, some legal rights already stipulated in relevant existing civil and commercial laws, such as easements, shareholders' right to know, shareholders' right to revoke resolutions of shareholders' general meetings, and shareholders' right to initiate derivative lawsuits, are credited as emerging rights for similar reasons above.

(b) Neither the past legal texts nor the current legal texts have clearly identified and stipulated certain legal rights in specific legal provisions. But the rights concerned can be logically derived from the texts in line with the spirit of the laws. In this regard, they are recognized as emerging rights. For example, the right to privacy can be acknowledged to exist as this type of emerging right in China. Other examples include prisoners' rights to marriage, the right to marriage for HIV patients,[9] and the sexual rights of transgender and homosexual people,[10] the right to digital interests,[11] among other things..

(c) The texts of any law established in the past did not have very clear legal provisions that explicitly or implicitly addressed relevant legal rights, but the amended texts of laws have specific legal provisions that make the rights concerned explicit or implicit. For that reason, the legal rights are emerging rights. For example, the legal rights arising from the purchase and sale of securities, including stocks and futures, the rights of fund purchasers, and the contractor's right to compensation (Article 286 of the Contract Law).

Similarly, the Seed Management Regulations promulgated by the State Council in 1989 did not explicitly provide the right to seed property, which was clearly established in the text of the Seed Law formulated in 2000 and revised in 2004. The promulgated Regulations on the Protection of New Varieties of Plants and the Implementation Rules for the Regulations on the Protection of New Varieties of Plants implemented in 1999 have confirmed the above seed rights by providing inventors with the right to "new varieties" of plants.[12]

Secondly, taking space as a benchmark, there are rights that have existed or been legally recognized for a while in foreign jurisdictions before being enshrined in laws recently enacted by Chinese legislatures. This sort of emerging rights consists of three subordinate varieties:

(a) The legal rights enshrined in the legal instruments at the international level (including treaties and conventions) formulated by the United Nations and its corresponding agencies or other international organizations. These legal documents explicitly or implicitly stipulate the legal rights concerned through corresponding specific provisions. For example, the International Covenant on Economic, Social and Cultural Rights, one of the international human rights

[9] Hakak and Pereda [9].

[10] Eyer [10].

[11] Hu and Xia [11].

[12] Fan [12].

treaties targeting the legal framework to protect and preserve the most basic economic, social, and cultural rights, embraces a cluster of rights relating to favorable conditions, including the right to adequate food, the right to clean drinking water, and the right to adequate housing.

(b) The rights enshrined in the legal instruments at the regional level or by regional inter-governmental organizations, including treaties, conventions, regulations, and directives formulated within the framework of the Treaty on European Union, the United States–Mexico–Canada Agreement (USMCA), and the Treaty Establishing the African Economic Community (the AEC Treaty).

(c) The rights that the laws of other jurisdictions expressly stipulate through specific legal provisions or imply in the specific provisions. Overall, these three varieties have to endure legal transplants before they are incorporated into Chinese domestic law and have legal effectiveness. For example, the unsafe right of defense in the field of civil and commercial law in China, the subrogation and rescission rights of creditors in the Contract Law, the right to request share repurchase in the Company Law, the investor's right to compensation arising from false claims in the Securities Law, and the right to easement in Property Law.

4 The Substantive Standards of the Emerging Rights

The substantive standards of emerging rights refer to the substantive contents of rights that cannot be categorized into any of the existing legal rights catalogues in China. Some of these rights are completely new, while others have undergone minimal changes to their contents, but the scopes or application conditions have significantly changed.

Regarding the substantive standards, the emerging rights include the following types of legal rights in contemporary China.

First, the purely emerging rights. This type of emerging rights refers to the right patterns which cannot be found any of the existing legal rights. For this consideration, not only the subjects of the rights concerned are brand-new, but also the objects are not seen before. This catalogue is regarded as the most representative type. The examples include the corresponding rights vis-à-vis freezing sperm, egg cells, fertilized eggs and embryos (whether as property rights or as personality rights),[13] various rights established in genes,[14] the rights of HIV/AIDS patients, the rights of homosexuals, the rights of transgender people, the consumers' right to personality stipulated in the Consumer Rights Protection Law, the deceased's right to reputation rights, the right to be forgotten and the data right,[15] etc.

Second, the emerging rights with new legal subjects. This type of emerging right refers to those rights for which the legal subjects have changed to some extent, while

[13] See generally Chen [13].

[14] See Ni [14].

[15] Chen [15].

the legal objects and application scopes remain unchanged. The changes are in the form of either an expansion or reduction of legal subjects. For example, the rights arising from group membership, the rights deriving from being part of a legitimate club, the rights arising from community membership, as well as the workers' right to claim payment directly from the original contractor of a project—with whom the workers have no contractual relationship—within the scope of the unaccomplished payment, according to judicial interpretations by the Chinese Supreme People's Court.[16]

Third, object-oriented emerging rights refer to new rights that emerge after changes to the scope of legal objects, while legal subjects remain unchanged. These changes are reflected in the expansion or contraction of the scope of legal objects, which are carriers of legal objects. It should be noted that legal objects of legal relationships and rights are intellectually interchangeable because they are both considered legal interests. Therefore, changes in legal objects or the scope of rights are actually changes in the objects or scope of rights. For example, the right to chastity, which includes strict abstinence from sexual relations before marriage and complete fidelity and loyalty to one's spouse after marriage, is not found in any legal provision in mainland China, but has been extensively discussed in Chinese academia and is clearly defined in the legal system of Taiwan, China. Other examples include the right to credit, the corresponding rights arising from frozen sperm, egg cells, fertilized eggs, embryos, and various rights established on issues of genes. These rights are undoubtedly object-oriented in nature because they involve new legal objects, and as a result, are categorized as emerging rights.

5 Rationale Behind the Emerging Rights

In contemporary China, the reason why emerging rights have been rapidly emerging and institutionalized with a high level of quality can be observed from various aspects, as follows:

First of all, any increase or decrease in the number of legal rights and any change in the connotations of legal rights in any society is a corresponding reflection of the legal system's response to the development of the society itself. This is in accordance with the Marxist theory's "economic base determines superstructure axiom" and Marx's statement in his Critique of the Gotha Program that "Right can never be higher than the economic structure of society and its cultural development conditioned thereby." In a deeper sense, legal rights change in response to the development of society. It can be argued that social changes lead to the differentiation and diversification of legal interests, which are reflected in the changes in the institutional design of legal rights, including the birth of emerging rights. This is the primary rationale.

[16] See Article 26 of the Interpretation of the Supreme People's Court on Issues Concerning the Application of Law in the Trial of Cases Involving Disputes over Construction Contracts [Fa Shi [2004] No. 14].

Second, in modern society, it is particularly important to pay attention to the significant changes in the reality of social relations brought about by the rapid development of science and technology, which can give birth to new rights. For example, the various rights arising from frozen sperm, egg cells, fertilized eggs, embryos, and genes.

Third, as mentioned above, any type of emerging rights ultimately originates from social development, which gives rise to the diversification of social interests and subjects themselves. The diversification of social interests leads to an increase in awareness of these interests, and the corresponding claims to legal protection cause competitions and struggles towards the legal recognition or even institutionalization of the rights concerned throughout society. This type of emerging rights includes, for example, the right to mental damage compensations due to the breach of contract, and the right to mental damage compensation due to the loss of ashes and photographic negatives, etc., according to the Chinese Contract Law.

Fourth, in contemporary China, an additional reason for the emergence of emerging rights is the Reform and Opening-Up policy implemented since the Third Plenary Session of the Eleventh Central Committee of the Communist Party in 1978. Given the fact that the all-round social-economic reform in China would inevitably lead to the development of the entire society and thus the development of legal rights as described above, rights that are legally recognized in other jurisdictions and viewed as producing good social, economic, political, and cultural outputs but did not exist in China, have impacted the formation of awareness in China, prompting China to seriously consider such effective rights in legal reform.

Fifth, for any right claim, including emerging rights, to acquire its social and formal institutionalized identity, namely to be recognized as a statutory right, there is a prerequisite that the claim must firstly be accorded with recognition and must be politically harmless. Demands for rights arise when the conscious awareness of individuals is agreed upon by the vast majority of society, signifying that communication and coordination of opinions have been reached to the greatest extent, and a basic consensus is formulated in society. This consensus demonstrates that the society as a whole has given recognition to the right appeal or has given a sufficient degree of rational tolerance to the negative consequences that might be brought forward by the right appeal. However, it must be noted that the consensus is reached not based on interests but on values and principles, because fundamentally speaking, rights involve values and principles.

According to Ronald Dworkin, the theory of rights sets out three presuppositions: (i) a rule-compliant society has some notion of political morality, that is, it recognizes moral constraints on governmental activities; (ii) the society's viewpoint vis-à-vis political morality—and the legal judgments derived from that view—is 'rational'; that is to say, it treats the same situation in the same way and does not allow contradictory judgments; (iii) the society believes that all its members are born equal, and they have the right to be cared for and respected equally.[17] From another perspective, any claim for rights based on interests is actually an expression of a political claim

[17] Dworkin [16].

from a certain social standpoint. At the same time, the social effect of any interest appeal would always present its political significance. If the claim for rights unilaterally pursues individual private interests, partial social interests, or interests of limited groups, it is very likely that the delicate equilibrium of various social interests would be undermined.

Laurence Friedman, an internationally renowned legal historian, formulated—on the basis of research by Willem Aubert—his argument that claims can be distinguished into two groups: interests and affirmations. Suppose two parties seek the same precious things, a conflict of interests arises, for example, two men falling in love with a woman; two politicians running for an office; two cities competing for a conference. Conflicts of interests arise because of rarity. In the above examples, both parties have legitimate demands to claim, while there are no conflicts of values or principles in these cases. Indeed, the conflict arises based on a certain kind of agreement, as reflected in the above-mentioned example of both men loving the same woman, and both candidates wanting the same office. On the other hand, claims of rights can be represented through lawsuits, for instance, both parties claiming ownership of land. In the defense, each party would insist on the legality of their claim and the illegality of the opposite party's claim. Debating would be centered on facts, norms, and rules of rights, instead of interests.

From a legal perspective, Friedman further argued that the distinction between conflicts of claims and conflicts of interests has corresponding consequences. His standpoint is that for conflicts of interests, the parties are easy to reach a compromise, while for conflicts of values, it is more difficult to do so. In a sense, a contract is seen as the resolution of the conflict of interests. One person wants to buy a horse at a low price, the other person is willing to sell but at a higher price. Both parties haggle and come to an agreement when they try to resolve disagreements over the price. Often, neither party is 'morally involved,' and courts do not resolve conflicts of interests. One party must translate their claims into values or facts. In a land ownership case, it would be a waste of time for the plaintiff to claim that they need the land for a business, a house, or simply because they like the land. Such a statement of interests is irrelevant. Instead, they must build their argument based on a certain kind of value or rule to justify their claim."[18]

Prof. Zhang Hengshan held the view that despite the fact that rights are sometimes connected with related interests, the essential attributes of both rights and legal rights are found in the legitimacy of the actions they refer to. This legitimacy is reflected in the attitudes of social members towards approving and approving such acts and opposing hindering and infringing such acts. To prove his viewpoint, he further argued that "rights, particularly legal rights, refer to legitimacy, which means that a certain subject can freely choose and put into practice three options about an action that are generally recognized by society. The meaning of extra-legal rights should be understood from the following aspects. First, the legitimacy here refers to the attitude of the whole society towards the act concerned. Second, when members of society view an act as a right, their attitude includes two aspects: on the one hand,

---

[18] Friedman [17].

it refers to the general approval by the majority of the members of a society, and on the other hand, it refers to their objection to actions that undermine the above act. Third, the legitimacy of rights refers not to the act itself, but to the nature of the act in the minds of other members of society. Fourth, an act is called a right not because it can bring benefits to the right holder, but because this kind of act will not cause harm to society and its members."[19]

Furthermore, he pointed out that "a legal right refers to the legitimacy of the right-holder's act conferred by the law. To put it completely, legal rights are the three states of a certain behavior—to do, to temporarily refrain from doing, or to permanently give up—recognized by the legal rules of the law, and by predetermined opinions representing society and the country in the context of that the conditions preset by legal rules are realized."[20]

The definition of legal rights includes the following points: first, legal rights are part of ideology, which refers to the legitimacy of an action. As mentioned above, the so-called "legitimacy" does not refer to the existence of the aspect concerning the objective facts of the act itself, but refers to the nature of the act concerned in the minds of social members. It can also be said that the so-called "legitimacy" refers to the attitude of social members towards this act concerned. This attitude includes two aspects: on the one hand, it refers to approval and support of the social members; on the other hand, it refers to the objection of the members of society towards the hindering or infringing acts against the rights. Second, legal rights, as a positive evaluation and recognition of a behavior, are ostensibly determined by the law, particularly by what the legal rules stipulate. Third, the legitimacy of an act expressed by legal rights—inviolability, unhinderability—comes from the confirmation of the members of society and the confirmation of the state. Fourth, the acts referred to by legal rights include acts and expressions of intention.[21]

In summary, for a claim for rights based on interest claims to be recognized in a legal sense and further institutionalized as legal rights, it must maintain its political innocence in a social sense. This means it cannot disrupt the balance between various social interests, nor cause chaos in social orders or the values and principles behind them. For instance, the right of an employee to terminate their labor contract by giving one month's notice to the employer, as stipulated in the Chinese Labor Contract Law, is an "emerging" right that arises only when the required conditions are met.

6 The Means of Confirming Rights as 'Emerging' Rights

The process by which a claim becomes a legal right may vary depending on the society in question, for the reason that the juridical, constitutional, and common law traditions of each human society, as well as the history of their sedimented interpretations and

[19] Zhang [18].
[20] Zhang [18].
[21] Zhang [19].

internal debates, will shape the legal articulation of human rights.[22] However, for any claim to become an emerging legal right in any jurisdiction or society, it must first demonstrate its legitimacy and validity in the sense of public ethics.[23]

It must also maintain its positive significance in the expected social effects arising from the different dimensions of a given society, including politics, economy, culture, and society. Additionally, it must demonstrate its rationality and practical feasibility. A crucial step towards the affirmation and confirmation of a right claim is the legal recognition of that claim. This process generally includes two aspects:

First, the creation and setting of legal rights through legislation and enactments. This formalizes the right and establishes it as an affirmative legal right. For example, the right to automatic renewal of residential land usage stipulated by Chinese law.

Second, the confirmation and transformation of legal rights through legislation, resulting in emerging rights. This process is applicable when there are corresponding rights demands in China, but the formulation of the right consciousness is based on a comprehensive understanding of the relevant laws and rights of other countries in the world, as well as the understanding of relevant rights set out in international legal documents formulated by international organizations and institutions. These rights are then transformed into domestic legal provisions through legislation, resulting in the establishment of corresponding legal rights. This method is also applicable in some other cases, such as the formalization of customary rights as specific provisions of corresponding legal texts, thus transforming them into emerging legal rights.

It is noteworthy that, to become a legal right, a customary right must generally meet the following conditions: (a) a fact that has been recognized and abided by people for a while; (b) its content is relatively of normativity; (c) there is no provision for this right in the current legislative framework; (d) it does not conflict with the basic principles of the existing law and existing legal rights; (f) it must be recognized by the national legislature and incorporated into the law, as proposed by Professor Guo Daohui.[24]

Third, through the judicial interpretation of 'legality' in judicial practices, exploring the connotation of rights stipulated by relevant laws and the extension or limitation of the subject of rights can help establish 'emerging' rights. This is another important way for the emergence of 'emerging' rights in contemporary China.

As a developing country, China faces the objective reality of many imperfections in its laws. Moreover, judicial officials in China differ in legal, social, political, and cultural literacy, as well as the corresponding legal skills that judicial officials should have. The gap is relatively large, and relying solely on judicial officials is insufficient to achieve the unity of law application and ensure the unity of the entire legal system. To address this reality, China has established a Chinese socialist legal system since the 1980s, taking into account specific conditions and the need to solve specific types of legal cases.

---

[22] Benhabib [20].

[23] Franck [21].

[24] Guo [22].

A crucial institutional arrangement in judicial practice is that the highest judicial organs, including the Supreme People's Court and the Supreme People's Procuratorate, and judicial supervision organs, have the power to make judicial interpretations on the specific application of law in judicial practice. Such interpretation empowerment is significant to the judicial practice of the entire judicial organs in China. Judicial interpretations have guiding and reference significance for judicial practice, and in essence, they have equal status as the related laws, and their specific provisions are in judicial practice. In some cases, judicial interpretations even have more important significance in China, although judicial decisions can only cite legal provisions and cannot directly cite the provisions of judicial interpretations. In many judicial interpretations, especially the judicial interpretations of civil and commercial laws, the highest judicial organs have independently created, properly revised, and strictly confirmed emerging rights. For example, the right to reputation of the deceased (protecting the personality interests of the deceased through the protection of the right to reputation by the surviving) and the right to inheritance by the fetus, as confirmed by relevant legal practices in China.

Fourth, emerging rights are created on the basis of reasonable and legal right presumption in daily life. Confirming the legitimacy of certain rights through the presumption as rights is viewed as a routine creation path of rights in any society, in theory or practice. In China, the presumption as rights is also a crucial way for the creation of rights, including the formation of emerging rights.

As a way of emerging rights, the presumption as rights must first meet the requirements of reasonableness, i.e., the common sense by members in society. The presumption as rights that meets the above conditions guarantees the social acceptability of the presumed rights conforming to the general ethical legitimacy of non-legal rights. It also guarantees the legitimacy of its ultimate legal significance and the rationality of its practical significance. The presumed rights not only have considerable social identity but also have complete legal identity and can be directly taken use of in legal practice.

According to Professor Guo Daohui's theories about the presumption as rights, rights exist in social life in the form of potential primitive rights before they are introduced by legal documents. Such potential primitive rights or human rights cannot be exhausted by law, and it is not necessary for all kinds of interests to be transformed into legal rights. However, except for those that cannot be transformed for the reason that they do not conform to the interests of the ruling class or are restricted by economic and cultural conditions, there are indeed some rights that should be transformed but are 'omitted' by law or 'new rights' that could not be predicted and are not yet transformed temporarily. For these rights, it is necessary and possible to confirm them by applicable law or recognize them. This kind of confirmation or recognition based on the fact of existing rights and corresponding rights is the presumption as rights.

He specifically lists out several main ways of presuming rights, namely, (a) 'presumption from legal rights'. This is seen as the most common way of presumption as rights, which is determined by one or some statutory express rights. There are several situations concerning presumption as rights as follows: First, a right derived from a fundamental right, such as supervision rights, recall rights, and by-election rights. Second, a right presumed from multiple rights, such as the right to know derived from the following rights including the right to criticism and suggestion in Article 2 of the Constitution, Article 3 of the right to supervise, Article 34 of the right to vote, and Article 41 of the right to criticism.[25]

The presumption of rights, as the major way in which 'emerging' rights can be generated, mainly occurs in specific legal practices. First, the parties of lawsuits and their lawyers present claims to non-statutory rights based on the legal facts concerned, and demonstrate and explain them from both theoretical and practical levels. Once the claims to non-statutory rights (presumed as rights) are taken into consideration by courts, they can be viewed as a legal recognition of emerging rights.

7 Emerging Rights and Impact on the Development of Rights

At all times, there has always been an extremely complex relationship between "emerging rights" and "conventional rights": on the one hand, any emerging right is more or less dominated by conventional legal rights, that is, whether recognized by Chinese law or by laws of other jurisdictions, or by international laws. The emerging rights are derived from the conventional rights. Therefore, the conventional rights and non-legal rights are, of course, functioning as the matrix giving rise to the emerging rights; on the other hand, after the identity of 'emerging' rights is confirmed by law, there might be dissonance arising in legal theories and practices, which is caused by tensions between conventional rights and emerging rights. Specifically speaking, emerging rights may attract attention because of their newness, which may lead to the development of legal theories and legal practices, for the reason that conventional legal rights are to some extent not consistent with the emerging rights.

This conflict between old and new rights is actually a normal phenomenon and a normal way of rights practice and rights development. Any mature legal right basically starts from "emerging" rights, which are gradually recognized, recognized and familiarized by the whole society in practice, and thus become part of the daily life of social subjects, especially the legal life. After considering the basic factors, these "emerging" rights gradually lose their "new" color and become regular legal rights. This process is the mature road that any legal right must go through.

Judging from the development process of rights, the conflicts and coordinations between conventional rights and emerging rights are frequently seen. From the perspective of the progress of the legal system, the positive significance of emerging rights vis-à-vis the system of legal rights is extraordinary. This significance can be mainly reflected in the following two aspects:

First, emerging rights can help the renewal of conventional legal rights in terms of the evolution of concepts and systems in both theory and practice, so as to gradually

[25] Guo [23].

realize the overall development of legal rights. As mentioned earlier, the reason why emerging rights are "new" is that, compared with existing legal rights, they have an obvious expansion or contraction in terms of the right holders and the objects. Such changes are themselves driven by the development of society, so they are also in line with the spirit of time, namely, the sum of the many trends that layer upon layer control norms, attitudes, and actions. In other words, the spirit of time can be reflected in the field of legal rights and the entire legal system by the emergence of new concepts of rights and awareness of rights. Such new concepts and new awareness not only in the aspect of rights but also in the entire legal field have the function of broadening the way of thinking, reforming the conventional concepts, and formulating theoretical development, and furthermore present challenges against the conventional rights. In addition, they have a substantial impact on the evolution of the concepts and systems of the conventional rights, so as to promote those conventional legal rights to be reformed in line with the spirit of time.

Second, emerging rights effectively promote the progress of rights in legal practice. Especially in difficult cases involving parties' rights confirmation and protection, the concept and awareness of emerging rights instill new legal awareness, legal concepts, and corresponding rights in judicial practice to relevant personnel involved in such legal practice. Concepts and awareness of rights inspire the legal thinking of the people involved in this legal practice, expand the theoretical and practical horizons as well, so that they can better deal with issues concerning rights confirmation and protection in difficult cases.

8 Conclusion

The emergence of rights with attributes of newness within a certain period of time is basically part of the social context of any jurisdiction. Especially in a transforming country like contemporary China, the new development of rights and the social popularization of rights discourse are primarily in a positive interaction. However, a negative consequence of the widespread social popularization of rights discourse is that the sanctity and seriousness of 'rights' are intentionally or unintentionally vulgarized. For example, when searching the word 'right', there are quite trivial or kitsch expressions such as 'the right to cry' and 'the right to be unhappy', which is a realistic example of the vulgarization of 'right'.

Therefore, starting from the individual emerging rights, this book will explore the common attributes and characteristics of the emerging rights as a composite type of rights, and investigate the differences and similarities between emerging rights and conventional rights. However, this topic itself is indeed complex and challenging because it is not only a theoretical issue but also a practical issue. In this regard, this research approaches the topic from a legal-theoretical perspective while incorporating the expertise of specific legal departments.

Acknowledgements After completing the initial draft of this section's outline, I reached out to Professor Cai Lidong and Professor Peng Chengxin from the Law School of Jilin University for their feedback and suggestions regarding the potential "emerging" rights discussed in this section, from the perspective of civil and commercial law. Following this, I invited Professors Cai Lidong, Peng Chengxin, and Yu Ying to engage in a lengthy discussion on the framework, views, ideas, and specific forms of rights discussed in this section. After three revisions and the completion of the official draft, I specifically requested Professor Cai Lidong's input, asking him to review and revise any expressions in the text that were not entirely accurate from the perspective of private law. I would like to express my sincerest gratitude to Professor Cai Lidong, Professor Peng Chengxin, and Professor Yu Ying for their invaluable contributions to this section.

References

1. Lucena, C. (2014). Human rights and development: An international political economy perspective. *Brazilian Political Science Review, 7*(3), 145–460.
2. Henkin, L. (1989). The Universality of the concept of human rights. *The ANNALS of the American Academy of Political and Social Science, 506*(01), 10–16.
3. Zhang, W. (2019). The modernization of social governance and the construction of the social governance Jurisprudence. *China Legal Science, 07*(05), 3. (in Chinese).
4. Zhang, W., & Yao, J. (2005). Theoretical landscape in the age of rights. *Legal System and Social Development, 5*, 13. (in Chinese).
5. Glendon, M. A. (1993). *Rights talk: The impoverishment of political discourse*. Free Press, preface, p. 3.
6. Glendon, M. A. (1993). *Rights talk: The impoverishment of political discourse*. Free Press, preface, p. 4.
7. Gorsuch, N. M. (1999). The right to assisted suicide and Euthanasia. *Harvard Journal of Law and Public Policy, 23*, 599–658.; Rudnev, M., & Savelkaeva, A. (2018). Public support for the right to euthanasia: Impact of traditional religiosity and autonomy values across 37 nations. *International Journal of Comparative Sociology, 59*(4), 301–318.
8. Shahid, M. (2017). The Right to same-sex marriage: assessing the European court of human rights' consensus-based analysis in Recent Judgments concerning Equal Marriage Rights. *Erasmus Law Review, 10*, 184–195.
9. Hakak, L., & Pereda, P. (2021). Marriage in the Time of the HIV/AIDS Epidemic. Available at SSRN: https://ssrn.com/abstract=3799554 or https://doi.org/10.2139/ssrn.3799554. Accessed 7 March 2021.
10. Eyer, K. R. (2019). Statutory originalism and LGBT rights. *Wake Forest Law Review, 54*, 63–75; Knauer, N. J. (2020). The politics of eradication and the future Of LGBT rights. *The Georgetown Journal of Gender And The Law, 21*, 615–670.
11. Hu, J., & Xia, J. (2022). As an emerging right, the data development authority certificate establishment and its realization. *Nanjing Social Science, 12*, 112–124. (in Chinese).
12. Fan, S. (2007). A Review of research on the legal system of biotechnology. In J. Yi (Ed.), *China Science and Technology Law Yearbook (2006)* (pp. 137–162). Huazhong University of Science and Technology Press. (in Chinese).
13. Chen, G. (2019). Systematic and localization thinking of new rights research: Take public law rights system as the domain. *Jianghan Forum*, (10), 129–136. (in Chinese); Ni, Z., Lu, Q., et al. (2005). *Introduction to Bioethics and Law*. Wuhan University Press. (in Chinese); Li, S., Ni, Z., & Liu, C. (2005). *Research on assisted reproductive technology law*. Law Press China. (in Chinese).
14. Ni, Z., Lu, Q., et al. (2005). *Introduction to Biolaw*. Wuhan University Press, Wuhan. (in Chinese); Liu, C., & Liu, Y. (2005). *Research on gene technology law*. Law Press, Beijing. (in

Chinese); Wang, Q. (2005). *Genetic discrimination' and its legal countermeasures*. Renmin University of China Press, Beijing. (in Chinese); Fan, S. (2007). A review of research on the legal system of biotechnology. In: Yi, J. (ed.) *China Science and Technology Law Yearbook* (2006). Huazhong University of Science and Technology Press, Wuhan, pp. 137–162. (in Chinese).

15. Chen, G. (2019). Systematic and localization thinking of new rights research: Take public law rights system as the domain. *Jianghan Forum, 10*, 129–136. (in Chinese).
16. Dworkin, R. (2013). Taking rights seriously. Bloomsbury, pp. 15–35.
17. Friedman, L. M. (1975). *The legal system: A social science perspective*. Russell Sage Foundation, pp. 258–298.
18. Zhang, H. (2002). *Essentials of Jurisprudence*. Beijing University Press, Beijing, pp. 374–377. (in Chinese).
19. Zhang, H. (2002). *Essentials of Jurisprudence*. Beijing University Press, Beijing, pp. 378–385. (in Chinese).
20. Benhabib, S. (2008). The legitimacy of human rights. *Daedalus, 137*(3), 94–104. https://doi.org/10.1162/daed.2008.137.3.94
21. Franck, T. M. (1987). Why a quest for legitimacy? *University of California Davis Law Review, 21*, 535–547; Benhabib, S. (2008). The legitimacy of human rights. *Daedalus, 137*(3), 94–104.https://doi.org/10.1162/daed.2008.137.3.94
22. Guo, D. (2005). *The Essence of Jurisprudence*. Hunan People's Publishing House, Changsha, pp. 98. (in Chinese).
23. Guo, D. (2005). *The Essence of Jurisprudence* (pp. 133–138). Hunan People's Publishing House.

Chapter 2
Generation of Emerging Rights: Taking the Right to Outdoor Advertising as an Example

Yahui Song

1 Introduction

The Shenyang Urban Construction Bureau (SUCB) and the Shenyang Commercial City Company (SCCC) concluded the Outdoor Advertising Publishing Rights Purchase Agreement, agreeing that the ten-year outdoor advertisement rights are sold to the SCCC, for the following sections of the public road network: the East–West Expressway, First Ring Road, Second Ring Road, Beiling Street, Yellow River Street, and Beijing Street (hereafter the Section), at a price of 50 million yuan from April 13, 2001 to April 13, 2011.

However, as early as the beginning of the year 2000, the Golden Dragon Hotel (GDH) had published advertisements on its own building franchise, and the location of the real property and the billboard is found to be within the scope of the above-mentioned Section area. Based on the agreement, the SCCC believed that the GDH was infringing its right to publish outdoor advertisements by publishing advertisements within the Section area without its permission, and filed a lawsuit with the Huanggu District Court of Shenyang City.

The Huanggu District Court held in the first instance that according to the advertisement agreement for the right to publish outdoor advertisements concluded between the SUCB and the SCCC, except for the Commercial City Company, no one else has the right to publish any outdoor advertisements in the Section area. The GDH published outdoor advertisements in the above-mentioned areas without the consent of the SCCC, which violated the SCCC's exclusive right to publish advertisements. Therefore, the GDH was ordered to compensate for the loss. The GDH was not satisfied with the decision and appealed to the Shenyang Intermediate Court.[1]

---

[1] See: Shenyang Huanggu District People's Court. (2004). Civil Judgment, Huangmin Yiquan Chu Zi No. 44.

Y. Song (✉)
Nanjing University Law School, Nanjing, China

J. Yao (ed.), *The Legal Issues of the Emerging Rights*,
https://doi.org/10.1007/978-981-97-0499-6_2

The Shenyang Intermediate Court held in the second instance that the SCCC legally possesses the right to publish outdoor advertisements within the Section area, and the nature of this right is contractual right. The GDH's advertisement publishing activity is arising from its own property, which is part of the possession and use of the ownership, and this right is a typical property right in nature. In this regard, there is currently a conflict of two rights concerning advertisement publishing. Since the legal effect of real property right is greater than that of the contractual right, the GDH's activity does not constitute any infringement. The SCCC's claim was correspondingly rejected in accordance with the law.[2]

The SCCC as the plaintiff filed a series of similar lawsuits afterwards, and the courts' decisions were found to vary. It is summarized as follows: first, regarding the nature of the dispute, some judicial decisions viewed it as a conflict between real property rights and contractual rights, while others viewed it as a conflict between state public powers; second, regarding the nature of the right to publish advertisements, some decisions viewed it as a contractual right, while others considered it a real property right.All the cases concerned are listed out in Table 1.

From a theoretical perspective, this chapter raises the following questions: What is the basis for the plaintiff's claim to the 'right to publish outdoor advertisements'? How did this new type of 'right' come into existence? There may be two ways of understanding these questions. Firstly, it could refer to rights in the sense of capabilities and qualifications, i.e. who is qualified to engage in outdoor advertising, addressing a qualification matter. Secondly, it could refer to rights that can be possessed and transferred. This chapter intends to use the term 'outdoor advertising right' in the second sense, unless otherwise specified.

The significance of probing into the emerging rights is that with the development of legal theories and judicial practices, the interests are increasingly transformed to be rights, which is called in this chapter as 'rightization'. Among them, some are ultimately recognized as legal rights, including for example land contract management rights and privacy rights.[3] Some others are not possible to be legalized, at least for the time being, for example the 'right to kiss' and 'the right to mourn'.[4] Facing the trend of rightsization of interests, the question of whether an interest can be raised to a right, and how it can be raised to a right, has become a theoretical issue that the legal academia should be dealing with. This chapter takes 'outdoor advertising publishing rights' as an example to deeply analyze how this emerging right has come into view, and whether it can be transformed to a legal right or statutory right, so as to theoretically analyze the borders of the rights of interests.

---

[2] See: Shenyang Intermediate People's Court. (2005). Civil Judgment, Shen Zhongmin Sanquan Zhong No. 59.

[3] As legal development progresses in China, the right to privacy has emerged as a new type of right that has gradually evolved from being considered an "interest" to being recognized as a "right". In 2001, the Interpretation of the Supreme People's Court on Several Issues Concerning the Determination of Liability for Mental Damage Compensation in Civil Torts confirmed privacy as a form of "personal interest" in Article 1. The Tort Liability Law, which was promulgated on December 26, 2009, clearly defines the "right to privacy" in Article 2.

[4] See: National Judges College & Renmin University of China School of Law [1].

Table 1 Overview of *Outdoor Advertising Rights* lawsuits brought by the SCCC and the judicial decisions

Judgement number	Lawsuit parties	Causes of action	Judicial decisions	Reasoning
Huanggu District Court [2004] Huangmin Yiquan Chu No. 44	SCCC versus GDH	Violation of outdoor advertising rights	Infringement	The plaintiff's right to publish advertisements is legal, valid, and exclusive, and the defendant's activities constitute infringement
Shenyang Intermediate People's Court [2005] Shen Zhongmin Sanquan No. 59	SCCC versus GDH	Violation of outdoor advertising rights	Noninfringement	The plaintiff's right to publish advertisements is a creditor's right, while the defendant's right to publish is a real property right. The effect of the real property right is of greater significance than the creditor's right. Therefore, the defendant's activities do not constitute infringement
Shenhe District Court [2004] Shen He Min Yi Fang Chu Zi No. 14	SCCC versus Business Bridge Company	Violation of outdoor advertising rights	Infringement	The plaintiff's claim to the outdoor advertising publishing rights, as acquired through the buyout agreement, is legal, valid, and exclusive, and therefore should be protected by law
Shenyang Intermediate Court [2005] Shen Min (3) Hezhong No. 327	SCCC versus Commercial Bridge Company	Violation of outdoor advertising rights	Noninfringement	The plaintiff has the right to publish advertisements. However, the defendant's activities are not illegal and do not constitute tort liability
Shenyang Heping District Court (multiple lawsuits)	SCCC (multiple)	Violation of outdoor advertising rights	Dismissed	The lawsuits were initiated due to power conflicts between the Urban Construction Bureau and the Industry and Commerce Bureau, which is beyond the scope of the court's jurisdiction

2 Emerging "Rights" Generated in Local Legislations

2.1 *Laws and Delegated Local Legislations*

As a national law, Article 33 of the Chinese Advertisement Law stipulates that the planning and management of outdoor advertising should be formulated by the local people's government at or above the county level. This is to organize advertising supervision and management, urban construction, environmental protection, public security, and other relevant departments. The Advertisement Management Regulations and the Implementation Rules for Advertising Management Regulations promulgated by the State Council are consistent with the provisions of the Advertisement Law in delegating local governments to enact outdoor advertising legislation. Therefore, the so-called emerging right type is not directly concerned at the national law level.

At the local level, various local governments have successively enacted "the right to use outdoor advertising facilities and the operating franchise rights" or "the paid use vis-à-vis the right to set up outdoor advertising" in accordance with the authorization of Article 33 of the Advertisement Law. They have also proposed the "outdoor advertising release system" and other similar types of emerging rights. It also stipulates that the competent authority of outdoor advertising can trade the rights by means of bidding or auction. As a result, outdoor advertising rights and related emerging rights have been made statutory at the local legislative level.

In practice, outdoor advertising is attached to specific carriers, which are referred to as 'slots' (Zhendi in Chinese) in advertising terminology, including public and private slots.[5] Public slots are owned by the state, and the government is authorized to sell the 'outdoor advertising rights' arising from public slots to third parties on behalf of the state, so there are no property rights disputes in such cases. However, with regard to private slots, it becomes more complicated, as when an outdoor advertising authority sells the outdoor advertisement publishing rights attached to private slots to a third party, a property right dispute between the third party and the slot owner (owner) may arise. The aforementioned case law is a typical property right dispute caused by emerging rights.

It can be seen from this that China's outdoor advertising publishing system mainly exists in local legislation. To study how the "outdoor advertising publishing right" came into being, it is necessary to examine the specific practices in local legislation and practice in detail.

---

[5] In advertising studies, the term "slots" refers to the various carriers used for outdoor advertising such as roads, bridges, buildings, subway stations, train stations, airports, vehicles, elevators, floating objects on water, and flying objects in the air. The Advertisement Management Regulations of China refer to "outdoor advertising sites and buildings," while the Implementation Rules for Advertising Management Regulations refer to "outdoor advertising media" and "outdoor advertising sites and facilities." For the sake of simplicity, this book will use "slots" and "slot usage rights" to refer to these carriers and their usage rights.

2.2 *The Evolution of Local Legislative Modes and the Generation of Emerging Rights*

This book focuses on the capital cities of 29 provincial jurisdictions in China, including provinces, autonomous regions, and municipalities directly under the Central Government, as the research objects.[6] The normative legal documents published by each locality are scrutinized, and the outdoor advertising management legal systems are approximately divided into four modes, based on how to obtain the right to use private and public slots.

2.2.1 The Traditional Mode of Outdoor Advertising Management

When examining early local legislations, we can see that China has a dualistic management system for outdoor advertising, which includes planning management and publishing registration management. This system is currently being used in provincial capitals such as Jinan, Ningxia, Zhengzhou, and Guiyang.[7]

Firstly, there is the planning set-up management system which governs the installation of outdoor advertising carriers or facilities. As outdoor advertising is typically attached to specific carriers located in downtown areas, this can impact public interests such as municipal landscape, public transportation, pedestrian safety, ventilation, and lighting. Article 12 of the Administrative Licensing Law stipulates that matters directly affecting significant public interests need to be subject to administrative licensing in accordance with the law. Therefore, some local legislations have implemented the administrative licensing system for setting up outdoor advertisements. The administrative licensing bodies mainly include market supervision departments, municipal landscape management departments, municipal management departments, and municipal administrative departments.

Secondly, there is the publication registration management system which governs specific outdoor advertising release activities based on planning set-up management. While the Advertising Law does not explicitly require the establishment of an outdoor advertising registration management system, the Outdoor Advertising

[6] Note: China has a total of 33 provincial-level administrative units. However, this study excludes Hong Kong, Macau, and Taiwan due to differences in their legal systems. Additionally, Lhasa city currently has no relevant regulations in this area, while Haikou city has abolished its regulations, and new regulations have not yet been enacted. Therefore, this book will focus on the remaining 29 provincial capital cities. The legislative documents for these cities were collected up to December 16, 2009.

[7] See "Interim Measures for the Management of Outdoor Advertisement Setting and Posting in Jinan City", Government Order No. 84 of 1994; "Regulations on the Management of Outdoor Advertising in Ningxia Hui Autonomous Region", promulgated by the Standing Committee of the People's Congress of the Autonomous Region in 1997; "Regulations on the Management of Outdoor Advertising in Zhengzhou City", Amended by the Standing Committee of the National People's Congress in 2005; "Guiyang City Outdoor Advertisement Management Measures", Government Order No. 3 in 2008.

Registration Management Regulations (promulgated by the State Administration for Industry and Commerce in 1995 and revised in 2006) clearly stipulate the system. This requires that all outdoor advertisements cannot be released before obtaining an Outdoor Advertisement Registration Certificate granted by the Market Supervision Bureau.[8] Some local legislations have also adopted this system, requiring the registration authority to be market supervision bodies.

Therefore, there is no such thing as an 'outdoor advertising right' or other emerging rights in the traditional management system. Specifically, the functions of the competent authority for outdoor advertising focus on implementing administrative licensing. As long as the outdoor billboards comply with municipal planning and meet relevant technical standards (including length, width, height, material, ventilation, lighting, etc.), the competent authority should allow the set-up of the outdoor advertising. As for the right to use outdoor advertising slots, the parties should negotiate sufficiently before being granted the right, and the competent authority needs only to examine whether they have the right. Therefore, there are no emerging rights in the traditional management mode of outdoor advertising except for the right to use the slot.

2.2.2 Differential Treatment Model Between Public and Private Slots

Table 2 distinguishes between private and public slots. Regarding private slots, the competent authority does not intervene except for administrative licensing matters, which is not different from the traditional mode mentioned above. Thus, there are no emerging rights in this regard. However, the issue with public slots is critical.

Outdoor advertising publishers must first obtain the right to use public slots. Since these slots are state-owned properties, the acquisition of usage rights requires consent

[8] According to the Regulations on the Administration of Registration of Outdoor Advertisements, the registration system for outdoor advertisements mainly focuses on the pre-examination of the advertisement content. The review of billboard specifications can be completed under "Setting Planning Management". The main difference between outdoor advertisements and other forms of advertisements is that they are published in different media. Advertisements published through other media do not require prior review of their content, except for special product advertisements. This raises the question of why outdoor advertisements require prior review. Furthermore, as commercial advertisements fall under commercial speech, they are protected by the freedom of speech in the Constitution. Local legislation is not authorized to infringe upon the field of freedom of speech, except for content censorship involving public interests (legal reservations). In the United States and Taiwan, China, the protection of commercial speech under constitutional freedom of speech has evolved from non-protection to protection. This can be observed in the 1967 case of Virginia States Board of Pharmacy v. Virginia Citizens Consumer Council, Inc.; It is arguable that based on the interpretations by the "Judicial Yuan" of Taiwan, namely Interpretation Zi No. 414, No. 577, No. 617, and No. 623, in the dual management system of outdoor advertising, setting planning and management is necessary as the setting of outdoor billboards is related to public interests such as pedestrian safety, city appearance, ventilation, and lighting. Additionally, outdoor advertising differs from other media advertising. Furthermore, except for special product advertisements (such as medicine, tobacco, wine, etc.), which require content review, the prior content review system for outdoor advertisements should be cancelled.

Table 2 The authorizations vis-à-vis public slots should be granted by means of auction[a]

Legal document	Competent authority	Rights	How to treat private slots	How to obtain the rights concerned
Beijing: Government Decree No. 200 of 2007	Municipal Administration	The right to use outdoor advertising facilities and operating concessions	Negotiation	Private slots: negotiation on their own; public slots: franchise rights granted by bidding and auction
Shanghai: Government Decree No. 43 of 2004	Municipal Sanitation Bureau	The right to use slots	Negotiation Bidding Auction	The Municipal Sanitation Bureau conducts bidding and auctions for public slots or applied private slots
Changsha: Government Decree No. 80 of 2002	Multi-departmental cooperation	Ad slot usage rights	Negotiation	The State-Owned Assets Supervision and Administration Commission (SASAC) organizes auctions for public slots
Chongqing: Standing Committee of the National People's Congress [2005] No. 17	Municipal Sanitation Bureau	Ad slot usage rights	Negotiation	The Municipal Sanitation Bureau only conducts auctions and tenders for public slots

[a] The legislative model is adopted by the following provincial capital cities: Wuhan City (Government Order No. 179, 2007), Nanchang City (Government Order No. 112, 1996), Chengdu City (Chengdu Municipal People's Congress Standing Committee Announcement No. 29, 2005), Kunming City (Kunzhengfa [2007] No. 36), Xining City (Government Order No. 81, 2007), and Hefei City (Government Order No. 96, 2002). However, the specific content is not listed anymore

from the state-owned assets management department. The practices of Changsha City in Hunan Province are perhaps the most representative. The city stipulates that the state-owned assets department should organize auctions for public slots, and all the proceeds from the auction will be turned over to public finance (see Changsha City Urban Outdoor Advertising Management Implementation Measures (Government Decree No. 80 in 2002)). Paragraph 2, Article 9 states that the right to use outdoor advertising space that occupies public spaces and uses public facilities shall be auctioned, and the auction shall be conducted by the municipal state-owned asset management department, which is responsible for organizing the implementation.[9]

[9] See "Changsha Urban Outdoor Advertising Management Implementation Measures" (Government Order No. 80, 2002), Article 9, Paragraph 2: "The right to use outdoor advertising positions that occupy public places and use public facilities shall be auctioned, and the auction shall be funded by the city's state-owned assets. The management department organizes and implements".

Moreover, from a value perspective, the income obtained from auctioning public slots is the consideration for the use of state-owned land or buildings, and no further consideration is given for any emerging rights. Therefore, such provisions do not involve emerging rights.

Furthermore, the outdoor advertising franchise system adopted in Beijing is also worth noting. It mandates that if the right to use outdoor advertising facilities in public places is granted by auction, a franchise of outdoor advertising facilities must be granted after the agreement is concluded. The so-called *operation franchise* is actually a new right that has emerged from the original slot use right and has become an independent transaction object. This can be seen as the first step taken by local legislation in the process of interest entitlement.[10]

2.2.3 Integrated Auction Mode Vis-à-Vis Public and Private Slots

The auction system for private slots requires careful analysis. According to local legislations listed in Table 3, the owner's consent must be obtained before auction or bidding procedures. This approach recognizes the owner's right to the outdoor advertising slot, which is the slot ownership or the right to use it. However, it is unclear whether there are any emerging rights associated with this ownership.

For instance, Nanjing and Hangzhou regulations state that after the auction of private slots, the income shall be turned over to the finance, after deducting the slot occupation fee and/or compensation to the owner. The slot occupation fee and compensation are the consideration for the right to use private slots. But why should the income from the auction of the right to use private slots be turned over to public finance? Whose consideration is it? Shijiazhuang City has adopted a particularly typical regulation, where the government and the owners are equally attributed.[11] If there are no emerging rights other than the right to use the position, the auction proceeds should all be given to the owner as the government's half of the income is groundless.

In addition, it should be noted that the half of the auction price given to the government is not considered as the auction fee (which has already been deducted according to regulations). Instead, it can be seen as the consideration for any emerging rights that may exist in addition to the right to use the slot. However, the nature of this new right has not been explicitly clarified in the regulations of Shijiazhuang City. In contrast, Tianjin City distinguishes between the right to use advertising space

[10] Articles 21, 23, and 24 of "Beijing Municipal Outdoor Advertisement Management Measures" (Government Order No. 200, 2007).

[11] See Shijiazhuang City Outdoor Advertising Installation Management Measures (Shi Zhengfa [2007] No. 5), Article 15 states that income from auctioning outdoor advertising locations must be deposited into a special account of the municipal treasury, after deducting the commission required for withdrawal according to auction regulations. For income derived from auctioning the right to use advertised locations on buildings, structures, and places with non-public property rights, the municipal treasury must allocate 50% of the auction transaction price to the owner unit within one month.

Table 3 The competent authority will conduct a joint auction of both public and private slots, and provide compensation to the owners[a]

Legal document	Competent authority	Rights	How to manage private slots	How to obtain the rights concerned
Shijiazhuang: Shi Zhengfa [2007] No. 5	Municipal Administration	Outdoor advertising slot usage rights	The Municipal administration shall first obtain the written consent of the owner, and then conduct a unified auction, and pay 50% of the auction income to the owner	The public and private slots are auctioned by the Municipal Administration. The income from public slots will be turned over to the state treasury, and for private slots, the income will be split at a 1:1 ratio between the owner and the Municipal Administration
Changchun: Government Decree No. 58 of 2002	Municipal landscape administration	Right to set outdoor advertising	There is no statutory stipulation, but the use agreement needs to be submitted for approval	For any advertising slot larger than 40 square meters, a bidding or auction procedure is required
Nanjing: Ning Zhengfa [2005] No. 108	Municipal landscape administration	The right to set up paid outdoor advertising	The Municipal landscape Administration shall negotiate with the owner to obtain the right to use the real estate	The Municipal Landscape Administration is responsible for bidding or auctioning public and private slots, and compensating owners with a portion of the income
Tianjin: Jinzheng Decree [2007] No. 114	Municipal landscape administration	Advertising slot use rights, franchise rights	The Municipal landscape Administration shall first obtain the consent of the property owner	The right to use advertising space can be obtained through bidding, auctioning, listing, and the franchising system

[a] Another provincial capital city that has adopted this legislative model is Hangzhou, see Hangzhou Measures for the Administration of Outdoor Advertising (Hangzhou City Government Order No. 128 of 1998)

(i.e., the right to use the slot) and the franchise right, which may be an emerging right.[12] If the franchise right is owned by the government, then it is reasonable for the government to share in the auction income as consideration for this right.

Therefore, in order to profit from auctioning private slots, the government has introduced the concept of emerging rights in local legislation and used it as an

[12] See Article 14 of the Tianjin Outdoor Advertising Installation Management Regulations.

object in the auction setting, providing a theoretical basis for sharing the profits. The relationship between emerging rights and outdoor advertising rights will be further analyzed below.

2.2.4 Visual Spatial Auctioning Mode

From the perspective of emerging rights, the fourth mode of local legislation is considered the most typical. Localities such as Taiyuan, Harbin, Xi'an, and Urumqi have all clearly defined concepts such as 'urban space resources,' 'urban effective visual space,' 'urban public space resources,' 'paid use of space,' 'public space resources,' and other similar terms (collectively referred to as public visual space).[13] It is believed that all outdoor advertisements occupy a certain amount of public visual space, of which the property rights belong to the government. The government proposed this concept for two purposes. First, to prove that the publication of outdoor advertisements involves resources of public nature that go beyond private or public slots, specifically, public visual space. Second, to propose an independent new right that goes beyond the right to use the slot, providing a basis for allocating or even monopolizing auction benefits. According to local legislations, the emerging right implied here is an independent right derived from public visual spaces, which the Urumqi legislature has put forward as a resource management right.[14] This means that all outdoor advertisements, whether set up on public or private slots, must be subject to a resource occupation fee paid to the government, which is the consideration for the emerging right.[15]

Therefore, the purpose of local legislation in proposing the concept of "public visual space" is to establish the foundation for the creation of emerging rights. If public visual space is recognized as a type of resource, it logically follows that new rights can be generated based on these resources, and the property rights belong to the government. Consequently, local legislation need not differentiate between public and private slots. If outdoor advertisements occupy any public visual space, the government can claim the corresponding property rights. As a result, the government

[13] See Lanzhou Interim Provisions on the Paid Transfer of Outdoor Advertising Space in Lanzhou City, Lan Zhengfa [2006] No. 100; "Interim Measures for the Management of Paid Use of Outdoor Advertising Positions in Taiyuan City" [2002] No. 25; "Harbin Urban Outdoor Advertising Installation Management Measures" [2006] No. 153; Regulations on the Administration of Outdoor Advertising in Xi'an, Announcement No. 40 of 2004 of the Standing Committee of the Shaanxi Provincial People's Congress; Measures for the Administration of the Collection of Space Resource Occupancy Fees for Outdoor Advertising Facilities, Wuzhengban [2007] No. 159.

[14] Articles 5 and 6 of the Administrative Measures for the Collection of Space Resource Occupancy Fees for Outdoor Advertising Facilities in Urumqi (Urumqi [2007] No. 159).

[15] Refer to Article 6 of the Regulations on the Administration of the Installation of Outdoor Advertising Facilities in Urumqi, which states that "all proceeds from the transfer of the right to set up outdoor commercial advertising facilities in public places shall be handed over to the treasury." In the case of non-public venues, a space resource occupancy fee for outdoor commercial advertising facilities shall be paid at a rate of 20% of the income derived from the transfer of the right to set up such facilities.

has the right to auction space resources or the emerging rights that arise from the space resources theory, and the proceeds from these auctions should be allocated to the national treasury.

3 Types of Emerging Rights

3.1 The Terminology as 'Right'

In this book, we examined the legislation of 29 provincial capital cities and found 18 different types of rights related to outdoor advertising.[16] When we consider the right to publish outdoor advertising, which was disputed in the case we mentioned earlier, there are a total of 19 types of rights. However, the creation of a new right should not only be based on practical needs, but also meet basic legal requirements. Therefore, it is necessary to critically evaluate the emerging rights proposed by local legislations. In general, emerging rights proposed by local legislations may fall into two categories. Firstly, there may be a misuse or abuse of the term "right". For instance, legal interests that have not yet been elevated to rights are expressed as rights due to misunderstandings about the relationship between rights and legal interests, leading to confusion in the terminology of rights. Secondly, the emerging rights may be created because the existing rights system is inadequate to protect certain interests. When new practical needs arise, traditional rights systems may not be sufficient to address them, requiring the creation of new rights. For example, the consumer right to know is an emerging right created in response to the consumer movement. Regarding the outdoor advertising publishing right, whether it can be recognized as an independent right is a theoretical issue that requires further exploration.

3.2 Integration of the Types of Emerging Rights

After a critical examination of the 19 proposed rights in local legislations, this research argues that the "right to use slot" is a statutory right, while the "right to outdoor advertising carrier setting" is merely a qualification under administrative

[16] The different rights related to outdoor advertising include: the use right of outdoor advertising carriers, the use right of advertising positions, the use right of advertising sites, the use right of outdoor advertising facilities, the use right of advertising space, the right to install and manage outdoor advertising facilities, the use right of outdoor advertising setting positions, the right to manage urban public space resources, the paid use right of outdoor advertising space, the use right of outdoor advertising installation positions, the use right of commercial outdoor advertising positions, the right to install and use commercial outdoor advertising facilities, the paid installation right of outdoor commercial advertising, the use right of outdoor advertising setting locations, the advertising space franchise, the right to set up outdoor advertising, and the outdoor advertising operation concession.

law. However, the "right to publish outdoor advertisements" is more complex due to the following reasons:

Firstly, regarding the "right to use slot", this refers to the right to use real estate such as land, houses, bridges, tunnels, and other forms of property that outdoor advertising must be attached to. This is an embodiment of the "base use right" in property law. Although expressed in various forms in local legislations, such as "use right", "facility use right", and "carrier use right", the right to use the slot is undeniable and based on the ownership or right to use property.

Secondly, the "right to set up outdoor advertising carriers" is a qualification for outdoor advertising activities from the perspective of municipal planning and management at the local legislative level. It applies to advertising reprints, advertising columns, neon light stands, LCD screens, etc. and is essentially an activity qualification obtained through administrative licensing, rather than an independent right.

Thirdly, concerning the "right to publish outdoor advertising", local legislations and judicial practices present new types of rights, such as the "outdoor advertising franchise", "outdoor advertising setting (publishing) right", "advertising space franchise", and "municipal public resources management", which cannot be seen as part of the traditional rights system.[17] These rights are recognized by local legislations as a new type of rights, collectively referred to as "outdoor advertising rights" in this Chapter. However, according to Chinese laws and regulations, publishing outdoor advertisements must be subject to the right to use the slot and the right to set up carriers. The local legislations have integrated the "right to use slot" and the "right to set up a carrier" by creating a new right, namely the outdoor advertising right, which is a derivative right.

3.3 "Outdoor Advertising Right" as an Emerging Right

3.3.1 The Evolution Paths of Four Outdoor Advertising Management Modes

Taking local governments' approaches to defining property rights into consideration, the evolution of the four modes listed above demonstrates strong characteristics.[18]

[17] Measures for the Administration of Outdoor Advertising in Hangzhou (Government Order No. 128 [1998]), Article 8; Tianjin Outdoor Advertising Installation Management Regulations ([2007] No. 114 Government Order), Article 14, Paragraph 3; Measures for the Administration of Outdoor Advertising in Beijing ([2007] No. 200 Government Order), Article 21; Measures for the Administration of the Collection of Space Resource Occupancy Fees for Outdoor Advertising Facilities in Urumqi (Urumqi Political Office [2007] No. 159), No. 6 Strip.

[18] The term "property rights" referred to here include the position use right, outdoor advertising carrier setting right, and outdoor advertising release right outlined earlier. As for the property rights of the billboard itself, they should be governed by the requirements of the property ownership system, and this book will not delve into this topic.

Among them, local governments incorporate all property rights of outdoor advertising by first clarifying their property rights in public slots in the second mode (Table 2), then further allocating part(s) of the property rights in private slots in the third mode (Table 3), and finally, in the fourth mode (Table 4), all outdoor advertising property rights are owned publicly or privately, and the rights are transacted by auction or bidding. Therefore, local legislations propose a new right to define the property rights of outdoor advertising to be granted to local governments themselves, whose theoretical basis is the effective visual space theory. This theory exerts an impact due to the huge volume of traffic and people flow. It is precisely because the government has invested large, if not immeasurable, upfront costs in the construction and maintenance of infrastructure such as roads, parks, and stadiums, that outdoor advertising has value. According to the principle of "who invests, who benefits," it is a matter of course to attribute to the government the power to define property rights implied in outdoor advertising.

As a socialist country like China, land in urban areas is owned by the state. Land ownership is a two-dimensional concept in the sense of property law, including both horizontal and vertical scopes. The vertical attribute includes a certain space above and below the surface of the land that can meet the needs of the right holder.[19]

The government's authority is limited to granting or transacting the right to use the land, and it's unclear how much control they have over the space resources on that land. Therefore, it's much easier for the government to claim the right to the visual space rather than the right to publish outdoor advertisements directly. Consequently, the right to outdoor advertising that arises from the visual space is enjoyed by the government. In fact, the theory of effective visual space is the basis for local legislations in various cities, such as Lanzhou, Taiyuan, Harbin, and Xi'an. To support this theory, some scholars use analytical tools from law and economics to argue that the government has the right to outdoor advertising not only in public slots but also in private slots. They argue that "defining it as a state-owned resource is conducive to the improvement of economic efficiency."[20] However, this argument is open to debate.

3.3.2 Doubts on the Theory of Effective Visual Space

The effective visual space theory, as proposed by local legislations, asserts that space resources are owned by the state, and that the outdoor advertising rights are a derivative of the effective visual space. Consequently, the state should also own the outdoor advertising rights. However, according to the theory of property law, unless otherwise agreed by the parties, the space above the land is part of the ownership or usage right of the land, and its scope is within the scope of the right holder's interests in

[19] Sun [2].

[20] Zeng [3].

Table 4 Emerging rights derived from effective visual space are owned by the government and granted through government auctions[a]

Legal Document	Competent authority	Rights	How to treat private slots	How to obtain the rights concerned
Taiyuan: Taiyuan Municipal Government [2002] Order No. 25	Municipal Planning Bureau	The right to use outdoor advertising slot	With the consent of the owner, the Municipal Planning Bureau can conduct bidding or auction, and the profits should be turned over to the governmental finance	As the outdoor advertising inhabits the effective visual space, the municipal planning bureau can conduct bidding or auction, and the profits should be turned over to the governmental finance
Harbin: Government Decree No. 153 of 2006	Urban space resource management unit	The right to set up outdoor advertisements, with a resource fee as its consideration	The government can collects space resource occupation fees after reaching a use agreement with the owner	Outdoor advertisements publishing are subject to urban space resource occupation fees, but the payment standards for public and private slots are different
Urumqi: issued by the Standing Committee of the Municipal People's Congress in 2006; Urumqi [2007] 159	Municipal Landscape Administration (entrusted by the Finance Bureau to collect resource fees)	The right to operate public resources in urban spaces, including outdoor advertising	The use of private slots should be subject to space resource occupation fee to the government, at a rate of no less than 20% of the auction income	All outdoor advertisements rely on space resources, and are subject to resource occupation fees. The right to set up outdoor advertisements should be granted through auction procedures
Xi'an: Announcement No. 40 [2004] of the Standing Committee of the Shaanxi Provincial People's Congress	Municipal Administration	The right to set up outdoor advertising with a consideration	a. obtain the consent of the owner b. sign a lease contract c. pay the government a fee for the use of advertising space	Public slots are transactioned by bidding, auction, and etc.; private slots are subject to additional fees for the use of advertising space

exercising that right.[21] Thus, the crucial issue is how to define the ownership of the land space.

The traditional view on land ownership is that the landowner is entitled to everything between the land, from the sky to the center of the earth. However, as technology develops and human activities expand, the space above and below the land have become scarce resources, leading to changes in legal norms for allocating these resources. The concept of space right was first proposed by American case law in the early twentieth century, and later, Japanese law, German law, and the law of Taiwan, China established a system of space rights where above-ground and underground spaces could be separately transacted.[22] Article 136 of the Chinese Property Law stipulates that "the right to use construction land can be established on the surface, on the ground, or underground." As a result, multiple cadastres have been created on a piece of land, making the attribution of space resources complicated.

Outdoor advertising must be affixed to land or buildings and occupy a specific area. The ownership of outdoor advertising rights is determined by the ownership of the space where the advertising is located. Article 348 of the Chinese Civil Code requires that when the right to use land for construction is assigned through bidding, auction, agreement, or other means, the parties must enter into a written contract that includes clauses regarding the space occupied by buildings, structures, and their ancillary facilities. However, in practice, most agreements on the right to use land are based on the segmentation of the area rather than the vertical space.[23] Since outdoor advertising occupies both horizontal and vertical space, determining the ownership of outdoor advertising publishing rights can be challenging when the vertical space is not specified under property law.

As a result, the space occupied by outdoor advertisements corresponds to the ownership or usage rights of the land or buildings to which they are attached. Local legislations' effective visual space theory is incorrect because it violates basic principles of property law.

3.3.3 The Essence of the Outdoor Advertising Right

For private slots, outdoor advertisements are physically attached to the slots and legally occupy the space that should be controlled by the slot's right holders (unless otherwise agreed during land transfer and allocation). The outdoor advertising rights derived from the slots are therefore naturally consistent with the ownership or usage rights of the slots. As an emerging right, the outdoor advertising publishing right is essentially the usage aspect of a real property right. Similarly, for public slots, the outdoor advertising right is an emerging right derived from the public slot, which is essentially a result of the realization of the power of the real property right, and its property rights should be owned by the government.

---

[21] See Xie [4].

[22] Chen [5].

[23] Liang [6].

4 The Theoretical Living Space of Outdoor Advertising Rights

4.1 The Process of Entitling Bundle Parts of Property Rights

The contradiction between the limitation of social resources and human desire to pursue resources highlights the need for the full utilization of resources, including rights resources. The bundle of property rights includes possession, ownership, use, disposition, enjoyment, and exclusion. Since Roman law, there has been a concern about separating ownership from the other parts of the bundle, resulting in the emergence of debt rights. In terms of real estate, such as land and houses, modern land law focuses not only on land ownership but also on land usage rights.

From a rights formulation perspective, real estate usage, such as land, may be legally transformed into a creditor's right to meet practical needs and provided with varying degrees of protection.

4.1.1 The Right to Use Set as a Creditor's Right

In the examined local legislations of the capital cities in 29 provinces, all localities that proposed the right to publish outdoor advertisements protected it in the form of creditor's rights, allowing the parties to set contents and scope through agreement. Creditor's rights are determined and confirmed through local legislations. Since creditor's rights have a definite nature, the parties can establish them freely without violating mandatory provisions.

Firstly, the acquisition of the outdoor advertising right should be based on being granted, in the manner of successive acquisition, the right to use the outdoor advertising slot since all outdoor advertising is attached to the use of advertising slots. The right to use the slot is incorporated into ownership and cannot, therefore, be independently transformed into a new type of right.

Secondly, the acquisition of outdoor advertising rights must be subject to the qualification to set up outdoor advertising carriers. Based on public interest considerations, the right to use the outdoor advertising position may give rise to the outdoor advertising publishing right only if it conforms to urban planning. In addition to the above two prerequisites, it must also meet the general requirements for establishing creditor's rights, such as agreement of intention and legality of the subject matter.

4.1.2 Part of the Bundle of a Real Estate Right to Be Transformed as an Independent Property Right

The outdoor advertising right could theoretically evolve to be part of the property rights. In order to protect the interests of creditors, the law can set up special provisions to make the creditor's right into a property right. Even though creditor's right has some property-right absoluteness, it needs to be protected against third parties. This protection can be achieved by registering lease rights or real estate sales contracts in advance.[24] Therefore, the question arises whether the outdoor advertising right can be legally recognized as a property right, and whether it is necessary to protect this right in the form of a property right in China.

4.2 Is It Necessary to Realise the Right to Publish Outdoor Advertisements?

4.2.1 The Implifications from the Land Contract Management Right

The management of land contracts in mainland China serves as a prime example of property rights that have evolved from a subset of real estate rights. This process has undergone a transformation, moving from the right to use land to the establishment of creditor's rights, and finally, to a full-fledged property right. From a historical perspective, this process can be divided into three stages.

(a) first stage: the evolution of land contract management rights in mainland China can be traced back to the late 1970s with the establishment of the land contract mode in Xiaogang Village, Anhui. The process continued until 1986 with the promulgation of the General Principles of Civil Law. During this period, the land contractual management right had a clear creditor's rights nature due to its formation process and specific contents.[25]
(b) second stage: the evolution of land contract management rights in mainland China continued from the promulgation of the General Principles of Civil Law in 1986 to the promulgation of the Rural Land Contract Law in 2003. During this period, the government recognized the importance of national economic development and rural social stability, leading to active efforts to provide more comprehensive and legally effective protection for land contractual management rights. However, this led to disputes among various theories regarding the nature of these rights, including the theory of creditor's rights, the theory of property rights, the theory of real estate rights and creditor's rights, and the theory of quasi-ownership.[26]
(c) third stage: The evolution of land contract management rights in mainland China continued from the promulgation of the Law of Rural Land Contract in 2003 to the present day. During this period, the nature of these rights has been comprehensively formulated. In 2005, the Supreme People's Court issued the Interpretation on the Application of Law in the Trial of Cases Involving Rural Land Contract Disputes, which clarified the property rights nature of land contract

---

[24] Wang [7].
[25] Chen [8].
[26] Ding [9].

management rights and the nature of creditor's rights under specific circumstances.[27] The Property Law, enacted in 2007, includes a special chapter on the system of land contract management rights, confirming the real rights results of land contract management rights in the form of law. These laws were later incorporated into the Civil Code enacted in 2020. As a result, the land contractual management right has finally achieved the status of a real right, having evolved from a subset of real estate rights related to land.

The establishment of land contractual management rights as property rights is the result of two major factors. Firstly, agricultural production requires the law to protect land contractual management rights as property rights. Secondly, the object of land contractual management rights has inherent property attributes. Specifically, agriculture needs sustainable development, the land system needs long-term stability, and land contract management rights need to be transacted independently. Therefore, these rights can be transformed into creditor's rights first and then into property rights. Some scholars have summarized the basic conditions required for the transformation of legal interests into independent rights from the perspective of rights formulation. These include the existence of an independent interest presented as legal interest, vulnerability to risks, insufficient protection under the existing interest protection regime in the legal system, and recognition as a right in line with the existing rights system.[28]

In conclusion, this chapter suggests that outdoor advertising has legal interests and objects that are similar to land contract management rights in terms of their property attributes, such as usefulness, manageability, and ease of registration. However, the question remains whether protecting outdoor advertising rights as creditor's rights is sufficient or whether they should also be recognized as property rights.

4.2.2 Is It Insufficient to Protect the Right to Outdoor Advertising in the Form of Legal Interests or Credit Right?

Article 2 of the Tort Liability Law lists the civil rights and interests that are legally protected. Unlike in Germany and Taiwan, the legislative approach of differential protection of rights and interests is not adopted.[29] The Chinese Tort Liability Law appears to provide equal protection to all rights and interests. However, in judicial practice, judges have become increasingly conservative. They only identify an act as an infringement when the specific type of rights infringed by the accused act is found. As a result, the degree of protection for interests in Chinese judicial practice

[27] The right to contract and operate land obtained through household contracting is considered a property right. Similarly, if an individual obtains the right to contract and operate through bidding, auction, or fair consultation and registers it in accordance with the law, it is also considered a property right. However, if it is not registered, it is considered a creditor's right. For details, see: Huang [10].

[28] See Li [11].

[29] Chen [12].

is much lower than that of legal rights. The approach to this issue is similar on both sides of the Taiwan Strait, where the perpetrator must deliberately violate good customs and cause harm for an infringement of legal interests to occur.[30] From a legal development perspective, interests are initially protected by tort law. When judicial precedents protect a particular interest for a certain period of time and the legislature deems it necessary to elevate such an interest to a right, it gradually ascends from being a protected interest under tort law to a specific civil right confirmed by the law.[31] In the context of outdoor advertising, the lack of clear definition in the Property Law regarding ownership and scope of property rights for above-ground space when land usership is allocated or transferred, makes it easy to infringe on the interests of outdoor advertising arising from privately-owned real estate. Transforming it into a legal right would be beneficial for the protection of this interest. The trend of local legislation regarding outdoor advertising has shown an inclination towards such entitlement.

If the methods of establishing creditor's rights are effective in protecting the "right to publish outdoor advertisements," then it may not be necessary to transform it into a property right. The local laws examined in the 29 provincial capital cities show that the entitlement process for outdoor advertising publishing rights is still in its early stages, and the creditor's rights have not yet been fully transformed. As a result, the creditor's rights system's legal protection function has not been fully realized. It is premature to make a judgment on the adequacy of debt law at this stage. Only after the creditor's rights protection system has been improved and practically tested can we determine if creditor's rights are sufficient to protect outdoor advertising rights. If it is found that creditor's rights are insufficient, then transforming it into a property right may be considered as an option to improve its protection.

5 Conclusion: Taking the Generation of Emerging Rights Serviously

From a legislative perspective, some local governments in China have implemented reforms to the management of outdoor advertising in order to obtain property rights. These reforms have gradually eliminated the property rights attributes of outdoor advertising rights, with the help of the generation of outdoor advertising rights. This approach is based on the public effective visual space theory. However, the research in this book shows that the urban effective visual space theory conflicts with prevailing property law theory and is therefore not feasible.

The outdoor advertising publishing right is, by nature, the result of the realization of real rights. Whether the Advertising Law should introduce the concept of 'outdoor advertising publishing rights' needs to be decided based on further research. As far as the research in this book is concerned, the auction system of outdoor advertising

---

30 Wang [13].

31 Yang [14].

publishing rights has become a common practice throughout the country with the continuous growth of the outdoor advertising market.

From a legal research perspective, it is important to take emerging rights proposed in local legislations and judicial practices seriously to avoid any potential confusion when introducing new rights to the existing legal regime and judicial practices. In a market economy, the emergence of a new economic sector can lead to new interests that require protection through a new right. The "right to publish outdoor advertising" is a typical emerging right resulting from the new market and interests. With the increasing awareness of rights, various "rights" have emerged, including the right to sunshine, the right to kiss, the right to mourn, the right to commit suicide, and so on.

The generation of new rights depends not only on legal confirmation but also on social and economic living conditions and people's concepts. If an interest is not deemed significant to people's social life or not recognized by the general concept of society, it may not be acknowledged by law as an independent right, but only covered by other rights.[32]

However, as social concepts change and people's understanding of the importance of the independent interest deepens, the recognition of such interests as an independent right becomes an inevitable law of legal development. From a legal research and judicial status perspective in China, the right to land contract management, the right to privacy, and the right to know consumers are successful examples of entitlement. In contrast, the entitlement process of the "outdoor advertising right" is still in its early stages, and the main task currently is to establish a sound creditor's rights protection system. However, this does not rule out the possibility of realizing real rights in the future.

References

1. National Judges College & Renmin University of China School of Law. (2008). *A survey of Chinese trial cases (2007 Civil Trial Cases Volume)* (pp. 168–178). Renmin University of China Press & People's Court Press. (in Chinese).
2. Sun, X. (2003). *A general introduction to china's property law* (p. 134). Law Press. (in Chinese).
3. Zeng, N. (2008). Discussion on the definition of property rights of outdoor advertising resources: A perspective of law and economics. *The Economist, 2*, 83. (in Chinese).
4. Xie, Z. (1992). *Revised edition of "Treatise on Property Rights in Civil Law" (Part I)* (p. 22). Self-published. (in Chinese).
5. Chen, H. (2004). *Property law* (pp. 247–250). Law Press. (in Chinese).
6. Liang, H. (2000). *Proposed draft of China's property law* (p. 453). Social Sciences Academic Press. (in Chinese).
7. Wang, Z. (1996). *Research on civil law doctrine and jurisprudence* (Vol. 7, p. 90). Self-Published. (in Chinese).
8. Chen, S. (1996). Materialization of land contracting and management rights and the establishment of the system of agricultural land use rights. *China Law Journal, 3*, 86. (in Chinese).

[32] Li [15].

9. Ding, G. (2007). *The basic issues of land contracting and management rights* (pp. 123–135). Zhejiang University Press. (in Chinese).
10. Huang, S. (Ed.). (2005). *Understanding and application of judicial interpretations of rural land contracting dispute cases of the supreme court* (p. 25). People's Court Press. (in Chinese).
11. Li, Y. (2008). The generation of economic law rights: Taking the right to know as an example. *Legal System and Social Development, 6*, 60–61. (in Chinese).
12. Chen, Z. (2008). *Contract liability and tort liability protection object* (pp. 40–41). Xin Xuelin Publishing Company. (in Chinese).
13. Wang, Z. (2001). *Tort law (Part I)* (p. 78). China University of Political Science and Law Press. (in Chinese).
14. Yang, L. (Ed.). (2007). *Research on types of tort law* (pp. 341–342). People's Court Press. (in Chinese).
15. Li, Y. (2004). *Research on human capital contribution* (p. 144). Renmin University of China Press. (in Chinese).

Chapter 3
Administrative Right to Know

Long Zhang

1 Introduction

According to Professor Louis Henkin, today is an age of rights,[1] and among the various claims of rights, the administrative right to know is increasingly receiving attention as a new right. In the first half of 2003, the Chinese people realized the importance of the administrative right to know and the urgent need to establish a corresponding legal system.[2] Looking back at the situation during the SARS epidemic, it was found that the transparency of government information was directly proportional to the public's psychological tolerance and inversely proportional to the spread of the epidemic.[3] In other words, the more open and transparent the epidemic information was, the less panic people would experience, and the easier it would be to control the spread of the epidemic. The professionalization and specialization of public administration, along with the secrecy of public administration and the independent status of public administrations in society, have increased the distance between citizens and public bodies. This has undermined the fundamental spirit of public administration in the context of totalitarian rule, enlarging the gap between the government and the public, causing tensions, strangeness, and even misunderstandings between citizens and the government. This deteriorating situation not only harms the interests of citizens but also erodes the prestige and efficiency of the government, which is viewed as an infringement of the spirit of public administration.[4]

[1] See generally: Henkin [1].

[2] For details, see Min, D. (2010, April 19). China's Internet in the SARS Crisis. Retrieved from http://www.people.com.cn/BIG5/14677/40628/3003430.html. (in Chinese).

[3] For the relationship between information transparency and the probability of SARS disease, see Feng [2].

[4] Wei [3].

L. Zhang (✉)
Law School of Beijing Technology and Business University, Doctor of Laws, Beijing, China

J. Yao (ed.), *The Legal Issues of the Emerging Rights*,
https://doi.org/10.1007/978-981-97-0499-6_3

SARS had a profound impact on Chinese society, leading to a realization of the necessity for a modern and transparent government that can guarantee citizens the administrative right to know. Following this, a series of incidents and scandals occurred that undermined the government's credibility, including the bird flu virus incident in 2004, the Sudan food additive scandal in 2005, the E71 virus infection incident in Fuyang, Anhui Province in 2008, the 3.14 Lhasa Riots in Tibet in 2008, the protest against the Beijing 2008 Olympic Torch Relay, and the 5.12 earthquake disaster in Wenchuan, Sichuan in 2008.

As a result, the Chinese people, the government, and the international community have increasingly focused on China's government information disclosure and the public's administrative right to know. This trend has been further strengthened with the implementation of China's Government Information Disclosure Regulations (hereinafter referred to as the Regulations) on May 1, 2008. The Chinese government is constantly striving to improve the openness of government information to promote and enhance credibility and authority. However, despite several theoretical and practical research efforts regarding the disclosure of government affairs in China in recent years, little attention has been paid to the legal system for the disclosure of government information (here, specifically referring to administrative organs).

The term 'right to know' was coined by American journalist Kent Cooper in January 1945. At the time, the US federal government was becoming increasingly bureaucratic and was treating the disclosure of government information arbitrarily while expanding the authority of confidentiality. Cooper argued that political freedom in a country, or even the world, would be undermined if citizens' right to know was not respected. From a democratic political perspective, he proposed that the right to know should be promoted to a constitutional right.[5] Since then, the term 'right to know' has gained widespread use and has become an international concept, driven by the 'right to know campaign' that emerged in the United States during the 1950s.[6] The legal protection of the administrative right to know can be traced back to the Swedish Freedom of the Press Act of 1766, which is considered the prototype. This act aimed to protect the right to publish and read official documents, granting the public the freedom to reprint official documents through newspapers and periodicals.[7] Statistically speaking, 68 countries around the world have enacted laws on the disclosure of government information. Legislation on government information disclosure has become an important component of governments around the world to promote the legalization of information.[8]

---

[5] See Song [4].

[6] See Pi [5].

[7] See Huang, T. (2010). On the Right to Know as a Constitutional Right. Retrieved April 20, 2010, from http://search.studa.net/guojiafa/090707/08314953.html. (in Chinese).

[8] Li [6].

The right to know, also known as the "right to information,"[9] encompasses the right of individuals, legal entities, and other organizations to access and acquire information. It comprises both the right to know under public law and the right to information under private law. The right to know under public law refers to the right of individuals, legal entities, and other organizations to access and possess information held by legislative, judicial, administrative organs, and other state organs based on public law, such as the Constitution, administrative law, procedural law, and other public laws. This is collectively referred to as the right to know in a public law setting. The right to know in a public law setting can be further classified as citizens' right to know, legal persons' right to know, and other organizations' right to know, depending on the right holders. It can also be categorized as the right to know legislation, the right to know the judiciary, and the right to know administrative information, depending on the content of the information. The right to know in a private law setting refers to the right of individuals, legal entities, and other civil and commercial entities to access information directly related to their interests based on private law, such as civil law and commercial law. For instance, it includes consumers' right to know, shareholders' right to know, and spouses' right to know.

Generally speaking, the right to know in public law and the right to know in private law are collectively referred to as the right to know in the broad sense, while the right to know in the narrow sense refers specifically to the administrative right to know, which falls under the public law setting. In this research, we will be focusing on the administrative right to know.

The administrative right to know refers to the right and freedom of natural persons, legal persons, and other organizations to obtain necessary administrative information. This right includes citizens' (including citizens and foreign citizens residing in a given jurisdiction, which is basically synonymous with natural persons here) right to know administratively, legal persons' right to know, and other organizations' right to know. However, Chinese scholars discussing and analyzing the right to know in administrative law setting often face difficulties. First, the right to know in public law and private law are not distinguished, making the ownership of the right to know in administrative information unclear. Second, the holder of the administrative right to know is not clearly defined, resulting in confusion between citizens' right to know administratively and the right to know administratively of the public (including citizens, legal persons, and other organizations). Third, the right to know in public law setting is equated with the administrative right to know, which excludes citizens' rights to know legislative information. Fourth, the right to know administrative information is improperly understood as the right to administrative information, resulting in an expansion of the right to know to all government information, contradicting the authentic definition of the administrative right to know.[10]

---

[9] For example, Article 1 of Chap. 1 of the Macao Publication Law stipulates: "This Law regulates the exercise of freedom of the press and the right to information, as well as the activities of enterprises such as newspapers, periodicals, editors and newsletters".

[10] According to the author's search on the China Periodicals Network, from 1998 to 2008, there were only 2 journal articles that directly used the term "Right to Access to Political Information" as the topic of the article.

Clear presentation and in-depth analysis of the administrative right to know and its related theoretical and practical issues can help to reduce the current confusions in the academic study of the administrative right to know.

2 The Ontology of the Administrative Right to Know

Note: The quotations related to foreign legislations in this chapter, unless otherwise noted, are taken from the book "Comparison of Foreign Government Information Disclosure Systems" edited by Zhou Hanhua and published by the China Legal Publishing House in 2003. For the complete text of China's Draft Expert Recommendations on Open Government Information Regulations, which are referenced in this chapter, please refer to Appendix II of "Open Government: A Study on the Legal System of Open Government Information" by Zhang Mingjie, also published by the China Legal Publishing House in 2003.

2.1 The Concept of the Administrative Right to Know

The term "administrative right to know" refers to the right of citizens, legal persons, and other organizations to access and obtain information that is produced or possessed by public organs, including administrative bodies and other organizations that are authorized by laws and regulations to perform administrative functions or provide public services in the course of their activities.

2.2 Analysis of the Constituent Elements of the Administrative Right to Know

2.2.1 Right Holder

The administrative right to know should be accessible to a wide range of individuals and organizations, including citizens, legal persons, and both domestic and foreign entities. This principle is in line with international standards and is enshrined in Article 1 of China's 'Regulations of the People's Republic of China on Government Information Disclosure'. The article specifies that citizens, legal persons, and organizations have the right to access government information in accordance with the law. It also aims to increase transparency in government work.

2.2.2 Obligation Holder

The holders of the obligation arising from the administrative right to know are government organs and organizations other than legislative and judicial organs, which are obligated to disclose government information in accordance with the law. In their information disclosure legislation, which stipulates the administrative right to know, various jurisdictions stipulate that the government or administrative organ be the holder of information disclosure obligations. However, the specific types of government or administrative organs vary from jurisdiction to jurisdiction, according to the following two general recognition standards:

(1) Functionalist standards

The vast majority of jurisdictions adopt functionalist standards when stipulating the types of holders of the administrative right to know. That is, the organs and organizations that actually exercise the administrative functions of the government, including administrative management functions and public service functions.

(2) Financial support standards

Given that the government information disclosure system can effectively enable the public to understand and supervise various activities, such as tax collection by the government, some jurisdictions consider whether the institution has received national financial support when defining the subject of information disclosure obligation. Jurisdictions that adopt financial support standards generally regard entities that receive government financing, such as state-owned companies, state-controlled companies, public schools, public hospitals, national libraries, and national museums, as the obligation holders in the context of the right to administrative information.

Article 2 of the Chinese Regulations defines government information as information produced or obtained by administrative organs during the course of performing their duties and recorded and preserved in a certain form. Article 36 states that the Regulations apply to organizations authorized by laws and regulations to disclose government information, including organizations with public management functions. Article 37 stipulates that the disclosure of information produced or obtained by public enterprises and institutions closely related to the interests of the people, such as education, medical care, family planning, water supply, power supply, gas supply, heating supply, environmental protection, and public transportation, in the course of providing social and public services, shall follow these Regulations, and specific measures shall be formulated by the relevant competent departments or institutions of the State Council. (Article 37).

The provisions mentioned above have adopted functionalist standards to determine the obligation-holders of information disclosure. This means that the administrative organs at all levels and quasi-administrative organizations that are legally authorized to exercise administrative functions or provide public services are subject to information disclosure obligations. This type of standard determines the obligation-holders of information disclosure based on whether they have administrative management functions or provide public services. As a result, a large number of quasi-administrative organizations can be compelled to be subject to information disclosure obligations, which effectively ensures that the obligated parties correspond to the public's administrative right to know in terms of breadth and accuracy.

2.2.3 The Contents

What is the government information that should be disclosed and can be disclosed? Below we will be focusing on the above issues to specifically analyze the contents of the administrative right to know.

The Carriers of Information

The information disclosure laws of various jurisdictions typically define government information as administrative information recorded in certain carriers, which generally include two types: written documents and/or records.

In contrast, the Chinese law does not specify the specific forms of information carriers. Instead, Article 2 of the Regulations broadly stipulates that the government should record and preserve information in a certain form, without providing further details. Some argue that this "certain form" provision may allow for improper interpretation, potentially leading to the withholding of administrative information.

The Relationships Between Information and the Government

Various jurisdictions use different methods to determine what information is considered government information and should be subject to disclosure. These methods include: (a) information currently held by the government, (b) information produced by the government, (c) information obtained by the government, and (d) information related to government administrative functions. In legislation aimed at protecting citizens' right to know in administrative matters, most jurisdictions use a combination of these methods to determine the relationship between the disclosed information and the government.

Government Information Disclosure

Generally speaking, unless otherwise provided by law, the information owned by government agencies should be disclosed, which is a basic principle of the legal system regulating the disclosure of government information. Therefore, it is necessary to clearly define what government information can be disclosed and what government information cannot be disclosed.

Government Information that Can Be Made Public

It is generally recognized that, in principle, all government information should be made public except for information that cannot be disclosed. However, this recognition alone is not sufficient to guarantee the effective realization of the administrative right to know. It is also necessary to establish clear guidelines on how the information that can be disclosed should be disclosed.

A. The principle of disclosure

In the process of disclosing government information, it is important to clarify the following fundamental principles: first, all information, except for that which is clearly stipulated as not to be disclosed, should be disclosed; second, information disclosure should be timely, sufficient, and consistent; and third, disclosure fees should be limited to the costs incurred.

This includes two aspects: on the one hand, the government needs to charge fees for information disclosure, and on the other hand, the government can only charge for the cost of information disclosure. According to Article 27 of the Regulations, administrative organs providing government information upon request shall not collect fees other than those for searching, copying, mailing, etc. Administrative organs are also prohibited from providing government information as paid services through intermediaries. The competent departments for pricing under the State Council shall formulate standards for administrative organs to collect costs such as retrieval, reproduction, and mailing.

B. Scope of disclosures

Various jurisdictions use two ways to define the scope of information disclosure: first, a vague generalization approach, which is rarely adopted, and second, a combination of affirmative generalization and negative enumeration approach. The Chinese Regulations take a unique approach. Article 9 stipulates that administrative organs should voluntarily disclose four types of government information. Article 10 lists 11 types of government information that governments at or above the county level and their departments should disclose, while Article 11 lists four types of government information that governments at the districted city level, county-level and their departments should disclose. Article 12 lists eight types of government information that township governments should disclose. Moreover, in accordance with Article 9, these government agencies may determine the specific contents of government information that should be voluntarily disclosed within the scope of their respective duties.

However, the approach has implicit disadvantages. Firstly, foreign governments usually adopt the principle of 'disclosure as the principle and non-disclosure as the exception,' clearly stipulating the scope of non-disclosure, while the rest is disclosed, allowing citizens to make concrete and rapid predictions when applying for government information disclosure. The Chinese Regulations do not clearly stipulate this principle. Secondly, Article 8 of the Regulations, particularly the provisions on social stability, is unnecessarily vague, potentially allowing for too much room for the interpretation of undisclosed information.

In the process of disclosing government information, three fundamental principles should be followed. First, all disclosures, except those explicitly not disclosed, are required. Second, information disclosure should be timely, sufficient, and consistent. Third, charges for disclosure should not exceed the cost of providing the information. Article 27 of the Regulations stipulates that administrative organs providing government information should only charge for searching, copying, mailing, etc., and not provide government information in the form of paid services through intermediaries. The competent departments for pricing under the State Council should formulate the standards for collecting costs such as retrieval, reproduction, and mailing.

Paragraph 4 of Article 14 of the Regulations prohibits the disclosure of government information involving state secrets, commercial secrets, or personal privacy. However, government information involving trade secrets or personal privacy can be disclosed with the consent of the right holders or if administrative organs view it as highly related to public interests.

C. The extent of disclosure

The information that can be disclosed can be divided into two categories based on the extent of disclosure: all-disclosed information and partially-disclosed information. In the practice of information disclosure in various jurisdictions, the vast majority of information that is disclosed falls under the category of all-disclosed information, while only a small proportion falls under partially-disclosed information.

D. Disclosure of Personal Information

To ensure that individuals have the right to access information related to themselves held by the government and the right to request correction of incorrect information, is a fundamental principle of the government information disclosure system.

There are three models for legal protection of personal information worldwide: first, enacting a separate personal data protection or privacy law to safeguard personal information; second, providing provisions on the protection of personal information in the information disclosure law; and third, including them in both the personal data protection and privacy laws. China currently adopts the third model.

Article 25 of the Regulations stipulates that when citizens, legal persons, or organizations apply to administrative organs for government information related to themselves regarding tax payment, social security, medical and health care, etc., they must provide valid identification documents or supporting documents. If citizens, legal persons, or organizations have evidence that the government information records provided by administrative organs related to themselves are inaccurate, they have the right to request that administrative organs make corrections. If the administrative organ does not have the authority to make corrections, the request shall be transferred to the administrative organ that has the authority to make corrections for handling, and the applicant shall be informed.

Government Information that is not Publicly Available

As mentioned earlier, disclosure legislation worldwide requires that information, except for non-public information, be disclosed. Therefore, defining the scope of non-disclosure information has become key to protecting the right to access government information.

A. The principle of non-disclosure of information

Corresponding to the principle of information disclosure, it can be argued that the non-disclosure of information should be defined according to the following two principles: First, the principle of legality, which means that the scope of non-disclosure of information must be prescribed by law. Second, the principle of rationality, which is also known as the principle of proportionality in administrative law. This means that the administrative body must choose the way that causes the least harm to the public.

B. Scope of Non-disclosure

Ensuring the right to access information while also protecting non-public information is a fundamental principle of government information disclosure systems. To achieve this, the scope of non-disclosure information must be clearly defined, based on the principles of legality and reasonableness. Legality means that the non-disclosure of information must be prescribed by law, while reasonableness requires administrative bodies to choose the least harmful way to protect public interests.

In addition to following these principles, the determination of non-public information must also clearly define the scope of exceptional information. The non-disclosure of information can be divided into two categories. The first is information related to public interests, which includes national security, national defense, foreign affairs, and other major national and social interests. Different countries have different approaches to defining this category, such as providing confidential documents or enumerating specific exceptions. In China, administrative organs are required to establish and complete mechanisms for confidentiality review of government information releases, including procedures and responsibilities for review. Administrative organs must not disclose government information involving state secrets, commercial secrets, or personal privacy. However, information involving trade secrets or personal privacy may be disclosed with the consent of the right holder or if non-disclosure may have a negative impact on the public interest.

The second category is information involving private interests, which includes personal privacy, trade secrets, and business information. Personal privacy is often protected by safeguarding personal information. Trade secrets are information that can generate competitive business advantages, and enterprises take confidentiality measures to protect them. Across the globe, trade secrets and quasi-trade secrets are generally considered non-disclosure information. However, the Regulations in China fail to provide for quasi-trade secrets, such as information provided by enterprises to government agencies on the condition that they are not disclosed.

In summary, the core purpose of both keeping secrets and making disclosures is to protect public interests most effectively. Therefore, the government must strike a balance between protecting non-public information and ensuring the public's right to access information.

C. Non-disclosure information

The government's non-disclosure of information can be categorized into two types: general non-public information and absolute non-public information.

General non-public information refers to information that administrative organs may choose not to disclose based on the principle of balancing interests. However, since there is no absolute prohibition on disclosure, this type of information can still be disclosed in exceptional cases, such as when the public interest outweighs the need for confidentiality. The majority of non-public information falls into this category, and different jurisdictions have their own rules and exceptions for disclosure.

Absolute non-public information, on the other hand, refers to information that is prohibited from disclosure under any circumstances. Examples of this type of information include certain criminal investigation and counterintelligence materials. The government has no discretion to disclose such information, hence the term "absolute" non-public information.

While some jurisdictions have clear and specific rules for both types of non-public information, China's regulations are somewhat vague in this regard. Article 14 of the Regulations specifies that government information involving state secrets, commercial secrets, or personal privacy must not be disclosed, but also allows for exceptions in certain cases. However, the Regulations do not directly address information that is absolutely non-public, and the general provision in Article 8 that administrative organs must not endanger national security, public safety, economic security, and social stability is open to potential abuse. Therefore, there is a need for more specific guidelines and safeguards to ensure that confidentiality powers are not misused.

2.3 *Realization of the Administrative Right to Information*

From the perspective of the individual who holds the right to know in an administrative setting, there are two ways to exercise this right: active information disclosure and information disclosure upon request.

2.3.1 Information Disclosure in an Active Manner

Active information disclosure refers to the process by which the obligated party discloses administrative information, as required by law, to realize the right to know without any request or fees from the right holder. In other words, the government proactively discloses information.

Most government information disclosure legislation includes a system for the government to proactively disclose information. This system requires the government to actively disclose specific information, such as information related to administrative organizations and their functions, procedural provisions, and bases of decision-making. By doing so, this system reduces the costs of individual requests for government information and minimizes the expenditures of government agencies in processing a large number of applications. Moreover, this system effectively ensures the realization of citizens' right to access administrative information, promotes democratic politics, and prevents administrative corruption.

According to Article 9 of the Regulations, government information reflecting institutional arrangements, functions, procedures, etc. of administrative organs must be actively disclosed. However, implementing active information disclosure requires several supporting measures, such as government information disclosure guidelines, information registers, and information disclosure reports.

Government Information Disclosure Guidelines

The purpose of government information disclosure guidelines is to provide the public with a clear understanding of their right to access administrative information and what measures the government should take to protect this right. These guidelines are essential in substantively restricting the abuse of discretion by administrative organs, preventing them from restricting or depriving the public of their right to administrative information through technical details, and ensuring that the public can access government information.

According to Article 19 of the Regulations, administrative organs are required to compile and publish government information disclosure guidelines and government information catalogs, as well as to keep them updated. Government information disclosure guidelines should include categorizations, arrangement systems, and access to government information, as well as the contact personnel, office address, working hours, contact telephone number, fax number, and e-mail address of the open government information disclosure department.

Government Information Disclosure Registers

The government information disclosure register is a directory of information created by the government to allow the public to retrieve information and access government information. This system promotes the efficient management of government information resources, improves administrative management efficiency, and facilitates the effective development of e-government.

According to Paragraph 3 of Article 19 of the Regulations, the government is required to compile a catalog of government information disclosure. The catalog of government information should include an index, name, content overview, date of generation, and other relevant information.

Information Disclosure Reports

Looking at the development of government informatization, it is arguable that most states establish specialized cross-departmental institutions responsible for managing government information resources and utilizing information technology. These government information management departments are tasked with implementing information disclosure legislations and reviewing, counting, and analyzing information disclosure reports submitted by government departments. Importantly, these government information disclosure reports must be made available to the public so that they can gain a comprehensive understanding of the exercise of the administrative right to information.

Article 31 of the Chinese Regulations mandates that administrative organs at all levels must publish annual reports on government information disclosures before March 31st of each year.

2.3.2 Information Disclosure upon Application

Information disclosure upon application refers to the process where the public's right to know is exercised through an application made by the right holder, and the government organ discloses the government information upon receiving the application. In other words, the administrative right to know is actively exercised through the government's disclosure of government information upon receiving an application.

Information Disclosure Applications Submitted by Administrative Right Holders of the Right to Know

Form of Application

Filing an application is the first step in exercising the administrative right to know in the context of the Information Disclosure Upon Application approach. There are two ways to apply: orally and in writing. Some jurisdictions allow for oral filing, while others require written forms of application, including those submitted electronically.

Paragraph 1 of Article 20 of the Regulations states that citizens, legal persons, or other organizations who wish to obtain government information in accordance with Article 13 of the Regulations must do so in writing (including data messages). If it is truly difficult to submit a written application, the applicant may do so orally, and the administrative organ receiving the application shall fill out the government information disclosure application on their behalf.

The Contents of the Applications

Paragraph 2 of Article 20 of the Regulations stipulates that an application for government information disclosure shall include the following information: (1) the name and contact information of the applicant; (2) a description of the government information to be disclosed; and (3) the formal requirements for the government information to be disclosed.

The Handling of the Application by the Government

After receiving an application for information disclosure, government agencies should make a corresponding decision within the legally prescribed deadline.

Providing Assistance in Supplementing Applications

If an application for information disclosure is incomplete, the government organ cannot simply reject it on the grounds that it does not meet the statutory requirements. Instead, the government organ shall make every effort to assist the administrative right holder in exercising their rights. This includes notifying the right holder to make supplementary or corrective submissions, and providing reasonable assistance to the applicant when necessary. According to Item 4 of Article 21 of the Regulations, if the application is unclear about the government information being requested for disclosure, the administrative organ shall inform the applicant to make changes or additions.

Transfer of Applications

The transfer of an application refers to the situation where the authority receiving the application is not the appropriate authority that can provide the information, and the receiving authority is aware of the due authority, it should transfer the application to the appropriate government agency. This provision is similar to the transfer of cases under procedural law. As the administrative agencies are interconnected in the context of the administration system, it is usually easier to determine which authority has the relevant information. Item 3 of Article 21 of the Regulations stipulates that if the requested information cannot be disclosed by the administrative organ in accordance with the law, or if the requested government information does not exist, the applicant shall be informed. If the appropriate government agency is known, the applicant shall be informed of the contact information of the relevant agency.

To Respond When It is not Necessary or Impossible to Disclose the Information

A response that indicates it is not necessary or impossible to disclose information refers to the government's reply to an applicant, stating that the requested information cannot be provided due to legal or practical reasons. The government is obligated to respond to any request for information disclosure, except for absolute non-public information. This rule enables the administrative right holder to be informed of the decision and take further measures to protect their rights. According to Items 2 and

3 of Article 21 of the Regulations, in case of non-disclosure, the government must inform the applicant of the reasons and provide an explanation. If the information cannot be disclosed by that administrative organ in accordance with the law or the requested government information does not exist, the applicant must be informed accordingly.

Decisions Concerning Public or Non-Public

This step will discuss the final decision made by a government agency regarding disclosure or non-disclosure of information after receiving an application, which was previously mentioned as the definition of the information part. The issues regarding the deadline and decision-making will also be addressed. The deadline rule is essential because it ensures that government authorities make decisions within a certain time frame. According to Paragraphs 1 and 2 of Article 24 of the Chinese Regulations, administrative organs must respond to government information disclosure applications within 15 working days.

Protection Vis-à-Vis Third Parties

The information obtained by government organs during administrative management may involve the interests of unspecified third parties, including natural persons, legal persons, or organizations. Therefore, if the government information requested is related to the legal interests of a third party, the government organ should notify the third party and provide them with an opportunity to express their opinions. In other words, when the government organ decides to disclose information related to the interests of a third party, it should notify them in advance of the decision and the deadline for initiating legal actions. During this period, the government shall not provide the information to the applicant.

Article 23 of the Regulations stipulates that where administrative organs believe that the government information requested for disclosure involves commercial secrets or personal privacy, and may negatively impact the lawful rights and interests of a third party, they shall solicit the opinions of the third party in writing. If the third party does not consent to disclosure, it shall not be carried out. However, where administrative organs find that non-disclosure may have a significant impact on the public interest, they shall disclose the information and notify the third party of the decision in writing. These Chinese provisions not only reflect respect for the rights and interests of third parties but also demonstrate reasonable protection of public interests.

Application Fees

The Principle of Cost Payment of Application Fees

Charging fees for information applications is a crucial issue in the government information disclosure system. Charging reasonable fees for applications, primarily in line with the costs, has become a common legislative practice. However, there are two approaches as to whether to require applicants to pay fees in advance. The first approach is that administrative agencies cannot charge fees in advance, except when the applicant has a relevant poor credit record. The second approach is that fees are paid first, and government information is provided later.

Article 27 of the Regulations stipulates that administrative organs providing government information upon application shall not collect fees other than the costs for searching, copying, and mailing, among others. Administrative organs must not provide government information in the form of paid services through intermediaries, whether organizations or individuals. The competent department for pricing under the State Council shall formulate the standards for administrative organs to collect costs such as retrieval, reproduction, and mailing.

Waiver of Application Fee

To ensure that fees do not become an obstacle to government information disclosure, fee reductions and waivers are provided to applicants in certain circumstances. In many jurisdictions, fee reductions are provided for disclosure applications that are in the public interest because such disclosure can enhance government transparency and strengthen public supervision of the government. According to Article 28 of the Regulations, citizens who apply for the disclosure of government information and have genuine financial difficulties may apply for a reduction in application fees.

2.4 Remedies for Administrative Right to Know

Rights are dependent upon remedies, meaning that without remedies, rights cannot exist. When it comes to the right to know, there are three theoretical forms of remedies: administrative remedies (which include administrative reconsideration and administrative appeal remedies), quasi-judicial remedies (such as administrative tribunal remedies), and judicial remedies (including administrative litigation remedies).

Administrative remedies are typically seen as legal pre-procedures for judicial remedies, and judicial remedies are usually considered the final option to ensure the right to know.

2.4.1 Administrative Remedies

This regulation clarifies that government offices at all levels are responsible for guiding, supervising, and accepting the reconsideration of failed government information disclosure. However, it's unclear which specific agencies are responsible for government information disclosure, other than the general offices of local governments at or above the county level.

Furthermore, the general offices of governments at lower levels often have many responsibilities and heavy workloads, so they may only be able to handle government information disclosure part-time. While the level of openness may be higher, the effectiveness of their work is concerning.

Administrative Reconsideration Remedy

Administrative reconsideration is an internal administrative supervision system in which a higher-level administrative organ reviews the legality and rationality of specific administrative acts of a lower-level organ according to legal procedures. The administrative review petition allows administrative subjects to express their dissatisfaction and initiate an adversarial proceeding. Administrative reconsideration is an effective means of supervising administrative organs, including the control of information disclosures by government organs. Compared to administrative litigation remedies, administrative reconsideration for the right to know has advantages such as shorter duration, simpler procedures, and being free of charge. However, there are also shortcomings such as concealing misconduct by subordinate organs. Administrative reconsideration is often a statutory pre-procedure before administrative litigation remedies.

For example, Article 33 of Chinese regulations allows citizens, legal persons, or organizations to report to the superior administrative organ, the supervision body, or the competent department for government information disclosure if they believe that administrative organs are not performing their government information disclosure obligations according to the law. The receiving organ must conduct an investigation. Citizens, legal persons, or organizations who believe that administrative organs' administrative activities during government information disclosure infringe upon their lawful rights and interests may apply for administrative reconsideration or file an administrative lawsuit according to the law.

Article 3 of the regulations clarifies citizens' right to petition, appeal, apply for reconsideration, and initiate administrative litigation in government information disclosure cases. Governments at all levels must strengthen organizational leadership over government information disclosure. The General Office of the State Council is the competent department for government information disclosure nationwide, responsible for promoting, guiding, coordinating, and supervising government information disclosure across the country. The general offices of local people's governments at or above the county level or other competent departments for government information disclosure designated by local governments at or above the county level are responsible for promoting, guiding, coordinating, and supervising government information disclosure in their respective jurisdictions.

This provision clarifies that governments at all levels and their general offices are the supervisory authorities for government information disclosure.

Other Forms of Remedies as Administrative Petition

In addition to submitting administrative appeals to the administrative organ that made the information disclosure decisions and its superior organ, the administrative right holder and relevant third parties may also choose to file petitions with specialized administrative appeal organs. These bodies include independent information commissioners and specialized information committees.

Independent Information Commissioners

An example of an independent information commissioner system can be found in English law. Independence means being self-governing from the state and its agencies. The independent Information Commissioner responds to complaints primarily by issuing three types of administrative instruments: a decision letter, a notice of provision, and a notice of enforcement. If the administrative authority refuses to implement the decision from the Information Commissioner, the Commissioner has the authority to notify a judicial body, which will carry out an investigation. If the applicant and the administrative authority are dissatisfied with decisions from the Information Commissioner, they may apply to the Information Tribunal for a ruling. The UK's independent information commissioner mechanism is a non-judicial remedy in case the administrative remedy fails. Its significance lies in the resolution of disputes through non-judicial procedures before administrative disputes enter quasi-judicial proceedings.

Special Information Committee

The Special Information Committee is a government organization established within the administrative system that operates independently of the administrative information authority. It is generally composed of administrative officials, such as heads of relevant governmental departments, as well as experts. Most of the positions on the committee are part-time and its duties include providing guidance to government organs, delivering advice to review bodies, and directly addressing complaints. The committee's independent nature helps to prevent undue influence from government departments, and its expertise can help ensure that disputes are reviewed based on scientific principles. However, it's important to note that the decisions made by the Special Information Committee are administrative in nature and are not legally enforceable through the judicial system.

2.4.2 Quasi-Judicial Remedies

The Information Tribunal is a type of quasi-judicial administrative tribunal that is independent of the administrative system, and can be found in legal systems such as those of the United Kingdom and Thailand. Adjudicators are selected from experts in the field, which has the advantage of providing low fees, high efficiency, and strong professionalism compared to administrative litigation remedies.

2.4.3 Administrative Litigation

Administrative litigation is a judicial remedy for the right to access information held by the government. The rule of law dictates that any legal right must be safeguarded through judicial procedures. Open government information legislation in many countries provide administrative litigation remedies as a final option to protect the right to access information. Article 33 of China's Regulations also provides that the public can enforce their right to access information through administrative litigation.

The principles governing remedies for the right to access government information typically include the principle of exhaustion of administrative remedies and the principle of independent review or adjudication.[11]

2.5 Legal Liabilities

Legal liabilities arise from violations of legal rights or obligations and are determined by judicial proceedings.[12] In the legal relationship concerning government information disclosure, government organs have an obligation to respond to the public's administrative right to know by disclosing government information. If a government authority fails to fulfill this legal obligation, it must be held responsible for the corresponding legal responsibilities. However, merely bolstering the administrative right to know through the three channels of administrative reconsideration, administrative appeal, and administrative litigation is not enough. Government information disclosure legislation should provide penalties for governmental bodies that passively deal with information disclosure and deliberately conceal or block government information. Legal liabilities mainly include administrative and criminal liabilities. Two approaches can be taken to regulate administrative liabilities: directly stipulating them in the information law or stipulating them in the general administrative procedure law. Criminal liability may result from intentional concealment, destruction, or blocking of government information.

---

[11] See Zhou [7].

[12] Zhang [8].

3 Resolutions to the Conflicts Between Administrative Right to Know and Civils Rights and Public Powers

As a fundamental right, the administrative right to know should be recognized and protected by law. However, this does not mean that the administrative right to information is absolute and superior to other legitimate rights and powers. Instead, it may conflict with them in many cases. The rights and powers that often conflict with the administrative right to know include, among others, the state secrets privilege, the right to trade secrets, and the right to personal privacy. Resolutions typically serve two purposes: first, to clearly define the boundaries of powers and rights that may conflict with the administrative right to know,[13] and second, to establish clear criteria for weighing and balancing conflicting powers and rights when the administrative right to know is involved.

3.1 The Right to Administrative Information and the State Secrets Privilege

The state secrets privilege is the authority of state organs to withhold state secrets. State secrets are classified as matters related to national security and interests, which are determined by specific organs in accordance with legal procedures, exclusively known to a certain range of personnel within a certain period of time, and for which the state implements confidentiality measures in accordance with the law. Specifically, state secrets include information concerning national defense, foreign affairs, national government information, military technology, cutting-edge technology information, as well as information on major political and economic decision-making related to national security and interests. A primary characteristic of state secrets is that they are closely related to national security and interests. Thus, ensuring the security of state secrets has become an imperative need to safeguard national security and interests.

3.1.1 The General Relationship Between the Administrative Right to Know and the State Secrets Privilege

It is generally accepted that the state secrets privilege predates the administrative right to know. Even in today's information society, the protection of state secrets is

---

[13] The key point that needs to be explained here is that, according to our consistent "rights-based" view, power originates from and serves rights, and is subordinate to them. The existence of power is necessary and rational only to the extent that it protects rights. Therefore, when power conflicts with rights, power is not automatically superior. Both power and rights need to be weighed and trade-offs made on an equal footing. For a discussion of the "rights-based theory", see Zhang [9]. Zheng [10].

still the primary concern of the government. State secrets are usually considered an exception to the principle of disclosure established by information disclosure laws. Therefore, it is common legislative practice worldwide to enact a confidentiality act (or national state secrets law) to protect state secrets. Although the open information law and the national state secrets law may seem to conflict with each other, their underlying purpose is the same—to protect the safety and interests of the public. The main reason for the frequent conflict between the two is that when the scope of confidentiality matters is too broad or ambiguous, the tendency of administrative organs to achieve administrative convenience through confidentiality becomes more prominent, and the corresponding protection of the administrative right to know is difficult to ensure.

Balancing public interests in administrative disclosure with those of non-disclosure is crucial. The balance of interests forms a fundamental basis of social life. In democratic politics, this balance is particularly important. It maximizes civil rights to participate in and supervise the administration while limiting the scope of bureaucratic clandestine activities.[14] To resolve conflicts, a possible solution is to clearly stipulate the classification system and decryption system in the state secrets law. The classification system can help define the scope and extent of secrecy more effectively. The declassification system may specify the period of secrecy for state secrets with different levels of secrecy. State secrets that exceed the secrecy period and should be declassified may then become subject to the right to know and be made public.

Secrecy, while necessary, must be subject to strict procedural limitations. Historical experience proves that more secrecy in government administration leads to more corruption. On the other hand, the more transparent the government is, the better the quality of its service.[15]

3.1.2 Deficiencies and Improvements in the Law of the People's Republic of China on Guarding State Secrets

Since its implementation in May 1989, China's Law on Guarding State Secrets (LGSS) has had limited impact on national secrecy and the promotion of socialist modernization. However, after more than 30 years, a re-examination has revealed that there are certain aspects related to the formulation and implementation of the law that require improvement.

[14] Wang [11, p. 975].

[15] Wang [11, p. 960].

Problems in the Formulation and Implementation of the LGSS

There are several issues with China's Law on Guarding State Secrets (LGSS). First, the classification process lacks standardization,[16] resulting in a broad scope of secrecy and unnecessarily high classification levels. Although Article 11 of LGSS aims to address this issue by requiring specific scope and classification levels to be formulated by relevant departments and made public, this provision is often violated in practice. As a result, many government organs classify secrets according to customs rather than law, leading to arbitrary and inconsistent classification practices.

Second, the supervision mechanism for classifying secrets is ineffective. Although LGSS allows for correction of wrong classifications by higher-level organs or relevant secret-guarding departments, this has rarely happened in practice.

Third, insufficient declassification has resulted in state secrets being kept classified rather than being declassified when their period of secrecy has expired. LGSS specifies that state secrets must be declassified once their period of secrecy has expired or through legally prescribed procedures. However, in practice, most classified information is not declassified.

Overall, the implementation of LGSS needs improvement in standardizing classification, strengthening supervision, and enhancing declassification efforts.[17]

Improvement of the LGSS and Its Implementation

To effectively balance secrecy and declassification, three areas need improvement.

First, a new concept that values both confidentiality and disclosure equally needs to be formulated. The traditional concept of secrecy leans excessively towards secrecy, resulting in information that doesn't necessarily require confidentiality being classified as state secrets. An example of this is the 2004 Central Document No. 1, which was widely distributed and studied, but still classified.[18] To establish balance and coordination between confidentiality and disclosure, a new concept needs to be developed.

Second, the system of classifying secrets needs improvement in three ways: (a) establishing a confidentiality review system before classifying secrets; (b) creating an

---

[16] China's Law on Guarding State Secrets, Article 1, outlines the classification of state secrets into three levels: "top secret", "secret", and "confidential". "Top secret" refers to the most crucial state secrets, the leakage of which can cause severe damage to the security and interests of the country. "Secrets" are also important state secrets, the leakage of which can cause significant harm to the country's security and interests. Lastly, "confidential" refers to general state secrets, the leakage of which can cause damage to the security and interests of the country.

[17] Details of this situation can be found in the Confidentiality Law Research Group. (2001). A Comparative Study of Confidentiality Law. Beijing: Golden City Press, pp. 379–389. (in Chinese).

[18] For details, see Xuefeng & Chen Youmou. (2010). Document No. 1 of the Central Committee turned out to be a "secret" document: revised Confidentiality Law. Available at: http://www.people.com.cn/BIG5/guandian/35560/2937582.html [Accessed 20 April 2023].

objection system for classifying secrets; c) allowing administrative reconsideration when corrections to the classification of secrets are refused.

Third, the declassification system needs improvement. This requires secret-guarding organs to set clear confidentiality periods, including maximum confidentiality periods, and declassification dates for each state secret. Strict review procedures for state secrets that require special extensions of the secret-keeping period should also be established. Additionally, authorities and procedures for declassification need to be strictly stipulated to prevent irregularities in declassification that may result in the improper disclosure of state secrets.

3.2 Administrative Right to Know and Right to Commercial Confidentiality

The right to trade confidentiality refers to the exclusive rights of entities engaged in commercial activities over their own trade secrets and quasi-trade secrets, which are commercial information other than trade secrets that can bring benefits to enterprises. In the process of administrative management, government agencies often hold a large amount of trade secrets and commercial information. When the administrative right holder applies to disclose government information, it often contains various types of commercial information, particularly trade secrets and quasi-trade secrets. These are information that enterprises do not want to be known to any third party, including specific business information such as business plans and financial information.

Enterprises may request the government to keep the trade secrets and quasi-trade secrets they possess confidential and not disclose them based on the right to commercial secrecy. On the other hand, the public and other commercial entities may require the government to disclose such commercial information through the administrative right to know. Although there is a contradiction between the administrative right to know and the government's obligation to protect specific commercial information, in essence, the public's right to know administrative information conflicts with the enterprise's right to commercial confidentiality.

Therefore, when responding to claims for commercial information disclosure, the government must first clarify the scope of trade secrets, quasi-trade secrets, and publicly available commercial information. The government should then make reasonable decision and trade-off criteria when conflicts between the two are inevitable.

3.2.1 Protection Vis-à-Vis Trade Secrets and Quasi-Trade Secrets by the Legal System of Information Disclosure

Trade secrets and quasi-trade secrets are valuable assets for enterprises, providing them with advantages in competitive markets. As a result, information disclosure laws typically exempt these types of information from disclosure. Therefore, it is crucial to have a precise definition of trade secrets and quasi-trade secrets to resolve the potential conflict between the right to know and the right to commercial confidentiality.

Definition of Trade Secrets

As mentioned earlier, trade secrets are proprietary information owned by an enterprise that can provide a competitive advantage, and the enterprise has taken appropriate measures to keep the information confidential. This information typically includes business plans, formulas, processes, designs, marketing plans, costs, profits, and so on. In jurisdictions that lack specific trade secret protection laws, general rules are typically provided in laws and regulations to identify trade secrets. In some cases, commercial practices and judicial precedents may also be referred to when necessary.

In the People's Republic of China, Paragraph 3 of Article 10 of the Anti-Unfair Competition Law (ACL) defines trade secrets as technical and business information that is not known to the public, can bring economic benefits to the right holder, is practical, and has been subject to confidentiality measures by the right holder to protect it. According to the Several Provisions of the State Administration for Industry and Commerce on Prohibiting Infringement of Trade Secrets (SPSAICPITS), technical information includes practical technical knowledge acquired from production practices, such as design drawings, research results and reports, general charts and calculation results related to a product, technological processes, production data, product formulas, schemes, operating skills, manufacturing techniques, test methods, etc. Business information refers to all confidential management methods related to enterprise marketing activities, and information and intelligence closely related to business management methods, such as management methods, know-how, production and marketing strategies, customer lists, source information, bidding prices, advertising, product formulas, production processes, production methods, bidding content, and expression content, etc.[19] The characteristics of trade secrets in China can be summarized as follows. First, trade secrets have a need for secrecy, meaning that the information must be kept confidential to maintain its economic value. Second, confidentiality measures must be taken by the right holder to protect the information, such as confidentiality agreements and systems. Third, the information must be practical and capable of bringing economic benefits to the right holder, which includes both actual economic benefits and potential competitive advantages. Fourth, the acquisition of trade secrets must be legal, through means such as self-research, legal licensing, inheritance, transfer, or gift. These characteristics are essential for determining whether information constitutes a trade secret under Chinese law.[20] Paragraph 4 of Article 19 of the SPSAICPITS states that trade secrets are not subject to disclosure, unless the right holder consents or the administrative organ believes

---

[19] See Several Provisions on Prohibiting Infringement of Trade Secrets2Strip.

[20] See Qiaoling and Xiuling [12].

that non-disclosure may negatively impact the public interest. The criteria for determining confidentiality, practicality, and legality can be used to define trade secrets under this provision.

Definition of Quasi-Trade Secrets

Quasi-trade secrets refer to information that enterprises provide to the government under the condition of non-disclosure, including business and financial information. Financial information pertains to the financial status of a business, while business information refers to any other information related to the interests of the enterprise, aside from trade secrets. Trade secrets and quasi-trade secrets are generally considered exceptional information that is not to be disclosed under information disclosure laws.

3.2.2 Restrictions on the Protection of Trade Secrets and Quasi-Trade Secrets in the Legal System of Information Disclosure

Unlike information classified as state secrets, trade secrets and quasi-trade secrets are not always considered completely confidential. The government has discretion to disclose trade secrets and quasi-commerce on a case-by-case basis depending on the purpose and motive of the disclosure application. In the context of conflicts between the right to administrative information and the right to commercial secrecy, the government needs to seriously consider two aspects.

Firstly, the government needs to determine whether the exercise of the administrative right to know is to obtain the private interests of commercial competition or to protect the public interest. When deciding whether to approve an application for disclosure of exceptional information, the government should not ignore the purpose of the application and must understand in detail what the purpose of the disclosure application is. If the purpose of the application for disclosure of information is only to obtain the business information of competitors to gain an advantage in competition, the government should not approve the application. However, if the purpose of the disclosure application is to protect the public interest, the government must take the application seriously and carefully consider whether there are sufficient grounds for disclosure of the exceptional information.

Secondly, after clarifying that the purpose of the application for information disclosure meets the requirements, the government needs to weigh the benefits of the public interest and commercial confidentiality rights associated with the administrative right to know. The government may disclose trade secrets and quasi-trade secrets only if the benefits arising from the non-disclosure of such information are less than the public interest involved in disclosing the information. For example, in times of war, the disclosure of military technologies that are not state secrets, and the disclosure of information on whether a medicine contains specific ingredients that may endanger health.

3.2.3 Administrative Right to Know and the Right to Privacy

Privacy refers to the ability of individuals or groups to seclude themselves or their information from others and express themselves selectively. It includes personal affairs that parties do not want others to interfere with and personal areas that parties do not want others to intrude upon. The right to privacy is a personality right enjoyed by individuals that has nothing to do with the public interest. Specifically, it includes the exclusive right to protect private information from acknowledgement, disclosure, and use by others.

The protection of privacy rights has received increasing attention since Harvard Law School professors Warren and Brandies explicitly proposed the concept of "the right of privacy" in the Harvard Law Review in 1890.[21] Many jurisdictions have formulated special privacy protection laws, and in recent years, the right to privacy has been recognized and protected as an international human right by important international human rights conventions. Foreign legislative experiences show that legal protection of privacy includes civil law protection, criminal law protection, administrative law protection, and constitutional protection. In recent years, China has paid more attention to the civil law protection of privacy, but insufficient attention has been given to other legal departments, including administrative law.

In the information society, through their powerful administrative power, the government can obtain almost all important information, even about citizens' life and death. Requests for information using the administrative right to know are likely to involve the personal privacy of others. Therefore, the protection of individuals' privacy by administrative law is particularly important.

The Personal Privacy Protection by the Legal System for Information Disclosure

The legal system for protecting personal privacy in the context of information disclosure focuses on safeguarding personal information or data. Personal information refers to any information that can identify an individual, while personal data generally pertains to electronic information automatically recorded through electronic devices, excluding personally recorded personal information. Therefore, it is more reasonable to frame the protection of personal privacy in the context of information disclosure as the safeguarding of personal information.

Around the world, there are two main approaches to protecting personal information (data) in information disclosure laws: Firstly, the information disclosure law explicitly outlines the protection of personal privacy (data); secondly, the Information Disclosure Law provides only general rules and concrete rules are adopted through a separate personal information (data) protection law or privacy law. In the United States, for example, the protection of personal privacy is provided through laws such as the Privacy Act of 1974, The Electronic Fund Transactions Act 1978, the Financial

[21] See Xianbo and Jiancheng [13].

Privacy Rights Act 1978, the Telecommunications Privacy Act 1986, the Electronic Communications Privacy Act 1986, the Video Privacy Protection Act of 1988, the Employees Protection Act of 1988, the Computer Competition and Privacy Protection Act of 1988, and the Children's Online Privacy Protection Act of 2000. Among these, the most influential laws are the Privacy Act, the Electronic Communications Privacy Act, and the Children's Online Privacy Protection Act.

In the United States, courts have extended privacy protection to various types of information, including marital status, legal status of children, welfare relief, family disputes and reputation, physical health, date of birth, religious belief, nationality status, social security number, criminal history, history of US citizens serving sentences abroad, sexual orientation, and economic situation.[22]

Restrictions on the Protection of Personal Privacy in the Legal System for Information Disclosure

Personal privacy needs to be protected, but this protection is not absolute. On the one hand, individuals have the right to access and correct personal information recorded by the government. On the other hand, there is a need to balance the public's right to know and personal privacy. For instance, the Dutch Government Information Act stipulates that information should not be published or disclosed if the individual's right to privacy outweighs the importance of the information.

The Chinese Regulations also provide protection for personal privacy information held by the government and exceptions to this protection. The exceptions include obtaining the consent of the person concerned or restricting disclosure when it has a significant impact on the public interest. However, defining the criteria for 'significant impact on the public interest' is a problem that can cause ambiguity and controversy. Professor Mo Yuchuan, one of the drafters of the Regulations, suggests that the scope of public interest is dynamically changing.

Based on the consensus and experience of academic and practical circles at home and abroad, the following six comprehensive criteria can be used to help locate the dynamically changing scope of public interest: legality and reasonableness, public benefit, fair compensation, open participation, power constraints, and unity of authority and responsibility. If the privacy right holder objects to the disclosure of personal information by a government organ on the grounds of public interest, they can seek relief through reporting and investigation, administrative reconsideration, or administrative litigation in accordance with Article 33 of the Regulations.[23]

---

[22] See Mingjie [14].

[23] See Chai Chunyuan. (2008, April 29). Government Information Disclosure Regulations: Several problems to be solved. Procuratorial Daily. (in Chinese).

4 The Status Quo and Reflections on the Legislations and Practices of Administrative Right to Know in China

4.1 The Status Quo and Reflections on the Legislations of Administrative Right to Know in China

4.1.1 The Status Quo of Legal Regulation of the Administrative Right to Know

The legal system in China does not provide direct provisions on the right to know of the administration. Instead, it establishes indirect provisions on the public's right to access administrative information.

Provisions of the Constitution

The principles of people's sovereignty, government oversight, and freedom of expression established in our Constitution imply the existence of the public's right to know as a constitutional right regarding administrative information.

The Presumption of the Right to Know of the Executive by the Principle of Popular Sovereignty

Article 2 of the Constitution of the People's Republic of China states that all powers in the country belong to the people, and these powers are exercised through the National People's Congress and local people's congresses. The people manage state affairs, economic and cultural undertakings, and social affairs through various channels and forms in accordance with the law. This confirms the principle of "popular sovereignty." The exercise of people's sovereignty involves the right to manage state and social public affairs, and this can only be realized if the administrative right to know is guaranteed.

The Administrative Right to Know as a Requirement of the Right to Supervise the Government

Article 27, paragraph 2, of the Constitution states that all state organs and functionaries must rely on the support of the people, maintain regular contact with them, listen to their opinions and suggestions, accept their supervision, and strive to serve them. Similarly, Article 41 stipulates that citizens of the People's Republic of China have the right to criticize and make suggestions to any state organ or functionary. However, the prerequisite for the public to exercise their right to supervise, criticize, suggest, appeal, accuse or report to administrative organs is that the public has access to information on the activities of administrative organs and their staff. Therefore, the administrative right to know is an inherent prerequisite right to these aforementioned rights.

The Administrative Right to Know as a Way to Bolster the Freedom of Expression

Article 35 of the Constitution guarantees the freedom of speech, press, assembly, association, procession, and demonstration for citizens of the People's Republic of China. The exercise of these freedoms, especially when it comes to expressing political opinions, inherently requires access to administrative information. Therefore, the administrative right to know is closely related to the protection of freedom of speech and expression under the Constitution.

Provisions of Relating Laws

Before the implementation of China's Government Information Disclosure Regulations, there were no specific provisions to protect the administrative right to know. As a result, the protection of this right was mostly expressed through the disclosure obligations of government organs in other laws. For instance, the principle of disclosing administrative punishments was stipulated in paragraph 3 of Article 4 of the Administrative Punishment Law. Additionally, the Legislation Law's Articles 62, 76, and 77 mandated the public publication of administrative regulations, departmental rules, and government rules. The Archives Law required the regular publication of archives catalogues, while the Law on Guarding State Secrets contained declassification provisions. Furthermore, the Anti-Unfair Competition Law had provisions for trade secrets, and the Statistics Law regulated the management and publication of government statistical data. These provisions are scattered throughout various laws in an unsystematic manner.

The Provisions in the Regulations on Government Information Disclosure

Article 1 of China's Government Information Disclosure Regulations, which came into effect on May 1, 2008, states that the regulations are formulated to ensure that citizens, legal persons, and organizations obtain government information in accordance with the law. The aim is to increase the transparency of government, promote administration in accordance with the law, and strengthen the role of government information in serving the people's production, livelihood, and economic and social activities.

Article 6 stipulates that administrative organs must promptly and accurately disclose government information. Additionally, a series of provisions in Chapter II, Scope of Disclosure, clarify the obligations of governments at all levels to disclose information. These provisions confirm that the public in China has the right to access administrative information.

Provisions of Local Government Regulations

China's government information disclosure legislation is unique in that it is carried out from the bottom up rather than from the top down. Before the enactment of a national government information law, some local governments had already implemented their own regulations. Guangzhou led the way by enacting the Guangzhou Municipal Government Information Disclosure Regulations, which, for the first time in China, proposed that the public has the right to access government information and clearly stated that "disclosure is the principle and non-disclosure is the exception" for government information. This was the first administrative rule formulated by a local government in China to comprehensively and systematically regulate government information disclosure. It was also the first time that relatively comprehensive provisions on government transparency were made in the form of legislation in China. This was followed by a surge of local legislation, including the formal implementation of the Measures for Online Disclosure of Information of the Shenzhen Municipal Government in April 2004, and both the Shanghai Municipal Government Information Disclosure Provisions and the Chengdu Municipal Government Information Disclosure Provisions in May 2004, and the Hangzhou Municipal Government Information Disclosure Provisions in October 2004, among others. The information disclosure legislation of local governments is viewed as having several advantages:

A. *They clearly stipulate the public's administrative right to know and the government's obligation to disclose information.*

Article 1 of the Provisions on Government Information Disclosure in Chengdu states that the Regulations were formulated to increase the transparency of administrative activities, standardize government information disclosure, and protect the right to know of citizens, legal persons, and organizations. The aim is to enable the public to supervise administrative activities in conjunction with the actual conditions of Chengdu.

B. *A relatively broad definition of the objects of information that can be disclosed.*

Article 2 of the Guangzhou Municipal Government Information Disclosure Regulations defines government information as any information produced, obtained, or owned by governments at all levels, their functional departments, and organizations that exercise administrative powers in accordance with the law.

C. *The following three principles of information disclosure have been established: the principle of disclosure, the principle of cost charging and the principle of fee reduction.*

For example, both Guangzhou and Hangzhou have established the principle of disclosure in Article 6 of their respective Government Information Disclosure Regulations, stating that government information should be disclosed as the principle, and non-disclosure should be the exception. Additionally, Paragraph 3 of Article 25 of the Provisions on Disclosure of Information of the Guangzhou Municipal Government establishes the principle of fee reduction by providing that fees may be reduced or waived for disclosure rights holders with special economic difficulties.

D. *Relatively clear provisions have been established on the procedures for government information disclosure.*

For example, Article 16 of the Chengdu Provisions on Government Information Disclosure stipulates that government information, which should be disclosed in accordance with these provisions, shall be disclosed by the obligated parties within 30 days from the date of production, acquisition, or possession of such information. In case the supervisory and management departments find that the obligated parties have not fulfilled their disclosure obligations within the stipulated time, they shall be compelled to rectify their actions in a timely manner.

E. *The supervision of government information disclosure is clearly stipulated.*

For example, Article 23 of the Chengdu Municipal Government Information Disclosure Provisions stipulates that the general office of the government shall conduct regular or irregular inspections of the obligors' government information disclosure and establish government information disclosure complaint mailboxes.

F. *The remedies for the administrative right to know are clearly stipulated.*

For example, Article 29 of the Guangzhou Municipal Government Information Disclosure Provisions stipulates that if the holder of the disclosure right is dissatisfied with the decision to disclose, they have the right to apply for reconsideration, file a lawsuit, or request compensation in accordance with the law.

G. *The legal responsibilities of the government not to disclose information are clarified.*

For example, Article 32 of the Hangzhou Municipal Government Information Disclosure Provisions states that if a disclosure obligor violates these Provisions by concealing or providing false government information or divulging trade secrets or personal privacy, and it causes damage to the parties, it shall be liable for compensation in accordance with the law. If relevant persons are suspected of committing a crime, they shall be subject to criminal prosecution.

4.1.2 Reflections on the Chinese Legal System of Administrative Right to Know

The Right of Citizens' (Administrative) to Know Should Be Clearly Stipulated in the Constitution

Although the Chinese constitution implies the presumption of citizens' right to know, this expression is still too vague. As a human rights claim based on constitutional concepts, the right of citizens to know should be clearly stipulated in the constitution to ensure the highest legal basis for the protection of the citizens' right to administrative information.

To Make Corresponding Amendments to the Government Information Disclosure Regulations Based on Experiences from Practice

Citizens' right to know should be explicitly stated in the Government Information Disclosure Regulations. Article 1 of China's Government Information Disclosure Regulations suffers from a similar problem to the Chinese Constitution in that it does not clearly stipulate that citizens have the right to access administrative information. In a regulation that upholds the principle of information disclosure and guarantees citizens' right to know administrative information, it is insufficient to make only implicit provisions. Therefore, it is recommended that the Regulations be revised to explicitly and clearly state that the purpose of the Regulations is to confirm and protect the public's full right to administrative information.

4.2 The Status Quo and Reflection on the Practice of Administrative Right to Know in China

4.2.1 The Status Quo of Administrative Right to Know in Practice

Before local governments formulate rules to clarify the administrative right to know, the implementation of the above-mentioned indirect provisions in the Constitution, laws, and administrative regulations constitutes the practice of the administrative right to know.

The principle of popular sovereignty, enshrined in the 1954 Constitution, is one of the fundamental principles of the Chinese political and legal system. According to this principle, the people have the right to know the information of the government. After the Third Plenary Session of the Eleventh Central Committee, with the deepening of the reform of the Chinese political system, the transparency of government affairs was clearly proposed. In 1988, the Secretariat of the CPC Central Committee proposed that leading government organs at all levels should implement the system of 'two disclosures and one supervision'—the administrative procedures should be made public, the governmental management should be made public, and all work should be subject to public supervision. In 1995, after the principle of 'governing the country according to law' was clearly proposed, some provinces and municipalities successively proposed regulations on the disclosure of public affairs that are closely related to the interests of the public. The system of 'supervision' has been incorporated into a system of openness. However, it is the disclosure of village affairs that has played a huge catalytic role in protecting the right to know of administrative information through government information disclosure in China.

With the development of organizations in villages, townships, and townships, a movement for government affairs has also been developing in various governmental departments. In 1999, the Ministry of Public Security issued the Notice on the Implementation of the System of Disclosure in Public Security Organs Nationwide, which stipulates that all matters should be disclosed in principle except for those that cannot be disclosed according to laws and regulations. This notice mainly includes the bases for law enforcement, institutional procedures, police disciplines, and law enforcement processes. In 2000, the State Administration of Taxation issued the Notice on Further Implementing the Eight Disclosures of Civilized Tax Handling in the National Tax System. The 'eight disclosures' refer to the disclosure of taxpayers' rights and obligations, tax policies and regulations, management service specifications, audit work specifications, tax violation and punishment standards, tax cadre integrity and self-discipline regulations, taxpayers' complaint departments and supervision and reporting telephone numbers, and accountability for violations of regulations. In addition, the then State Administration of Industry and Commerce also issued the Notice on In-depth Implementation of the Administrative Affairs Disclosure System in the same year.

As the government affairs disclosure has developed, the public has shifted their focus from broad government affairs disclosure (including the disclosure of administrative acts and administrative information) to specific government information disclosures. Everyone has a deeper understanding of the contents of government information disclosure, and due to the influence of the information society, the form of government information disclosure has begun to diversify, especially with the use of the internet. The government Internet project, which began in 1999, has effectively promoted the realization of the administrative right to know by using the internet as one of the most efficient means of disclosure.[24] As of June 2002, there were 128,362 domain names registered under CN. The number of domain names registered under GOV has reached 5,181, representing 4% of the total number of domain names. Government websites have become an essential way to access government information, and have played an irreplaceable role in the realization of the administrative right to know.

As government affairs disclosure and government Internet projects advance, there is growing public demand for the enactment of government information disclosure legislation. Before the promulgation of the Government Information Disclosure Regulations, some local governments began to establish and protect the public's right to know administrative information by formulating local administrative rules.

The preparation period for the Chinese Government Information Disclosure Regulations was comparatively long, taking more than a year from promulgation to implementation. This indicates that legislators foresaw the difficulty of implementation. The problem is manifested in the fact that many government departments are not prepared for government information disclosure, and there are also implementation issues caused by the unclear and imperfect formulation of the Regulations.

First, the competent authorities for government information disclosure need to be determined. Although most local governments have established a leading body for government information disclosure headed by a deputy leader (often called a "leading group for information disclosure"), the promotion of government information disclosure still needs to rely on a competent regular department, namely, the

[24] See Hanhua [15, pp. 31–32].

general office or office of the local government. Before the implementation of the Regulations, most of the work relating to disclosing government affairs was handled by the Communist Party's discipline inspection departments (which are co-located with the government's supervision departments), and the central government did not clarify how this power should be carried out by discipline inspection and supervision departments after the promulgation of the Regulations. When the general office of the government is in charge of government information disclosure, it faces the problem of overlapping powers with discipline inspection and supervision departments.

Second, in some regions, vertical leading departments have become obstacles to promoting the implementation of open regulations. According to the Chinese administrative system, the central vertical systems such as customs, national taxation, finance, and foreign exchange administration, as well as the vertical systems below the provincial level such as local taxation, industry and commerce, quality supervision, and land management are not subordinate institutions of local governments (sub-provincial level). Local governments are in most cases powerless to promote, guide, coordinate, and supervise the government information disclosure work of these departments.

4.2.2 Reflections on the Practices of Administrative Right to Know in China

To Effectively Promote the Government's and Public's Awareness of the Importance of the Administrative Right to Know

It is important to recognize the importance, urgency, and significant value of establishing and safeguarding citizens' right to access information about administrative administration. By realizing the right to know, citizens can compel the government to fulfill its obligation to disclose information. The government's administrative philosophy should shift from being based on power to being based on rights, and the government's administrative role should transform from being administration-focused to being service-focused. Those who possess information must fully respect the right to know in order to uphold the values of service, convenience, humanism, and democracy embodied in the Regulations.

To Enrich the Means and Methods of the Government Affairs Disclosure, and Actively Promote and Improve the Government's Internet Access Project

In today's information society, the online publication of government information has become the most effective way to achieve government transparency. The accuracy, comprehensiveness, and authority of government information provided on official government websites is the most significant aspect of information disclosure. Through these websites, the public can obtain government information in the most effective way possible. However, the construction of government websites in China is not up to par. Some government websites function as commercial websites or professional portals, and do not adequately fulfill their information disclosure functions.[25] Some government websites are focused on broadcasting news, while others have outdated information. Unfortunately, very few local government websites post information in a timely manner. Therefore, it is recommended that the effectiveness of government website construction be considered a specific and significant indicator for promoting government information disclosure.

To Formulate and Clarify Standards for Administrative Information Disclosure

The initial stage of the construction of the Chinese government's website was carried out spontaneously, without unified planning and normative requirements. Due to this lack of planning, information systems of governments at various levels are composed of different databases, operating systems, and even different networks. This results in an inability to effectively share information between websites, creating so-called 'isolated information islands'.

To address these issues, improvements can be made in the following areas:

Firstly, standards for information disclosure classification systems and core metadata standards for information disclosure need to be formulated.

Secondly, a set of technology standards should be developed to extract and classify information according to grammar and semantics, meeting the needs of management, identification, positioning, discovery, evaluation, and selection of government information resources from multiple perspectives such as themes and applications.

Thirdly, under the technical support of the central government for information disclosure, local governments should build a government information disclosure directory system that meets the needs of the local people in light of their own actual conditions.

Currently, the state has formulated the national standard for the government information resource catalog system (GB/T 21,063–2007), which clarifies the overall framework, technical requirements, and specifications such as core metadata, classification of information resources, and technical management requirements. Existing technical standard requirements may be referred to in the process of compiling the government information disclosure catalog.

To Strengthen the Training of Personnel to Have a Good Competency to Disclose Information

To ensure that government agencies and staff have sufficient competency, they must receive systematic, comprehensive, and long-term training. The General Office of the

---

25 See Hanhua [15, p. 48].

State Council and the general offices of governments at other levels should prioritize providing relevant training to truly implement the requirements of the Regulations.

To Accelerate the Political System Reform and Promote Government Information Disclosure

To promote the disclosure of government information and ensure the realization of the administrative right to know, it is essential to accelerate political system reform, which will help to streamline the relationship between various government departments. By clarifying functions and powers, the corresponding subjects of obligations and rights regarding the right to know administrative information will become clearer. Therefore, it is necessary to clearly define the specific scope of responsibilities of government departments and agencies, and to straighten out their powers and responsibilities. This can be achieved through collaboration between the general offices of governments at all levels. Only by doing so can the disclosure of government information be effectively and efficiently promoted.

To Improve Legal Remedies for Non-disclosure of Information

After the implementation of the Regulations on May 1, 2008, there was an increase in the exercise of the right to access administrative information throughout China. However, a subsequent problem arose when the public requested government information and encountered rejections based on reasons such as "the information does not exist," "the information is of an internal nature," or "the information is highly related to social stability."[26] For instance, a Southern Weekend reporter questioned 25 land and resources bureaus in 21 cities in China to disclose real estate information that should have been made public, but only four bureaus provided the information. In other words, according to the survey, only 16% of administrative agencies comply with the Government Information Disclosure Regulations.[27]

5 Conclusion

The saying "Sunlight is one of the best disinfectants" emphasizes the importance of transparency and good governance as essential components of a strong civil society.[28] The citizens' right to know, including the administrative right to know, is a basic

---

[26] For details, please refer to Cai, Y. (2008, July 10). Implementation of the New Information Disclosure Law Encounters Initial Difficulties. Southern Weekend.

[27] For details, please see Su, L. et al. (2008, July 10). Journalists experience: information is not public. Southern Weekend.

[28] Wang [16].

human right in the modern world and a prerequisite for the realization of many other civil rights. In today's rapidly developing information society, the right to administrative information, which is closely related to government information, holds a unique and irreplaceable value as the most crucial social resource.[29] To strengthen our understanding of this right, we should study and draw on experiences from advanced foreign systems, and build a legal system that upholds the right to know by the Chinese government. By doing so, we can promote the development of China's constitutional and human rights undertakings.

References

1. Henkin, L. (1990). *The age of rights*. Columbia University Press.
2. Feng, X. (2003). Reflecting on government information transparency from SARS cases. *Journal of the National Academy of Administration, 2003*(4). (in Chinese).
3. Wei, N. (2002). Democratic administration with citizen participation. *Journal of the National Academy of Administration, 2002*(3), 19. (in Chinese).
4. Song, X. (1994). Freedom of information act: The legislative history of the united states. *Journalism and Communication Studies, 1994*(2), 14. (in Chinese).
5. Pi, C., & Liu, J. (2000). The right to know and the system of information disclosure. *Journal of Shanxi University (Zheshe Edition), 2000*(3), 17. (in Chinese).
6. Li, S. (2008). Regulations on open government information of the People's Republic of China: Background, main content and catalogue compilation. *E-Government, 2008*(5), 21. (in Chinese).
7. Zhou, H. (Ed.). (2003). *Expert proposal draft on open government information regulations* (p. 168). China Legal Publishing House. (in Chinese).
8. Zhang, W. (2001). *Studies on the scope of legal philosophy (Revised Edition)* (p. 122). China University of Political Science and Law Press. (in Chinese).
9. Zhang, W. (1990). From the obligation standard to the rights standard: The development law of law. *Social Science Front*, (3). (in Chinese).
10. Zheng, C. (1989). Rights-based theory. *Politics and Law*, (4). (in Chinese).
11. Wang, M. (1995). *American administrative law (Part II)* (p. 975). China Legal Publishing House. (in Chinese).
12. Qiaoling, W., & Xiuling, L. (2004). Legal protection of trade secrets. In *Information age: Scientific and technological information research, academic papers of scientific and technological journal editing* (p. 387). China Science and Technology Press. (in Chinese).
13. Xianbo, L., & Jiancheng, Y. (2003). On the coordination of freedom of expression and the right to privacy. *Chinese Law, 2003*(5), 88. (in Chinese).
14. Mingjie, Z. (2003). *Open government: A study on the legal system of open government information* (p. 158). China University of Political Science and Law Press. (in Chinese).

[29] The author agrees with the following views regarding the study and adoption of the Western legal system. It cannot be blindly transplanted or copied without proper analysis. Instead, the right approach should be based on the following three principles. First, we should selectively learn from each other. Second, we should consider the compatibility and feasibility of the system. Finally, we must carry out transformation and adaptation tailored to our national conditions. See Shi [17].

15. Hanhua, Z. (2003). China's government informatization and its practical problems. In Z. Hanhua (Ed.), *Practice and exploration of China's government affairs openness* (pp. 31–32). China Legal Publishing House. (in Chinese).
16. Wang, M. (1995). *U.S. administrative law (Part II)* (p. 960). China Legal Publishing House.
17. Shi, S. (2003). On the view of reform in judicial reform. *Journal of the National College of Public Prosecutors, 2003*(4), 104.

Chapter 4
Right to Information

Xiaohui Li

1 Introduction

Since the 1960s, the wave of information technology represented by computer technology has triggered a new round of technological revolution, which has significantly impacted the whole world. In recent decades, social life has undergone an unprecedented process of informationization. Almost everything has the information attribute, especially the appearance of electronic and digital information. Informationization does not only disguise itself behind the informatic symbols in social life; it has also profoundly affected people's behavior patterns and social structure, triggering tremendous changes within our societies. With the continuous development of this information society, sufficient information resources and convenient access to information are viewed by most people as being equivalent to a good life in which they can enjoy high efficiency, democracy and freedom.

The information issue has condensed the irresistible charm of the times and theoretical potential. Issues relating to information have, since the twentieth century, attracted attention from various theoretical fields, and have led to in-depth studies in respective areas. These include the economics of information, a branch of microeconomic theory that studies how information and information systems affect the economy and economic decisions; another is the philosophy of information, a branch of philosophy that studies topics relevant to computer science, information science and information technology. In this regard, it is hard to imagine that in an era dominated by information, a theoretical study can turn a blind eye to information issues. However, legal research, which has always regarded practicality as one of its attributes, has made little response to information issues. For a long time, information was not seen as an object on which the law has impact and it was not recognized as a legal concept. It was not until the 1970s to 1980s that legal research emerged and began to regard information as an independent subject of study, concerning

X. Li (✉)
Beijing Foreign Studies University Law School, Beijing, China

J. Yao (ed.), *The Legal Issues of the Emerging Rights*,
https://doi.org/10.1007/978-981-97-0499-6_4

issues in the field such as information freedom, information governance, information control, and rights to information. In international academia, discussions on topics including 'information law', 'information and law', 'information, law and information technology' emerged during this period.[1]

Nevertheless, the legal research on information issues is still in its infancy as it is lacking in basic theories and methodologies. What is information from a legal perspective? Can the law regulate information? How does the law realize this kind of regulation? Basic questions such as these still lack in-depth research and have not yet been sufficiently answered. At present, legal studies on information, especially in Chinese domestic legal studies, is often limited to a specific legal field or departmental law and lacks a general understanding of theoretical methodologies. The slow theoretical development in this field contributes to the legal system being ill-equipped to confront the repeated emerging issues and problems concerning information, thereby leading to inadequate legal regulation in the information space. At the same time, the public is being harassed by calls, flyers, cell phone text messages, and internet spams. Moreover, incidents such as corporate credit scandals, fake information disclosures, disputes over database property rights, arbitrary collections and abuse of personal information, and information monopoly by public institutions have increased with high frequency. People are deeply troubled by the various problems arising from the information abuse but lack the necessary legal knowledge and systematic institutional solutions to deal with them.

Rights are legal, social, or ethical principles of freedom or entitlement, and are of essential importance in such disciplines as law and ethics, especially theories of justice and deontology. In this information society, numerous information-based claims also reflect that rights are the key to legal access to information issues. The

[1] Nowadays, Chinese legal academia mainly pay their attention to the following aspects of the information issues. First, information law studies. In this field, it is argued that information law is an independent legal department, and the systematic framework of information law has been primitively established. Second, the studies of related issues are scattered in different law departments, such as intellectual property law in the era of knowledge economy, e-commerce law, information control in the securities market, distortion of accounting information, privacy and the right to know, government information disclosure, press and publication law, etc. Third, theoretical legal information issues, such as freedom of expression and freedom of information, internet political and legal issues, information technology and legal issues, etc. Since the 1990s, information issues have aroused continuous and widespread attention. In Western academia, especially British academia, academic discussions have been carried out in two trajectories: the overall theoretical understanding (what information is, the legal meaning of information, the framework for solving information problems by law, etc.), and the discussion about specific issues (privacy, information disclosure, intellectual property rights, the right to know, etc.) Discussions in Western legal academia have reached agreements on some basic issues: information is a major issue and topic that contemporary law must be confronted with; the purpose of law to regulate information is to ensure sufficient balance freedom and order for information; law must provide cognitive models and institutional norms for information control. In parallel, Western legal scholars have also debated on the legal meaningfulness of information, legal theoretical models for understanding information issues. They have proposed different methods and approaches for the confirmation, mutual relations, and remedies of information rights.

theoretical presupposition from the perspective of legal rights is to realize the legitimate value and legitimate interests in the rights through the legal protection of legitimate rights, and to prevent possible damage to legitimacy, so the goal of the rule of law can be achieved. Legitimacy is crucial to, and the theoretical prerequisite for, the right to information.

'*Legitimacy*' is actually a concept concerning the affirmation of rights formed by people: a legitimate behavior is neither a behavior required by other members of society nor a behavior prohibited by other members of society; instead, it is a freedom accorded to the right holder to choose to carry out a behavior or not, namely, self-government. This kind of freedom that is labeled 'being righteous' is a right. In practice, when the term 'right' is used to express a certain legal freedom, this usage is carried out on the basis of its legitimate aspect.'[2] This book aims to approach the issue from the perspective of the constitution of rights and demonstrate the legitimacy of the right to information. As such, it shall be protected by law to provide a theoretical framework for the legal research on information issues and related regulatory issues.[3]

2 Information as a Legal Term

The starting point of the research on the right to information is information per se. It is arguable that a good conceptual analysis of information is the basis of this entire research. Initially, information was understood as a 'daily language' in practice. Theoretically speaking, it is, in this regard, merely a dependent concept to describe the physical world and its contents. With the increasing awareness of the value of information in life practice and the continuous advancement of informationization in human society, it is being gradually realized that information can solve crises, promote knowledge sharing, and eliminate the uncertainty of interpersonal behaviors. It is not surprising to find it has been acknowledged that information has become an important resource in the twenty-first century and is an overriding social structural factor.[4]

However, as an institutional arrangement, law ought to respond to the information issue, namely, provide answers to the question of what information is from a legal perspective. Information in a legal sense is an independent object of human cognition rather than a representation of the physical world and its contents; it must be of a

[2] Zhang [1].

[3] Right is a concept commonly used by multiple disciplines. It has far-ranging meanings and possesses various attributes such as morality, religion, customs, and law. Although legal research focuses on the studies of legal rights, the meanings could be quite different when the concept of right is used. In most cases, legal rights are conferred by the law. This research aims at studying legal rights from the perspective of legal development. The core concern is the emergence of new rights. Therefore, the rights referred to in this research are all legal rights. Other forms of rights (such as moral rights, due rights, etc.) will be pointed out when they are used.

[4] Li [2].

concrete and existing nature. In this sense, the items that can harbor information mainly include news, intelligence, signals, data, materials, knowledge, and symbols. Symbols are, by essence, information in artificially coded forms. Functionally, they are expressers of meanings and are in material existence. 'Every information is made up of symbols.'[5] It is viewed that messages, intelligence, signals, and materials can all be represented by symbols. The difference between them lies in that these symbols may have different functions for the information receivers, respectively. Data is nothing more than a symbol expressed in the form of data. In addition to the form of data alone, information can also be given in the form of graphics or through other kinds of symbols. Meanwhile, some scholars would like to use knowledge to define information. This is, at least, legally infeasible. The knowledge information is an epistemological concept. It cannot make information a more precise and clearer object. In the opposite, it would make the concept of information vaguer and more abstract. Therefore, it is appropriate to use symbols to define legal information.

In a general sense, information represented by symbols has characteristics that are different from those presented by physical objects:

2.1 *Independence*

Information can exist independently. That is, it can be distinguished conceptually and institutionally from the media that carries the information and has an independent legal interest orientation. For example, movie image information and films are different carriers of legal interests. People can obtain movie information by using camcorders to secretly record, not necessarily by obtaining copies of a film. The independence attribute of information is also reflected in its independence from the objective realities it reflects. For example, in a picture of a flower, the visual information it conveys about the flower is different from that of the flower in nature or reality. The images of flowers in the picture can be processed into a variety of colors and even shapes, which can be changed by modifying the data concerned. However, the colors and appearances of flowers in nature are predetermined. Therefore, information and objective reality are not necessarily completely consistent. In fact, a large amount of information is artificially processed. Whether the information is consistent with the objective truth does not affect the independent attribute of the information in a legal sense.

2.2 *Intangibility/Invisibility*

Compared to physical objects with a physical appearance, information is invisible, that is, it does not have a physical shape, mass, or weight. At the same time, the

[5] Jacobson [3]. Cited in: Li and Xu [4].

intangibility of information also refers to the fact that any changes to information rights cannot be made by carrying out changes to information carriers. Information, such as a piece of work, can appear in multiple versions in multiple contexts, but the ownership of the information right itself, such as copyright, is exclusive to the right holder. However, the intangibility of information does not mean that it is completely invisible or uncontrollable. Instead, it represents a symbolic system that has obtained an objective form and can be reproduced through encoding and in a media format, for instance, information about flowers, which have to be presented in the form of photos or videos. The purely objective reality that is completely unknown to human beings can only be a natural existence outside of human society and knowledge because it cannot be communicated or perceived by humans.

2.3 Sharing

Sharing is the joint use of a resource or space. Information is a 'commodity' in economic terms. As a public product by nature, it has two characteristics: first, one's consumption does not reduce or negatively affect the consumption of others, which is the so-called 'non-competitive consumption'; second, the costs of preventing infringement of the right are viewed as being quite high. The sharing of information means that 'in short, the same information can be attached to multiple different substances at the same time, and exist in multiple places at the same time; or in other words, the same information can have multiple carriers, and the change of carriers do not have impact on the content of the information. That is to say, the information carried by different carriers is the same. This is the sharing of information, which brings forward losslessness and reproducibility. And it is also one of the main differences between information and physical materials.'[6]

The characteristics of information as being public goods are related to its attribute of reproducibility, spreadability, and intangibility. For these reasons, there are differences between information and the traditional 'commodities' as studied in economics, including, for example, municipal public facilities and street lamps. It is precisely because of these information characteristics that the degree of information sharing is higher than that of tangible 'commodities' in traditional economics. Because the sharing attribute would undermine the basis of the exclusiveness of rights in traditional jurisprudence theories, it is quite difficult to confirm and protect the right of information as a legal object. The confirmation and protection of the rights of traditional tangible property are often accomplished by directly linking the rights system with the object of rights. For example, the protection of movable property rights is accomplished through possession and transfer, whereas, the protection of real property rights is accomplished through possession plus registration and insurance systems. In traditional property law theories, the principle of 'one property, one right' in civil law tradition especially embodies the exclusiveness of rights through

[6] Zhu [5].

the exclusiveness of the possession of objects. The emergence of intangible property, for example, intellectual property, has broken away from previous theories, which believed in the absolute link between the exclusiveness of things and the exclusiveness of rights. When it becomes possible for carriers of rights to be possessed, used, and benefited by multiple subjects at the same time, the foundation of the exclusiveness of rights is strongly impacted. The intellectual property right itself is the core part of information rights. The form of rights based on information needs to break away from the inevitable connection between the exclusiveness of rights and the exclusiveness of objects, as mentioned above. It also becomes possible to establish multiple types of and multiple (same type) legal rights on the same information, thereby mitigating the connection between the exclusiveness of the object and the exclusive right, or establishing a relatively new legal system of the objects' exclusiveness.[7] Of course, the protection of information rights would also address the connection between different legal rights and rely more on the protection arising from the development of information technology.

2.4 *Time-Sensitivity*

Once information is generated, the value is proportional to freshness. That is to say, in the sense of freshness, the newer the content, the greater its value; as time passes, its value decreases correspondingly. Naturally, time-sensitivity is not the only criterion for measuring the value of information. Information with significant social and scientific value may have value for a while, and for longer than many other types of information. At the same time, factors such as authenticity, scientificity, and artistry also affect the value of information. Compared with tangible objects, the value measurement system vis-à-vis information is more complicated. In the context of extensive information in the modern day, people often need to spend a lot of time identifying the value and effectiveness of information. However, in light of encouraging the creation and dissemination of information, the protection of information throughout legal rights cannot be without time limitations, which means that the protection of information is also time-sensitive. Information that is free from legal protection would be available to the public for use and, as such, becomes the common information for mankind. Not all symbolic information with the above characteristics is information in a legal sense. Legal information is a symbolic system that should meet certain conditions. In other words, legal information ought to be subject to certain legal requirements in order to become the object of legal adjustment and a constituent element of rights in a legal setting. These legal requirements effectively specify the qualifications of legal information.

[7] For example, the argument that object sharing and interest exclusiveness as the principle of intellectual property protection, put forward by Dr. Zhu Xiequn, reflects the concept of information rights protection, that is, the legal system should allow the sharing of legal objects (a certain type of specific information). And, at the same time, the binding effectiveness of law can protect the benefits derived from the specific information. See: Zhu [5].

These requirements were put forward mainly in consideration of the limitation arising from the adjustment scope of the legal system and the operability of law. The provisions concerned mean that any legal system that takes information as the object of adjustment and the object of rights needs to consider these fundamental principles, to provide standards for all legal systems that take information as the object of regulation at a macro level. The establishment of these standards also has impact on how the law views information, and, thus, plays a role in shaping the concept of information in law. After comprehensively considering the feasibility of a legal regulation on information, it is arguable that the specific standards for information should include codability, dissemination, and compliance and sociality. Of course, those requirements mentioned above are per se still very vague by nature and can only be used as preliminary principles in establishing a primitive information legal system. Nevertheless, on the purpose of establishing a comprehensive legislative framework, these requirements still need to be further reconstructed and improved on the basis of incorporating the elements as follows:

A. *Codability: a potential approach to regulate information by law*

'We use the word *information* extensively. Essentially, anything that can be encoded in the digitized form, namely, presented in digital unit (for the most notable example, Byte)'.[8] Information can only be disseminated after being encoded. The encoding and decoding processes vis-à-vis information within the scope of legal adjustment should be mastered and under control by humans and could also be interpreted and reproduced. The encoded information must be attached to certain mediums, and the content and meaning of the information can be understood through those mediums. The mediums could take various forms, including, for example, newspapers, telephones, CDs, disks, and the internet. These mediums make invisible, intangible, and non-objectified information concrete and objectified; viewed in this way, it has a form that can be controlled and described. Varieties arising in the mediums themselves may lead to differences in the existing forms of information: sound information, text information, image information, data information, and multimedia information.

Paying attention to information mediums and the encoding and decoding process can, to a certain extent, help overcome the difficulties caused by the intangibility of information, thereby making it possible to locate the scope, content, and forms of information. Information law that combines technology and legal norms can regulate the process of information dissemination by controlling information mediums and coding and decoding technologies. In other words, the settings of information rights must be managed by means of the regulation of information media and the encoding and decoding process. The specific systems of information rights also have their own characteristics due to the differences that exist in media forms and coding and decoding technologies. There is obviously a considerable difference between the legal norms vis-à-vis the information dissemination via paper mediums and that via electronic data.

[8] Shapiro and Varian [6].

With the development of information technology, the trend of the multimedia transformation of information is becoming more obvious. At present, laws governing information dissemination in various countries and jurisdictions around the world can be roughly classified into two different regulatory approaches; the first approach is to govern information on the basis of the forms of the mediums, including, for example, China's *Regulations on the Administration of Audiovisual Products*, *Regulations on the Administration of Radio and Television*, *Interim Measures on the Administration of Cable Television*, and *Regulations on Publication Administration*. From the titles, one can tell that the laws regulate information, respectively, according to what medium it utilizes. The second approach is targeted at the patterns for information dissemination, such as Germany's Multimedia Law, which regulates the conditions for information and communication services. Experience gained from the research on internet information dissemination proves that it is not appropriate to simply transplant the legal expressions applied to traditional information dissemination channels into internet information dissemination regulations. Compared with other communication channels, the internet is fundamentally different in terms of the form of medium and the existing patterns of information, reflecting the diverse forms of information disseminations. Therefore, the arrangements of legal rights must respond to the differences mentioned above.

B. *Transmissibility: the time and space limits to information regulated by law*

Information can be transmitted and disseminated, and, as such, it is valuable to humans. Although the dissemination of information depends on the material medium that carries it, information is different from its material medium. As a result, to some degree, it has an independent nature. For example, the textual information recorded in books and the physical form of paper books themselves are independent of each other.

Regarding the process of information dissemination, Claude E. Shannon—an American mathematician, electrical engineer, and cryptographer known as 'the father of information theory'—published two influential papers in the late 1940s, entitled, respectively, *A Mathematical Theory of Communication* and *Noisy-channel coding theorem*, which focused on this issue and proposed the mathematical model below (Picture 4.1).

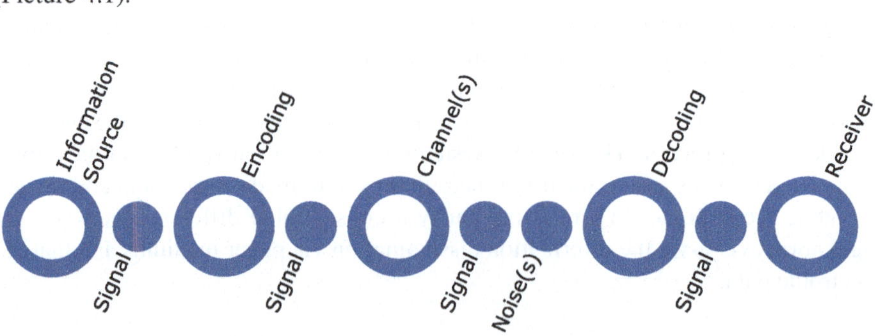

Picture 4.1 Shannon's model for the communication system

He argued that communication is the behavior and procedures whereby people use symbols communication media to exchange information.[9] Information starts from an information source and can be effectively transmitted through the channel(s) after being encoded. The encoded information is interfered with by noises from the environment during the transmission process and must be decoded in order to present its contents when the information reaches the receiver.[10]

Shannon's theory focuses on the process of information disseminations, which proposed an appropriate point for the law to intervene in information issues. Undoubtedly, information is highly dependent on disseminations. The reason that all kinds of information are meaningful to society lie in its apparent or potential communicability. The spreadability of information also distinguishes information from static signals and symbols. The encoding and decoding processes of information distinguishes information effectively from unencoded and unserialized data. In this context, the information in a legal sense (namely, what the legal rights can be legitimately ascribed towards) should also be information that can be disseminated by means of mediums; legal rights are concerned with, but not with all information-related issues, the legal interest relationships and contradictions arising from the processes of information disseminations.

During the entire information dissemination process, the information to be disseminated, the information in the dissemination, and the information after the dissemination can all become the objects of legal relationships within which rights and obligations arise. The information society relationships regulated by the law are, in essence, social relationships formed during the dissemination of information. These relationships may occur during the pre-dissemination stage (information generation, collection, etc.), during the dissemination stage (information transmission, on-going and reception), and the post-dissemination stage (the possession and utilization of information, etc.). The time and space limits applied to information dissemination are essentially the limits arising from legal governance vis-à-vis information. The legal provisions can only achieve the effect of information regulation by strictly regulating (namely, controlling) all stages of information dissemination. Applying relevant provisions of information law to different stages of information dissemination and focusing on key issues at different stages is an important starting point for the establishment of a sound and effective information legal system. These key points can be summarized as follows: subject conditions, content and purpose restrictions, methods, and legal responsibilities. For example, during the pre-dissemination stage, attention should be paid to determining who has the right to collect, store, and manage what kind of information at what time and under what conditions, and what kind of legal responsibility/responsibilities should be prescribed for violations of statutory or agreed obligations. At different stages of information dissemination, the

[9] Cited from: Yan [7].

[10] For example, if a person speaks, the person who speaks is the source of information, and the words in his speech are encoded into a piece of wording, and the language is transmitted to another person listening to his speech through sound waves in the air (mixed with various environmental noises) (carrier), the sound waves are restored to meaningful information in the process of decoding by the listener's ears.

following should be established: which subject(s) has/have the right to disseminate what kind of information at what time, place, or in any other conditions, and what kind of legal responsibilities should be borne by the violator for violating statutory or agreed obligations. During the post-dissemination stage, attention should be paid to determining who can possess, store and use different types of information obtained at what time or place, and for what purpose(s); it should be established which method should be used and what kind of legal responsibility should be prescribed for the violation of statutory or agreed obligations. These are the key elements that would enable an information legal system to competently regulate the entire process of information transmission.

Modern information technologies enable the information transmission to break through the limits of time and space, thus, infinitely extending the time and space scope of information dissemination. This presents unprecedented and unparalleled challenges for a legal regulation towards information. In spite of that, it is not impossible to define the scope in relation to how far legal rights and obligations can regulate information dissemination. Accompanied by the scientific development of information law and the improvement of related research methodologies, it is possible to govern the control over information dissemination from a legal perspective. Therefore, the temporal and spatial challenges concerning information dissemination can be dealt with via legal means, although some remain technically unresolved. For example, in the context of internet information regulation, it becomes possible to locate and prosecute the person responsible for distributing illegal information on the internet, because firstly, the existence of positioning coding technologies such as an IP address, a numerical label assigned to each device connected to a computer network that uses the Internet Protocol for communication and, secondly, the existence of the management system of network service providers, and the development of technical instruments to discover and store electronic evidence, although this is not seen as being significantly difficult.

C. *Sociality: the scope of information under legal regulations*

According to different content attributes, information can be generally divided into natural information and social information. The former refers to unrecognized biological information as well as that being studied, which are mainly subjects in the field of natural science research; the latter refers to economic information, political information, and cultural information. Economic information includes trade secrets, securities market information, listed company operating information, e-commerce information, and financial data information. Political information consists of government management and decision-making information, information about candidates in election activities, state secrets and national security information, information about national conditions and circumstances, and statistical information. Cultural information includes information on intellectual achievements in scientific and technological fields, namely, intellectual property information, technical standardization information, personal information, information related to news and publications, and postal communication information. The information in the legal setting is, in most cases, social information that has a substantial and direct impact on people's social lives, as opposed to information relating to natural sciences or all other information. Of course, the content of information is not only related to sociality, but also the various stages in the communication processes as well as means (channels) of communication. The law's governance on the dissemination of different information also reflects the impact the information has on people's lives. The social aspects or attributes of information in a legal setting emphasize the sociality of the legal system that is embodied in information regulations, to inscribe the sociality of people in a comparatively deeper way.

During the final analysis, the need to regulate information is related to human social life and social welfare, rather than humans' scientific pursuits to understand nature. Therefore, what kind of information the law protects and how it can be protected are related to specific social values and ethical mechanisms, rather than to the authenticity and scientific value of the information. It is also arguable that there will always be differences in information protection systems formulated on the basis of different ideologies and in the context of different ethical backgrounds. Those regulations that are closely related to social values can always become the focus of debates inside and outside of the systems concerned.

D. *Regulatability: The Effectiveness of Legal Regulation Towards Information*

Information is a set of meaningful data, and the spread of the data is equivalent to the spreading of the meaning of its contents. This is very important for the understanding of information issues from a legal perspective. Communication researchers Charles Kay Ogden and Ivor Armstrong Richards created a communication model that focuses on the meaning of information. They argue that the understanding of information is dependent on elements such as 'reference', 'referent' and 'symbol'. 'Reference' refers to the meanings and thoughts contained in information; 'referent' is an objective thing represented by information; symbol is the manifestation of information used to connect 'reference' with 'referent'.[11] The comparison between the information dissemination model created by Ogden and Richards and Shannon's model highlights the close connection between information and meaningfulness. As a legal object that connects legal subjects to legal relations, information refers to 'all valuable and meaningful knowledge or data'.[12] Unlike natural sciences, electronic information technology, legal science and law are more concerned with the contents and meanings of information than the form of information. For example, when sending an e-mail, information technology is concerned with how to make the rapid and convenient dissemination of information through technical means possible, while the law is concerned with whether the content of the e-mail contains illegal information, whether it has been illegally obtained (e.g. information theft), who should be charged with legal responsibilities, and what those legal responsibilities are. All the issues above are directly related to the content and meaning of the

[11] For example, the linguistic information of 'table', its 'signifier' is an abstract table, and it 'refers to' is a kind of furniture supported by legs on which there is a flat surface where objects can be placed; its symbol is the two Chinese characters 'table'.

[12] Wenxian [8].

information. Meaningfulness in the legal rights setting is also different from that in the communication science setting. The law focuses on the part of the information content that is related to the scope of legal adjustments, that is, the meaningfulness of legal effects, rather than the meaningfulness (on the surface) of languages and symbols.

Theoretically speaking, the meaning is related to the content and the interpretations of the content. As people in various historical and social contexts set different goals for the legal regulation of information, the focus of legal regulation towards the meaningfulness would also be correspondingly disparate. In autocratic societies, where supreme political power to direct all the activities of the state is concentrated in the hands of one-person, legal attention would be paid to ways to control the dissemination of information and, in some cases, keep the public in the dark; the public disclosure of information is prohibited and information is kept secret. By comparison, in democratic societies, more transparency is accorded when regulating information communications to promote a so-called 'open government'. In parallel, Eastern culture is more inclined to disseminate information through informal channels, and information communicated through private channels usually attracts more attention than through public channels. Western culture, by contrast, is inclined to institutionalize information dissemination channels. Private information, being linked to individuals directly, is viewed as being bound by preventing unauthorized disclosures, and, thus, shall be kept in the 'secret box', while public information must be disclosed in broad daylight, ensuring the public has access to public information. Customs, traditions, cultures and regional arrangements affect the legal perspective and focus on the content of information. Some information content is recognized as legal objects in one jurisdiction but not in another. Therefore, if the meaning of information requires the intervention of the law, the social and cultural context concerned must be considered. It should be noted that culture as discussed above is a broad term, which is used to refer to a heritage of social norms, ethical values, traditional customs, belief systems, political systems, and specific artifacts and technologies.

3 Information Rights

3.1 Information as a Legal Object

Locating an emerging legal object is, in many cases, a prelude to the development of new rights systems and the formulation of new rights norms. Information that meets certain conditions can become the object of rights.

First, as a meaningful and communicable symbol system, information is an important resource in the information society and is a 'useful thing' that has value to the subjects of social relations. In the context of economic activities, information can reflect market changes in a timely manner. Sufficient information can ensure the safety and efficiency of production and trading activities; from a social and cultural perspective, information sharing and communication strengthens social cohesions, enhances mutual understanding and promotes tolerance; from a political perspective, information freedom and open information policy promote political democracy and the rule of law. Therefore, information embodies comprehensive aspects of the values within society. With the development of the information industry and the prosperity of the information economy, information control brings forward wealth, opportunities, and satisfaction. However, compared to people's needs, information is always limited. As a scarce resource, information will inevitably lead to competitive interests. When acquiring a larger amount of information, transmitting information more quickly, and analyzing information more accurately, there are continual conflicts of interest among different society members. Solving these disputes has become a new subject of law.

Second, information is a 'thing for me' that can be controlled by the legal subject. Highly developed information technology provides unprecedented means for humans to control information. With the help of various advanced sciences and technologies, human beings obtain more knowledge information from the environment and use various possible tangible means (information carriers) to express them. The process of encoding information gives the information an objective form. Under the aegis of the media to display and copy symbols, people have been able to control information, as necessary. Moreover, accompanied by the rapid development of technology, the possession of the means by human beings to uncover and control information would continuously intensify. Needless to say, a lot of information still exists that humans cannot administer, control, or disseminate. This type of information exists in reality but has no legal significance. Therefore, it does not constitute the legal object of an information rights system. Simultaneously, by controlling the processes of information dissemination, the law can also regulate information in terms of time and space, although it should be noted that the regulation mechanism concerned is relatively complicated.

Third, information can exist as a 'thing in itself', separated from its carriers in the process of understanding, known as separation. Information is an objective existence independent of human will, and is an objective manifestation of human cognition, concept, and knowledge. The coding process of information transforms people's subjective cognition into a symbol system with public significance. With these symbols, information has, to some extent, become an autonomous form, not being subject to the rule or control of another. Information with an objective existence form can be possessed and transferred due to its independent nature. The encoding and decoding processes allow information to be possessed by different people and/or entities concurrently. The same method is applied to the encoding and decoding processes and the same information (in another words, reproduction of the information) can be obtained. Certainly, the above-mentioned separation requires the use of media and technical means. The encoding process of information also distinguishes the information from the source(s) of the information itself. A steed (a horse used or trained for riding) is an animal, but a picture of a steed is information about the horse that is encoded into an image. They are objects of different legal rights. Based on the above analysis, the information completely meets the basic standards required to be a legal object in a law setting and can be regarded as a legal object.

3.2 Right to Information and Its Functions

Information can become the legal object over which a legal subject may hold rights. Namely, there is the right to take information as the object, that is, the information right. Drawing from the previous theoretical investigations of information and the examinations and reviews of existing different understandings of information rights,[13] it is argued that information rights are the types of legal rights in which information meets certain conditions to become the legal object; and, the information right is a rights system; that is to say, it is composed of multiple subordinate rights. Subordinate rights include information property rights, the right to know, the right to information privacy, the right to freedom of information dissemination, the right to an information environment, and the right to information safety. Specifically, the concept of information rights we use has the following meanings.

[13] At present, the concept of information rights is used in the following settings: (1) Information rights are rights emerging in the information society, as a result of profound changes in the structure of rights, awareness of rights, and rights norms in the information society. (2) Information rights are the informationization of rights. Comprehensive informationization of the subject, object, and content of rights. (3) Information rights are ethical intermediary that communicates between the real and the virtual. In this sense, the right to information is an ethical right. (4) Information rights are individual rights related to information: the rights and obligations of individuals related to information can be summarized into four categories, namely ownership, confidentiality, privacy, and freedom. (5) Information rights are the rights to use information as a legal object. (6) Information rights are the rights to possess information as content. (7) Information rights mainly refer to rights in an internet context. (8) Information rights refer to intellectual property rights, the right to obtain information, and the right to information security. (9) Information rights are rights within information law. Information law consists of two major parts: first, the legal system for the regulation of the information industry; and second, the regulation of information activities and behaviors. Information activities mainly refer to activities related to the acquisition, processing, dissemination, storage, and transfer of information. For example, information law is used to regulated information activities, or the law of social relations concerning information technology and the information industry. Information activities include various information interaction behaviors between people concerning information; information has special characteristics. See Qinghua and Jianzheng [9]. The information law in the viewpoint of academia abroad (particularly in common law countries) is not seen as a strictly independent legal department, but a legal approach for theoretical understanding and systematic formulation. The research scopes of information law studies at home and abroad are not the same. Generally speaking, the latter is comparatively much wider, and includes various information-related legal systems, such as postal law, intellectual property law, trade secrets and computer crimes, etc.; in China, the research scope is relatively limited and only includes network knowledge property rights, online privacy, freedom of the press and the right to know, etc.

3.2.1 Right to Information as Legal Right

Legal rights are statutory rights. In a nutshell, they are rights provided by law, that is, rights that are legally effective in specific jurisdictions. They are essentially fundamental normative rules, the exercise of which are binding on the obliging parties. Legal rights are directly related to the will of the state and are, in this regard, the unitarity of the will of the state and the will of bearers of juristic rights. Accordingly, legal rights are clearly rights that exist under the rules of legal systems and are safeguarded by the systematic protection enshrined in legal systems. The information right that is to be justified is not a moral right but a legal right. According to collectivist ethics—which is characterized by the emphasis on cohesiveness among individuals—the legitimacy of moral rights lies in the existence of the moral obligation that the subjects owe to others. It is viewed as a legal interest return (a benefit, precisely speaking) that the moral subject should objectively be granted after fulfilling a certain moral obligation. In general, moral rights are requirements or claims that are legitimately bolstered by ethnical values, and moral rights have universal informal normative significance only in the social context of moral identity. Since the functioning of moral rights is mainly dependent on the internal self-discipline of people as well as supervision through public opinions, and there is no compulsory means of remedy, in most cases, they exist instead in the form of natural rights. The information right we are discussing is not a factual right in a sociological sense. Legal rights can be descriptive, but they should be more than descriptive, indeed normative. Its objective is aimed at constructing a system of behavior patterns in law and adjusting and regulating social relations. The information right, which is a macro description of an emerging right in the information society, is not a legal concept and cannot be the goal of rights reasoning.

3.2.2 Right to Information as a Metrix of Rights

Legal rights can be defined and described from multiple perspectives. In linguistic analysis, the expression of '*X* rights' is seen as an inflectional phrase, and prefixes with different meanings can be added to the structure of the expression of rights. These different prefixes emphasize various aspects of the rights structure. The prefix of the right term can be the subject of the right, such as 'human rights' and 'consumer rights', specifying the rights to a definite subject, focusing on highlighting the hierarchical status and particularity of the rights of a certain subject. A subject might be accorded multiple rights. Accordingly, most of the rights defined by subjects constitute an array of multiple specific rights; the X can be the content of the right, such as the 'right to live', the 'right to appeal', and the 'right to education'. These types of rights are ones that oblige the party to carry out certain actions, namely fulfilling certain obligations and enabling right-holders to enjoy certain benefits, thereby emphasizing the different content of rights. Rights defined by content are mostly specific rights. Therefore, such rights are often legally institutionalized; the X can also be the carrier of rights, namely the legal objects of rights, including, 'property rights', 'personal rights', and 'intellectual property rights'. These types of rights refer to the general term of rights established by law with respect to a specific carrier, highlighting the significance of the legal object in the context of a specific right and the special interests of the related right associated with it. The different legal objects of rights directly lead to deviations in the content and exercising of rights. In the context of information rights, information is not a lawful subject that can provide legal intention. At the same time, the information right is not a right to 'de-information'. As a term, information cannot express the content of specific legal actions and interests. In a semantics setting, the right to information can only be a positive phrase with the object of the right as a modifier, which signifies the information as the legal object. As a specific legal object, information is something in respect of which some rights can be held. Owing to the rights development and system control functions of the right to information, the right framework established on the basis of information has a particular structure and form. Even so, since there are multiple forms of legal interests arising from information, information rights include a variety of individual sub-rights, for example, the information right, the right to know, and the right to information security in a network setting. Therefore, information rights not only refer to a type of rights but represent a specific group of specific information rights.

3.2.3 Right to Information Right as a Right Type[14]

Unlike the concept of rights that refers to a specific type, information rights represent a group of sub-rights. The difference between type and group is that a type refers to a category of rights having common characteristics; it is a more abstract term. A group might refer to a collection of individual rights as being a more concrete term. Professor Karl Larenz, one of the greatest German jurists of the twentieth century, mentioned the divergences in the designation of types and groups when discussing the recognition of legal facts in judicial cases from the perspective of legal methodology, by stating that under the aegis of definitions, to an extent, types can be specified as follows: 'if and only if' all the elements of the definition are comprehensively presented in a specific event or case, the 'type' concept can apply. The various factors proposed to describe the type do not need to be all present, they can also appear to varying degrees; and, the type cannot be defined but only described.[15] As a consequence, the concept of 'group' is comparatively much more open and flexible compared to that of 'type'.

The group of rights is a model of the basis on which the rights are constructed. This marks a functional divergence from the type of rights. The clarification of the

---

[14] Article 38 of the Uniform Computer Information Transactions Act of the United States provides: 'Informational rights' include all rights in information created under laws governing patents, copyrights, mask works, trade secrets, trademarks, publicity rights, or any other law that gives a person, independently of contract, a right to control or preclude another person's use of or access to the information on the basis of the rights holder's interest in the information. See: Ruihua [10].

[15] Chen [11].

concept of rights is directed by the system for the application of legal rules and principles. Therefore, the concept of legal rights must be unclouded, explicit, accurate, standardized, and unified. Types of rights cannot generally be directly employed as a reference system for applicable laws. Its function is mainly to provide theoretical explanation and institutional guidance for the specific sub-rights under its type of rights. Consequently, compared with the specific concept of rights, the types of rights appear in the form of loose bundles of rights, open legal right structures, or macroscopic frameworks. For example, as a type of rights, intellectual property rights cannot be directly applicable as copyrights, trademark rights, or patent rights. Instead, its function is mainly to make the concepts of various intellectual property sub-rights theoretically consistent, thereby establishing a unified understanding system, and then providing a consistent institutional arrangement. The intellectual property right, as a type of rights, integrates its sub-rights in the sense of intellectual property protection. These sub-rights have temporal and regional characteristics. The existence of the types of rights provides not only an appropriate and unified explanation for these originally scattered concepts of specific legal rights, but also an ideal orientation for the institutional arrangements of these specific rights. Types of rights can be transformed from theory into practice by virtue of the institutionalization of the concepts of specific rights. To be sure, the formulation of the types of rights is not arbitrary. It comes not only from the generalization and sublimation of specific rights with certain common elements, but also from the limitation of legal order goals under specific values. The key to the way of thinking about the types of rights lies in the discovery of common typical factors from some specific rights concepts, the correlation between these typical factors, and the clues of value ideas behind them. In the context of legal development, the evolvement of types of rights is an important stage in the establishment of new rights systems and new legal systems. The type of rights as an open legal theoretical structure provides potential room for the development of rights. On the contrary, legal systems that lack types of rights are often scattered and unintelligent.

For various purposes, there are different definitions of types of rights, which are not, theoretically speaking, necessarily related to specific departmental laws. This purports that the same concepts of rights can be interpreted within the institutional frameworks of different types of rights. For instance, ownership can be explained within the framework of civil rights, private rights, and general human rights. These coexisting interpretation frameworks exist for different purposes and do not conflict with each other. Indisputably, a certain correlation between the types of rights is found in the context of a specific legal tradition and a specific legal system. They may form a system from a macro level to a micro level, or they may be parallel to each other instead of one being subordinate to the other. The purpose of the types of rights is to unify the concept of rights with common elements, making the legal rights system more understandable, comprehensible, and reasonable.

Regarding the connections between legal objects and the types of rights, Prof. Joseph Raz holds the view that people have certain types of rights vis-à-vis something or the actions of others. In some respects, 'the ownership of real property is different from the ownership of movable property… not only different types of rights (ownership, possession rights, etc.) must be distinguished, but also different types of legal subjects and objects.'[16] The information right is, first of all, a theoretical type of rights. It can provide an interpretation based on a new object of rights—information for the rights of intellectual property rights, the right to know, and the right to information privacy. Behind this interpretation is the historical requirement of the information society to treat information as an independent legal object, and it reflects a reasonable and clear definition of the rights of information in stimulating the creation and production of information and promoting its convenient circulation. In terms of value, all information rights are aimed at solving the tensions caused by the structural contradictions of information itself and the structural conflicts of the information society. Through the arrangements of rights, the amount of information is sufficiently rich and not excessive; the communication of information is convenient and not distorted; information production is sufficiently active without losing incentives; and the information space is broad enough to maintain proper distinctions between public and private domains. One core element of information rights is a specific legal object, that is, information that meets specific conditions. The exercise of rights is mainly to realize benefits arising from information through actions concerning information (including information production, collection, sorting, dissemination, and utilization). The characteristics of information actions are not only pertaining to the carrier of the actions, which are different from the aforementioned, but also the characteristics of the information actions themselves. Regarding the system advantages embodied by information rights as a type of rights, examples, including information property rights, are given as follows: Information property rights are a form of rights developed on the basis of intellectual property rights. As such, it generally presents the original characteristics of intellectual property rights. However, the concern is that the legal object of information property rights is not knowledge, or any result(s) of intellectual workings, but instead, information. Although information is intangible, it can be reproduced through its carriers and can spread through the reproduction of different carriers. Established on the same information content, multiple independent property rights can exist simultaneously, and information property rights can be realized across time and space. The characteristics of these rights can be understood only by means of taking a look into the specific meanings of information as the carrier of specific rights and can only be fully explained in the franchise of the new type of information rights. Only under the dominance of information rights, as a new type of rights, can the relevant information property rights system be institutionally consistent and in line with a higher level of unity in value orientation. Take 'the right to know' and the 'right to freedom of speech' as examples. Within the framework of the right to information, this relatively abstract concept of rights, which is aimed at restricting public powers, especially political powers, can be explained more specifically; the right to know is the right to access information; the right to freedom of speech is embodied in the right to publish and disseminate information. In the information society, considering it does not matter whether it is the right to know or the right to freely disseminate information, there is an implicit basis that

[16] Wu [12].

effective and adequate information circulation is an effective means of bolstering political civilization and social progress. In parallel, the right to information effectively transforms the right to know and the right to freedom of expression from an abstract form into a concrete form, which has a direct advantage when building a rights system. The existence of information types of rights can encompass new rights concepts such as information environment rights and information security rights and provides a legitimate basis for these new rights concepts. Therefore, as a type of rights, information rights can not only provide a sounder interpretation of the legal system and an institutional control for existing forms of rights, but it can also provide a rational argument for the creation of a new rights system in the setting of legal rights development.

3.2.4 Right to Information as Being Both Institutional and Explanatory

Traditional legal thought views law as an institutional system with the main purpose of establishing and maintaining order. The law is institutional and its rights are institutional and normative. The core purpose of legal studies, including those focused on legal rights, is to regulate social life and achieve specific legal goals. The practical nature of law means it is seen as a problem-solving technology, focused on "how to do it" rather than "why." This is why law has historically been excluded from science as a systematic endeavor that builds and organizes knowledge through testable explanations and predictions about the universe. The latter's main purpose is to explain the world, so legal science is considered more of a governance field.

This research holds the viewpoint that, in a general sense, law is truly of prescriptive and institutional nature, but, at the same time, it can also be explanatory just like other social sciences. Law is explanatory, which means that the basic concepts, principles, and methods of law are not only institutional norms that regulate the relations between legal subjects, but it can also be used to explain social phenomena and theoretical issues. Therefore, legal rights are not only institutional norms, but they also have explanatory functions. The interpretability of legal rights means not only that the theories and systems of legal rights relations could reflect out the causes of legal actions and social relations, but also that the types of rights abstracted for different purposes can be used as tools to explain specific rights systems and become the frameworks of institutional constructions.

For example, an intellectual property right as a type of right is a theoretical interpretation of trademark rights, copyrights, and patent rights. Intellectual property rights can explain the purpose(s) of copyright and other specific rights in general, namely, to stimulate intelligent creation, and provide general principles for the formulation of its system. Another example is the type of property rights, which can be used to provide explanations for the group of economic rights established for different tangible and intangible objects, which are not person-related. In reality, both ownership rights and other property rights are legal means by which the control and domination of properties can be carried out to pursue economic interests.

Theoretically speaking, the emergence of new types of rights occurs to satisfy the need for optimal explanatory power. 'For any explanatory theories, the appropriateness of explanation is the ultimate criterion ... There are two criteria for measuring the superiority of one explanation to another: first, a better explanation can encompass and explain more features of the phenomena to be studied; second, it can explain the other's theory, including its standpoints and shortcomings.'[17] Although, to some extent, the law has always been conservative, it still needs to be developed. Discovering and abstracting new types of rights is an important way for the development of the law per se. The motivation to seek the best explanation in theory has always been an inexhaustible driving force for legal development. Of course, any legal right cannot be merely an description at a theocratical level, it should also be something relate to the system, and must be institutionalized and standardized, in spite of the fact that the realization of this standardization cannot be made without the help of specific legal arrangements under the type of rights concerned. In addition, it should be noted that the meaningfulness of all theoretical types of rights often has an apparent purpose in the system setting and can reach a new harmonization of institutional norms in terms of function. For example, a private right is a more general type of right abstracted from civil rights. As a concept opposite to rights in public law, it provides an opportunity to understand the differences in concepts and systems between people's rights in a public setting and their rights in private setting. Private rights are characterized by autonomy, are self-governing, and are seen as the foundation of legal systems in civil society. Consequently, any rights systems governed by private rights ought to embody this spirit. Therefore, when thinking about a type of right, you need to take it into account the purpose behind it.

As a type of right with a sound explanatory function, information rights embrace the elements of the existing information-based rights. Moreover, information rights effectively place these elements in a brand-new environment as an information society for reflections, thereby enriching and developing these elements. The advantage arising from the explanatory function of information rights bolsters further the original types of rights and the reasonable elements of the concept of rights to a certain extent and unified these specific rights systems under the new goals of expanding information freedom and maintaining information order. As a new type of rights, information rights are both explanatory and institutional. They are embodied in form as an umbrella of rights formed by specific concepts of rights with specific information as the carrier (legal object); in essence, they reflect the tension between guaranteeing information freedom and establishing information order in the information society.

The existence of the types of information rights provides a new interpretation approach for some specific rights in theory; it also embodies the specific and clear trend of rights development in the system. Recognizing this new type of rights not only means that many complex legal relations in information society can be properly regulated, but also that a possible path can be found for the development of rights in the information society. As a new type of rights, information rights have creative

[17] Zhou [13].

and supplementary functions; on the premise of recognizing that information as the legal object of rights, new rights can be further developed, including for example, information environment rights and information security rights. At the same time, by making use of the flexibility and tolerance of information, new rights can emerge, for example, information property rights. By overlapping the functions of information rights and other types of rights in terms of interpretation, it is difficult to simply incorporate it into any branch of law according to the current divisions of legal fields. Information rights include both positive rights, for example information property rights, and negative rights, for example privacy rights and information security rights. It also includes both private rights, for example, information property rights and information privacy rights, and public rights, for example the right to know. These two types of information rights coexist. Individuals in a legal setting can be accorded information rights in the sense of both public rights and private rights at the same time, and can be empowered to seek legal remedies in both public law and private law.[18] Seeing information rights as only either public rights or private rights cannot bring forward a comprehensive interpretation of information rights.

It should be noted that since information rights are a type of rights, the rights system cannot function in good order without the assistance of specific sub-rights. Therefore, bolstering the legitimacy of information rights as a type of rights cannot be accomplished without both reasoning the individual sub-rights in the system or, theoretically, demonstrating that information that satisfies certain conditions can become the object of rights. Only by reasoning the sub-rights of information rights can the comprehensive essence of information rights be understood as a whole and a general understanding of information rights be reached.

[18] According to an episode (on September 12, 2003) of a well-known TV program by China Central Television entitled *Legal Report* (Jin Ri Shuo Fa), a manager of a steel-wire rope company for coal mines based in a county in Shaanxi Province discovered that the wall advertisement he commissioned to an advertising company for tens of thousands of dollars was tampered with by competitors based in the neighboring county. The competitors changed the address and contact phone number with their own. This resulted in a sharp drop in turnover of the aforementioned steel-wire rope company, causing serious losses. However, the Administrative Department for Industry and Commerce (ADIC) was competent merely to impose administrative penalties on owners who tampered with the contents of advertisements in accordance with the Advertising Law, the Anti-Unfair Competition Law and the Administrative Punishment Law, while the losses caused by illegal tampering with advertisements cannot be compensated. Even if a civil lawsuit is filed, what rights can the parties claim? There is no contractual relation between the parties, and it is difficult to find a legal basis in the civil rights system. However, this kind of tampering with information violates the completeness and accuracy of the information and causes false guidance. It violates not only the right of the advertising audience to know correct information, but also the protection of the advertising company and owners of advertisements to ensure that the information is true and accurate. This act of tampering violated the principle of equality, honesty, and credibility, and misled consumers, causing actual damage. This case presented that information rights can be of public law nature. Precisely speaking, they are viewed as rights protected by administrative law. Nevertheless, it disclosed the problems that there are only remedies arising from public law (advertising law, anti-unfair competition law). In cases of the infringement of information rights and remedies, especially economic compensations, cannot be exercised on a timely basis.

4 Individual Information Rights

4.1 *Information Property Rights*

4.1.1 Information Property Rights as the Result of In-Depth Intellectual Property Theory and System Expansion

Article 4 of the Individual Information Protection Law 2021 views Personal information as various information that is recorded electronically or by other means and is related to identified or identifiable natural persons. It does not include information that has been anonymized (Article 4). Alvin Toffler, an American sociologist, argues that while tangible properties such as land and machines are still necessary in the third wave of technological development, information has become the main form of property. Information property is viewed as the symbol of symbols, and the concept of property has changed accordingly.[19] Throughout human history, forms of property have become increasingly diverse, from tangible properties such as land and houses to intangible properties. The term "intellectual property" has become a common term for identifying intangible property rights. The rise of the knowledge economy and information society has led to a preference for the intellectual property system, resulting in its expansion despite its theoretical basis or capacity. This trend has expanded the theoretical and institutional space of intellectual property as a legal right but also highlighted its limitations. It is based on this recognition of limitations that the concept of information rights has emerged in the development of intellectual property, reflecting a process of reasoning for legal rights.

(1) *Rethinking the Theoretical Basis of Intellectual Property*

Legal object theories form the foundation of the intellectual property system. Currently, there are various opinions in the field of intellectual property regarding the subjects of intellectual property, including the intangible property theory, the intellectual property rights theory, the intellectual rights theory, and the information rights theory. The intangible property theory generally follows the legal-philosophical approach derived from the tangible property theory, particularly the property right theory in the civil law system. Although it appears logical, its theoretical basis is relatively weak. The main drawback of the intangible property theory is that it can only explain what intellectual property and its objects are not, not what they are. The advantages of intellectual achievement rights and the intellectual rights theory are that they go beyond traditional property law theories and propose that the legal object of intellectual property is distinct from tangible intellectual works or knowledge. However, concepts such as intellectual achievement and knowledge are abstract, presenting logical and institutional difficulties in developing an effective

---

[19] Cited from: Chen [11].

system based on them. Upon comparing the three concepts of intellectual achievement, knowledge, and information, it is found that information is superior in terms of explanatory effectiveness, inclusiveness, and operability.

Intellectual achievements refer to the results of human intellectual creation activities. Recognizing that humans, like other creatures, cannot exist without matter, energy, and information (basic elements from a modern physics viewpoint), these achievements can be seen as the result of the movements of the human brain and its interaction with the objective world. The "trace" produced from these interactions can be considered a form of information. Creativity is the key factor in intellectual achievements. Without creative work, merely copying and repeating existing information cannot be considered an intellectual achievement. As a result, trademarks, geographical indications, and other forms of information used to differentiate goods and services and reduce the cost of product selection, are considered lacking in creativity.

The claim that the legal object of intellectual property rights is knowledge demonstrates that the knowledge of objectively existing information is knowledge per se.[20] However, after careful analysis of this argument, it is not difficult to determine that it does not regard information as part of knowledge. Instead, it demonstrates that knowledge is part of information for the reason that it views information as an objective existence and, as a result, some can be recognized by humans and some cannot.

This demonstrates that information is broader than knowledge in terms of extension. It can be seen that the definition of knowledge by Peter Drucker, one of the most widely-known and influential thinkers on management, as a type of information, is arguable. This type of information can be the prerequisite for certain behaviors or actions. It can also make an individual (or an institution) engage in different and more effective behaviors to change something or to have an impact on someone. The distinction between knowledge and information is essential for a reasonable understanding of the legal objects of the intellectual property system. As an objectively existing concept of information, it has a broader extension than the concept of knowledge. Not only is knowledge part of information, but also information can be taken as the legal object of rights to provide more justification for the intellectual property system. It is helpful to understand the different goals of the two in the sense of theoretical instruments, that is, their existence can clarify their disparate nature. In essence, knowledge, as a concept, belongs to the epistemology and field of thinking, which aims to address the innovation and accumulation by human beings in terms of knowledge and practical ability. This concept is used as a way to understand the thinking process that occurs in the process of human cognition. Information is an objective existence. It is also the embodiment and carrier of knowledge activities. The value of information lies in understanding things by means of precise descriptions and making it possible for communications through media. All this above effectively provides resources and nourishment for knowledge creation and production. Objective knowledge is an integral part of information, and subjective knowledge can only be the object of subjective cognition because it cannot be expressed via a tangible

[20] Liu [15].

carrier, and cannot be clearly described or accurately controlled. As the legal object of rights, the concept of knowledge is, indeed, relatively too vague and has the strong nature of subjective cognition. It is difficult to use an objective and tangible carrier to definitively present it. As an objective existence, information can be reproduced via a tangible carrier, and the spread of meaning cannot be made without the help of media. Therefore, compared with knowledge in the sense of epistemology, information is more an object of rights.

With the advent of the knowledge economy and information society, the values of intellectual property, including inspiring the creation of intellectual works, can no longer meet the requirements of social progress for systematic change. In the context of the development of the information society, it is no longer enough to provide sufficient motivation for intellectual innovation and creation. Further provision of an abundant and orderly information legal environment for intellectual creation is require, that is, a legal system ensuring that intellectual work can obtain sufficient beneficial returns through the creation of rights. Moreover, it is required to ensure that intellectual creation activities will always have rich information resources and convenient and active information circulation conditions. Therefore, making use of intellectual achievements and knowledge to identify the intellectual property system obviously cannot meet the requirements of social development. Instead, it is essential to extend the scope of the legal object of intellectual property to encompass information. More critically, replacing intellectual property rights with information rights can meet the needs of social development for information resources, which are vital for intellectual creation and knowledge production.

4.1.2 Justification of Information Property Rights

Information property rights are the legal manifestations of various information products in the information society, encompassing the rights held by information owners over the results of their original intellectual work. These rights include intellectual property rights, related information rights, and other non-intellectual information rights. As such, traditional intellectual property rights cannot fully capture the essence of information property rights, with the latter being a broader concept that encompasses the former. This distinction in meaning and understanding necessitates a reevaluation of whether a new information property rights framework should be constructed, based on traditional intellectual property rights, to better suit the information society.[21]

---

[21] Chen Ying, in his article "The Conflict between Information Property Rights and the Connotation and Extension of Intellectual Property Rights," published in China Intellectual Property News in 2003, highlights two possible interpretations of information property rights. The broader interpretation encompasses all rights that a rights holder may possess concerning information, including both personal and property rights. In this context, information property rights can be seen as an expanded interpretation of intellectual property. On the other hand, the narrow interpretation of information property rights refers specifically to the property rights that a rights holder can establish over information. Since our discussion revolves around rights issues within the framework of

The theory of "information property rights" was first proposed in 1984 by Australian scholar Professor Michael Pendleton in his monograph The Law of Industrial and Intellectual Property in Hong Kong.[22] He elucidated the intrinsic connection and unity between traditional intellectual property rights and information property rights, interpreting patents as "technical information reflecting the depth of invention and creation," trademarks as "information enabling people to identify product marks in trade activities," and copyrights as "fixed and long-lasting forms of information." In 1987, Professor Chengsi Zheng provided a comprehensive discussion on information property rights in his book Legal Protection of Computers, Software, and Databases, which garnered attention in the international academic community.[23]

4.2 The Right to Information and the Right to Freedom of Expression as Information Rights

4.2.1 Right to Information

The process of reasoning behind the right to information,[24] from its inception to its broad application, serves as an excellent example of how this right has evolved and been widely applied. The right to information directly embodies the principles of autonomy and informed consent in information ethics. In a deeper sense, it is connected to democracy and the rule of law as a legal right to know.[25]

One of the fundamental principles of the rule of law is the knowability of the law. This means that the law must be public and accessible, not kept secret and monopolized by a select few. As the most typical form of public information, the law must be made available to everyone. Social subjects have the right to be informed about the implementation of legal provisions, and the right to know the law is a crucial aspect of the right to information. The rule of law is a system of governance based on rules. It requires not only that the rules themselves are open and knowable, but also that the application of the rules is transparent. Procedural principles further clarify the application of the rules, making them clear and transparent. The embodiment of procedural values requires a functional information circulation system where people

information rights, the term "information rights" captures all rights that a rights holder may have with respect to information. However, for the purpose of this analysis, we will focus on the narrow aspects of information property rights, that is, property rights concerning information.

[22] Pendleton [16].

[23] See Zheng [17].

[24] The right to information can be broadly or narrowly defined. In a broad sense, it refers to the right of citizens to access and receive information about all aspects of social life, including consumer rights, the workings of state power organs, and the election process. In a narrow sense, it is the right of citizens to access government work and affairs. The right to information is often discussed as a fundamental human right and a fundamental political and economic right. It generally refers to the right of social subjects to know and access relevant information.

[25] Regarding the information ethics, please see: Li [18].

can exchange ideas and reach agreements. The right to information ensures that information is easily obtainable and effectively controlled, making it a necessary means of ensuring the transparency of procedures. By promoting transparency and accountability, the right to information helps to uphold the principles of the rule of law and protect the rights of citizens.

Democratic principles form the cornerstone of modern politics, which is based on acknowledging the choices made by the majority. However, to make an informed, independent decision, a comprehensive understanding of relevant information is crucial. Without access to information, independent and rational judgment is impossible, leading to blind and arbitrary choices or mere repetition. Democracy is a system of self-governance,[26] and the public must equip itself with the power of acquired knowledge if it wants to be in control. If the government fails to provide sufficient information to the public or if the public doesn't have access to clear information channels, the idea of a transparent government becomes a farce, tragedy, or comedy.[27] It is the responsibility of any state that claims to be democratic to provide adequate information guarantees for the exercise of democratic rights. Without openness, democracy cannot exist. If democratic rights are only written into law and information is effectively blocked, monopolized, and distorted, such politics cannot be considered democratic. The right to information is fundamental to democracy. In this regard, Stiglitz believes that participants in the democratic process can only participate meaningfully if they are fully informed. On the other hand, secrecy reduces the quality and quantity of information available to the public, hindering public participation. Therefore, there can be no genuine democracy or rule of law without the right to information.

Stiglitz argues that the right to information is justified from the perspective of property economics. He believes that the public, who have paid for the collection of government information through taxes and other means, should benefit from this information just as they own government facilities such as tables, chairs, and buildings. Today, the importance of intellectual property is widely recognized, and information generated, collected, and processed by governments is considered as valuable as patentable inventions. Therefore, using public information property rights as private property is no different from misappropriating other public property for private use.[28] Moreover, Stiglitz asserts that the public pays for information and that government officials who use it for personal gain or to present a positive image, are committing theft just as they would if they were stealing other public property. While the need for collective action is understood, individuals have the fundamental right to understand how power works in the context of collective action. In summary, Stiglitz's argument emphasizes that the right to information is not just a moral principle, but also a matter of property rights, and that the public has the right to benefit from the information generated through their collective investment.

---

[26] Cohen and Rogers [19].

[27] Padover [20].

[28] Stiglitz [21].

The right to information is often seen as an implicit contract between the governed and the ruler. Property rights, which are considered private rights, are deemed equal and subject to the law of equal exchange.[29] While the right to information is typically viewed as a political right under public law, some argue that it can be seen as a property right. This perspective reflects the evolution of the liberal concept of rights, which has progressed from private rights to public rights centered on private rights. According to the public choice theory, the lack of the right to know can cause harm, and disclosing government information to protect this right benefits the public interest. Secrecy, on the other hand, can serve the hidden interests and demands of government officials and interest groups. Making more information public can enable people to make more informed judgments about government actions. Secrecy can breed corruption and undermine public trust in democracies. The scarcity of information, like other artificial scarcities, can lead to rent-seeking behavior.[30]

In this regard, Stiglitz argues that secrecy in information leads to a decrease in active public participation in the democratic process, as many voters are no longer able to pursue their own interests. As a result, media and public opinion cannot form a healthy check and balance mechanism to prevent government abuse of power. Moreover, secrecy in information also leads to a reduction in the quality of decision-making, as the government limits decision-makers to a small circle to keep information confidential. This creates a vicious cycle, where the government's decision-making errors increase, leading to fear of responsibility among officials and self-protective behavior, causing more information to be kept secret. This, in turn, leads to a smaller circle of decision-makers and further deterioration in the quality of decision-making.[31]

The principles of information economics demonstrate that better quality and timely information can lead to more efficient allocation of resources in the market. As the information industry continues to evolve, more employees are involved in collecting, processing, and disseminating information. Ironically, these employees often seek to collect and publish information that should be made public by government agencies, but is kept secret. The government's monopoly on information is not beneficial for the allocation of market resources and hinders the vitality of the market.[32] Under the guise of secrecy, individual rights are frequently violated. Therefore, it is important to establish a culture of openness where all information held by public officials belongs to the public and using it for personal gain is equivalent to stealing public property. The drive for secrecy often stems from the desire to conceal the actions of interest groups.[33] Sharing information between government departments and between the government and the public can reduce the costs of repeated information collection, organization, and editing, while also greatly improving decision-making and behavior selection efficiency. It can fundamentally

[29] See Stiglitz [21].

[30] Yu [22].

[31] See Stiglitz [21].

[32] See Stiglitz [21].

[33] Stiglitz [21].

improve the organizational mode of public power organs, making the traditional image of the high-ranking manager approachable in networked information exchange and enhancing the government's credibility.

In most societies, government information is the most authoritative and efficient source of information for the entire society. It serves as the foundation for ensuring the truthfulness, security, and orderly management of information resources throughout society. Government information is generated, obtained, preserved, collated, utilized, and disseminated by government agencies in the performance of their duties. This information includes legal and normative documents, administrative procedures, and social information such as statistical data, information on epidemics and disasters, population flow information, resource usage status, and industrial structure information. Government agencies also collect and collate information about individuals, operators, and social organizations during official activities. Some of this information is disclosed to the public, providing basic information and source material for social activities such as general social information, industrial and commercial registration, property rights transfer, and transfer registration. The information that should be disclosed pertains to the public's general right to know.

If government information is inadequate, late, or incorrect, it can increase the cost of acquiring information for the public, making it difficult to obtain effective or even accurate information. This can have far-reaching consequences, from affecting national macro decision-making to hindering the public's ability to make informed choices, resulting in economic chain reactions. For example, if the Ministry of Industry and Commerce reports false asset values for a company, it can make it difficult for companies with which it has established economic relations to assert their claims, leading to chain debts. In some social crises, the failure to protect the right to information can also lead to rumors and social chaos, as demonstrated by the 2003 SARS outbreak in China.

The other aspect of government information is kept confidential to protect state secrets and personal privacy. However, even this information is related to the right to know. Government-collected information that may influence its behavior towards the public or impact the judgment of others about the public should be disclosed to the source of the information. This allows individuals to verify the accuracy of their personal files, and companies to access accurate punishment records of government agencies. The right to information should be exercised by the person concerned, and government agencies should provide reasonable procedures to ensure that parties have access to this information and can initiate review procedures when they object to the legality and authenticity of the information. If a person's right to information is not protected in accordance with the law, they can seek judicial remedies.

In Western countries, such as the United States, the right to know is a fundamental principle rooted in democracy and the rule of law, often referred to as freedom of information. In the US, the Freedom of Information Act of 1966 requires federal government agencies to disclose government information, with the principle being that open government information is the norm and non-disclosure is the exception. This means that citizens have the right to access and use information from a variety of sources, including government archives, libraries, media outlets, and scientific research institutes. The Act recognizes that most archives in the possession of the federal government can be examined and photocopied by anyone, with a few exceptions. These exceptions include documents relating to national defense, foreign policy, investigative files carried out in accordance with the law, private information, trade secrets, and secrets protected by other statutes. If a government authority unjustifiably refuses to release a document, affected individuals can file a lawsuit in federal court. In addition to the Freedom of Information Act, the Government in the Sunshine Act sets information disclosure obligations for the government and protects privacy issues involved in information disclosure through the Privacy Act.[34] This ensures that the right to know is effectively protected and promotes the efficiency of government work. Countries around the world have adopted "freedom of information" as a legal term to protect citizens' right to know and set information disclosure obligations for the government. For example, France (1978), the Netherlands (1978), Canada (1983), Australia (1983), New Zealand (1983), and the United Kingdom (2000) have enacted Freedom of Information Acts. Other countries, such as Finland, Norway, Denmark, Ireland, and Japan, have also adopted information disclosure laws, such as the Information Disclosure Act in Japan, to protect the public's right to know. Some Nordic countries and Canada have also created a special "Information Commissioner" position to help federal courts deal with disputes over access to information. These laws typically include important information, such as scientific and technological information, national condition information, epidemic information, disaster information,

[34] In 1974, the Privacy Act was enacted to regulate how US administrative agencies handle personal records. The law requires that personal records be disclosed to individuals and restricts disclosure to third parties. Along with the Freedom of Information Act, it falls under the Administrative Disclosure Law. However, there are some key differences between the two laws. The Privacy Act applies only to personal records, while the Freedom of Information Act applies to all government records. The Privacy Law focuses on protecting citizens' personal privacy, while the Freedom of Information Act focuses on protecting the public's right to know. The Privacy Act seeks to restrict the availability of certain government documents, whereas the Freedom of Information Act seeks maximum openness of government documents. Despite their close relationship, the two laws are independent of each other in application. When it comes to the disclosure of personal records systems by administrative organs, both laws apply. However, if a document is exempt from disclosure under one law, it does not necessarily mean that it is exempt under the other law. For example, an administrative agency cannot rely on the exemption from disclosure in the Freedom of Information Act to refuse to provide an individual with documents available to them under the Privacy Act. Similarly, administrative organs may not rely on the provisions of the Privacy Law to refuse to provide publicly available documents under the Freedom of Information Act. The Freedom of Information Act is compatible with other laws that prohibit the disclosure of a document. When the public requests documents from administrative agencies under the Freedom of Information Act or the Privacy Act, and the administrative organ refuses to provide it, exemption from disclosure can only be relied upon by the Act itself. The Freedom of Information Act and the Privacy Act effectively balance the rights of individuals. The right to privacy defines the scope of the right to information, while the right to information provides a reverse constraint on the right to privacy. These rights define and depend on each other. It is this reciprocal setting of rights that makes the boundaries of rights clearer and avoids abuse of rights. Thus, a reasonable power structure is constructed. Concerns have been raised about the conflict of rights between the right to information and privacy. However, when viewed from the opposite angle, this conflict pushes the boundaries of rights and clarifies the essence of each individual right.

and emergencies, in the scope of information that should be known to the public, with a corresponding disclosure system in place.

Of course, the right to information is not limited to the political sphere. Extending democratic principles from political life to the economic and cultural spheres means that the right to information extends to these areas as well. Democracy is based on trust in humanity, respect for the legitimate choices of each individual, and rejection of the oppression of free will by power. In economic life, however, the existence of dominant groups presents a threat to democratic principles. Large corporations have distinct advantages, including information superiority, as providers of goods and services. If they distort information and exaggerate propaganda, consumers will not be able to make rational decisions. In line with democratic principles, consumers are rational subjects and have the right to make independent decisions about the goods and services they need based on the availability of true and sufficient information. As a result, the right of consumers to information has become an essential requirement for extending democratic principles to economic life. Culturally, democratic principles require audiences to have the right to information, especially between the mass media and the public. This ensures that cultural choices align with the true wishes of the audience. The right to know for consumers, patients, small and medium-sized shareholders, and job seekers are all outcomes of advocating for democratic principles in information issues. As the state retreats in certain areas of social governance, some public organizations, industry associations, and large enterprises have taken on the role of state agents and autonomous social organizers, thereby concentrating information in the economic and social fields. To balance the interests of both the strong and the weak in society, it is important to maintain a necessary level of vigilance against their information superiority.

4.2.2 The Right to Freedom of Expression

Article 19 of the 1948 United Nations Universal Declaration of Human Rights provides legal protection for the right to freedom of expression. This right encompasses the freedom to hold opinions, seek, receive, and impart information and ideas, and express one's opinions through meaningful information and symbols. However, if an individual only holds an opinion internally and does not express it, it does not have the characteristics of a legal act and falls under the purely spiritual realm. Freedom of expression includes both freedom of speech and freedom of the press, with the main focus being the freedom to gather, publish, and impart information. The legitimacy of the right to freedom of expression is based on the "free market doctrine of ideas," where truth emerges from a free exchange of ideas. Judge Hand also believed that the wisdom of the crowd is more likely to lead to the correct conclusion than any authoritative decision.[35] Freedom of speech, expression, and the press are essential civil liberties and closely linked to freedom of thought, morality, and religion. Without the opportunity to express thoughts, the freedom to hold thoughts

[35] Dworkin [23].

becomes meaningless. Therefore, the right to freedom of expression is crucial for the development and maintenance of democratic societies.[36]

The public nature of information dissemination, along with its ease of access, makes it prohibitively expensive to curb the free flow of information through laws. Throughout history, political power has often been afraid of the right to freedom of expression, fearing that the spread of unfavorable information will undermine political stability. However, once information is objectified and symbolized, its diffusion becomes almost inevitable, and it is futile to try to prevent its spread artificially. For example, in 17th-century England, the Constellation Court tried to block newspaper publication, and in Nazi Germany, many books were burned, and speech that was different from the government was strictly forbidden. Despite these efforts, information continued to be transmitted through various informal and secret channels. In the information age, the development of network-represented information media and the independence of information technology make it difficult for any organization to achieve comprehensive and effective control of information. People can now obtain information through multiple channels and provide feedback on it in the form of interactive information, communicating with others without barriers. Blindfolding and gagging people's mouths is no longer possible, and the operating logic of contemporary politics and economics is no longer one-way domination but two-way interaction. Democratic political governance must listen to people's judgments based on rational analysis of information, not stifle people's minds through information blockades. The internet, a new interactive medium, has become a stage where the right to freedom of expression truly triumphs. On the network, the voices of countless people converge into a deafening roar. Netizens' centralized feedback on a piece of information not only reflects public opinion and sentiment but also makes democratic demands almost ubiquitous. Online surveys have become an essential source of news media, an important part of official statistics, and can even directly affect legislation. For example, the 2003 tragedy of Sun Zhigang, who was beaten to death at a Guangzhou custody and repatriation station, sparked a wave of criticism on the internet about the custody and repatriation system. This eventually led to the banning of the unreasonable system and its replacement with a humane vagrant rescue system.

The concept of freedom of expression and information can be better understood in the context of the right to information. In essence, the right to express oneself and disseminate information is realized through the objectification of ideas and opinions into symbolic information that can be made public through various channels. The object of the right to freedom of expression is information that has an objective form, can be transmitted, and has meaning that can be understood. As such, freedom of expression can be understood through the lens of the right to information, which extends to freedom of information dissemination. The right to freedom of information dissemination provides a more objectified basis for defining, realizing, and remedying rights compared to the vaguer concepts of the object of the right to freedom of expression, which are ideas and opinions. It also extends the scope of the right

[36] Bogdanor [24].

beyond the realm of politics and allows for its application in other spheres of social life such as the economy and culture.

Incorporating the right to freedom of information dissemination into the information rights matrix can help us build a more reasonable rights structure system by analyzing the relationship between different types of information rights. These rights are interrelated and form a chain, where the right to freedom of expression is a key link. The construction of the information rights chain and the entire process of information generation, sending, transmission, and reception have an intrinsic logical connection and objective regularity. The right to freedom of expression is closely related to the right to send and disseminate information and determines the degree of realization of the public's right to know. It is also closely related to the right to freedom of thought and academic freedom.[37] The right to freedom of expression determines the value and form of information. Once information is known to others through free expression, it becomes challenging to control the channels and scope of dissemination. Additionally, the right to freedom of expression is closely related to other rights, such as the right to privacy, the right to assembly and association, and the right to vote. In some cases, the process of realizing certain rights is a form of free expression, such as the right to vote.

However, based on the special nature of these rights, general legislation separates them from the right to freedom of expression for protection in the form of lex specialis. In fact, these special protections are the detailed regulations of the conduct involved in the expression of specific information.

The right to freedom of expression in the sense of the right to information demonstrates the contemporary understanding of freedom of expression in the information society. Traditional freedom of expression pays more attention to the content of expression, while the right to freedom of expression as an information right focuses on the way of expression and dissemination of information in an all-encompassing manner, and aims to achieve protection of freedom of expression by clarifying possible legal protection methods and removing barriers in the dissemination process. The focus of controversy in many contemporary freedom of expression cases is not only on the legality of the expression's content (i.e., the information), but also on debates surrounding the legality of expression methods and information dissemination methods. The right to freedom of information dissemination includes not only the right to publish ideas in the form of information and make them public, but also the right to disseminate them through various information networks. Ideas and concepts are easily transformed into information, and this information is more widely disseminated.[38] The information age is an era of "crowding gold and destroying bones," and ideas are spread at high speed through efficient information media in the symbolic space. People need to express themselves freely and convert their ideas into information symbols while demanding wider dissemination through different

[37] Chen [25].

[38] Questions have arisen regarding the legality of certain forms of expression, such as burning the flag or displaying a placard in one's garden that denies the Holocaust. It is important to determine whether these forms of expression are legal or not.

media, especially computer networks, for far-reaching impact. The focus of freedom of expression has shifted from traditional fields like press freedom and freedom of the press to a broader space for information dissemination. It is no longer just concerned with media, professional journalists, and political and business people and organizations. The network has broken the dependence on traditional media like newspapers and books, fully liberating public information expression and dissemination. This makes the general public's right to freedom of expression the focus and challenge in rights protection.

Balancing interests and protecting rights in a highly developed and fast information technology environment requires considering the characteristics of freedom of expression as an information right. It starts by defining the object of the right—information—and regulating the methods and channels of information generation, publication, and dissemination. The first issue in the institutional setting of freedom of expression is the content, scope, and exceptions of information protected by this right. This may include political information (political views, opinions on political events, etc.), economic and commercial information (business conditions, economic events, etc.), and art and ideas. Political expression is the strongest in the protection of freedom of expression worldwide due to its importance in democratic societies. Ideological and artistic expression and business messages are weaker. The content of information protected by freedom of expression should adhere to the principle of "harmlessness," meaning it does not conflict with the public interest, national security, and the legitimate rights of others. Illegal exposure of state secrets, personal privacy, trade secrets, promoting apartheid, hatred, fascism, xenophobia, racism, and information on obscenity, pornography, violence, etc. is not protected by freedom of expression. It is not necessary for the information expressed to be completely correct or accepted by the majority. The second issue is regulating the manner and method of expression. Laws should restrict harmful forms of expression and specify legal means of expression like print media, radio and television, film, painting, leaflets, banners, and slogans. The means of expression should be coordinated with the time, place, and occasion of expression and limit violence, offensive or immoral acts, and other illegal expressions. Finally, those responsible for infringing on the right to freedom of expression should bear legal responsibility, and victims of infringement should have access to remedies.

4.3 The Right to Information Relating to Personal and Personal Interests

4.3.1 Information Privacy Rights

The right to privacy is one of the basic rights of citizens that should be guaranteed in a society ruled by law. In the past, the existence of privacy was mainly reflected in private living spaces isolated from the public sphere and private acts and private lives that had nothing to do with the public interest. The destruction of privacy is also mainly reflected in the invasion of private living space and interference with the freedom of individual action and life. For example, the mass media's reporting and dissemination of personal privacy behavior, the illegal monitoring and tracking of personal space by public power, and the illegal dissemination of other people's private information.

In the information society, an individual's ability to control information not only determines their position in society but also affects the maintenance of their personality and dignity. The right to information privacy has become an important manifestation of privacy in the information society. This means that the protection of private information has become the top priority of privacy protection, and personal information exists in various forms, such as personal credit information, genetic information, medical history information, marriage history information, personal telephone call records, emails, personal image information left in ubiquitous monitoring devices, and so on.

The infringement of privacy is achieved by illegally acting on private information, and it is difficult for the privacy information protection system to play a role when the law has not given private information an independent status. With the in-depth development of the privacy system, the protection of private information has an expanding trend. Personal data protection laws developed from the legal system of privacy have included more personal information in the scope of protection. Law is an institutional copy of the times, and the expansion trend of privacy protection is a dynamic response of the legal system to the crisis of privacy protection in the information society.

Understanding the right to information privacy from the perspective of information rights refers not only to the personality rights to private information, but also to the rights to private activities and private spaces that have been informationized in the information society. People in the information society have both a biological existence and an information existence, and their private activities and private spaces also have an information form. Hence, the right to information privacy includes the personality rights to these informationized private activities and spaces.

Due to the widespread use of recording equipment, people are increasingly recording their private activities in the form of information. As a result, more and more human activities have image information copies, and the privacy protection of personal activities must extend to these copies. At the same time, the abuse of private activities is increasingly being carried out through information, making it necessary to use technology to stop these abuses.

The comprehensive informatization of the social structure has also led to the emergence of private information spaces, such as personal computers, personal emails, network private chat rooms, and private telecommunications spaces. These private information spaces provide new opportunities for invasions of privacy, and violations of privacy are spreading to these personal information spaces. Invasion of private computers and personal network mailboxes, snooping and recording of personal activity information, and the dissemination of these personal privacy information, have resulted in a new privacy protection crisis. The recent reports of the "cell phone surveillance master" alone are shocking and highlight the need for better protection of privacy.[39] Setting protection for private information spaces is an urgent need to solve the privacy crisis in the information society. With the widespread use of internet applications, online privacy concerns have become a pressing issue. In 2001, Enonymous.com and PC Data jointly released a comprehensive report on online privacy. The report showed that 22,000 out of 30,000 websites had no measures in place to protect user privacy. A Washington-based privacy research firm, EPTC, found that 86% of the online companies tested used software programs known as "privacy spying" to collect personal information.

Individuals are often unaware of their personal information being used without permission and lack the means to prevent it. Litigation is also expensive. The current situation of online information privacy protection is not promising. A 2006 report by the China Internet Network Information Center (CNNIC) showed that 45.4%, 19.3%, and 7.2% of the 111 million mainland Chinese netizens were dissatisfied with privacy protection. The report listed privacy leaks during internet usage as one of the main objections of netizens.[40]

4.3.2 Personal Data Rights

Today, biotechnology has made it possible to create a complete reproduction of a person by recording their genetic information, physical characteristics, and internal biological structure.[41] People's "information existence" encompasses not just biological information, but also social and cultural information, such as religious beliefs, ethnicity, work experience, marriage history, political leanings, consumption habits, and so on. In the information age, nearly all human activities leave a record in the form of information, resulting in a comprehensive representation of a person. This "information existence" gives a dual meaning to the human body and also provides a new form of expression for spiritual and intellectual aspects beyond the physical body.

t the end of the twentieth century, a legal system specializing in the protection of personal information emerged to more effectively safeguard personal interests arising from the existence of information based on individuals. Personal information

---

[39] The "Mobile Listener King" is an electronic device that allows the user to pre-implant a set of phone numbers into the monitor. Once a phone number is entered, the device can intercept and store the voice of the call according to the program. It has a recording time of up to 20 hours or more.

[40] See China Internet Network Information Center (CNNIC) [26].

[41] In 2002, the first digital data collection of the human body in China was completed. The study involved integrating cross-sectional data from thousands of individuals into a computer to reconstruct a three-dimensional image of the human body. Using a computer, it is now possible to reproduce the data and images of the "visual person" that was collected. The resulting digital "visual human" is incredibly realistic, with muscles, bones, blood vessels, nerves, and internal organs appearing clearly on the computer monitor. Arteries and veins are distinguished by their red and blue colors. This achievement represents a significant milestone in Chinese digital imaging technology. available at: http://edu.beelink.com.cn/20021025/1229913.shtml, 2010-04-18.

encompasses all data and information about an individual, including information generated by the individual, such as name, gender, age, blood type, health status, height, weight, address, marital status, family members, social relationships, work, position, degree, birthday, income, hobbies, etc. and information not generated by the individual, mainly evaluations by others, such as credit ratings given by banks. The purpose of using personal information is to "identify" an individual and distinguish them from others. Personal information and privacy protection information have similarities and differences. There is overlap in the content of the two, but private information mainly refers to information that individuals do not want to disclose to the outside world, such as family life or sensitive information, or information that they do not want others to know, such as height.

Information privacy focuses on protecting the private information space of individuals. Of course, the scope of this space is related to social and public cognition, as well as personal sensitivity. The concept of personal information, on the other hand, focuses on "identification," that is, the independent recognition of an individual through personal information.[42] The concept of personal information has expanded beyond the definition of private information. For instance, the UK's Data Protection Act defines personal information as "data about a living person that can be used to identify them and includes an assessment of the individual." The EU Data Protection Regulation views personal data as "any information about an identified or identifiable individual." Proposed amendments to the 1992 Council Data Protection Regulation of the Council of Europe define personal data even more broadly, encompassing not only information in a formal form, but also personal information of deceased individuals.[43]

The legal protection of personal information, particularly personal data and privacy, demonstrates that the personal rights system in the information age has taken on a new form. The aim of this protection is to prevent the improper use of personal information for commercial or other purposes, preserving personal life and ensuring the healthy growth of e-commerce.

Even commentators who support the property rights model to protect the right to privacy have to admit that the prevalence of network technology poses a great challenge to protecting personal information privacy. The fundamental problem is not just a simple dispute such as "who owns the information," but the use of digital technology has changed the way individuals understand and perceive themselves and has had a profound effect on the interaction between individuals and groups. Ultimately, the key to untangling the relationship between digital technology and personal information privacy lies in our view of both the individual and society.[44] Moreover, protecting privacy through privatizing information may create confusion

[42] For instance, Section 1 of the German Federal Personal Data Protection Act 2 states that "personal information" refers to all information related to an identifiable natural person. Similarly, Taiwan's Law on the Protection of Personal Data Processed by Computer Processing (1978) and France's Data Protection Act state that the purpose of personal information is to "identify" an individual. Du and Tang [27].

[43] See Zhu and Yang [28].

[44] Post [29]. See also Unger [30].

between two legal rights and even run the risk of dissolving the right to privacy with property rights. Currently, the international community has rich legislative and judicial experience in information privacy protection and has provided valuable experience for reference in the protection of personal information and network privacy. This provides a basis for comparison and reference in the development of China's information privacy protection.[45]

4.4 *The Right to Information Environment and Information Security*

As an objective phenomenon, information has inherent structural contradictions, including "the contradiction between the objective independence of information and its dependence on media," "the contradiction between the exclusivity and sharing of information," "the conflict between the fidelity and distortion in the dissemination of information," and "value judgments of 'good' and 'evil' based on different value judgments of the information being disseminated." When analyzing the interests related to information, it becomes clear that its positive value is not absolute and that information can bring wealth and satisfaction but can also result in negative factors such as information pollution, information security crises, and other indirect or direct damages. This leads to a new value crisis and harm to interests, causing a new imbalance in the social interest structure. To mitigate these information damages, it is necessary to detect them and use legal rights to reduce or avoid them.

---

[45] Here are some legal references for the direct protection of the right to privacy. In the United States, the Privacy Act was established in 1974; Canada also has the Privacy Act of 1982. In Germany, the interpretation of Paragraph 1 of Article 823 of the Civil Code of 1954 provides direct legal protection for privacy. France implemented the No. 70-643 law on July 11, 1970, which added Article 9 to the Civil Code providing for privacy protection, stating that "everyone has the right to inviolability of his or her personal life." After World War II, Japan revised its civil code and established "personal dignity and substantive equality between the sexes" as the highest standards for the interpretation of civil law, which includes the right to privacy. In terms of the protection of personal data, the following legislation can be referred to: the German Data Protection Act of 1976; France's personal data protection laws passed in 1978; the EU Directive on the Protection of Individuals in the Processing of Personal Data and on Their Free Movement of 1995; the EU Directive on the Protection of Electronic Communications Data of 1996; the Electronic Data Protection Act of 2002; the Italian Personal Data Protection Act of 1996; the UK Data Protection Act of 1984; and the Personal Information Protection and Electronic Documents Act enacted by the Government of Canada in October 1998. As for the protection of internet information privacy, the following legislation can be referred to: the Electronic Communications Privacy Act of 1986 in the United States; the Information and Communication Services Act promulgated in Germany in 1997; the EU's adoption of the General Principles of Personal Data Protection in 1999; the Directive on the Protection of the Operation and Free Movement of Personal Data of 1995; the First Directive on the Transfer of Personal Data to Third Countries—Possible Ways of Assessing Adequacy of 1997; and the Directive on the Protection of Personal Data Collection and Transmission on the Information Superhighway of 1999.

4.4.1 Information Environment Rights

Since the information revolution, "the problem of the social information environment has become increasingly prominent and has become a global issue. This is mainly manifested in the widening of the information gap, the imbalance in the distribution of information resources, and the imbalance in information circulation. Additionally, there is information flooding, serious information pollution, the intensification of information barriers, an increase in information crime, and a heightened global conflict over information. The battle for control of information is also intense."[46] In the vast amount of information, there is a considerable amount of false, outdated, redundant, excessive, and harmful information, including dirty, harassing, and defective information. This type of information is not only worthless to people but can also harm the information ecology, causing the destruction of the entire information environment and the pollution of the information ecosystem. The term "information ecology" refers to the sum of the information environment that is crucial for human survival and development, while the "information environment" specifically refers to the conditions created by the exchange of information between individuals, organizations, and the individuals and organizations that center around specific people or organizations. The destruction of the information ecology results from an imbalance in the various systems, links, and factors that make up the information environment that is crucial for human survival and development. The pollution of the information environment is caused by harmful and defective information, introduced by human factors, which can damage the environment and have negative effects on people's information lives. This type of pollution is similar to environmental pollution and is caused by short-term actions that can harm people's physical and mental health. Once the information environment is polluted, it is difficult to recover, which will seriously affect the sustainability of the information society. Information pollution not only limits people's information choices but also poses a threat to social security and order by misleading, inducing, and abetting information. It can be seen that information pollution damages both individuals and society. Controlling information pollution is a long-term and ongoing task, much like controlling environmental pollution.

Information pollution refers to the act of causing harm to others through the creation or dissemination of false or harmful information. The control of information pollution can be achieved through laws that prohibit its occurrence. This also gives injured parties and potential victims the right to a safe information environment, free from illegal information pollution. The damage caused by information pollution can be categorized into two types: defective information damage and harmful information damage. Defective information damage refers to moral and economic harm caused to others by intentional or accidental creation and dissemination of false, duplicate, outdated, harassing, or irrelevant information. On the other hand, harmful information damage refers to the creation and dissemination of information with undesirable content, such as pornography, violence, incitement of crime, terrorism, extremism,

[46] Lin [31].

incitement of separatism, cults, endangering national security, leaking state secrets, computer viruses, or other damaging information.

The dissemination of harmful information can be used for economic gain, such as distributing pornographic content to attract internet users, or for the purpose of seeking excitement or for illegal activities that threaten the stability of the state and society. The negative information presents a serious threat to national and social interests, individual and organizational rights, corrupts social customs, and leads to criminal activity, hence it is subject to legal restrictions and enforcement. The harm caused by such information to people's physical and mental health has been confirmed through sociological surveys, such as the 1982 publication of "Television and Behavior: A Decade of Scientific Progress and Its Impact on the Eighties" by the National Institute of Mental Health. This publication summarizes 2,500 independent studies and finds that there is a direct link between television violence and aggressive behavior, heavy TV viewers are more timid, apprehensive, and untrustworthy than light TV viewers, and children who watch pro-social shows are more likely to exhibit responsible behavior.[47] In real life, the problems of mental illness and crime among teenagers resulting from browsing pornographic websites and making pornographic voice calls demonstrate that exposure to harmful information can harm people's physical and mental health.

Compared to harmful information, people's awareness of defective information is far from adequate. Defective information doesn't directly cause obvious physical or mental harm, unlike harmful information. Thus, its effects often go unnoticed until later. However, this doesn't mean that the damage caused by defective information should be ignored. False information within defective information can lead to incorrect behavioral decisions, resulting in direct economic losses and missed opportunities. Furthermore, redundant, repetitive, outdated, and valueless information not only wastes time but also occupies a large amount of storage space, causing information transmission systems to become congested or even paralyzed and causing significant economic losses. A prime example of defective information pollution is the current flood of spam on the Internet.[48] In August 1985, the world's first recorded junk email appeared. Since then, spam has plagued email users. According to statistics, there are currently about 1.4 billion emails sent and received daily worldwide, with more than 10% being spam. In China, over 50% of the sent and forwarded spam is processed by mail servers. A survey in December 2002 showed that Chinese netizens received an average of 7.7 normal emails and 8.3 spam messages per week. By July 2003, the average number of normal emails per week had dropped to 7.2, while the number of spam messages had increased to 8.9. This resulted in a ratio of spam to normal emails increasing from 108:100 to 124:100. Internationally, ISPs

---

[47] Biagi [32].

[48] The Anti-Spam Specification of the Internet Society of China defines spam as follows: "An email that includes the following attributes: First, the recipient has not requested or agreed to receive promotional emails such as advertisements, electronic publications, and various forms of publicity materials in advance. Second, email messages that recipients cannot reject. Third, emails that hide information about the sender's identity, address, header, and more. Fourth, email messages with fake information about sources, senders, routing, and more."

such as AOL, Yahoo, and Hotmail already account for over half of the emails they manage.[49] Due to the absence of effective technical measures, the proliferation of spam has resulted in a massive waste of network resources, affecting the normal functioning of the internet and infringing upon the personal rights of users. The Anti-Spam Act, enacted in 2004, was the first legislation aimed at regulating spam since the emergence of the internet, and has had a significant impact on the daily lives of many people. The act aims to reduce spam by specifying and limiting the manner in which it is sent and received, effectively giving email recipients the legal right to refuse to receive it. This right to refuse spam is a fundamental right to control one's information environment. Anti-spam legislation represents a major milestone in the development of legislation protecting information environmental rights.

Bad and defective information consume a significant portion of information space, and identifying this information requires a lot of human effort, contributing to the already severe problem of information overload. According to calculations by Frederick, a scholar of American studies, the total amount of information in human society doubled approximately every 1500 years since the first year of the Common Era. In the 1990s, the amount of human information doubled annually. At this rate, by 2025, the rate of information growth is expected to double every month, no longer on an annual basis. On February 13, 2006, Google, the largest search engine, had indexed over 8 billion pages (according to Google's homepage). However, with current search technology, no search engine can cover more than 60% of Internet pages, highlighting the enormity of information available on the Internet. In the face of massive information, people struggle to collect information comprehensively and effectively identify relevant information, which also requires effort to sort through repetitive and false information. The existence of information overload leads to individuals being overwhelmed by the sea of information and spending time and effort screening and selecting information. Excessive information can cause mental diseases such as information phobia, anxiety, and allergy, and physical diseases such as decreased vision and increased blood pressure. Removing or filtering bad and defective information is a concern for search engine technology and security software technology. Doing so will improve people's information use efficiency and enhance the overall information environment of society.

Some jurisdictions have introduced legal systems to maintain the information environment, particularly in the governance of the Internet, the hardest-hit area of information pollution. For example, the UK's "3R Internet Cybersecurity Act," with "3R" standing for "graded identification, reporting, and responsibility," establishes a comprehensive mechanism for rectifying the Internet information environment by linking content censorship, netizen rights protection, and the responsibility of violators. The United States has also enacted protection laws, such as the Children's Online Privacy Protection Act and the Protection of Children from Online Pornography Act, to safeguard children who are vulnerable to information pollution and establish an effective mechanism for netizen supervision. Volunteer organizations, such as "Cyber Angels," have been established to protect teens from harmful information.

[49] See Du [33].

Australia restricts young people from accessing websites containing inappropriate information through its online content rating system and online identity authentication technology, serving as a model for legislation. In the Chinese mainland, while a basic legal system has been established to maintain the information environment, there is still a need for a more systematic, targeted, and comprehensive approach.[50] People are still eagerly awaiting the right to refuse harassment from faulty information, such as advertising leaflets and inexplicable text messages claiming to offer prizes. A good information environment is as essential to people in the twenty-first century as the natural environment. The social structure has become informationized, making people's work and life more reliant on information. This has made the information environment an integral part of human existence and a necessary condition for living, working, self-development, and enjoying the fruits of progress. People have the right to demand that the state and society provide a good information environment through legal means, freeing them from physical and mental harm and financial losses caused by information damage.

The right to an information environment encompasses citizens' and organizations' right to live in a healthy information environment, the right to reasonable use of information resources, and the right to participate in managing the national and social information environment (such as knowledge, participation in decision-making, reporting information infringements, etc.). It also includes the right to request cessation of information damage, compensation for losses, and other remedies. The legalization of the right to the information environment will effectively combat information pollution and create a good information environment. However, controlling information pollution is a complex task that requires contributions from information technology, legal punishment, and the legal rights system. Nonetheless, the legitimization of the right to the information environment is the most proactive and fundamental approach to governance, as it enables broad social participation.

4.4.2 Right to Information Security

Security refers to a state of stability, preservation of property, and protection of human dignity. The right to security is a negative right, meaning freedom from intrusion and freedom from loss. The development of informatization and information security presents a paradox, as the faster informatization progresses, the greater the

---

[50] For instance, the "Interim Provisions of the People's Republic of China on the Administration of National Networking of Computer Information Networks", "Interim Provisions on the Administration of Telecommunications Business Markets Liberalized for Business", "Measures for the Administration of International Networking of Public Computer Internet in China", and "Measures for the Implementation of the Interim Provisions of the People's Republic of China on the Management of International Networking of Computer Information Networks" are some of the laws and regulations that impose a licensing system for network operators, an electronic censorship system for cyber police, and a reporting system for harmful information to curb its spread. However, currently, China's legal responsibility for the publication and dissemination of harmful information is restricted to administrative penalties, and it applies only to network operators, not to other users of the network.

potential for security problems. Protecting individuals', society's, and the state's fundamental interests in the realm of information has become imperative for the positive development of informatization. Valuable information recorded, processed, stored, shared, transmitted, and received on electronic media must be systematically protected against threats such as theft, inaccessibility, alteration, or deliberate disclosure, which can result not only from accidents or errors but also from intentional acts like fraud.

The right to information security encompasses the protection of both the security of information and the security of information systems. This right requires the assurance of integrity, objectivity, availability, and confidentiality of both the information and telecommunications infrastructure and the information itself, against any unauthorized interference or infringement. Availability refers to the accessibility and usefulness of information when needed, as well as the ability of the system providing it to withstand and recover from any relevant attacks. Confidentiality dictates that information can only be viewed by those with the appropriate permissions. Integrity involves the inability to modify information without authorization. Authenticity and non-repudiation ensure that business transactions and information exchanges are trustworthy. The use of information, telecommunications systems, and information resources in violation of established regulations, laws, or norms of international law, as well as unauthorized interference in collecting, possessing, storing, displaying, searching, disseminating, or using information, and interrupting the normal operation of information systems, is prohibited by law.

Information security has long been viewed as a hindrance, providing no value. However, with the growth of global networks and the expanding reach of businesses beyond traditional boundaries, information security has become a source of value and opportunities, particularly in terms of boosting the trust of IT stakeholders. In today's digital society, information security is crucial in all aspects, including enterprise management, daily office work, business transactions, and even personal communication. Information is often considered a company's most valuable asset, with 70% or more of a business's worth derived from its intellectual property. A loss or theft of this data can result in serious consequences for the enterprise, potentially threatening its market position. The 2002 CSI/FBI Computer Crime and Security Survey found that information security breaches caused the most financial losses for the 26 respondents, who reported a combined total of over $170 million.[51] A joint survey of 643 businesses by the Computer Security Association and the FBI found that 43% of the surveyed businesses suffered losses of $265 million due to hacking. A study by Bush-Kugel at the University of Minnesota in the United States also pointed out that, in the absence of available information, the financial industry can only operate for up to 2 days, while businesses can only survive for 3.3 days, the industry for 5 days, and insurance for 5.6 days. In terms of economic conditions, 25% of companies may go bankrupt immediately due to data damage, and 40% will

[51] See Sun and Hao [34].

declare bankruptcy within two years. Less than 7% of businesses survive for five years.[52]

At present, information systems are widely utilized in both business and government organizations, but security remains a concern as no system or technology is foolproof. Despite advancements in technical and non-technical security measures, such as physical security, background checks, user identification, password protection, smart cards, biometrics, and firewalls, the state of information security is still not ideal. No technology is perfect and the compatibility requirements for computer security are yet to be perfected. The open design of personal computers makes it easy for anyone to learn about the internal structure and operation of the operating system, leading to the discovery of vulnerabilities. In the internet age, security issues have become more pressing as communication through personal computers increases. On one hand, the most widely used network protocol, TCP/IP, is designed for interconnection and interoperability rather than security and is known to have vulnerabilities. On the other hand, limitations in software design methodologies often result in important security vulnerabilities that are only addressed by frequent security patches from software companies.

The worldwide damage caused by computer viruses is even more shocking. According to the Computer Research Company in Carlsbad, California, the estimated damage in 2001 was $10.7 billion due to virus attacks on information systems. The company reported that computer viruses caused $17.1 billion and $12.1 billion in losses in 2000 and 1999, respectively. According to the 2003 National Computer Virus Epidemic Investigation Report released by the Public Information Network Security Supervision Bureau of the Ministry of Public Security, the proportion of computer users infected with viruses in China reached 85.57%, an increase of 1.59% points from 2002 and 25.57% points from 2001. The proportion of computer viruses causing losses to users accounted for 63.57% of surveyed users.[53] Cyber attacks against systems are becoming increasingly prevalent globally. In 1996, the U.S. General Accounting Office (GAO) reported that the U.S. Department of Defense faced 250,000 attacks on 15,000 systems annually, with 65% being successful. The cost of preventing and repairing damages amounted to hundreds of millions of dollars. Notably, only 400 of these attacks were identified and 20 were reported. Back then, the issue of information security was largely a weakness in the system, but today it is a significant threat. As shown by the FBI's investigation into 100 extortion cases targeting e-commerce websites, attackers not only threaten to release customer information, but they follow through if their demands are not met.[54] Many governments have recognized the importance of information security and have taken active measures to improve it. For example, the U.S. government has listed 53 information security priorities and included information security in its national strategy after the 9/11 incidents. In 2003, the U.S. government invested more than $50 billion to

---

52 See Sun and Hao [34].

53 See Ministry of Public Security: This year, China's computer virus infection rate is about 85%, available at: http://news.21cn.com/domestic/guoshi/2003/10/21/1308718.shtml, 2010-04-18.

54 See Sun and Hao [34].

improve its IT infrastructure and performance, with government agencies spending about $3 billion on cybersecurity alone, which is an increase of 64% compared to previous years.[55] In the world, China is ranked in the lowest "fourth category" for information security and is on par with some backward African countries. Its information and network security protection capabilities are very weak and many application systems are in an undefended state, which poses an extremely high risk. In recent years, China has witnessed a number of information security incidents, such as the computer system failure at the capital airport that caused over 6,000 people to be stranded and delayed more than 150 flights. The computer ticketing system of Nanjing Railway Station also crashed, causing ticket sales to come to a halt. The Industrial and Commercial Bank of Guangdong Province experienced a system failure that resulted in the entire line being shut down for one and a half hours. Additionally, there has been an outage in the securities trading system of the Shenzhen Stock Exchange.[56] These accidents not only result in substantial direct economic losses, but also have a significant adverse impact on society. Although the economic losses can be compensated, the crisis of public trust in the information society, caused by the vulnerability of information networks, is difficult to recover from in a short span of time.[57] The newly developed computer "receiving and restoration equipment" can receive any computer screen information that has not taken protective measures, even from a distance of hundreds of meters or kilometers. Perhaps the next generation of computers will be defined not by speed, but by security.

Information security is of significant importance to personal life. With the growing importance of information exchange in personal matters, protecting personal information from illegal interference and infringement is a common concern. Computer viruses, home appliance viruses (such as mobile phone viruses), and the theft of personal account information can lead to the destruction of information and negatively impact the safety of personal life, causing worry and anxiety and affecting the stability and order of society. The issue of personal information security is becoming more pressing due to the widespread use of computer networks. According to the "Report on the Development of China's Internet Network" released by the China Internet Network Information Center in January 2006, only 4.3% of internet users are very satisfied with network security, with 20.2% relatively satisfied, 44.6% average, 23% less satisfied, and 7.9% very dissatisfied. The most unpleasant aspect of the internet for users is related to information security issues such as online viruses (19.9% of respondents), online charging traps (12.8%), cyber intrusions/attacks (including Trojans) (11.7%), decoys/fraud/Phishing (6.1%).[58]

In order to respond effectively to global information security threats, countries have enacted laws and regulations that prohibit behaviors that compromise information security and grant rights to information holders to maintain security. Penalties for violating information security are severe, with cyber criminals facing up to five years

[55] See Bai [35].

[56] See Cai [36].

[57] See Cai [36].

[58] See China Internet Network Information Center (CNNIC) [26].

and as little as six months in prison in the United States. Repeat offenders may face up to ten years in prison and fines ranging from $250,000 to twice the total damage of the affected website. Other countries such as Singapore, South Korea, Germany, and Japan have also introduced relevant laws to address the growing issue of hacking. China's Ministry of Public Security has also taken positive legislative measures, including the 1997 Measures for the Security Protection and Management of International Networking of Computer Networks and the 1999 amendment to the Criminal Code criminalizing illegal intrusion into computer information systems. These laws not only increase penalties for damage but also give people the legal right to protect their own information security. The Organisation for Economic Co-operation and Development (OECD) published Policy VIII on electronic data encryption in March 1997, and U.S. Congressman Kerrey-McCain and others proposed the Public Cybersecurity Act, which defines terms and affirms the private sector's right to ensure information security through encryption and other means while also protecting privacy rights, intellectual property rights, and network users' personal security. If there is an infringement, the victim may use legal means to pursue the responsible party and seek compensation for losses.

However, China's current information security laws and regulations are limited to controlling illegal political and pornographic content on the Internet, with no clear punishment measures for information damage to the economy. The legislation is prohibitive in nature and lacks clear rights setting, often expressed through accountability language. For example, Article 25 of China's Regulations on the Security Protection of Computer Information Systems states that organizations or individuals who violate the provisions and cause losses to the state, collectives, or others will be held liable in accordance with the law. However, the limited resources of the regulatory authorities and their weaker incentive to maintain information security compared to the victim result in limited monitoring and timely discovery of dangers and abuse. By using rights language in information security norms, every subject that may be threatened by information security can become a defender who consciously maintains information security. This will establish safety valves throughout the information dissemination and society to effectively maintain order.

Information security can be considered a legal right. This right applies to both government and public administration, as well as private entities such as individuals and companies. The meaning of this right varies depending on the subject. For governments and public administration organizations, the focus is to maintain the stability and integrity of the information system necessary for public order. For private entities, information security concerns the security of transactions, information property, and privacy.

In China, several legal documents have been established to regulate information security, including the Law of the People's Republic of China on Guarding State Secrets, the National Security Law of the People's Republic of China, the Electronic Signature Law of the People's Republic of China, the Regulations of the People's Republic of China on the Security Protection of Computer Information Systems, and various local regulations. These laws cover aspects of information security such as facility security, Internet security, virus prevention, and legal liability for information crimes. However, there is a lack of specialization, systematization, and effectiveness in the application of these laws, leading to inconsistencies in information security at both the national and private level.

To address these issues, the National Informatization Leading Group has prioritized the study and drafting of the Information Security Law. This law should clarify the legal right of information security, specify the subject, content, and rights protection mechanism of this right. With a clear legal framework in place, the rights protection and remedy mechanisms will have a clear orientation and institutional basis. Only when the Information Security Law protects the right to information security can it effectively ensure information security.

The Information Security Law should clearly establish that the right to information security is a legal right that applies to state organs, public management organizations, citizens, enterprises, and other legal persons. This right encompasses the protection of the integrity, objectivity, availability, and confidentiality of information and protection from illegal infringement. Public information security and private user information security are treated differently under this law.

To safeguard the right to public information security, the law shall provide rules for the establishment and maintenance of public information platforms and systems, the sharing of responsibility for their security, the rights and responsibilities of individual and corporate users, technical standards for categorical protection of public information based on its importance and confidentiality, the establishment of specialized information security assessment and management bodies, mechanisms for early warning and resolution of information security crises, legal liability, and other relevant content.

Regarding private information security, the law shall clarify that civil legal subjects have the right to maintain the integrity, objectivity, availability, and confidentiality of the information they collect, collate, and store. It shall define the types and scope of protected information, and provide procedures for relief when rights are infringed, including stopping the infringement and compensating for losses. Unlike privacy protection, the right to private information security does not require confidentiality of information or the parties' unwillingness to disclose it. It places more emphasis on protecting individuals' information platforms and information storage and utilization from illegal interference, such as protecting personal computers from hacker attacks.

It is important to recognize that not only can rights be established based on information, but the holders of these rights also have corresponding obligations and responsibilities. They must properly manage the relationship between information rights and other factors. When protecting personal privacy information legally, the restrictions posed by national security and public interests must also be taken into account, as well as the needs of relevant authorities (such as state security agencies) and professionals (such as pastors, lawyers, doctors, counselors, etc.).

The ultimate aim of information rights is not to expand private information endlessly. In some cases, personal and even private information (such as military experience, credit records, real estate registration records, transaction behavior records, etc.) may need to be disclosed for the purpose of national security, market transaction security, and social welfare. For example, many countries have established personal credit file and assessment systems.[59]

5 Conclusion

Of course, these forms of rights are not exhaustive but rather typical forms of information rights, such as the National Information Resources Management Law (Public Information Management Agency). For instance, the operating rules of information resource management institutions, such as libraries and industry information centers, and the information rights involved in the Information Industry Operation and Management Law (such as the Telecommunications Law and the Postal Law), are highly specialized and often intersect with other departmental laws, such as administrative law. However, this does not mean that the right to information that may exist in these legal norms is disregarded. The right to information is an open system and has always been so. It is also crucial to note that the right to information, as a type of right, has a close relationship with its specific sub-rights and other rights. They can provide reciprocal explanations and are linked together in institutional functions. For instance, there is a symbiotic relationship between the right to information and the right to freedom of expression: "Freedom of expression is essential for the effective functioning of a democratic society, but without the right to information, it also becomes a source of water that cannot reflect its core values and functions."[60] However, the explanatory functions that exist between specific information rights do not imply that they can replace each other's autonomous status. This is due to differences in the objects they protect and the methods of protection, as well as variations in the orientation of interests.

Understanding the right to information involves a change in legal concepts in the entire information age, and the demand for theoretical and institutional innovation is unprecedented. However, we are still stuck in traditional thinking frameworks and institutions. However, the pace of development of the information society will not stop, and its footsteps will continue to challenge the ability of human beings to

[59] The protection of personal information varies depending on the content of the information and its impact on the individual's life. Therefore, it is necessary to provide hierarchical and categorical protection of personal information, instead of making generalizations. For example, personal information can be categorized into five levels of protection: (a). Publicly available information that can be freely used, such as directories, telephone yellow pages, and publicly published member directories. (b). Information whose disclosure would not obviously harm personal interests and can be acquired and used with the consent of the owner of the data, such as degrees and social positions. (c). Information whose misuse may harm personal interests and reputation, such as marital status, beliefs, employment experience, and income. (d). Information whose misuse can clearly cause serious harm to personal interests and reputation, such as medical history, criminal record, and financial status. (e). Information whose misuse could harm the health, life, or freedom of an individual, such as personal emotional life information, witness identity, and news provider identity. For the above classification, please refer to Wang [37].

[60] Stiglitz [21].

innovate systematically. Thus, only by making innovations can we be worthy of this ever-changing era.

References

1. Zhang, H. (2001). The justification of property ownership rights. *Modern Law, 6*, 11–19. (in Chinese).
2. Li, X. (2006). *Information rights research* (pp. 9–15). Intellectual Property Press. (in Chinese).
3. Jacobson, R. (1971). *Selected writings (Vol. 2)* (p. 689). Mouton.
4. Li, G., & Xu, A. (2000). *Analytical positivism law* (p. 58). Wuhan University Press. (in Chinese).
5. Zhu, X. (2004). Information and intellectual property. In J. Du & J. Tang (Eds.), *Legal exploration in the internet era* (p. 58). Law Press.
6. Shapiro, C., & Varian, H. (2000). *Information rules: A strategic guide to the network economy*. Zhang, F. (Trans.) (p. 2). Renmin University of China Press. (in Chinese).
7. Yan, D. (2001). *Information culture and human information behavior research under its influence* [PhD Dissertation, Peking University], p. 15. (in Chinese).
8. Wenxian, Z. (2001). *Study on the categories of legal philosophies* (revised edition), p. 109. China University of Political Science and Law Press. (in Chinese).
9. Qinghua, Z., & Jianzheng, Y. (Eds.). (2001). *Information law tutorial* (pp. 17–20). Higher Education Press. (in Chinese).
10. Ruihua, H. (Ed.). (2004). *Information law* (p. 7). Publishing House of Electronics Industry. (in Chinese).
11. Chen, A.-E. (Trans.). (2003). *Methodologies of the legal sciences* (Methodenlehre der Rechtswissenschaft) (p. 100). The Commercial Press. (in Chinese).
12. Wu, Y. (Trans.). (2003). *The concept of a legal system by Joseph Raz* (p. 210). China Legal Publishing House. (in Chinese).
13. Zhou, L. (2003). Explanatory humanities: From Taylor's views on social science. *Journal of Social Sciences of Shanxi Colleges and Universities, 5*. (in Chinese).
14. Chen, Y. (2003). *The conflicts between information property rights and the connotation and extension of intellectual property rights*. China Intellectual Property News, 2003-10-17. (in Chinese).
15. Liu, C. (2003). Analysis of intellectual property rights. *Chinese Social Sciences, 4*. (in Chinese).
16. Pendleton, M. (1984). *The law of intellectual and industrial property in Hong Kong*. Butterworths.
17. Zheng, C. (2010). *Information, information property rights and their relationship with intellectual property rights*. Retrieved from http://vip.chinalawinfo.com/newlaw2002/SLC/slc.asp?gid=335573229&db=art. 18 April 2010.
18. Li, X. (2006). *Study on the right to information* (pp. 81–87). Intellectual Property Press.
19. Cohen, J. M., & Rogers, J. (1988). *On democracy*. (Chongxin & Z. Xiuxian, Trans.) (p. 6). Commercial Press.
20. Padover, S. (Ed.). (1953). *The complete madison*. Harper.
21. Stiglitz, J. E. (1999). *On liberty, the right to know, and public discourse: The role of transparency in public life*. Retrieved on March 2, 2023, from https://internationalbudget.org/wp-content/uploads/On-Liberty-the-Right-to-Know-and-Public-Discourse-The-Role-of-Transparency-in-Public-Life.pdf
22. Yu, B. (2004). On transparent government. *Journal of Chizhou Teachers College*, 3. (in Chinese).
23. Dworkin, R. (2001). *Freedom's Law: The moral reading of the American constitution* (L. Liu, Trans., p. 285). Shanghai People's Publishing House.
24. Bogdanor, V. (Ed.). (1992). *Blackwell encyclopedia of political science* (D. Zhenglai et al., Trans.) (2nd ed., p. 274). China University of Political Science and Law Press.

25. Chen, X. (2003). *Legal guarantees for freedom of expression* (p. 9). China Social Science Publishing House.
26. China Internet Network Information Center (CNNIC). (2010). [Online]. Available at: http://www.cnnic.net.cn/images/2006/download/2006011701.pdf. Accessed 18 April 2010.
27. Du, J., & Tang, J. (Eds.). (2005). *Informatization and law* (p. 69). Beijing.
28. Zhu, Q., & Yang, J. (Eds.). (2001). *Information law course* (p. 54). Beijing.
29. Post, R.C. (1995). The social foundations of privacy: Community and self in the common law wrong. In R. C. Post (Eds.), *Constitutional domains: Democracy community management* (p. 51).
30. Unger, R. (1987). *Social theory: Its situation and its task* (p. 26).
31. Lin, J. (2002). *From the sea of books to the internet: The evolution of communication technology* (p. 287). Jiangxi University Press.
32. Biagi, S. (2000). *Media impact: An introduction to mass media* (Z. Jingsong, Trans.), p. 314. Northeast University of Finance and Economics Press.
33. Du, Z. (2003). *Anti-spam legislation should be enacted*. Retrieved from http://www.blogchina.com/2003082512598.html on April 19, 2023.
34. Sun, Q., & Hao, Y. (2010). *Information security governance: Creating a new strategic competition mechanism*. Retrieved from http://industry.ccidnet.com/pub/article/c35_a100948_p1.html on April 18, 2010.
35. Bai, X. (2008). *Research on enterprise IT risk management framework based on IT governance*. Master's thesis, Ocean University of China.
36. Cai, C. (2009). *Zhongshan power grid EMS: Research on system information security management and security policy*. Master's thesis, University of Electronic Science and Technology of China.
37. Wang, Z. (2003). *Introduction to information law* (p. 273). China Legal Publishing House.

Chapter 5
Genetic Rights

Hongzhen Liu

1 Introduction

Genes, as pieces of DNA that carry genetic information, are the basic factors that control life traits and determine life phenomena. Since ancient times, the structure and function of genes have remained hidden, naturally and silently encoding the story of life and reproduction. But the rapid development of genetics and genetic technology in the mid- to late twentieth century changed this. The hidden code of life in genes was unmasked and deciphered, and genes became objects that could be manipulated, intervened, and modified. Based on the interpretation of the molecular mechanism of heredity, genetic diagnosis, gene therapy, gene pharmaceuticals, genetically modified crops, genetically modified foods, and other marketable products have been introduced and improved through the detection, isolation, splicing, and recombination of genes in humans, animals, plants, microorganisms, and other organisms with specific genetic effects. An emerging economic sector, known as the "gene economy," is rising and becoming one of the main battlegrounds for economic forces to seize the commanding heights of the global market.[1]

At this point, genes are no longer just submerged in organisms and nature as the genetic material of life, but have become raw materials or products that can attain economic value in laboratories and markets—a fulcrum for sunrise industries to grow, a new type of production resource that characterizes sky-high commercial interests, and a new medium of law and benefit with scarcity.

The rebirth of this medium of law and benefit is bound to be accompanied by frequent disputes between law and benefit. Driven by the logic of capital, major scientific research institutions and commercial companies engaged in gene product research, development, and investment compete to explore, occupy, and seize genetic

[1] See Zhang [1].

H. Liu (✉)
Theoretical Legal Research Center, Law School of Jilin University, Changchun, China

J. Yao (ed.), *The Legal Issues of the Emerging Rights*,
https://doi.org/10.1007/978-981-97-0499-6_5

resources, genetic information, and genetic knowledge that may bring wealth and benefits in any possible corner and any possible field in the world. In contrast, the owners (providers) of genetic resources, genetic information, and genetic knowledge are fighting and resisting to share the economic benefits of genes, opposing "gene plunder" and "gene piracy", and defending the personality and ecological legal interests "materialized" and "colonized" by capital. The conflict between investors in gene product research and development and the owners of genetic resources has increasingly escalated into a major issue in forums such as trade, human rights, and the environment around the world, as well as in microlife fields such as medicine, agriculture, and food.[2]

Legal interests of freshmen in the field of law and interests of intensification are legally confirmed claims that will inevitably arise. R&D and investors in genetic products demand recognition of their monopoly interests through "intellectual property" rights in order to repay their costs and inputs. They tend to extend the scope and intensity of "intellectual property" protection to the maximum. Owners of genetic resources, genetic information, and genetic knowledge (providers) put forward demands for rights such as "gene property rights", "gene privacy rights", "farmers' rights", and "traditional knowledge protection". In this way, they claim that the benefits of property law, personality law, and ecological law are attached to genes and used to counter and constrain overly inflated intellectual property rights.

However, in the process of confirming rights, a difficult question arises: Can living organisms such as human genes, genetically modified animals and plants, and microorganisms become patentable subjects? If so, does it mean the alienation of man and the privatization of nature? Can basic research results, such as functional genes, be protected by intellectual property rights? If so, is it consistent with the principles and conditions under traditional patent law, which do not grant patents for natural phenomena or discoveries and require the subject to have an "inventive step" and "novelty"? Do people have property rights to genetic resources and genetic information? If not, is it against basic human morality and a sense of fairness to allow intellectual property to monopolize huge profits? If so, does it mean the "objectification" of people and the debasement of personality? Can farmers and indigenous peoples at the center of biodiversity include their traditional knowledge in the protection of intellectual property rights? If so, what techniques are used to interpret the collective extension of anonymity as the subject of intellectual property? In short, various types of claims have encountered difficulties and obstacles in both the basis of legality and the design of the protection mechanism.

The solution to the above difficult problems seems to have exceeded the ability of modern legal theory to answer. Or, rather, the above conundrum is caused by the failure of the paradigm of modernity theory. Modern legal theory follows the approach of the philosophy of consciousness, based on subjective/objective, subject/object, internal/external, and person/thing/personality. The logic of binary opposites, such as property, culture/nature, makes an absolute distinction between personality

[2] See Rifkin [2].

rights and property rights, discovery rights and invention rights. However, the characteristics of gene technology challenge and blur this binary distinction to some extent. On the one hand, DNA cutting, recombination, modification, and other technologies enable genes that determine specific traits in living organisms at the most fundamental physiological functions to be transferred and expressed across species at the molecular level. Thus, the human gene fragment that controls the production of a specific protein may be introduced into the cells of a transgenic animal or plant to produce a genetic product with a specific performance. In this way, with a certain strange feeling, the absolute distinction between people and things seems to be quietly dissolved somewhat in the deepest part of the mystery of life.[3] On the other hand, gene technology has a strong "social constructivity". The detection of gene structure and function, the masking, and decryption of genetic mechanisms are all realized by scientists under the guidance of specific cognitive interests in expensive laboratories. According to carefully constructed theoretical models and with the help of high-end complex instruments and equipment. Here, cognitive achievements are not so much the revelation of objective truths, but rather "contaminated" by theory and "made" by money and power. They are not so much "discoveries" as "inventions".

What is more prominent is that, due to the commercial applications of gene diagnosis, gene pharmaceuticals, gene therapy, and other technologies, human genes, genetic resources, and gene information are increasingly detached from their integration with the human body and are being functionalized, becoming independent, externalized, and property.[4] Here, the human body and its components are no longer strictly distinguished from external objects as a whole. They represent a personality that cannot be derogated or degraded from each other, and the line that originally divided man from external objects seems to have moved inward to man. The human body is fragmented and becomes both "inside" and "outside," both "person" and "thing," both "personality" and "property."

It can be seen that the solution to the problem lies in the paradigm shift of rights theory, that is, moving beyond the dualist framework of modern jurisprudence. This involves reinterpreting the legal attributes of genes in the mixed zone of opposing categories and reconceptualizing and institutionalizing the legal interests of personality, property, and ecology that they carry. In fact, the discourse of rights is simply a struggle and game between interests and power. The pattern of interests and power changes with events, and the structure of power naturally adjusts accordingly. As far as genetic rights are concerned, the technological innovation of rights theory is politically subject to the contest and compromise of relevant interest groups. It depends on economic/ethical, utilitarian/rights, and efficiency/value considerations, and requires a balance between these goals for fairness.

[3] Myerson [3].

[4] Knorr-Cetina [4].

2 Genetic Property Rights

Property claims on animal and plant, microbial genetic resources and genetic information are mainly confirmed by the sovereign national ownership of the common heritage of mankind and the protection of intellectual property rights for traditional knowledge. This varies depending on the ethical and jurisprudence involved. This section focuses on the legality basis and protection model of property rights for human genes (information).

2.1 Personality or Property: Confusion Between Law and Interest

2.1.1 Paradigm Failures, Value Conflicts and Practical Dilemmas

During the Enlightenment, when medical knowledge and diagnostic methods could not divide the parts of the human body into functionally independent components, people were related to the outside world as a whole. Taking the criterion of "inside" or "outside" to a man's free will, the relationship between man and the outside world is divided into the relationship between "person" and "thing," "subject" and "object."[5] The complete human body is the dwelling place of man's free will, capable of undertaking the acts imposed on him as the "subject," and constitutes the carrier of "personality rights." Things, which are objects of the free activity of the will, refer to those things that cannot be held liable as subjects, and are considered "objects" that constitute the carriers of "property rights."[6] In order to establish the supreme subjective status of human beings and ensure that human dignity and freedom are not violated and degraded by the logic of power and money, the whole human person is the boundary. Man, as the owner of foreign objects, can transfer his property through contract. However, "a person can be his own master, but not his own owner, and he cannot deal with himself arbitrarily, let alone have such a relationship with others." For he is responsible for his humanity within himself.[7]

According to this classical theory, human organs, tissues, genes, and other body components are related to human integrity and the dignity they carry. They belong to the scope of "personality rights" and cannot be commercialized or marketed. For a long time, to meet the needs of organ transplantation and genetic research, even if not strictly following Kant's prohibition that "man cannot deal with himself arbitrarily", Locke's thesis that "each person has a kind of ownership of his own person" was adopted. Thus, the right of a man to dispose of his body freely was

[5] Kant [5], pp. 25–30.

[6] Kant [5], pp. 80–101.

[7] Kant [5], pp. 18–25.

recognized.[8] However, the practice in this field still adheres to the bottom line of "non-profit." That is, human organs, tissues, genes, and other body components can only be donated as "gifts." But they cannot be bought or sold as a "commodity."[9]

However, as medical procedures like organ transplantation, genetic diagnosis, and gene therapy become more common, body components such as organs, tissues, and genes are acquiring more value in the transfer and replantation between individuals. This fragmentation of the body from a functional whole to its isolated parts is causing it to become anonymous in circulation. What's more concerning is that the high demand and profit potential of this market is leading medical institutions, genetic technology research and investment companies, to treat the providers of organs, tissues, and genes as depersonalized functional bodies, mere storage units, and valuable resources.[10]

Biological and genetic technology is exploring the power of cognition and transformation, along with the influence of the market, on the deep mechanisms of human beings and their lives. As a result, the criteria used to distinguish between "people" and "things" become ambiguous. The human body and its components, as the carriers of "personality," begin to evoke the notion of being certain "property," even without strong capitalistic intrusion.

On the subject of "human nature," the debate over whether the organs, tissues, genes, and other body components of the "physical nature" variation should be considered a "personality right" or a "property right" under the law, and whether they can be monetarily traded for benefit, has become a contentious issue. This is particularly relevant in a time where market profits from such products have become an indisputable fact, driven by the scarcity and uniqueness of the donor's "vital material." Donors are expected to act altruistically and donate for free, but greedy R&D institutions and commercial companies are allowed to profit through "intellectual property." Is this unfair? Does this encourage for-profit medical institutions and biotech companies to prioritize profits over the greater good? Does it result in the exploitation and oppression of the human body by those with the advantage of knowledge and capital? Has the original intention to honor the supremacy of personality led to the paradoxical result of personality degradation? And will the imbalanced distribution of benefits and resulting personality alienation reduce the incentive for donors to participate, slowing the development of biological and medical technologies due to a shortage of "raw materials" such as organs, tissues, and genes?[11] The answer is: Of course, these negative consequences are happening in reality. Apparently, traditional methods of personality rights protection are unable to balance the relationship between donors and developers of vital materials in legal disputes. They also fail to balance the conflict of values between personality and utility. But is the failure of this approach to the protection of personality rights an indication of the superiority of property rights protection methods? As we have reasonable concerns that most

[8] Locke [6].

[9] See Marchant [7].

[10] See Sharp [8].

[11] See Qiu [9], pp. 57–62.

national systems strive to avoid, if the theory of economic analysis is adopted and price and market mechanisms are introduced for everything that is based on utility, scarcity, and selectivity, the trade-off of benefits would define property rights.[12]

So, the consequences can be catastrophic. People will be incentivized to sell organs, tissues, genes, and other body components for money. In particular, the poor will be reduced to the means and tools of the rich to restore their health. Meanwhile, according to the principle of operation of property rights, once organs, tissues, genes, and other body components are transferred, the most hidden life information loaded on them will circulate in the market, out of the donor's control. On the one hand, it constitutes a serious damage to the donor's personality. On the other hand, donors may face discrimination or unfair treatment in basic aspects of life, such as social attitudes, employment, medical care, and insurance. This is visible where there is no power in the way property rights are protected. The modern theory of personality rights, which is the binary opposition of property rights, exposes its dysfunction and stretched dilemma.

The conflict between law and interests, the conflict of values, and the failure of theory are reflected in law. This is expressed through the trial-and-error and uncertainty of the institutional arrangements of various countries in the game between interest groups. This trial-and-error and uncertainty, whether it's for maintaining ethical values, promoting economic development, or protecting the interests of life resource providers or life technology developers, is not beneficial.

2.1.2 Limits Arising from the Moore Rule and the Revelation of the PXE Model

"Moore v. Board of Regents of the University of California" is a seminal case in which the providers of genetic resources assert genetic property rights. The denial of these rights served as an important reference and had an impact on subsequent cases involving similar claims.[13]

In 1976, John Moore was treated at UCLA Medical Center by his attending doctor, Dr. David W. Golde. He was diagnosed with a rare form of leukemia called hairy-cell leukemia and had his spleen removed during treatment. In the following years, Moore was asked to return to the medical center for follow-up visits, during which Dr. Golde took his blood, serum, skin, bone marrow, and semen samples. Suspecting that his body tissues were being used for purposes other than his personal medical treatment, Moore repeatedly questioned Dr. Golde, who claimed that the samples were necessary to monitor his condition. However, it was later revealed that Dr. Golde and his assistant, Shirley G. Quan, had cultured cell lines from Moore's spleen and other samples and obtained a patent for the cell lines, which was held by the University of California, Los Angeles. This patent was estimated to be worth over $3 billion. In subsequent collaborations with industry, Dr. Golde and UCLA profited

[12] See Becker [10]; Posner [11].

[13] Moore v. Board of Regents of the University of California [12].

from Sandoz Pharmaceuticals Corporation, received sponsorship of at least $330,000 per year from the Genetics Institute, and Dr. Golde also became a paid consultant for the Genetics Institute. He acquired 75,000 stock rights.

In 1985, when Moore learned the truth, he accused the University of California of absent of informed consent, breach of fiduciary duty, and conversion of property. He filed lawsuits in a California court seeking monetary damages. However, the California Supreme Court ultimately affirmed Moore's breach of fiduciary duty but denied his claim of misappropriation of property. The denial was based on California's Uniform Anatomical Gift Act and the federal Health and Safety Code. The former prohibits the receipt of any valuable consideration in the context of body donation, while the latter prohibits the buying and selling of human blood. The court held that, since the law on human tissues prohibits the sale of human tissues, allowing Moore to obtain compensation for the use of his cells would be tantamount to admitting that the sale of human tissues was contrary to the intent of existing law. Furthermore, the court also held that the social benefits of human tissue contributions to the development of new drugs should take precedence over personal interests. If it were to be admitted that Moore's "property" was illegally taken, scientists would have to assume the obligation to verify the origin of all human cell samples, which would negatively impact the biotechnology industry.[14]

The Moore ruling did not clarify the legal nature of human genes, not because it failed to recognize Moore's property rights, but because it sidestepped the issue of the nature of genes themselves by defining them as "human tissue." This interpretation ignored the differences in legal meaning and implications between genes and "human tissue" in the context of extraction and transplantation. Ultimately, one of the primary reasons for prohibiting the sale of body parts, organs, and tissues is to prevent harm to health and life for financial gain or self-harm.[15] However, the extraction of gene fragments and the culture of cell lines, because they are performed at the molecular level, do not require large amounts of human tissue, or even very small amounts. Most of this work is carried out using diseased and discarded tissue, so the behavior is not significant enough to pose the risks and harms that may result from allowing the buying and selling of organs and tissues. The disregard for the unique qualities of genes has prevented the court in Moore's case from addressing the core of the dispute, greatly reducing its persuasive power and guidance. Furthermore, the ruling does not perform a negative analysis of the legal property status of human genes.

However, public policy cites the suppression of the property rights of genetic material providers, while also favoring the affirmation of the intellectual property rights of gene technology developers. It is unclear what negative ethical consequences this ruling, dominated by economic considerations, will have on the scientific and technological progress and economic development it is meant to promote, as Moore

---

[14] See Liu & Liu [13].

[15] Of course, it also contains important reasons for protecting personality. This is consistent with the arguments against the recognition of full genetic property rights. However, in this case, the California Supreme Court makes an analogy between human tissue and genes; it is clear that the shared personality elements between the two are not taken into account, nor will it devise a verdict of one-way protection of property rights in the biotechnology industry.

himself claims. Gene technology developers will be encouraged to continue to "claim my humanity, my genetic essence, their inventions and property." They see me as a mineral deposit that can be extracted from biological material, and I am their harvest.[16]; With a sense of dehumanization and alienation, how can a gene resource provider actively supply the gene technology industry with the necessary raw materials? As the California Court of Appeals stated in Moore's case, "If science were solely driven by profit, there would be no justification for excluding patients from sharing in the profits."[17]

If the case of Moore is not suitable as a guiding principle, the PXE model serves as an example. PXE (Pseudoxanthoma Elasticum) is a rare and incurable genetic disease that weakens elastic fibers in the skin and blood vessels, potentially leading to blindness, gastrointestinal bleeding, heart disease, and a shortened lifespan. The non-profit organization, PXE International, which provides support for families affected by PXE, has collected blood and DNA samples from over 2,000 PXE patients. Researchers may be granted access to these samples from the Tissue Bank if they meet certain conditions set by PXE International. These conditions include sharing any intellectual property and profits derived from their use of the samples. PXE International's requirement of becoming a patentee aims to ensure that genetic testing for PXE remains affordable and accessible to all. It appears that researchers working with PXE do not object to this requirement.[18]

The PXE model is respected by both researchers and patients for its core emphasis on the right of genetic resource providers to enter into benefit-sharing contracts. This right is derived from the recognition of genetic property rights. By focusing on the protection mechanism of property rights and maximizing the benefits of gene technology, the model provides a way for both genetic resource providers and gene technology developers to balance their interests. It also allows for a reconciliation between preserving moral fairness and promoting the science and technology economy.

2.1.3 Exploring a Pragmatic Solution

As previously analyzed, the power of technology and the logic of the market have irrevocably and irreversibly imposed the elements of property law on top of the genetic benefits of personality law. This confusion between personality law interests and property law interests makes it possible to simply adopt either end of the dual concept system of personality rights/property rights, which will lead to self-contradictory consequences and will not be enough to resolve the resulting conflicts of interest and values.[19] Perhaps, as Moore suggests and the PXE model demonstrates, the solution to the problem lies in abandoning the either/or distinction between personality rights

[16] Quoted from Qiu [14], p. 58.

[17] Quoted from Qiu [14], p. 58.

[18] Marchant [15].

[19] See [16].

and property rights. Instead, pragmatism creates a new comprehensive category in the middle ground where these two rights are intertwined.

2.2 *Personality Property Rights: A New Approach*

2.2.1 Intersection of Personality and Property Rights

As a form of discourse, the binary opposition between personality rights and property rights is similar to the boundaries between subjectivity and objectivity, consciousness and matter, inner and external, subject and object, and nature and civilization. These boundaries form the basis of its logic and were created by Enlightenment thinkers who advocated for and promoted anthropocentrism. The ideal picture of politics, economics, and ethics was shaped by the tools and facilities of rationalism and liberalism.

However, even during the period of the abuse of modern thought by classical thinkers, the rights of personality and property were not fundamentally separated.

Following a similar approach to Kant's argument, Hegel defined man as a being of ideas and free will. He regarded things that are different from the free spirit, whether to the spirit or in itself, as lacking subjectivity, something unfree, impersonal, and powerless. As man exists as an idea and attains the fixation of personality, his freedom must be given an external realm, allowing man the right to embody his will in everything, making everything his own. This is man's absolute right to possess everything for himself and ownership is rational, not in satisfying needs, but in rejecting the pure subjectivity of personality. Ownership can be transferred because the property is mine only because my will is embodied in it, but personality rights cannot be transferred. The welfare of my personality, universal essence of my sense of self, ethics, and religion are non-transferable and their right will never lapse.[20] However, in Hegel's seemingly absolute distinction, the relationship between property and personality, and property rights and personality rights, remains inextricable. According to Hegel's logic, before a person can impose their free will on an external object, they must be considered an "absolutely infinite will in this initially or completely abstract provision." Only through the possession and domination of things, or the acquisition and exercise of "ownership," can an individual abandon the "pure subjectivity of personality" and "the fixation of reaching personality."[21]; It appears that something may be so closely tied to the composition of "personality" that it can be considered an integral part of it. As a result, the recognition and protection of this thing is separated from "ownership." This leads to the creation of a new concept called "personality property rights" as the central area becomes a part of the periphery of "personality rights."[22] Additionally, Hegel's analysis of the

[20] Hegel [17], pp. 40–83.

[21] Hegel [17].

[22] Radin [18], pp. 60–92.

distinction between slavery and employment relationships highlights the limitations of the division between personal and material, personal rights and ownership[23]: In any case, criticizing the former solely on the basis of workload as an alienated transfer of personality while endorsing the latter as legitimate always gives the impression of exhaustion and lack of conviction.[24]

In addition to Hegel, Locke also experienced incompleteness and paradoxism. Locke believed that every individual has ownership of their own body and that any labor or work performed by their hands rightfully belongs to them. When someone takes something from its natural state and incorporates their own labor into it, they have created their own property. This is because they have added something to it through their own labor, thereby excluding the common rights of others.[25] According to Locke, a person has ownership of their own body, and this ownership cannot be claimed by anyone else. The ownership of oneself extends to the ownership of one's actions or labor, and then to the ownership of the result of that action or labor. In other words, the human body forms the foundation of ownership[26]; According to this reasoning, does the entry of property into the circulation and transfer process through the medium of money mean that the person and personality it is based on also enters the circulation and transfer through money? Thus, how can one logically argue that the transcendent nature of the white personality is not accessible or enjoyed by others?[27]

2.2.2 Personality Property Rights as a New Concept

The commodity logic of the free market, high-tech, and consumer economies expands to all fields, including ethics. Interest groups and human moral sentiments often fight against the colonization of commodity logic to protect fairness, justice, and human dignity. The struggle between economy and ethics creates a mixture of "personification of property" and "propertyization of personality." The traditional concepts of "property rights" or "personality rights" are not sufficient to protect these mixed forms, leading to the adoption of the new concept of "property rights for personality" by American jurist Margaret Jane Radin.[28]

Inspired by Hegel's ideas that "a person's personality is inseparable from certain object relationships" and that a person can only fully realize their true self through establishing property relationships with external things, Margaret Jane Ruidan developed the concept of "property rights for the sake of personality". She argues that society should be based on the external moral reality of the community and recognizes the importance of self-identity through things, which are either fixed or constructed

---

[23] See Hegel [17].

[24] See Radin [19].

[25] John Locke [6].

[26] John Locke [6].

[27] See Frow [20].

[28] See Radin [18].

according to the personality of things. Margaret Jane Ruidan divides things into two categories: "fungible property" and "personality property." Fungible property has no connection or is far removed from a person's personality and is valued in money according to property rights mechanisms. It is freely and anonymously traded in the market. On the other hand, personality property is more strictly protected because it is related to the core value of human personality and dignity. Margaret Jane Ruidan defines "residence" and "factory" as personality property related to human survival, privacy, freedom, and dignity. She has made institutional suggestions on government regulation in special circumstances, such as leasing, expropriation, and bankruptcy, prioritizing personal rights and welfare rights.[29]

Subsequently, Margaret Jane Ruidan deepened her theory of "personality property rights" by discussing issues such as blood and child sales, organ transplantation, sexual services, surrogacy, and more. She acknowledges that the logic of capital is increasingly being applied to the human body, but argues that a blanket ban on any form of economicization of the body and its components could worsen the plight of those who are already disadvantaged. Therefore, in her opinion, the highest value goal and code of conduct should be "human flourishing", based on its impact on human well-being and human dignity. Using the concepts of "property", "personality property", and "personality" as tools, she proposes a "market inalienability" protection and regulation mechanism, which allows for free or indirect paid transfers such as donations based on its "property" and prohibits commercialization and profit-making based on its "personality".[30]

Margaret Jane Ruidan's theory conceptualizes and types "personality property rights" to protect celebrities and their name rights, portrait rights, and other right to publicity. This is the confirmation of "personality property rights" in specific systems and judicial practices. As postmodern consumer economy, represented by advertising, brands, symbols, etc., continues to develop, celebrities' names, images, voices, and other personality symbols are increasingly given commercial value and used as an economic factor in market competition. These commercialized personality symbols do acquire certain "property" characteristics, such as a certain degree of separability from the human body, inheritability, investment, licensing, and transfer. However, the characteristics of "personality" remain, as personality symbols are still just embodiments and expressions of personality. The commodification of personality symbols changes the direct possession of the "body," rather than the "personality" by the person. Various countries have adopted a comprehensive protection mechanism for "personality rights" and "property rights" with regard to "personality property rights" such as portrait rights and name rights.[31]

[29] See Radin [18].

[30] See Radin [19].

[31] See Xiaoyao [21]; Sharp [8].

2.2.3 Legitimacy Argument Vis-À-Vis Genetic 'Personality Property Rights'

First of all, genes and genetic information carry and express irreplaceable, non-dilutable, and non-derogable personality values. They are the building blocks of life and the most fundamental substances that make it possible. Genes contain the mysteries and potentials of life, encoding all aspects of an individual's history, future, traits, and processes, as well as those of their population and species. Genes and genetic information are linked to the core, most basic, and most intimate aspects of human personality values, such as individuality, uniqueness, and pluralism. Improper manipulation, pre-fertilization, and use of genes and genetic information can cause serious harm to people's sense of dignity as human beings, as well as their freedoms and equality in society. Even with gene technology able to break down the human body into functional cell lines and anonymous data information at the molecular level, and even with cell lines and genetic information being able to be transferred and used according to market mechanisms, the personality value carried by genes cannot be obscured, ignored, or devalued. The personality rights of genetic data providers must be protected more seriously and strictly than the property rights of gene technology developers.

Second, the development of the gene economy has become an irreversible trend. The economic value of genetic information and the development of human genes has become an undeniable fact. Gene diagnostics, gene pharmaceuticals, and gene therapy have created a huge profit market, which has become a key industry supported by various countries. To repay the investment of gene technology developers and stimulate the development of the gene economy, intellectual property is increasingly pushing the boundaries of bioethics and is being granted more ergonomic projects. Human genes with special functions have become more and more economically valuable, making them increasingly the object of exploration, search, and scramble in the genetic industry. In this context, if traditional ethical taboos are adhered to, the possibility of genetic data providers profiting from their cooperation is categorically denied. On the one hand, this violates basic moral fairness, denying the contribution and value of genetic data providers to R&D projects and weakening their enthusiasm to participate in scientific and technological progress. On the other hand, it will also encourage gene technology developers to further instrumentalize and dehumanize donors. Especially in developed countries, "gene theft" of patients in less developed countries rich in genetic resources, large medical institutions, and biopharmaceutical companies, is becoming increasingly rampant. As such, appropriate recognition and protection of the economic interests of genetic resource providers is all the more necessary.

Third, recognizing the genetic "personality property rights" and protecting them with the dual mechanism of personality rights and property rights provides a pragmatic channel for balancing the conflict between personality values, scientific and technological progress, and economic development. After all, genes are a medium for the mixing of personality and property law interests, and the protection mechanisms of personality and property rights ensure the control and domination of the donor's use of genetic materials and information, while also maintaining reasonable sharing of the benefits of scientific and technological progress. Motivating the efficient allocation of genetic resources is beneficial.[32]

2.3 *Dimensions of Protecting Genetic "Personality Property Rights"*

2.3.1 Primary Empowers

Due to the fusion of genetic personality and property legal interests, the personality rights mechanism that protects its personality legal interests is subject to alteration based on its property factors. Simultaneously, the property rights mechanism that protects its property legal interests is limited by personality considerations. In turn, the genetic "personality property right" breaks through the usual inalienable, transferable, and economic traps of personality rights. This allows genetic data providers to donate, transfer, and obtain returns from their data. However, when exercising their genetic "personality property rights," genetic data must not be commercialized, sold, or circulated in the market for money.

Additionally, hospitals and gene technology developers must obtain informed consent from the genetic data provider before sampling, extracting, or using the data, even if it has already been donated or transferred. This ensures the genetic data provider maintains control and authority over their genetic profile and information.[33]

2.3.2 Informed Consent

Informed consent is a fundamental principle of bioethics. Individuals have the right to make informed decisions regarding their bodies, including those involved in scientific research and experiments. This means that those receiving physical manipulation should have full access to relevant information and be able to make voluntary, free and autonomous decisions. Informed consent is essential in preventing expert tyranny and protecting autonomy and dignity.

Genes are a person's "personal property" and they have the right to possess, dominate, control, and reap rewards from them. At the same time, they are also a coveted resource and wealth by the biotechnology industry. Extracting, mediating, and utilizing human genes can cause harm or infringe upon the personal and property interests of donors. As such, when collecting, storing, and using human genes, special attention must be paid to the protection of the donors' "right to informed consent". In response, the Human Genetics Organization recognizes that "it is important for participants to understand the nature, risks, and benefits of research as well as any

[32] See Marchant [22].

[33] See Radin [19].

other available options" and "any choice made by participants regarding the storage or other use of materials or information obtained or derived from them should be respected, as should the choice to know or not know the accompanying research results"[34]; The United Nations Educational, Scientific and Cultural Organization (UNESCO) is present in its Universal Declaration on the Human Genome and Human Rights, which states that "in all cases, prior consent from the person concerned must be obtained" and that "the person should have the right to be notified of their genetic test results and this right must be respected".[35]

According to the regulations or practice of most countries, the actor must provide informed consent to the recipient before collecting, storing, and using any genetic material and information. This consent must include written information on the confidentiality measures taken after collection, the extent to which the donor has control over the genetic data, the ability to withdraw from the study, the length of time the genetic data and information will be stored, the ability to obtain information related to their genes and whether this information can be used for medical treatment, secondary use of genetic data and information, and use by third parties in the future. The recipient then independently decides whether to agree and participate in the relevant operation.[36]

2.3.3 Benefit Sharing

Since the provider has the "personality property rights" over its genetic material and information, it is the raw material or object of the genetic products or methods on which the gene technology developer obtains intellectual property rights. The beneficial power inherent in property rights, and their contribution to related engineering projects, gives the provider of genetic information a natural right to share in the benefits of the results.

Based on the personality traits of genetic property, the benefit method for property owners does not take the form of direct and immediate receipt of money. The models under exploration mainly include: concluding a benefit-sharing contract and agreeing to share a certain percentage of expected profits; becoming one of the owners of the prospective patent right (in addition to receiving patent royalties, they can control low-cost licensing to specific beneficiary groups); enjoying the products or services of the Participating Program free of charge or at a low price; and in the case of the use of ethnic genes, helping the community to build healthcare technology or investment.[37]

[34] The Human Genome Organization [23].

[35] UNESCO, translated by Zhi [24].

[36] See Weir [25], p. 100.

[37] See Andrews [26]; Marchant [22].

3 Gene Patent Rights

3.1 Legitimacy Argument and Ethical Critiques

The traditional patent right system grants the right holder the privilege of monopolistic possession, use, benefit, and domination over an invention—product or process—for a certain period and scope. Gene patent right is similar, but it applies to qualified gene technology methods and products, taking into consideration the unique attributes of gene technology and its social consequences.[38]

At present, when considering relevant international agreements (e.g., TRIPS) and the practices of various countries, the patentable subject matter for gene patent rights mainly includes gene technology methods, functional gene sequences, transgenic microorganisms, new varieties of transgenic plants, new varieties of transgenic animals, and biological products.[39]

Despite the wave of opposition to the patenting of life, the lobbying and pressure activities of the gene technology industry to seek government authorization have not decreased, and the behavior of developed countries to use trade as a threat to force latecomer countries to improve their level of patent protection has become more and more direct. After all, genetic engineering has brought about revolutionary development in the agriculture, medical, pharmaceutical, and other industries, with gene economy having the potential to catch up with the information economy and become the future economic leader. With research and development of gene technology having the characteristics of high investment and high risk, the monopoly profit mechanism of patent rights has become indispensable for rewarding and stimulating the innovation and commercial application of gene technology. John J. Doll, head of the biotechnology examination team at the USPTO, defended that "the granting of patents not only facilitates the dissemination of technical information within the scientific community as a basis for further research, but it also stimulates investment in the research, development and commercialization of new biology. Only by patenting DNA technology can some companies, especially small ones, raise enough venture capital to produce market-friendly products or fund follow-up research. Strong US patent protections prevent the dissemination of information about the components of DNA sequences into the public domain.[40] It is clear that, especially in international trade,

[38] See Handong [27], p. 187.

[39] The so-called biological products are made by processing microorganisms, microbial metabolites, animal toxins, human or animal blood or tissues, etc. They are immunological agents used for the prevention, diagnosis, and treatment of specific infectious diseases or other related diseases, such as vaccines, antivenoms, toxoids, and antibiotics. These products also protect personality, as argued against the recognition of full genetic property rights. The California Supreme Court has analogized human tissue and genes, but failed to take into account the shared personality elements between the two and to devise a verdict of one-way protection of property rights in the biotechnology industry. See Qingkui [28]; Yongming, & Canjun [29].

[40] Doll [30].

the acquisition and protection of gene patents has commercial, economic and political significance. It is an important factor in economic superiority.

It is undeniable that the economic incentive mechanism of patent rights for intellectual property has, to a certain extent, contributed to selfishness, greed, ruthlessness, and bullying of technological capital. In any profitable area, even if it violates ethical boundaries, forcibly seizes and plunders, and harms the interests of the public and future generations, the gene technology industry will go to any lengths to use "power" for personal gain. Repeated attempts to legalize reproductive gene therapy and cloning, efforts to privatize the common heritage of mankind such as the human genome, attempts to promote "terminator" technology, and "biopiracy," "bio-colonization," "bio-enclosure," and "bio-exploitation" of patients and subjects have all led to gene patent rights being subjected to surging ethical criticism.[41]

Gene patent rights are like a double-edged sword: when pointed in the right direction, it can act as a "fuel" and "accelerator" for technological progress and economic development, ultimately leading to improved human health and wellbeing. However, misuse of these rights can lead to abuse, with endless disasters for mankind, the environment, and future generations. Since patent rights are a legal right granted by the state, their protection and degree of protection are dependent on the competition and games between economic, political, ethical, and cultural forces in any given place.

Gene patent rights are still in the early stages of conceptualization and institutionalization, so the interpretation and modification of the basic principles of patent rights in the context of gene technology are still being tested and explored. The debate on the acceptability of gene technology and its patent protection will inevitably influence the theoretical innovation and institutional change of gene patent rights. It is clear that gene patenting can be beneficial, but it should be strictly regulated when it provokes and violates moral and ethical taboos.

4 Practical Problems and Theoretical Innovation

4.1 Controversy and Crux

The core challenge of gene technology to the traditional patent system is the "non-obviousness" requirement of the patent subject matter. The "inventive step" requirement stems from the patent law's distinction between "invention" and "discovery." A patent can only be granted to an "invention" and not a "discovery," as the knowledge involved in "discovery" is too basic and extensive; granting it a "monopoly right"

---

[41] The Terminator technique, also known as the Seed Suicide Technique, was developed by Monsanto, an American biochemical company, to protect seeds from being reproduced. The principle is to implant a gene with self-toxic properties into a seed. When the seeds are replanted the following year, the self-poisoning genes are expressed, resulting in the seeds' death. At one point, the Terminator technology was patented; however, due to international and domestic condemnation, the patent was revoked. See: Brac de la Perrière, & Seuret [31].

would impede the dissemination of knowledge and hinder scientific and technological progress. Additionally, patenting is intended to motivate the modification of nature and the commercial application of practical technologies, not to reward scientific discovery. According to this law, naturally occurring phenomena (including life) and the purification, aggregation, or minor alteration of pre-existing substances cannot be patented.[42]

Genetic technology has challenged and undermined the requirement of an "inventive step" by blurring the distinction between "invention" and "discovery". The essence of genetic engineering is to recognize, reveal, intervene and modify life processes and forms with the decoding and recoding of the code of life (DNA). Discoveries like the analysis of DNA molecular sequences and the localization of functional genes rely on the "double deoxystrand end termination method" or "inventive" technologies such as the "chemical degradation method". Inventive activities on genetically modified microorganisms, animals, plants, and biological products are based on discoveries such as sequencing and functional localization of DNA molecules. Furthermore, no matter the type of "creative" activity such as cutting, splicing, and recombining DNA molecules, or the completely new varieties or products it "invents", the results of genetic engineering technology are based on the genetic information of life in nature and implement the working principle of natural life mechanisms.[43] When invention and discovery are so closely intertwined, how can one identify and judge the inventive nature of gene technology? And when it is difficult to determine whether it has inventive attributes, how can one decide whether gene technology and its basic research can be patented?

As the line between patentable and non-patentable subject matter becomes blurred, the conflict between those who benefit from patent rights and those who lose out intensifies. This is particularly evident with those who suffer a financial loss, such as patients who are subject to genetic exploitation without their informed consent, farmers whose traditional knowledge or biodiversity is stolen without recompense, and communities whose environment is contaminated by genetic engineering. Advocates for ethics, morality, and ecology have vocally opposed gene patents, while also denying any possibility of confirming their rights.[44] Conversely, the beneficiaries of patent rights—mainly genomic research institutions, medical institutions, biomedical and chemical companies—have sought alternative interpretations of the "inventive step" requirement. They are removing theoretical and technical barriers to the confirmation of gene patents while advocating for the extension of its protection to topics such as genetically modified microorganisms, life forms such as animals and plants, and even the human genome.[45]

[42] See Demaine & Fellmeth [32].

[43] Yongming & Canjun [33].

[44] See Shiva [34].

[45] See Demaine & Fellmeth [35].

4.1.1 Theoretical Resolutions

The crux of the problem lies in the use of genetic technology, which erases the boundary between "invention" and "discovery" and thus fails to meet the criteria of "creativity". What strategies should be adopted to address this issue? Is it possible to forgo the binary distinction between "invention" and "discovery" and the condition of "inventive step"? This approach is extremely risky, as it could lead to the appropriation and privatization of naturally occurring genetic resources and knowledge that belong to the public domain. This could result in the stifling of technology, the stagnation of the economy, the formation of an oligarchy of technological capital, and the exploitation and colonization of the poor and weak.[46] However, if the traditional dichotomy and the substantive elements of creativity are maintained, the problem returns to square one. How do we incorporate new technologies that embody the characteristics of rebellion within existing principles and institutional frameworks? How do we identify which items, such as functional genes, can be interpreted as creation at the intersection of discovery and invention? And what items, such as the human genome, cannot be included in the scope of patentable subject matter in any case?

When technical characteristics are an immutable premise, only the theoretical framework can be changed. This includes the binary distinction between "invention" and "discovery" as well as the reinterpretation of the "inventive" element.

Like people and things, inside and outside, subject and object, personality and property, culture and nature, and consciousness and material, the invention/discovery dichotomy on which the patent system is based is a tool of the narrative of modernity, intended to establish and celebrate the supremacy of man as the spirit of all things in nature. This narrative, driven by rationalism, utilitarianism, liberalism, pragmatism, and consumerism, encourages people to understand and control nature. However, resource depletion and ecological destruction serve as a powerful blow to the narrative of modernity, including the invention/discovery dichotomy, in terms of factual consequences. The linguistic turn of epistemology is a narrative method that exposes this binary opposition on the philosophical paradigm and theoretical frame of reference, revealing the power relations between man and nature, the strong and the weak, and the elite and the ordinary. Gene technology specifically disintegrates the narrative of modernity modeled by the binary conceptual system of invention/discovery, personality/property, and person/thing from the inside and micro in practice.[47]

The questioning and critique of the narrative tools of modernity, in the context of genetic patents, seems to illustrate the assertion that the binary distinction between invention and discovery, property and personality, etc., does not necessarily mean that this is indeed the case. If it is not a discursive construction that covers specific power relations, then there is no need to mechanically apply the clear distinctions between "invention" and "discovery" to the debate surrounding the legitimacy of gene patent rights. While downplaying the opposed concepts of the two, it is necessary to judge

[46] See Jaffe, & Lerner [36].

[47] See Pottage [37].

the "inventiveness" and "patentability" of relevant projects more according to the struggles and games between various economic, political and cultural forces taking place in reality as expressed through discourse. Additionally, since intermediate states and "hybridity" that straddle the two ends of the binary concept have undeniably occurred and existed, it is necessary to abandon the attempt and effort to continue to drag it back to a certain end point and instead to "mix" and judge the presence or absence of the "creativity" of the object involved according to the degree and balance of forces in the time and place.

4.1.2 Practical Problem Resolutions

On the issue of inventive step and patentability of the human genome map, the Human Genome Project working draft was completed in June 2000. It covered 83% of the genome sequence, including the autochromatin region 90%. This map provides information on gene sequencing, localization, and expression.[48]

The completion of the human genome map is akin to compiling a biological dictionary or periodic table that reveals the metacode of human heredity and life mechanisms, allowing us to gain a greater understanding of the evolution of life, the laws of biological evolution, and the mysteries of human birth, aging, illness, and death, as well as the diagnosis of genetic diseases.[49]

First, the development of therapeutics and gene-based pharmaceuticals has revolutionized commercial value and profit potential. Before the mapping of the human genome was completed, UNESCO issued the Universal Declaration on the Human Genome and Human Rights, which declared that the human genome is the common heritage of all mankind and should benefit all humankind.[50] Upon announcing the Human Genome Project, then-U.S. President Bill Clinton and British Prime Minister Tony Blair declared that the raw data of the human genome should be accessible to scientists worldwide.[51] The specific sequencing information of the working sketch, the method used for sequencing, and the analysis results of the sequence were published, reducing the possibility of filing a patent application for the human genome map with the disclosure of various types of raw data. However, the working sketch only draws the rough structure and sequence of the human genome, leaving endless space to be discovered and interpreted on the human DNA chain, which can be stretched around the earth for three weeks. In fact, the gene technology industry, including one of the participants in the Human Genome Project, the private American company Celera Genomics, has not ceased patenting gene structures and fragments. Therefore, it is still important to further elucidate or refute the issue of patentability of the human genome map. Although, according to the basic principles of patent law, it is possible to apply for a patent for the method of discovering genes and

[48] See Wikipedia [38].

[49] Zhenjiang, & Yinliang [39].

[50] UNESCO, translated by Zhi [24].

[51] Quote from: Jida [40].

extend it to its products, this is only an indirect confirmation of the gene fragment, and its scope of protection should be strictly limited. Ultimately, the human gene map "only indicates the order of proteins, and does not know which bases play what role in life, meaning it is not inventive and therefore cannot be patented."[52] The EU Directive on the Legal Protection of Biotechnological Inventions states that a "simple DNA sequence that does not specify its function" is not patentable. Wu Handong et al.'s Intellectual Property Law Towards the Knowledge Economy (2002) makes it clear that protecting the human genome map with patents would stifle and restrain the advancement of gene technology and economy.[53] It is understandable that the protection of the human genome map, being the fundamental accomplishment and upstream product of gene science and technology research, through patents, could stifle and restrain the future development of gene technology and economy.

Second, the inventiveness and patentability of basic research results such as functional genes is noteworthy. Not every segment of the DNA chain has the ability to control protein production and expression to determine specific traits and life phenomena. Genes without this ability are referred to as "junk genes," while those with this ability are called "functional genes." Functional genes are of particular value in bioengineering and the manufacture of genetic products and their commercial applications. Unlike the discovery of simple gene structures and fragments, the discovery, extraction, cloning, and recombination of functional genes requires more creative technical operations. Therefore, functional genes are generally considered to be both "inventive" and "patentable."

Third, the "inventive step" and patentability of genetically modified microorganisms, animals, plants, and biological products have historically been met with resistance due to ethical considerations. This is because living beings exist naturally in nature and matters without an "inventive step" are not patentable. However, with the broad uses of GMOs in environmental protection, winemaking, food, agriculture, animal husbandry, pharmaceuticals, and medical treatment, patent applications with genetically modified organisms as the subject matter have become increasingly common. The primary challenge to patenting GMOs, aside from moral and biodiversity concerns, is proving their "inventiveness." This is because the creation of such organisms is based on natural genetic information and follows natural life mechanisms. Nevertheless, the introduction of gene recombination technology has added innovative elements that are distinct from natural substances and processes, thereby making GMOs patentable. This idea was established in the U.S. Supreme Court case, Diamond v. Chakrabarty,[54] which granted patents on genetically modified

---

[52] Handong [27], p. 193.

[53] Quoted from Handong [27].

[54] In this case, "Chakra Bhattiyu1972to the United States Patent and Trademark Office (PTO) File a patent application, The invention comes from bacteria with pseudo-single-celled biological genes, The bacteria of this artificial heritage project are able to break down crude oil and various components. It is valuable for oil spill treatment. PTO The application was rejected,The reason is:(1)Microorganisms are products of nature; (2) In accordance with U.S. patent law, Living organisms are not patentable... After a series of legal arguments. The case went to the U.S. Supreme

microbes.[55] More patents are being granted to genetically modified microorganisms, biological products, plants, and animals.[56]

4.2 *Power Conflicts and Confrontations*

The creation and realization of genetic benefits can be logically described as: the genetic technology industry engineering pre-fertilization and modification of genetic resources or information to produce genetic products with specific properties or uses, which are then sold on the market or licensed. Genes serve as legal and beneficial mediators, and the subjects and rights associated with them mainly include the property rights and privacy rights of gene resource and information providers, the patent rights of gene technology or gene product research and development and producers, and the rights of consumers of gene products. Technological capital contributes the most to the value of products, so patent rights are the most powerful and expansive. These can crowd out and suppress the legal interests and rights of the other two, so sufficient attention and emphasis must be given to the potential conflict between patent rights and other forms of rights, and how they should be confronted by other forms of rights.

4.2.1 Conflict and Confrontation Between Gene Patent Rights and Gene Property Right

As previously explained, providers of genetic resources and information have personal property rights over their living materials, which entitles them to request informed consent from the producers of gene technologies and products and enter into benefit-sharing contracts. Correspondingly, if a manufacturer of gene technology and product obtains a gene patent without the informed consent of the gene resource and information provider, does not give any compensation, and privately embezzles its benefits, it constitutes "gene encroachment" or "gene theft", which may lead to the revocation of the gene patent right.[57]

Court.". The Supreme Court ruled that a patent should be granted to the subject matter. See Handong [27], pp. 194–195.

[55] Naigen [41].

[56] See Xiaofeng [42].

[57] There are many cases in which patents have been revoked for "theft" and "exploitation" of indigenous genetic resources by multinational biotechnology companies. The most famous of these include American medical anthropologist Carol Jenkins and Papua New Guinea Hagahai. A toxin contained in the blood of the people was cultivated into a cell line that treats leukemia, and the National Institutes of Health (NIH) was granted a patent for the cell line. This action provoked outrage, and Papua New Guinea summoned the U.S. ambassador for explanation. Third-world countries also strongly condemned such acts as "genetic imperialism". Under pressure, the NIH announced the waiver of the patent. See Pottage [37].

4.2.2 Conflict and Confrontation Between Gene Patent Rights and Gene Privacy Rights

Genes encode the most secretive and central information about human traits and life processes, which is directly related to human dignity and equal treatment in society. Therefore, those who provide genetic resources and information should enjoy absolute privacy rights to their data, even if they submit it to scientific and technological research and development institutions, such as biobanks, with the informed consent of the provider. In this case, the provider should remain in control and dominance over their genetic data, and the holder of the patent right should treat the subject matter anonymously and unidentifiably, without the informed consent of the provider. Furthermore, they should not buy, sell, transfer, or disclose their genetic information to third parties, such as insurance companies and employers.[58]

4.2.3 Conflict and Confrontation Between Gene Patent Rights and Farmers' Rights

As a result of the development model of modern capitalism over the past four hundred years, the economically and technologically advanced countries of the Northern Hemisphere are relatively poor in biodiversity, while those of the Southern Hemisphere are rich in biodiversity yet economically and technologically backward. This has led to the phenomenon of large biotechnology multinational corporations and scientific research and experimental institutions competing to explore, collect, develop, and commercialize genetic resources and traditional knowledge from late-developing countries and communities that have been isolated for a long time and have thus kept their biodiversity intact. These organizations "acquire and use knowledge by analyzing plant and other biological samples provided by the national community or by observing the traditional craftsmanship of the national community, and they research, develop, reproduce, and treat materials originating in the national community as objects of property rights"; finally, these materials are put on the market. On the other hand, communities and national communities at the center of biodiversity are limited by a lack of knowledge, experience, and negotiating power, though they have been provided with these but were not compensated for their use by transnational corporations and scientific institutions until recently.[59]

Genetic resources or traditional knowledge that have been "patented" by biotechnology multinational corporations and scientific research and experimental institutions embody the wisdom and experience of ethnic groups and communities that have fostered and developed them for generations. When these resources are used on a large scale for commercial purposes such as agriculture and medicine, and bring immense wealth to biotechnology multinational corporations and scientific research and experimental institutions, the original rights holders and founding contributors

---

[58] See Greely [43].

[59] Zelda-Sarmiento, & Freiro-By Pineda [44].

are not only not given fair returns but also lose access to their resources and knowledge since they cannot pay large licensing fees.[60] This prompted latecomer countries and ethnic groups, as well as the international or non-governmental organizations acting as their representatives, to denounce such "genetic piracy", "genetic exploitation", and "genetic imperialism".[61] Consequently, the concept of "farmer's rights" emerged as an alternative to genetic patent rights.[62]

The concept of "peasant rights" aims to protect genetic resources and collective knowledge from areas that have been exploited of their "common heritage of mankind". Before the Convention on Biological Diversity, plant genetic resources were seen as a "common heritage of mankind" by international conventions, similar to the high seas and the Antarctic continent, which are to be used equally, freely, and gratuitously. However, this has resulted in the exploitation of the biological resources of less developed countries by economically and technologically advanced nations. The Convention on Biological Diversity establishes the sovereignty of nations over plant genetic resources within their territories. "Peasant rights" seek to defend the property and legal interests of indigenous peoples and communities, who protect and develop the genetic resources and traditional knowledge. Depending on the degree of institutionalization of "farmers' rights", the types of rights mainly consist of "seed rights" and "collective intellectual rights", and the content of rights includes "informed consent rights", "benefit sharing rights" and "research and management participation rights".

In terms of the type of rights, "seed rights" are a revolt against the "breeding rights" of the science and technology industry, especially "gene protection technology" (also known as "terminator technology"). It seeks to protect the right of farmers to harvest and keep the seeds they have sifted and cultivated. "Collective intellectual property rights" is the protection of the knowledge related to biodiversity that has been accumulated by national communities and collectives over generations. It breaks through the individualistic constraints of the modern intellectual property system, and is a new form of intellectual property.[63] Since each member of the community is a successor, practitioner, user, developer, and contributor to the relevant knowledge system or lifestyle, the collective right to knowledge (TK) exists in the public domain of the community and not in the private property of any individual member. The community as a whole, not any one individual, is the holder, beneficiary, and custodian of this intellectual right. The establishment of the collective right to knowledge provides not

[60] For example, Food and Agriculture Organization of the United Nations, Economic Cooperation Organization of the United Nations, etc.

[61] For example, W. R. Grace & Company patented Indian farmers for the use of neem trees as traditional methods; And the University of Mississippi in the United States patented the method of Indian healing with turmeric.

[62] Peasant Rights: The earliest origin of the concept dates back to 1979, when a discussion was held within the Food and Agriculture Organization of the United Nations. After five years, it was clearly stated in the resolution that peasant rights should be recognized. In 1992, the Nairobi Final Act of the Convention on Biological Diversity and the United Nations also set out an achievement plan of action on the century agenda to address the peasant rights issue. See Wenting [45], p. 107.

[63] See Brac de la Perrière, & Seuret [31].

only tools and weapons for self-defense, but also encourages communities to better cooperate with biotechnology companies and research institutions, allowing them to benefit more productively from their knowledge.

With regards to the content of their rights, Farmers' Rights seeks to recognize and protect the equitable benefits of original rights holders from scientific and technological progress, and to enhance their ability to control resources and negotiate with technological capital. Consequently, the collection, commercial development, and patent application of genetic resources or traditional knowledge by biotechnology multinational companies and scientific research and experimental institutions can no longer be considered as free and unrestricted use of "common human resources". Instead, they must obtain informed consent from the original right holder and share patent profits or research benefits in monetary or non-monetary ways as per agreement. Moreover, they should allow the original right holder to enjoy more management and control rights as a joint patentee.[64]

4.2.4 Conflict and Confrontation Between Gene Patent Rights and Health Rights

Expensive licensing fees for patent rights can limit access to specific drugs, diagnoses, and treatments for the general public. To address this issue, there are various mechanisms within the patent right to compromise with the public domain and the public interest (e.g. time, territory, patentable subject matter, limitation of the scope of rights, as well as statutory licenses, compulsory licenses, reverse engineering, etc.). When there is an urgent need for public health, gene patent rights must yield to the public's right to health, and the state can require the provision of its patent objects through compulsory licensing or other measures. At the international level, the Doha Declaration seeks to address the strong protection of pharmaceutical patent rights in developed countries under the Agreement on Trade-Related Aspects of Intellectual Property Rights (TRIPS). It proposes a compulsory licensing system for patented drugs, allowing developing countries without the capacity to produce drugs to obtain affordable drugs for the treatment of diseases such as AIDS, malaria, and tuberculosis, regardless of the intellectual property rights of drugs.

4.3 Boundaries and Restrictions on Confirming Rights

In essence, technology is a typical form of instrumental rational knowledge, instigated by the incentive mechanism of patent law, which allows it to break free from the reins of value rationality and swing in any profitable, even unknown, moral, and social direction. Therefore, even in a discourse system dominated by technical terms, it is

---

64 See Margulies [46]; McManis [47].

not difficult to find provisions of ethical or policy-mandated norms in patent law at any stage of development.

Gene patenting is a complex field with significant implications for bioeconomics, biopolitics, and bioethics. Improper operation can have adverse consequences on human ethics, freedom, dignity, fairness, and justice. On the other hand, genetic engineering is a far from mature technology, and its prediction and alteration of life processes and even genetic mechanisms on people, animals, plants, and microorganisms can have unpredictable and potentially harmful effects on the environment, species, and people themselves. For this reason, the recognition and protection of gene patent rights must be carefully and resolutely restricted.

The European Patent Office agrees that any invention involving higher life forms must be thoroughly examined for ethical implications, and the merits, technological advances, and potential adverse effects must be carefully weighed against each other.[65] At present, for reasons of public morality, health, safety, and order, patents are not granted for human cloning, eugenic and reproductive gene therapy, gene technology protection, and transgenic technologies that may result in "gene escape" and "gene contamination".

5 Genetic Privacy

5.1 Basis of Legality

Privacy refers to matters and information that are not related to others. According to the degree of privacy, it can be classified into personal information, personal affairs, and personal domain. Generally speaking, the personal domain is the outer layer, personal affairs are secondary, and personal information and data belong to the core level.[66]

Accordingly, the right to privacy is "a fundamental right of individuals to control their personal information, private activities, and private sphere unrelated to the public interest." This right is intended to protect the dignity, freedom, and autonomy of the individual, and the closer it is to the core of human subjectivity, the greater the legal protection it receives.[67]

Genetic information is at the core of personal privacy and human dignity. It holds the life code that reveals basic information about human history, future, family and ethnic relations, physiological and psychological tendencies, birth, old age, illness and death. It has a high degree of identification for a person's individuality, almost like a "biological identity card."

---

[65] Quoted from Qingkui [48].

[66] Liming [49], pp. 480–482; Dahong [50].

[67] Liming [49], p. 487.

It is precisely because of the constitutive significance and recognition function of genes and genetic information to the uniqueness of people that the protection of gene privacy is of great social significance. Human genes are diverse, containing both 'good' and 'defective' genes. Under the erroneous concept of genetic determinism, the disclosure of personal 'disease-making' genes could lead to discrimination and unfair treatment in society. Furthermore, with the advancing development of gene technology and the gene economy, it has become easier and more common to collect genetic samples, as well as genetic information, for commercial purposes. This puts the personality and property legal interests loaded on personal genetic information in an increasingly precarious position. Therefore, preventing the privacy of personal genetic information from being illegally collected and maliciously used, and enhancing individuals' control over their genetic privacy, has become one of the most important topics in ethical, legal, and social research related to gene technology.

5.2 Jurisprudential Implications

With the emergence of the information, symbol and consumer economies, items such as names, portraits, and non-personal data and information, which once only had personal and legal benefits, have become commercially viable and now have an economic value that can be quantified.[68]

Correspondingly, the nature and legal meaning of the right to privacy are undergoing a shift—from valuing human "dignity" alone to emphasizing human "freedom" and "autonomy," from emphasizing static control and inaccessibility of data and information to allowing access and free disposal.[69] Shift from purely personality rights attributes to limited absorption of certain features of property rights.[70]

The legal implications of genetic privacy are especially prominent. The development of property law has stimulated the benefit of genetic personality law, and this has been proposed in opposition to the "colonization" of the human person by commodity logic. However, as the development of gene technology and gene economy has become an unstoppable and irreversible trend, and the search and collection of human genetic resources and information by various bio-banks and biotechnology companies has become ubiquitous and pervasive, the only rational choice is to accept the reality of the property of genetic information on a limited basis and build a system of norms that is most conducive to the personality and economic interests of genetic resources and information providers.[71]

---

[68] This has even evolved into a new category of "publicity" (right of publicity). As a sibling of the "right to privacy," if the latter still focuses on static and negative connotations, then the "right of disclosure" recognizes and protects the dynamic and commercial use of "privacy" matters.

[69] The right to privacy was first proposed in the United States, given the negative connotations of "comfort" and "undisturbed" by American jurist Louis Brandeis in 1890.See Warren, & Brandies [51].

[70] See Liming [52].

[71] See Valerio Barrad [53]; Everett [54].

Therefore, genetic privacy has a double legal meaning: it not only defends the legal interests of personality, but also protects the legal interests of property. It emphasizes the static control of genetic information, prohibiting it from being spied on, obtained, and transmitted without permission. Additionally, it emphasizes the dynamic use of genetic information, allowing providers to benefit from discretion.

5.3 Power and Protection

5.3.1 Right to Confidentiality

Because genetic information is related to all aspects of human life processes, relationships, and traits, it directly impacts the most private and core part of human freedom, dignity, uniqueness, and self-identity. If adverse information is leaked, it is directly related to people's psychological anxiety and harm, as well as social discrimination and unequal treatment. Therefore, individuals have a right to strict confidentiality of their genetic information. When collecting personal genetic resources and information, biobanks and biotechnology product departments must ask providers whether they allow disclosure of the obtained data. Without public consent, it shall not be disclosed to any third party, other than family members in a sick situation, and the obtained material must be anonymized and de-identified in compliance with the providers' confidentiality requirements.[72]

5.3.2 Right to Informed Consent

Providers of genetic resources and information have complete control over data related to their genes. They must be informed of their options regarding genetic testing, including whether or not to accept it, the results of testing, and the status of use, transfer and dissemination of their genetic information. Their opinions and choices should be faithfully heard and respected.[73]

[72] In 1997, before the mapping of the human genome was completed, UNESCO issued the Universal Declaration on the Human Genome and Human Rights, warning that "data relating to or stored and processed by individuals for research or any other purpose must be kept confidential in accordance with the law." Genetic data must be kept secret in accordance with the law's requirements. See UNESCO [55].

[73] Sato [56].

5.3.3 Right to Benefit Sharing

Providers of genetic resources and information have property rights to their genetic information and the right to receive a share of relevant research interests and commercial profits through contractual agreements.[74]

5.3.4 Anti-Discrimination and Unequal Treatment

This is the most painful part of genetic privacy protection. Genetic information has anthropological implications[75] and can lead to discrimination, ostracization, and unequal treatment of certain groups of people due to their genetic traits that may predispose them to negative consequences such as violent tendencies or personality defects. This is a tragedy and can even lead to real hatred and revenge. In the field of microlife, there have already been cases of genetic discrimination: some insurance institutions, employers, schools, and other departments require their customers or recruits to undergo genetic testing and charge higher insurance premiums for those with certain disease-causing genes, or even refuse to recruit or raise the conditions for recruitment. The bias and insensitivity of genetic determinism is evident here.[76]

In fact, human life traits and processes are not determined by genes alone. Environmental factors have a significant impact on the expression of functional genes and methods of expression. Furthermore, some disease-causing genes may not always lead to diseases as predicted by genetics. Additionally, genetics and gene technology are far from mature. The interpretation of human genes and the mysteries of life is far from reaching the level of "truth". The diversity of human genes means that genes that do not express certain traits may have other unique properties and functions. Thus, genetic discrimination, which is based on a lack of scientific evidence, is unfair and should not be used to treat people unequally.

In terms of system design, insurance providers, employers, and schools should be prohibited from requiring genetic testing. Confidentiality of individuals' genetic information should be strictly protected to prevent it from being leaked or disseminated through any channels.

References

1. Zhang, T. (2001). *The gene age and the gene economy* (pp. 1–71). Democracy and Construction Press (in Chinese).

---

[74] See Everett [54].

[75] In the World Declaration on the Human Genome and Human Rights, UNESCO warns that no one should be discriminated against on the basis of their genetic characteristics. Failure to do so would violate or have the effect of violating human rights, fundamental freedoms and human dignity.

[76] See Jensen [57]; Kim [58].

2. Rifkin, J. (1999). *The Biotech century: Harnessing the gene and remaking the world* (Trade Ed edition, pp. 39–70).TarcherPerigee.
3. Myerson, G. (2000). Donna Haraway and genetically modified foods. In: *Icon* (pp. 43–58). Totem Books.
4. Knorr-Cetina, K.D. (1981). The *manufacture of knowledge: an essay on the constructivist and contextual nature of science* (pp. 1–88). Elsevier Ltd.
5. Kant, I. (1790). *The Science of Right. E-BOOKARAMA*, 2022.
6. Locke, J. (1689). *Two treatises of government*. Cambridge University Press.
7. Marchant, G.E. (2005). Property rights and benefit-sharing for DNA donors? Jurimetrics Winter:159–164.
8. Sharp, L. A. (2000). The commodification of the body and its parts. *Ann Rev Anthropol, 29*, 303–311.
9. Qiu, G. (2008). *Analysis of human genetic property rights*. Academic Forum (6) (in Chinese).
10. Becker, G.S. (1976). *The economic approach to human behavior* (pp. 5–25). The University of Chicago Press.
11. Posner, R.A. (1998). *Economic analysis of law* (5th ed., pp. 3–40). Aspen Publishers.
12. Moore v. *Board of regents of the University of California*. (1990). 793 P.2d 479 (Cal.).
13. Liu, C., & Liu, C. (Year). *Laws and property rights on the application of human tissue in biotechnology*. http://myweb.ncku.edu.tw/~sts1/wine/021216.doc, accessed on 2010–04–18. (in Chinese).
14. Qiu, G. (2008). *Analysis of human genetic property rights*. Academic Forum, (6) (in Chinese).
15. Marchant, G. E. (2005). Property rights and benefit-sharing for DNA donors? *Jurimetrics, 2005*(Winter), 163–164.
16. Pottage, A. (2004). Instructions: The Manufacture of Persons and Things. In A. Pottage & M. Mundy (Eds.), *Law, Anthropology, and the Constitution of the Social: Making Persons and Things* (pp. 1–39). Cambridge University Press.
17. Hegel, G. W. F. (1821). *Philosophy of right. Batoche Books Kitchener, 2001*,
18. Radin, M. J. (1982). Property and personality. *Stanford Law Review, 34*, 957–1015.
19. Radin, M. J. (1987). Market-Inalienability. *Harvard Law Review, 100*(8), 1849–1937.
20. Frow, J. (1995). Elvis fame: The commodity form and the form of person. *Cardozo Studies in Law and Literature, 7*(2), 131–171.
21. Xiaoyao, X. (2005). The right to commodity: expansion and equity of personality symbols. *Law and Business Studies, 2005*(3), 81–86. (in Chinese).
22. Marchant, G.E. (2005). Property rights and benefit-sharing for DNA donors? Jurimetrics Winter:163–164.
23. The Human Genome Organization. (2000). Statement on the Principled conduct of genetics research. Rev Derecho Genoma Hum, Jan–Jun(12):253–5.
24. Zhi, Z. (1998). World declaration on the human genome and human rights. *Medicine and Philosophy, 1998*(3), 114.
25. Weir, R.F., & Horton, J.R. (1995). DNA banking and informed consent. *IRB: Ethics and Human Research* 17(5/6):1–8
26. Andrews, L.B. (2005). Harnessing the benefits of biobanks. *Journal of Law, Medicine and Ethics*, Spring.
27. Handong, W. et al. (2002). *Intellectual property law towards the knowledge economy* (p. 187). Law Press (in Chinese).
28. Qingkui, Z. (2001). *On new challenges in biotechnology patent protection*. Intellectual Property Press.
29. Yongming, L., & Canjun, P. (2003). Patent protection for gene technology. *Journal of Zhejiang University, 2003*(1), 136–140.
30. Doll, J. J. (1998). The patenting of DNA. *Science, 280*, 690.
31. Brac de la Perrière, R.A., & Seuret, F. (2020). Brave new seeds: The threat of GM crops to farmers (Global Issues, pp. 20–50). Zed Books.
32. Demaine, L. J., & Fellmeth, A. X. (2002). Reinventing the double helix: A novel and nonobvious reconceptualization of the biotechnology patent. *Stanford Law Review, 55*(2), 10.

33. Yongming, L., & Canjun, P. (2003). Patent protection for gene technology. *Journal of Zhejiang University* (1):137 (in Chinese).
34. Shiva, V. (1998). *Biopiracy: The plunder of nature and knowledge* (pp. 7–11). Green Books Ltd.
35. Demaine, L. J., & Fellmeth, A. X. (2002). Reinventing the double helix: a novel and nonobvious reconceptualization of the biotechnology patent. *Stanford Law Review, 55*(2), 3–6.
36. Jaffe, A.B., & Lerner, J. (2004). *Innovation and its discontents* (pp. 56–207). Princeton University Press.
37. Pottage, A. (1998). The inscription of life in law: Genes, patents, and bio-politics. *Modern Law Review, 61*(5), 740–765. https://doi.org/10.1111/1468-2230.00177
38. Wikipedia. (2010). *Human genome project.* http://baike.baidu.com/view/22966.htm?fr=ala0_1_1 [Accessed 18 April 2010]
39. Zhenjiang, Z., & Yinliang, L. (2001). Research on the Legal Issues of the Human Genome Project. *Chinese and Foreign Law, 2001*(4), 435.
40. Jida, R. (2006). *Human gene Atlas completed.* Beijing Youth Daily
41. Naigen, Z. (Ed.). (1995). *Selected cases under U.S. patent law* (pp. 66–76). China University of Political Science and Law Press.
42. Xiaofeng, H. (1996). Origin and development of intellectual property protection issues in biotechnology. *Intellectual Property Rights, 1996*(2), 16.
43. Greely, H.T. (1998). Legal, ethical and social issues in human genome research. *Annual Review of Anthropology*
44. Zelda-Sarmiento, A., & Freiro-By Pineda, C. (2002). Intellectual property issues of knowledge in national communities. *International Social Science Journal, 2002*(1), 99–114.
45. Wenting, Z. Farmers' Rights Perspective on Access to Plant Genetic Resources and Benefit-sharing. http://www.riel.whu.edu.cn/article.asp?id=27705
46. Margulies, R.L. (1993). Protecting biodiversity: international intellectual property rights in plant genetic resources. *Michigan Journal of International Law* 14(322), Winter:323–356
47. McManis, C. R. (2003). Intellectual property, genetic resources and traditional knowledge protection. *Cardozo Journal of International and Comparative Law, 157*(547), 547–580.
48. Qingkui, Z. (2001). *On new challenges in biotechnology patent protection.* Intellectual Property Press (in Chinese).
49. Liming, W. (Ed.). (1994). *New Theory of Personality Rights Law.* Jilin People's Publishing House.
50. Dahong, L. (2002). Gene technology and the protection of privacy. *Chinese Law, 2002*(6), 75. (in Chinese).
51. Warren, S. D., & Brandies, L. (1980). The right to privacy. *Harvard Law Review, 5*, 193–222.
52. Liming, W. (2010). The development of the privacy system in the united states and its enlightenment to China's legislation. http://www.govyi.com/lunwen/2007/200711/147433_5.shtml
53. Valerio Barrad, C. M. (1993). Genetic information and property theory. *Northwestern University Law Review, 87*(3), 1037–1086.
54. Everett, M. (2007). The I in the gene: Divided property, fragmented personhood and the making of a genetic privacy law. *American Ethnologist* 34(2), p. 375.
55. UNESCO. (1998). World declaration on the human genome and human rights. Medicine and Philosophy (3):115 [Translated by Zhi, Z.] (in Chinese).
56. Sato, T. (2003). On the legal protection of privacy in the age of genes. *Jurisprudence, 12*, 100.
57. Jensen, P. (1999). Genetic privacy: The potential for genetic discrimination in insurance. *Victoria U. Wellington L. Rev., 29*, 347–369.
58. Kim, P. T. (2002). Genetic discrimination, genetic privacy: rethinking employee protections for a brave new workplace. *Northwestern University Law Review, 96*(4), 1497–1551.

Chapter 6
Sexual Rights

Yongjun Li

1 Introduction

The concepts of "sex" and "rights" are familiar, but when combined, "sexual rights" doesn't have the same familiarity. Despite this, we have thoroughly reviewed official international human rights documents and China's domestic laws and regulations, and the term "sexual rights" isn't explicitly mentioned anywhere, nor is it used in any article. Rights are a fundamental aspect of the law, and the theory of rights is a crucial component of China's legal education. However, in traditional legal textbooks, whether in jurisprudence or departmental law, one can find concepts such as "human rights," "property rights," "creditors' rights," "litigation rights," "intellectual property rights," and "freedom of speech rights," but the term "sexual rights" is notably absent.

Sexual rights are often seen as unfamiliar and precarious in practice. Professor Li Yinhe has stated that "Of all the civil liberties rights, sexual freedom and sexual rights are the most vulnerable and fragile in China." While people may hesitate to publicly oppose other freedoms, the right to sexual freedom is often treated as one that some people are comfortable rejecting.[1]

Sexual rights are inherent human rights that reflect freedom, equality, and independent subjective status. They are closely related to human survival and development. Despite their importance, sexual rights have been suppressed by various forces due to the fundamental position of sex in human society. Sex plays a crucial role in the development of human society, including the release of human sexual desires and instincts and the reproduction of the human race. Sexual pleasure is a core part of human happiness, and for society, sex is the most important way to regenerate social human resources. Gender relations are the most basic social relations in human society, as human blood relations are generated through sex, and marriage and family

[1] Li [1].

Y. Li (✉)
Theoretical Legal Research Center, Law School of Jilin University, Changchun, China

J. Yao (ed.), *The Legal Issues of the Emerging Rights*,
https://doi.org/10.1007/978-981-97-0499-6_6

are established based on these relations. The sexual order is the basis of human social order, and the norms of sex constitute the core of the moral ethics of human society. However, the control of sex has always been an important task of the state, as sex that does not operate according to established rules will fundamentally subvert social order. In traditional societies, state control of sex became extreme suppression of it. In order to subordinate sex, various forces such as public opinion, custom, morality, religion, law, and even science were mobilized to suppress it in all directions.[2] This is specifically manifested in the rejection of women's sexual freedom in the male-centered subject of rights, the exclusion of sexual autonomy in the center of power and identity in sexual selection, and the prohibition of interrupting marriage relationships and re-selecting sexual partners centered on ultra-stable marriages in sexual relations. The function of sex is centered on reproduction, rejecting sexual behavior in the form of pleasure, and so on. Under this extreme suppression of sexuality, there is no living space for sexual rights. Because of this, in a sense, in the history of human civilization for thousands of years, sexual rights are the most uncharted rights, and sexual freedom is the freedom that society is most unwilling to grant to the people.

From tradition to modernity, along with the changes in society, the way sex exists in society and people's attitudes towards it have also undergone fundamental changes. With the development of sex science, human beings began to observe themselves rationally and objectively. With the use of contraceptive technology, the recreational function of sex began to separate from the reproductive function and became the main function of sex. With the use of transportation and information technology, people's communication channels are expanding, and the exchange of sexual information is becoming more and more frequent. With the deepening of the market economy, people's concepts of individualism, utilitarianism, pragmatism, and liberalism have gradually strengthened. With the rise of the feminist movement, women became increasingly aware of their rights and waged many forms of struggle for their sexual freedom. In particular, the "sexual revolution" that emerged in the 1960s and swept the Western world more powerfully dissolved the conservative nature of traditional sexual culture. As a result, human sexual culture is being renewed. Under the new sexual culture, the mystery and guilt of sex are dissolving, the binding power of marriage is weakening, the quality of sexual life in the marriage and family is improving, and the way people have sex is expanding. The idea of pursuing sex for

[2] Science does not exist in a vacuum. The ideologies of the time, particularly the mainstream ideology, often influence scientists' thinking. Even some scientific conclusions are the result of catering to the rulers' needs. As sex perception has long been surrounded by prejudice and ignorance, this bias and ignorance also infiltrate the scientists' minds to varying degrees. Therefore, some science itself or some fallacies have joined the ranks of slavery in human history in the name of science. For example, in the 19th century, the medical profession generally believed that semen loss could cause neurasthenia and even lead to mental breakdowns, blindness, and epilepsy as a revenge for masturbation. At the beginning of the 20th century, psychiatry and psychology even considered pregnancy out of wedlock to be a manifestation of mental retardation. Consequently, many girls in Britain were sent to correctional homes and psychiatric hospitals. Wang [2], Giddens [3].

pleasure is becoming generally accepted, and the idea that the pursuit of sex is a fundamental human right is beginning to take shape.[3]

Since the reform and opening up, China's market economy has developed in depth, democratic politics have steadily advanced, and society has enjoyed long-term peace and stability. People's living standards have greatly improved, and society has become increasingly equal and pluralistic. People began to pay attention to sex, and they now have the ability and energy to pursue sex and enjoy it. The proportion of sex in people's lives is becoming increasingly prominent, and the trend of sexual needs and behaviors diversification is taking shape. Practice also works according to this logic. According to the surveys and research of Chinese sexual sociologists, since the reform and opening up, China's "sexual revolution" has also quietly risen. In this process, the philosophy of "reproductive teleology" has been completely discredited. The divorce rate has increased, sexual "tutoring" has relaxed, sexual knowledge can now be openly preached, pornography has increased dramatically, and sex stores have become popular in cities. The proportion of sex life in marriage has increased significantly, premarital sex is widespread, polyamorous sex and its tolerance have increased, and women's awareness of sexual autonomy has increased.[4] In such a process and environment with diverse sexual needs, the traditional concept of sexuality has gradually declined, and the concept of sex as an independent right is beginning to take shape. With the increasing pluralism and openness of society, this concept of rights will become more mature, and the demand for rights will become more urgent. Specifically, in recent years, there has been an increasing trend in judicial practice of cases claiming compensation for damage to sexual rights or "sexual well-being" due to damage to sexual organs or sexual functions, as well as cases of divorce due to disharmony in sexual life[5,6]; The awareness of protecting sexual rights is increasing, and some minor sexual offenses that were only recognized as immoral in traditional society are now included in the category of "sexual harassment" and are legally held accountable for violating sexual rights.[7] As society becomes more diverse, the demand for sexual rights of marginalized groups has also emerged, such as the sexual rights of migrant workers, prisoners, and homosexuals.[8]

[3] In the United States, the discourse that accompanies the "sexual revolution" of the 20th century began to take shape in the 1960s and 1970s. See Hedge [4].

[4] Pan et al. [5].

[5] Cao [6]; Wu [7, 8].

[6] A survey conducted by Zero Point Research found that lack of sexual happiness leads to overall unhappiness. Additionally, according to a domestic report, around 30% of divorced couples cited discord in their sex lives as a cause for their separation. For more information, see Zhou [9].

[7] In recent years, there has been a rise in reported cases of sexual harassment and abuse. To address this issue, the Law of the People's Republic of China on the Protection of Women's Rights and Interests was amended in 2005, and in 2006, the Law of the People's Republic of China on Administrative Punishments for Public Security was enacted with provisions specifically prohibiting sexual harassment.

[8] See "Shenzhen Migrant Workers Demand the Right to Live as a Husband and Wife." (2005, June 29). Southern Metropolis Daily; "Saying that the prison sets up a 'mandarin duck room'." (2005, February 14). Star Online. Retrieved from http://www.csonline.com.cn, Li [10].

Social changes have posed challenges to contemporary sexuality legislation in China. Due to the particularity of sex, in the process of China's legal reform and modernization, the reform of sexual law is undoubtedly lagging behind. In a sense, China's current legislation and practice of sexual behavior are still governed by traditional thinking, which establishes various rules centered on human sexual responsibility and sexual obligation. "Prevention" is greater than "protection" of sex, and more suppression than channeling. As a result, there has been a certain degree of disconnect and contradiction between law and reality. For example, with the increasing development of printing, audio-visual, the Internet and information technology, the demand for pornography is becoming more and more widespread. The practice of completely prohibiting the dissemination of pornography without distinction of grade or age is to some extent neither possible nor feasible. Moreover, it violates citizens' right to sexual appreciation and access to sexual information.[9] For example, China's Criminal Law and Public Security Administration Punishment Law still treat sexual acts between multiple people in private based on their consent as the crime of gathering a crowd to commit sexual immorality and the illegal act of gathering a crowd to commit sexual immorality. For example, in recent years, the number of homosexuals in China has been growing. According to expert estimates, the number of homosexuals is currently between 39 million to 5200. In the face of such a large group, China's law has not responded as it should from the perspective of rights.

As Marx said, "Only the unknowable of history do not know that monarchs have to submit at all times to economic conditions and can never dictate to them." Both political legislation and civic legislation are merely requirements for indicating and recording economic relations.[10] Contemporary Chinese sexual legislation should reflect this right demand in a timely manner and take it as the goal and value orientation of sexual legislation. It is true that due to the particularity of sex and the characteristics of law as a norm, sexual law must be more manifested as a regulation and restriction of human sexuality at the actual level. But legislators must be clear that these regulations and constraints exist only as a means to better meet human needs and realize human rights. Therefore, China's contemporary sexual behavior legislation should arrange various systems and norms centered on sexual rights. Only in this way can our legislation be closer to the people, more in line with the people's feelings, more suitable for society, and more respectful of human nature. Only laws that conform to the people's feelings, adapt to society and respect human nature have permanent vitality. This is also at the heart of human-centered legal thinking.

[9] Li [11].

[10] The Complete Works of Marx and Engels [12].

2 Ontological Interpretation of Sexual Rights

2.1 Conceptual Definition of Sexual Rights

To define sexual rights, we must first define "sexuality". In Chinese, the word "sex" is generally used in three senses: first, "sex" in the biological sense, that is, "sex" used at the level of sexual behavior and sexual intercourse. In the Modern Chinese Dictionary, "sexuality" is interpreted as "related to the reproduction or sexual desire of living things". In the English Webster College Student's Dictionary (fifth edition), it is also explained as "the functions of men and women in activities related to reproduction". It is equivalent to the word "sex" in English. Second, the use of "sex" in the sense of gender refers to differences in the characteristics of men and women, which is equivalent to the word "gender" in English. Of course, in English, the word "sex" is also sometimes used to denote gender. Third, "sex" refers to people's "nature", "disposition", and "habits", which the ancient Chinese said: "Food color, sex also." "Sex" here means "nature", which is equivalent to the word "nature" in English. These three meanings of "sex" are related: the division of sex is based on biological "sex", biological sexual behavior is usually carried out between the sexes, and the pursuit of sexual behavior is a human nature.

"Sex" in sexual rights is "sex" in the first sense. Therefore, we define sexual rights as a general term for various rights in the sexual field that arise around human sexuality, are related to human sexuality, and are related to human freedom, equality, pursuit of happiness, freedom from infringement, and so on.

2.2 Types and Contents of Sexual Rights

As mentioned earlier, the Declaration on the Rights of Sexuality was adopted at the 14th World Congress of Sexology, held in Hong Kong, China, in August 1997. The Declaration on Sexual Rights stipulates 11 major rights, including the right to sexual freedom, sexual autonomy, sexual integrity and sexual safety, sexual privacy, sexual fairness, sexual pleasure, sexual expression, sexual free union, independent responsibility for reproductive choice, the right to sexual information based on scientific investigation, the right to comprehensive sex education, and the right to sexual health care. It is the most detailed and authoritative interpretation of sexual rights in human society so far. Although the Universal Society is only a civil society organization, and the Declaration of Sexual Rights does not have the effect of a formal international legal document, its adoption marks that the concept of sexual rights has developed considerably, injecting vitality into the theory and practice of sexual rights. It also provides a useful reference for the development of international and domestic official legislation and practice for the protection of sexual rights.[11] The specific definition of sexual rights in the Declaration on Sexual Rights is as follows:

(a) The right to sexual freedom, which encompasses the possibility for individuals to express their full sexual potential while excluding all forms of sexual coercion, exploitation, and abuse.
(b) The right to sexual autonomy, sexual integrity, and sexual safety, which allows individuals to make autonomous decisions about their sexuality in the ethical context of individuals and society, and the right to control and enjoy their bodies while being free from any abuse, injury, or violence.
(c) The right to sexual privacy, which permits individuals to make their own decisions and conduct autonomously regarding their intimate relationships, provided they do not violate the sexual rights of others.
(d) The right to sexual fairness, which refers to the right to be free from all forms of discrimination based on sex, gender, sexual orientation, age, race, social class, religion, or physical or emotional disability.
(e) The right to sexual pleasure, which includes autoeroticism and is a source of physical, mental, conceptual, spiritual, and healthy well-being.
(f) The right to sexual expression, which allows individuals to express their sexuality through communication, contact, emotional expression, and love.
(g) The right to free sexual association, which implies the possibility of marriage, non-marriage, divorce, and other responsible sexual unions.
(h) The right to be responsible for reproductive choices, which includes the right to decide whether or not to have children, the number and spacing of births, and the right to adequate birth control measures.
(i) The right to sexual information based on scientific investigation, which must be generated through unrestricted and scientific inquiry and disseminated in an appropriate manner to all segments of society.
(j) The right to comprehensive sexuality education, which must involve all social organizations and cover the process of sex education from birth to death.
(k) The right to sexual health, which includes sexual health care used to prevent and treat all sexual worries, sexual problems, and disorders.

While the Declaration of Sexual Rights lists 11 sexual rights, the author argues that an important sexual right has been omitted: the right to sexual relief, which is the right to remedies through self-reliance or legal means when the above sexual rights are violated. Referring to the definition method of sexual rights in the Declaration on Sexual Rights, the author adds the right to sexual relief to the list, resulting in a total of 12 sexual rights, which include the right to sexual freedom, sexual autonomy, sexual integrity, and sexual safety, the right to sexual privacy, sexual fairness, sexual pleasure, sexual expression, sexual free union, independent responsibility for reproductive choice, the right to sexual information based on scientific investigation, comprehensive sex education, sexual health care, and sexual remedies.

[11] Perez-Conchillo and Coleman [13]. For Dr. Zhao Hejun's translation of this, see Zhao [14].

3 Human Basic Instincts for the Existence of Sexual Rights

Marx said: "Man, as a natural being and a living natural being, on the one hand, has natural force, vitality, and is a dynamic natural being. These powers exist in man as gifts and talents, as desires." Sexual rights are rooted in human nature, stemming from human needs, and this need is rooted in man's natural impulses as a pluralistic and sensual animal. However, man is not an ordinary animal; he is an intelligent and thoughtful animal, which determines that his needs and impulses must not be the simple mechanical physiological response of animals, but rather a more active, higher pursuit of happiness and well-being. Therefore, we say that the human source of sexual rights is the rational basis for their recognition and protection by law.

3.1 Sexual Needs

Like animals, human sexual needs come from their own sexual desire, determined by physiological characteristics. With the arrival of puberty, the number of sex hormones in the body gradually increases, followed by the formation of "sexual impulse" desire. This creates the need for "sexual catharsis," which leads to sex. But humans are different from animals. Except for humans, animals that rely on sexual reproduction have estrus, which means they only have sexual desire and sexual needs during the estrus period of the year. Many female animals have a very short estrus period.[12] Humans gradually disappear in estrus in the long evolution, and because there is no restriction of estrus, people who grow to sexual maturity have sexual needs almost all the time. This shows that humans are much larger than animals in terms of both the degree of demand for sex and the actual amount of sex that occurs. It also reflects that humans need sex more than animals.

Harmonious sexual life is not only the process of enjoying pleasure of sexual subjects but also the process of sexual energy discharge. Modern medicine shows that the inability to discharge sexual energy smoothly will inevitably lead to dysfunction in all aspects of the human body, and dysfunction is the cause of disease. According to Freud's theory, if the sexual instinct is blocked and repressed, it will find another way to find a substitute, and psychoneurosis is a substitute when this instinct is not satisfied.[13] Relying on Xi's theory, sexual repression is also the root cause of aggressive sexual crimes, and a "sexually hungry" person is more likely to ignore the rules, take risks, and commit violent sex.[14] Therefore, from the perspective of human nature, in the adjustment of sex, we cannot blindly "block," "control," and "punish," and "channeling" in a specific environment is more conducive to individuals

---

[12] Scientists examined the sexual behavior of primates, the closest to humans. All female primates were found to have estrus. These animals only need to engage in sexual activity during estrus. (See Fisher [15].).

[13] See He and Yu [16].

[14] See Chen [17].

and society than "blocking." This can be illustrated by both positive and negative examples from ancient and modern times.

The Middle Ages in Europe were an extremely ascetic society, and not only all kinds of pre-marital and extramarital sex, so-called "unnatural" sex for pleasure purposes were severely punished by the Church and the law, but even normal sexual behavior between couples within marriage was interfered with.[15] As a result, on the one hand, the whole society turned almost into a "madhouse," and many suffered from hysteria due to the unfulfilled many normal sexual needs.[16] On the other hand, the ruling class and even within the church could not put an end to illegal and promiscuous sexuality, so much so that the clergy of the Middle Ages became synonymous with hypocrisy at that time or for a long time thereafter.[17] For example, traditional society has always considered so-called pornography to be the root cause of sexual crimes, so the law has always adopted a strict attitude towards them. But the Danish social experiment came to the opposite conclusion. Denmark first opened the market for pornographic literature in 1967 and then pornography in 1969, providing for the production and sale of pornography to citizens over the age of 16. As a result, the opening of the sex market, far from leading to an increase in sexual crimes, has led to a marked decline in sexual crimes.[18]

Animal sexuality is a simple, mechanical physiological response. In contrast, humans can experience sex as a physiological response and develop it to the level of emotions and aesthetics. During human evolution, when people began to walk upright, genitals changed from downward to forward, particularly in males. Human sexual intercourse transformed from "posterior" to "forward," which was epoch-making. Using the pre-entry sexual intercourse method, men and women can communicate with each other more directly and richly, infecting each other with attachment. Sexual behavior in conscious individuals involves aesthetics, which affects the quality of sexual behavior. Human sexual intercourse is not merely a mechanical physiological activity but a social behavior that integrates physical, psychological, and spiritual behaviors. It may eventually develop into exclusive sexual behavior between specific people, which is why only humans have love. With anterior sexual intercourse, human females are entirely likely to resist and prevent intercourse against their will, rather than being passive like female mammals who adopt post-occupancy intercourse. Thus, only human beings have sexual rights, which is the fundamental right to engage in sexual activity of their own will, and just as rape arises only in

[15] Medieval canons and laws regulated the position of sexual intercourse between husband and wife. Except for the male and female postures, all other poses were prohibited. Otherwise, once reported, the participants were subject to penalty for years of hard labor. (See Tannahill [18].).

[16] During that time, there was a prevalent condition known as hysterical spasms, which affected mainly female patients. It was characterized by sudden, generalized convulsions at the onset, with the body sometimes stiffening and lying flat on the bed. Patients may also arch their abdomen, resembling sexual intercourse movements. (See [19].).

[17] At that time, many church organizations became secret places of sexual immorality. See Fourks [20].

[18] See Gagnon [21].

human beings.[19] When someone forcibly has sexual intercourse against their will, the harm to the human spirit is often much greater than the physical body. Therefore, the crime of rape set by the law focuses more on punishing the perpetrator from the perspective of mental assault and protecting the sexual rights of the violated party.[20] Because human beings can elevate the physical level of sex to the spiritual level, they know how to enjoy and cherish sex. Therefore, they invest a lot of time and energy in pursuing sex and business. Human sexual activity is more elaborate and complex than that of animals. As a physiological response, animal mating time is generally very short, only 8 s for baboons and 90 s for chimpanzees. Human sexual activity combines physical, psychological, and spiritual components and occurs after the subject object is specified, making it incomparable to animals in terms of time and quality. As the famous British anthropologist Morris described, human partners engage in prolonged sexual activity rather than the typical baboon's rapid and cold mating process of up to 8 s. Intercourse is also much longer when these long periods of libido reach orgasm. Although humans can complete sexual intercourse as quickly as apes, as long as their health allows, and with enough privacy, they would rather spend at least 100 times longer than most apes on sexual activity.[21] For this reason, humans have been trying to find ways and technologies to prolong sexual intercourse for thousands of years. Sexual dysfunction is treated as a disease by modern people, and when this disease cannot be cured, the relationship between husband and wife and family harmony are threatened, and cases leading to divorce are not uncommon.

3.2 *Personality as a Social Attribute of Men*

Man is considered superior to animals because he is conscious, thoughtful, and passionate in pursuing his purpose. Nothing happens without conscious intention, without intended purpose. On the other hand, the animal is directly identical to its life activity, with no distinction between itself and its own life activity. It is precisely this life activity that sets it apart from humans. Humans become the object of their will and consciousness in the very activity of their life. Their life activities are conscious, and this directly distinguishes between human and animal life activities.[22] Humans are animals capable of thinking, and their behavior is governed by consciousness. Humans can not only produce according to the scale of any species, that is, according to the laws of the object to be transformed, but also use the intrinsic inherent scale to measure the object anytime and anywhere, that is, engage in the behavior of transforming the object according to their own needs and purposes. It is precisely

---

[19] See Pan [22].

[20] Rape is a sexual act that occurs without the consent of one of the parties involved. Even if no obvious physical harm is inflicted on the victim, it is still considered a crime. Therefore, the focus of the law is to punish the psychological harm caused by the assault.

[21] Morris [23].

[22] Selected Works of Marx and Engels [24].

this purposefulness and regularity, the unity of "human scale" and "material scale" that shapes the unique existence of humans. In the practice of this unity, humans realize their own development and transformation of the world.

Animals, on the other hand, can only replicate themselves from generation to generation according to the "scale of things", and therefore have no "history" and "development" of their own. It is precisely because humans are conscious and thoughtful animals that they have a personality. Within the scope of personality, everyone has their own needs and different behaviors under the guidance of their own needs. Relevant studies have shown that ants formed a highly hierarchical, orderly, and organized group 30 million years ago, and all ants of this group moved in unison, acted in unison, and went to the same place to eat the same food, do the same things, and respond the same to the same stimuli. However, the model of ant society can only be the product of the nature of the ant, since it has no different needs, no individual personalities, and therefore, the history of ants has not advanced in 10,000 years. Man, as an animal completely different from the ant, cannot suppress his own personality, personality, dignity, and rights if he wants to establish his own relationship structure according to the pattern of ants. In contrast to all animals that are enclosed within the boundaries of nature and have no way out, humans are unique because they liberate rather than suppress their individuality. There can be 10,000 identical ants, but no two identical humans. To bring countless living humans into a society like an ant colony, history stops.[23] From this point of view, personality is a fundamental feature that distinguishes humans from animals and is the essential prescriptiveness of humans as social animals.

Since people have personalities, their needs in the sexual sphere should be diverse. This manifests in various ways: first, the object of sexual behavior is specific, and the quality of the copy and material used to achieve sexual attraction is independent. Beauty and ugliness are subjective and can be described as "out of the eyes of the lover." Second, the forms of sexual activity are diverse, including not only intercourse between the genitals of both sexes but also oral sex, anal sex, bestiality, instrumental intercourse, masturbation, and all other activities for sexual purposes and desire. Any form can result in orgasm. Third, the way to achieve sexual pleasure is also specific. Different sexual behavior methods, postures, means, and timing, place, and environment of sexual acts will have different effects on the experience of sexual pleasure. Sexual needs are specific to the individual and can only be satisfied in specific ways.[24] Therefore, sexual relationships must be based on mutual consent and agreement. Engaging in "pulling and matching" is not acceptable. Modern laws protect people's right to sexual choice and freedom, prohibiting rape, indecency, sexual harassment, and other sexual acts against one's will. Laws also protect the freedom of marriage, oppose arranged marriages, and punish forced marriages by

---

[23] Cheng and Wang [25].

[24] According to Article 16 of the Universal Declaration of Human Rights, adult men and women have the right to marry and start a family without any restrictions based on race, nationality, or religion. Both partners should have equal rights during the marriage and at the time of dissolution. The article emphasizes the importance of free and complete consent from both parties for a valid marriage.

violent means.[25] Article 16 of the Universal Declaration of Human Rights states that "adult men and women have the right to marry and start a family" and "during the marriage and at the time of dissolution, there should be equal rights." In this sense, there should be no unified copy, method, standard, or norm in satisfying sexual needs and realizing sexual pleasure. Sexual behavior should not be judged by the criteria of others, and sexual union should not be limited to opposite-sex relationships. For a person, as long as they can achieve sexual pleasure without hindering others, all sexual behavior should be allowed. Private sexual behavior should be treated with respect for the choices of the parties involved and with an emphasis on the diversity of sexual behavior. Traditional society is sexually repressive because it excludes the sexual choices of individuals and stifles the diversity of sexual behavior. The American scholar Ger J Robin pointed out that "difference is the fundamental nature of all life, from the simplest basic biological organisms to the most complex constructs of human society." Sexuality should also be seen as diverse, and there should not be a single standard. The belief that there is a "best" way to engage in sexual activity is an ideological root of sexual domination that has persisted for thousands of years.[26]

3.3 *Diversity and Sexiness*

Sociologists refer to humans as "multi-sexual" animals. They are considered "sexy" because, according to behavioral and biological studies, humans are the most sexually motivated species among primates. In the words of the famous British behaviorist Morris, "humans are the sexiest primates."[27]

Firstly, human beings have a well-developed information processing system that can receive sexual information widely. Under the stimulation of this information, humans may have more sexual desire and sexual behavior. Animal sexual stimulation systems are simple and mainly come from direct stimulation by the opposite sex, with at most a first signal system after the formation of conditioned reflexes. This system involves specific stimuli that act directly on various senses, such as sound, light, air, and electricity. Because humans are intelligent animals, their sexual stimulation system and sexual information processing functions are much more complex than those of animals. In addition to the direct stimulation of the opposite sex and the first signal system, human sexual stimulation channels also include a second information system—language and images. Therefore, humans can experience sexual excitement not only through direct, real sexual organs and acts but also through indirect, virtual, and replicated sexual acts depicted in language, writing, and pictures. Even without these stimuli and signal stimuli, people can experience sexual excitement through their imagination of sexual behavior scenes.[28] Secondly, animal sexuality is only

[25] Kinsey [26].

[26] Gore et al. [27].

[27] Morris [28].

[28] See Tan [29].

instinctive and limited to reproductive sex, and it is also limited by a long period of estrus. In contrast, human sexuality is conscious, autonomous, and emotional. Humans can choose sexual partners and behaviors according to their preferences, love, and desires.[29] Therefore, human sexuality is diverse, emotional, and purposeful. Sexual behavior can serve not only pleasure and health but also the expression of emotions, the establishment and maintenance of relationships, and livelihood. This makes human sexuality incomparable to animal sexuality. Starting from this "sexy" biological characteristic, the law's concern for human nature should be reflected in at least two aspects. Firstly, it should strive to respect the sexual needs and choices of individuals. Secondly, it should strictly prohibit aggressive sexual behavior against the will of others. These two aspects form the basis of sexual rights.

It is said that human sexiness is diverse because people have a tendency to like new things and dislike the old, which is a trait inherited from our primate ancestors. According to Morris's research, naked apes (humans) have a strong desire to explore, which increases from infancy to adulthood, unlike young monkeys whose desire to explore gradually decreases as they grow older. This tendency to be interested in new things is called "liking new things". In the sexual field, this habit and tendency manifest as the "new impulse" for sexual objects.[30] The impulse for everything familiar decreases, while the impulse for the new opposite sex increases. This "urge to seek novelty" is the biological basis for the variability of human sexuality.[31] The highly erogenous physiology of human beings, combined with this "urge to seek novelty", makes it possible for them to have sexual relations with multiple sexual objects in their life. Although human beings have also formed the habit of marrying, this coupling is often interrupted by phenomena such as the "four-year itch" and "seven-year itch". Sociologists believe that human divorces are regular, and the peak of divorce often occurs around four or seven years after marriage, hence the terms "four-year itch" and "seven-year itch".[32] While the institution of monogamous marriage is the main form of sexual regulation in countries around the world, modern law advocates both freedom to marry and freedom of divorce. The monogamous marriage it establishes is only a kind of "continuous monogamy" marriage, that is, a marriage institution that allows reunion after divorce. If the coercive and sacred nature of marriage is overemphasized, and people's feelings are severed, it can be inhumane to try to monopolize a person's lifelong sexual behavior with all of them in one marriage. The law that makes such provisions can easily become an evil law that suppresses human nature.[33]

---

[29] See Li [30].

[30] Morris [31].

[31] See Tan [32].

[32] Sociologists believe that human divorces are common. Some scholars suggest that the peak of divorce occurs around four years after marriage, while others argue that divorce occurs around seven years after marriage. Therefore, it is referred to as the "four-year itch" and "seven-year itch". See Fisher [33].

[33] See Zhang [34].

3.4 Happiness Persuit

Seeking benefits and avoiding harm, avoiding hardships and seeking pleasure, are instincts of human beings and a natural part of human nature. As an intelligent animal, humans exist on both physical and spiritual levels, and their pleasure-seeking nature takes a higher form, the pursuit of happiness. Happiness is defined as being happy, comfortable, and free from pain. It is divided into two levels: sensory happiness and spiritual happiness, with the latter being the advanced level. While sensory happiness is essential, spiritual happiness is more indispensable as it better reflects human characteristics and is the main component of happiness. Many thinkers, including those from the ancient Greek period, believed that the pursuit of pleasure and happiness is a human right and an essential aspect of human nature. Democritus believed that pursuing happiness as much as possible and avoiding pain was the basic way to achieve happiness in life. Epicurus believed that happiness in life is the pursuit and acquisition of happiness, with spiritual happiness being superior to sensual happiness.[34] However, during the Middle Ages, Christianity oppressed human nature and opposed people's pursuit of earthly happiness. In response, Renaissance thinkers raised the banner of humanism, which called for humanity, opposed divinity, and advocated the enjoyment of the present world. Humanism and liberalism have become mainstream discourse in the West, which regard the pursuit of happiness as a basic human right.

As mentioned earlier, an essential difference between humans and animals is that humans have consciousness, intelligence, and thought. Therefore, human happiness in the sexual sphere is not only physical but also spiritual. In the face of nature, as people's autonomy improves, and their spiritual world becomes fuller and more perfect, their concept and practice of pursuing sexual happiness will inevitably move from low-level physical happiness to high-level spiritual happiness. Maslow's hierarchy of needs demonstrates that everyone has physical, security, belonging, love, respect, beauty, and self-realization needs, which are realized step by step from low to high. The realization of these needs is a progressive process from physical to spiritual. These needs also apply to the realm of sexuality, and as humans progress from satisfying physical needs to self-realization, the physical component gradually decreases, and the spiritual component gradually increases. Pursuing sexual happiness is the process of constantly satisfying these needs. As a result, the process of pursuing happiness in the sexual field is the process of continuous sublimation of feelings and the process of continuous progression from sexual desire to eros, which is an advanced form of sexual desire. Sexual desire is simply the desire for the relationship between the sexes, while eros is rich in content. Sexual desire is only a partial, short-lived pleasure for the individual, while eros gives the individual full, lasting pleasure and helps society establish a new relationship. Human advanced sex is an activity full of self-love and rich emotions of loving oneself.[35] Maslow once

[34] Quoted from Tang [35].

[35] It is generally believed that Eros is an advanced form of sexual desire. Marcuse believed that sexual desire is simply the desire for the relationship between the sexes. Eros, on the other hand,

said, "The enjoyment of sex is a major characteristic of self-actualizers."[36] Love is based on and directed by sexual behavior, and sex behavior takes love as a guarantee of harmony. When the physical and spiritual body and spirit reach a high degree of integration and unity, people will feel great happiness. Engels discussed this incisively in "The Origin of the Family, Private Property and the State."[37] Love affects the frequency and amount of sexual intercourse. If neither spouse loves the other anymore, there will be less sex between them. If both parties are still in love, they will have more sex. If one party loves the other more, there will be a little more sex.[38]

4 Social Basis for the Existence of Sexual Rights

The form of the existence of sex is subject to certain socio-economic conditions, so sex will take on different forms under different social conditions. In traditional agricultural economies and societies, due to the limitations of material living conditions, people's independence, autonomy, and freedom in the field of sex are greatly restricted. Sex is more manifested as obligations, responsibilities, and privileges, and it is difficult to form a systematic concept and practice of sexual rights. Correspondingly, sexual law is necessarily obligation-based. In modern market economy societies, the improvement of material living standards has promoted an increase in human sexual demand. The renewal of production and lifestyle has changed the individual mode of sexual behavior, and the development of science and technology has expanded the autonomous space of sexual behavior. Under such social conditions, people's awareness of sexual rights began to rise and mature, and the existence of sex in the form of rights has a solid social foundation.

---

is rich in content. Sexual desire is only a partial, short-lived pleasure for the individual, while Eros gives the individual a full, lasting pleasure and helps establish a new relationship in society. See Wang and Gao [36]; Marcuse [37].

[36] Quoted from Yongyi and Xiaohua [38].

[37] From August 1999 to August 2000, a social survey conducted by Professor Pan Suiming and others found that love has a significant impact on the frequency and amount of sexual intercourse between partners. If neither the husband nor the wife loves each other, they are likely to have less sex, with the average score being 18, and some reaching as low as 44. On the other hand, if both partners are still in love, they are likely to have a lot more sex, with an average score of 59. Regardless of who loves whom, the frequency of sexual intercourse is generally similar. However, if one partner loves the other more, there may be slightly more sex, with an average score of around 62 min. See Pan et al. [39].

[38] Selected Works of Marx and Engels [40].

4.1 Improvement of Material Living Standards

The degree of tolerance towards sexuality and the recognition and protection of sexual rights in a society are closely related to the general living conditions of its people. Generally, they are directly proportional to the standard of living of people in a society. The stronger the demand for sex, the higher the degree of social tolerance towards sex, the greater the degree of freedom of people in the field of sexuality, the more mature the awareness and concept of sexual rights, and the more developed the practice of sexual rights. People can only pursue physical happiness and spiritual enjoyment when they live without worry, according to Maslow's hierarchy of needs. That is, people can have higher spiritual needs only after their lower needs such as survival and security are satisfied.

Due to the influence of ascetic culture, ancient Chinese often used the phrase "full of warmth and lust" to devalue sex. However, this statement objectively reveals the relationship between material living standards and human sexual needs. The reason why the ancient Roman period had a developed concept and practice of sexual rights, and the relative tolerance towards sex in the Chinese High Tang Dynasty, all had something to do with the strong social strength, prosperity of the people, and high material living standards of the society as a whole. When discussing the reasons for the lack of traditional social rights concepts and practices, we tend to pay more attention to the ascetic culture and the suppression of sex by religious, moral, legal, and other power networks. In fact, the poor material living conditions at that time also played a considerable role in restraining them.

There is no more repressive era of sex in human history than the feudal era in Europe, and this era is also an era of considerable backwardness in the state of productive forces and people's living standards. Western scholars have described the living conditions of European peasants around the 16th century as, "Their situation is very sympathetic and very difficult; they lived separately, very deferential, with relatives, livestock. The huts were constructed of clay and planks, were low, and had a roof made of straw. This is their house. Very little bread, oatmeal, cooked vegetables are their food, water, and whey are their drinks." The peasant, though also human, is less cultured and vulgar than others... Eat without a fork, put five fingers in a basin, squeeze lettuce and sauerkraut juice and put it back in or stuff it into your mouth to chew. Wipe the snot and water droplets hanging from the nose with your sleeve, and the dregs from eating are left on it. What people saw in the village were children running half-naked, shouting handouts from passers-by. The parents' bodies were almost just a few rags, covering only the lower body... They look stunted and miserable.[39] Although this depicts the living conditions of European peasants in the 16th century, it is actually a microcosm of the life of the entire medieval European population. This remains true even in cities, where infrastructure is dilapidated, urban environments are filthy, and crowded living conditions are widespread. People have little knowledge of indoor hygiene and sanitation, and infectious diseases are rampant. Many urban areas are infested with rats, which can spread various

[39] von Diermann [41].

diseases.[40] According to the History of European Weathering, personal hygiene was a major problem during that time. People had completely forgotten about proper washing. Even Louis XIV only sprayed some flower dew on his hands and face in the morning, and even after washing, "the stench on his body made people want to vomit at ten paces". Noble women combed their hair only once a week or two, and most women of the middle and lower classes combed their hair only once a month. Women had piles of lice on their heads, giving off a strange smell of broken balm. In addition, bad breath was common because there was no concept of dental care. Most people had poor teeth or tooth decay.[41] In such living conditions, experts speculate that before the 16th century, sexual activity was probably far less attractive than in modern life. Even in the early modern period, according to Lawrence Stone, young men and women rarely met very sexually attractive people or people who had spare energy to engage in sexual activity. People had lice in their hair, foul breath due to lack of dental hygiene, broken or decayed teeth, they rarely bathed, and their skin was covered with eczema, scabies, ulcers, sores, and bleeding, among other disorders that made sexual intercourse uncomfortable, painful, or impossible altogether. Sexual intercourse caused a variety of sexually transmitted diseases, such as James Boswell, an 18th-century biographer, who had at least 17 cases of gonorrhea.[42]

In a society with extremely poor material living conditions, the foundation for the realization of sexual rights is also extremely weak, because when people's basic survival needs have not been met, they cannot have excessive passion for sex and cannot afford to waste their energy on non-productive activities.[43] Although sex is necessary for everyone from a physiological or reproductive standpoint, due to the limitations of living conditions, it often remains only at the level of physical satisfaction. It is enough to stop and rush, and the actor does not have the ability or energy to break off the existing marriage according to their own will to change partners frequently, or operate the sexual act as delicately as an important undertaking. Scholars' research also reveals that in the early modern period of the West, people's sexual intercourse generally lasted only a few minutes, and most people had not heard of sexual preparation movements, only using male and female positions. Women rarely experienced sexual pleasure.[44] In such a state of sexual existence, it is difficult for the individual to value and respect their own sexuality. When they cannot see the need for sex as a primary need and cannot view the suppression of sex by society as a deprivation of their important interests, it becomes difficult to regard the infringement of their own sexual freedom by others as a major injustice. Thus, the

[40] This unsanitary condition eventually led to the 14th-century pandemic of the plague (Black Death) throughout Europe. It is estimated that the plague was endemic by the year 100, and the Black Death alone claimed the lives of around 24 million people, which accounted for one-fourth of the population of Europe. For more information, see Xiao [42].

[41] Fourks [43].

[42] See Li [44].

[43] "Libido" is a fundamental concept in Freud's theory of sexuality. It refers to the power and energy in the human body that drives itself to find satisfaction due to sexual instinct. Freud often called it "sexual force." See He and Yu [45].

[44] See Li [46].

concept and practice of sexual rights are hindered from maturing and developing. For example, in early capitalist society, the working class lived and worked in poor conditions. Workers of different genders and ages worked together in crowded, hot, and stuffy environments. Women had to wear minimal clothing in almost all industrial sectors, while in other sectors such as coal mines, both men and women worked semi-naked. Workers lived in cramped housing with children and adults crowded into small living spaces. Therefore, under these social conditions, violations of the sexual rights of women and minors were commonplace, but victims found it difficult to elevate it to the perspective of sexual rights protection. As Edward As Fourx describes, "A tired and paralyzed female worker collapses on her bed in a daze and can do whatever she wants. Most of the time, she didn't even know if she was meeting her husband, her brother, or a young man who rented a corner."[45]

Foucault put it succinctly: 'The sudden increase in the nutritional intake of a population is, in a sense, much more significant than a change in the constitution or a transition from a monarchy to a republic.' Changes in material living conditions often constitute the driving force behind deeper social transformations.[46] The ancient Chinese expressed it well: "If you have adequate food and clothing, you can be content with the simple pleasures of life and understand the difference between right and wrong." In modern Western society, the concept and practice of sexual rights have truly matured and become complete due to the developed level of productive forces, high material living standards, and a stable social environment. The existence of a developed social security system and medical and health system is inseparable from this. When people no longer have to worry about their basic needs, they can focus on pursuing happiness. When people view sexual needs as an essential requirement for adults and have the passion, energy, and ability to continuously pursue sex, take sex seriously, and manage it delicately, and view freedom in the sexual realm as an indispensable interest, the concept and practice of sexual rights will inevitably mature and develop.

4.2 Changes in Production and Lifestyle

Although pluralism and sexuality are human biological qualities, this character is constrained by social conditions from the beginning. This is manifested in the fact that people must marry in society, and sexual relations must be controlled between marriages composed of specific subjects. In traditional agricultural economic societies, the monogamous form of marriage was greatly developed and firmly defended, and it was precisely through this form of marriage that society suppressed sex.[47] The

[45] Fourks [47].

[46] Quoted from: Li [48].

[47] The form of marriage in ancient China differed slightly from that of medieval Western Europe. Western Europe, under the influence of Christianity, strictly adhered to monogamy for both nobles and serfs. However, there existed a lover phenomenon outside of marriage that was regulated. In

use of marriage and family to solidify sexual behavior is ostensibly an artificial political means used by the power machine in agrarian societies. However, in fact, there are deep economic roots behind this political method, namely, the production and lifestyle of this society have a decisive influence on the individual patterns and official strategies of sexual behavior.[48]

Agricultural society is characterized by a sedentary lifestyle and agricultural production, so the model of family-by-household, male and female cooperation is the main mode of production and lifestyle of people. Under such production and lifestyle, marital status must be characterized by high stability. Western scholar Helen Fisher analyzed the reasons for the low divorce rate in Europe during the agrarian era, stating that "Agrarian couples must rely on each other to survive. The woman living on the farm had to rely on her husband to move stones, cut down trees and cultivate the land, while her husband needed her to order, weed, gather, prepare and store vegetables, and they worked together on the land. More importantly, whichever spouse chooses to end the marriage will bring barren land, and neither party can cultivate half of the land or resettle it. Agrarian men and women are bound to the land and bound together, forming a symbiotic and coexisting blood relationship. In this ecological state, divorce is of course an impractical and irrational act." The situation in China's agricultural society also confirms this. China's agricultural society is a typical small-scale peasant society where men cultivate and weave, men lead women to assist, and men lead women outside the house.[49] Although women had a low status, they were not dispensable. In the relatively backward productivity situation at that time, husbands and wives relied on each other and had their own responsibilities, working together to solve the common problem of survival. The saying "men are the rake for money, and women are the boxes for managing accounts" illustrates this point.

The form of marriage in agrarian societies is characterized by authoritarianism and high stability, and there are other factors at play. The agricultural mode of production requires a large amount of labor, and the reproduction and nurturing of labor can only be done through the cooperation of both men and women. Physiological experience shows that women carry a pregnancy for about 280 days until the fetus matures in the womb, and it generally takes about 700 days to cultivate a child into adulthood. In contrast, most mammals have obvious advantages over humans,

contrast, wealthy men in ancient China were allowed to take concubines, but the status of a wife and concubines in the family was very different. Concubines were generally only slightly higher than maids, and the process of marrying and renouncing them was not as grand and cumbersome as it was for formal wives. Therefore, the ancient Chinese system of marriage cannot be accurately described as "polygamy"; instead, it should be expressed as "—polygamy." Moreover, the scope of existence for these concubines was also limited to those whose wealth was strong to a certain extent. The vast majority of common people did not have the ability to take concubines, making the ancient Chinese form of marriage essentially monogamous.

[48] In this context, the author's "lifestyle" refers to the overall term for a society's mode of production, social structure, and the forms of interaction and lifestyle of its people. This is equivalent to the concept of "relations of production" in Marxist philosophy.

[49] See Fisher [49].

with either a short pregnancy, a short growth period, multiple litters, or a combination of these factors. Although the formation of a fertilized egg requires sexual activity between a man and a woman, conception and childbirth are physiologically a woman's own responsibility. Conception and childbirth place an additional burden on women compared to men, reducing their viability. This physiological characteristic of humans determines that women cannot complete the task of reproducing and raising offspring alone, and they must rely on men's support for a long time to provide nutrition for themselves and their children. Men must provide for women and children if they want to obtain their own heirs and labor.[50] Men cannot and are not allowed to provide for children who are not related by blood, so women can only immobilize their spouses in exchange for a fixed source of nutrition. Under the productivity conditions of the time, the average man did not have much capacity to support multiple spouses and their children. In this way, both men and women can only fix sex in an authoritarian marriage. Of course, in this system of provision, it is not that women are only passively supported, but only that they are in a secondary position in the direct creation of material wealth. Therefore, we say that this system of support is a mode of production and life in which men and women are assisted and must work together.

This model of absolutist or monogamous marriage, which is centered on the man, with the wife and children being, in fact, a kind of his property, emphasizes the stability of the family's power structure and the purity of the blood lineage. Premarital and extramarital sex is strongly rejected. The characteristics of agricultural production and life are obtaining means of subsistence from fixed land, and settling life centered on land. Therefore, the agricultural society is a society in which order is supreme, and the family is the foundation of the whole society. Blood and marriage are the basic ties of social ties, and the instability of the family will be directly related to the stability of the country. Impurity of blood ties can confuse the basic order of inheritance, and fornication before marriage and adultery outside marriage directly pose a serious threat to marital stability, family power structure, order of dignity and inferiority, and blood lineage. Sexual conduct that cannot be included in marriage is naturally prohibited by law.

More importantly, the characteristics of agricultural production and life determine that agricultural society is an acquaintance society, which expands outward and imitates various relationships centered on blood relations, and arranges the order of production and life with identity as the center.[51] In such a society, direct blood,

[50] The system of provision has existed in primitive societies, where men would offer offerings solely in exchange for the right to have sexual intercourse with dependent women. However, in agrarian societies, men had a twofold purpose. They offered offerings to acquire sexual intercourse with a dependent woman and to acquire heirs and labor. The Chinese folk proverb "get married, get married" and the saying "Dress and eat" accurately describe this system of subsistence in an agrarian society. This is in contrast to the system of support in primitive societies. see Pan [50].

[51] The social relations of acquaintance societies are centered around blood relations, which are known as "source relationships." These relationships are considered the most intimate. Although the relationship between husband and wife and in-laws is not biologically related, it is a relationship formed by the union of men and women. This union creates new kinship, and the relationship

collateral blood, quasi-blood, fictitious blood, and general acquaintance relationships are connected in an orderly manner, and the hierarchy of elders and younger, nobility, and proximity is clearly arranged. In such a network of relationships, the choice of sexual partners is very limited, and emotional involvement between men and women can lead to forbidden territory. Once this boundary is crossed, it not only destroys the original relationship between the individuals involved, but also causes disturbances in the relevant social structure. Ordinary people living in such a society may find it difficult to cope with the resulting social disorder and psychological gap, leading to a moral degradation that invites public criticism. This "prohibition" applies not only to close relatives, but even to distant ones, and the discomfort caused can be quite obvious. Mr. Fei Xiaotong gave an example of this phenomenon, stating that "for instance, a distant relative who was originally referred to as 'elder' or 'younger,' once married, often caused a very unnatural mood when others changed their words to him. We may have experienced this situation and felt the unnatural mood due to small disturbances in the social structure."[52] It is not necessary to mention whether such a sexual union that is disordered and bad will be punished by the law, as the pressure from public opinion alone is often enough to make it difficult for such a union to survive.[53]

It is precisely because of this characteristic of an acquaintance society that marriage has high stability once it is concluded. This is because marriage and subsequent fertility can generate a variety of new social relationships, and once the marriage relationship is dissolved, these relationships are also dissolved or even deteriorated. This will cause considerable damage and shock to the complex network of relationships and social structures that have been formed. In addition, in an acquaintance society, various relationships are actually exchanges and games between various interests, and the dissolution of marriage relations often brings about the loss of various interests. Neither the parties nor their relatives will be indifferent to this. Moreover, in an acquaintance society, marriage is a major event for everyone and every family. The payment of dowry, the holding of wedding banquets, and various cumbersome etiquette are time-consuming, laborious, and costly. This achieves the effect of publicity and credibility. If a man and a woman dissolve their marriage at will, it means that he and other families will have to pay more economic costs

between husband and wife and in-laws is a relationship that is mediated by this union. Therefore, we call it quasi-kinship. For instance, the child's uncle and the child's uncle's wife are not related by blood, but they are both related to the child. This creates a kinship between them known as quasi-blood relations. Ordinary social relations aim to achieve the degree of intimacy of blood relations, and a new kinship can be formed through artificial blood fiction. Examples of such relationships include those formed through Jinlan marriage, blood alliance, and recognition of relatives. We call this pseudo-kinship. Even the most ordinary acquaintance relationships are often framed by blood in acquaintance societies to demonstrate their intimacy. This is why there are Chinese sayings such as "master and apprentice are like father and son" and "friends are like brothers and sisters."

[52] Fei [51].

[53] In the novel "Thunderstorm," there is a plot where Lu Shiping discovers that Zhou Ping and Sifeng had engaged in incest and that Sifeng is pregnant. Her immediate response is to help them flee quickly. This may reflect the reality of the situation because she knew that based on this taboo behavior, it would be difficult for them to survive in the acquaintance society.

and public opinion costs. Neither the person concerned nor his relatives will remain indifferent to this.

The acquaintance society also leaves very little space for the implementation of illegal sexual acts such as premarital and extramarital affairs, because the eyes of acquaintances are the best tools for enforcing traditional sexual morality. It is difficult for these acts to remain hidden from the many acquaintances, and any discovery would immediately become the subject of public opinion and moral evaluation. Therefore, the more acquaintances a person has, the greater the psychological pressure on them to conform to traditional sexual norms, and the greater the scrutiny of any offending sexual behavior. This pressure and supervision are even greater in an era where humans are still unable to control the outcome of births.[54]

In today's era of industrialization, urbanization, and informationization, people's production and lifestyle have undergone fundamental changes under the conditions of a mature market economy. The market economy is characterized by the full circulation of production factors such as talents, commodities, and goods. The development of transportation and information technology has accelerated this circulation, breaking down the traditional acquaintance society. As Marx said, commodities are inherently egalitarian, and market economies allocate resources with factors of production and establish various relationships with contracts as ties, thus breaking the traditional identity society. The life of the market lies in competition, and the life of competition lies in diversity. Different subjects compete together, and various commodities, resources, and needs are exchanged with each other, breaking down the traditional monolithic society. In such a high-speed circulation society, as the frequency of people's communication increases, the space for choosing sexual partners also increases. As the frequency of circulation of goods and information increases, so does the stimulation for sexual activity, and so does the demand for sex. In such an egalitarian contractual society, blood and identity relations are broken, and people's sexual selection objects are relatively increased, and sexual forbidden areas are relatively reduced. People are relatively free to arrange their sexuality of their own volition, without having to think more about the interests of the family, the village, and various complex relationships. In such a diversified society, people's sexual needs, sexual behavior methods, and marriage patterns also show diverse characteristics, and various sexual needs are more easily satisfied through an open market. Diverse patterns of sexual behavior and marriage are more likely to be respected as long as they do not interfere with others. More importantly, in a society of strangers, it is difficult for a person's vision and words to spread and form public opinion, and under the conditions of the increasing maturity of contraceptive technology and abortion technology, human beings are fully able to control the fertility caused by sexual behavior. Therefore, the safety factor of illegal sexual acts such as premarital

[54] This can be inferred from Qin Keqing's death in "Dream of Red Mansions". Although she died of illness, according to the twelfth and thirteenth episodes, her death was directly linked to the excessive psychological pressure caused by her long-term affair with her father-in-law. Her stress levels increased when this affair was accidentally discovered by two maids, and when she learned that her mother-in-law might know about it. This sudden increase in psychological stress may have accelerated her death.

and extramarital sex has increased significantly, resulting in more violations in the traditional sense.[55] When such violations become commonplace and integrated into the lives of most people, it ceases to violate them, because the rules no longer exist, and it becomes a human right to engage in such violations. The growing acceptance of premarital sex in modern society is a case in point.

4.3 Development of Science and Technology

Since mankind entered modern society, science and technology have begun to develop rapidly, and so far, mankind has experienced three scientific and technological revolutions. The development of science and technology has brought about major changes in people's lifestyles and social structures. Among these changes, the impact on the sexual field is also very obvious. Traditional sexual concepts, sexual norms, and sexual behavior systems have encountered fierce challenges and provided a broad space for the development of sexual rights.

Advances in science and technology have led to unprecedented emancipation for women. On the one hand, due to the application of science and technology, many heavy manual tasks have begun to disappear, and women can take on or even perform better than men in many jobs that can only be performed by men in traditional societies. This way, a large number of women began to go out of the house and into society, thus expanding their social interactions. On the other hand, the application of contraceptive technology, abortion technology, and artificial insemination technology has separated sex and reproduction, and women can artificially control the timing of childbirth, the number of children, and choose whether to have children. The physiological burden brought about by pregnancy, childbirth, and parenting has been significantly reduced, so that women's dependence on men has weakened, and women's sense of independence has gradually increased. In this way, the marriage model of male and female heads in traditional society began to disintegrate, and a new type of equal marriage model is taking shape, in which women's sexual freedom increases. This makes it possible for women to choose partners of their own will, arrange the timing of sex, choose the way of sex, refuse to have sex against their will, etc., both within and outside of marriage.

The development of science and technology has increased people's sexual desires, expanded their sexual communication channels, and provided them with greater sexual freedom. Contraceptive technology and abortion methods have significantly reduced the risk of pregnancy and childbirth resulting from sexual activity. This not only increases the privacy of premarital and extramarital affairs but also reduces the stress and negative consequences for those involved, leading to a more carefree

[55] According to a recent survey of college students in the United States, 94% of boys and 80% of girls have had premarital sex. Additionally, current statistics show that in the United States, the proportion of women who engage in sex outside of marriage is between 30 and 36%, while for men it ranges between 40 and 50%. (Source: Li [52]).

and enjoyable sexual experience. The progress in transportation has also expanded the geographic scope of sexual activity, allowing people to avoid the prying eyes of acquaintances and "keep things private" even from a distance[56]; The application of information and network technology has broadened people's horizons, providing increased communication opportunities and the ability to connect across geographical barriers. This allows people to engage in long-distance relationships and explore sexual encounters beyond their immediate surroundings. The development of printing and imaging technology has provided people with more and higher-quality sexual stimuli, which can serve as a partial substitute in the absence of a real sexual partner. The research and development of sex-enhancing drugs and tools, as well as sexual dysfunction treatments, have overcome physiological obstacles, improved sexual performance, and enhanced sexual pleasure. Paternity testing technology has also solved the confusion caused by traditional reproductive models, where it is difficult to determine a child's biological father. Men can now identify their biological roots, even in situations involving multiple sexual partners, clarify their blood lineage, and establish property succession. This provides men with more options and tolerance for premarital and extramarital sexual relationships.

The development and application of science and technology have transformed traditional sexual structures and behavior patterns, as well as the way humans approach sexual relationships. On one hand, technological advancements have replaced human labor in production and warfare, leading to a reduced role of labor in society. On the other hand, contraceptive and abortion technologies have allowed for a separation of sexual intercourse and fertility, with artificial insemination, IVF, and various surrogacy technologies offering alternative fertility options that do not rely on sexual intercourse. This separation of fertility and sexual pleasure has led to a change in the way people approach sexual relationships, with pleasure function becoming more dominant than reproductive function. As a result, people have become more accepting of a wider range of sexual behaviors that promote individual happiness, including anal sex, oral sex, sexual intercourse with hands or tools, masturbation, caressing, and even sadomasochism. This has led to a shift in the patterns of sexual relationships, with same-sex unions and heterosexual unions having equal meaning under the pleasure function. This increased selectivity has allowed individuals to choose the sexual behaviors and relationships that bring them the most happiness, promoting a greater sense of personal independence and choice.

---

56 Some scholars believe that the growth of premarital and extramarital sex in Western society in the early to mid-century period is directly related to the rapid development of the automobile industry. Allen explained this relationship as follows: "The car provides people with an almost ordinary means of escaping from the world. People no longer have to be monitored by their parents and bridesmaids and are no longer influenced by neighborhood opinion. Young men and women can now jump into their car and travel 20 km away to another city to go dancing. There, they are strangers and can enjoy freedoms that are difficult to find among their neighbors." Russell believes that young Americans have more premarital sex than the British because of cars. He said, "Since the vast majority of girls own their own cars, they can easily avoid the eyes and ears of their parents and neighbors and elope with their lovers. See Liu [53], Russell [54].

5 Legal Approaches to Sexual Rights

Rights are not only a conceptual existence but also a practical existence. Although rights are more than just a form of legal rights, a right, no matter how morally and traditionally justifiable it may be, must ultimately be confirmed by law before it can be realistically justified and feasible. Legal rights are therefore a typical manifestation of this practical existence. The same is true of the practice of sexual rights. Because it is determined by the characteristics of the coercive force of the law, the law is the most important and obvious means of the state's adjustment of sex. Thus, in modern society, the attitude of the law towards sex reveals the fate and direction of sexual recognition and protection in the law, truly representing the freedom of human sexuality.

Since the law of modern society aims to maximize the realization of human freedom, legal norms of sex in modern society should be based on sexual rights, care for human nature, respect for consent, oppose violence, tolerate pluralism, and strive to achieve sexual freedom, independence, and liberation. This is the development process and basic trend of modern social sex legislation. In this process, the expansion of sexual freedom by law and the recognition and protection of sexual rights are achieved in two ways: tolerance and intolerance. The law is increasingly tolerant in treating consensual sexual behavior that does not interfere with others and increasingly intolerant in treating violent sexual acts against others.

5.1 Increasing Legal Tolerance Vis-À-Vis Sex

5.1.1 Confirmation of the Right to Be Naked

Scientific studies have shown that, unlike humans, any animal, especially female animals, has an estrus period. This means that the sex hormone endocrine system of animals only plays a role in certain seasons or periods of the year, which may promote the animal's sexual desire and lead to sexual intercourse. Outside of estrus, animals not only lack sexual desire and do not have sexual intercourse, but some even live apart and do not communicate with each other.[57] As a high-level animal, humans differ from ordinary animals in that they have no restrictions on estrus. As long as there is desire, humans can engage in sexual activity with the opposite sex anytime and anywhere. Human intercourse is not only a physiological response but is also integrated into the psychological and spiritual component. In the long process of human evolution, humans have not only learned to walk upright but have also lost body hair, which exposes their genitals. For extremely sexually stimulating species, the exposure of genitals is the greatest sexual stimulation and attraction, which can lead to a large number of illegal sexual activities that pose the greatest threat to

[57] See Pan [55].

the sexual order of society. This behavior is intolerable by the power system.[58] So humans must dress and cover even if they don't need protection from the cold. As the British anthropologist Morris points out, "It is clear that in the increasingly large and unnatural naked ape society, there is a real need to take measures to prevent the sudden increase in non-spousal behavior caused by frequent social activities."[59] In his view, dressing is the most basic precaution. The covering of sexual organs and related parts increases the mystery surrounding sex, which subconsciously stimulates nudity and sexual desire. The heightened stimulation instills a greater fear of nudity within the power system. Therefore, the first step to abstinence is to "ban nakedness," which has become the habitual thinking of traditional social rulers. Controlling physical nudity between opposite sexes within a specified range is the main objective of abstinence, making the prohibition of nudity between opposite sexes an important aspect of traditional social taboos. Revealing private parts in public is considered a mortal sin against decency. Even in orthodox Jewish law, nude sex between husband and wife is prohibited. It is no wonder that after the ancestors of mankind, Adam and Eve, felt ashamed of eating the fruit of wisdom, their first action was to cover their lower bodies with leaves.

According to traditional Christian theory, women have been viewed as the source of lewdness and the culprit of hedonism, and as a result, traditional ascetics often focus their "abstinence" on women. During the conservative Victorian era, women were expected to dress modestly and cover themselves up in order to maintain purity. The American scholar Hunter described this period as follows: "In the 1820s, British women began to wear clothes with lace belts, tight bodices, straight sleeves, and hoops that made movement difficult. By the 1830s, British actress Fanny Kemble wrote from Pennsylvania that American women also bound themselves in immobile clothing. From the 1840s to the 1860s, padded floor-length dresses turned 19th-century women into fantasy angels rather than real people. They always walked with cautious steps, sliding forward with a gentle creeping sound."[60] The German scholar Fourx provided a more incisive comment on the clothing of this period, stating: "Vulgar morality requires that a wall be formed with skirts, enclosing women's bodies like a bunker." Women were not only protected from all kinds of abuses, but also sealed from top to bottom. The layers of dresses were so thick that even the strongest wind could not reveal any part of the body.[61] Between a husband and wife, while it may not be necessary to enforce the principle of "no nakedness", those who adhere to this practice are respected by society as models of high morality. There are accounts from the Victorian era of women who married and had several children, but lived to old age without ever seeing a man's nudity. It is said that even the most affectionate lovers, the Brownings, never saw each other's naked bodies.[62] According to this principle, even in medical procedures, gynecological examinations

---

[58] See Tan [56].

[59] Morris [57].

[60] Hunter [58].

[61] Fourks [59].

[62] Hunter [60].

should only be performed on female patients in very special cases and under special circumstances, such as in dark rooms and under sheets. However, many doctors often encouraged this pathological practice. For example, a Philadelphia professor proudly proclaimed in his 1852 "Brother Women's Reader" that he was proud of American women who would rather endure extreme danger and pain than give up modesty concerns that would allow for a full examination of their diseases. He saw this as evidence of "virtue."[63] As a result, many women refused to see a doctor and ultimately delayed treatment, which led to their deaths. Furthermore, in order to avoid using the word "sex," many families during this time wrapped piano legs in cotton and cloth to avoid any association with human legs. Additionally, many nude sculptures were only allowed to be displayed if they had cloth bands wrapped around the waist or other adornments, as any depiction of nudity without these coverings was banned.[64]

With the wave of "sexual liberation" in the 20th century, the social and cultural suppression of nudity gradually relaxed, and the law became more tolerant of public nudity. As a result, the right to nudity began to be seen as a right to freely dispose of one's own body.[65] The United States was founded on Puritanism and has traditionally been a more conservative country when it comes to sex. Until the 1950s and 1960s, many state governments in the United States considered public nudity to be "indecent behavior." For example, the Model Penal Code of the United States from 1962, Section 213, Article 5, stipulated that "anyone who reveals their genitals for the purpose of stimulating or satisfying their own sexual desires or those of a person who is not a spouse or another person, knowing that it causes disgust or consternation, commits a misdemeanor."[66] Since the Model Penal Code does not have the mandatory force of uniform enforcement, nudity is not regulated differently in state law, and the concept of "genitals" varies from state to state, with many states using the concepts of "private parts," "body," and "intimate parts," among others. Although this brings difficulties and arbitrariness to the determination of the crime of nudity, it also creates conditions for breaking through traditional sexual suppression and affirming the emerging right to nudity. In recent years, there have been cases in many states where women have been prosecuted for public toplessness, but many of them have been acquitted by courts on the grounds that female breasts are not genitals or private parts. Feminists are also active in campaigning for their rights on the grounds of sexism. In 1992, five women in New York State went completely naked to publicly challenge a provision in the New York State Criminal Code that prohibited people from exposing their private parts in public, arguing that men could be naked and women could not. They invoked the Equal Protection Clause of the Constitution to protect themselves, and finally, a federal appeals court found the state's law unconstitutional and acquitted the five women of showing their breasts. This greatly expanded the space for people's

[63] See Tannahill [61].

[64] See Liu [62].

[65] The following information and discussion on the right to nudity can be found here: Zhang Zherui United Law Firm [63].

[66] Xiao [64].

naked freedom in the form of case law. In recent years, various nude movements have sprung up across the United States. According to statistics, about 60,000 Americans participate in various nude societies, and nudity on the beach becomes so natural and common on hot summer days that some states have begun to implement zoning management, allowing people to choose whether or not to dress in a given area. At this time, the right to nudity in the right time, place, and object becomes a human right.

5.1.2 Decriminalization Against Premarital and Extramarital Sex

The most important manifestation of sexual control in traditional society is to confine sex to the scope of marriage and give strict control over the conclusion and dissolution of marital relationships to the state. This control is manifested in the fact that, on the one hand, the parties are not free to enter into marriage, and on the other hand, once the marriage is concluded in accordance with the will of the ruling class, it cannot be arbitrarily dissolved. In the Middle Ages, according to Christian theory, marriage was an "unbreakable relationship between a man and a woman," a "formal lifelong contract placed under the protection of religious enterprise." The self-restraint in sexual relations, as a moral standard of life, took precedence over all other rules of life. Such contracts could not be easily abrogated, so that divorce was almost completely prohibited by medieval European law.[67] In ancient China, there was no free divorce system. Although a man could repudiate his wife in the case of "seven outs", it was only possible when the wife had serious ethical and moral defects. If the wife had special experiences or circumstances that conformed to feudal ethics, the husband must not abandon his wife, which is known as "three do not go".[68] Therefore, even in ancient China, even in a patriarchal society, men actually had almost no right to divorce on their own. It is precisely for this reason that in the traditional Chinese concept, the behavior of "Qin Xianglian" is morally reasonable and sympathetic, while "Chen Shimei" is the embodiment of a morally inferior person It has always been condemned.

In traditional societies ruled by asceticism, the state monopolized the right to have sex within marriage, and natural premarital and extramarital sex was considered morally and legally unacceptable. Therefore, the crime of adultery has always been an essential element of traditional social crime legislation. For example, the laws

---

[67] Hunter [65].

[68] "Seven Out" refers to the seven reasons that ancient Chinese men could repudiate their wives, as described in "The Book of the Great Daili·The Natal Book": "There are seven reasons for repudiating a wife: disobedience to parents, lack of virtue, childlessness, lewdness, jealousy, malignant diseases, and theft." "Three Don't Go" refers to the three reasons why ancient Chinese men were not allowed to repudiate their wives, as explained in "The Legend of the Ram·Zhuang 27 years of He Xiu Note", "Confucius Family Language·Honmei Solution" and "The Book of the Great Daili"·Honmei: "Do not repudiate a wife who has mourned for three years, is not ungrateful; do not repudiate a wife based on her cheapness or expense, as it is not against virtue; and do not repudiate a wife for having no family property, as it is not poor."

of Burgundy and Lombard in medieval Western Europe, as well as the laws of the Ming and Qing dynasties in China, had provisions allowing husbands to kill their wives and adulterers who committed adultery.[69] For example, during the British Republic, Puritanical revolutionaries passed a law which stipulated that unmarried men and women would be sentenced to three months' imprisonment for fornication, while married individuals would be punishable by death for committing adultery.[70] As another example, in early American society, adultery was also punished severely, with punishments ranging from expulsion from the local area to naked public display, branding with fire, and even lynching in some places.[71] Even in the late last century, the tradition of adultery as a crime still gained some degree of preservation in the United States. According to 1983 statistics, 10 states provide for adultery, private adultery, and unlawful cohabitation in their criminal laws. Eight states have laws prohibiting only adultery, not fornication and unlawful cohabitation. Three states provide only for adultery and unlawful cohabitation. Two states provide only for adultery, not private adultery. Only two states have neither adultery, nor private adultery, nor unlawful cohabitation.[72]

In the 20th century, there were significant changes in social norms. The widespread use of contraceptive technology and abortion has greatly reduced the chance of unintended pregnancy and childbirth due to sexual activity. This has not only increased the secrecy of premarital and extramarital sex but also reduced the negative pressure and consequences for the parties involved. The development of transportation has greatly expanded people's opportunities for sexual activity, and the application of information technology has increased people's communication opportunities and expanded their horizons. The most important factor is the development of the market economy, which has increased people's sense of freedom and pluralism. As a result, people have begun to see sex as a form of entertainment, rather than solely as a means of procreation. Consequently, people no longer want to confine sex within the bounds of marriage, and sex that occurs outside of marriage is quite common in modern society.[73]

In such social conditions, the concept of adultery is disappearing, and the criminalization of adultery is being removed from the law, leading to a tendency to decriminalize premarital and extramarital sex. In the United States, the first draft of the Model Penal Code of 1955 did not include provisions for adultery and private adultery, but it did include the crime of unlawful cohabitation, which was abolished

[69] See Li [66], Zhang [67].

[70] See·Hunter [68].

[71] See Pan [69].

[72] According to the provisions of canon law, when a married person has sexual relations with someone who is not their spouse, it is considered adultery. If someone who is not the spouse has sexual intercourse with the spouse, it is called private adultery. However, in the usual sense, we refer to both situations as adultery. See Chu [70].

[73] According to a survey of college students in the United States, 94% of boys and 80% of girls reported having engaged in premarital sex. According to statistics, the proportion of women who have sex outside of marriage in the United States is between 30 and 36%, and for men, it is between 40 and 50%. See Li [71].

in the 1962 text. Many scholars believe that since the 1960s, the crime of adultery has rarely been punished in American legal practice, and some people use adultery as a tool to blackmail others, which undermines the prestige of the law.[74]

Adultery and concubinage are criminalized in traditional Italian criminal law, which the Italian Constitutional Court declared in 1961, 1968 and 1969 to violate Article 3 of the Constitution and Article 29, which eventually abolished the crime.[75] The crime of adultery was also provided for in the traditional German Penal Code, but ended up with the 1st Penal Reform Act in 1969 and the 4th in 1973 The Ministry of Penal Reform Law completely abolished the crime of adultery.[76] Article 183 of Japan's 1907 Penal Code provided for adultery, which was abolished in 1947.[77] Article 194 of the former Austrian Penal Code provided for adultery, which expired on 1 March 1997.[78] According to the author's incomplete statistics, at present, the criminal laws of Western countries basically no longer provide for the crime of adultery. At present, the criminal code of Taiwan's region still retains the provisions on the crime of adultery, but its application space has also been greatly limited, and its vitality is also in danger.

In order to adapt to the changing social situation, many countries have had to change their marriage and family laws to reduce the constraints of marriage. Legal reforms on divorce were initiated as early as the middle of the 19th century. In 1857, England's new Marriage Act was introduced, which transferred the power to grant divorce from Parliament to the relatively private civil courts, and also abolished the procedure of pre-judgment by the church. Although the conditions for divorce were still as harsh as ever, people could file for divorce when conditions permitted, and the cost of divorce was significantly reduced. Similarly, in the United States, the general trend of divorce at this time was to transfer the power to decide divorce from the judicial organ to the special court. This was because the judicial department deciding divorce cases was embarrassing, laborious and costly, and to a certain extent, was constrained by the political system. In addition, the conditions for granting divorce in the United States were relaxed compared to the past. Even Catholic France, where the divorce clause that had been abolished by the Napoleonic Code was restored in a conservative form in 1884, relaxed its conditions for granting divorce.[79]

In the second half of the 20th century, the revolution in marriage law became even more rapid. In 1970, the California Divorce Act was the first to abolish the traditional principle of fault as a ground for divorce. The act stipulated that if one of the parties submits that "irreconcilable differences have caused irreparable breakdown of the marriage," they can obtain a divorce. Since then, many states in the United States and many Western countries have followed suit and enacted no-fault divorce laws, greatly

[74] See Chu [72].

[75] See Huang [73].

[76] See Xu and Zhuang [74].

[77] See Makino [75].

[78] See Xu [76].

[79] See Hunter [77].

reducing the difficulty of divorce.[80] In addition, many countries have simplified divorce procedures and made them more efficient. For instance, in California in the 1970s, a radical divorce measure was implemented, allowing individuals who had been married for less than two years and had not accumulated significant joint property to end their marriage through mail. If the spouses agree on the distribution of joint property, they can file for divorce within six months of receiving a reply letter for less than $50, and there is no need to appear in court or hire a lawyer. Currently, many states in the United States are introducing a faster method of divorce by mutual agreement, which is suitable for couples who recently married, have no children, and have very little joint property.[81] For example, a Texas judge presided over a "collective divorce ceremony" that set a record of 54 couples in just 24 min. When divorce becomes easier and cheaper, the binding force of marriage is greatly reduced, and the number of so-called illegitimate children increases sharply. Currently, in the Nordic countries, cohabitation is considered an acceptable alternative to marriage, and the benefits of motherhood are substantial and not related to marital status. By 1983, over 40 percent of children born in Sweden were born out of wedlock.[82] In Denmark, the rate of children born out of wedlock is as high as 45 percent. Consequently, the government had to take a series of measures aimed at protecting their rights. For instance, instead of calling them "illegitimate" with disdain as in the past, they are referred to as "children born out of wedlock." Similarly, Swedish legislators grant cohabitants and married couples the same status, and children born to them have the same legal rights.[83] The Registered Family Partnership Act is currently being introduced or has been introduced in many US states and some other Western countries to allow cohabitants to enjoy the same rights as married individuals.[84]

5.1.3 Unbanning of Pornography

Although the concept of "pornography" is controversial, one thing is certain: the information conveyed through pornography has a strong stimulating effect on human sexual desire. Man is a diverse and sexual creature, not limited by the mating season like other animals. When properly stimulated, he can engage in sexual activities with objects of desire at any time and place. In this way, individual sexual behavior inevitably conflicts with the established sexual norms of society. Therefore, in order to control individual sexual behavior within a specified range, the power mechanism must control the source of sexual stimulation. This control in traditional ascetic societies is usually achieved by prohibiting the open circulation of pornography. In traditional ascetic societies, sex is solely for reproduction, and instinctive attraction between spouses is sufficient for reproductive purposes, without the need for

[80] Tan [78].

[81] See Liu [79].

[82] Posner [80].

[83] See Liu [81].

[84] See Li [82].

additional stimulation. Therefore, seeking erotic stimulation for pleasure is considered inappropriate, and the dissemination of pornography is a grave offense in such societies.

Needless to say, even in relatively open modern times, the prohibition of the spread of pornography was an important part of the power mechanisms' sexual control. In Britain, the Obscene Publications Act was passed in 1857 at the initiative of Lord Campbell, establishing Victorian norms. The law granted magistrates throughout the country considerable powers "to order the destruction of pornographic books being sold and distributed before the court is about to decide". In the British "Sickling case" of 1868, the presiding judge arbitrarily disregarded the book's intention and banned it if it contained even one or two obscene words or a sexual description. In the United States, the United States Anti-Obscenity Act was passed in 1873 at the initiative of Postal Inspector Comstock, which prohibited the mailing of pornographic publications, obscene advertising, and the dissemination of contraceptive information in the United States. Under this Act, mailing and receiving obscene literature is a felony punishable by a fine of $5,000 for a first offense and a sentence of up to five years. Repeat offenders face a fine of $10,000 and a sentence of up to 10 years. During Comstock's tenure, he achieved great success, incarcerating over 3,600 offenders against public decency and seizing a total of 160 tons of pornography.[85]

After entering the 20th century, with the development of printing, photography, and information technology, it became relatively easy and convenient to produce, reproduce, and disseminate pornographic information. Coupled with the renewal of sexual concepts, appreciation of pornography and information is increasingly seen as a substitute and compensatory means of sexual activity, and a sense of rights. Producers and disseminators see it as a legitimate act of freedom of expression. In fact, the sex industry in the United States, which is now developed, uses the free speech provisions of the First Amendment of the US Constitution to protect itself.[86] As a result, the legal control of pornography began to loosen. In 1968, the U.S. Congress established a national advisory committee to provide responses on how the nation should deal with pornography and obscenity. The committee conducted a special study that lasted two years and cost $2 million, and ended with 12 out of its 18 members supporting the motion that "the prohibition of the sale, distribution, and display of sexual material to adults should be lifted."[87] According to Posner, Western sexual customs underwent dramatic changes between 1920 and 1980, and one important manifestation of this was the widespread dissemination of even the most secular publications with little legal interference.[88] While national laws generally tend to be tolerant of pornography, the degree of tolerance varies considerably

[85] See Liu [83], Li [84].

[86] Bob Guccione is the founder of the renowned American pornographic publication, "Penthouse". His success with the magazine brought him immediate fame and enduring notoriety, eventually establishing him as a tycoon in the American adult entertainment industry. Throughout decades of legal challenges, Guccione protected himself through the freedom of speech enshrined in the U.S. Constitution. See Zhang Zherui United Law Firm [85].

[87] Quoted from: Liu [86].

[88] See Posner [87].

between countries. Denmark was the fastest country to liberalize the sex market, allowing the sale of pornographic literature in 1967 and pornographic photographs in 1969, with citizens over the age of 18 able to produce and sell pornography. Surprisingly, instead of increasing the number of sexual crimes, the liberalization of the sex market in Denmark led to a marked decline in the sex crime rate. The most conservative country in this regard was the United Kingdom, which enacted the Obscene Publications Act in 1959. Although it was a marked improvement over the Obscene Publications Act of 1857, it is still quite conservative compared to other countries, and the law is still in force.[89]

There have also been twists and turns in the anti-ban process of the American market. Some feminists associate pornography with gender oppression, arguing that the theme of pornography is to express the violence, aggression, exploitation, and oppression of men against women, and the more they consume, the higher the degree of sexism and oppression in society. In 1983, at the initiative of prominent feminists Dworkin and McKinnon, the Anti-Obscene Act was passed in Minneapolis, Minnesota. Since then, similar bills have been passed in other cities in the United States, but opposition to these laws was heard. In 1986, the U.S. Supreme Court rejected the anti-obscene proposal on the grounds that the Act violated constitutional principles of free speech in the case of the American Booksellers Association and the American Publishers Association v. Mayor of Minneapolis. Justice Buchanan himself, after years of involvement in the debate over anti-obscenity laws, came to the conclusion that all obscenity laws should be repealed. At present, the United States has conditionally opened up to adults in terms of text, film, theater, photography, and painting.[90] That is, there is already a focus on management, specifically in circulation, while the appreciation link is relatively relaxed. In terms of audience, it is relatively liberal for adults. For example, in the United States, the current film rating system is implemented, which means that the government classifies movies according to the degree of pornographic content they contain for people of different ages.[91]

5.1.4 Acceptance of "Abnormal" Sexual Behaviors

In traditional ascetic culture, the sole purpose of sex is reproduction, which can only be achieved through sexual intercourse between the genitals of both sexes. Therefore, in traditional society, only such sexual acts are considered normal, and sexual acts such as oral sex, anal sex, masturbation, and bestiality, which do not directly help reproduction, are considered abnormal and prohibited. Traditional Christianity believes that all kinds of abnormal sexual acts are manifestations of hedonism, the source of sexual immorality, and must therefore be severely punished by law. Even in the Victorian era of the 16th to 18th century, and even in the 19th century after

[89] Liu [88].

[90] See Li [89].

[91] See Gegnon [90].

the Middle Ages, this idea was still guiding, and Protestantism and Old Christianity, which had many differences in other aspects, reached a surprisingly consistent agreement in this regard. Governed by this thinking, many countries in Europe and early American society regarded bestiality, anal sex, oral sex, etc. as felonies and severely punished them.[92]

In modern society, on one hand, with the emancipation of human thoughts, people increasingly regard the pursuit of happiness as their right. On the other hand, with the enhancement of human ability to control fertility, the pleasure function of sex and reproductive function are separated and gradually become the main function of sex. For reproduction, people must rely on intercourse between the genitals of both sexes. But for happiness, it is not necessary to stick to this, and any way that helps the actors to be happy should be among the choices. Therefore, in modern society, the ways people have sex are diversifying.[93] As a result, the law has begun to accept activities that were traditionally considered "abnormal sexual acts". On one hand, the law has redefined the concept of "sexual intercourse" to include all kinds of traditional abnormal sexual acts. For example, Section 213 of the Model Penal Code in the United States, Article 1, stipulates that sexual intercourse includes oral or anal intercourse. Section 213 of the Norwegian Penal Code is more specific, stating that "the term sexual intercourse includes vaginal and anal intercourse in this chapter. The insertion of the penis into the mouth and objects inserted into the vagina or rectum are equivalent to sexual intercourse."[94] The Spanish Penal Code provides that sexual assault constitutes rape if it is committed through physical channels such as the vagina, anus, or oral cavity or by vaginal and anal contact. This expands the conceptual connotation of sexual intercourse by establishing the crime of rape. On the other hand, society's tolerance for non-coercive sexual behavior has increased, prompting many countries and states in the United States to no longer criminalize it. Even in places where it is still prohibited, law enforcement is inconsistent.[95] In fact, religious forces are also loosening their views on sexuality. In 1977, a group of Catholic theologians issued a document and statement expressing their position on

[92] There were precedents in the Middle Ages where punishments were given for sexual acts considered taboo at the time. For example, if a man ejaculated in a woman's mouth, he could be sentenced to three years of penance. If it became a habit, the sentence could be extended to seven years. In cases of anal sex, punishments could be even more severe. One case resulted in a sentence of ten years of penance, while another resulted in a sentence of fifteen years. In the 16th century, European and American societies were marked by records of executions or burnings related to what was considered perverse behavior. See Pan [91], Rice [92].

[93] In the 1990s, the 20th century was faced with the threat of AIDS, which led to the invention of sexual activities that did not involve the exchange of bodily fluids. Examples include masturbation with other men, telesexual activity, and other forms of non-penetrative sex. Additionally, the popularity of sadomasochism has been on the rise. See Li [93]; See generally Li [94].

[94] Ma [95].

[95] See Posner [96].

sexuality. They believed that sexual intercourse, in whatever form, can be considered moral if it is "self-relaxing, satisfying, honest, happy, socially responsible, and necessary for life."[96]

Of particular note is the fundamental change in the attitude of the law towards homosexuality. It is well known that same-sex sex was discriminated against and punished as a serious anomaly in the Middle Ages and later days. Now, it has gained legal status in almost all Western countries. In 1973, the American Psychiatric Association officially removed homosexuality from its list of published sexual disorders, and in 1988, Denmark enacted the world's first same-sex marriage law. In 1982, San Francisco passed the Cohabitation Act, which legalized homosexual families. In 1991, the Mayor of New York recognized long-term commitment and loving relationships for homosexuals. Many U.S. states and some other Western countries are currently introducing or preparing to introduce the Registered Family Partnership Act, which aims to give same-sex partners the same rights as male and female couples. In some countries, homosexuals also operate through their own organizations and have become an important force capable of influencing the political scene.

5.2 *Increasing Intolerance vis-à-vis Sex*

As mentioned earlier, human society is, in a sense, centered around sex, and if basic social order is to be maintained, illegal sexual behavior must be regulated and punished, even in modern society. Therefore, in modern society, the law also has an increasingly strict side to the regulation of sex, which is mainly manifested in the "intolerance" of sexual acts carried out against the will of others, and the degree and scope of this "intolerance" are increasing.

5.2.1 Regulation of Sexual Assaults

Although rape has been considered a serious sexual crime since ancient times, there are significant differences between traditional and modern ways of regulating it. In traditional patriarchal societies, rulers did not raise it to the level of a violation of human rights for regulation, so the scope and extent of its regulation were limited. In modern society, with the liberation of women and the awakening of people's awareness of their rights, rape is increasingly seen as intolerable by society, and the regulation and punishment of rape are being strengthened and improved. It is an important aspect of strengthening the protection of citizens' rights.

In traditional Western societies, due to the prejudice that women are the source of sexual immorality, the law often blamed the woman for sexual violations. In handling rape cases, the law set up many obstacles for victims to defend their rights, resulting in many rapists in the modern sense not being punished by the law at that time. For

---

[96] See Tannahill [97].

example, there was a common consensus in the legal profession during the pre-French Revolution dynasty that "If a man alone wants to rape a woman who is determined to resist, it is impossible from the point of view of physical strength alone." This suggested that women have enough strength to protect themselves and find a way to do so.[97] In the United States, for centuries, the judiciary has often cited a classic saying about rape: "If the needle is moving, it cannot be threaded," which seems to imply that women bear some responsibility for rape. It is not surprising that such a verdict has emerged under the guidance of this judicial philosophy.[98] In a rape case tried in 1840, Rachel was kidnapped by two gangsters. Miss Lee admitted that when resistance seemed to be of no help to her, she deliberately put aside the modesty of chastity and shouted to the two gangsters: "Come on, I can't wait!" Due to her actions, the judge immediately acquitted the two men accused of rape, and the audience in the gallery unanimously supported the judge's verdict.[99] Based on this concept, rape is interpreted very narrowly in the law, and at one point, New York State law required victims to provide eyewitnesses to the rape. Such a system design is quite favorable to the defendant's escape of guilt and quite detrimental to the protection of the victim's rights.[100] It is also based on this concept that the "principle of resistance to the end" and the "theory of implied consent" have dominated Western judicial practice for a long time. That is to say, if during a rape crime, the victim does not resist at all, or when the rape first occurs, resists a little but later still has the ability to resist and there is no significant danger of continuing to resist, the abandonment of resistance shall be deemed to be the woman's eventual consent to sexual intercourse with a man and therefore not constitute rape. Because this theory is incompatible with the modern concept of human rights, it has been attacked and resisted by most people in contemporary Western society.[101] So far, most Western countries no longer adopt this principle and system, and the Model Penal Code of the United States does not support it. Especially under the promotion of the sexual revolution and feminist movements in the West, there has been a fundamental change in the way rape is determined. That is, from the original notion of "not saying that you agree is agreeing" to the current idea of "not saying that you agree is not agreeing".[102]

Influenced by the central view of male dominance, the traditional theory of Western legislation holds that the subject of the crime of rape can generally only be men, and women can constitute the instigator or accomplice of the crime of rape. However, women cannot constitute an offender or commit the crime themselves, and the victim can only be a woman.[103] More than two hundred years ago, Blackstone, the founder of common law, summarized the basic elements of rape in common law countries as "forcible sexual intercourse against the will of a woman." Based on this

[97] Vigalello [98].

[98] Qiu and Chen [99].

[99] See Hunter [100].

[100] See Gegnon [101].

[101] Sevetez [102].

[102] Suiming et al. [103].

[103] See Mingkai [104].

logic, laws such as the British Sexual Offences Act of 1956, the Model Criminal Code of 1962 in the United States, and the Criminal Code of the former Federal Republic of Germany in 1975 only stipulate that sexual assault committed by a man against a woman can constitute rape. However, with the rise of feminism and the advancement of science and technology, the traditional male-dominated and female-subordinate way of sexual behavior is being challenged. In real life, women can complete sexual acts with the help of sexual drugs or other scientific means even without the man's agreement. Additionally, with the increase of homosexuality, sexual assault between people of the same sex is also inevitable. As a result, reality has impacted traditional theory and practice, and Western countries have amended their sex crimes legislation to meet the needs of the present time. In 1983, Canada began to replace "rape" with "sexual assault" in its sexual offenses law reform, characterized by the absence of prescribing the gender of the victim and the accused, and it protects sexual rights in all sexual relations.[104] The new German Penal Code of 1998 deleted the term "forced woman" from the 1975 Federal Criminal Code and replaced it with the term "forced person."[105] The Sexual Offences Act of Michigan, which came into effect in 1974, extended the protection of rape laws to include men as well as women.[106] Currently, the penal codes of France, Sweden, Finland, Norway, Denmark, Spain, Austria, Italy, and other countries describe the victim as "another person" when providing for rape and other crimes of sexual violence. They use "any person" or "a person" in the English version, instead of "woman." Only the criminal codes of Switzerland, Japan, and other countries explicitly express it as a woman.

The expansion of the scope of subjects and victims of offensive sexual crimes is also reflected in the establishment of "marital rape". In the West, there was a long history of "no adultery in marriage". Article 213 of the French Civil Code of 1804 stipulates that "The husband shall protect his wife, and the wife shall obey her husband." Article 214 stipulates that a wife has an obligation to cohabit with her husband. Traditional Western theory holds that marriage is actually a contract, and sexual life is included in the life of the husband and wife. Once the marriage relationship is established, it means that the wife has agreed to fulfill the obligation to meet the sexual needs of her husband during the marriage. In 1763, the famous British jurist Maffei Sir Hale famously introduced the theory of "immunity from marital rape", which states that "husbands are not convicted of raping their wives because they have given their lives to their husbands under their marriage contract." This commitment is irrevocable".[107] Guided by this theory, traditional criminal law in Western countries generally did not recognize sexual assault by a husband against his wife as a crime. In the United Kingdom, for example, the 1976 Act defined rape in statutory law for the first time, prohibiting "unlawful sexual intercourse," i.e., intercourse outside of marriage.[108] In the United States, for example, even the Model

[104] See Ao and Caixia [105].

[105] See Jiusheng [106].

[106] See Yumei and Ruchun [107].

[107] Quoted from Ao and Caixia [108].

[108] See Smith [109].

Penal Code of 1962 defines rape as follows: "A man ... having sexual intercourse with a woman who is not his wife constitutes rape." As of 1977, the laws of 29 states clearly stated that husbands could not be prosecuted for the rape of their wives.[109] In Germany, for example, article 177 of the former Federal German Penal Code of 1975 stipulates that "rape is committed when a woman is forced to commit extramarital intercourse with herself or another person by force or coercion", which explicitly denies the existence of marital rape.[110] With the development of society, the progress of science and technology, and especially since the middle and late 20th century, more and more women have been liberated. The sexual revolution and the new wave of feminist movements in the 60s and 70s of the 20th century have brought unprecedented improvement to women's awareness of rights and subjectivity. As a result, the traditional marriage commitment theory has been fiercely criticized. In a conjugal relationship, the wife is no longer a mere subject, and she can refuse her husband's unreasonable sexual demands, which has increasingly become the mainstream view in Western society today. As Lord Judge Kings of the Supreme Court put it in the 1991 R case in England, "The modern wife is no longer a submissive sexual slave under her husband but an equal sexual partner."[111] Driven by this reality, especially in the past 20 years, Western countries have abandoned the theory of "marital adultery" and affirmed the actionability of marital rape in legislation. In the United States, in the 1970s, the New Jersey Code stipulated: "No person shall be presumed to be incapable of rape because of old age or sexual impotence or marriage to the victim," breaking with the common law tradition of "no adultery in marriage." In 1984, Judge Wachtler of the New York State Court of Appeals stated: "The promise to always agree to have sex with a husband is irrational and ridiculous. Marriage should never be considered to give a husband the right to force his wife to have sexual intercourse as needed. Therefore, a marriage certificate could not be regarded as a permit for a husband to rape his wife with impunity."[112] By 1993, North Carolina became the last state in the nation to abolish marital rape immunity.[113] In the United Kingdom, in 1991, the Court found in R that "there is no rule that a husband cannot be convicted of raping his wife"[114]; In 1992, the British House of Lords made it clear in Appeal No. 599 that a husband may have committed rape of his wife; Sexual Offences (Amendment) Act 1994 The phrase "unlawful sexual intercourse" was deleted, i.e. the "immunity from marital rape" was indirectly abolished.[115] In Germany, the Penal Code, as amended in 1998, deleted the reference to "sexual intercourse outside marriage" from Section 177 of the former Federal Criminal Code on rape.[116] The penal codes of Austria, Switzerland, and other countries also explicitly hold spouses, husbands,

[109] See Escherman [110].

[110] See Xu [111].

[111] Quoted from Ji [112].

[112] Quoted from An and Yang [113].

[113] See Gross [114].

[114] Smith [109].

[115] Ji [115].

[116] See Xu and Zhuang [116].

or cohabiting partners criminally liable for rape, but only if it is explicitly stated in their laws.[117] According to the author's investigation, currently, only one country, Denmark, has a provision regarding extramarital sexual intercourse in its criminal code on rape. However, this provision only applies to the following three situations: sexual intercourse with a person who is mentally ill or mentally deficient, facilitating sexual intercourse with a person who cannot resist, or taking advantage of another person's subordination or economic dependence.[118]

The increasingly robust regulation of sexual assault is also reflected in modern laws that regulate "sexual harassment". In traditional patriarchal societies, sexual assault by men, especially high-ranking men, against lower-ranking women was often recognized or went unpunished by law. As early as medieval Europe, customary law recognized the right of feudal lords to the first night of newlywed serfs' wives. In modern times, the sexual assault of working-class women in Europe by factory owners was still commonplace, as Engels wrote in the book "The Condition of the British Working Class": "It goes without saying that the dependence of factories is greater than any other dependence. At least, it was given to the master of the jus primae noctis. In this respect, the factory owner was also the master of the body and beauty of female workers. Nine out of ten threats of dismissal, or even ninety-nine out of a hundred, were enough to destroy any resistance of girls, not to mention that they did not value their virginity in the first place."[119] Before the founding of New China, the phenomenon of female workers being raped by foremen and experiencing other forms of sexual assault was more common. This was confirmed by Hornig's investigation of female bonded workers in Shanghai spinning mills in the 1930s, as well as He Xiao's survey of the lives of female workers in Tianjin in 1949.[120] The law does not always cover serious sexual assaults such as rape, and even minor sexual assaults are less likely to be punished. In the United States, until the 1970s, judges mostly considered sexual harassment to be a private matter outside the scope of the law. Thus, someone harassing a woman was at most considered morally problematic.[121] Today, with the rise of feminism, the mainstream concept of modern justice positions sexual harassment as gender discrimination, and the violation of women's sexual rights. This is now recognized by most national laws. The Law of the People's Republic of China on the Protection of Women's Rights and Interests, amended in 2005, and the Law of the People's Republic of China on Administrative Punishments for Public Security, which came into effect in 2006, both prohibit sexual harassment. This shows that in modern society, even minor sexual assault is not tolerated by the law, indicating the increasing sophistication of sexual rights protection in modern law.

[117] See Xu [117], Xu and Zhuang [118].

[118] Articles 218 and 220. See Xie [119].

[119] Quoted from Fourks [120].

[120] See Honey [121], Hershatter [122].

[121] See Zhang [123].

5.2.2 Protection of Minors

Although sexual abuse of minors is considered more serious than that of adults in traditional societies, such as during the dynasties before the French Revolution, where the rape of an unmarried girl was deemed more serious than the rape of an adult woman. If the raped person was a virgin and the woman was not yet of marriageable age, the rapist would be sentenced to death, or even subject to castration.[122] For example, in 16th and 17th century Britain, those sentenced to death for rape were only those who raped virgins and underage girls, while the rape of adult women was treated as a general crime against property. However, the mechanism behind such legislation was not to protect the rights of minors, but to treat them as the property of the father to be sold at a price, and if she was "lost" as a result of rape, the value of her property would greatly decrease. It is precisely because legislators did not have the idea that the rights of minors should be specially protected that when minors violated the basic order of society, the law did not have special leniency measures. For example, in medieval and Protestant Europe, and early America, bestiality was punished by death, including for minors.[123] Incest was also punished, often involving minors.

The concept of modern rights generally assumes that the rights of minors should be specially protected. This is because, on the one hand, minors are physically and psychologically vulnerable members of society, whose rights are more easily violated, and the theory of social justice requires special protection for them. On the other hand, because minors are in a period of development, sexual abuse can greatly damage their physical and mental health, and have extremely detrimental effects on their later growth, both psychologically and physically. As the French scholar Georges Duby said, "The violation of children becomes the first fear of society; it is an extreme violence that allows us to see in an unprecedented way the contrast between two images of society: either there is a demonic deviation in society, or people's sensitivity and fear of this crime have become so acute that people's attention to suffering and evil has been put first. Once it touches children, isn't this a heinous crime?"[124] Based on this, contemporary Western countries' sex crime legislation pays special attention to the protection of minors. In the United States, Texas legislation provides for the world's first crime of rape of underage men, and in 1998, the Children's Online Privacy Protection Act was specially enacted and passed to prevent pornographic websites from harming minors. In 2002, France added a section on the "use of minors for prostitution" to chapter V of the Penal Code, "Crimes against human dignity". Japan enacted the Child Prostitution Punishment Act in Heisei 11, and the Spanish Penal Code devotes a special chapter to the eighth episode "the crime of inducing a girl to prostitution". The criminal laws of Germany, Italy, Canada, and other countries criminalize sexual acts, bestiality, and the display of obscene materials in front of minors. Canadian criminal law also makes it an offence to touch,

---

[122] See Vigalello [124].

[123] See Pan [125], Rice [126].

[124] Vigalello [127].

directly or indirectly, any part of a person's body with a part or object of the body for the purpose of adultery.

As mentioned earlier, although the right to nudity has been recognized to some extent and the market is being liberalized, it is not absolute, at least in the presence of minors. "No nakedness" and "prohibition" are the most typical and widespread protection of minors. The provision of the "voluntary age line" is that sexual relations with minors below the voluntary age line, whether the person concerned is voluntary or not, is considered sexual assault.[125]

5.3 *Tolerance Versus Intolerance: Basic Approaches to Sexual Rights*

The preceding paragraphs provide a general overview of the evolution of laws related to sexuality from the Middle Ages to modern times. It is apparent that the adjustment of laws regarding sexuality has progressed along two parallel paths of "tolerance" and "intolerance". Specifically, the law has become increasingly tolerant of consensual sex that does not interfere with others, while simultaneously becoming stricter with regards to sexual violence and violations of the rights and freedoms of others. From the perspective of regulating illegal acts, modern laws tend to be more lenient in cases where no harm is caused to others, while being more severe in cases where others are victimized.[126] It can also be said that in matters of sexuality, modern law has become tolerant in dealing with conflicts between the individual and the social order, and harsh in dealing with conflicts between people. It is under this development that people's naked space has increased, premarital and extramarital sex has been acquiesced, the market has been liberalized, and all kinds of abnormal sexual behavior have been accepted; The law has tightened the regulation of sexual assault, and the sexual protection of minors has become more perfect.

If we dig deeper, it is not difficult to see that behind this development trend and the overall picture, there is a red line that is extending and working. That is the rise and growth of sexual rights. The two paths of "tolerance" and "intolerance" rely on this red line so that there will be no contradiction and unification. The two attitudes of the law towards sexual "tolerance" and "intolerance" are actually the two modes of operation

---

[125] In today's America, under the Prohibition of Child Pornography of Minors Act, it is an offense to possess child pornography. See Zhang Zherui United Law Firm [128]. According to the current provisions of the Swedish Constitution on freedom of the press and expression, it is not illegal to possess child pornography. However, in May 1998, the parliament overwhelmingly passed a bill that outlawed the possession and sale of child pornography. If the circumstances are serious, the offender may face a punishment of up to 4 years in prison. See Liu [129].

[126] According to the current provisions of the Swedish Constitution on freedom of the press and expression, it is not illegal to possess child pornography. However, in May 1998, the parliament overwhelmingly passed a bill that outlawed the possession and sale of child pornography. If the circumstances are serious, the offender may face a punishment of up to 4 years in prison. See Gegnon [130], Li [131].

of the law to confirm and protect sexual rights. Specifically, it is a "permissive" model and a "prohibitive" model. The "permissive" model allows consensual sexual acts that do not harm others, while the "prohibitive" model prohibits violent and aggressive sexual acts. In the process of "permissive" operation, the traditional sexual order is giving way, the shackles of oppressive power are being broken, and the sexual freedom of individuals is increasing. In the process of "prohibitive" operation, the sexual freedom of the individual is established and the sexual independence of the private is maintained. Implemented in law, these two models are manifested as two normative means of determining rights and setting obligations. The tolerance of law on sex means that the law recognizes the subject or sets rights for it, and the intolerability of sex in the law means that the law sets obligations for others other than the subject of rights. The subject of rights obtains freedom and benefits from the former, and the latter is protected from the encroachment of others, thus ensuring the realization of freedom and interests. The operation mode of "permissive" means that the subject of rights is expanding space for its own interests, and the power system is returning to the territory that has long been usurped by itself but belongs to private individuals. The operation mode of "prohibitive" means that the power system is delineating boundaries and making marks for the existence of rights, stipulating the reasons for resistance for the intervention of others, so that the scope of interests of the right holder forms a relatively closed space, and the distinction between "yours" and "mine" arises in people's concepts. Each person can only dominate the interests in their own space and cannot step out of this space to dominate the interests of others, otherwise, it constitutes an abuse of power. The counterparty cannot step into the territory of the right holder to exercise its rights, otherwise, it constitutes an infringement. Both abuse and infringement of rights can lead to negative evaluations of society and law. In this sense, the wider the space for "permissive" operation and the greater the intensity of "prohibitive" operation, the richer the content of sexual rights and the more mature the development of sexual rights. The more autonomous people are in the sexual sphere. The rise and growth of sexual rights is fundamentally an aspect of the increase in the overall freedom of modern people, a reflection of the modern rule of law principle that "the code is the Bible of people's freedom".[127] Therefore, in value, modern legislation on sex should be based on sexual rights. From a macro perspective, the attitude of modern law towards sex should be guided by the spirit of rights.

6 Sexual Rights from the Legal Perspective

Freud believed that civilization and instinct are opposites, and that the development of human civilization is achieved through the suppression of human instincts.[128] In a sense, human civilization is manifested as a series of systems and rules, an

[127] The Complete Works of Marx and Engels [132].

[128] See Freud [133].

institutionalized order, which is achieved through the suppression of human instincts. The pursuit of sexual pleasure is a natural human instinct, and although human reproduction, social development, family harmony, and personal growth all depend on this instinct, if these instincts cannot operate according to certain rules, they can transform into a huge destructive force, directly threatening the normal social order of human beings. Therefore, from the point of view of social maintenance, the public power of any society will not allow sexual behavior to be entirely free and must impose the necessary constraints on sexuality. However, this constraint is expressed with different intensities between tradition and modernity. Even in modern society, the marriage system, the punishment system for sexual assault, the incest prohibition system, the regulation system for pornography, the disease management system, the sexual privacy preservation system, etc., are still common systems in all countries in the world, and they maintain the proper social order. Therefore, in this sense, human sexual civilization is manifested in the institutionalization and standardization of sexual behavior. Human sexual rights and sexual freedom can only be rights and freedoms within the framework of order and permitted by rules. While people have sexual rights, they also have sexual obligations that must be fulfilled.

The rules governing sexuality have been gradually formed over the course of history, both spontaneously and through artificial construction. They represent not only a manifestation of society's self-balance and self-consistency in response to the interplay of various forces, but also the result of the ruling class acquiescing to, processing, and transforming this spontaneous form in order to maintain social order and protect its own interests. These rules were initially expressed in the form of various sexual taboos in early societies, as well as through a chaotic mix of social norms such as customs, morality, religious doctrines, and primitive legal practices. During this time, sexual rules, like other rules, had no clear rights and obligations. With the accumulation of social management experience and the evolution of civilization, people became better able to distinguish the nature and extent of different behaviors affecting society. Legal, moral, religious, customary, and other norms began to become independent and increasingly clear. While the maintenance of society relies on the joint effect of various social norms, such as morality, religion, customs, and law, it is undeniable that, in the development of human civilization, law has become the most widely used and practical norm due to its clarity, universality, and coercive characteristics.[129] Various official institutions in society are supported by law. Therefore, the various regulations governing sexuality must be established through legal rules, and the functioning of institutions must be realized through the implementation of legal rules.

Any legal rule or system can be broken down into certain rights and obligations at the empirical level, and rights and obligations are the core elements and central categories of law.[130] Sexual legal rules or regimes are no exception, and they can also be broken down into sexual rights and obligations. Sexual rights represent the

[129] Fuller [134].

[130] See Zhang [135].

freedom, autonomy, and interests of people in the sexual sphere, and sexual obligations represent the constraints, restrictions, burdens, and responsibilities of people in the sexual field. Sexual rights and sexual obligations, as two contradictory aspects, together constitute the whole picture of the existence and operation of sexual rules or systems. Although rights and obligations are the two core elements of legal rules or systems, if we consider any rule or system from an empirical point of view, it exists as a rational form of human perceptual constraints. Therefore, the so-called "no rules are not square circles." In this context, it is not rights but obligations that best embody the characteristics of rules or systems. In the case of a law, only the provision of rights without the provision of obligations cannot be made into law, and at best, can only be described as a declaration and initiative. However, only the provisions of obligations without rights can sometimes become law, for example, laws whose main function is prohibition and punishment. Thus, a legal rule or system represents both a set of freedoms defined by obligations and a set of obligations that limit human freedoms. In this sense, legal rights and obligations imply certain limitations and constraints, obligations are limitations and constraints themselves, and rights are the result of human freedom being limited by obligations. This is what Montesquieu's famous phrase "freedom is the right to do everything permitted by law" really meant. In the field of sexuality, sexual rights are not equivalent to sexual freedom; sexual rights are only sexual freedom after being recognized by law, only sexual freedom limited by sexual obligations, and only limited sexual freedom within the framework of sexual rules and systems.

As a rule, its effect is universal. From the perspective of evolutionary theory, the generation of a rule depends on the acceptance of the group, so an effective rule itself represents a kind of "cooperation", representing the limitation and sharing of interests between individuals. The American anthropologist Hobel, in his discussion of the nature of social order, argues that everyone living in a group should become a "social scientist with practical experience". They must be able to anticipate what others will do and adjust their behavior based on their past experience, expectations, and in harmony with the behavior of others so that the group can be sustained. If everyone acts on their own impulse, the group will cease to exist.[131] From this perspective, sexual rights in rules are actually the result of long-term human evolution in which people have continued to compromise with each other and cooperate in order to achieve success. While everyone has natural sexual freedom, if each individual fully exercises their sexual freedom, conflicts are inevitable, and this will eventually lead to the loss of everyone's interests and freedom. Therefore, through constant conflicting interaction, people have realized that only through cooperation, conceding a part of their own interests and freedoms, and appropriately recognizing the interests and freedoms of others, can they preserve some of their own interests and freedoms. In this mutual recognition of interests and freedoms, the rules of rights arise. Singh describes the process by which rights arise: "In doing so, they establish the basis for mutual recognition. To recognize that I have rights is to recognize that you also have rights, and vice versa. So, if any of us can be arbitrarily deprived of this right,

[131] See Hobel [136].

then it is not actually a right. I can therefore realize that defending your rights is in my interest, and I can show you that defending my rights is also in your interest."[132] When public power emerges, legal recognition is given to social norms that do not conflict with reality, and sexual legal rules that identify and qualify human interests arise. Sexual rights and sexual obligations have their own division of labor in sexual rules and systems.

Sexual rights, with their unique interest-oriented mechanism, contribute to the realization of human sexual freedom, while sexual obligations, with their unique restraint mechanism, help to establish social sexual order. Because freedom occupies the highest value in human society, sexual rights lead the value trend of sexual rules or systems and determine the good and evil qualities of sexual rules or systems. Because order is the prerequisite for the development of human society, sexual obligations ensure social cooperation and create an orderly environment for people. The reason why traditional society became a society of sexual autocracy and sexual oppression is precisely because it set sexual rules centered on the element of obligation, completely excluded people's subjective status, and deprived people of sexual freedom and sexual autonomy. Sexual law in traditional society was obligation-based. However, it must be reiterated that the reason why we reject traditional social laws is not because there are sexual obligations in the sexual laws of traditional societies, but because the configuration and implementation of sexual obligations deviate from the humanistic direction led by sexual rights. Rules and institutions without humanism are evil rules and evil institutions.

In a sense, the political process of human society is a gradual unfolding of rights from different fields and perspectives, and the discourse on rights is constantly strengthened. In today's world, rights have become a universal and dominant political discourse and legal term. The legitimacy of various interests often has to resort to the language of rights to prove it, and the guarantee of various freedoms often has to be realized through rights. Rights have become the cornerstone category and core value of modern law and jurisprudence. The American scholar Louis A. Professor Henkin once said, "Our time is the age of rights."[133] In the field of sexuality, with the "sexual revolution" in the West, the discourse of sexual rights began to emerge in the West in the 1960s and 1970s. Sexual rights bills and declarations of a civil nature were introduced during this time. For example, the American Humanist Association asked Lester Kirkendall, a prominent sexologist and professor of family life at Oregon University, to draft a bill of sexual rights. This bill was then signed by a group of humanists and published in The Humanist magazine in January–February 1976 under the title "A New Bill of Sexual Rights and Responsibilities."[134] As mentioned earlier, in August 1999, the 14th World Congress of Sexology held in Hong Kong, China, also adopted the Declaration on Sexual Rights (Declaration on Sexual Rights). The Declaration stipulates 11 major rights, including the right to sexual freedom and declares that "sexual rights are basic and universal human rights." In contemporary

---

[132] Singer [137].

[133] Hengkin [138].

[134] See Hejun [139].

Western society, some scholars have even elevated the importance of sexual rights to the level of the foundation of the existence of democratic states, arguing that "sexual self-expression is rooted in the social contract that forms the philosophical basis of free nations."[135]

It is undeniable that the formation of the discourse on sexual rights has played a significant role in the progress of sexual civilization and the expansion of people's sexual freedom. However, we must reaffirm that most of the discourse on this right still remains at the level of ideas and slogans. It is still just a "claim" or a demand, not a real legal "right". At best, it can only be called a "moral right" or a "natural right." At the empirical level, this kind of demand or claim that stays at the slogan level can only be regarded as a "semi-finished product" or a "blank" of a right because the creation and existence of a right requires two core elements: First, the subject of rights must put forward the requirements and claims of interests; Second, this proposition must be recognized by society. Although there are many ways of social identification, such as mainstream morality, traditional habits, etc., in today's society ruled by law, legal recognition is the most effective and operable social identity. In a society governed by the rule of law, a claim that is not legally recognized is at least not a right that can be safely enjoyed or justiciable. Even in modern society, it is always much more difficult for a claim or demand to be legally accepted than to make such a claim or demand. This is because a claim or demand is merely made without regard to the cost of implementation, and there is no need to design special obligations to correspond to it, nor bear the responsibility of trial and error. In contrast, the establishment and implementation of a certain legal right must consider important factors such as the acceptance of the people, the operability of the system, historical and cultural traditions, and the cost and effectiveness of law implementation, and bear the responsibility of trial and error of the system. Therefore, the responsibilities of jurists and legislators concerned with legislation and justice are far heavier than those of the thinkers who make these claims and demands. As such, the former should be more conservative and prudent than the latter. Foucault argued that there was no essential difference between punching a person in the face and inserting a penis into a person's vagina; both forms of injury or tort, and that it was problematic to classify rape as a more serious crime.[136] It is true that there is no essential difference between the two in appearance, but from the beginning of human civilization, sex has been a special problem and domain. Although it is not fundamentally different from human activities such as dressing, eating, and sleeping, it is impossible for any culture to treat it equally. It may be true that inserting a penis into a person's vagina is much less physically damaging than hitting a person in the face with a fist, but the former is more psychologically damaging to the victim and their family than the latter can be in any way. This may be the result of cultural trends, but it is an undeniable fact. This is something that legislators or judges must consider when making operational legal rules. It is true that, as humanist thinkers have proclaimed, freedom in the sphere of sexuality is rooted in human nature and is a natural right that human beings should

---

[135] Abramson [140].

[136] See Foucault [141].

enjoy. However, jurists, legislators, and judges do not deal with it as lightly as the former because they have to think about rights in terms of rules or institutions. In Kelson's words, "A statement of the existence or absence of a right is impossible without prejudging a general norm regulating human conduct." If there is a question of legal rights, a legal rule must be presupposed".[137] Since sex is a special field, and since rights need to be taken seriously, sexual rights, especially sexual rights under legal rules or systems, need to be taken more seriously.

References

1. Li, Y. (2003). *The Question of Sexuality: Foucault and Sex* (p. 76). Culture and Art Press. (in Chinese).
2. Wang, Y. (2004). *Sex·Civilization and Absurdity* (pp. 246–247). Kyushu Publishing Company.
3. Giddens, A. (1992). *The Transformation of Intimacy: Sexuality, Love, and Eroticism in Modern Societies* (p. 102). Polity Press.
4. Hedge, P. (1999). *Consent: Sexual Rights and the Transformation of American Liberalism* (p. vi). Cornell University Press.
5. Pan, S., Bai, W., Wang, A., & Lawman, S. (2004). *Sexuality and Sexual Relations in Contemporary China* (pp. 9–22). Social Science Literature Publishers.
6. Cao, F. (2003). China's first "sexual rights" lawsuit trial begins and ends. *Rule of Law and Society, 8*.
7. Wu, Z. (2007, September 3–9). Wife's appeal for "sexual rights" triggers discussion on sexual rights. *Legal Weekly, 9*.
8. The absence of the law behind husband and wife's demand for 'sexual rights'. (n.d.). Retrieved April 18, 2010, from http://news3.xinhuanet.com/comments/2004-11/13/content_2209253.htm.
9. Zhou, Y. (2005). *Sex and Society* (p. 173). Wuhan University Press.
10. Li, Y. (2005, November 7). *Li Yinhe Dialogue Volunteer: It is not far off to legalize same-sex marriage in China*. Southern Metropolis Daily.
11. Li, Y. (2003). *The Question of Sexuality Foucault and Sex* (pp. 77–81). Culture and Art Press.
12. *The Complete Works of Marx and Engels* (Vol. 4, 1st edn., pp. 121–122, Chinese Translation, 1958). People's Publishing House. (in Chinese).
13. Perez-Conchillo, M., & Coleman, A. (Eds.). (2000). *Sexuality in the New Millennium: Proceedings of the 14th World Congress of Sexology, Hong Kong SAR, China*, 23–27 August 1999 (p. xii). Publishing Composers. Preface.
14. Zhao, H. (2002). Sexual and human rights—"Declaration of sexual rights": Speaking of which. *Global Law Review* (Spring issue).
15. Fisher, H. (1992). *Anatomy of Love: The Natural History of Monogamy, Adultery and Divorce* (pp. 110–135). Norton.
16. He, Z., & Yu, F. (Eds.). (1999). *Freud: The Price of Civilization* (p. 65). Liaohai Press.
17. Chen, X. (1995). *Sexual Revolution* (p. 96). Taiwan Yangzhi Cultural Business Co., Ltd.
18. Tannahill, R. (1980). *Sex in History* (pp. 130–190). Stein & Day.
19. Fenggao, Y. (2004). *The Changing Concept of Sexuality in the West* (p. 56). Hunan Literature and Art Publishing House.
20. Fourks, E. (2000). *History of Sexuality in Europe: The Renaissance* (H. Huanhong, Trans., pp. 357–377). Liaoning Education Press.
21. Gagnon, J. (1973). *Sexual Conduct: The Social Sources of Human Sexuality* (pp. 294–358). Aldine Books.

137 Kelsen [142].

22. Pan, S. (1998). *The Social History of Sexuality* (pp. 48–49, 52). Henan People's Publishing House.
23. Morris, D. (1994). *The Human Animal: A Personal View of the Human Species* (pp. 150–198). BBC Publications.
24. *Selected Works of Marx and Engels* (vol. 4, 2nd ed., p. 241, 1995). People's Publishing House.
25. Cheng, L., & Wang, R. (1998). *Rights and Remedies* (p. 66). Shandong People's Publishing House.
26. Kinsey, A. C. (1998). *Sexual Behavior in the Human Male* (Reprint ed., pp. 10–25). Indiana University Press.
27. Gore, R. et al. (2003). *Queer Theory* (Y. Li, Trans., p. 22). Culture and Art Press. (in Chinese).
28. Morris, D. (1994). *The Human Animal: A Personal View of the Human Species* (pp. 153–210). BBC Publications.
29. Tan, D. (1998). *Sexual Culture and Law* (p. 46). Shanghai People's Publishing House. (in Chinese).
30. Li, Y. (2003). *The Question of Sexuality·Foucault and Sex* (p. 9). Culture and Art Press. (in Chinese).
31. Morris, D. (2003). *The Naked Ape: A Zoologist's Study of the Human Animal* (L. Wenrong, Trans., pp. 111–112). Wenhui Press. (in Chinese).
32. Tan, D. (1998). *Sexual Culture and Law* (pp. 469–470). Shanghai People's Publishing House. (in Chinese).
33. Fisher, H. (1992). *Anatomy of Love: The Natural History of Monogamy, Adultery, and Divorce* (p. 112). Norton.
34. Zhang, D. (2004). *From Bestiality to Humanity: Man's Re-understanding of His Own Behavior* (p. 144). Shandong People's Publishing House.
35. Tang, D. (2002). *Ethics of Interests* (pp. 14–15, 29–30). Peking University Press.
36. Wang, W., & Gao, Y. (1992). *Sexual Ethics* (p. 86). People's Publishing House.
37. Marcuse, H. (2005). *Eros and Civilization* (H. Yong et al., Trans., p. 4). Shanghai Translation Press.
38. Yongyi & Xiaohua (Eds.). (1988). *The Love Theory of World Masters* (p. 227). Hunan Literature and Art Publishing House.
39. Pan, S., Bai, W., Wang, A., & Lawman, S. (2004). *Sexuality and Sexual Relations in Contemporary China* (p. 191). Social Science Literature Publishers.
40. *Selected Works of Marx and Engels* (Volume 4, 2nd ed., p. 75, 1995). People's Publishing House.
41. von Diermann, R. (2004). *Modern Life in Europe* (Y. Wang, Trans., pp. 18–19, 20). Oriental Press. (in Chinese).
42. Xiao, H. (2005). The plague almost ruined Europe. *Disaster Reduction in China, 10*. (in Chinese).
43. Fourks, E. (2000). *History of Sexuality in Europe: The Renaissance* (H. Huanhong, Trans., pp. 357–377). Liaoning Education Press. (in Chinese).
44. Li, Y. (2003). *The Question of Sexuality: Foucault and Sex* (p. 20). Culture and Art Press. (in Chinese).
45. He, Z., & Yu, F. (1999). *Freud: The Price of Civilization* (p. 121). Liaohai Press.
46. Li, Y. (2003). *The Question of Sexuality: Foucault and Sex* (p. 19). Culture and Art Press.
47. Fourks, E. (2000). *History of Sexuality in Europe: The Renaissance* (H. Huanhong, Trans., pp. 50–137). Liaoning Education Press.
48. Li, Y. (2003). *The Question of Sexuality: Foucault and Sex* (p. 267). Culture and Art Press. (in Chinese).
49. Fisher, H. (1992). *Anatomy of Love: The Natural History of Monogamy, Adultery, and Divorce* (pp. 85–137). Norton.
50. Pan, S. (1998). *The Social History of Sexuality* (pp. 61–68). Henan People's Publishing House. (in Chinese).
51. Fei, X. (1998). *Native China Fertility System* (p. 143). Peking University Press. (in Chinese).

52. Li, Y. (2003). *The Question of Sexuality: Foucault and Sex* (pp. 98, 103). Culture and Art Press. (in Chinese).
53. Liu, D. (1999). *World Contemporary Sexual Culture* (p. 104). Shanghai Sanlian Bookstore. (in Chinese).
54. Russell, B. (1988). *Marriage and Morals* (pp. 105–106). China Youth Publishing House.
55. Pan, S. (1998). *The Social History of Sexuality* (p. 53). Henan People's Publishing House. (in Chinese).
56. Tan, D. (1998). *Sexual Culture and Law* (pp. 1–4, 26). Shanghai People's Publishing House. (in Chinese).
57. Morris, D. (2003). *The Naked Ape: A Zoologist's Study of the Human Animal* (W. Liu, Trans., p. 71). Wenhui Press. (in Chinese).
58. Hunter, M. (1988). *Natural History of Love* (Y. Zhao & J. Li, Trans., p. 429). Writers Press. (in Chinese).
59. Fourks, E. (2000). *History of Sexuality in Europe: The Renaissance* (H. Huanhong, Trans., pp. 175–224).Liaoning Education Press. (in Chinese).
60. Hunter, M. (1988). *Natural History of Love* (Y. Zhao & J. Li, Trans., p. 426). Writers Press. (in Chinese).
61. Tannahill, R. (1980). *Sex in History* (pp. 323–389). Stein & Day.
62. Liu, D. (1999). *World Contemporary Sexual Culture* (pp. 19, 366–367). Shanghai Sanlian Bookstore. (in Chinese).
63. Zhang Zherui United Law Firm (Ed.). (2005). *The Right to Be Naked: American Law and Sex* (pp. 7–18). Law Press. (in Chinese).
64. Xiao, R. (Ed.). (1998). *Selected Codes of the World·Criminal Code Volumes* (p. 65). China Democracy and Legal System Press. (in Chinese).
65. Hunter, M. (1988). *Natural History of Love* (Y. Zhao & J. Li, Trans., pp. 150–151). Writers Press.
66. Li, X. (2005). *Studies in Germanic Law* (pp. 207–208). Commercial Press. (in Chinese).
67. Zhang, Z. (1987). A treatise on the crime of adultery in Chinese feudal society. *Journal of Nanjing University, 3.* (in Chinese).
68. Hunter, M. (1988). *Natural History of Love* (Y. Zhao & J. Li, Trans., pp. 298–299). Writers Press.
69. Pan, S. (1998). *The Social History of Sexuality* (p. 392). Henan People's Publishing House. (in Chinese).
70. Chu, H. (2005). *U.S. Criminal Code* (3rd ed., pp. 195–196). Peking University Press. (in Chinese).
71. Li, Y. (2003). *The Question of Sexuality·Foucault and Sex* (pp. 98, 103). Culture and Art Press. (in Chinese).
72. Chu, H. (2005). *U.S. Criminal Code* (3rd ed., p. 196). Peking University Press. (in Chinese).
73. Huang, F. (Trans.). (1998). *Italian Penal Code* (p. 158). China University of Political Science and Law Press. (in Chinese).
74. Xu, J., & Zhuang, J. (Trans.). (2004). *German Penal Code, Preface* (p. 19). China Founder Publishing House. (in Chinese).
75. Makino, E. (2003). *General Meaning of Japanese Criminal Law* (C. Chen, Trans., pp. 4, 174. China University of Political Science and Law Press. (in Chinese).
76. Xu, J. (Trans.). (2004). *Penal Code of the Federal Republic of Austria* (p. 79). China Founder Publishing House. (in Chinese).
77. Hunter, M. (1988). *Natural History of Love* (Y. Zhao & J. Li, Trans., p. 447). Writers Press. (in Chinese).
78. Tan, D. (1998). *Sexual Culture and Law* (p. 153). Shanghai People's Publishing House. (in Chinese).
79. Liu, D. (1999). *World Contemporary Sexual Culture* (p. 220). Shanghai Sanlian Bookstore. (in Chinese).
80. Posner, R. (2002). *Sex and Reason* (L. Su, Trans., p. 76). China University of Political Science and Law Press. (in Chinese).

81. Liu, D. (1999). *World Contemporary Sexual Culture* (p. 325). Shanghai Sanlian Bookstore. (in Chinese).
82. Li, Y. (2003). *The Question of Sexuality·Foucault and Sex* (pp. 104–105). Culture and Art Press. (in Chinese).
83. Liu, D. (1999). *World Contemporary Sexual Culture* (pp. 387–388). Shanghai Sanlian Bookstore. (in Chinese).
84. Li, Y. (2003). *The Question of Sexuality·Foucault and Sex* (p. 92). Culture and Art Press. (in Chinese).
85. Zhang Zherui United Law Firm (Ed.). (2005). *The Right to Be Naked: American Law and Sex* (pp. 49–51). Law Press.
86. Liu, D. (1999). *World Contemporary Sexual Culture* (pp. 382–385). Shanghai Sanlian Bookstore. (in Chinese).
87. Posner, R. (2002). *Sex and Reason* (L. Su, Trans., pp. 73–74). China University of Political Science and Law Press. (in Chinese).
88. Liu, D. (1999). *World Contemporary Sexual Culture* (pp. 393–394). Shanghai Sanlian Bookstore. (in Chinese).
89. Li, Y. (2003). *The Question of Sexuality·Foucault and Sex* (pp. 146–150). Culture and Art Press. (in Chinese).
90. Gegnon, J. (1994). *Sociology of Sexuality: Human Sexuality* (Y. Li, Trans., pp. 322–325). Henan People's Publishing House. (in Chinese).
91. Pan, S. (1998). *The Social History of Sexuality* (pp. 321, 379). Henan People's Publishing House. (in Chinese).
92. Rice, E. (Ed.) (2004). *American Sexual History* (D. Yang et al., Trans., pp. 14–45). Oriental Press. (in Chinese).
93. Li, Y. (2003). *The Question of Sexuality·Foucault and Sex* (p. 212). Culture and Art Press. (in Chinese).
94. Li, Y. (2002). *Sadomasochistic Subculture*. China Friendship Publishing Company. (in Chinese).
95. Ma, S. (Trans.). (2005). *Norwegian General Civil Code* (p. 44). Peking University Press.
96. Posner, R. (2002). *Sex and Reason* (L. Su, Trans., p. 74). China University of Political Science and Law Press. (in Chinese).
97. Tannahill, R. (1980). *Sex in History* (pp. 412–482). Stein & Day.
98. Vigalello, G. (2000). *History of Sexual Assault* (S. Zhang, Trans., p. 63). Hunan Literature and Art Publishing House.
99. Qiu, Y., & Chen, R. (2004). A comparative study of rape in criminal law in the United States. *Journal of Henan Political and Legal Management Cadre College, 6*, 123.
100. Hunter, M. (1988). *Natural History of Love* (p. 412). Writers Press.
101. Gegnon, J. (1994). *Sociology of Sexuality: Human Sexuality* (p. 272). Henan People's Publishing House.
102. Sevetez, L. D., et al. (1988). *Sexual Crimes Research (Compiled by Chen Z)* (pp. 17–18). Wuhan Press.
103. Suiming, P., Weilian, B., Aili, W., & Lawman, S. (2004). *Sexuality and Sexual Relations in Contemporary China* (p. 304). Social Science Literature Publishers.
104. Mingkai, Z. (1999). *Outline of Foreign Criminal Law* (p. 520). Tsinghua University Press.
105. Ao, A., & Caixia, Y. (2005) *A Comparative Study on Crimes Infringing on the Rights of Citizens* (p. 141). Chinese Public Security University Press. (in Chinese).
106. Jiusheng, X., & Jinghua, Z. (Trans.). (2004). *German Penal Code* (p. 93). China Founder Publishing House.
107. Yumei, Q., & Ruchun, C. (2004). A comparative study of rape in criminal law in the United States. *Journal of Henan Political and Legal Management Cadre College, 6*, 124.
108. Ao, A., & Caixia, Y. (2005). *A Comparative Study on Crimes Infringing on the Rights of Citizens* (p. 142). Chinese Public Security University Press.
109. Smith, H. (2000). *English Criminal Law* (G. Li et al., Trans., p. 513). Law Press.

110. Escherman, J. R. (1991). *Introduction to the Family* (Y. Pan et al., Trans., p. 407). China Social Science Publishing House
111. Xu, J. (Trans.). (1991). *Criminal Code of the Federal Republic of Germany* (p. 119). China University of Political Science and Law Press.
112. Ji, X. (2005). *Marital Rape Study* (p. 78). People's Court Press.
113. An, A., & Yang, C. (2005). *A Comparative Study on Crimes Infringing on the Rights of Citizens* (p. 147). Chinese Public Security University Press.
114. Gross, H. (1999). *Family Law* (pp. 147–148). Law Press.
115. Ji, X. (2005). *Marital Rape Study* (p. 72). People's Court Press.
116. Xu, J., & Zhuang, J. (Trans.). (2004). *German Penal Code* (p. 93). China Founder Publishing House.
117. Xu, J. (Trans.). (2004). *Penal Code of the Federal Republic of Austria* (pp. 81–82). China Founder Publishing House.
118. Xu, J., & Zhuang, J. (Trans.). (2004). *Swiss Federal Penal Code* (p. 65). China Founder Publishing House.
119. Xie, W. (2005). *Danish Penal Code and Danish Criminal Enforcement Act* (pp. 58–59). Peking University Press.
120. Fourks, E. (2000). *History of Sexuality in Europe: The Renaissance* (p. 80). Liaoning Education Press.
121. Honey, E. (1986). *Sisters and Strangers*. Stanford University Press.
122. Hershatter, G. (1986). *The Workers of Tianjin, 1900–1949*. Stanford University Press.
123. Zhang, S. (2003). *Fighting Back Sexual Harassment* (p. 6). China Procuratorial Press.
124. Vigalello, G. (2000). *History of Sexual Assault* (p. 22). Hunan Literature and Art Publishing House.
125. Pan, S. (1998). *The Social History of Sexuality* (pp. 392–393). Henan People's Publishing House.
126. Rice, E. (Ed.). (2004). *American Sexual History* (D. Yang et al., Trans.) (pp. 25–26). Oriental Press.
127. Vigalello, G. (2000). *History of Sexual Assault* (p. 298). Hunan Literature and Art Publishing House.
128. Zhang Zherui United Law Firm (ed.). (2005). *The Right to Be Naked: American Law and Sex* (p. 66). Law Press
129. Liu, D. (1999). *World Contemporary Sexual Culture* (p. 396). Shanghai Sanlian Bookstore.
130. Gegnon, J. (1994). *Sociology of Sexuality: Human Sexuality* (Y. Li, Trans., p. 267). Henan People's Publishing House.
131. Li, Y. (2003). *The Question of Sexuality·Foucault and Sex* (p. 41). Culture and Art Press.
132. *The Complete Works of Marx and Engels* (Vol. 1, 2nd ed., p. 176) (1995). People's Publishing House.
133. Freud, S. (2000). *Civilization and Its Discontents* (Y. Xu et al., Trans.) (pp. 2–3). International Culture Publishing Company.
134. Fuller, L. L. (2005). *The Morality of Law* (pp. 55–111). Translated by Zheng G. Commercial Press.
135. Zhang, W. (2001). *Studies in the Scope of Philosophy of Law (Revision)* (pp. 325–332). China University of Political Science and Law Press.
136. Hobel, E. A. (1993). *The Law of Primitive Man: A Study in Comparative Legal Dynamics* (p. 12). China Social Science Publishing House.
137. Singer, B. J. (2001). *Pragmatism, Rights and Democracy* (p. 38). Shanghai Translation Press.
138. Hengkin, L. (1997). *The Age of Rights* (p. 1). Knowledge Press.
139. Hejun, Z. (2002). Sexual rights as human rights. In X. Xianming (Ed.), *Human Rights Studies* (p. 217). Shandong People's Publishing House.
140. Abramson, P. R. (2003). *Sexual Rights in America: The Ninth Amendment and the Pursuit of Happiness* (pp. 74–75). New York University Press.

141. Foucault, M. (1988). *Politics, Philosophy, Culture: Interviews and Other Writings of Foucault, 1977—1984* (Kritzman (Ed.), pp 200–202). Routledge.
142. Kelsen, H. (1996). *General Theory of Law and State* (p. 89) (Shen Zongling trans). China Encyclopedia Publishing House.

Chapter 7
The Right of Homosexuals to Marry

Hao Feng

1 Introduction

Homosexuality is not a modern invention, and its history is as old as the history of heterosexuality. However, historical encounters of homosexuals have been much different from those of heterosexuals. In China, due to historical reasons and discrimination, the behavior and identity of homosexuals are secretive. The close association of homosexuals with AIDS has further complicated their sexual, emotional, and marital lives. Moreover, the contradiction between the demands of homosexuals and their social disapproval has led to problems. The legal status of homosexuals has not been recognized, and their legitimate rights and interests have not been equally protected. In 2005, two lesbians, Miao Hongxiu and Wang Lanying, were sentenced in a bloody case for pursuing "freedom" in love.[1] In August 2006, a man in Shanghai filed for divorce because his wife was gay. The Shanghai Pudong New District Court held that the couple's relationship had broken down and ruled in favor of the man.[2] While love and marriage are taken for granted by every heterosexual person, homosexuals face difficulties in living together for a long time due to the lack of recognition by society, which seriously violates their rights.

Throughout history, in China and abroad, it has seemed self-evident that the person who enters into marriage should be of the opposite sex, and this fact is currently undergoing great challenges. Social pluralism and moral liberalization have made it possible for homosexuals to "come out," and increased knowledge and understanding of sociology, biology, and psychology has helped to recognize homosexuals

[1] See Song [1].

[2] "The First Case of Homosexual Divorce in Shanghai: Wife and Homosexual Husband Divorce as per His Wishes" (2006) Available at: http://www.sznews.com/news/content/2006-10/11/content_421705.htm (accessed 5 March 2007).

H. Feng (✉)
Tongji University Law School, Shanghai, China

J. Yao (ed.), *The Legal Issues of the Emerging Rights*,
https://doi.org/10.1007/978-981-97-0499-6_7

as a sexual identity. Society's tolerance and acceptance have prompted homosexuals to demand more: they want to be allowed to marry like heterosexual couples. Ms. Li Yinhe submitted a Proposal to Legalize Same-Sex Marriage in China to the National People's Congress three times. Although the proposal was not submitted to the General Assembly due to nominations, there was more support for sexual rights for homosexuals.[3] We must face the question: Is it legitimate and possible for homosexuals to have the right to marry when non-marital cohabitation, sex trafficking, and sexual promiscuity are all inconsistent with mainstream morality?

Same-sex sexual behavior is prevalent in the animal kingdom, particularly among mammals, such as macaques, baboons, and chimpanzees,[4] which are the primates closest to humans. This demonstrates that same-sex tendencies are not "against nature." Homosexuality has also existed in human societies for a long time. Professor Li Yinhe has stated that "if homosexual behavior patterns were not a universal phenomenon and if this phenomenon was not observed in other animals, and only a very few humans exhibited it, then its significance would be diminished." In our society, the proportion of adults who identify as homosexual is 3% to 4%,[5] with an absolute number of 39 million to 52 million.[6] The study of this relatively small but still significant number of individuals has important academic and practical implications.

The study of homosexuality in foreign academic circles began in modern times, and numerous academic monographs and papers have been published in the past century. As of December 2006, a search for "Homosexual Rights" in the ARL (Academic Research Library) database found 12,043 papers. A search for "Same-Sex Marriage" found 484 papers. In the web.lexis-nexis.com search for "Same-Sex Marriage," 125 papers were found. Foreign research on homosexuality has been extensive and in-depth. In China, it was not until the 1980s that the medical community began to study this issue, and the first sociological monograph was published in the early 1990s. As of December 2006, on the China Journal Network (www.edu.cnki.net), a total of 206 papers were found by searching for "Homosexuality," including 51 legal papers. A search for "Gay Rights" found 12 articles, including three legal papers. Clearly, domestic research on gay rights lags behind that of foreign countries in terms of breadth and depth, and legal research on gay rights is mostly theoretical analysis with less empirical research. To address this gap, we intend to study their lifestyles, values, and claims from anthropological, medical, sociological, psychological, ethical, and legal perspectives.

[3] See "An Open Letter from Homosexuals to NPC Deputies" (2007) Available at: http://post.baidu.com/f?kz=174743042 (accessed 4 January 2007).

[4] See Ellis [2].

[5] Li [3].

[6] See Liu [4].

2 Homosexuality as a Social Existence

Homosexuality refers to the sexual orientation and behavior of individuals towards the same sex.[7] Homosexuals are individuals of the same sex who have a homosexual orientation, experience same-sex attraction, and have a desire to have sexual relationships with people of the same sex. This includes gay men and lesbians.

2.1 Homosexuality in the Social Setting

In order for the phenomenon of homosexuality to be the object of our study, it must be considered a social fact. A social fact is defined as "all modes of conduct, whether fixed or unfixed, that can be restrained by individuals from the outside, or in other words, pervasive and inherent in all parts of society." Regardless of its manifestation in the individual, it is called a social fact. Social facts have three basic characteristics: universality, externality, and coercion.[8] A social fact is universal because it is social, not because it is universal. It is external to personal consciousness and produces or tends to coerce an individual's consciousness.

2.1.1 Prevalence of Homosexuality

Archaeology and anthropology tell us that homosexuality as a mode of behavior has been widespread throughout human history and cultures, ancient and modern.

(1) The phenomenon of homosexuality in world history

According to records, in ancient Mesopotamia, there was a large number of homosexual phenomena, and many male prostitutes specialized in serving homosexuals. In the temples of Babylon, male prostitutes gathered in special brothels, supervised by the Church and administered by bishops.[9] The ancient Egyptians regarded sex between men as a sacred thing, and in the Mayan civilization, homosexuality was considered a human nature.[10] Ford and Beech studied existing anthropological literature and found that 49 out of 76 primitive tribes considered homosexuality to be normal. Two-thirds of the tribes considered adolescent homosexuality to be normal and acceptable. In the Amazon basin of Kuber, Moharve, Chuni, and other parts of North America, it exists in a habitual manner. Two-thirds of societies in the 20th-century world seemed to acquiesce to homosexual activity. In fact, it is almost impossible to find a society completely free of homosexuality.[11]

---

[7] Yinhe [5].

[8] Durkheim [6].

[9] See Yinhe [7].

[10] See Runxian [8].

[11] See Yinhe [9].

The Greeks believed that men were near-perfect creatures, and therefore there was love between two men, which went beyond the purely physical realm and became an elegant and aesthetically meaningful taste. Plato even believed that "divine love" existed only between men, and that only love between men was a true form of nobility and knighthood. For the ancients, love between two rational beings was the highest type of love. Both the Sacred Band of Thebes in Sparta and the general Asibiades in Athens testified to the splendor of homosexuality in Greek civilization with their actions.[12,13]

Homosexuality in Japan is similar to that in ancient Greece, where homosexuality was considered sacred. The earliest record of same-sex love in Japan is found in the Chinese "Nihon Shu" (written in 720), which tells the story of the Shengong Empress (third century AD) and the tale of Kotakesu and Amano Zhu, recorded in February of the first year of the regent. Amano was so saddened by Kotake's death that he threw himself onto Kotake's body and killed himself, and they were later buried together. During the tenth century AD, there was an ancient Greek tradition of anal sex among Buddhists in Japan. They admired the ancient Greek master-apprentice relationship, with older monks acting as teachers and protectors while young monks reciprocated with love and devotion. During the Edo period, homosexuality became popular among the samurai class. By the mid-seventeenth century, the classical form of anal sex was replaced by homosexuality between adults, and by the mid-nineteenth century, there were tea rooms offering male prostitutes in Japan.[14]

In medieval Europe, homosexuality was brutally treated. By the time of the urban revival in Europe in the eleventh century, the homosexual community had developed. However, by the second half of the twelfth century, society had turned to homophobia, which persisted for centuries to come. In the eighteenth century, during the reign of Louis XIV of France, a gay and lesbian community formed primarily among the upper classes of society.[15]

(2) The phenomenon of homosexuality in Chinese history

Ji Xiaolan of the Qing Dynasty wrote in volume 12 of the "Notes on Reading Wei Caotang": "Miscellaneous sayings call child prostitutes the first Yellow Emperor," and in this context, "pederasty" refers to homosexuality. "Shang Shu · Yizhong" records the "urchin boy" and considers it a "chaotic wind." The "Book of Zhou" states: "Beautiful men break old (birth), beautiful women break their tongues (residence), and martial arts are destroyed." Both "urchin" and "beautiful man" here refer to homosexuality. Therefore, we can infer that in the Shang and Zhou dynasties, homosexuality not only existed but also became more popular.[16] The first example

---

[12] See May [10].

[13] See Yinhe [11].

[14] See "Same-Sex Love Culture in Japan." (2010). Accessed April 18, 2010. http://www.xici.net/main.asp?url=/u6194199/d45439947.htm.

[15] See Liyong [12].

[16] See Runxian [8].

of homosexuality is the story of the "Yuren" admiring Qi Jinggong, recorded in "Banquet Spring and Autumn." It also includes the story of Longyang Jun as the "pillow seat" for the King of Wei, Mi Zixian and Wei Linggong "dividing the peach and eating it," and Emperor Han Moi sleeping with Dong Xian, with Dong Xian pressing Emperor Han Moi's sleeve. Emperor Han Moi could not bear to wake him up, so he "broke his sleeve and rose." As a result, "Long Yang," "Yu Tao," and "Broken Sleeve" became code words for homosexuality in later generations.[17]

The earliest record of lesbianism is in the "Hanshu · Foreign Qi Chuan," which states that Empress Chen, during the reign of Emperor Wudi of Han, "later blackmailed women to flatter, quite aware." In the fifth year of Yuan Guang, the woman Chufu and others sat down to worship the queen's witch shrine, and more than 300 people were involved in the curse. Chu Fu was in the city."[18] During the Jin Dynasty and the Six Dynasties, homosexuality was quite popular and openly discussed. "The Jin Dynasty and the Six Dynasties were an era of great character… Among the various qualities, the most recorded is posture and grooming, and men also talked about grooming,"[19] which serves as evidence of male homosexuality.

From the Sui and Tang Dynasties to the Five Dynasties, it is difficult to find official historical records of homosexuality. However, during the Song Dynasty, homosexuality was once again openly practiced, as evidenced by the phrase "To this day, between Jingshi and Junyi, rogue men are used for food and clothing, and the old is not forbidden." Emperor Huizong began to crackdown, offering a reward of fifty guan for information leading to the arrest of male prostitutes, and imposing a sentence of one hundred lashes on those caught.[20] The phenomenon of homosexuality seems to have no official historical record in the Yuan Dynasty, but it became prominent in the Ming Dynasty with the Zhengde Emperor who "spoiled the young handsome little internal minister". There was also "Day Feijin (male drama)" where officials did not eat or sleep at night, and Confucian students "drowned in male favors and did not care about their wives, old or young". After the Qing Dynasty succeeded, the male color continued to be popular for a while. Chen Weisong in the late Ming and early Qing dynasties publicly acknowledged his relationship with his male pet Yun Lang, and seeking joy in the "Xianggong Hall" also became a trend.[21] "Xianggong Tangzi" was an organization in the Beijing drama industry in the middle and late Qing Dynasty. Due to the prevalence of male officials engaging in same-sex sexual activities with male dan performers, some people considered Xianggong Tangzi as a form of male prostitution. In modern times, China refers to the homosexual subculture as "tongzhi" or "comrade culture", and it is also known as "nanfeng" or "southern wind", which is

[17] See Yinhe [13].

[18] Book of Han·Legend of Imperial Clansmen.

[19] Ellis [14].

[20] Pingzhou Chronicles.

[21] See Shufen [15].

said to be particularly strong in Fujian and Guangzhou.[22] Gay men refer to each other as "Chego Chidi", while lesbians are referred to as "Cam Ranh". After the Xinhai Revolution in 1911, the police of the Republic of China began to close down the male brothels that were left over from the Qing Dynasty. In China, homosexuality was not particularly discriminated against or viewed with as much hatred before modern times, which is very different from the situation of homosexuality in the West.

(3) The current state of homosexuality

In contemporary times, homosexuality is widespread worldwide. According to a 1948 survey by Professor Kinsey of Indiana University, 37 percent of the 5,300 white adult men surveyed had had a homosexual experience, and 4% were absolutely homosexual. In 1953, Professor Kinsey conducted another survey of adult white women. The results showed that 13 percent of the 5,940 adult white women surveyed had had a homosexual experience, including 3 percent who were absolutely homosexual. In 1972, a U.S. government publication published Giberhard's estimates. Jiberhard estimated that 10% to 12% of adult women have had homosexual experiences, and the incidence of male homosexuality is double that, at about 20% to 24%. Dr. Schneibel in Germany also proposed in the 1970s: "Many countries have carried out a large number of surveys, and homosexuality accounts for about 3% to 4% of the entire population. By this standard, at least 100 million people in the world are homosexual."[23]

In China, the issue of sex is a relatively obscure issue, so many homosexuals dare not openly admit their sexual orientation, and we can only grasp the number of homosexuals in China by speculation and estimation. Sociologist Li Yinhe estimated in 1998 that the proportion of homosexuals in China was about 3%–4%, with a total of 36 million to 48 million.[24] According to recent surveys of college students in China, 16.6% of boys have had same-sex sexual experiences, 8.4% of boys have had only psychological tendencies towards homosexuality, and 4.2% of boys have both homosexual and heterosexual tendencies.[25] According to some surveys of college students in China in recent years, 16.6% of boys have had same-sex sex, and 8.4% of boys have only psychological tendencies, with both homosexual and heterosexual tendencies at 4.2%. Another survey showed that between 7.0 and 8.3 percent of college boys had same-sex sex.[26] Although the results of these two surveys are somewhat different, they both reflect the signal that the proportion of homosexuals among male students in our universities is not small. On November 30, 2004, the Office of the Working Committee for the Prevention and Control of AIDS of the State

---

[22] "Gay people in China are gradually being accepted by the public. Same-sex marriage remains the biggest challenge." (2006). Available at: http://www.phoenixtv.com/phoenixtv/83887282590842880/20050915/636371.shtml. Accessed December 9, 2006.

[23] Quoted from Dalin and Longguang [16].

[24] See Dalin and Longguang [17].

[25] See Suiming [18].

[26] See Dalin [19].

Council and the United Nations AIDS Task Force in China jointly issued the 2004 Epidemic Task Force Joint Evaluation Report on HIV/AIDS Prevention and Control in China. According to the report, the proportion of sexually active male homosexuals in China accounts for about 2 to 4% of the sexually active male population. In other words, there are between 5 and 10 million gay men in China.[27] From the above materials, we can see that the phenomenon of homosexuality as a mode of behavior has been widespread in human society from ancient times to the present day, without interruption.

2.1.2 External Coercion of Homosexuality

The externality of social facts refers to the fact that certain ways of behaving, thinking, and feeling are independent of the individual. Homosexuality, as a mode of behavior and sexual orientation, is independent of the individual, and it is not a psychological phenomenon that exists only in and depends on the consciousness of the individual. When a person is born, homosexuality is a way of acting that already exists for the person. It does not exist independently of the individual's will, and this situation can be observed in every member of society. In relation to the individual, it has become a social "landscape" that is external to the consciousness of the individual.

Coercion of social facts means that an independent act or thought has a coercive force that must be obeyed, imposing on the individual whether they wish to accept it or not.[28] Homosexuality has flourished and declined throughout history. When it is accepted, we do not feel its power, but when it is opposed and suppressed, it does not become extinct. On the one hand, the phenomenon of homosexuality as a mode of behavior does not become extinct by repression. As mentioned earlier, when homosexuality is socially repressed, it does not die because of public hatred towards its perpetrators, nor is it eradicated through harsh punishment or being buried alive, but simply "hidden".[29] After the twelfth century, there were incidents of homosexuals being buried alive in Britain. In the late 1940s of the twentieth century, there were also instances of gay men being captured by the police and paraded through the streets. However, homosexuality did not become extinct. Based on the foregoing, we can conclude that homosexuality is neither a product of the decay of some society nor of the vices peculiar to a certain people. Rather, it is a common and recurring part of human sexual activity and exists as a basic social fact.

---

[27] See "2004 China Joint Assessment Report on HIV/AIDS Prevention and Treatment Released." (2006). Available at: http://www.people.com.cn/GB/14739/14740/21474/3023446.html. Accessed December 4, 2006.

[28] Durkheim [20].

[29] See Qinghui [21].

2.2 *Causes and Classification of Homosexuality*

2.2.1 Causes of Homosexuality

"What causes homosexuality?" This question forms the basis of self-identification for homosexuals and legitimizes their identity and lifestyle. The explanation of the phenomenon of homosexuality mainly has the following levels[30]:

(1) Innate formation. The idea is that homosexuality is caused by physiological factors such as genetics, hormone levels, brain structure, and so on. Doctors were among the first to study homosexuality, followed by geneticists and biologists. According to the research conducted by these professionals, homosexuals have had same-sex sexual orientation throughout history, but the means to satisfy their desires have varied according to time and place. To some extent, all of our actions require a biological basis, and discussing the relationship between homosexuality and biological factors is as convincing as discussing which came first, the chicken or the egg. At the legal level, homosexuals are a minority and if homosexuality is natural, protecting their basic rights is an expression of the idea of human rights.
(2) Psychological theories. Freud believed that homosexuals planted seeds of terror towards the opposite sex in their subconscious minds during childhood, and in adulthood, they either feared sexual contact with the opposite sex or were afraid of them. Therefore, homosexuality is a pause at some stage in psychosexual development. The psychoanalyst Bibo also pointed out that cowardly fathers and domineering mothers are two important factors in the development of homosexual tendencies. The underlying assumption of these studies is that homosexual behavior is abnormal and must be explained as a consequence of neuroses. As a result, normative psychoanalytic treatment methods for homosexuals and electroshock therapy to suppress homosexual tendencies were developed based on psychological theories.[31]
(3) Constructivist theory. The hypothesis that homosexuality is a disease blurs the distinction between behaviors and types that Kinsey and comparative anthropology have fully proven, and this idea is falsified by practice. As a result, explanations of homosexuality are beginning to shift towards the historical circumstances that led people to believe in such a hypothesis. The constructivist theory holds that the idea of sexual orientation is artificially created by social and cultural forces, which vary greatly according to historical and social conditions. Homosexuality had different meanings in ancient Greece, the Japanese shogunate era, and the late Ming and early Qing dynasties in China. "Constructivism" focuses on the history of the construction of the social identity of the

[30] See Qinghui [21].

[31] Douglas [22].

homosexual community, arguing that homosexuality is not a unique experience of a specific minority.[32]

(4) "QUEER" theory. "QUEER" is a transliteration of a derogatory term for homosexuals in mainstream Western culture, meaning "weird". Later, radicals of sexuality used it to summarize their theory that sex is a continuous, divergent experience. "Queer" means challenging the dichotomy of heterosexuality and homosexuality, opposing both homosexual assimilation and heterosexual oppression. It encompasses all those marginalized by power.

2.2.2 Classification of Homosexuals

Homosexuals are still discriminated against even without engaging in sexual behavior. Furthermore, sexual behavior is not necessarily related to sexual orientation (identity). The criterion for distinguishing homosexuality and heterosexuality is sexual orientation rather than sexual behavior. People who have engaged in same-sex sexual behavior are not necessarily homosexual, and people who have homosexual tendencies do not necessarily have to engage in same-sex sexual behavior.

At present, scholars tend to classify homosexuals into three types: (1) true homosexuality, also known as absolute homosexuality; (2) concurrent homosexuality, which is equivalent to variable homosexuality; and (3) pseudohomosexuality, which mainly refers to situational or casual homosexuality. "True homosexuality" is irreversible, and individuals with this sexual orientation take the same sex as the object of sexual behavior and satisfaction throughout their lives.[33] The legal challenge mainly affects such individuals, and they are the ones researchers want to study—homosexuals.[34]

Homosexuality is a fundamental social fact that exists in all societies, although some cultures recognize it while others abhor it. Since homosexuality is neither natural nor a disease, the question is not how to explain the phenomenon of homosexuality, but rather whether homosexuals can be accepted as members of society. If so, what are the reasons that allow people to accept homosexuals?

3 Social Recognition of Homosexuality

The term "homosexual" was first used by the German physician Benkert in 1869 to refer to sexual attraction and behavior between people of the same sex. In 1890, the sexologist Havelock Ellis introduced the word to the English-speaking world.[35] In the nineteenth century, the basic paradigm of sexual activity shifted from religion to

---

[32] See Qinghui [21].

[33] See Dalin and Longguang [23].

[34] Runxian [8].

[35] See Chang-do [24].

science, and the power to judge the legitimacy of sexuality shifted from the church to academia and society at large. This was an irreversible process from the start. Initially, homosexuals were often seen as having a pathologically deviant sexual orientation. "In addition to being a personality, a way of life, it also becomes a character, an experience, a problem, and a childishness... Sodomy is just a few heretics, while homosexuals are now a category."[36] So "homosexuality" in the modern sense emerged, and homosexuality became an identity.

Identity is an individual's affirmation of their sense of self, that is, the answer to the question "who am I?" A person's sense of survival is often determined by their sense of identity, as "in the social jungle of human existence, there is no sense of survival without a sense of identity." Therefore, seeking out and establishing an identity is a way for individuals to validate their own existence.[37] Identity is an important concern that is indispensable to individuals at every stage of their lives. Sociology divides identity into self-identification and social identification. "Self-identification refers to an individual's self-affirmation of their role,[38] which is the unity of a series of personalities of an individual, and the overall identity that distinguishes one person from another." Self-identity is formed through the interaction of "I look at people and see me".Social identity is the common identity of a collective, and the process of defining "we" is also the process of defining a series of "them". Self-identity is the basis of social identity, and the identity of all people is social identity in a certain sense.[39]

3.1 Self-identification of Homosexuals

The self is the starting point for most complex interaction processes, and our understanding of social behavior begins with the self. In the nineteenth century, after the Enlightenment in Europe, individualism and liberalism emerged. As a result, all people were thought to have roughly the same rationality, and the idea that homosexuality was a pathology completed the transformation from dehumanization to humanization, so that homosexuals changed from being seen as "non-human" to being seen as "human". Based on rational presuppositions, everyone is endowed with the same freedom, equality, and dignity. At this time, the concept of the "self" was born out of the free will of humans. Homosexuals also realized that they are ends in themselves, not mere means to others.

From the perspective of freedom, people have the right to choose their sexual orientation, as being homosexual does not harm others. With the emergence of the concept of sexuality, human beings became defined by the way they experience and express their sexuality. As one homosexual individual put it, "Homosexuality is

[36] Foucault [25].

[37] Erikson [26].

[38] Xiangdong [27].

[39] See Wrightsman [28].

not only a way of expressing my feelings and desires, but also a major part of my identity. If I were no longer gay, I would feel fragmented and lose myself. I really can't imagine not being gay."[40]

The establishment of a homosexual identity is mostly determined by the self-identification of homosexuals, which is the internal driving force of their life practices. The development of a homosexual identity depends on the meaning that the individual assigns to the concepts of homosexuality and homosexual behavior. This can be verified through the history of the gay rights liberation movement in the United States.

In the years after World War II, the gay rights movement in the United States began, and the "minority consciousness" of urban gay men began to awaken. From 1950 to 1952, homosexuals searched for identity; from 1952 to 1953, there was outrage over their longstanding injustice. From 1953 to 1960, the gay movement intensified information exchange and paid attention to the field of education. In the 60 s, the civil rights movement led to the gay movement, and in 1969, a mass gay movement began. The period from 1973 to 1979 was a period of dialogue between the gay movement and the government through official channels. The entire 70 s ended with the union and successful consciousness of the gay movement.[41] Most American cities now have gay communities. By the end of the twentieth century, the gay rights movement in the United States had a huge impact on Western countries, and homosexuals in many countries gained equal or near-equal rights with heterosexuals.

Through an investigation of the history of the gay rights movement in the United States, it can be seen that: (1) social discrimination and oppression of homosexuals actually cultivated their sense of identity and contributed to the formation of the concept of homosexuals. Because they have been oppressed and discriminated against, homosexuals tend to strategically and emotionally believe that they share certain personality traits, upbringing, and even certain genes, and that they have their own values and lifestyles. (2) Today's homosexuals are a vulnerable minority that can be distinguished from other ethnic groups. The idea that homosexuals are the result of the planting of trees by predecessors, and the collective identity of homosexuals is not innate.[42] (3) The identity of homosexuals is not a visible identity, and is not considered valid if it is not disclosed. The characteristics (sexual orientation) of this vulnerable group are not visible from appearance, and "appearance" is a peculiar appearance strategy for homosexuals. (4) The meaning of "appearance" is that homosexuals accept their sexual orientation and identify with themselves, and disclose their sexual orientation to society. This "debut" strengthens group communication, makes society face up to homosexuality, helps eliminate misunderstanding and prejudice against homosexuals, and makes them realize the rights and claims of homosexuals as a social group.

In China, the depathologization of homosexuality is underway, and homosexuality is no longer considered a mental illness. Unlike in the West, there is no

---

[40] Quoted from Qinghui [21].

[41] Quoted from Yinhe [29].

[42] See Marcus [30].

history of oppression of homosexuality in China, which is more conducive to the self-identification of homosexuals. In China, same-sex sex is viewed as "a fetish, as long as it does not reach the point of 'losing the mind of a plaything' and not having children, it is tacitly approved by Chinese Taoists."[43] Moreover, the development of network technology and transportation has broken the boundaries of traditional time and space, promoting the self-identification of homosexuals. The internet has become the main carrier of gay culture, strengthening the connection and communication between Chinese homosexuals, allowing them to think more about their rights and social status. Furthermore, the "coming out" of some celebrities has allowed the public in China to discuss the issue of homosexuality widely, enhancing the understanding of the mainstream culture of the gay community, and laying a good foundation for the further social identity of this group. This also provides a good background for in-depth academic research. Changes in the social environment have contributed to the increase in the social identity of homosexuals, with a more open environment for discussing sexuality, an increasing number of books and periodicals disseminating information about homosexuality, and a more liberal stance on sexuality through the media. All these contribute to the creation of a new community of knowledge among the homosexual community.

3.2 Social Identification of Homosexuals

The social identity of homosexuals promotes the self-identification of homosexuals. It is a mutual process, where social identification is more likely to promote the self-identification of a homosexual person. In the case of social identification, it is easier for them to become a true homosexual. After that, a person who self-identifies as homosexual (even if they may just be a masculine gay person) will be given greater recognition by society.

3.2.1 Non-pathological Identification of Homosexuality

Homosexuality, as a behavioral tendency, has been erroneously labeled as a sexual perversion and mental illness, but such attempts to discredit it have been unsuccessful. Certain religious organizations and pseudo-mental health groups in Britain and the United States have launched "pre-gay movements" with the belief that homosexuals could change their sexual orientation through repentance, religious devotion, Bible study, and "restorative healing."[44] However, despite these efforts, scandals continued to emerge. On April 14, 2003, PlanetOut.com reported that John Paulk, Chairman of the Board of Exodus International, was stepping down from Focus on the Family. Even the two founders of Exodus International, Michael Bussee and Gary Cooper,

---

[43] See Marcus [31].

[44] Qinghui [21].

eventually left their wives and lived together for more than a decade, until Gary Cooper's death.[45]

After investigating more than 20,000 cases of homosexuality, the research team led by American sexologist Kinsey published the "Report on Male Sexuality" in 1948 and the "Report on Female Sexuality" in 1953. Their findings suggested that there is no scientific basis for labeling homosexuals as pathological simply because they are a minority. In 1955, American anthropologist Evelyn Hooker experimentally found no difference in the psychological status of homosexuals and heterosexuals,[46] proving that homosexuality does not exist as a unit of disease. She concluded that the "pathology" of homosexuals is the result of social repression, and that the best way to help them is through tolerance rather than "treatment". The American Psychiatric Association removed homosexuality from its list of disorders in 1973, and the American Psychological Society followed suit in 1975. Subsequently, France's Ministry of Health in 1982 and Japan in 1995 removed homosexuality from the classification of diseases. In 1999, the American Psychological Association, the Psychiatric Association, and the Australian Psychological Association strongly spoke out against "curing" homosexuality. The World Health Organization's International Classification of Diseases (10th edition) excluded homosexuality from the category of mental disorders in 1992. On April 20, 2001, the Chinese Classification and Diagnostic Criteria for Mental Disorders also removed homosexuality from the list of mental disorders, recognizing it as a non-pathological condition. Only when same-sex behavior leads to psychological contradictions and anxiety, which seriously affects normal life and study, is it considered a sexual psychological disorder in China. "The failure of 'conversion' and 'treatment' of homosexuality proves that the idea that homosexuality is a disease and a mistake, and its extension, are wrong." The international scientific community now generally views homosexuality as a natural condition for a minority, parallel to heterosexuality.[47]

3.2.2 Morality of Homosexuality

Throughout human history, especially in the West, homosexuality has been treated with extreme cruelty. Although people's perceptions have changed, prejudice remains:

(1) Homosexuality has been considered to go against the laws of nature. Western homophobia is rooted in the Bible. The Old Testament says, "Men and men do shameful things… God decreed that those who do such things deserve death." The existence of homosexuality is often evaluated as a moral evil as it is believed

[45] See "Focusing on his own family-Far Right-John Paulk leaves Focus on the Family." (2003, May 27). Available at: http://www.findarticles.com/p/articles/mi_m1589/is_2003_May_27/ai_102105232. Accessed December 9, 2006.

[46] See "New Standards for Psychosis: Homosexuality is not pathological." (n.d.). Available at: http://love52h9.blog.sohu.com/124772628.html. Accessed December 9, 2010.

[47] Qinghui [21].

to not be beneficial for the survival of society, especially when society needs labor. In China, homosexuality that does not challenge Confucian sexual culture and allows for marrying and having children is simply viewed as absurd or a fetish. However, homosexuality has existed since ancient times, and from the perspective of innate formationism, homosexuality is a "natural attribute" of humans.

(2) Homosexuality has been perceived as offensive. This is due to the way people imagine homosexuality and the way in which they believe homosexuals have sex. The image of feminine men and masculine women and their way of having sex is often viewed as despicable. However, homosexuality is simply different from heterosexuality in terms of sexual orientation, meaning that the object of sexual activity is more likely to be someone of the same sex, regardless of biological sex, psychological gender, and social gender. Homosexuality is difficult to observe from the outside, and feminine men or masculine women are not necessarily homosexuals.

(3) Sexual behavior and reproductive order have been at the center of society's regulation of sex. Traditional culture assumes that sex is sinful, and only reproduction and marriage are grounds for exemption. Currently, the standard of sexual morality in China has changed from marriage to love, meaning that sex based on love is justified. This is evidenced by the proliferation and tolerance of phenomena such as cohabitation based on love, which are not aimed at marriage. In this case, same-sex sex based on love is morally justified.

(4) Homosexuality has been thought to be a hotbed of AIDS. AIDS is caused by the human immunodeficiency virus (HIV), which is transmitted through sexual contact, contaminated blood or blood products, and vertical mother-to-child transmission. Safe sex is an effective way to prevent AIDS. AIDS was first seen in homosexuals in the United States, and out of fear of AIDS, the already existing homophobia became even stronger. Homosexuals became a black sheep until other groups also became affected by AIDS. However, homosexuals are not necessarily linked to AIDS. It is only because they may have more sexual partners, frequent sexual intercourse, and different sexual intercourse styles than heterosexuals, that the incidence of AIDS is higher. The "2004 China AIDS Joint Assessment Report" jointly issued by the Office of the State Council AIDS Prevention and Control Committee and the United Nations AIDS Task Force in China stated that there are currently 840,000 people living with HIV in China, of which 43.9% were drug addicts, 24.1% were previously paid for blood collection, and 11.1% were gay men. The HIV prevalence rate among gay men reached 1.35%.[48]

Moral liberalization has made it possible for same-sex relationships to be morally justified. The implementation of a market economy has led to the differentiation of social group interests, and economic individualism has gradually transformed

[48] See "Putting homosexuality in perspective is an important part of HIV/AIDS prevention." (2003, December 31). Available at: http://eladies.sina.com.cn/2003-12-31/130984.html. Accessed December 9, 2006.

into ethical individualism. Due to technological advancements, there can now be non-sexual reproduction and non-reproductive sex. For the sake of social survival, homosexuals are no longer restricted. Sexual morality has begun to liberalize, and sexuality is becoming increasingly viewed as a morally neutral behavior.

The change in public perception of homosexuality in China mainly stems from scientific research and the popularization of scientific knowledge. The first peer health education organization composed of gay volunteers in China, the Zhejiang Gay Love Working Group, was established on August 12, 2005. Society is also increasingly accepting and confronting homosexuality.[49] In August 2005, CCTV's investigative news program aired "In the Name of Life" to discuss homosexuality. In September 2005, Fudan University launched a public elective course "Homosexuality Studies" for undergraduate students. On September 29, 2005, Southern Weekend published "Two Men's 20-Year Marriage." Society's attitude towards homosexuality has shown a certain degree of seriousness and tolerance.[50] However, tolerance is not the same as acceptance, and a change in perception takes time. The relative security required by social order, pressure from dominant culture, and various societal and familial pressures can lead to "phobia" towards homosexuals, while the high incidence of AIDS among homosexuals can also contribute to their social stigmatization.

3.3 Homosexuals in the Legal Setting

With a gradual deepening of our understanding of homosexuality, social attitudes have also shifted from oppression and discrimination to tolerance and acceptance. Correspondingly, the law has also come to recognize the subjectivity of homosexuals.

1. Relaxation of severe punishments. From the Middle Ages to modern times, homosexuality in the West was severely punished, and church courts imposed hard labor and the death penalty on homosexuals, a practice that continued into modern times. However, at the beginning of the nineteenth century, the Napoleonic Code recognized that sexual acts voluntarily and privately committed by adult men were not subject to legal prosecution. This law had a significant impact on 19th-century Europe, particularly in countries such as Italy, Belgium, and the Netherlands, although it was not enforced for a long time.[51] The British Criminal Law Amendment Act of 1885 stipulated that all sexual activity between men, except sodomy, was deemed "indecent and unnatural" and punishable by up to two years of hard labour. The Act served to draw a clear distinction between "legal" sex (sex between spouses within marriage)[52] and "illegal" sex (sexual behavior deemed

[49] See "Gay Caring Working Group: Zhejiang established the first non-governmental gay organization." (2005, September). Available at: http://www.21cbpc.com/Article/gnxw/zspl/200509/680.html. Accessed December 9, 2006.

[50] See Dalin and Qiang [32].

[51] See Ellis [33].

[52] See Weeks [34].

to threaten the emotional stability of the family and the traditional roles of men and women, and subject to social punishment). Homosexuality was seen as a threat to stable sexual relations in bourgeois families, which were increasingly viewed as important pillars of social stability during that time.

2. The law should not be moralized—the revelation of the Wolfenden report.

In 1957, the British Research Committee on Homosexuality and Prostitution produced the Wolfenden Report, which distinguished between morality and law, arguing that the function of law is to regulate social order rather than defend traditional morality. The report advocated avoiding the establishment of morality through public regulations that regulate or prohibit sexual acts that are offensive to decency or harmful to social order.

Given the guiding principle that homosexuality is pathological, the report recommended that consensual homosexual acts between adults should not be included in the scope of criminal punishment. Under this guiding ideology, the United Kingdom's Offences in Sexual Relations Act 1967 stipulates that "it is not an offence to engage in male same-sex sexual conduct in private if the participant is over 21 years of age and consenting." This legislation sets the legal boundaries for sexual acts, including whether minors are involved, whether both parties are consenting, and whether it is public. This standard is still used today, and at this point, same-sex sex has been decriminalized.[53] Switzerland decriminalized homosexuality in 1941, Sweden in 1944, Canada and the former Federal Republic of Germany in 1969, and Israel in 1988.[54]

3. Homosexuals Need Equal Protection. In the late twentieth century, some industrialized countries enacted laws protecting the general rights of homosexuals. By the end of the twentieth century, Denmark, Sweden, Norway, the Netherlands, Germany, France, Belgium, and other countries enacted laws that granted homosexuals equal rights with heterosexuals. The most representative of these laws is the enactment of the "Same-Sex Couples Act" or the "Same-Sex Marriage Act." These laws recognize that homosexual unions can enjoy the same rights as heterosexual marriages, such as social benefits, insurance, immigration, inheritance, and more.[55]

Before modern times in China, legislation on homosexuality was rare, and the regulation of same-sex sexual behavior relied more on moral norms, in addition to regulating male prostitutes. The only legislation related to homosexuality was the "crime of sodomy" under the Great Qing Statute of 1740. However, the law was only a symbolic clause and had no practical effect. After the founding of the People's Republic of China, in 1957, the Supreme People's Court issued a document stating that adult consensual same-sex sexual activity "should not be criminalized." However, later legal nihilism reduced the homosexual issue to "hooligan" activity,

---

[53] See Weeks [34].

[54] See "One Hundred Years of Humanity: Facing Homosexuality." (2010, April 10). Available at: http://tieba.baidu.com/f?kz=8648132.

[55] See Qinghui [21].

and during the Cultural Revolution, many homosexuals were punished for "hooliganism" and "sodomy."[56] The Criminal Code, as amended in 1997, abolished the principle of analogy and introduced the principle of "criminalization of crimes," decriminalizing homosexuality in China. From the perspective of judicial practice, currently in China, the judicial department will not pursue homosexual sex if it does not involve the following four situations: (1) rape; (2) sex trafficking; (3) targeting minors; and (4) conducted in public or in the same room.[57]

Throughout the history of homosexuality, mainstream society's attitude towards homosexuality has undergone three stages of severe punishment, reflection, and dialogue. Correspondingly, the law has also undergone a transition of criminalization, decriminalization, and recognition of legal rights in dealing with homosexuality. However, there is often a gap between the rights that should be enjoyed and the rights actually enjoyed. This is similar to the experience of black Americans in fighting for equal rights, which requires a difficult dialogue process.

In the era of commodity economy and today's pluralistic subjects, tolerance has become the most basic value, and society's tolerance of homosexuals has become the boundary for measuring the rights of homosexuals. However, even when homosexuality is not considered a sin or a disease but a normal way of life, challenges still exist. For example, when non-marital cohabitation and sexual promiscuity are inconsistent with mainstream morality and sex needs to be regulated, when AIDS wants to reduce the sexual partners of homosexuals without affecting their other legitimate rights, when countless homosexuals enter heterosexual marriages and cause unhappiness or even death for at least one party, and when homosexuals are discriminated against and struggle to find a stable home, homosexuals demand the right to marry members of the same sex. As the code of conduct governing social relations, the law must also answer these questions.

4 Legitimacy of the "Marriage" of Homosexuals

The reason for the law's denial of same-sex marriage is very simple: marriage is a union of a man and a woman, and it does not apply between people of the same sex. In the case of Juliet Joslin et al. v. New Zealand, the lesbian couple failed to obtain a "marriage permit" in their country. In the absence of domestic remedies, they turned to Article 23 of the International Covenant on Civil and Political Rights. However, the Human Rights Committee (HRC) argues that "Article 23, paragraph 2, of the Convention is the only article in the Convention that uses 'men and women.' Instead of 'everyone' and 'all persons' to define the substantive provisions of rights. This use of 'man and woman' rather than the general term (elsewhere in Part III of the Convention) has been uniformly and consistently understood as defined by States parties in article 23, paragraph 2, of the Convention. The treaty obligation

[56] See Jie [35].

[57] Qinghui [21].

under this paragraph is only to authorize marriage between a man and a woman who wish to marry."[58] Similarly, the European Court of Human Rights, in the cases of Mark Rees v. United Kingdom (1986) and Cossey v. United Kingdom (1990), also held that "the right to marry protected by Article 12 of the European Convention on Human Rights applies to traditional marriages in which biological sex is opposed".[59] The law's response depends to a large extent on the historical context of the time and the limits of people's awareness of homosexuality. As people's understanding of the phenomenon of homosexuality deepens and tolerance grows, homosexuals once again challenge the law. Should same-sex marriage be legally justified? The first question to clarify is: what is marriage?

4.1 Nature and Purpose of Marriage

Marriage is an institutional arrangement for men and women to choose a mate, and as a social system, it is a historical category, not an inherent part of human beings. The question of why people should enter the institution of marriage begins with what marriage actually is. It is a social relationship between people, and if a relationship between individuals of different sexes is not recognized by society, it cannot be called marriage.

The German sociologist Müllerier once summarized the motives of human marriage into three types: economy, children, and love. He believed that in ancient times, the economy came first, children second, and love third; in the Middle Ages, children came first, economy second, and love third; in modern society, love comes first, children second, and the economy comes third. Although he does not exhaust all the motives of marriage,[60] it illustrates the transformation of values in marriage in modern society.

In ancient societies, marriage was closely linked with childbearing, and the purpose of marriage was mainly for procreation. From the era of slavery to the bourgeois revolution, the legal system of ancient societies encompassed a "trinity" of marriage, sexuality, and reproductive norms. Marriage was aimed at procreation, sex was the means of procreation, and marriage served as a regulation of sex. These norms were reflected in the fact that marriage ensured sexual legitimacy and imposed restrictions on procreation. Sex outside of marriage was considered illegal, and the concept of "no heir" was one of the reasons for the dissolution of marriage in ancient laws. Sex without reproductive purpose was deemed impure, and childbearing outside of marriage was stigmatized. In the pursuit of the value of marriage, the purpose of

[58] Quoted from Xiao An, "Protection of the Rights of Homosexuals", available at: http://www.tongxingai.com/Html/sdbd/161313607.html, 2006-12-04.

[59] "Gay people in China are gradually accepted by the public. Same-sex marriage is the biggest problem." Available at: http://www.pfc.org.uk/legal/rees.htm, 2010-04-18; http://www.pfc.org.uk/legal/cossey.htm, 2010–04-18.

[60] See Dalin [36].

childbearing was placed higher than the happiness and mutual respect of the parties involved in the marriage.[61]

Since modern society, marriage and childbirth have become relatively separated, and childbearing is no longer the primary purpose of marriage. With the development of science and technology and the social economy, marriage and childbearing have been separated. The expansion of China's population has promoted family planning and has been a realistic driving force for the separation of marriage and childbirth. First, advances in contraception and reproductive technology separated sex and reproduction. The invention of condoms and contraceptives made sex no longer subordinate to fertility, and fertility methods have also changed, with IVF, embryo transfer, cloning technology, etc., making fertility asexual. Secondly, with the change of sexual concepts, the purpose of sex has become pleasure. Sexual behavior is diversified, and other sexual acts except traditional vaginal sex have nothing to do with fertility. Sex within marriage also no longer implies procreation. Third, children have lost their economic utility, and in the case of a perfect social security system, it is no longer necessary to raise children to prevent old age. A 2002 survey showed that 12.4 percent of households in Shanghai were voluntarily infertile after marriage.[62] At the beginning of 2003, a survey in Shenzhen showed that DINK (double income, no kids) families accounted for about 10 percent of households. To a certain extent, this shows that procreation is no longer the primary purpose of marriage.[63] The normative approach to the "trinity" of marriage, sexuality, and reproduction began to disintegrate, and marriage and procreation were theoretically and institutionally separated.

Marriage, even when separated from procreation, remains necessary for society and individuals. In terms of the social value of marriage, it serves as a stabilizer of social relations. Marriage without fertility is still considered marriage because it institutionally guarantees the stability of gender relations, thereby maintaining the basic order of social life. This can be confirmed by the following two aspects:

4.1.1 Marriage as an Institutionalization of Sexual Relations

From ancient times to the present, sex has been seen as a highly destructive force that requires regulation. In primitive society, where there were no sexual taboos, sexual promiscuity led to sexual jealousy and disorder, which had a direct impact on human productivity. Blood intermarriage resulting from sexual promiscuity could lead to impotence in offspring and threaten the survival of the human species. Therefore, humans had to invent a system to limit the disorderly nature of sex, and that system was marriage. The preference for new things and rejection of old ones is an unavoidable tendency for many people, and monogamy in the marriage system ensures the

[61] See Burguière [37].

[62] See Aishu [38].

[63] See "Proportions Up to 10%, Approaching the 'Dink' Family in Shenzhen," available at: http://news.21cn.com/guangdong/tq/2003-01-27/922710.htm. Accessed on 2006-12-04.

equal distribution of sexual resources, preventing society from descending into sexual injustice and chaos. While marriage may be separated from procreation, it still serves as a stabilizer of social relations, and the marriage institution guarantees the stability of gender relations, thereby maintaining the basic order of social life. It is these institutional functions of marriage that make a marriage without fertility and sex still worthy of being called marriage.

4.1.2 Marriage as a Stabilizer of Social Relations

The family plays an important role in the understanding of marriage. Logically, the family is derived from marriage, and from the origin of marriage, marriage actually stems from the family. The distinction between marriage and purely sexual relationships is that it involves the parties living together for a long period of time, whereas men and women originally lived together in order to raise the next generation. According to research, "... Marriage is considered by law to be non-binding until there are children".[64] As Mr. Fei Xiaotong said, "It is not so much that because of the hobbies of both sexes, they are willing to raise their children together, but rather, because they want to raise their children together." The sexes need a lasting emotional connection.[65] Later, economic factors were added to make the relationship between the sexes stronger. The key reason why the Punalua family and the dual family stage were eliminated by history was that they had to achieve the same social effect as monogamy, but the running cost was too high. However, for the family, it does not necessarily mean sex and reproduction. The institution of marriage focuses on the creation and revocation of identity (marriage, divorce, paternity) and the legal consequences of the creation and cancellation of identity, as well as the protection of family members.

The purpose of modern marriage for the parties involved is the pursuit of happiness. While order is essential for human life, it may not necessarily be the ultimate goal for the individuals involved. As people's private views of marriage and family become more prominent and modern life becomes more hectic and stressful, people have higher spiritual expectations and requirements for marriage. On the spiritual side, people seek to relieve the stress of their lives through marriage and emphasize the role of love in marriage. Marriage provides not only material support but also emotional support and care, and happiness is a combination of material and spiritual satisfaction.

At the level of values, the institution of marriage balances order and freedom in the private sphere. Order has become a fundamental value goal in human life, and history has shown the superiority of an orderly life over chaotic states. However, everyone needs space to develop, and freedom is a basic human desire and right. To prevent its abuse, it must be limited. Therefore, the law strives to balance social order and individual freedom. Through the marriage system, individuals can pursue

[64] Westermarck [39].

[65] Xiaotong [40].

happiness and be protected by law while society achieves stability in the form of meeting individual needs, achieving the dual compatibility of personal and social purposes, which is unique to the institution of marriage.

Homosexuals also pursue stable order and emotional mutual support in life, just like heterosexuals. However, in China, the quality of heterosexual marriage for homosexuals is inherently deficient compared to that of ordinary people. One party usually accommodates the other and bears the burden alone, or the marital relationship becomes disorganized until it breaks down. Homosexuals usually have little or no sexual relations with opposite-sex partners and may have difficulty developing romantic relationships. Therefore, their family relationships are relatively weak, and they often seek sexual satisfaction and emotional support in society. Without institutional constraints, they move around frequently, seeking novelty and difference, making them vulnerable to deception, blackmail, and robbery. Homosexuals desire a secure home with people of the same sex.

Academics believe that the basis of marriage roughly includes physiological, psychological, emotional, and life needs. As part of human emotions, homosexuality has the same needs as heterosexuals, so the law should protect marriage between homosexuals.[66] Indeed, the relationship between homosexuals and their partners is no different from that between heterosexual marriages: psychological mutual support, emotional affection, and care in life, as well as sexual gratification. Everyone has the freedom to live with someone they like, the only difference is that the object of sexual activity is different, and such sex is harmless to others.

The moral basis of marriage is love. "Human marriage is different from animal mating. It is not only a physical union of people, but more importantly, a spiritual union. If men and women could not have sex with each other, they would marry not on the basis of their biological instincts, but on the basis of their feelings."[67]Love is the ultimate goal of marriage, a pure spiritual connection. Hegel made a clear distinction between love and sexual desire, emphasizing the importance of a "beautiful soul" in love. He believed that in love, the highest principle is the subject's surrender of their independent consciousness and individuality to feel that they can only truly know themselves in the consciousness of the other person. This unity of self-consciousness with the other person is love, and this love is ethical love with the significance of law. Human marriage typically evolves from no love to some love[68] and eventually to a marriage that is solely based on love. "Only marriages based on love are moral" and "if it is true that the affection has disappeared or has been squeezed out by new passionate love, it will make divorce a blessing for both parties and for society".[69] There are real emotions between homosexuals, as shown in the film "Lan Yu". Although it abandons the entanglement of struggle and opposition between homosexuality and heterosexuality, the film constructs the beautiful and normal side of homosexuality

[66] See "Experts call for new marriage law to protect same-sex marriage rights", available at: http://news.eastday.com, 2006-12-04.

[67] Runxian [8].

[68] Hegel [41].

[69] Marx and Engels [42].

with humanistic ideals that transcend reality. Two men in the film have proved the vow of "the sea is rotten, the heart will never change, the white head will grow old, and the tradition will be challenged" with 20 years of devotion to each other. This proves to a large extent that the qualities of true love are indifference between the two. The demand for marriage by homosexuals based on genuine human love should be morally justified.

At the legal level, marriage is essentially a contract. The law can only regulate people's external behavior, not human emotions. Legally, marriage is not based on love as the basis of legitimacy. From a modern legal perspective, human society has transitioned from identity to contract, and the marriage relationship has become a contractual relationship. The legal definition of marriage is "the union of a man and a woman with the intention of becoming husband and wife and living together for life." This definition can be extended to include same-sex marriage, which is the union of two people of the same sex with the intention of living together for life.[70] As long as the parties are qualified and the intention is genuine, their marriage is legally valid and should be protected by law. Marriage does not give equal rights to everyone, but only to those who remain in long-term relationships.

Restrictions on the principle of freedom of marriage should not include restrictions on sexuality. Freedom of marriage is a specific application of the principle of autonomy in the field of marriage. Autonomy is required by the basic principles of private law, and only in this way can people's enthusiasm be mobilized and human society can develop healthily. Looking at the legislation of various countries in the world, most restrictions on the freedom of marriage do not have other prohibitions except incest affecting childbearing and the age and capacity of the subjects. Homosexuals are eligible to enter marriage as long as they have the age and ability to express meaning, and the law allows homosexuals to enter into heterosexual marriage. Gays are protected from living with people they do not like, but it is ridiculous that homosexuals are not protected from living with people they like.

4.2 Homosexual Marriage from a Legal Right Perspective

Our era is the age of rights, and human rights are the concept of our time - the only political and moral concept that has been universally accepted. Human rights are the birthright of all human beings,[71] and are rights that all people enjoy equally. Human rights seek human dignity as human beings and abstract equality between human beings. The concept of human rights is the basis for the protection of the value of "marriage" for homosexuals.

The right to marry refers to the right of the parties to a marriage to enter into marriage, exercise their spouses' rights, and dissolve their marriage. The right to

[70] Yanman [43].

[71] See Hengkin [44].

marriage has been recognized as a fundamental human right by international legislation, and Article 23, paragraph 2, of the International Covenant on Civil and Political Rights stipulates that "the right of men and women of marriageable age to marry and to found a family shall be recognized." This article is the only provision in the International Covenant on Civil and Political Rights that requires States to establish institutional safeguards. This is because marriage assumes the function of the survival of human society, maintains the stability of social order, and provides institutional guarantee for the long-term happy life of every member of society.[72]

4.2.1 Personality Autonomy of the "Marriage" of Homosexuals

As mentioned earlier, a homosexual is not a psychopath. They are not irrational beings but rational entities, and reason is a way of being. Their happy life must be supported by reason, and everything that contributes to a happy life is chosen by reason. A person's ability to choose their way of life and style makes them a rational fixation that transcends all animals and fulfills the cause of personal happiness or self-love. "The pursuit of happiness must be the aspiration of every rational but limited being", and therefore an inevitable basis for their desire for capacity.[73] Personality is a philosophical summary of the nature of humans. On this basis, the ethical values internalized by human beings are endowed with freedom, dignity, life, and health because of their inner rationality. Only in this way can social progress and prosperity be ensured. For homosexuals themselves, they are people of intrinsic value, and they themselves are an end, not just a means for others to pursue an end. Homosexual "marriage" means that homosexuals themselves pursue their own happiness, which is an autonomy based on the personality of homosexuals. Ethically, there is no legislator but themselves. Marriage is the institutional guarantee for the most cherished emotions in human society, and homosexuality as a component of human emotions should also be given the same legal status as heterosexual marriage and family in the new era. The law should not evade or avoid it.

4.2.2 Selectivity of Interests in the "Marriage" of Homosexuals

The realization of interests is at the core of rights, and the right to marry is essentially a reflection of marital interests. The interest in marriage is not a physical category that exists independently of the individual. Rather, it is the result of the combination of the subjective needs of the parties involved in the marriage and the objective outcomes of marriage. It is the satisfaction that marriage brings to both homosexuals and heterosexuals. As established in the Baehr v. Miike case,[74] marriage is of interest to both

[72] Immanuel Kant [45].

[73] See Liping [46].

[74] Baehr v. Miike [47].

homosexuals and heterosexuals for reasons such as parenting, achieving relationship stability and mutual commitment, personal intimacy, monogamy, establishing a permanent relationship, realizing personal value, and obtaining legal and economic protection and benefits. The right to marry legally means the protection of practical interests such as spousal rights, custody, inheritance rights, guardianship rights, visitation rights, and so on.[75] Furthermore, it also means the social recognition of the relationship between homosexual partners. For homosexuals, its spiritual interests are more important than the practical ones.

"Because interests vary according to individuals' preferences, the right to marry must first be based on the subjective will of homosexuals, and they must be free to choose according to their own will. As long as their behavior aligns with their inner will, it is difficult for others to judge whether it is beneficial or not. The parties themselves are the best judges of their own interests. The right to marriage is an active pursuit of establishing and sustaining human married life, which first embodies human free will. Free will is the initial driving force of rights, and a person cannot pursue rights that are not aligned with their will or interests. Therefore, a person's choice to enter marriage, what kind of marriage to choose, and what interests to pursue must go through the decision of free will. Rights have a purpose, which is not directly conferred by the material relations of the economy, but rather mediated and regulated by the free will of individuals. Without a purpose, there can be no talk of rights. In this sense, the right to marry is an external expression of people's free will to choose interests, and it is a means for homosexuals to realize themselves and pursue happiness in married life."

4.2.3 Harmlessness of Homosexual "Marriage"

In order for the subject's actions to be justified in the eyes of the law, they must meet socially harmless standards. Regarding homosexual "marriage", it must first be harmless to the parties involved. Homosexuals have a higher incidence of AIDS due to social pressures and constraints, and their relationships can be extremely unstable, leading them to pursue only momentary pleasure and have multiple sexual partners. However, if homosexuals enter into a marriage, they have a certain obligation of sexual fidelity to their partners, which greatly reduces the incidence of AIDS among them.

Homosexual "marriage" is also harmless to society. Restrictions on the right of homosexuals to marry cannot be based solely on the moral preference of the majority, but must consider the actual public interest. The view that homosexual marriage is harmful can be summarized as follows: (1) Some argue that homosexual marriage will have a huge impact on the traditional human concept of the family and may be a destabilizing factor. However, same-sex marriage has existed since ancient times, such as among the Transcot Indian tribes in North America, who had the custom of marrying men to men. Additionally, the tradition of "female husbands" exists

[75] Liping [46].

among the Dahomey tribes in Africa,[76] and traditions are not immutable. (2) Some argue that same-sex marriage is like sex trafficking, as homosexuals often change sexual partners and are seen as unstable without true feelings, thus undermining moral standards and endangering social harmony, indirectly damaging the interests of third parties. Kinsey once said: 'If there were no social customs and legal prohibitions to strengthen and continue marriage, heterosexual sexual relations would have lasted much less or for a much shorter time than they actually exist today. In contrast, same-sex sexual relations would not have had such favorable external conditions and external sustaining forces.' Kinsey argued that same-sex relationships are constantly troubled by personal inner conflicts and personal and social conflicts, resulting in the vast majority of these relationships lasting only one or two times[77](3) Some people believe that homosexuality has a negative impact on children and can make them more likely to develop homosexual tendencies. However, studies have shown that children who grow up in homosexual families do not differ significantly in psychological development from children who grow up in heterosexual families. For instance, a study compared 40 children raised by homosexual and heterosexual mothers and found that the mother's sexual orientation did not differ in the number and form of feelings between the two groups of children. There was also no evidence that the children of homosexual mothers had gender confusion, increased homosexual tendencies, or difficulty in emotional development. Experts have pointed out that if children's sexual orientation is simply a matter of imitation, why do some heterosexual parents have homosexual children?[78] For the past 25 years, dozens of psychologists have devoted themselves to researching the physical and mental health of children from gay families. They have come to an almost unanimous conclusion that children from gay families do not have a more difficult upbringing than those from heterosexual families. Even the most rigorous American pediatric medical schools have had to admit that gay families are growing in number, gaining power, and becoming more organized.[79] (4) While some argue that homosexuals cannot be competent parents, research has shown that the sexual orientation of the parents itself cannot be a criterion for judging their ability to raise children. Homosexual parents and couples also have the potential to raise their children well, and should not be discriminated against based on their sexual orientation.[80]

4.2.4 Social Justice in Homosexual Marriages

Rights not only imply the harmlessness of the free will and actions of the right holder but also meet the requirements of social justice. The essence of justice means equality, and the right to equality is the most fundamental human right. Article 2

[76] Wenyi [48].

[77] Quoted from Yinhe [49].

[78] See Liping [46].

[79] See Editorial Article. (2005). Triumph of Homosexuality. World Expo, 1.

[80] Liping [46].

of the Universal Declaration of Human Rights declares that 'Everyone is entitled to all the rights and freedoms set forth in the present Declaration without distinction of any kind, such as race, colour, sex, language, religion, political or other opinion, national or social origin, property, or other status.' Both the Charter of Fundamental Rights of the European Union and the Directive against all forms of discrimination in employment, including discrimination based on sexual orientation, prohibit discrimination on the grounds of a person's sexual orientation. The marriage regime should provide homosexuals with the same or similar protections as heterosexuals. Prohibiting homosexuals from the right to marry on the grounds that marriage is an intersex mechanism discriminates on the grounds of "sex",[81] as this gender classification restricts homosexuals from enjoying the same marriage rights as heterosexuals. This unduly curtails the equal rights of homosexuals to marry with heterosexuals and unduly curtails the constitutional rights of homosexuals. If the marriage law applies only to heterosexuals, it becomes a privileged law for heterosexuals, and homosexuals are denied their right to marry.[82]

Formal equality transcends class, gender, religion, and other differences in the granting of rights and pursues abstract equality, giving people equal opportunities. However, it ignores that people differ in the degree to which freedom is realized, and that absolute formal equality creates widespread inequality, making the rich richer and the poor poorer. Therefore, substantive equality must supplement formal equality. Article 27 of the International Covenant on Civil and Political Rights clearly declares that 'In States where ethnic, religious, or linguistic minorities exist, such minorities may not be denied the right to enjoy their own culture or to profess and practice their own religion or to use their own language.' A group of 'minorities' who have long been subordinate in political, economic, or cultural life due to prejudice, discrimination, or deprivation of rights have a low social status due to disparities in the enjoyment and realization of rights. Homosexuals exist as a special 'minority' group, and their particularity is reflected in the non-superficial cognition of sexual orientation.[83] In other words, the judgment of minority groups such as minors, women, the elderly, and the disabled can be based on their appearance, but the same cannot be done for homosexuals. Once their sexual orientation is exposed to the public, the loss of profit is incalculable. In real life, homosexuals suffer from discrimination in employment, education, housing, and other areas. Therefore, only by providing positive protection for homosexual marriages can the 'vulnerability' of homosexuals not be submerged in the general personality.[84]

[81] EC No 78 Directive, 2000 Gazette, L303/16.;See Waddington, Lisa and Mark Bell. "More Equal than Others: Distinguishing European Union Equality Directives." Common Market Law Review (2001): n. pag.. 577–611.

[82] Zhendong [50].

[83] Runxian [8].

[84] See Runxian [8].

5 Practical Obstacles to the Marriage Rights of Homosexuals

For a moral right to be elevated to a legal right, it must be evaluated by the majority of the members of society, and a right that has not been evaluated by the legitimacy of the majority of the members of society cannot become a legal right. Chinese society, which is on the road to the rule of law, also faces various conceptual and institutional obstacles in the process of legalizing the marriage rights of gay people.

5.1 Conceptual Barriers

Although I have refuted some misconceptions in the previous article, it cannot be denied that traditions are not easily changed. It is arguable that there are mainly the following problems on the issue of homosexuality in China at present.

5.1.1 Self-identification of Homosexuals

Influenced by traditional culture, there are not many openly homosexual individuals in China. Homosexuals have not yet formed a strong interest group, and the homosexual rights movement is also in a moderate state. As a result, they tend to express their rights more conservatively. The extreme imbalance in the development of Chinese society has made it more difficult for homosexuals to openly identify themselves. The imbalance between urban and rural development has led to a higher degree of self-identification among homosexuals in open areas and highly urbanized areas. Gay bars, clubs, fraternities, and related organizations have sprung up in major cities such as Beijing. In rural and more isolated areas, the stigma against homosexuality is stronger. As depicted in the novel, "There is no government, no constitution, no recognition, no respect. All we have is a bunch of rabble nationals."[85] When homosexuals complain about Chinese "homophobia"[86] and are afraid that others will find out that they are gay, there are many instances where alcohol is involved. This fear is not necessarily caused by outsiders, but rather reflects their own anxiety and worry about their living conditions.

---

[85] Yinhe et al. [51].

[86] Xianyong [52].

5.1.2 Public's Failure to Have a Comprehensive Understanding of Homosexuality

The medical profession and schools have shown relatively large tolerance for homosexuality, but due to the late start of research on homosexuality in China, the public's understanding of homosexuality has not yet been unified. A 2004 survey showed that 57.2% of medical personnel considered homosexuality to be pathological, while 77.2% considered homosexuality worthy of sympathy and understanding. Moreover, 62% of those surveyed believed that homosexuality should be accepted in society in the future, and only 19.4% of respondents had come into contact with homosexuality. On the other hand, college students are more open to homosexuality than medical staff.[87] Another survey showed that a stratified group of 250 medical specialists were selected, and a higher proportion of male and female respondents answered that they wanted to know more, at 58.95% and 71.83%, respectively. The proportion of those who answered that they knew a lot or knew everything was a total of 15.19% for both genders.[88] Despite this level of knowledge among professionals, public awareness remains low.

5.1.3 Negative Guidance by the Media to the Public

Since very few people have had contact with homosexuals, most people's stereotypes are created by public opinion. The impact of AIDS has improved the social living environment of homosexuals, and the media generally adopt an external perspective, from the standpoint of the self-interest of heterosexual audiences, and use AIDS as an entry point to connect the two groups of urban homosexuals and heterosexuals. The excessive focus of non-homosexuals on self-interest and the lack of internal perspective can equate homosexuals with AIDS. The external perspective only stays at the level of "they need care," making it easy to become a condescending gesture of charity.

The exclusion of homosexual partnerships from being recognized as marriages is dependent on many social and political factors. Although attitudes towards sex have become more secularized, marriage, as a social institution that has been extended by humans for thousands of years, still carries a sacred connotation in the eyes of many. Morality is a product of changing times, and even if it is recognized that homosexuals need marriage, emotional acceptance takes time. People's reliance on tradition has a rational side after all. To change society's attitude towards homosexuality, "the 'appearance' of homosexuals themselves is the premise, the guidance of the media, the gradual recognition and acceptance of the public is the foundation, and the attention of political and academic circles is the key."[89] First of all, homosexuals should actively "come out", show their positive aspects to society, and help society

[87] See Songyu et al. [53].

[88] See Jong-yan and Guangxiang [54].

[89] Runxian [8].

understand, tolerate, and accept them. Second, governments should take on the task of disseminating knowledge, advocating for acceptance. From the perspective of social perception, the government is the best force to change the misunderstanding, discrimination, and stigmatization of homosexuality.[90] On the premise of reaching a consensus in the academic community, grassroots workers should be trained, psychiatrists and psychological counselors working at the grassroots level should have their knowledge updated, and the process of depathologization of homosexuals should be promoted. The government should take on the task of joining hands with homosexuals in the fight against AIDS. Finally, the media should highlight the internal perspective and describe the positive feelings and experiences among homosexuals, as well as the various difficulties they face under social pressure. They should also depict the understanding and acceptance of homosexuality, even marriage, by family and friends of homosexuals, and present a positive portrayal of the spiritual outlook of the homosexual community to clarify the stereotype of "gay" in the public mind. Through the guidance of the law, the general public can accept homosexuals, allowing them to truly enjoy the rights they are entitled to.[91]

5.2 *Institutional Obstacles*

In the West, the issue of same-sex marriage was dealt with within the framework of the rule of law. However, in China, during the transition period, the imperfection of the legal system makes it difficult for the law to recognize gay marriage. As far as the existing system is concerned, neither legislative nor judicial recognition of the right of homosexuals to marry is possible.

From a legislative point of view, China's constitution itself is not highly normative, and the connotation of the confirmation of citizens' right to equality and marriage is not clear. China's current constitution lacks general provisions to protect basic rights, and the principle and generalization of the basic rights norms of the constitution itself are not high. Article 33 of the Constitution alone stipulates that "all citizens of the People's Republic of China are equal before the law," and Article 49 stipulates that "marriage, the family, mothers and children shall be protected by the State… It is forbidden to undermine the freedom of marriage." There is no clear definition of the subject of rights and the content of rights. Thus, the right to marry recognized in the Constitution can only be concretized by ordinary laws and realized through the implementation of ordinary laws. The task of allowing homosexuals to marry falls on the Marriage Act as a sectoral law. The only way to legalize same-sex marriage is to ask the legislature to amend the Marriage Act. However, it still requires a certain number of people to identify as homosexual for same-sex marriage to be on the legislative agenda.

[90] Runxian [8].

[91] Runxian [8].

At the judicial level, the absence of constitutional proceedings makes it difficult for the judiciary to confirm the right of gay people to marry. The irregularity of the Constitution also weakens the judicial applicability of the Constitution. Affirming and guaranteeing the basic rights of citizens is one of the basic spirits of the Constitution, and constitutional litigation is an important means to achieve this spirit. The so-called constitutional litigation means that when citizens' basic rights are violated, citizens should have the right to initiate constitutional litigation when they cannot be safeguarded through other litigation means or there is no other way to obtain effective remedies so that the damaged rights can be restored. As far as China is concerned, on the one hand, abstract administrative and legislative acts cannot be prosecuted in the courts, and homosexuals cannot ask the legislature to amend the Marriage Law on the grounds that the current Marriage Law contradicts the Constitution. On the other hand, the Constitution itself cannot be used as the basis for judicial decisions after all remedies have been exhausted, and homosexuals cannot seek constitutional remedies based on the Constitution after their application for marriage has been rejected by the civil affairs authorities.[92] Thus, homosexuals cannot pass constitutional review nor guarantee their right to marry through specific constitutional proceedings.

6 Legal Guarantees for Homosexuals' Right to Marry

The legal protection of the right of homosexuals to marry has been a challenging process. In 1989, Denmark became the first country to recognize same-sex unions and allow same-sex couples to register. In April 2001, the Netherlands became the first country to legally recognize same-sex marriage, providing families with all the benefits of traditional marriage. In 2002, several countries such as Norway, Sweden, Iceland, Germany, France, and Switzerland registered same-sex unions, granting them rights traditionally enjoyed by heterosexual families. On December 13, 2002, the Parliament of Buenos Aires, Argentina, set a precedent in conservative, Catholic Latin American countries by adopting civil union laws legalizing same-sex marriage and heterosexual cohabitation following a five-hour debate.[93] On January 30, 2003, Belgium became the second country in the world to legalize same-sex marriage, after the Netherlands. On June 28, 2005, marriage was allowed nationwide for homosexuals. On June 30, 2005, Spain adopted the Act Legalizing Same-Sex Marriage. On December 21, 2005, the UK's Same-Sex Marriage Bill came into force. On November 14, 2006, the South African Parliament approved a proposal to legalize "same-sex marriage," officially becoming the sixth country in the world and the first

[92] The legalization of same-sex marriage in the United States is achieved through constitutional review by the courts. See Liping, W. (2004). Same-sex marriage: Denial, acceptance or dialogue? Journal of Chinese Humanities, (4).

[93] See "Homosexual 'Couples' Legal," available at: http://www.godgivc.com/book/knowhow/focus20.html (last accessed December 8, 2006).

in Africa to legally recognize same-sex marriage.[94] In front of lawmakers, the emergence of same-sex marriage is perhaps the biggest legal problem that mankind has ever presented to itself. Regardless of the attitude of lawmakers, the issue cannot be avoided. The author believes that the legal protection of the marriage right of homosexuals can be specifically divided into two aspects: legislative protection and infringement remedies.

6.1 Legislative Protection of the Right of Homosexuals to Marry

The right of homosexuals to marry should be recognized at the constitutional level as a fundamental right of citizens. The Constitution guarantees everyone the right to marry someone of his or her choosing. This right is only limited by the legal capacity and legal capacity of civil subjects and the autonomy of will.

In civil law, specific protection of the right of homosexuals to marry is also established. Professor M. Kerstel summarized the current legislative model of same-sex marriage in various countries into the following four basic models.[95]

The first is the sporadic rule model, which establishes special rules for cohabiting partners, for example, regarding the common home, social insurance, debt liability arising from their partnership, and inheritance rights.[96] In this pattern of sporadic rules, individual specific rules are not systematized.

The second regulatory model is the domestic partnership legislative model. In this legislative model, the legislature decides to establish an internally harmonious legal system for cohabitants, which emphasizes not sexual partnership or a commitment to lifelong bonding between them, but the fact that they have formed or have formed a stable union in life.[97]

The third is the registration of partnerships. Homosexuals, in addition to demanding specific rights or privileges that have been integrated into an internally harmonious legal system, also ask the public to recognize their relationship as a highly respected institution in the same way as the institution of marriage. The legislation of all Scandinavian countries, as well as France, Belgium, Vermont in the United States, and Taiwan, follows this model, although the legal terminology may differ (registered partner, civil partnership, or civil association, integrated agreement).[98]

The fourth model is the marriage relationship. For example, the Dutch legislature, three years after enacting legislation on registered partners, decided to apply the same

[94] See "South Africa's Proposal to Approve Legalisation of Same-Sex Marriage," available at: http://old.jfdaily.com/gb/jfxww/xinwen/node1220/node9800/userobject1ai1499724.html (last accessed December 9, 2006).

[95] See Coester [55].

[96] See Coester [55].

[97] See Coester [55].

[98] See Coester [55].

institution of marriage to same-sex partners. Section 30, paragraph 1, of the Dutch Civil Code, which entered into force on 1 April 2001, provides that: "Marriage is a contractual relationship between two people of the opposite sex or the same sex."[99]

In the Netherlands, same-sex marriage differs from heterosexual marriage in only two aspects: intercountry adoption of children and the presumption of paternity. Firstly, intercountry adoption of children. The law on same-sex spouse adoption prohibits intercountry adoption by same-sex spouses mainly due to objections from the sending country. However, this provision may be phased out as some countries of origin already allow same-sex couples to adopt children. Secondly, the Dutch Civil Code stipulates that the husband is the father of a child born to his wife, which does not apply to same-sex couples of the biological mother. Later, the legislation was amended to provide that lesbian spouses automatically had joint parental authority over children born to one of them. Same-sex couples of birth mothers can protect their legal parenthood through the adoption process. However, during this procedure, the biological father can assert his legitimate rights and interests.

The differences between marriage and registered partnerships lie mainly in the presumption of paternity, adoption by second parents, and joint adoption. Although the steps taken by European countries are carried out in their own legal, social, and political contexts and processes, surveys show that a trend towards harmonization between marriage and registered partnerships is gradually emerging.[100] However, legal reasoning alone cannot lead to significant changes in public policy, and other determinants such as politics, morality, experience, etc., must also be taken into account.

It is not yet possible to apply the institution of marriage to same-sex and opposite-sex couples without distinction. However, it is necessary to establish a system of rules that cannot deny protection simply because the parties are not registered, and social order must be maintained within the framework of basic security. Even if marriage were applied to same-sex and opposite-sex couples without distinction, a significant number of people would not register their relationship, and de facto cohabitation would still become a social problem. For this reason, more efficient legislation would adopt a piecemeal rule model. With existing legal resources, it is neither necessary nor possible to provide adequate protection for de facto cohabitation. The parties do not register precisely to avoid the mutual obligations arising from registration. Therefore, at present, legal adjustments should be made mainly to the property relations of these de facto cohabitants, such as the property regime during the period of living together, mutual support obligations, mutual inheritance rights, the right to claim compensation in the event of personal injury suffered by the other party, and the right to claim maintenance after the termination of the registered relationship.

For homosexual couples intending to live together for a long time, it is advisable to adopt the registered partnership (civil union) model. This is because marriage is a social mechanism that has lasted for thousands of years, and any change requires a process. Conceptually, "same-sex marriage is difficult for most people to accept, and

---

[99] See Coester [55].

[100] See Cortina and Festy [56].

it is much easier to respect serious commitments of shared responsibility and mutual care, regardless of whether the parties making the commitments are of the same or opposite sex."[101] According to Kester's research, establishing a domestic partnership model requires defining the boundaries of the "scope of individual requests." Before the law applies, there should be a formal ceremony or starting point for the time of cohabitation. For example, Article 1, paragraph 1, of the law of Catalonia provides a waiting period of 2 years for opposite-sex partners, while Article 2 stipulates that same-sex partners must formally declare that they wish their relationship to be regulated by law before they can be considered "cohabitants" unless they have given birth to a child. The registered partner model creates a new legal identity.[102] Under the registered partnership model, same-sex couples who wish to live together are registered by a special registration authority to protect their legal rights against interference and discrimination by third parties. Same-sex couples who desire to live together must have the corresponding civil capacity, i.e., they must be of a certain age. Same-sex couples who are related by consanguinity or who have already registered a partnership or who are in a heterosexual marriage may not be registered.

Our current law does not recognize the validity of de facto unions. Article 8 of the Marriage Act includes a provision stating that "in accordance with the provisions of this Act...where marriage registration has not been completed, a supplementary registration shall be made." This provision positively reaffirms the need for marriage registration. The registered partner is protected by law from the date of registration, and both parties have the obligation to respect and be faithful to each other. If one party fails to comply with these obligations, the other party may request the termination of the registration relationship and obtain corresponding compensation as appropriate. Unless otherwise agreed, the property acquired by the parties during the registration period shall be jointly owned by both parties. During this period, the parties have mutual support obligations, the right to inherit each other's inheritance, the right to claim compensation in case of personal injury suffered by the other party, and the right to claim maintenance after the termination of the registered relationship. After five years of living together, the couple may adopt a child jointly.

The partnership cannot be dissolved on its own, but must be applied for and dissolved by a statutory authority, such as a court. Due to the special nature of same-sex registered partnerships, once accepted by the court, it should issue a dismissal judgment without the need for substantive examination, and the principle of conciliation does not apply.

At the legislative level, reference can be made to Article 2, Paragraph 3 of the Marriage and Family Law in the Draft Green Civil Code organized and drafted by Mr. Xu Guodong, which stipulates that "The civil union concluded between same-sex persons with each other shall be within the scope of a suitable nature, and all provisions of this subpart shall apply."[103] Same-sex unions are defined as marriages, and

---

[101] See Coester [55].

[102] See Coester [55].

[103] Guodong [57].

their equality with heterosexual marriages is defined through principled provisions, while their differences from heterosexual marriages are clearly defined.

6.2 Remedies for Infringement of Homosexuals' Right to Marry

The saying goes, "no remedy, no right," and having a remedy for one's rights is more important than empowerment itself. Remedies for rights can be divided into litigation remedies and non-contentious remedies. In modern society, the expansion of administrative power has led to its undertaking more tasks related to rights relief, so the right of homosexuals to marry also needs to be protected in relevant administrative regulations.

"Judicial remedies are the core and final channel for the remedy of rights",[104] and domestic law bears the primary responsibility for the remedy of individual rights. This requires clear and specific protection of the right of homosexuals to marry in procedural law. Constitutional proceedings can only be sought if specific laws cannot be applied. Under the premise that the constitution recognizes the right of homosexuals to marry, the establishment of a constitutional litigation system is an effective way to remedy the right of homosexuals to marry.[105] By protecting the right of homosexuals to marry, the court is not anti-democratic, but fulfills the highest mission of the court to protect the fundamental rights of every Chinese.

In cases where domestic remedies have been exhausted and prove to be ineffective, individuals may consider seeking human rights protection under international law. While there is no regional court in Asia similar to the European Court of Human Rights in Strasbourg, complaints can still be submitted to the UN Human Rights Council. Homosexual individuals are recognized and protected by the law. Due to societal changes, the definition of family is expanding to include living together, economic ties, or other forms of close and fixed relationships.[106] Therefore, a homosexual partnership that meets these criteria can be considered a family relationship. Article 23, paragraph 1, of the International Covenant on Civil and Political Rights stipulates that "the family is the natural and fundamental unit of society and shall be protected by society and the State." Although the United Nations Commission on Human Rights does not include the family of homosexuals in the "family" of Article 23, paragraph 3, of the Convention, it does include it in Article 23, paragraph 1, where "the family" is recognized and protected. Such protection is the protection of the "existence of the family."[107] In the broadest sense, these rights and obligations

---

[104] Jianzong [58].

[105] See Xiaofei [59].

[106] See Nowak [60].

[107] See Nowak [61].

include the right of family members to live together, financial assistance, tax benefits, family assistance, etc. This protection of rights is less extensive than that of the registered partnership model and only maintains the existing "family" status.

7 Conclusion

Gays and lesbians fighting for the legalization of same-sex marriage are part of a broader quest for identity. In countries governed by the rule of law, the law must give equal protection to the right to marry, regardless of whether the object of marriage is of the same sex or the opposite sex. In China, which is moving towards the rule of law, the right to marry of homosexuals still needs to be demonstrated in theory. We still discuss the marriage rights of homosexuals on the basis of liberalism to provide preliminary answers to the questions raised by homosexuals.

Life must be fluid and passed on, and it is equally dangerous to hold on too tightly or to tear apart. In any case, the growing demands of gay people in reality cannot be ignored, and the answer to the question of homosexuals' pursuit of their own happiness will change over time. At the very least, expanding the scope of dialogue and thinking rationally should be our basic gesture. Because the law carries not only care for people in the sense of survival but also care in the sense of life. Humans are "kind" beings and have their own special belonging and attachment to "human beings." As one disabled person said, "I study blind people because they teach me how to observe; I study political refugees because they teach me how to campaign; I study homosexuals because they taught me how to love…".[108]

References

1. Song, Y. (2006). Legislative perspectives on same sex marriage starting with a bloody case caused by homosexuality. *Procuratorial Storm* (7). (in Chinese).
2. Ellis, H. (1987). Studies in the psychology of sex. *Translated by Pan Guangdan.* Beijing: life·study·New Knowledge Triple Bookstore, 1987, p. 297.
3. Li, Y. (2002). *Gay subculture* (p. 9). China Friendship Publishing Company.
4. Liu, D., & Lu, L. (eds.). (2005). *Studies on Homosexuality in China.* Beijing: China Social Publishing House, p. 44.
5. Yinhe, L. (2002). *Gay subculture* (p. 5). China Friendship Publishing Company.
6. Durkheim, E. (1995). *The rules of sociological method.* (Yuming, D., Trans.). Commercial Press, Beijing, p. 34.
7. Yinhe, L. (2002). *Gay subculture* (p. 9). China Friendship Publishing Company.
8. Runxian, L. (2005). *On the legality of same-sex marriage.* Master's thesis, Jilin University.
9. Yinhe, L. (2002). *Gay subculture* (p. 16). China Friendship Publishing Company.
10. May, H. (2014). *On Socrates.* (Xutong, Q., Trans.). Chung Hwa Book Company, Beijing, pp. 31–32.
11. Yinhe, L. (2002). *Gay subculture* (p. 11). China Friendship Publishing Company.

[108] Quoted from Qinghui [62].

12. Liyong, C. (1996). *Survey of Homosexuality in China*. Guangming Daily Press, Beijing, preface.
13. Yinhe, L. (2002). *Gay subculture* (p. 17). China Friendship Publishing Company.
14. Ellis, H. (1987). *Studies in the psychology of sex*. (Guangdan, P., Trans.). Life·Study·New Knowledge Triple Bookstore, Beijing, p. 732.
15. Shufen, S. (2001). From the relationship between Chen Weisong and Yun Lang, on the good reasons for the male favorites of the early Qing Dynasty. *Journal of Soochow Chinese*, (5).
16. Dalin, L., & Longguang, L. (Eds.). (2005). *Studies on Homosexuality in China*. China Social Publishing House, Beijing, p. 44.
17. Dalin, L., & Longguang, L. (Eds.). (2005). *Studies on Homosexuality in China* (p. 46). China Social Publishing House.
18. Suiming, P. (1995). *The current situation of sexuality in China* (p. 411). Guangming Daily Press.
19. Dalin, L. (1995). *Contemporary Chinese sexual culture* (p. 113). Shanghai Sanlian Bookstore.
20. Durkheim, E. (1995). *The rules of sociological methodologies*. (Yuming, D., Trans.). Commercial Press, Beijing, p. 24.
21. Qinghui, Z. (2003). *The History, Theories, and Current Situation of Homosexuality: Characterized by "Gone with the Wind"*. Master's thesis, Sichuan University.
22. Douglas, J. D., Smith, D. C., & Wender, J. (1987). *Introduction to the sociology of deviance*. (Ning, Z., & Xinmin, Z., Trans.). Hebei People's Publishing House, Shijiazhuang, p. 132.
23. Dalin, L., & Longguang, L. (Eds.). (2005). *Studies on Homosexuality in China* (p. 47). China Social Publishing House.
24. Chang-do, L. (2004). The turmoil over the draft "same-sex marriage" in Canada. *Journal of Henan Political and Legal Management Cadre College*, (1).
25. Foucault, M. (2000). *History of sexual experience*. (Biping, S., Trans.). Shanghai People's Publishing House, Shanghai, pp. 32–33.
26. Erikson, E. H. (1998). *Identity: Youth and Crisis*. (Mingzhi, S., Trans.). Zhejiang Education Press, Hangzhou, p. 115.
27. Xiangdong, Z. (2006). *Conceptual analysis of identity*. Hunan Social Sciences, 2006(3).
28. Wrightsman, L. S. (1988). *Social psychology of the eighties*. (Min, P. et al., Trans.). Life·Study·New Knowledge Triple Bookstore, Beijing, p. 65.
29. Yinhe, L. (2002). *Gay subculture*. China Friendship Publishing Company, Beijing, p. 17.
30. Marcus, E. (1997). *Making Gay History: The Half-Century Fight for Lesbian and Gay Equal Rights*. (Xianxiu, L., Trans.). Happy Sunshine Publishing Company, Beijing, p. 19.
31. Marcus, E. (1997). *Making Gay History: The Half-Century Fight for Lesbian and Gay Equal Rights*. (Xianxiu, L., Trans.). Happy Sunshine Publishing Company, Beijing, p. 13.
32. Dalin, F., & Qiang, L. (2006). *Hey, Comrades*, In "The People", (4).
33. Ellis, H. (1987). *Studies in the psychology of Sex*. (Guangdan, P., Trans.). Life·Study·New Knowledge Triple Bookstore, Beijing, p. 313.
34. Weeks, J. (2002). *Making sexual history*. (Wenwei, S. et al., Trans.). Jiangsu People's Publishing House, Nanking, p. 35.
35. Jie, Z. (2004). Legal provisions on same-sex crimes in the qing dynasty and enlightenment to current relevant legislation. *Chinese Sex Science*, (3).
36. Dalin, L. (1998). *The sociologist's point of view: Changes in Marriage and Family in China* (p. 83). China Social Publishing House.
37. Burguière, A. (1998). *A History of the Family, Volume II: The Impact of Modernity*. (Shuren, Y. et al., Trans.). Life·Study·New Knowledge Triple Bookstore, Beijing, p. 136.
38. Aishu, X. (2005). *Research on the marriage system in China in the 20th Century* (p. 283). Intellectual Property Press.
39. Westermarck, E. (2002). *The history of human marriage*. (Bin, L. et al., Trans.). Commercial Press, Beijing, p. 711.
40. Xiaotong, F. (1999). *Native China Fertility system* (p. 120). Peking University Press.
41. Hegel, G. W. F. (1991). *Aesthetics: Lectures on Fine Art* (2nd Volume). (Guangqian, Z., Trans.). Commercial Press, Beijing, p. 333.

42. Marx, K., & Engels, F. (1995). *Selected works* (2nd Edition, Vol. 4). People's Publishing House, Beijing, p. 81.
43. Yanman, Y. (2002). On the essential attributes of marriage in modern and modern law. *The Law Review*, (3).
44. Hengkin, L. (1997). *The Age of Rights. Xin Chunying, Wu Yuzhang, Li Lin (trans.).* Beijing,Knowledge Press, preface I.
45. Immanuel Kant. (1999). *Critique of Practical Reason. Zhang Mingding (trans.).* Beijing,Commercial Press, p. 24
46. Liping, W. (2004). Same-sex marriage: Denial, acceptance or dialogue? *Journal of Chinese Humanities*, (4).
47. Baehr v. Miike (1996) WL 694235, Haw. Circ. Ct. Quoted in Liping, W. (2004). Same-sex marriage: Denial, acceptance or dialogue? *Journal of Chinese Humanities*, (4).
48. Wenyi, H. (2005). Legal and Philosophical Inquiry on the Basis of Marriage Legitimacy. In S. Xianzhong (Ed.), *Lecture on Philosophy of Departmental Law (Part I)* (p. 91). Higher Education Press.
49. Yinhe, L. (2002*). Gay subculture* (p. 104). Beijing: China Friendship Publishing Company.
50. Zhendong, S. (2002). Study on the protection of the human rights of homosexuals. In Beam-comet, C. (Ed.), *Civil and Commercial Law Series* (Vol. 24, p. 625). Beijing: Golden Bridge Culture Publication (Hong Kong) Ltd.
51. Yinhe, L. et al. (2002). On Self-Identity, Gay Rights, Rights of Homosexuals and 'Coming Out'. Available at: http://www.homosky.com/inews/NEWS/news_1/gaynews_2/2002-04/1018384140.html. Accessed December 9, 2006.
52. Xianyong, B. (1988). *The Sinner* (p. 37). People's Publishing House.
53. Songyu, D., Lin, T., & Yingxia, L. (2004). Investigation and Research on the Attitude of Some Medical Staff to Homosexuality in Shenzhen. *Chinese Journal of Health Psychology*, (5).
54. Jong-yan, L., & Guangxiang, R. (2006). Survey and analysis of homosexual awareness of medical specialists. *Journal of Qiannan Ethnic Medicine*, (6).
55. Coester, M. (2002). Same-sex relationships: a comparative assessment of legal developments across Europe. *European Journal of Law Reform, 4*, 585–601.
56. Cortina, C., & Festy, P. (2020). Same-sex couples and their legalization in Europe: Laws and numbers. In M. Digoix (Ed.), *Same-Sex Families and Legal Recognition in Europe* (pp. 45–71). Springer.
57. Guodong, X. (Ed.). (2004). *Draft green civil code (p. 185).* Social Science Literature Publishers.
58. Jianzong, Y. (Ed.). (2006). *Jurisprudence: General legal science (p. 176).* China University of Political Science and Law Press.
59. Xiaofei, G. (2005). Seeking common ground while reserving differences and seeking differences while reserving common ground. The constitutional dimension of same-sex marriage. *Global Law Review*, (5).
60. Nowak, M. (2003). UN Covenant on Civil and Political Rights. CCPR Commentary (Xiaoqing, B., & Shiyan, S., Trans.) (p. 401). Beijing: Life·Study·New Knowledge Triple Publishing House.
61. Nowak, M. (2003). UN Covenant on Civil and Political Rights. CCPR Commentary (Xiaoqing, B., & Shiyan, S., Trans.) (p. 402). Beijing: Life·Study·New Knowledge Triple Publishing House.
62. Qinghui, Z. (2003). *The History, Theories and Current Situation of Homosexuality: Characterized by "Gone with the Wind"*. Master's thesis, Sichuan University.

Chapter 8
The Right to Euthanasia

Jingfang Wen

1 Introduction

Euthanasia is the act or practice of killing or permitting the death of hopelessly sick or injured individuals in a relatively painless way. The word evokes emotions, regardless of the way it is used. When pronounced, separate camps of irreconcilable proponents and opponents are drawn up. Debate over euthanasia is not a recent phenomenon.[1] The debate around euthanasia has been ongoing since the concept was first proposed. Today, due to advances in life sciences and the inevitability of death, the discussion of euthanasia will not cease. It is a wide-ranging question, which can be explored from multiple angles, such as medicine, sociology, theology, philosophy, economics, and psychology. The reason why euthanasia has become such a hot topic is not only because of the loss of life, but also because that life could still exist and the helper's behavior in the process of euthanasia is judged. It is a difficult thing to do.

We will explore the objective existence of euthanasia in the real life, analyze the basic trends of countries when it comes to this unavoidable issue, outline the various arguments for and against the legitimacy of euthanasia, and clarify the appropriate basis for euthanasia.

[1] Obi [1].

J. Wen (✉)
Dalian Radio and Television University, Beijing, China

J. Yao (ed.), *The Legal Issues of the Emerging Rights*,
https://doi.org/10.1007/978-981-97-0499-6_8

2 De Facto Euthanasia

2.1 Concept and Practice Abroad

In the seventeenth century, the famous British philosopher Francis Bacon advocated for people to have control over their own bodily processes, either to prolong life or end it in a painless manner. In his writing, he often referred to "painless lethal surgery". He believed that prolonging life was the noble purpose of medicine, and also viewed euthanasia as an important field of medical technology that can be used to relieve the suffering of patients.[2] In the 1930s, many people began to actively advocate for euthanasia. Sigmund Freud, the founder of psychoanalysis, ended his life through voluntary euthanasia. After the Second World War, with the advancement of science and technology, and the re-evaluation of concepts, people became more aware of death and euthanasia, making it a hot topic of general concern. According to some foreign opinion polls on euthanasia, the majority of people support it rather than oppose it.

In 1952, a Gallup poll in the United States revealed that 36% of people supported euthanasia regardless of category. In 1972, Life magazine conducted a poll of 4,100 people, with 90% expressing the right of dying patients to refuse life-supporting measures. Three years later, a survey showed that 53% of people backed active euthanasia. More recently, polls in the United States have indicated that the public, including medical professionals, is largely in favor of euthanasia. In 1994, worldwide media reported the "poetic death" of an elderly woman with a terminal illness who passed away peacefully during a song of peace sung by her children.[3]

In the Netherlands, 80% of the 240,000 people in voluntary euthanasia associations are in favor of the practice. In the UK, support for the legalization of euthanasia has grown over the years. Statistics from the 1950s show that less than half of people in the UK were in favor of its legalization, but this proportion has now risen to 82%. In a 1991 poll, 72% of the 36,000 surveyed doctors indicated that euthanasia should be made legal under certain conditions. Moreover, 1 in 7 doctors admitted to having interrupted a patient's treatment or provided medication to help them die. In 1998, The Times reported that euthanasia had not yet been legalized, but that 2.7 thousand people had been euthanized with the help of doctors.[4] In Japan, when a poll asks, "What if you have a terminal illness?" 40% choose to die decently; 12.2% chose to declare their efforts to "end their lives" in advance. Most Germans are also in favor of euthanasia. A 1994 survey of 1,004 Germans by a German poll showed that 83% were in favour of euthanasia, 30 As many as 88% of people under the age are in favour of euthanasia. In Germany, the membership of euthanasia associations reached 44,000 in 1994.[5] In France, a poll in late 1987 revealed that 76% of the

---

[2] See Shi [2].

[3] Yuxia [3].

[4] See Yuxia [3].

[5] See Yuxia [3].

population wanted to amend the law so that euthanasia would no longer be illegal. In Sweden, a poll on the same issue showed that 68% were in favor, 19% were against, and 13% had no opinion.

Although the majority of the population has accepted and approved of euthanasia, countries have shown patience and caution in their legislation of it.

2.1.1 Netherlands

The Netherlands was the first country in the world to enact legislation on euthanasia in 1973. Giltruda Dr. Postma's mother, who had advanced cancer and could no longer endure the pain, had repeatedly expressed her desire to die, so Postma was arrested and tried for using morphine to euthanize her. At the time of the trial, eighteen doctors issued an open letter to the Dutch Ministry of Justice, admitting that they had performed the same act at least once. The court sentenced Postma to one week in prison, suspended for a year. In this judgment, the judge specifically stated that euthanasia must be carried out under prescribed conditions, which marked the Netherlands' first acquiescence to euthanasia.[6] In 1988, the Royal Pharmaceutical Administration set out the criteria for euthanasia in a report. On February 9, 1993, the Dutch Parliament's upper house passed the bill by a narrow margin of 37 to 34. This bill stated that "a patient who has no hope of a cure has the right to request that their life be ended," making the Netherlands the first country to regulate active death assistance by doctors.[7] It is worth emphasizing that the bill does not legalize euthanasia; it merely allows doctors to perform active death assistance for patients in strict compliance with official regulations. The Act outlines 20 conditions for the strict implementation of euthanasia and related restrictive provisions. On October 20th, 1994 in Amsterdam, the capital of the Netherlands, nearly a million citizens witnessed the process of euthanasia through a television program called "He Chose His Own Death." A 63-year-old person underwent the procedure. On August 10th, 1999, the Netherlands adopted an amendment that permits 16 and older terminally ill patients to decide whether to undergo euthanasia. For adolescents between 12 and 15, parental consent is required.[8]

On 10 April 2001, the upper house of the Dutch Parliament voted 46 in favor and 28 against; as a result, the euthanasia bill was passed due to abstention. The bill conditionally recognizes active euthanasia, and sets out strict and detailed conditions to avoid the abuse of euthanasia and unnatural death. Firstly, the patient must be an adult and must make an unwavering, voluntary decision to pursue euthanasia after careful consideration. Secondly, the patient must only apply for euthanasia when they are unable to bear the pain any longer. Thirdly, the patient's disease must be diagnosed by two doctors, and the method of euthanasia must be carefully determined. Lastly, the Act does not stipulate that only persons of Dutch nationality can apply the law;

---

[6] See Ni et al. [4].

[7] See Zhang [5].

[8] See Ni et al. [6].

anyone in the Netherlands can use the Euthanasia Act.[9] Thus, the Netherlands was the first country in the world to legalize euthanasia. Today, about 25,000 people in the Netherlands die by euthanasia annually.[10]

2.1.2 United States

The United States is an active but conservative participant in the euthanasia legislation movement, with varying laws between states.[11] As early as 1938, the United States established the "Society for Death Without Pain". The main focus of this society was on "passive death assistance," which removes or terminates life support systems. In 1975, the Karen Ann Quinlan incident occurred and drew the United States' attention to the issue of vegetative death assistance. This led to the California State Legislature passing the Natural Death Act on August 30, 1976. The Act permits individuals to sign a document indicating that death is imminent and authorizes a doctor to stop life-sustaining measures. The directive states, "My life will not be artificially prolonged" and that "there is an incurable disease, two doctors certify that I am in a terminal condition, and life-sustaining measures are being used". The Act also specifies that the doctor must comply with this directive fourteen days after the patient is deemed to be in a dying state, unless the patient withdraws the directive.[12] At the same time, there has been a controversy over "assisted dying" in the United States. Notable of these is Oregon's Death With Dignity Act of 1994. The U.S. District Court declared the Oregon Act unconstitutional in 1995. In 1996, both the U.S. Circuit Court of Appeals ruled that laws prohibiting physician-assisted suicide in Washington and New York were unconstitutional and overturned the federal district court's decision on Oregon's Death With Dignity Act.[13]

In 1997, the Federal Supreme Court ruled on whether the Constitution allowed for physician-assisted suicide for terminally ill patients. The Court held that states have the right to prohibit assisted suicide in order to protect the population. This is because legalizing assisted patient suicide may create a risk of abuse, thus making a law

---

[9] See Ni et al. [7].

[10] See Xu [8].

[11] See Hou [9].

[12] See Zhang [10].

[13] In the 1996 case of Vacco v. Quill, the Federal Court ruled that Washington State's law prohibiting physician-assisted suicide was unconstitutional. Similarly, in Washington v. Glucksberg, the court ruled that New York State's law prohibiting physician-assisted suicide was unconstitutional. The defendants in both cases—Quill and Glucksberg, along with four other doctors in Washington and New York States respectively—sought to be able to provide euthanasia services to their terminally ill patients. However, the laws of both states made aiding another person in committing suicide a crime. The Supreme Court of the United States ultimately overturned the decisions of the Ninth Circuit Court of Appeals and the Second Circuit Court of Appeals in both cases, ruling that the bans did not violate the Equal Protection or Due Process Clauses. For further discussion of the functional appeal of crime composition and the conflict resolution mechanism in the criminal field, see Lao, D. (2001). "On the Functional Appeal of Crime Composition: Rethinking the Conflict Resolution Mechanism in the Criminal Field." Jinling Law Review, 47, 1–47.

prohibiting doctor-assisted suicide not unconstitutional. In 1999, Congress passed the Pain Relief Promotion Act, which authorized doctors to prescribe painkillers that may increase the risk of death, yet the doctor must not have the intent to cause death or help others to die. As a result, active euthanasia is illegal in the United States.[14]

2.1.3 Australia

In May 1996, the Northern Territory passed the Rights of the Terminally Ill Act (also known as the Critically Ill Rights Act), which came into effect on July 1st. It was the world's first legislation to legalize voluntary and active euthanasia. This differed from other pieces of legislation in that it allowed for active and proactive death assistance. In order to be eligible, a patient must be determined to be terminally ill by two physicians and a psychiatrist licensed by the local government in the Northern Region. The diagnosis must be supported by both physicians, and the patient must sign a written document expressing their wish to die, which must be witnessed and signed by a second physician. Additionally, the Act stipulates a 48-h cooling-off period and a seven-day waiting period so that the patient may further seriously consider the decision. The Act has sparked widespread controversy in Australia, with unconstitutional lawsuits brought by religious groups, such as Wake v. Northern Territory of Australia. On July 24th, 1996, the Full Court of the Northern Territory Supreme Court dismissed the plaintiff's suit by a two-to-one vote.

On September 22nd, 1996, two months after the Terminal Patients' Bill of Rights took effect, 66-year-old Bob Dent was in Darwin, Northern Australia. He became the first person in the world to die from euthanasia after being injected with lethal drugs by a computer. Bob's death sparked intense controversy over the Terminal Patients' Bill of Rights. On December 1996, the Australian House of Representatives voted 88 to 33 to end the Act. Then, on March 25th, 1997, the Australian Senate voted 38 to 33 to repeal the euthanasia law, which had allowed four people to legally perform euthanasia during the time the bill was in force.[15]

2.1.4 United Kingdom

There is still no legislation in the UK legalizing euthanasia, but the UK was the first to establish a euthanasia organization. In 1936, the Voluntary Euthanasia Society was founded and presented a euthanasia bill to Parliament. The bill requires individuals to submit an application form if they are over 21 years of age and have an incurable, painful condition. Two references must be present when signing the form and it must be reviewed by a "euthanasia examiner" appointed by the Ministry of Health. In 1961, the Suicide Act was passed, which carries a maximum sentence of 14 years

---

[14] See Zhang [11].

[15] See Ni et al. [12].

in prison for aiding and advising someone else to commit suicide. However, since 1980, UK courts have been notably lenient with instances of euthanasia in real life.[16]

On February 4, 1993, the UK Supreme Court ruled on the country's first euthanasia case, granting the application of the parents and doctors of a 21-year-old patient to stop providing them with nutrient solution. On April 24, 1996, the court granted permission to perform euthanasia on 53-year-old Janet M. Johnson, who had been in a vegetative state for more than four years.[17]

These two cases are not related to euthanasia, however, they demonstrate the UK's stance on the matter. Euthanasia is still not legalized in the UK, but there is increasing demand for it to be made so.[18]

2.1.5 Japan

Euthanasia has been conditionally recognized in Japan through court precedents, and the case law regarding it has developed gradually.[19] In 1950, the Tokyo Court ruled in a euthanasia case that an act of ending a patient's life as a last resort to eliminate physical suffering could be considered equivalent to an "emergency evacuation act" under Japanese criminal law.[20] On December 22, 1962, in the Nagoya High Court judgment case, the defendant's father had been bedridden for years due to a cerebral hemorrhage. Knowing that his father had no chance of recovery, the defendant mixed organophosphorus insecticide with milk for him to drink, resulting in his death by poisoning. This case established the conditions for legalizing euthanasia. These conditions include: (1) according to modern medical knowledge and technology, the victim is suffering from an incurable disease and death is imminent; (2) the victim is experiencing unbearable physical pain; (3) the purpose is to alleviate the pain of the victim's death; (4) the victim is conscious and is expressing sincere consent; (5) the act is done by a doctor in the absence of any special circumstances; and (6) the method chosen is ethically appropriate. If all of these conditions are met, the act of taking human life is a "legitimate act" under the Japanese Criminal Code.[21]

In the Tokai University incident, the physician of the Affiliated Hospital and School of Medicine of Tokai University accepted the patient's family's request to "terminate treatment if the patient's death is imminent". The family then strongly requested Doctor A to pull out the drip to alleviate the patient's pain, which Doctor A accepted. Subsequently, the patient was injected with large doses of sedatives several times, resulting in cardiac arrest and death. On 28 March 1995, the Yokohama District Court sentenced Dr. A to two years' imprisonment and two years' probation

---

[16] See Hou [9].

[17] See World Euthanasia Memorandum. (n.d.). Available at: http://www.southcn.com/law/fzzt/200307300345.htm. Accessed April 18, 2010.

[18] See Hou Hou [9].

[19] See Hou [9].

[20] See Ni et al. [13].

[21] Zhang [14].

for ordinary homicide. The court listed four elements of an unlawful obstruction of active assistance in death: (1) the patient was tormented by unbearably intense physical pain; (2) the patient's death was inevitable and imminent; (3) attempts to eliminate and alleviate the patient's physical suffering by various means had been unsuccessful; (4) the patient had expressed an intention to shorten their life.[22]

The court's judgment gradually shaped Japanese case law on euthanasia; however, Japan has yet to adopt a written law on the subject.

2.1.6 Denmark and Israel

On October 1, 1992, Denmark implemented a law regulating euthanasia for incurable patients. This has been widely accepted, with 45,000 people making wills in the first four months stating their willingness to accept euthanasia if needed.

In 1998, an Israeli court approved the first case of euthanasia when a doctor in Jerusalem injected a 49-year-old terminally ill patient with a lethal dose of anesthetic. In 1999, the German Surgical Society included the restriction and termination of treatment in certain circumstances as part of its principles of medical care. On 26 October 2000, the municipality of Zurich in Switzerland decided to allow assistance to elderly people who wish to end their lives through "euthanasia" in nursing homes, effective from January 1, 2001.[23]

2.1.7 First International Euthanasia Conference

In 1976, the first international euthanasia conference was held in Tokyo, Japan. Representatives from the United States, Japan, Australia, the Netherlands, and the United Kingdom signed the Tokyo Declaration, which equated human rights with life and death, marking a new stage in human understanding of life and death. In 1980, the International Federation of Associations for the Rights to Die was founded, furthering the process of legalizing euthanasia.[24] Foreign forms of legislation on euthanasia mainly include case law and statutory law. We can observe that worldwide, euthanasia legislation is progressing slowly. Even in countries with relevant euthanasia legislation, the main legal recognition is for passive euthanasia. Active euthanasia, however, is typically prohibited by law.[25]

[22] See Zhang [14].

[23] See Qiang [15].

[24] See Dingquan [16].

[25] See Jiawei [17].

2.2 Concept and Practices in China

In China, euthanasia is no longer an unfamiliar concept. The discussion of euthanasia in China began in the late 1970s. In 1986, Hanzhong City, Shaanxi Province, China saw its first case of euthanasia. A man named Wang Mingcheng asked Dr. Pu Liansheng to euthanize his terminally ill mother, and both Pu and Wang were then charged. On June 25, 1992, the Hanzhong Intermediate People's Court ruled in accordance with the law, upholding the original judgment, and declaring Pu and Wang as not guilty. However, this does not mean that euthanasia is legal. The verdict still considered their actions as intentional deprivation of life, but the drugs prescribed by Pu Liansheng to the patient were not the direct cause of death and the harm caused was minor. After the case was publicized by the media, it sparked a great discussion about euthanasia in China. In 2003, Wang Mingcheng, who had previously performed euthanasia on his terminally ill mother, requested euthanasia for himself due to advanced stomach cancer. However, due to a legal gap, no doctor had the courage to carry out the act. Wang Mingcheng passed away on August 3, 2003, leading people to once again discuss the issue: Should euthanasia be legalized?

Since the euthanasia incident at Hanzhong Hospital in Shaanxi Province, euthanasia has attracted widespread attention and discussion in China's medical, legal, sociological, ethical and public circles. In 1987, the Institute of Philosophy of the Chinese Academy of Social Sciences and the Beijing Medical Philosophy Research Association jointly initiated a "Discussion on the Issue of Euthanasia". National euthanasia symposiums were held in Shanghai in July 1988 and October 1994.[26] On December 24, 1987, the Institute of Philosophy of the Chinese Academy of Social Sciences, the Beijing Medical Philosophy Research Association, and the Chinese Natural Dialectics Research Association jointly invited thirty medical and philosophical figures to discuss the issue of euthanasia. On January 22, 1988, Central People's Radio broadcast an audio recording of the discussion on the program "Half an Hour at Noon". After the program was broadcast, the program group received a letter from Comrade Deng Yingchao. In the letter, Comrade Deng Yingchao said: "Today, you bravely broadcasted the issue of 'euthanasia' and sought to start a discussion. I agree with it. I think the issue of 'euthanasia' is a materialist point of view. A few years ago, I made a will stipulating that when my life is coming to an end and there is no need to prolong it with labor and drugs, I will not use salvage methods. That is my comment and I have joined your discussion as an audience."[27]

A questionnaire survey of 200 elderly people willing to euthanize conducted in Shanghai revealed a support rate of 72.56%. Similarly, a survey in Beijing showed a support rate of 79.8%. Health News reported that a survey of nearly 1,000 people in

[26] See Jiawei [17].

[27] Kemin [18].

Beijing showed an even higher support rate of 91%, with 85% believing euthanasia should be legislated.[28]

Beijing Medical University surveyed 384 medical staff and 79 nurses in 8 hospitals, and 93.6% were in favor of euthanasia. According to an online survey conducted by "Tianhu.com" on the issue of euthanasia, as of 18 pm on April 24, 2001, Nearly 32,000 people participated in the survey, and the results showed that about 74% were in favour and the remaining 26% of netizens have a negative attitude towards euthanasia.[29]

At present, in some cities such as Shanghai, some people are secretly practicing "euthanasia". The premise of this "euthanasia" is that the patient makes a request and leaves a suicide note: "I died of unbearable pain, I have nothing to do with others, I have no basis for my words, and I have a license." It is then quietly carried out by the doctor with the consent of the family. A large hospital in Shanghai investigated and counted the deaths of critically ill patients in the past three years and found that 28% of the 563 patients who died in internal, external, and gynecological departments had died because they or their family members had voluntarily requested to give up treatment. Relevant surveys conducted in some large cities show that passive euthanasia accounts for about 20% of all deaths. This form of euthanasia has become a routine practice in the medical profession and has not been opposed. In judicial practice, passive euthanasia is generally not held liable. However, active euthanasia is not allowed under the current laws of China and, if someone complains, the perpetrator will be punished by law. There have been several such cases in China in recent years, but from the point of view of the punishment imposed on the perpetrator, it is clearly different from other intentional homicides and is lenient. At the same time, there have also been cases of patients' families requesting approval from relevant authorities for euthanasia or notarizing euthanasia. In 1989, the Department of Justice of Anhui Province submitted to the Ministry of Justice the "Request for Whether the Notary Public Can Handle the Notarization Certificate of 'Euthanasia'", and the Ministry of Justice clearly stated in its reply that there is no legal provision for euthanasia in China. Therefore, notary authorities are not allowed to handle notarization matters related to euthanasia without legal basis.[30]

At the National People's Congress, deputies have repeatedly introduced bills on euthanasia legislation. In 1989, the General Office of the Standing Committee of the National People's Congress reported to the sixth meeting of the Seventh National People's Congress Standing Committee that 11 deputies had proposed the formulation of a 'euthanasia law'. After careful consideration, the Ministry of Health concluded that euthanasia is a complex medical, legal, social, and ethical issue of special significance. The regulations surrounding euthanasia are still incomplete, but we must hasten preparations for its legislation and actively promote 'death education'

---

[28] See "Legalization of Euthanasia in the Netherlands Sets Off a Chain Reaction." (2001). [Online]. Available: http://www.china.com.cn/zhuanti2005/txt/2001-04/15/content_5029142.htm. [Accessed April 18, 2010].

[29] See Wenmei and Xiaomin [19].

[30] Jiawei [20].

in the future.[31] Since 1992, the Proposal Group of the National People's Congress has received yearly proposals on legalizing euthanasia.

Professor Cui Yitai, Secretary of the Party Committee of Tianjin Medical University and "Father of Hospice in China", and Professor Hu Yamei, Honorary President of Beijing Children's Hospital and pediatric expert, are both sponsors of the euthanasia bill. They are not only working to legalize euthanasia, but also saying that they will implement it when necessary. In October 1998, the euthanasia research group led by Professor Zhu Shine of Shandong University of Traditional Chinese Medicine proposed the "Interim Regulations on Euthanasia (Draft Draft Recommendation) and its Notes". This groundbreaking proposal included many new ideas.[32]

From the examples above, we can see that although caution is necessary when discussing euthanasia, it is an unavoidable issue.

3 Definition of Euthanasia

As one scholar has pointed out, "Euthanasia is a confusing and ambiguous term, and it can be divided into different types, each with a different ethical reproachability." Therefore, it is essential to define the euthanasia discussed here and explore its basis of rights accordingly.[33]

3.1 Existing Discussions on Concept and Classification

Most scholars believe the word 'euthanasia' is derived from the Greek words 'eu' (good) and 'thanatos' (death), which originally meant a comfortable or painless death. There is still no uniform and complete definition of euthanasia in the modern sense, though Black's Law Dictionary defines it as "the act or practice of putting to death a person suffering from an incurable disease and extreme suffering, out of mercy."[34]

The Encyclopedia of China defines euthanasia as: "For patients who are irreversibly close to death and for whom modern medicine has no cure, a doctor, with the patient's voluntary consent, may take steps to reduce unbearable suffering and end their life prematurely."[35]

[31] Jiawei [20].

[32] See Zhengmao et al. [21].

[33] Sanmu and Zaixiang [22].

[34] Jiawei [23].

[35] Jiawei [23].

The American Medical Association defines euthanasia as "the act of causing the death of a person suffering from an incurable disease or illness in a relatively rapid and painless manner, out of benevolence."[36]

Scholars define euthanasia as: "The act of ending a patient's life early in a benevolent way, when a terminally ill or seriously disabled person is in a state of critical condition and dying due to extreme mental and physical suffering, at the request of themselves or their relatives and friends, out of compassion to avoid pain."[37]

Dr. Xiaomei Zhai proposed the following definition: "Euthanasia is an active medical intervention that is carried out by a doctor at the express request of a dying patient in order to relieve their unbearable suffering."[38]

Professor Ni Zhengmao and colleagues proposed that euthanasia is the death of a patient who is near the end of their life and is suffering from severe physical pain. In these cases, the doctor can end the patient's life as painlessly as possible, while following the proper legal protocols, at their own request.[39]

In academic discussions, the theoretical classification of euthanasia has always been mixed. For the needs of this discussion, two basic classifications will be provided.

3.1.1 Voluntary vs. Involuntary Euthanasia

Voluntary euthanasia, also known as benevolent assisted death, refers to a situation where both the patient and those involved have willingly agreed to end the life of the patient. In contrast, involuntary euthanasia, also known as mercy killing, is euthanasia that is carried out despite the patient not being able to express their wishes in the matter. This mainly applies to those who are incapacitated, such as infants, premature infants, brain-dead patients, unconscious patients, mentally ill people, and mentally retarded patients. It should be noted that some scholars believe that involuntary euthanasia should also be included in this classification, even though the patient did not agree to their death. The most famous example of involuntary euthanasia is the 'euthanasia plan' of Adolf Hitler. Such deaths, decided against the wishes of the person in question, can be seen as nothing more than murder.[40] In the author's opinion, the "involuntary euthanasia" mentioned does not belong to the category of euthanasia carried out to relieve the unbearable suffering of seriously ill and endangered patients. It will only add to the already complex euthanasia discussion.

36 Jiawei [23].

37 Peizhi [24].

38 Xiaomei [25].

39 Zhengmao et al. [26].

40 See Sanmu and Zaixiang [22].

3.1.2 Active vs. Passive Euthanasia

This is a classification of euthanasia based on the criterion of action or inaction. Active euthanasia refers to when doctors take measures to hasten the death of patients in order to relieve them from the unbearable suffering of a terminal illness. For example, this could involve injecting a large amount of morphine to end the life of a patient with terminal cancer. Passive euthanasia, on the other hand, refers to when doctors suspend life-sustaining measures for terminally ill and dying patients, allowing them to die on their own. An example of this would be allowing a patient in a vegetative state to succumb to pneumonia without antibiotic treatment. Active and passive euthanasia are also known as voluntary and involuntary euthanasia, respectively.

Of course, the concepts and academic classifications of euthanasia in the discussion are much more than that, and our theme is to explore whether there is a right basis that can support euthanasia. Therefore, we will only summarize some of them. From this, it is clear that none of us were consistent in our discussions. I will not delve into the divergence of opinions here, except to indicate that the euthanasia I am addressing is necessary for the basis of my further discussion. However, I will set out the elements of euthanasia discussed here, and it may be more useful to express them based on distinct elements.

3.2 Discussions in This Chapter

Given the complexity of the definition of euthanasia in many discussions, we will use the following elements as the basis for continuing our discussion: Euthanasia.

3.2.1 Who Implements Euthanasia

Euthanasia should be performed on patients who meet all four of the criteria listed below:

(1) Terminally Ill and Unsupported in Current Medical Care

The emphasis here is on being diagnosed and treated for an incurable disease in the current medical context, rather than being deemed incurable due to a medical condition, in order to avoid desecrating a part of life due to the unequal distribution of medical resources. This should serve as a standard when discussing the operational aspects of euthanasia, by qualifying the subject who made the judgment that there is no rescue in the current medical context.

(2) At the End of Life

Death is imminent, and the concept of time cannot clarify what is meant by "imminent" or "compulsed". Near-death is considered when a patient has received a death verdict from a doctor, but death may not come for up to one year. Even if the patient is in extreme pain, medical treatment should still be administered in an effort to prolong life and to provide hope. Euthanasia is not about allowing a life to choose the path of life or death, but about choosing the way to go on the road of death. Of course, one year is not a definitive criterion; instead, the patient's current condition and the progress of related medical fields must be evaluated by life sciences.

(3) Experiencing Severe Pain

What is "extreme pain"? This is a question that needs to be explained. Extreme pain here should include both physical and mental suffering, as mental suffering often derives from physical pain. Physical suffering should be considered extreme when a patient is unable to stay mentally happy despite enduring the physical pain. In this case, euthanasia may be discussed as an option. To determine whether the physical pain is extreme, medical evaluation may be used. For example, if an advanced cancer pain index in the clinical medical pain index ranking is 95, and the pain index of slashing on the palm of one's hand with a blade is only 8, we can refer to the degree of pain of the disease.[41]

(4) Possessing Full Capacity for Civil Action

This is a very important condition: we exclude euthanasia for incapacitated patients, such as infants, premature infants, brain-dead patients, unconscious patients, mentally ill people, and mentally retarded patients. These patients cannot express their wishes, so if euthanasia is used to relieve the mental suffering of others, it would be unfair to them. We cannot take it upon ourselves to send them down the road to death. Instead, we should dedicate ourselves to promoting the development of life sciences and trying to make them embrace life. Furthermore, if euthanasia is accepted for these patients, it implies that life is being measured by some value. This has been identified by scholars as being very dangerous, as it could lead to the conclusion that if a person does not have a so-called "value", they are not considered a person. This raises the questions of who judges "value" and who sets the standard for measuring it.[42] The author strongly agrees with this view, and the aforementioned problems are indeed alarming. We must not relativize the value of life, so that one may determine if the lives of others have value. Life can be valued in multiple ways, but the primary reason is that the living organism is the essence of life.[43]

3.2.2 Purpose of Euthanasia

In 1988 and 1994, China held two academic seminars on euthanasia, reaching the consensus that it is a manifestation of social civilization and progress, and the general

[41] Extracted from the clinical report of the Department of Anesthesiology at First People's Hospital Affiliated to Suzhou Medical College, accessed from http://www.0717boke.com/dispbbs.asp?boardID=29&ID=8404&page=19, on April 18th, 2010.

[42] See Ni et al. [27].

[43] Rachels [28].

trend. It is also beneficial in relieving the patient's physical and mental suffering, reducing the burden on their family in terms of economic, emotional, and artificial aspects, and allowing for fairer and more efficient distribution of social health resources.[44] When many articles discuss the issue of euthanasia, they often emphasize that euthanasia can save limited medical resources and reduce the mental, economic, emotional and artificial burden on the family. However, it should be noted that these are not the purposes of euthanasia. The sole purpose of euthanasia is to relieve the unbearable suffering of the dying patient. The other factors mentioned are only possible consequences of euthanasia and should not be taken into consideration when making decisions about euthanasia.

3.2.3 Subject of Euthanasia

The subject of euthanasia can only be a doctor, and the act of performing euthanasia should be within the scope of professional conduct. This is due to the need to take seriously this act of hastening death, and to provide a last guarantee for "incurable" conditions. Furthermore, it can offer professional conditions for fulfilling requests for a "quick and peaceful death".

3.2.4 Initiation Conditions for Euthanasia

Euthanasia can only be carried out voluntarily and at the request of the patient, and must be done when the patient is fully capacitated. In the first example given of euthanasia in China, the doctor was merely following the request of Wang Mingcheng and not of the patient themselves, and so does not qualify as true euthanasia. In a hospital in Delft, Netherlands, an 87-year-old woman was surrounded by a group of people, including two doctors, a nurse, a pastor, two children and six grandchildren. The doctor asked the patient in a calm, firm tone, "Do you wish to have an early death?" The patient nodded in reply with a smile and kissed each relative goodbye. After the farewell ceremony, the doctor gave the patient a morphine injection to make them fall asleep quickly. After 15 min, it was determined that the patient's spirit was suppressed, and the doctor injected a fatal poison, leading to the patient's passing within 10 min. This is an example of euthanasia.[45]

It can be said that the setting of each element of euthanasia helps to understand it. In this context, euthanasia generally refers to voluntary euthanasia, which includes both active and passive euthanasia. Most people consider passive euthanasia permissible, whereas the moral debate about euthanasia centers around active euthanasia. It is important to note that euthanasia does not equate to the choice between life and death; rather, it is the choice between euthanasia or a painful death that everyone may face.

---

[44] See Meng [29].

[45] Quote from: Hou [30].

3.3 *Justification of Euthanasia*

Patients do not have a self-evident right to ask for assistance with euthanasia. The current legal system does not provide a right to support euthanasia, but this does not mean that it will not exist in the future. Is there a due right to request euthanasia? If so, does this due right translate into a legal right?

People around the world are paying attention to the topic of euthanasia. The number of people in support of it is increasing, but the theoretical community is still divided in their opinion, with some for it and some against it. There is a lot of discussion surrounding the issue.[46]

Due to people's different life concepts, value orientations, and religious beliefs, there are various understandings and attitudes towards euthanasia. There are many arguments for and against this issue, but it is evident that the reasons supporting these views are not on the same level. Therefore, the author believes that we should divide the discussion into two levels. The first is the justification argument for euthanasia as a due right. The second is the question of whether due rights should be legalized, meaning, whether they should be transformed into legal rights. In this article, we will examine the arguments for and against euthanasia at both levels in an effort to clarify the discussion.

3.3.1 Arguments Supporting Euthanasia

(1) The Theory of the Dignity of Life. The Theory of the Dignity of Life states that human dignity has the highest value, and it is better to die with dignity than to live without it. Respecting the right of patients to die with dignity is consistent with principles of medicine and ethics. Euthanasia is not a harm to the patient, but rather a preservation of the dignity of life. Terminally ill patients often suffer immense pain that robs them of their dignity. Euthanasia can bring this life worse than death to an end quickly. Statistics show that more than one million people in China die each year in extreme suffering due to illness or old age. Death is inevitable for everyone, yet peaceful death is not accessible to all. This painful death greatly diminishes the dignity of life.[47]

(2) To alleviate suffering. The requirement to alleviate pain. According to this view, doctors have the responsibility to help patients alleviate their suffering, as well as their responsibility to save lives. When a person's quality of life is greatly reduced and he can only wait to die in great pain, it is actually an inhuman act for a doctor to try to prolong his life and make him suffer great pain. In a general sense, man's life is heavier than the pain he endures, but when a person's suffering makes it impossible to do anything meaningful with his dying life, leaving only the feeling that life is better than death, The responsibility of "alleviating pain"

[46] Han [31].

[47] Li [32].

can be greater than the responsibility of "saving life", only then will it be in the best interests of the patient at this time.[48]

(3) The right to self-determination of life. The right to self-determination of life is the belief that life belongs solely to the individual and that everyone has the right to decide what to do with it, including the right to end their own life.[49] Modern science and technology may be able to prolong life, but they cannot make people immortal. Medical treatments that may prevent death can also significantly extend the life process. If there is no hope of recovery and it is accompanied by great suffering, then the choice of euthanasia should be allowed and respected. In terms of civil rights, the right to life belongs to the individual, and they have the full right to decide to end their life when terminally ill and suffering from unbearable pain. As long as their actions do not harm the interests of others, we should respect the decisions made with the full knowledge of the facts, which is the respect and protection of the individual's rights. The act of euthanasia is the ultimate expression of the self-determination of the terminally ill patient's life interests.

(4) The principle of autonomy. The Principle of Autonomy in the medical field refers to a patient's right to make independent and voluntary decisions regarding their diagnosis and treatment. Medical ethics dictate that the purpose of medical personnel's obligations to the patient is to benefit them and never to cause harm. Patients, who are the ultimate goal of all medical activities, have the right to choose between various options, especially when it comes to potentially harmful medical measures. Ultimately, it is the patient who must bear the consequences of any medical activities; therefore, they have the right to decide independently whether or not to use these measures.[50] According to this principle, the patient's request for euthanasia should be respected as it is the result of a voluntary choice.

In addition, there are arguments in favor of euthanasia, such as saving medical resources and reducing the burden on third parties. However, this alone is not enough to justify it.[51,52] Compared to human life and death, saving resources is often insignificant. Whether or not to spend money on maintaining a short life is the freedom of the patient and their relatives, and society should not intervene in their judgment. These considerations are not included in the euthanasia element set up above, so they are not listed here as separate views.

---

[48] See Hou [9].

[49] Chen [33].

[50] Helun and Weixing [34].

[51] The view is that health resources should be seen as social wealth, and its distribution should prioritize equal rights, opportunities, and rules. It should be equally owned and used by members of society. However, maintenance treatments are given to those who are medically irreparable and have pain, and who voluntarily request relief. Both of these patients occupy beds, medical equipment, and a large number of medical personnel. With euthanasia legislation that has strict norms, the euthanasia of eligible patients is allowed. This can free up beds, medical equipment, and medical personnel to apply to patients who need them more, and free up more time and energy for medical staff to treat patients who are more likely to be cured.

[52] See Li [35].

Targeted objections to the above views exist. Some scholars have questioned the first view, asking "What is dignity?"[53] The death throes of terminally ill patients frequently involve both physical and psychological torture. If we accept that patients who willingly euthanize without enduring physical and mental anguish retain their dignity, does it not follow that those who are willing to suffer such torment and do not want to euthanize are not dignified? Additionally, physical and mental suffering is not exclusive to terminal illnesses; some curable or controllable diseases can also bring physical and mental anguish to patients. If these patients do not choose to euthanize, is it still considered a loss of dignity?[54]

Some scholars have proposed a second view: "If euthanasia is intended to avoid the painful experience prior to death, and if a doctor's postponement of death is an abuse of the patient, then are doctors not abusing chronically ill patients by prolonging their suffering?"[55] However, the author believes that both doubts overlook two starkly different experiences—one ending in accepting death and the other embracing life. With such a vast difference in expectations, how can the best interests of patients truly be the same in this situation? It is safe to say that there is no comparison between the two.

From the third perspective, there are various arguments to support euthanasia, such as the "right to end one's own life" or the "right to prioritize one's own interests." While these claims offer a compelling argument for euthanasia, the author does not agree with this line of reasoning. In our fourth part, two questions are posed: First, does this argument imply that all "death-seeking" behavior is acceptable? This is highly questionable, as the evaluation of suicide prevention and treatment is complex. Second, is there a risk of normalizing euthanasia as a "courting" of death? The essence of euthanasia should not be seen as "courting death."[56]

With regard to the principle of autonomy, the main consideration was the prioritization of principles. Among the many principles of medical bioethics, the general order is: the value of life is the most basic, followed by the principle of benefit and no harm, again the principle of justice and public welfare, and finally the principle of patient autonomy.[57]

In different realities, the precedence of principles may vary. The theoretical basis of the principle of autonomy is that personal rights are the most basic rights of people in modern society. Thus, patients with independent personality and normal rationality have the right to make their own medical decisions. In the case of euthanasia, however,

---

[53] Zhang [36].

[54] Han [31].

[55] Zhang [36].

[56] Currently, there is a debate in the academic community concerning the nature of euthanasia. One opinion is that its essence is "happiness", while the other is that it is "causing death without pain". Both of these views oppose the idea that euthanasia is essentially "lethal". See Zhu [37].

[57] See Huang et al. [38].

patients relinquish their right to live; this abandons the premise of autonomy. Therefore, the author agrees that medical professionals must make their own medical choices based on humanitarian respect for life, between life and autonomy.[58]

3.3.2 Main Arguments Against Euthanasia

(1) The Theory of the Sanctity of Life. It holds that human life is sacred and supreme, and thus medical and humanitarian ethics require that doctors do all that is possible to save the lives of their patients. Allowing doctors to end a patient's life would be contrary to the fundamental principles of humanitarianism and the ethical and professional responsibilities of doctors.[59]

(2) Landslide argument. The claim is that the two forces of patient autonomy and pain relief will cause us to slide down a slippery slope from physician-assisted suicide to active voluntary euthanasia, and then to involuntary/non-voluntary active euthanasia. In other words, if we allow doctors to help patients who wish to die, then soon they may end up "assisting" those who do not want to die.[60]

(3) The hindrance of development in medicine. It is based on the idea that if a disease cannot be treated, it does not contribute to the advancement of medical science and technology. Throughout history, there have been no diseases that have been deemed incurable and the purpose of studying medicine is to reveal the secrets of diseases and find ways to overcome them. If euthanasia is adopted, it will be damaging to the growth and progress of medical technology.[61]

(4) Violation of traditional ethics. Violating traditional ethics is viewed as an insurmountable moral dilemma. People cannot bear to see their loved ones suffer from illness, but it is also cruel to let them die artificially. Elderly people make up the majority of those to whom euthanasia applies. This is a serious violation of the concept of filial piety. As one scholar observed, "In Chinese tradition, ethics hold that 'the body is skinned, and the parents dare not destroy it.'" Children and family must accompany their parents or relatives to the end of any terminal illness and must not urge them to die early, for the sin of being unfilial can never be forgiven.[62]

(5) Concerns about abuse of rights. Concerns about abuse of rights arise from the view that the law allows euthanasia to be abused by people with ill-intent. Some relatives or doctors of patients may use euthanasia to achieve their own goals, causing harm to unwilling victims.[63]

(6) Possible loss of access to treatment can be concerning. Many believe that irreversible diagnoses may not necessarily be accurate and that the development

[58] He and Shi [39].

[59] See Zhang [40].

[60] Dworkin [41].

[61] Wen and Yang [42].

[62] Zhang [43].

[63] Zhu [44].

of medicine can make terminal diseases treatable. In reality, there are many cases that cannot be explained by medicine, and patients should still have the opportunity to be treated. Euthanasia can lead to three missed opportunities: the possibility of the patient improving naturally, chances of recovery from continued treatment, and the potential for new technology or approaches to give the disease a chance to be treated.[64]

Regarding the opponent's first point of view, the author believes that euthanasia is still involved. Allowing doctors to euthanize patients is not an act of "disguised killing" but rather a way to help terminally ill patients free themselves from unbearable suffering. Under strict conditions, this is in line with the professional ethics of medical personnel to alleviate the patient's suffering and respects the basic principles of humanity.

Regarding the objection to the landslide argument, here is a quote from American philosopher Frey: "Are we stagnant on the landslide? Our opposition still believes that if we legalize physician-assisted suicide, there will be horrific consequences. But why can't we prevent these consequences? We can find ways to regulate physician-assisted suicide and ensure that it is only used in cases where it is absolutely necessary."

If these arguments establish normative requirements for those who meet the prerequisites for assisted dying, then the burden of proof is on those who disregard or deny such requirements to provide evidence that the horrific 'slope effect' is likely to occur. We need evidence that the consequences of this fear are likely to happen; the mere possibility of these consequences is not sufficient evidence.[65]

The third view of the opponent is that "not treating terminally ill patients is not conducive to the development of medicine", which some consider untenable. However, from the history of medical development, it cannot be said that the development of modern medicine is mainly driven by the treatment of terminally ill patients. Furthermore, even if it were, euthanasia of dying patients cannot be equated to not treating all terminally ill patients. Generally, terminally ill patients go through three stages: diagnosis, a relatively stable period under active treatment, and a deterioration period when treatment control fails. Euthanasia is only administered to terminally ill patients in the third stage, so it does not have a major impact on the development of medicine. Additionally, doctors cannot help patients end their lives simply because medicine is the only reason.[66]

When considering the fourth point of view from the opposing side, it's easy to forget our original goal. Filial piety is for one's relatives, and the consideration of the "crime of unfilial piety" is ultimately for oneself. Additionally, "urging someone to die early" is not synonymous with euthanasia. Traditional morality can be changed, as is evident in the acceptance of divorce by the new moral and social collective consciousness. We do not evaluate whether this change is better or not; it simply

[64] Dong [45].

[65] Dworkin [46].

[66] Han [31].

exists.[67] For euthanasia, social morality must be taken into account, and the demand for traditional morality to accept it immediately is also rigorous.

Regarding the fifth point of the opponent, that is, the fear of abuse of rights, we can counter it this way: if euthanasia is allowed by law, some relatives or doctors may have maligned intentions and use it for ulterior purposes.[68] In this case, the act of ending a life is no longer helping the patient relieve suffering, but murder. We cannot ignore the potential for abuse, however, we can reduce this possibility by having strict euthanasia implementation procedures in place. The existence of any system has both advantages and disadvantages, but we should not abandon the benefits that can be obtained because of the shortcomings that may exist and that we can try to control. For example, although a plane may crash after liftoff, the convenience of travel is still preserved. The right to determine the kind of death one wants is a very serious right, and to deny it may leave the patient in great suffering and loss of dignity.[69] Thus, as long as we can control the probability of abuse through strict legislation, this issue should not be an obstacle.

The sixth view can be valid. In clinical practice, the bankruptcy of some doctors' predictions of the death of terminally ill patients and the miracle of survival of some terminally ill patients are all things that have happened. This again demonstrates that euthanasia is a conflict between two goods, and regardless of whether we practice euthanasia or not, we will pay a price that is difficult to give up.[70] Everyone will have countless choices throughout their life, and many opportunities will be lost in the process, which is the price of choice. Euthanasia is the last choice of an unfortunate patient's life, and even if this choice is later deemed wrong, we do not have the right to say anything about the patient's decision at the time.

Opponents of legalizing euthanasia come from those who believe it is immoral, those who fear its consequences, and those who believe that, while the idea may be good in theory, it is impossible to provide any effective law to that effect.[71] Of the six points of opposition, only (1) and (4) are moral arguments, while the other four are fears of adverse consequences if it were to become a legal right. When viewed from both positive and negative perspectives, there is no strong reason to justify the prohibition of euthanasia.

Dworkin said: "In most cases, when we say someone has the right to do something, we mean that if someone else interferes with that action, then the intervention is wrong. Unless, of course, there are special reasons that can be used to justify the interference."[72] There has been much debate about whether there are any legitimate grounds that could be used to restrict euthanasia, with analyses based on principles of harm, offense, paternalism, and welfare. It is generally accepted that no matter what principles are used, there is no sound justification for prohibiting euthanasia.

---

[67] Han [31].

[68] Han [31].

[69] Dworkin et al. [41].

[70] Han [31].

[71] See Rachels [47].

[72] Dworkin [48].

As such, euthanasia has the elements of freedom necessary for it to be considered a right.[73]

The author believes that, although a complete justification for euthanasia is not presented here, the analysis above shows that it has a moral basis and can be supported by due rights. Despite the fear of negative consequences of legalizing euthanasia, we are not powerless and there is not enough evidence that it would be worse than the current situation in which the law does not regulate it and allows people to act arbitrarily. This process requires patience and caution, as matters concerning human life are complex and the law is reluctant to address them. Nevertheless, the law's nature will not allow the spread of disorder, which makes it inevitable for euthanasia to be regulated and its due right to be affirmed. The author does not argue the necessity of transforming this due right into a legal right here, but the reasons presented are sufficient to make it so.

The next step is to identify a foundation in the legal framework that can be used to support euthanasia. Much of the debate will employ a methodology akin to Popper's trial and error approach.[74]

4 Basis of the Right to Euthanasia

One of the most famous jurists of the twentieth century, Oliver Wendell Holmes Jr., famously said, "There is no greater difficulty in jurisprudence than defining rights."[75] Immanuel Kant remarked on the difficulty of defining rights, saying that asking a jurist to do so is like asking a logician to define truth. In response, jurists try to avoid repeating synonyms but instead acknowledge that the law of a given country at a given time is the only thing that can be considered true, without giving a positive answer to the general question.[76]

There have been many scholarly discussions regarding the right to euthanasia, and this author will examine these discussions and offer their own opinion on the matter.

---

[73] See Cao [49].

[74] Karl Raimund Popper, a famous philosopher in the fields of British and American philosophy in the twentieth century, is renowned for his research interests in the philosophy of science, political philosophy, and metaphysics. His theoretical system is centered around the principles of falsification and trial and error.

[75] Quoted from Cheng and Wang [50].

[76] Kant [51].

4.1 Discussion on the Right to Die

Some scholars have proposed that the legal considerations of legalizing euthanasia hinge on whether individuals have the right to end their own lives. This is the key crux of determining the legality of euthanasia.[77] At around the same time, it was argued that people should have the right to die.[78,79] They all believe that from the perspective of life sciences, life refers to the entire process from the formation to the end of human life. Accordingly, the right to life should include three specific elements: the right to birth, the right to live, and the right to die near the end of life. That is to say, the right to life inherently includes the content of the right to death and is recognized as one of the most basic human rights. From a legal standpoint, rights are the confirmation and protection of interests and freedoms, and the right to death is the confirmation of the dying patient's freedom to die. However, life not only belongs to the individual but also to society. This means that when one's disposal of their own life may bring danger or damage to society, society can restrict the individual's right to dispose of their own life, and the law will become the most effective means of restriction. Therefore, an individual has the right to dispose of their own life only when it is harmless or beneficial to society, and this right to death should be respected, recognized, and protected by law. Thus, the right to death reflects the respect and protection of an individual's will by the law.

In view of the characteristics of the right to die, Liu Changqiu summarized it as follows: (1) the right to die is a very ethical right; (2) the right to die is to a large extent a natural right; (3) the right to die is a non-litigable right; (4) the application of the right to die has a very limited subject scope. They all agreed that the right to void was a reasonable way to legally regulate the right to die.[80]

Other scholars have expressed the opinion that the right to euthanasia is a right to die, and is an integral part of human rights.[81]

Matthew Father Harbinger once said, "It is now easy to sketch out a detailed plan for a thoroughly anti-life philosophical movement: from contraception to abortion to euthanasia." Once life is not seen as a divine gift from God, it is inevitable that a society will embrace death in various forms. "Therefore, embracing death in the form of euthanasia is the realization of the right to die?".[82]

Milne stated, "No one can possess a right simply because of their personal status." Does the right to die truly exist?[83]

The right to life is universally acknowledged as one of the most fundamental rights inherent in all humans. But should this right include the right to birth, life, and death? Both authors here simply made a judgment without offering any argument. When it

---

[77] Cheng [52].

[78] Liu [53].

[79] See Cheng [52], Liu [53].

[80] See Liu [54].

[81] Ni et al. [55].

[82] Dworkin [56].

[83] Milne [57].

comes to the right to birth, it is already quite confusing given that we have no control over our own birth, and that the intentional obstruction of birth is not automatically seen as an infringement or unfavorable evidence. Therefore, the judgment of this right to life is debatable.

Secondly, if the right to death is considered to be a component of the right to life, meaning it exhibits the qualities of human rights, is it in accordance with the origins and characteristics of human rights?

The concept of human rights asserts that all people have inherent and inalienable rights simply for being human. These rights apply regardless of nationality, religion, sex, social identity, occupation, wealth, property, or any other racial, cultural, or social identity. All people are born with these rights, and they remain with them throughout their lives, everywhere they go.[84]

Article 3 of the Universal Declaration of Human Rights states: "Everyone has the right to life, liberty, and security of person." This reflects the universality of human rights. The right to death is limited, however, and only applies to those who have an incurable illness and no chance of recovery, as specified by law.[85] Milne said: "A statement of human rights cannot stand up to rational debate if many of them are irrelevant to the majority of people."[86] Limiting the subject of a human right to such a narrow scope is a violation of the equal enjoyment of human rights and their universality. Furthermore, the author himself has stated that "the right to die is a natural right, innate and existing independently of the recognition and protection of the law".[87] Therefore, on what basis are the majority of people being denied rights that they already had when this natural right is elevated to a legal right?

We think that if we don't qualify this right to death, things could be more troublesome. Imagine this: Person A attempts to exercise their right to death and chooses to hang themselves. Person B then uses almost "violent" means to untie them from the rope. Has Person A's right to die been violated? Even if a "dying patient who has suffered from illness and has no real hope of cure and has seen through death" exercises their right to die, do they have an obligation to receive assistance from a doctor? If a doctor who believes in God refuses to provide the most basic help, making it impossible for the right holder to realize their rights, does this constitute an infringement? Perhaps in foresight and consideration of such issues, the designers of the right to death proposed that "the right to die is a non-litigation right" and that "legislation should not provide corresponding judicial remedies for this right when providing for the right to death". But let us be clear: when it comes to any right, it must be possible to identify what act or omission would constitute a violation of it, and if there is no such act or omission to prove it, then there is no right.[88]

[84] See Milne [58].

[85] Liu [53].

[86] See Milne [58].

[87] Liu [53].

[88] See Milne [59].

From the scope of the subject to the restrictions on actionability and the configuration of remedies, one can describe the designer of the right to death as well-intentioned. But is this unrecognizable thing still what we consider a right?

2. Human rights are the basic needs and freedoms of every human being, essential for their wellbeing and fulfillment. These rights include the right to a good material, spiritual, and social public health life. But how do we understand the right to die in relation to these rights?[89] It is important to note that the pursuit and realization of the right to die is not only impossible to meet the aspirations for a good material, spiritual, and social public health life, but even to meet the basic requirements for such a life.

Finally, the author intends to provide a path for further reflection. Starting from the formal structure of the phenomenon of rights, Beck has extracted ten elements of rights: (1) right holders, (2) obligors, (3) the relationship between right holders and obligors, (4) acts, omissions, status, or benefits owned or claimed by right holders, (5) moral grounds for claims, (6) elements constituting infringement, (7) circumstances under which infringement is condoned, (8) appropriate remedies, (9) methods of obtaining relief, and (10) who can enforce relief.[90]

We may consider these ten elements when debating the right to death. In conclusion, it is clear that the statement "people have the right to die" is inaccurate and thus, the legalization of euthanasia cannot be expected to be realized by it.

4.2 Discussion on Human Dignity

In the editorial note of a paper, I read this text: People do not come into this world of their own volition; they arrive with no dignity. This can be confirmed by observing the scene of everyone crying and making a fuss when they are born. However, once in this world, most of us refuse to leave. When it is impossible to avoid death, we must strive for dignity, as a means of claiming back the lack of dignity when we enter this world. In essence, the right to die with dignity is the final human requirement in life.[91]

In 1976, the International Symposium on Euthanasia, held in Tokyo, Japan, declared that people should be respected in their right to "die with dignity". Many scholars have argued that euthanasia is a dignified death, and some have pointed out that in this era of human rights, respecting the right of patients to decide the time and manner of death is not only in their fundamental interests, but also reflects the ultimate purpose of legislation. When the dying confront the extremely low meaning of life and the choice to preserve their dignity, the right to choose "superior death" to maintain their dignity is the true respect for life.[92] In November 1994, the Death with

---

[89] See Li [60].

[90] Yong [61].

[91] Editor's Note [62].

[92] See Yanglao.com.cn [63].

Dignity Act was passed in Oregon, United States, by a narrow majority of 51%. The bill stipulates that terminally ill patients have the right to request a humane death, as long as they have been diagnosed by two doctors and have not lived for more than 6 months.

First of all, it should be noted that although many people use the term "human dignity," it is used in different aspects, from traditional ethical and religious philosophies to legal terms. Human dignity is discussed from the perspective of human rights.

Kant believed that dignity was the result of human autonomy,[93] and his view of human nature "taking man as an end" undoubtedly had a great influence on the interpretation of the concept of human dignity. Scholars disagree on whether human dignity is a fundamental right and how it relates to it. Most scholars believe that human dignity is the main basic right in essence; the basic point of basic rights, the starting point of the basic rights system, and the value system of constitutional basic rights. This means that the human dignity clause is the norm within the norm of fundamental rights, because one of the important purposes of most fundamental rights is to protect and respect human dignity. Various types of basic rights with the function of protecting human dignity are, in fact, a separate part of human dignity. But this does not mean that human rights are a copy of human dignity; rather, human dignity is a fundamental right. Mr. Li Zhenshan positioned human dignity as one of the basic human rights after using "strong reasons".[94,95]

Secondly, Building on Mr. Li Zhenshan's view, if we accept the use of human dignity as the basis of the right to euthanasia, we must consider the conflict of human rights between the right to life and human dignity. This is the kind of conflict of rights faced by the same subject of rights under certain conditions. Such conflicts are becoming increasingly common due to the expansion of the list of human rights and the growth of their subjects. To resolve these conflicts, there are generally two outcomes: one of the parties is silenced or the parties to the conflict reach a compromise. What course do we take?[96]

In human rights practice, the resolution of conflict is a common occurrence. International human rights treaties provide clear guidance by recognizing certain non-derogable rights. For example, Article 4 of the International Covenant on Civil and Political Rights (ICCPR) states that a State may take certain measures derogating from its obligations under the Covenant when a state of public emergency threatens the life of the nation and is officially proclaimed. However, these measures must not conflict with other obligations the State has under international law, nor can they involve discrimination on the basis of race, color, sex, language, religion, or social origin. Moreover, no derogation may be made from Articles 6, 7, 8, 11, 15, 16, and 18 of the ICCPR, which safeguard the right to life, freedom from torture, slavery/forced servitude, debt imprisonment, retroactive criminal laws, equality before the law, and

---

93 Zhenshan [64].

94 See Zhenshan [65].

95 See Zhenshan [66].

96 See Xiaobing [67].

freedom of thought, conscience, and religious belief, respectively.[97] Similar provisions are found in the 1950 European Convention on Human Rights and Fundamental Freedoms. As such, these non-derogable rights are deemed absolute human rights under international law. The division of human rights into absolute and non-absolute, or the establishment of a hierarchy of rights, is one way of resolving human rights conflicts. In contrast, philosopher J.L. Mackie argued that all human rights should be equally respected and that no unilateral concessions should be made when equal rights conflict. One potential solution to this problem is the concepts of range and weight, which have been proposed to explain the academic thought of philosopher John Rawls.[98]

Is it possible to resolve the conflict between the right to life and human dignity in light of the many approaches mentioned? Let's explore if different levels can be assigned to each. Since the right to life has been granted a "non-derogable right", which is an absolute right, can human dignity be "derogated"? We have previously stated that "the human dignity clause is a norm within a norm, a fundamental right within a fundamental right"; thus, it seems too arbitrary to place it at a lower level. If the notion of absolute equality of all sovereignty is observed, the same concessions made by both parties should be closer to "hospice" or "palliative care", and in any case should not support euthanasia. To apply the concept of weight, the weight of a right is the determination of its importance, and the determination of the weight of conflicting human rights depends on the priority of the multiple obligations associated with conflicting human rights. If one considers the obligations associated with the right to life and those associated with human dignity, it does not necessarily take precedence over the obligation not to infringe upon the right to life, since the right to life is the basis of human dignity and the prerequisite for all fundamental human rights. Alternatively, we can think of it in another way: human dignity and the right to life should be rights enjoyed by everyone. If human dignity must take precedence over the right to life, then does the beggar have a reason to live? Mr. Li Zhenshan also pointed out: "We believe that it is not easy to establish the presumption that the legal interest of protecting human dignity is superior to the legal interest of the right to life, and based on the existence of life, there is an opportunity to strengthen the protection of human dignity in other ways." Therefore, it is believed that the guarantee of the right to life takes precedence over the guarantee of human dignity.[99]

From this, we can see that advocating for the realization of human dignity cannot completely suppress the right to life. In other words, while human dignity calls for euthanasia, it cannot support it.

[97] Yong [68].

[98] See Xiaobing [67].

[99] Zhenshan [69].

4.3 Discussion on the Right to Life

Life embodies the highest interests of the personality and has the right to be the fundamental right of all human beings.[100] Throughout history, three concepts have emerged to explain human understanding of their own life: the sacredness of life, the quality of life, and the value of life. The belief that human life is the most sacred and priceless was the first concept to arise. The quality of life theory emerged at the beginning of the twentieth century, where it was believed that different individuals possess different qualities, characteristics, and properties. This theory then led to the value of life, where individuals with higher quality of life require more resources to support them. Eugenics then developed, involving the self-regulation and control of production, fertility, birth control, health, life extension, and even death. The aim was to achieve a level of mastery over life and death that was no longer resigned to fate.[101,102]

Article 3 of the 1948 Universal Declaration of Human Rights states that "everyone has the right to life, liberty, and security of person", which clearly demonstrates that the right to life is the most fundamental human right of any individual. In conversations concerning euthanasia, due consideration must be given to the right to life. The debate centers around whether euthanasia preserves the right to life or undermines it. It is essential to recognize the importance of clarifying the right to life in order to resolve the issue of euthanasia.

Question 1: Is the right to life fully vested in the individual?

Some scholars have pointed out that the current misconception of the right to life is that it belongs completely to the individual, the state, and the person who has the right to life. This has been criticized for attributing the right to life entirely to the individual.

In 1992, Mrs. Rhoderigs, who had been fighting for the legalization of euthanasia after suffering from a terminal illness, asked at a hearing in Canada: "Gentlemen, who owns my life? Who is the owner of this shell of mine? Could I not approve myself to die?" This was her cry and struggle before she died.[103] So, is the right to life fully vested in the individual?.

Critics of the exclusive attribution of the right to life to the individual argue that there are two major issues with this view. Firstly, how is the individual's right to life obtained? Secondly, is it conducive to the survival and development of society that the right to life belongs exclusively to the individual? It is proposed that the life of the individual has a continuation of the life of the parents, and thus the parents should have a vested interest in the individual's life. If the right to life exclusively belongs to the individual, it deprives their relatives of any compensation from perpetrators who violate the individual's right to life.[104]

---

[100] See Dongping [70], Zhenshan [71].

[101] Zhenshan [71].

[102] See Xianghu [72].

[103] See Xixi [73].

[104] See Xianghu [72].

Regarding how the right to life is obtained, the commentator pointed out that the common view of the United States' Declaration of Independence, the French Declaration of Human and Citizens' Rights, and the Universal Declaration of Human Rights is that the right to life is a natural right enjoyed by natural persons. Of course, this view is only a value judgment, or so-called innate human rights view; not a scientific analysis or argument. It believes that the view of innate human rights cannot be used as a theoretical basis for legislation. Rights can only be granted to individuals by law and, if the right can be granted, it can also be withdrawn. It is also possible to grant individuals only the ability to use life in socially acceptable ways. Furthermore, it is possible that the right to life is not granted to individuals, and the realization of these possibilities depends on the will of the legislator.[105] Due to space constraints, I will not provide a comprehensive response to this argument, but only a brief reminder. Even if respecting the thinking of the commentator, since there are already so many international laws and domestic laws that recognize the right to life, it is of course enjoyed by the individual.

The theorist raises the question: "Should human behavior promote the survival and development of society, and is stipulating that the right to life belongs exclusively to the individual conducive to this aim?" This clearly states that people are an end, not a means.[106] Thus, stipulating that the right to life is exclusive to the individual does not necessarily promote the survival and development of society, as it is ultimately aimed at promoting human survival and development.

Regarding his statement that "if the right to life belongs entirely to the individual, when the individual's right to life is unlawfully taken away, the individual's relatives cannot receive compensation from the perpetrator of the infringement of the individual's right to life because they have no right to life," scholars have proposed numerous theories to address this, such as the theory of transformation of civil rights capacity, the theory of the perpetrator's obligation to compensate, the theory of the same personality subrogation, the theory of the right to claim between the gaps, the theory of double direct victims, and the theory of blood relations.[107]

The commentator's view that "the right to life should be shared by the individual, the state, the individual's main relatives, and those who have a direct and significant interest in life" is very imaginative. It is hard to imagine that a right with such a strong personal dependency could be controlled by so many subjects.

At the end of the day, a person's life can only be enjoyed by themselves, and the right to life belongs to the individual.

Question 2: Does the right to life include the right to control one's interests in life?

If the answer is yes, can the right holder exercise dominance and achieve suicide or euthanasia? The author disagrees with this answer. Civil law theory typically classifies rights into rights of domination and rights of claim. Rights of domination are those that allow the right holder to control interests, and the content of the right

---

105 See Xianghu [72].

106 See Xianghu [72].

107 See Bin [74].

can be realized by the will of the right holder alone. However, this division between domination and claim rights is derived from German civil law theory, which is mainly based on property rights and the clear division of property rights and claims. The law's purpose in creating personality rights is not to give natural persons the right to dominate and exploit their personal interests, but to protect basic elements such as life, health, and reputation that define a person's humanity from illegal infringement.[108] Therefore, "dominance" is not the "primary power" and fundamental characteristic of personality rights. Additionally, some commentators have argued that the act of dedication does not embody the right to control life, and that constitutions in various countries directly or indirectly recognize the sanctity and inviolability of the right to life. However, inviolability does not equate to exclusive dominance.[109] Finally, if it is determined that the subject of the right to life has the right to control the interests of life, there will be difficulty when the subject claims the right—such as being prevented from committing suicide—making it difficult to determine if infringement has occurred.

Question 3: Can the right to life be waived?

Hart argues that the essential function of legal rights is to respect the choices of rights holders. Rights express personal choice about what is considered good in life.[110] Ferguson commented, "Sometimes it is good to preserve life, while at other times it might be better to give it up."[111] The renunciation of life can often be a moral decision, so can the right to life as a fundamental human right be forsaken?

Legal rights are formally manifested as certain acts made by the subject in pursuit of their own interests. This behavior is the result of the subject's independent, free choice between "doing", "not doing", and "abandoning" the three forms of behavior. All of these are reasonable and no other subject can interfere or hinder them.[112] Of course, this freedom of choice is not unlimited, but the minimum freedom should be preserved, and restrictions should not be without boundaries.[113] Mill explained this boundary when he pointed out in his book On Liberty that any person's action is

---

[108] See Tian [75].

[109] See Bin, Z. (2003). Review of the Content and Status of the Right to Life. Jurisprudence, 3. Commentators think: First, if devotion is considered to be a rule of law, it is very difficult to identify the act of devotion. Is it determined by the civil subject's own judgment of the value of life or by the judgment of the public? According to the former view, the self-immolation of Falun Gong addicts can actually be counted as an act of devotion, which is patently ridiculous. According to the latter, does it mean that the public decides that a person should dedicate his life? If the man does not dedicate himself, will he be negatively evaluated by public opinion and even the law? It is not determined by other social norms, which would be more reasonable. Secondly, if the recognition of devotion is the exercise of the right to control life, it doesn't make sense. Domination is the ability to exercise autonomy without the consent of others, and exclude all rights to interference by others. Even if the standard of public recognition is adopted to determine that the right to life is dominant, could it be that those who prevent the senseless sacrifice of warriors on the battlefield violate the right to life of soldiers?.

[110] Wellman [76].

[111] Ferguson [77].

[112] See Jianzong [78].

[113] See Mill [79].

only responsible to society if it involves others; in the part that concerns them alone, their independence is absolute in rights.[114]

We are familiar with the state of right waiver, from creditors voluntarily relinquishing their claims to citizens giving up their right to vote and to be elected. As long as such disposition does not impede the realization of other rights, the law will positively assess it.[115]

According to basic principles of jurisprudence, basic human rights are an inherent, inalienable and non-transferable part of human rights. This is also known as the absolute right to life. It is clear that the subject of deprivation is not the subject of rights, and non-transferability is beyond reproach due to the personal nature of the right to life and there is no exclusion of renunciation. Absolute rights are the justification for an action that is equally enjoyed by all members of society.[116] According to Milne: "The right to life is an optional right that the right holder may give up, and he may voluntarily victimize others to escape for some purpose that can be achieved if he succeeds. He may also voluntarily engage in some dangerous act that no authority without any power commands him to do."[117]

A scholar once pointed out that the renunciation of fundamental rights is based on the principle that the right to life and human dignity cannot be abandoned, as this is the minimum standard required by the state's obligation to protect.[118] This "minimum standard" can be discussed in terms of the state's protection of people's basic rights and obligations. The triangular relationship between the perpetrator, the victim, and the state suggests that an appropriate balance should be sought. Some commentators have excluded self-harm from the state's obligation to protect.[119] Current legal situations, such as war, the death penalty, eugenics, abortion, and more, allow for soldiers, policemen, doctors, and judges to legally deprive others of their lives. This means that the protection of the right to life has been relativeized by national legislation. How is this reflected in the state's obligation to protect? The state's exercise of its duty to protect the right to life is the embodiment of social civilization. However, if the subject of the right to life must endure extreme factual suffering, what is the justification basis? Ancient Roman philosopher Sekar once said, "If I could choose between a painful death and a comfortable death, why wouldn't I choose the latter? When I was able to free myself from all pain, why should I endure the pain and struggle desperately?" These words demonstrate that it is not appropriate to invoke the "minimum standard" as an excuse to deny the renunciation of the right to life.

---

[114] See Mill [79].

[115] If the waiver of rights hinders the realization of the rights of other rights subjects,The law will give a negative evaluation,For example,Design of the right of avoidance in the contract preservation system.

[116] See Jianzong [80].

[117] Milne [81].

[118] See Zhenshan [82].

[119] See Zhenshan [83].

Now let's revisit the "boundaries" we just mentioned. Does the renunciation of the right to life violate that boundary? In the case of acts involving him alone, the principle of liberty asserts that every person is "sovereign over himself, of his own body and mind".[120] Thus, to anyone who is able to perform an act of suicide independently, they undoubtedly have the personal freedom to choose death. What about euthanasia? Commentators have suggested that "since a patient who voluntarily euthanizes must resort to the actions of others, his freedom to die is no longer an act that involves him 'only himself'".[121] The author believes there is an inaccurate understanding here, and it should be made clear that the renunciation of the right to life and the end of life should be considered two separate issues. Although in many cases, such as a suicide by throwing themselves into the river, these two occur simultaneously (the person renounces their right to life and their biological life ends), it cannot be assumed that they will necessarily be linked. For example, a girl in a family had a puppy that was inseparable from her. One day, the girl died, and her mother was heartbroken and unable to bear the pain of seeing the puppy every day. In desperation, the mother posted a notice outside, giving up her rights to the puppy and anyone could take it and raise it. A few days later, the puppy was nowhere to be seen. Euthanasia has a similar situation: the subject of the right to life can renounce the right, but they do not have the ability to make their biological life disappear. However, as far as the waiver of rights itself is concerned, the actions of the subject of rights "only involve the person" and should therefore have absolute independence.

We can conclude that the right to life should be waived, but only under specific conditions. This waiver should be expressed in a variety of ways, such as a suicidal person or a patient wishing to perform euthanasia. In either case, it should be a conditional renunciation, allowing for a peaceful and swift way of dying. Moreover, we should bear in mind what Hegel said: "All rights that can eventually be recovered after abandonment are non-property rights; Whatever cannot be recovered after renunciation is a property right."[122] Therefore, the subject can revoke their expression of renunciation of the right to life at any time before their life ends.

At this point, we have only demonstrated that the right to life may be conditionally renounced. However, this does not help those who have suffered so much to give up their experience of suffering. Before committing suicide in 1961, world-famous physicist Percy Williams Bridgman wrote a note: "It's not decent for society to let a person do it himself. Probably the last day I can do this myself."[123] In Part III of our discussion, we have concluded that this right exists. However, none of the above rights are what we are looking for. We must therefore believe that the development of society has brought forth a new claim, which we might as well call the right to die peacefully.

[120] See Mill [79].

[121] Yutang [84].

[122] Quoted from Guangyou [85].

[123] Holton [86].

5 Design of the Right to Die Peacefully

5.1 Nature of the Right to Die in Peace

In the eighteenth century, German jurist Christian Wolff integrated Pufendorf's system of natural law obligations with Jakob Thomasius' original theory of rights. In his book Institutiones Juris Naturae et Gentium, Wolff listed specific personality rights, including the right to life, the right to body, the right to reputation, the right to honor, and the right to value assessment in general. He also recognized rights to eat, drugs, dress, use organs, obtain, maintain, and expand pleasure, and all the rights to bodily comfort. Wolff's system of personality rights had a great influence, which was epitomized by its impact on the drafting of the Austrian Civil Code. Carl Anton von Martini, the drafter of the Austrian Civil Code, accepted Wolff's theory of personality rights almost entirely and listed his vast and complex list of specific personality rights almost step-by-step.[124] It is from these rights to bodily comfort that the right to die in peace should derive.

Although this personality right is not established in our current civil legislation, it does not prevent the protection of such rights. Property law implements the principle of statutory, meaning that without legal provisions, new types of property rights and their content cannot be confirmed. Contrary to this, the Personality Rights Law does not rely on legalism, as it recognizes and protects both personality rights provided for by law and those not provided for in the law. The law on personality rights protects all personality interests and, therefore, the absence of a clear legal framework does not lead to the neglect of certain personality rights.[125]

5.2 Characteristics of the Right to Die

5.2.1 Right to Die Peacefully

The right to die in tranquility refers to the right of natural persons to have the autonomy to choose their own deaths. This right is a part of the personality rights granted to individuals, and is an absolute right that is not affected by any external factors.[126] Natural persons have the right to die in tranquility as long as they exist in society, and cannot be deprived of this right for any reason. This right allows individuals to make decisions about their own death and to die with dignity.

[124] Liming [87].

[125] See Lixin [88].

[126] See Liming [89].

5.2.2 Contents of the Right to Die Peacefully

Tranquility

The right to maintain tranquility refers to the right of a natural person to be free from suffering and to maintain physical comfort of their own free will when they are in a state of imminent death. This right is equally enjoyed by all natural persons and is a legitimate requirement of every right holder. To alleviate suffering, measures must be taken, but there are still factors that make people suffer when they are in a near-death state. Dr. Kathleen Foley and colleagues have proposed a "classification of suffering" which includes seven shortcomings in the care of the dying patient: inadequate treatment of physical symptoms, undiagnosed depression or anxiety, unaddressed psychological grief of the patient, unaddressed psychological grief of family members, lack of recognition of the exhaustion and/or mental grief of family members, lack of effective communication skills, and lack of recognition of the exhaustion and/or mental grief of medical professionals.[127]

Control Over the Death Process

Control of the process of death refers to the right of individuals to exert influence over their own passing. We all have the power to control our lives, even when serious illness strikes. Though we cannot escape death, we can decide how we face it. This right to maintain control is especially important when it comes to avoiding pain and suffering. The more autonomy a person has to make choices in life, the more they should be empowered to extend that autonomy to the end of their lives.[128]

Right to Confidentiality

The right to confidentiality refers to an individual's right to demand the privacy of the course of their death and the confidentiality of any relevant medical information. This protection ensures that the person's interests are more favorably secured during the process of death. There are areas where protection overlaps with privacy. The only exception to granting the right to confidentiality is if the damage done to the individual, others, or society by continuing to protect this right outweighs the loss of rights suffered by giving it up.

5.2.3 The Object of the Right to Die Peacefully

The right to die peacefully is a personal interest, not bringing material benefits or social interests. Medicine is constantly advancing, allowing us to save lives, but sometimes our ignorance in the life sciences leads to cruelty and despair. Death is the ultimate destination, and every natural person with civil capacity has the right to claim a peaceful death. Euthanasia is one way to adjust the death process, eliminate

[127] Chermyl et al. [90].

[128] See Dworkin et al. [91].

the pain of death, optimize the state of death, and achieve a peaceful death. Thus, it is a way for people to realize their right to die peacefully.

5.3 Exercising the Right to Die Peacefully

The right to die peacefully is a personality right and an absolute right that can be realized by any right holder without the action of any other obligated subjects. When the realization of this right is unsatisfactory, the right holder can claim the right to a peaceful death. This right to a claim is a right to a claim for personality rights, which refers to the right of a civil subject to request a perpetrator or a court to perform a certain act or not perform a certain act when their satisfactory state of personality rights is hindered or threatened. This could be to restore the satisfactory state of their personality rights or prevent obstruction.[129] The right to claim a hospice claim, or euthanasia, is only applicable to those who meet four conditions: they must be terminally ill, have no possibility of help in the current medical context, be "on the verge of death" and "enduring extreme pain". As long as these conditions are met, anyone can claim the right to die peacefully.

It can be clarified that although every natural person has the right to die in tranquility and can exercise the right to die at peace without restrictions, not everyone can be the object of euthanasia, and only the subject of the right to die at peace can apply for euthanasia. That is, the implementation of the euthanasia application is the right holder claiming the right to die in peace. Subjects who meet the four conditions should apply for euthanasia in accordance with the prescribed procedure, which completes the "conditional renunciation of the right to life". The significance of this is that the right to life is the highest ranking right among personality rights, and any other personality right cannot impair the right to life, including the right to die peacefully. In the application process of euthanasia, the right to life is conditionally waived by the subject, and there will be no conflict of rights. The applicant is claiming a personality right at the same time, and is obliged to realize its claim to help achieve tranquility in the process of death.

References

1. Obi, M. C. (2016). A critical appraisal of euthanasia under Nigerian laws. *Nnamdi Azikiwe University Journal of International Law and Jurisprudence, 5*, 75–88, 2276–7371. http://www.ajol.info/index.php/naujilj/article/view/136296
2. Shi, H. S. (2004). *The confusion of life: An introduction to clinical bioethics* (p. 365). Southeast University Press.
3. Yuxia, L. (1999). Unavoidable Topic: Euthanasia. Available at: http://news.sina.com.cn/society/1999-11-26/35481.html. Accessed April 18, 2010.

[129] See Yang [92].

4. Ni, Z., Li, H., & Yang, T. (2005). *Euthanasia law research* (p. 61). Law Press.
5. Zhang, C. (2010) Legislative Attitudes and Judicial Practices of Death Assistance Abroad. Available at http://www.chinacourt.org/public/detail.php?id=244480. Accessed April 18, 2010.
6. Ni, Z., Li, H., & Yang, T. (2005). *Euthanasia law research* (p. 62). Law Press.
7. Ni, Z., Li, H., & Yang, T. (2005). *Euthanasia law research.* Beijing: Law Press, p. 62; Zhang, C. (2010). Legislative attitudes and judicial practice of death assistance abroad. Available at http://www.chinacourt.org/public/detail.php?id=244480. Accessed April 18, 2010.
8. Xu, X. (2003). *The Netherlands: Euthanasia in accordance with the law.* Southern Weekend, July 17.
9. Hou, J. (2005). Review and analysis of Euthanasia: Rights and interests of the elderly. *Population of the Northwest*, (1).
10. Zhang, C. (2010). *Legislative attitudes and judicial practices on assisted dying abroad.* Available at http://www.chinacourt.org/public/detail.php?id=244480. Accessed April 18, 2010.
11. Zhang, C. (2010). *Legislative attitudes and judicial practice of death assistance abroad.* Available at http://www.chinacourt.org/public/detail.php?id=244480. Accessed April 18, 2010.
12. Ni, Z., Li, H., & Yang, T. (2005). *Euthanasia law research* (pp. 61–62). Law Press.
13. Ni, Z., Li, H., & Yang, T. (2005). *Euthanasia law research* (p. 59). Law Press.
14. Zhang, C. (n.d.). *Legislative attitudes and judicial practices of death assistance abroad.* Available at: http://www.chinacourt.org/public/detail.php?id=244480. Accessed April 18, 2010.
15. Qiang, W. (2000). Switzerland Stumbles to Relax 'Euthanasia'. People.com.cn. Available at: http://www.people.com.cn/GB/channel2/702/20001102/297385.html. Accessed April 18, 2010: Jiawei, H. (2005). Review and review of euthanasia—on the rights and interests of the elderly. *Population of the Northwest*, (1).
16. Dingquan, H. (2007). *Medical law and bioethics* (p. 108). Law Press.
17. Jiawei, H. (2005). Review and analysis of Euthanasia: Rights and interests of the elderly. *Population of the Northwest*, (1).
18. Kemin, Y. (2004). Research on Euthanasia. Master's Thesis, China University of Political Science and Law.
19. Wenmei, C., & Xiaomin, Q. (2005). *Bioethics and new health* (p. 226). Jinan Press.
20. Jiawei, H. (2005). Review and review of euthanasia—on the rights and interests of the elderly. *Population of the Northwest*, (1).
21. Zhengmao, N., Hui, L., & Tongdan, Y. (2005). *Euthanasia Law research* (p. 66). Law Press.
22. Sanmu, L., & Zaixiang, W. (2004). Discussion on some controversial issues concerning Euthanasia. *Law Review*, 6.
23. Jiawei, H. (2005). Review and review of Euthanasia: On the rights and interests of the elderly. *Population of the Northwest*, (1).
24. Peizhi, Z. (2002). Thoughts on Euthanasia and Its Legislation. *Science·Economy·Society*, (1).
25. Xiaomei, Z. (2000). The conceptual issue of Euthanasia. *Dialectics of Nature Newsletter*, 2000(3).
26. Zhengmao, N., Hui, L., & Tongdan, Y. (2005). *Euthanasia Law research* (p. 39). Law Press.
27. Ni, Z., Li, H., & Yang, T. (2005). *Euthanasia Law research* (p. 35). Law Press.
28. Rachels, J. (1975). Active and passive Euthanasia. *The New England Journal of Medicine, 292*, 78–80.
29. Meng, X. Euthanasia from the Right to Life. Retrieved April 18, 2010, from http://www.law-lib.com/lw/lw_view.asp?no=1473.
30. Hou, J. (2005). Review and review of Euthanasia: On the rights and interests of the elderly. *Population of the Northwest*, (1).
31. Han, D. (2005). On the Euthanasia controversy. *Hunan Social Sciences*, (4).
32. Li, M. (2000). Euthanasia: The dignity of life. *Journal of Southwest University for Nationalities* (Philosophy and Social Sciences Edition), 2000(10).
33. Chen, S. (2007). Euthanasia and the protection of the right to life. *Journal of Nanjing Medical University* (Social Science Edition), 2007(2).

34. Helun, S., & Weixing. (2004). *The confusion of life: An introduction to clinical Bioethics.* Nanjing: Southeast University Press, p. 161.
35. Li, H. (2006). The collision of love and law: A study on the naturalness and reality of Euthanasia in China. *Journal of Shanghai University* (Social Science Edition), 2006(5).
36. Zhang, Y. (2001). Do We Have the Right to Die? Jurisprudence on the Euthanasia Controversy. *Jurisprudence*, (5).
37. Zhu, H. (2005). The Nature of Euthanasia: 'Death' or 'Happiness'? *Journal of Ningbo University*, 2005(3).
38. Huang, G., He, L., & Shi, W. (1997). *Biomedical Ethics*. Zhejiang Education Press, p. 15.
39. He, L., & Shi, W. (2004). *The confusion of life: An introduction to clinical bioethics*. Southeast University Press, p. 168.
40. Zhang, Y. (2001). Do we have the right to die: Jurisprudence on the Euthanasia Controversy. *Jurisprudence*, (5).
41. Dworkin, G., Frey, R. G., & Bok, S. (1998). *Euthanasia and physician-assisted suicide-for and against*. Cambridge University Press, pp. 25–75.
42. Wen, D., & Yang, H. (2005). Euthanasia should be discussed with caution. *Modern Hospital Management*, (2).
43. Zhang, Y. (2001). Do We Have the Right to Die? Jurisprudence on the Euthanasia Controversy. *Jurisprudence*, 5.
44. Zhu, H. (2005). Should Euthanasia Be Legalized? *Chinese Medical Ethics*, 5.
45. Dong, S., & Wang, Y. (2002). An Ethical Analysis of Euthanasia. *PLA Nursing Journal*, 6.
46. Dworkin, G., Frey, R.G., & Bok, S. (1998). *Euthanasia and physician-assisted suicide-for and against*. Cambridge University Press, pp. 25–75.
47. Rachels, J. (1975). Active and passive Euthanasia. *The New England Journal of Medicine, 292*, 195–248.
48. Dworkin, R. (1977). *Taking rights seriously*. Harvard University Press, pp. 220–265.
49. Cao, G. (2005). *What kind of right is Euthanasia?* Ethical Studies, 2005(1).
50. Cheng, L., & Wang, R. (2002). *Rights and remedies*. Shandong People's Publishing House, Preface: p. 2.
51. Immanuel Kant, Metaphysical Elements of Justice (2nd ed.), trans. John Ladd, Hackett Publishing Co., Inc., 1999, p. 39.
52. Cheng, Z. (2003). The right to death and the legislative issues of Euthanasia in China. *Clinical Misdiagnosis and Mistreatment*, (4).
53. Liu, C. (2003). On the characteristics of the right to death and the legislative design of the right to death in China. *Journal of Tongji University (Social Science Edition)*, (3).
54. Cheng, Z. (2003). The right to death and the legislative issues of Euthanasia in China. *Clinical Misdiagnosis and Mistreatment*, (4); Liu, C. (2003). On the characteristics of the right to death and the legislative design of the right to death in China. *Journal of Tongji University (Social Science Edition)*, (3).
55. Ni, Z., Li, H., & Yang, T. (2005). *Euthanasia Law research* (pp. 24–25). Law Press.
56. Dworkin, R. (1996). *Freedom's law: The moral reading of the American constitution* (pp. 191–245). Harvard University Press.
57. Milne, A. J. M. (2016). *Human rights and human diversity: An essay in the philosophy of human rights* (pp. 88–142). Palgrave Macmillan.
58. Milne, A. J. M. (2016). *Human rights and human diversity: An essay in the philosophy of human rights* (pp. 1–10). Palgrave Macmillan.
59. Milne, A. J. M. (2016). *Human rights and human diversity: An essay in the philosophy of human rights* (pp. 87–130). Palgrave Macmillan.
60. Li, B. (2004). On the origin of human rights. *Political and Legal Forum*, (2).
61. Yong, X. (2004). *Chinese philosophy of civil rights* (p. 315). Triptych Bookstore.
62. Editor's Note. (2004). The Right to Humane Death—Euthanasia Campaign Worldwide. Studies in Comparative Law, 3.
63. Yanglao.com.cn. (2009, May 15). Euthanasia Pilot Expected to Solve Legislative Dilemma. [Online]. Available: http://www.yanglao.com.cn/news/zonghe/yp/2009/0515/326399.html. Accessed: April 18, 2010.

64. Zhenshan, L. (2001). *Human dignity and human rights protection* (p. 4). Yuanzhao Publishing Ltd.
65. Zhenshan, L. (2001). *Human dignity and human rights protection* (p. 8). Yuanzhao Publishing Ltd.
66. Zhenshan, L. (2001). *Human dignity and human rights protection* (p. 9). Yuanzhao Publishing Ltd.
67. Xiaobing, X. (2005). Human rights conflict and the coordinated realization of human rights. *Jurisprudence,* (11).
68. Yong, X. (2004). Basic problems of the philosophy of rights. *Journal of Legal Studies*, (3).
69. Zhenshan, L. (2001). *Human dignity and human rights protection* (p. 139). Yuanzhao Publishing Ltd.
70. Dongping, C. (1980). Planning to die: Dying in the pursuit of happiness. Commercial Press, Taipei, pp. 16–18; Cited in: Zhenshan, L. (2001). Human Dignity and Human Rights Protection. Yuanzhao Publishing Ltd, Taipei, p. 30.
71. Zhenshan, L. (2001). *Human dignity and human rights protection* (p. 30). Yuanzhao Publishing Ltd.
72. Xianghu, M. Euthanasia from the Right to Life. Available at: http://www.law-lib.com/lw/lw_view.asp?no=1473. Accessed April 18, 2010.
73. Xixi, P. (1995). Towards death: Who has the final say? *Social Work*, (4).
74. Bin, Z. (2003). Review of the content and status of the right to life. *Jurisprudence*, 3.
75. Tian, Y. (2004). Legal discussion on the specific personality rights of natural persons. *Journal of Henan Provincial Political and Legal Management Cadre College*, 3.
76. Wellman, C. (2002). The concept of fetal rights. *Law and Philosophy, 21*(1), 65–93.
77. Ferguson, A. (2010). Principles of moral and political science. Gale ECCO, pp.82–132.
78. Jianzong, Y. (2004). *Jurisprudence: General legal science* (p. 123). China University of Political Science and Law Press.
79. Mill, J.S. (2017). On liberty. CreateSpace Independent Publishing Platform, pp.8–22.
80. Jianzong, Y. (2004). *Jurisprudence: General legal science* (p. 124). China University of Political Science and Law Press.
81. Milne, A. J. M. (2016). *Human rights and human diversity: An essay in the philosophy of human rights* (pp. 110–172). Palgrave Macmillan.
82. Zhenshan, L. (2001). *Human dignity and human rights protection* (p. 143). Yuanzhao Publishing Ltd.
83. Zhenshan, L. (2001). *Human dignity and human rights protection* (p. 153). Yuanzhao Publishing Ltd.
84. Yutang, Z. (2001). Do we have the right to die? Jurisprudence on the Euthanasia Controversy. *Jurisprudence,* (5).
85. Quoted from Guangyou, H. (2010). Waiver of civil rights from the perspective of contract cases. Available at: http://www.btophr.com/s_mfile/3660.shtml.
86. Holton, G. (1962). Percy Williaams Bridgman. *Bulletin of Atomic Scientists, 18*, 22–23.
87. Liming, W. (2006). On the new development of personality rights. *Law and Business Studies*, (5).
88. Lixin, Y. (2005). *Monographs on personality rights law* (p. 8). Higher Education Press.
89. Liming, W. (Ed.). (1994). *New theory of personality rights law* (p. 11). Jilin People's Publishing House.
90. Chermyl, N. I., Coyle, N., & Foley, K. M. (1994). Suffering in the advanced cancer patient: A definition and taxonomy. *Journal of Palliative Care, 10*(2), 57–67.
91. Dworkin, G., Frey, R. G., & Bok, S. (1998). *Euthanasia and physician-assisted suicide-for and against* (pp. 50–95). Cambridge University Press.
92. Yang, L. (2005). *Monographs on personality rights law* (p. 71). Higher Education Press.

Chapter 9
The Right to an Adequate Standard of Living

Zhihang Zheng

1 Introduction

The right to an adequate standard of living is an internationally recognized human right, appearing in the form of welfare rights as early as the Constitution of the Weimar Republic. This right is enshrined in several international legal instruments, most prominently in Article 25 of the Universal Declaration of Human Rights, Article 11 of the International Covenant on Economic, Social and Cultural Rights, and Article 27 of the Convention on the Rights of the Child. Generally, the right to an adequate standard of living includes the right to freedom from want, the right to housing, the right to health, the right to care, and other related rights.[1] This right is directly linked to the daily lives of all people.

At the heart of the right to an adequate standard of living lies the eradication of poverty by imposing certain obligations on governments. As far as the causes of poverty are concerned, they include at least two aspects: on the one hand, due to a scarcity of natural resources; on the other, due to our view of poverty as a quantifiable lack of natural resources. Governments are thus only passively reducing poverty, rather than actively eliminating it. Therefore, if poverty is seen as a violation of human rights, it will undoubtedly increase the government's responsibility, changing their response to poverty from passive to positive.[2] This basic position is mainly reflected in the following aspects:

First, the right to an adequate standard of living addresses the satisfaction of people's most basic daily needs. It entails providing human food, clothing, and

---

[1] See Eide [1].

[2] The question of what causes poverty is not the main focus of this chapter. The author is simply referencing Pierre Sané's conclusion. However, the author disagrees with Sané's view that the government's inactivity is the primary cause of poverty. Specific discussions can be seen in: Sané [2].

Z. Zheng (✉)
Shandong University Law School, Jinan, China

J. Yao (ed.), *The Legal Issues of the Emerging Rights*,
https://doi.org/10.1007/978-981-97-0499-6_9

shelter, which are the essential elements for human survival. As Mr. Liu Hainian stated, "Since nobody is immortal and all humans need food, clothing, and shelter for survival, these are the basic needs and basic human rights of human beings."[3]

Second, the right to an adequate standard of living is concerned with the support and protection of vulnerable groups and is intended to promote social justice and equality. It emphasizes the progressive obligation of states to fulfill this right to the best of their resources and capacity.[4] Thus, the right to an adequate life can achieve substantive equality for a larger number of people, as it places an emphasis on government responsibility. In this sense, the right to an adequate standard of living itself serves as a regulator of interests in society, which not only guarantees the basic material needs of humans as biological beings, but also, more importantly, makes resources secondary in society, thereby embodying the essential attribute of humans as a "class existence."

Finally, the author would like to emphasize that the right to an adequate standard of living is an essential part of the International Covenant on Economic, Social and Cultural Rights. The preamble of the Covenant states: "In accordance with the Universal Declaration of Human Rights, only if conditions are created that enable human beings to enjoy their economic, social, and cultural rights, as well as their civil and political rights, can the ideal of free human beings enjoying freedom from fear and want be realized."[5] Here, the "want" refers to the content of people's standard of living[6]; thus, the right to an adequate standard of living is the foundation and cornerstone of the International Covenant on Economic, Social and Cultural Rights.

2 Debate on the Right to an Adequate Standard of Living as a Fundamental Human Right

International legal instruments, such as the Universal Declaration of Human Rights, the International Covenant on Economic, Social and Cultural Rights, and the Convention on the Rights of the Child, state that the right to an adequate standard of living is a fundamental human right. Our analysis and research will focus on the legal practice in South Africa. South Africa has made significant efforts to uphold this right, as it has included the basic elements of an adequate standard of living, including the right to housing and health, in its Constitution. These elements are monitored by the Human Rights Commission. The country has also established several integrated policies, such as integrated nutrition plans and rural development strategies, to address this right.[7] Additionally, South African courts have provided guidance

---

[3] Liu [3].

[4] See Zhang [4].

[5] The Institute of Law, Chinese Academy of Social Sciences (ed.) [5].

[6] See Liu [6].

[7] See the right to an adequate and adequate standard of living: Results of six case studies", available at: http://www.fao.org/DOCREP/MEETING/008/J2475C.HTM, 2009-02-03.

on how to enforce the right to an adequate standard of living through cases such as Subramoni v. Minister of Health, Government of the Republic of South Africa et al. v. Grootbum, and Therapeutic Action Campaign v. Ministry of Health. However, there is still a debate in South Africa on whether the right to an adequate standard of living should be considered a fundamental human right. This discussion will be the main focus of the author, who will also provide brief comments on it.

2.1 Right to an Adequate Standard of Living as a Justification for Fundamental Human Rights

Despite the South African government's efforts to uphold the right to an adequate standard of living, there is ongoing debate over whether this should be considered a fundamental human right. Those who support this viewpoint argue for the importance of the right in relation to poverty alleviation, access to food, the fight against hunger and its role in promoting democracy. They also highlight the relationship between the right to an adequate standard of living and other human rights, as well as its significance in international human rights law.

2.1.1 Right to an Adequate Standard of Living and the Fight Against Poverty

In South Africa, hunger has been a persistent problem for the government, and addressing it is seen as an important aspect of promoting social progress. However, there are differing opinions on the root cause of hunger in the country. Some believe it is due to a lack of resources and materials, while others believe that it is caused by government policies and measures. At a national level, South Africa has achieved food security, producing enough food to meet the needs of its growing population and exporting surplus food. Despite this, a significant number of people in South Africa are still food insecure and suffer from hunger, malnutrition, and undernourishment.[8] This suggests that poverty in South Africa is a structural issue and cannot be resolved simply through the availability of resources and materials.

Structural poverty refers to the idea that poverty is not just caused by a shortage of natural resources, but also by societal structures and the lack of government action in certain areas. From this perspective, poverty has two main causes: firstly, a scarcity of natural resources, and secondly, the view that poverty is only a quantitative lack of resources, leading to passive government measures rather than proactive solutions.

---

[8] See the right to an adequate and adequate standard of living: Results of six case studies", available at: http://www.fao.org/DOCREP/MEETING/008/J2475C.HTM, 2009-02-03.

If poverty is viewed as a violation of human rights, it places a higher level of responsibility on the government to address the issue. This shift in perception can lead to a change in government response, from a passive approach to a proactive one.[9]

Indeed, the recognition of the right to an adequate standard of living as a fundamental human right has important implications for the government's responsibility to address poverty and promote social justice. The historical legacy of apartheid in South Africa has contributed to ongoing economic and social inequalities that continue to affect large portions of the population, particularly in terms of access to land and other resources.[10] The right to an adequate standard of living provides a framework for holding the government accountable for addressing these inequalities and ensuring that all individuals have access to the resources necessary for a dignified life. The South African court's decision in the Government of the Republic of South Africa, et al. v. Grootboom case, which held that the government has positive obligations to take action to meet the basic living needs of its citizens, is an example of how the recognition of the right to an adequate standard of living can influence government behavior. Without this recognition, the government's efforts to address poverty and ensure food security may lack legal standing, making it more difficult to hold the government accountable for ensuring the well-being of its citizens.

2.1.2 Right to an Adequate Standard of Living and the Availability of Food

Amartya Sen's views on the right to an adequate standard of living and food availability have had a significant impact on South Africa. He argues that there is a difference between the right to an adequate standard of living, which includes access to food, and the actual availability of food. The right to an adequate standard of living is a fundamental human right, and the availability of food is just one aspect of it. While calculating the availability of food in a country can give us an idea of the food situation, it does not guarantee that everyone in the country is free from hunger. Sen's views emphasize the importance of addressing the root causes of poverty, rather than just providing food to those who are hungry. This includes addressing social and economic inequalities and ensuring that everyone has access to resources and opportunities. In South Africa, where structural poverty remains a significant issue, Sen's views highlight the need for the government to take active measures to address the root causes of poverty, rather than relying on passive measures such as food distribution.[11]

The work of Amartya Sen has been highly influential in South Africa and the idea of the right to an adequate standard of living as a fundamental human right is central to his approach. Sen emphasizes the importance of focusing on individuals and families, as they are the ultimate beneficiaries of rights. This perspective is particularly relevant

---

[9] See Sané [2].

[10] Chen [7].

[11] See Friedmann et al. [8].

in the context of food security, as it requires individuals to have access to available food or the means to produce it. In South Africa, the landmark case of Government et al. v. Grootboom has had significant implications for the realization of the right to an adequate standard of living, including the right to food security.[12] The Court held that the government's focus on medium- and long-term housing needs was not enough, and that it needed to provide short-term relief measures for those in extreme need. This ruling has provided important guidance for the implementation of the right to an adequate standard of living in South Africa and has helped to shift the focus from a purely charity-based approach to a more rights-based approach.[13]

In the 2004 case of Mashava v the President of the Republic of South Africa, Mashava, a disabled person, applied to the local government for a disability grant but did not receive support. As a result, Mashava filed a lawsuit with the South African Constitutional Court. The court recognized the High Court's decision to invalidate the central government's decision to delegate the implementation of the Social Assistance Bill to local governments. Furthermore, the Constitutional Court held that since Mashava could not earn income through employment, disability benefits were the only way he could obtain food. The court ruled that the state must effectively fulfill its obligation to respect the right to an adequate standard of living by eliminating obstacles to its realization.[14] As a result, South African scholars generally agree that the right to an adequate standard of living, as a fundamental human right, provides a legal basis for food availability. This recognition elevates food availability from a moral requirement to a legal claim, providing a solid theoretical foundation for judicial proceedings, particularly constitutional proceedings, on this matter.

2.1.3 Hunger, Democracy and Rights

The relationship between hunger and democracy is a new area of research on hunger in recent years. In this regard, Amartya Sen's research is representative. He believed that famine was unlikely in a free and democratic society, because public opinion ensured that the government acted accordingly to the crisis.[15] On this basis, he argues that "all famine in the modern world can indeed be prevented by human action; Many countries—even some very poor—work tirelessly to prevent them; When people die of hunger in large numbers, there is almost no exception some kind of major social failure."[16]

He argues that democracy can help avoid hunger because governments must have people's support and face public criticism, creating a strong incentive to take a range

[12] See Brand and Heyns [9].

[13] See *Government of the Republic of South Africa and Others v Grootboom. (2001). 2001(1)HIS 46(CC).*

[14] See *Mashava v the President of the Republic of South Africa*, 2004 12 BCLR1243(CC).

[15] See *Michael Massing, Does Democracy Avert Famine*? at http://www.nytimes.com/2003/03/01/arts/does-democracy-avert-famine.html, 2009-04-06.

[16] Friedmann et al. [8].

of measures to prevent hunger and other disasters. However, he also stresses that "the belief that democracy can solve the problem of hunger is a misunderstanding of the relationship between democracy and hunger."[17] A democratic society is a necessary condition, but not a sufficient one for solving the problem of hunger.

Some scholars in South Africa agree with Amartya Sen's view that the media in their country has not effectively played its role in monitoring the government and society to urge the necessary corrections to certain policies regarding food security. However, democracy in South Africa has often been driven by racism, resulting in terrible outcomes. For instance, the country's existing land system is the product of democracy being usurped by racists, which directly affects the realization of the right to an adequate standard of living for the poor. Therefore, they believe that some united guilds and political parties are needed to speak for the poor. The most notable feature of a genuinely democratic society is its ability to elevate a series of the most basic needs of human beings to legal rights, thereby preventing democracy from depriving minorities of their rights. Based on this recognition, South Africa allows the public to actively participate in government action on food through a hearing process aimed at eradicating hunger and famine.[18] For example, the South African Parliament held public hearings on food security and requested the government to submit a Food Security Bill. In their view, elevating the need for food as a basic human right is necessary to ensure a democratic social environment. They aim to establish a virtuous relationship between democracy and the eradication of hunger through the bridge of rights discourse.

2.1.4 Relationship Between the Right to an Adequate Standard of Living and Other Human Rights

It has been argued that people's fundamental right to food cannot be viewed in isolation. Its enjoyment and realization depend on the enjoyment and realization of other rights. The right to education and the right to healthcare are particularly important to the right to food. The importance of education lies not only in its ability to provide opportunities for earning a living but also in the fact that it teaches people about nutrition and the value of different foods. The right to food is a prerequisite for the realization of other rights, such as the right to education. The right to health and the right to food are also interdependent, and the level of human health determines the degree of nutritional needs of people, and nutritional status is an important determinant of health.[19] At the same time, the right to an adequate standard of living is closely linked to civil and political rights. The right to equality and the prohibition of unfair discrimination are considered important aspects of the guarantee of the

[17] *Michael Massing, Does Democracy Avert Famine*? at http://www.nytimes.com/2003/03/01/arts/does-democracy-avert-famine.html, 2009-04-06.

[18] See the right to an adequate and adequate standard of living: Results of six case studies", available at: http://www.fao.org/DOCREP/MEETING/008/J2475C.HTM, 2009-02-03.

[19] See Brand and Heyns [10].

right to an adequate standard of living. Equality and non-discrimination in food are themselves concrete manifestations of the right to equality.

2.1.5 Right to an Adequate Standard of Living as a Fundamental Right Under International Human Rights Law

During the drafting of South Africa's new constitution, the drafters believed that the provisions of international human rights law on economic and social rights should greatly guide the formulation of the Bill of Rights in South Africa. They required that the South African constitution include "universally accepted fundamental rights" because the relevant specific human rights provisions of international human rights law are historically progressive. The drafters consulted the interpretation of "universally accepted fundamental rights" in international human rights law, which includes not only civil and political rights, but also economic, social, and cultural rights. Moreover, the United Nations International Covenant on Economic, Social and Cultural Rights is integrated with the International Covenant on Civil and Political Rights, and since the set of rights set forth in the International Covenant on Civil and Political Rights is fundamental in domestic law, the International Covenant on Economic, Social, and Cultural Rights should also be recognized in domestic law. The Committee of Constitutional Drafting Experts, therefore, recommended that the South African Constitution adopt the terminology of rights in the International Covenant on Economic, Social, and Cultural Rights.[20]

2.2 Examining the Controversy Surrounding the Right to an Adequate Standard of Living as a Fundamental Human Right and Its Implications

The development of the right to an adequate standard of living in South Africa has faced resistance from various sides, making it a bumpy journey. For instance, the South African Parliament held hearings on food security and requested the government to submit a Food Security Bill. However, by 2004, the bill was not yet submitted. While there have been some cases concerning the right to an adequate standard of living, they are not significant, particularly regarding human rights implications. Additionally, the courts do not protect the right to an adequate standard of living to the same extent as the right to housing. The primary obstacle to the development of the right to an adequate standard of living is doubts about it being a fundamental human right.

[20] See Fitzpatrick and Slye [11].

2.2.1 Negative Nature of Fundamental Human Rights

"No remedy, no right." This is one of the biggest differences between moral rights and legal rights. Legal rights can often obtain remedies through judicial channels, while moral rights are often not justiciable, so moral rights have more of a "declaratory significance." Legal scholars also tend to divide rights into positive rights and negative rights according to whether they are justiciable. The so-called positive rights refer to the rights that require certain actions by the government to be realized by individuals, while the so-called negative rights emphasize the right that can be realized by the government without interfering with the actions of individuals. According to Stephen Holmes, Keith Smith, and Cass Sunstein, "Negative rights prohibit government and keep it out; positive rights require and invite governments warmly. The former requires public officials to stagger, while the latter requires public officials to act vigorously. Negative rights are characterized by the protection of freedoms, while positive rights are characterized by the promotion of equality. The former carves out a private sphere, while the latter redistributes taxes. The former is deprivation and hindrance, the latter charity and devotion."[21] The concept of basic human rights derives from the concept of natural rights, which emphasizes the confrontation between the individual and the state, meaning that the state should not interfere in the private domain of the individual. If it does, individuals have the right to ask the court to rule in their favor, thus limiting the expansion of government.

As a fundamental human right, the right to an adequate standard of living implies that it is justiciable. Marius Pieterse argues that social rights are a sensitive issue and should be resolved through political means, rather than through law. This is because if social rights are fundamental human rights, positive action by the government is required to guarantee the realization of this right. Such action inevitably involves the decentralization of powers and democracy. If social rights are guaranteed through the judiciary, it may have anti-democratic tendencies.[22] This view of Pieterse has also been used to challenge the argument that the right to an adequate standard of living is a fundamental human right. Pieterse's views are also reflected in specific judicial practices. In the case of Minister of Health v. Treatment Action Campaign, the court held that the purpose of the review was not to require the government to "directly rearrange the budget". This is because it may violate the principle of separation of powers and create a direct conflict with the government department.[23] For this reason, South Africa imposes an obligation on the State with respect to the right to an adequate standard of living, which is not an immediate obligation, but embodies a 'principle of non-retrogression', namely, 'Governments must not adopt regression policies that lead to a deterioration in access to food'.[24]

[21] Holmes and Sunstein [12].

[22] See Pieterse [13].

[23] See *Minister of Health v. Treatment Action Campaign*, 2002(5)HIS 721(CC).

[24] Jean Ziegler. Report by the Special Rapporteur on the right to food. Available at: https://www.un.org/unispal/document/auto-insert-185061/.

2.2.2 Right to an Adequate Standard of Living and Economic Development

Some people believe that access to food is directly related to a country's level of economic development. Although South Africa is the most economically developed country in Africa, due to various reasons, its economic development level is still very different from that of developed countries in the world. Economic, social, and cultural rights, including the right to an adequate standard of living, are based on a high level of economic development in a country. Therefore, for the demand for food to rise to a basic human right, it must be backed by solid material resources. In other words, the right to an adequate standard of living is closely linked to the welfare state. However, judging by the level of economic development of South Africa, the country is still in the stage of industrialization and democratization.

This perception of the relationship between the right to an adequate standard of living and economic development has a direct impact on how the right to an adequate standard of living is perceived. According to the South African Government, "everyone in South Africa has the right to adequate food and water, and this right is to be realized progressively. States also have a direct obligation to ensure that every child and every person detained has the right to adequate food, a right that cannot be progressively realized, since children and detainees cannot feed themselves."[25] The right to an adequate standard of living cannot simply be understood as the right to adequate food. This view of the relationship between the right to an adequate standard of living and economic development was demonstrated in the Grootboom case. The South African Government argued that they did not provide the corresponding housing for the plaintiffs because providing housing for each applicant would inevitably increase the financial burden on the Government, which is beyond its financial resources. They argued that the realization of a right is subject to the level of economic development. Ultimately, the Constitutional Court stated that "There is a difference between those who can afford housing, even if it is only the most basic adequate housing, and those who cannot afford it." For those who can afford adequate housing, the main obligations of the Government are to provide access to housing and to establish a legal framework to facilitate self-construction by citizens. More importantly, for those who cannot afford to provide housing for themselves, the issues of development and social welfare are crucial. Government policies must take into account both groups, and the needs of the poor, who are disadvantaged, deserve special attention.[26]

Guided by the "Grootboom" decision, the interpretation of the right to an adequate standard of living generally emphasizes the following factors: First, policies related to the right to an adequate standard of living should adjust to people's immediate consumption needs to varying degrees according to different circumstances. Second, the requirement for the right to an adequate standard of living is only justified if it is

[25] Jean Ziegler. Report by the Special Rapporteur on the right to food. Available at: https://www.un.org/unispal/document/auto-insert-185061/.

[26] Quoted from Zhang [14].

consistent with the relevant policies of the state in the agricultural, health, and social development sectors.[27]

2.2.3 An Ideological Critique of the Right to an Adequate Standard of Living as a Fundamental Human Right

South Africa is a country that has long been oppressed by colonialism. It was once subject to Dutch and British invasions. At the beginning of the twentieth century, South Africa was a British autonomous territory. It was not until 1961 that South Africa withdrew from the Commonwealth and established the Republic of South Africa. After freeing itself from colonial oppression, South Africa has always been vigilant of the outside world, especially regarding the use of human rights by developed countries to interfere in their internal affairs.

In the drafting of the new Constitution, the drafters of the section that opposed the right to an adequate standard of living as a fundamental human right argued that the economic and social rights enumerated in Articles 22–30 of the Universal Declaration of Human Rights, as well as the Articles 1–30 of the International Covenant on Civil and Political Rights, embody the values and institutions that characterize the "welfare state." They questioned the reference to "universally accepted fundamental rights." In their view, the concept of "universally accepted fundamental rights" is nothing more than a global deduction of Western liberal thought, a global expansion of ideology, and objectively not "universally accepted." Since the rights specified in the International Covenant on Economic, Social and Cultural Rights are not "universally acceptable," the elevation of a need to a fundamental right depends on the specific circumstances of the country and the country's basic awareness of the need. Moreover, the inclusion of the right to an adequate standard of living as a fundamental human right may provide a pretext for Western countries to accuse their own human rights.

"For this reason, in September 1996, during a meeting with visiting Iranian President Rafsanjani, President Mandela publicly stated that 'the United States will not be allowed to dominate South Africa's diplomacy and destiny.' President Clinton visited South Africa in late March and early April 1998, and Mandela openly criticized the United States and other Western countries for interfering in the internal affairs of African countries and reducing aid to African countries under the pretext of human rights and other issues."[28] This is one of the reasons why South Africa signed the Convention as early as 1994, but has not ratified it to date.

---

[27] See *Right to Food Case Study: South Africa*, at www.fao.org.righttofood, 2009-02-03.

[28] Zeng [15].

2.2.4 Right to an Adequate Standard of Living and the Work Ethic

One of the major challenges facing the welfare state is the perception of laziness. Therefore, worldwide, there is an argument against the welfare right as a fundamental right, as it is believed that recognizing this right could encourage social laziness to some extent. For instance, in the American tradition, 'poor people' are often considered 'lazy,' and unearned 'hitchhikers' who take advantage of other people's hard work are resented. If the right to welfare is considered a natural right under the law, it could undermine the virtues of "hard work and bravery" in the United States and cultivate dependence among the poor, which contradicts the principle of self-reliance of modern citizens. This understanding of the relationship between welfare rights and laziness has also influenced South Africa's perception of the issue.[29] Although the current black government encourages black employment and requires companies and enterprises to prioritize hiring black people, there are still many black individuals who choose not to work and prefer to idle around. Most black individuals have little education and can only find work in manual labor jobs. In South Africa, an average black worker earns 1,230 rand per month (one rand is about 1.30 yuan), with about eight or nine hundred rand left after transportation expenses for commuting are deducted. Currently, South Africa's unemployment benefit is 700 rand per person per month, which means that many black individuals do not feel the need to work and rely on this benefit to live.[30] Opponents in South Africa who disagree with the right to an adequate standard of living argue that elevating this right to a fundamental or legal right could potentially discourage vulnerable groups from working and ultimately affect their access to adequate food.

2.3 A Brief Review of the Right to an Adequate Standard of Living as a Fundamental Human Right Debate

The debate in South Africa regarding whether the right to an adequate standard of living is a fundamental human right has had a significant impact on the realization of this right in the country. As a result of this controversy, South African courts have adopted a more cautious approach in cases related to the right to an adequate standard of living.[31] An objective and impartial assessment of the views of both

---

[29] Hu and Song [16].

[30] African Memorabilia·South Africa, available at: http://xuzhihong2008.blog.sohu.com/84791456.html, 2009-04-03.

[31] Professor Zheng Xianjun pointed out that the first economic rights case was heard by the Constitutional Court of South Africa in 1998, four years after its establishment. Since then, the Constitutional Court has heard several cases relating to socio-economic rights. The primary method used by the court in these cases is the test of reasonableness. The meaning of this standard is that the court recognizes that the power to make policy choices and resource allocation rests with the legislative and executive branches. The role of the courts is only to examine the reasonableness of the methods adopted by the legislative and executive organs. Therefore, if the approach of the legislative and

parties is therefore useful in our understanding of the right to an adequate standard of living. In summary, this debate involves three fundamental issues: the interpretation of the universality of "universally accepted fundamental rights," how to understand the relationship between the enjoyment of rights and economic development, and the role of government in this context.

2.3.1 How to Recognize the Universal Acceptance of Basic Human Rights?

The universality and specificity of human rights have been long-standing debates in academic and theoretical circles. The universality of human rights emphasizes that human rights are a value derived from the West but have universal applicability in the sense of Giddens' "de-domain" and should become a universal value recognized worldwide. The particularity of human rights places more emphasis on the cultural attributes that human rights should have, representing what Gierz calls "local knowledge". Supporters of the right to an adequate standard of living argue from the perspective of the universality of human rights, while opponents do so from the perspective of the specificity of human rights.

However, I believe there are certain problems with both the universal and specific perspectives of basic human rights, held by supporters and opponents alike. To truly understand human rights, we need to see beyond the institutional provisions and grasp the universality and "universality" of the values and meanings carried by these provisions themselves. Understanding specific human rights provisions is the first step in comprehending the universality of human rights. The universality and "universality" of the values and meanings that play a supporting role behind these human rights provisions are the true meaning of the universality of human rights. Although international instruments and international law specifically regulate human rights in various forms, they are mostly principled provisions that require the ratification of member States to be effective. Reservations and adaptations are even possible in some cases. This is also a prerequisite for the embodiment and realization of the particularity of human rights.

As far as the importance of food is concerned, it is the most basic daily need of life and the material basis for human existence. Therefore, the right to an adequate standard of living is undoubtedly a fundamental moral right. However, due to the specific nature of economic, social, and cultural development of countries, the right to an adequate standard of living must have a certain specificity in the process of realizing the transformation from moral rights to legal rights. This specificity is mainly reflected in the specific criteria for the right to an adequate standard of living. The realization of the right to an adequate standard of living is likely to become a

executive branches is reasonable, the court would not consider it unconstitutional. However, if their methods are obviously irrational, the court would deem them unconstitutional. Zheng Xianjun: Jurisprudence and Methods of Social Rights Remedies in the Constitutional Court of South Africa, available at: http://www.falvfagui.com/fagui/falv/Article/xianzhengzhaunti/xueshuwenzhang/200603/Article_943075.html, 2009-04-12.

luxury if the specific criteria of the right to an adequate standard of living are not taken into account.

2.3.2 How to Understand the Relationship Between the Enjoyment of Rights and Economic Development?

Regarding the first question, opponents of the right to an adequate standard of living as a fundamental human right are hindered by a misunderstanding of the universality and specificity of fundamental human rights. They tend to equate the enjoyment of the right to an adequate standard of living with its realization. In fact, any right encompasses two aspects: the enjoyment of rights and the realization of rights, and remedies are an essential part of the realization of rights. The enjoyment of rights is a prerequisite for the realization of rights, and if a person enjoys a right, it means that they are eligible to realize that right. However, from an empirical standpoint, the enjoyment of rights is mainly linked to the division of interests among different parties, which means that rights must take into account various factors in the process of allocation, and balance and coordinate between various interests. The realization of rights is to implement the form of rights, expressed as a system, specifically to the subject of rights, based on the enjoyment of rights. Although the subject of rights is also subject to various factors during the stage of realizing rights, the impact of resource allocation on them is indirect. In other words, the realization of rights is carried out on the premise that resource allocation has already been completed. The stage of realizing rights is the process of implementing the existing form of rights.

In the context of the right to an adequate standard of living, the appropriate standards adopted by a country are indeed influenced by the redistribution of national income. This impact mainly occurs at the level of national legislation, and the realization of the right to an adequate standard of living, particularly remedies for the right to an adequate standard of living, presupposes a breach by the State or Government of its obligations. In this sense, the primary role of the courts in the remedy process is not to test the legitimacy of the standard of the right to an adequate standard of living in the country itself, but to examine whether the Government has fulfilled its basic commitments regarding the right to an adequate standard of living, as enshrined in the law. Thus, the financial situation of the State has little impact on the remedy for the right to an adequate standard of living.

2.3.3 How to Position the Functions of the Government?

In this debate, both sides have touched on the issue of the positioning of government functions. Proponents position government functions more from the standpoint of the welfare state, while opponents tend to stand in the traditional liberal position that the government interferes as little as possible in social life and limits the government's power to the smallest possible extent. In their view, the right to an adequate standard of living, as a basic human right, means that government intervention and control over socio-economic life will inevitably be strengthened, and the space for free social competition will be reduced. The arguments of the opponents are not unreasonable, and this is reflected in South Africa and other high-welfare capitalist countries. "From cradle to grave" is the most straightforward expression of this phenomenon. At the same time, opponents agree that excessive judicial review by the courts on the right to an adequate standard of living may also violate the principle of separation of powers. This involves the question of how the Court's competence is controlled, since South Africa is a country with relatively developed case law, which means that the Court is in a stronger position in the overall political framework. To a certain extent, this strength will affect the performance of government functions.

However, structural poverty is also an indisputable fact in South Africa and requires positive government action to effectively eradicate it. Therefore, elevating the right to an adequate standard of living from a moral right to a basic or legal right necessarily helps to mobilize the general public to monitor the Government's efforts to address structural poverty. In this sense, South Africa wants to both expand the functions of the government and limit it to a certain extent. In the specific judicial practice of South Africa, this point is mainly reflected through the "reasonableness standard" in judicial review, and the court achieves a balance between expanding government functions and limiting government power through the flexible application of the "reasonableness standard".

3 Appropriate Standards for the Right to an Adequate Standard of Living

Traditional legal research has primarily focused on domestic law, resulting in insufficient research on international law. Additionally, the right to an adequate standard of living was only incorporated into international legal documents after World War II, which has resulted in both domestic and foreign academic research on this topic being insufficient. In the domestic context, there are few writings that focus on the right to an adequate standard of living, and the existing papers or teaching materials mainly describe the sub-rights included in the right and their relationship to social development. Consequently, the level of research on the right to an adequate standard of living in the country remains at a low level. The question of adequate standards for the right to an adequate standard of living has been neglected and has been used as a prerequisite for studying other related issues without question. As far as the situation abroad is concerned, to the author's knowledge, researchers on this issue mainly include A. Ed, S. Leckie, B. Tobis, and others. They have discussed the composition of the right, state obligations, adequate standards, redress procedures, and other related issues. However, they have not made a strong argument for the basis of legitimacy of the right to an adequate standard of living, and there is also a suspicion of raising the bar on the issue of appropriate standards.

In fact, the standards adopted by theorists regarding the appropriate standards of the right to an adequate standard of living directly affect current relevant international legal documents and specific operations on the right. Based on relevant legal documents and practical practice, the Committee on Economic, Social, and Cultural Rights has also adopted a higher and specific standard concerning the right to an adequate standard of living. This specific criterion is not achievable for the vast majority of developing countries in the short term. On the one hand, it ignores the understanding of the cultural diversity of countries for adequate living itself, and on the other hand, it is easy for developed countries to use the right of adequate living to criticize the human rights situation in developing countries, thus forming a new type of dominance. Therefore, the author believes that if the issue of appropriate standards for the right to an adequate standard of living is to be truly clarified, it is necessary to further question whether there is an appropriate standard for the right to an adequate standard of living. There are also several questions regarding how states can reach a basic consensus on such appropriate standards and what principles can determine appropriate standards.

3.1 Deconstructing the Right to an Adequate Standard of Living Through Appropriate Standards

The right to an adequate standard of living holds a fundamental place in human rights. In order to ensure that this right can be realized at the domestic level, certain specific standards of the right to an adequate standard of living are provided for in relevant international legal documents and legal practice. However, these specific criteria are significantly higher than the level of development of many developing countries.

3.1.1 Evaluating the Adequate Standard as a Demonstration of the Right to an Adequate Standard of Living: An Academic Exploration

The right to an adequate standard of living and the right to housing are essential components of human rights. International legal provisions specify their appropriate standards and have had a significant impact on specific legal practices. In the following section, the author reflects on the problems associated with the right to an adequate standard of living through the specific standards of the right to an adequate standard of living and the right to housing.

To reach a consensus in the international community and facilitate specific operational practices of states, the UN Committee on Economic, Social and Cultural Rights has concretized the abstract standards mentioned above. Adequate food can be broken down into several elements, such as the adequacy of food supply, which means that the type of food generally available (within the country, in local markets, and eventually at the household level) should be culturally acceptable, and conform to a generic food or food culture. Additionally, the overall supply should meet the overall nutritional needs (providing all important nutrients) in terms of quantity (energy) and quality, including micronutrients, such as vitamins and iodine. This concretizes the appropriate standard of the right to an adequate standard of living primarily through the term "daily dietary needs." The "daily dietary needs" refer to those dietary needs necessary for physical and mental development and physical activity. Moreover, the food supply should be safe (free of toxic ingredients and contaminants) and of good quality (e.g., taste, texture).

The stability of food supply and access presupposes environmental sustainability, which implies wise public or community management of the natural resources associated with the food supply. It also refers to ensuring economic and social sustainability in terms of the conditions and mechanisms by which food is obtained. Economic and social sustainability involves public income distribution, efficient markets, and a variety of public and informal support and safety nets. This support can range from public social protection planning to various forms of community transactions, self-help, and networking, which become even more important when people need to respond to crisis situations.[32]

The right to housing and the right to an adequate standard of living are closely related, and the United Nations Committee on Economic, Social and Cultural Rights has defined the content of the right to housing based on a review of numerous national reports. The right to housing includes, among other things, (a) legal security of tenure, which applies to all types of housing, such as rented, residential (public and private), partnership dwelling, lease, owner's dwelling, emergency dwelling or informal dwelling. All individuals should have a degree of security of tenure that provides legal protection against forced evictions, harassment, and other threats. States should take immediate action to provide legal security of tenure to individuals and families who currently lack it. (b) Availability of services, materials, equipment and infrastructure. Good housing must include certain facilities that are essential for health, safety, comfort, and nourishment: sustainable access to natural and general resources, safe drinking water, energy for cooking, heating and lighting, sanitation and washing facilities, food storage, waste disposal tools, drainage, and emergency service facilities. (c) Affordability. Housing-related personal and household expenses should not threaten or undermine access to and satisfaction of other basic needs. (d) Habitability. Residents should have adequate space and facilities to withstand cold, humidity, heat, rain and water, and be able to prevent other threats to health, structural hazards, and diseases. (e) Accessibility. Vulnerable groups, including the elderly, children, the physically disabled, the terminally ill, AIDS patients, the medically needy, the mentally ill, victims of natural disasters, those living in disaster-prone areas, and other groups, should have sustainable access to housing resources and receive some degree of priority in the field of housing, etc.[33]

---

[32] See Simonides [17].

[33] See Simonides [17].

3.1.2 Appropriate Standards and "Modernization Theory" Govern

In terms of the appropriate standard of the right to an adequate standard of living, there are two main effects. Firstly, there is the "demonstration effect," which means that all countries, regardless of their level of development, are expected to move towards this standard. Secondly, there is the effect of sanctions, where if a country fails to meet this standard, individual countries, regional organizations, and even the United Nations Security Council may impose economic sanctions on that country. However, the pressures on existing standards on developed and developing countries are quite different. Developed countries have already achieved these standards, or the standards themselves are based on their own actual conditions. However, for the vast majority of developing countries, meeting these standards is indeed quite difficult. Therefore, developed countries have more say in the issue of the right to an adequate standard of living.[34] According to the theory of the famous sociologist Zimmer, in the situation of social interaction, the superior party has the ability and opportunity to influence, determine and control the inferior situation, leading to "structural or coercive domination" of developed countries over developing countries. Milne, a famous contemporary British philosopher of human rights, pointed out in the introduction to his book "Human Rights and Human Diversity" that the economic and social rights enumerated in Articles 22–30 of the Universal Declaration of Human Rights embody the well-known values and institutions that characterize the "welfare state". In other words, the standards of these economic and social rights, including the right to an adequate standard of living, embody the values and institutions of a liberal democratic industrial society, implicitly calling on all countries in the world to become liberal democratic industrial societies, and requiring relatively backward countries to strive towards becoming "domestic, democratic, and industrial societies," taking incremental steps towards the goal of a liberal democratic industrial society in the West.[35]

Regarding the right to an adequate standard of living, the dominance of the "modernization theory" is mainly reflected in the views of states by the Committee on Economic, Social and Cultural Rights. In 1994, the Committee issued its final observations on the report of the Dominican Republic on the right to housing. In that opinion, the Committee requested the reporting government to apply the existing provisions of its Constitution on the right to housing and to take facilitation and promotional measures to that end. These promotional measures may include: (a) the development of comprehensive legislation on housing rights; (b) legal recognition of the right of affected residents to be informed about government programs that have actual or potential impact on their rights; (c) enactment of legislation on urban reform that recognizes the contribution of civil society to the implementation of the Convention and provides for issues such as security of tenure and arrangements for the management of land ownership. The CESCR urged reporting governments to consider a range of initiatives aimed at promoting the housing environment of

[34] Deng [18].

[35] See Milne [19].

their populations. These initiatives may include: (a) a formal commitment to facilitate public participation in the urban development process; (b) legal recognition of community-based organizations; (c) establishment of a community housing finance system aimed at increasing access to credit for poor segments of society; (d) strengthening the role of municipalities in the field of housing; (e) improving coordination among the various government agencies responsible for housing issues and considering a single government housing agency.[36] The promotion measures and implementation initiatives of the Committee on Economic, Social and Cultural Rights highlight two issues. First, both measures emphasize the role of law. In other words, the committee attempts to address the issue of the right to housing through legal means. The deeper demand behind this is that the state must initiate a judicial review process to conduct constitutional proceedings concerning the right to housing. This undoubtedly requires a change in the existing political system within a state. Second, the committee seeks to engage states in the process of urbanization in order to meet appropriate standards. Whether it is the way to realize constitutional litigation or the process of choosing urbanization, it deviates to a certain extent from the independent choice of the development path of each country.

3.1.3 Practical Problem of Achieving Appropriate Standards

The existing appropriate standards of the right to an adequate standard of living are dominated by the "theory of modernization", which has a certain impact on specific relevant legal practices and is not conducive to the realization of the right to an adequate standard of living. Therefore, further revealing the reality of the implementation of existing appropriate standards is a prerequisite for us to redefine appropriate standards. Specifically, these practical problems are mainly reflected in the following two aspects:

On the one hand, the established standards of adequacy of the right to an adequate standard of living are strongly scientistic, thus ignoring the impact of cultural diversity on the standard of living itself. From the perspective of the way established standards are determined, it emphasizes the important role of science and technology, excluding or ignoring religious factors, conceptual factors, and other cultural factors. Therefore, it is, in fact, contrary to the true way of life. For example, people's understanding of food is not only from a nutritional point of view, but also emphasizes the psychological acceptability of food.

On the other hand, at the international level, the international community has sought to exert pressure on Governments, especially those of third world countries, to eradicate poverty through the right to an adequate standard of living, so that the right to an adequate standard of living is clearly goal-oriented. The level of the goal also determines, to some extent, the specific standard of the right to an adequate standard of living. In terms of existing goals, the 1974 World Food Conference

---

[36] See UN resolutionsE/C.12/1994/15; International Human Rights Law Course Project Leader [20].

declared that "everyone, men, women, and children, has the right to be free from hunger and undernutrition, to develop one's physical and mental abilities. These rights may not be arbitrarily deprived." Governments agreed on a goal to address hunger, food insecurity, and undernutrition within a decade. Yet as late as 1996, there were 800 million undernourished and hungry people in the world.

In 1996, world leaders attended the World Food Summit convened by the Food and Agriculture Organization of the United Nations in Rome. At the meeting, leaders of all governments jointly issued the Rome Declaration on World Food Security. The Declaration expressed their desire to guarantee the right of all people to an adequate standard of living and to eradicate hunger in all countries. These include halving the number of undernourished people by 2015 and bringing the number of hungry people in the world to 400 million. However, with current developments, this goal is difficult to achieve. Such impossible goals necessarily affect and even distort the appropriate standard of the adequate standard of living, thereby giving the right to an adequate standard of living a short-term effect. The direct consequence of this short-term success is that if the overall goal is not achieved, confidence in the right to an adequate standard of living as a fundamental human right is shaken, and ultimately, the authority of the relevant legal provisions of international law is diminished.

3.2 The Right to an Adequate Standard of Living, the Reconstruction of Appropriate Standards

The existence of problems with the standards for the right to an adequate standard of living, both in theory and in practice, forces us to further reflect on whether the right to an adequate standard of living as a human right is universal. If it is universal, how should we perceive it? These issues are prerequisites for us to reconstruct appropriate standards for the right to an adequate standard of living.

3.2.1 The Universality of the Right to an Adequate Standard of Living

The concept of human rights, according to common understanding, refers to the rights that every human being possesses. It includes two dimensions: the first is the dimension of man as an individual, that is, man exists as a "class"; the second is the real-life situations of real people. In other words, human rights are established under the premise that the universal needs of the concept of "man" are combined with the needs that society can fulfill. As such, human rights represent a unity of universality and particularity.

The question of the universality and specificity of human rights has been the subject of debate in legal circles. Some scholars believe that the universality of human rights necessitates that they should be universal and that they should transcend any regional and national cultural forms to become a common moral pursuit and value choice of all humanity. In essence, the universality of human rights, as the natural attribute of human rights, the essential attribute of human rights, can be understood in two ways: First, from the perspective of rights, the universality of human rights means that the human rights of any person are the same as those of any other person in terms of their content; Second, from the perspective of subjects, the universality of human rights means that every human being is entitled to the same human rights. In other words, the universality of human rights is the universality of the subject of human rights, and every human right should belong to everyone without exception.

From such discussions, we can see that their understanding of the universality of human rights adopts a "realist" or "institutional" position. What they emphasize is the universalization of the system as a concrete form of human rights, i.e., the content of human rights should be the same for all. However, in the specific practice of international human rights law, this understanding of the universality of human rights requires the unreserved acceptance by States of a particular form of right. This also loses the dimension of locality of human life to a certain extent.

Some scholars have taken a negative approach to the universality of human rights. In their view, the so-called universality of human rights means that human rights standards and the system for realizing human rights should be universal. Therefore, the essence of Western countries' emphasis on the universality of human rights lies in using the universality of human rights to put pressure on countries with different social systems to promote Western-style democracy and freedom. They have the insight that Western countries use human rights to promote Western-style democratic freedoms, but they mistakenly reverse this domination as a cause, that is, adopt a consequentialist proposition, because the West uses the universality of human rights to put pressure on countries with different social systems. However, the author believes that the universalization of human rights standards and their realization systems, and the consequent use of human rights by Western countries, do not constitute grounds for opposing the universality of human rights. At best, we can only say that there is a certain problem with the way in which universality is achieved.

Given the problems with the previous two understandings of human rights, it is necessary to ask whether human rights have universality and in what sense this universality is applicable. Marx identifies three basic "forms" of human society, progressing from group and individual standards to class standards. This development is an inevitable trend in human history. Human beings are intrinsically social creatures and individualized life can only exist within a unified and integrated relationship with others. Similarly, human nature can only exist in an integrated relationship with the external world, i.e., the existence of human objects. This integrated relationship not only constitutes the object of human conscious activity but also is a fundamental principle of human self-activity.[37] Therefore, man does not exist only as a citizen of a sovereign state but also as a member of a "class", and people in different countries have the same "quasi-nature". However, this "quasi-nature" is not intended to obliterate the particularity of human beings but emphasizes that

[37] About the "Quasi-Being" of People, Mr. Gao Hai has made incisive statements, See Gao [21].

"the actual 'concrete', 'special', 'person' must produce the feeling of belonging and attachment as a 'kind', and the anxiety emotion of 'self' as a 'kind' individual." Such feelings of pity and concern for the 'self' of the individual as a 'kind' to other individuals as 'same' and 'kind'.[38] This is reflected in the Vienna Declaration and Programme of Action adopted by the World Conference on Human Rights in June 1993. In Part 2, paragraph 1, of the Declaration, it states: "The World Conference on Human Rights reaffirms the solemn commitment of all States to fulfill their obligations to promote universal respect for, observance and protection of all human rights and fundamental freedoms for all, in accordance with the Charter of the United Nations, other international instruments relating to human rights and international law." The universality of these rights and freedoms is indisputable. Paragraph 3 states: "All human rights are universal, indivisible, interdependent and interrelated, and the international community must treat human rights in a fair and equal manner with the same emphasis, taking a comprehensive view of human rights." Although human rights in all their forms are specified in international instruments relating to human rights and in international law, their validity requires the ratification of Member States. There were even cases where reservations and adaptations could be made by member States. This is also a prerequisite for the embodiment and realization of the particularity of human rights. It can be seen that the relevant international instruments on human rights and international law are more of a principled provision. In order to achieve the goal of truly understanding human rights, it is necessary for us to see through these institutional provisions the universality and "universality" of the values and meanings they carry. Therefore, insight into specific human rights provisions is the first step in understanding the universality of human rights, and the universality and "universality" of the values and meanings that play a supporting role behind these human rights provisions is the true meaning of the universality of human rights.

Regarding the right to an adequate standard of living, the relevant international instruments and international law highlight "the right of everyone to a standard of living necessary for the maintenance of his own health and that of his family." "The standard of living necessary to maintain the health and well-being of individuals and their families is universal, as understood in the text. However, the universal or "relegatable" value and significance of this provision at least contains people's yearning for what they think is a better living situation, while the external evaluation actually obtained is irrelevant. In other words, the premise of the aspiration for a better living situation itself is universal, and what kind of living standard is appropriate, and the choice of means, methods, and institutions to achieve such a better living situation should be determined by each country according to its own actual situation.

[38] Yao [22].

3.2.2 What is the Meaning of the Appropriate Standard of the Right to an Adequate Standard of Living

Human rights are a controversial concept both in theoretical and practical circles. One of the most important reasons for this controversy is the issue of human rights standards, and the right to an adequate standard of living is no exception. During the drafting of the International Covenant on Economic, Social and Cultural Rights, States disputed the appropriate criteria. The former Soviet Union stated that "States should take all necessary steps, in particular legislative measures, to ensure that everyone has access to housing worthy of human values". The United States proposed that "the States parties to the Convention recognize the right of everyone to adequate housing". Australia proposed that "the States parties to the Convention recognize the right of everyone to an adequate standard of living", among others.

The reasons for this divergence are mainly twofold. Firstly, as I discussed above, both theoretical and practical circles have adopted an "institutionalism" stance on the universality of human rights. This means that the understanding of the universality of human rights focuses more on the universality of the institutional level, without paying attention to the universality or "universality" of the values and meanings behind the system. Secondly, even if the universality or "universality" of the values and meanings of the human rights system is observed, the appropriate standard for the right to an adequate standard of living may be set too high or be an ideal standard. Many countries have not been able to meet this standard for a certain period of time.

On this issue, Milne has made a wonderful statement. He argues that the development of modern science and technology has made our era an era of global interdependence, and therefore, we need a moral standard that can be applied to all human relations. Since the eighteenth century, Western notions of human rights have been promoted as such a moral standard. But if this idea is to stand up to rational argument, it must confront human diversity. As Milne puts it: "If the concept of human rights is to be both understandable and scrutinized, it can only be a minimum standard concept."[39] To support this notion, Milne critiques the pre-existing notions of human rights. He argues that regardless of the ideal standard, the concept of human rights has historically ignored cultural diversity. For ideals to be coherent, they must arise from a particular cultural and civilized tradition. People belonging to another tradition have no reason to accept ideal standards that are too high for them. Regarding existing standards, human rights are composed of both freedom-democratic rights and modern society-welfare rights. However, this criterion ignores the diversity of cultures and the social basis for the existence of human individuality. Minimum standards, on the other hand, are rooted in the moral imperatives of a certain social life and can be applied to all cultures and civilizations.

On an operational level, given the "finitude of reason," it is impossible to establish the highest standards. The highest standard is an ideal that is meaningful to reality, but its establishment requires that our reason fully grasp the various situations that have been encountered, are present, or will be encountered in the future. Such certainty is

---

[39] Milne [23].

beyond the reach of our reason. Moreover, the meaning of life to the future is itself uncertain, and the ideal standard is likely to speak for the future in isolation from the existing life. This poses a certain challenge to the existence of a conservative institutional existence in the law itself.

It can be seen that the highest standards are oriented towards the future in terms of purpose. As for minimum standards, although they are not fully certain given the "finitude of reason," they take into account past and present situations. Therefore, the minimum standard has a smaller time span relative to the maximum standard and contains fewer desirable components. In other words, the minimum standard questions the unsatisfactory aspects of people's lives in the past from the standpoint of people's real life. The minimum standard points to the past, that is, to change the unsatisfactory aspects of people's lives in the past. Thus, the minimum standard implies the thinking that one should live the life one should have and ignores the better life that one has already lived than one should have.

In addition, most internationally accepted standards use certain "quantitative standards," and this process of "quantification" itself to some extent ignores the "specific details" of different countries. Since human beings are "concrete people" living in different cultures, they may continue to argue over what constitutes good, or we may not be able to find the highest and most appropriate standard for the right to an adequate standard of living and adopt it as an ideal for states to strive for. But we can still agree on what kind of life is intolerable and unquestionably wrong. Only when the right to an adequate standard of living is consciously minimal can the universal values and significance of the right to an adequate standard of living, and the universal responsibilities above it, live in harmony with the various ways of life.[40] The right to an adequate standard of living can only win universal acceptance as a firm "thin" theory of "what is right" (the fundamental definition of the minimum conditions common to all life). If an idealistic or supreme standard rule were chosen for the appropriate standard of the right to an adequate standard of living, it would probably not be met in most countries for a certain period of time. Such a situation may run counter to the original purpose of the right to an adequate standard of living or to its intended purpose.

3.3 Determination of "Adequate Standards" for the Right to an Adequate Standard of Living

Based on the above analysis, the author believes that the appropriate standard of the right to an adequate standard of living cannot be quantified at the level of international human rights law. Thus, international legal instruments on the right to an adequate standard of living can only be presented in a more abstract manner. However, this does not imply that countries cannot strive for an adequate and feasible standard of living at the domestic level.

[40] See Junren [24].

3.3.1 Negative Determination of Appropriate Criteria

First of all, it must not go against the basic way of life or living habits of people. Lifestyle or living habits are an important part of culture. Taylor, a famous British cultural anthropologist, believes that "culture or civilization is a composite whole including knowledge, beliefs, art, morality, law, habits, and other abilities and habits acquired by human beings as the essence of society."[41] The American cultural anthropologist Crookhorn defines culture as a way of life and a way of being. "The term culture used by American anthropologists is, of course, a term that must not be confused with ordinary language and more limited concepts in history and literature." This anthropological definition refers to those aspects of the entire human environment that are created by humans, both tangible and intangible. By 'a culture', it refers to the unique way of life of a certain human group, their entire set of 'lifestyles'.[42] Therefore, lifestyle or living habits represent not only the "material way of being" of people but also the support behind this "material way of being".

Secondly, human dignity must not be violated. In fact, dignity is also a very abstract and vague concept. In bioethics, human dignity mostly refers to the dignity and solemnity enjoyed by human life forms in the biological sense, which is different from things and other life forms. In physiology, human dignity often refers to people's sense of self-esteem and self-worth. In the sociological sense, human dignity is the recognition and respect given to the individual by others, groups, and societies with whom the individual has established social relations. It results in the esteemed and revered status or identity of the individual in people's minds.[43] The dignity I am referring to here is more from the sense of bioethics, that is, human life cannot be subject to other subjective criteria (such as morality, political position, social status, social relations, etc.) in addition to the objective standard of individual life. Besides the existence of such a minimum condition as individual life, no higher conditions (such as race, sex, physical integrity, genetic uniqueness, intelligence, physical ability, etc.) can be imposed.[44] In other words, the appropriate criterion for the right to an adequate standard of living must adhere to the "negative criterion," which means it must not violate human dignity and must emphasize that the human person is an end in itself and never a means to an end. Therefore, "every human being must meet his or her basic requirements of life with the dignity of the human person. In other words, no one may be compelled to meet his basic needs by reducing or being forced to deprive him of his fundamental freedoms, such as begging, prostitution or hard labor."[45]

Finally, it must not contradict the context in which society as a whole exists. This negative principle primarily relates to the international community's assessment of a country's right to an adequate standard of living. At the heart of this principle is

[41] Tylor [25].

[42] Crookhorn [26].

[43] See Yuehong and Shuxing [27].

[44] See Yuehong and Shuxing [27].

[45] Liu [3].

the understanding that when we evaluate the right to an adequate standard of living in another country, we must consider the living conditions of its inhabitants in the context of that country as a whole. The context here refers to two aspects: first, the overall development of the country; second, the country's place in the world structure. Regarding the former, the lives of the inhabitants do not exist in isolation but are subject to the country's geographical conditions, objective material base, cultural conditions, political reasons, and other aspects. To change the living conditions of a country, it is necessary to change all other aspects related to it. These factors must, therefore, be taken into account in evaluating a country's right to an adequate standard of living. Regarding the latter, poverty in the world today is more of a kind of "structural poverty." We must be aware that nearly 3 billion people receive only about 1.2% of the world's total income, while the 1 billion people living in rich countries do 80%. Ignoring this premise and evaluating the right to an adequate standard of living in another country would undoubtedly be biased.

3.3.2 Specific and Appropriate Standards for the Right to an Adequate Standard of Living—The Case of the Right to Housing in South Africa

In the case of South Africa, the decision of the Constitutional Court of South Africa v. Government of the Republic of South Africa and Others v. Grootboom guarantees citizens' right to housing judicially in practice. The Grootboom case not only provides a judicial avenue in practice to guarantee citizens' right to housing but also sets minimum standards for the right to housing in South Africa in the form of jurisprudence.

Grootboom, who lives with 389 adults and 510 children, resides in extreme poverty and extremely poor conditions. Faced with such living conditions, which were unbearable, they moved en masse to a privately-owned land used to build low-cost houses. Shortly after moving to the land, they were forcibly evicted by the government and, under pressure from the government, had to move en masse to a sports ground in the same area. They could not afford to build houses there, so they erected shacks. However, at the request of the site's owner, the government forced them to leave the land and bulldozed their temporary residence the day before the expiry of the prescribed period. The government also burned their shacks, leaving these people with nothing. They then filed a lawsuit in the High Court of the Cape Region, asking the court to issue an emergency order to the government, requiring them to provide immediate temporary accommodation or houses until they are granted permanent accommodation. The Cape District High Court, pursuant to section 28, paragraph 1 (3) of the South African Constitution, held that children should have an absolute right to a residence and their parents have the right to live with their offspring. As a result, the court ruled that the government was obliged to immediately provide tents, mobile toilets, and a regular supply of water to families with children. Subsequently, the government appealed to the Constitutional Court, dissatisfied with the court's decision. The South African Human Rights Commission and the Socio-Legal Centre became involved in the proceedings of Grootboom et al. They invoked article 28, paragraph 1, item 3 of the Constitution concerning the right of children to live and article 26 of the Constitution on the right to housing for all members of society.[46]

In Grootboom, the Constitutional Court of South Africa did not adopt the concept of "minimum core obligations" proposed by the UN Committee on Economic, Social and Cultural Rights. The appellant requested that the Government fulfill the United Nations Committee on Economic, Social and Cultural Rights' requirement in its general comment No. 3, which states that "each State party has a minimum core obligation to ensure the realization of each right reaches a minimum minimum level".[47] The Constitutional Court of South Africa held that while the concept of "minimum core obligations" was instructive, it was up to the court to determine the minimum core obligations of the legislature and the executive in a given situation, and the court needed a great deal of relevant information. While housing conditions in South Africa varied widely between regions and between urban and rural areas, it was very difficult for the courts to determine the minimum core elements of the right to adequate housing. Thus, Article 26, paragraph 1, of the Constitution of the Republic of South Africa, "Everyone has the right to adequate housing", did not include the minimum core obligation of the State to provide the right holder with direct basic accommodation, upon request. However, the Constitutional Court held that Article 26, paragraph 1, of the Constitution of the Republic of South Africa should be read in conjunction with paragraph 2. Paragraph 2 provides that "States must take reasonable legislative and other measures, within the limits of their available resources, for the progressive realization of the right to housing". The Court held that Section 26 of the Constitution of the Republic of South Africa, while not giving individuals the right to request housing directly, gave individual citizens the right to request that the State formulate reasonable policies within the limits of the resources available to them. Citizens may, on the basis of this provision, request the State to adopt reasonable legislation or other policy measures to ensure the genuine realization of citizens' right to housing.[48]

Through the analysis of the Grootboom case, we can see that the right to housing for South African citizens is a legitimate policy claim. In other words, the emphasis of the right to adequate housing in South Africa is on the government's legislative or other measures to improve the living conditions of South African citizens, rather than on the right of citizens to adequate housing. Thus, the criterion for the right to housing in South Africa does not guide the actual enjoyment of housing by non-citizens, but rather sets a minimum standard for the reasonableness of legislative or other measures to promote the improvement of citizens' living conditions. To further clarify the scope of citizens' legitimate policy claims in relation to the right to housing, the Constitutional Court of South Africa stated that "reasonable policy

---

[46] See *Grootboom v. Ostenberg Municipality and Others*, 2000(3)BCLR(C).

[47] *Committee on Economic, Social and Cultural Rights. (1990). General Comment No. 3. In HRJ/GEN/I/Rev.6 (p. 16). 12 May 2003.*

[48] See Yang [28].

claims means that individuals may petition the State in court if they do not have laws and policies in place to protect an economic and social right", including the right to housing. This means that citizens have the right to request that the legislative and executive bodies of the government take reasonable legislative and other measures, within the resources available to them, to ensure the genuine realization of citizens' right to housing. If the measures taken by the State are considered unreasonable, individuals may also request the court to review them.[49] Regarding the criterion of reasonableness, it mainly includes the following aspects: adopting a comprehensive and coordinated policy; implementing progressive realization measures if necessary to promote the realization of rights; ensuring that policies are balanced, flexible, and do not exclude a significant portion of society.[50]

There is a significant gap between the housing rights standards in South Africa and the ECOSOC housing rights standards, and it can be said that the minimum housing rights standards in South Africa are clearly lower than those promoted by the Economic and Social Affairs Committee. Why did the South African Government choose a minimum standard of housing rights that was significantly lower than that promoted by the committee? There are two main reasons for this.

On the one hand, South Africa's demographic structure has an important impact on the establishment of minimum standards for housing rights in the country.[51] According to the South African Bureau of Statistics, the proportion of white South Africans barely reaches 11%, and in terms of birth rate, the birth rate of whites is lower than that of blacks. The income and living standards of whites are significantly higher than those of blacks, which means that blacks are often at the bottom of the social ladder. In terms of employment, 50% of white employed people are in managerial or professional roles, while 47% of blacks work as mechanics and operators, with about 57% of black women and 41% of women of color engaged in manual labor. Black women also earn less from employment. Twenty-six per cent of workers in South Africa earn less than R500 a month, and 48% of black women workers are in this low-income bracket, while white women make up only 4% of this group. In terms of educational attainment, the proportion of whites with higher education is 20%, much higher than the 2% figure for blacks. Of South Africa's 6 million people who have never received any education, the majority are black. Among South Africans over the age of 20, 10% of black men have never received any education, compared to 0.5% for whites, and 14% of black women have never received any education. Overall, the above statistics highlight the vast disparities in living conditions, education, and employment opportunities between whites and blacks in South Africa. These disparities have a direct impact on the establishment of minimum standards for housing rights in the country.

Such a demographic structure has led to two outcomes. First, the structural gap between whites and blacks has widened, resulting in a situation where whites are becoming richer while blacks are getting poorer. Second, whites have more political

---

[49] Huang [29].

[50] See *Grootboom v. Ostenberg Municipality and Others*, 2000(3)BCLR(C).

[51] For the discussion of this part, the author refers to Ma [30].

say, and it is challenging for blacks to express their interests and demands politically and legally. Regarding housing in South Africa, 18% of the population lives in old, traditional houses, while 17% lives in humble shanty towns. More than 5.5 million households have piped water in their homes, but over 1 million South Africans still need to draw water from rivers. While 58% of households have access to electricity, 29% are using candles for lighting and 13% are using kerosene lamps. Most of these people living in poor housing conditions are black. Therefore, there are significant obstacles and difficulties in solving the housing problem for blacks by raising the minimum standards of housing rights.

On the other hand, South Africa's tax strategy has played a crucial role in establishing minimum standards for housing rights in the country. A country's tax strategy and tax situation directly affect its fiscal situation and expenditure. In this sense, the adequacy of the right to housing depends on the tax situation in the country. "On the eve of the enactment of the new Constitution of South Africa in 1996, the South African economy was going through difficult times. The fiscal deficit accounted for 7.2% of GDP, and between 1985 and 1994, the investment level decreased by 2.9% per year. The inflation rate remained high at 9–14%. Due to imbalances in the balance of payments and international sanctions on investment and trade, South Africa's economy grew at an average annual rate of −1%. Against this background, and with the objective of stabilizing the macroeconomic situation and establishing a sustainable growth model, the South African government urgently needed to broaden public revenue sources and strengthen debt management to meet growth and development needs. To this end, the South African government carried out a series of fiscal and tax reforms. These fiscal and taxation reform measures mainly include: (1) Unifying the tax structure of personal income tax and reducing the 10-level tax bracket to 6; (2) Implementing several large-scale reductions in personal income tax; (3) Reforming additional welfare tax arrangements to promote fairness; (4) Reducing corporate income tax rates and secondary income tax rates; (5) Taxing taxpayers' worldwide income tax; (6) Introducing the 'Retirement Fund Tax'; (7) Introducing the 'Income Tax Capital Gains Tax'; (8) Introducing new taxes such as the 'Skill Development Tax' and 'Air Travel Tax'; (9) Exempting paraffin and basic foodstuffs from value-added tax; (10) Ensuring the stability of tax collection, simplifying various tax tools, and improving the efficiency of tax collection and administration; (11) Creating a sufficiently attractive investment environment; (12) Reducing transaction taxes to improve the efficiency of the investment market; (13) Introducing strategic investment tax incentives, such as accelerated depreciation of equipment for large-scale investment projects; (14) Expanding the scope of depreciation subsidies for small enterprises."[52]

Although South Africa has noted the reform of additional welfare tax arrangements in the process of fiscal and tax reform, in general, the direction of fiscal and tax reform is to stimulate the overall growth of the domestic economic level through tax adjustment. In other words, South Africa's economic development in the past decade has been guided by "efficiency first, balance equity". We can see this from

[52] Mu [31].

the adjustment of personal income tax, corporate tax rate, and corporate additional tax rate. Since 1994, the South African government has reduced personal income tax by R63 billion. As a percentage of GDP, it fell from 10.2% in 1994/1995 to around 8% in 2003/2004. In order to further integrate with international standards, South Africa lowered its corporate tax rate from 40 to 35% in 1994. In 1999, it was lowered to 30%, which also applied to enterprises engaged in gold mining. The corporate surtax rate was reduced from 25 to 12.5% with effect from 4 March 1996.[53]

Although the fiscal and taxation reform in South Africa has stimulated domestic economic development on the whole, it has also weakened the regulatory and balancing role of taxation to a certain extent, thereby widening the gap between the rich and the poor in South Africa. Relative poverty in South Africa has not decreased but increased. The direction of using fiscal and tax reform to stimulate economic growth determines that the proportion of finance that can be used to invest in food, medical care, sanitation, housing, and other public welfare undertakings will not be too high. Therefore, the appropriate standard of housing rights will not be set too high, and it is impossible to give citizens the right to claim means of living to increase the financial burden of the government.

4 Remedies for the Right to an Adequate Standard of Living

The issue of remedies for the right to an adequate standard of living is increasingly a concern in human rights theory and practice. Subject to the influence of the traditional "human rights generation", the political rights of citizens are often regarded as first-generation human rights and economic, social, and cultural rights, including the right to an adequate standard of living, as second-generation human rights. The core difference between the first generation of human rights and the second generation of human rights is that the first generation of human rights is justiciable, and when the first generation of human rights is illegally violated, citizens can seek relief with the help of certain judicial means. Second-generation human rights do not have such attributes. Therefore, in this sense, second-generation human rights have a more "declaratory meaning". With the expansion and justification of welfare rights and the strengthening of the concept of the welfare state, there is increasing attention to the importance of economic and social rights in the daily lives of citizens. The remediability of the right to an adequate standard of living has become a hot topic in both theoretical and practical circles.

[53] Mu [31].

4.1 The Fallacy of the Inadmissibility of the Right to an Adequate Standard of Living

Although many countries around the world have constitutionally affirmed the right to an adequate standard of living, there has been strong questioning and denial of the justiciability of this right.

4.1.1 The Relationship Between Economic Development and the Right to an Adequate Standard of Living

The recognition of the right to an adequate level of water as a human right has undergone a complex process of controversy and proof. The concept of the right to an adequate standard of living first emerged in the form of the right to welfare, with the Weimar Republic's Constitution being one of the earliest examples. However, the fundamental law adopted by Germany after World War II did not consider the right to welfare as a fundamental right. In the United States, "welfare rights" were included in Roosevelt's proposed Second Bill of Rights in 1944, and subsequent legislation such as Title 42, U.S.C. Public Health and Welfare, covered a wide range of welfare interests. Nevertheless, there is considerable controversy over whether "welfare" is a right. In the 1960s, the U.S. Supreme Court gradually applied due process provisions to certain welfare payments.[54] From the perspective of international law, the right to an adequate standard of living is affirmed in Article 25, paragraph 1, of the Universal Declaration of Human Rights, which states that "Everyone has the right to a standard of living necessary for the maintenance of his own health and that of his family." Article 11 of the International Covenant on Economic, Social and Cultural Rights recognizes "the right of everyone to an adequate standard of living for himself and his family," while Article 27 of the Convention on the Rights of the Child recognizes "the right of every child to a standard of living adequate for his or her physical, mental, spiritual, moral, and social development." These binding international treaties are the main sources of law for the right to an adequate standard of living, including the right to water.

A brief review of the process by which the right to an adequate standard of living gained legal status shows that its emergence is a product of a certain stage of socio-economic development and reflects state intervention in laissez-faire economic life. Most scholars argue that the right to an adequate standard of living is not justiciable because it is based on a certain degree of economic development in a country. However, this view is untenable in statutory law countries.

Regarding the right to an adequate standard of living, the appropriate standards adopted by a state are indeed influenced by the redistribution of national income. For example, South Africa places more emphasis on policy claims in the context of the right to housing, while it has a higher standard of adequacy in relation to the right to

---

[54] See Yu [32].

health, which gives the person concerned both a right to claim policy and a right to a means of subsistence. South Africa is doing so mainly on the basis of its domestic fiscal situation. However, remedies for the right to an adequate standard of living presuppose a breach by the state or government of its obligations. In this sense, the primary role of the court in the remedy process is not to test the legitimacy of the right to an adequate standard of living in the country in terms of the standards themselves, but rather to examine whether the government has fulfilled its commitments regarding the right to an adequate standard of living enshrined in law. Therefore, the financial situation of the state has little impact on the remedy of the right to an adequate standard of living.[55]

4.1.2 The Confusion Between the Right to Claim Policy and the Right to Claim Subsistence Materials

The right to an adequate standard of living is a right to freedom from material deprivation, which includes both a reasonable policy claim and a reasonable claim for means of subsistence. However, those who advocate that the right to an adequate standard of living is not justiciable have, to some extent, confused the two claims or placed greater emphasis on the content of the right to an adequate standard of living in terms of policy claims while ignoring the right to claim means of subsistence. The direct result of this misconception of the right to an adequate standard of living is that if the right to an adequate standard of living is to be litigated, it will inevitably challenge the established judicial system of a country.

The right to reasonable policy claims means that if the state has not enacted laws and policies for the protection of an economic and social right, individuals may request the state (mainly legislative and executive) in court to "take reasonable legislative and other measures within the resources available to it"; if the measures taken by the state are considered unreasonable, the individual may also request the court to review them.[56] The so-called reasonable direct right to claim subsistence materials is the right of individuals to directly request subsistence materials from the government when their survival conditions are threatened. If the government does not provide them, the individual has the right to file a lawsuit before the Constitutional Court. In 2001, in Government of the Republic of South Africa et al. v. Grootboom, the Constitutional Court of South Africa denied individuals the right to claim housing directly under the relevant provisions, but recognized the constitutional right of individuals to reasonable policy claims.[57] Moreover, we can infer from

[55] South Africa is a developing country; however, it is at the forefront of implementing remedies for the right to an adequate standard of living. A series of cases have emerged to address this issue, including Subramoni v. Minister of Health (Soobramoney v. Minister of Health), Government of the Republic of South Africa et al. v. Grootboom (Government of the Republic of South Africa and Other v. Grootboom), and Therapeutic Action Campaign v. Ministry of Health (Treatment Action Campaign v. Minister of Health).

[56] Huang [29].

[57] See *Government of the Republic of South Africa and Others v. Grootboom*, 2001(1)HIS 46(CC).

the 1996 case of Subramoni v. Minister of Health that an individual has a right to reasonable medical treatment in relation to the right to health.[58] The South African Government therefore has an obligation to provide reasonable medical care directly for the purposes of the right to health.

In fact, there are differences in the nature of these two kinds of claims: reasonable policy claims are a kind of claim enjoyed by individuals against abstract administrative acts of the government; the reasonable right to claim personal subsistence materials is a claim enjoyed by individuals against specific administrative payments from the government. As far as China is concerned, abstract administrative acts cannot be litigated in administrative law, but concrete administrative acts can still be litigated. We can fully rely on administrative proceedings to obtain judicial remedies in the established judicial system relating to the right to an adequate standard of living, the right to reasonable means of subsistence, and the right to claim it.

4.1.3 The Fallacy of the Rights Dichotomy

Thanks to Isaiah Berlin's dichotomy between negative freedom and positive freedom, the legal profession also distinguishes rights into negative rights and positive rights. Civil and political rights are often positioned as negative rights, emphasizing that the State's obligation is merely omission; Economic, social, and cultural rights, including the right to an adequate standard of living, are considered positive rights. This dichotomy of rights has two problems:

First, civil and political rights also require active action by the state. In its 1982 general comment No. 6 on the right to life, the United Nations Human Rights Committee noted the need for States parties to take positive measures to reduce infant mortality and increase life expectancy, particularly by eradicating malnutrition and epidemics.[59]

Second, from the perspective of the types of obligations of the right to an adequate standard of living, it broadly includes three obligations: respect, protection, and enforcement. These obligations are both negative and positive in the traditional dichotomy. We can take General Comment No. 14 on the International Covenant on Economic, Social and Cultural Rights, published by the Committee on Economic, Social and Cultural Rights, as an example. It provides for breaches of obligations: breaches of the obligation to respect include "violations of Covenant 12" The standard of State conduct, policy or law established by this Convention and which is likely to cause bodily harm, unnecessary morbidity, and preventable death"; Violations of the obligation to protect include "a State's failure to take all necessary measures to ensure that the right to health of its citizens within its jurisdiction is protected from harm by third parties"; Violations of the obligation to implement include "failure by

[58] *Soobramoney v. Minister of Health*, 1997(12)BCLR 1696(HIS).

[59] See Wu [33].

States parties to take the necessary steps to realize the right to health". The obligation to respect is a clear negative obligation of the Government.[60] It is, therefore, a mistake to generalize the right to an adequate standard of living as a positive right and to assert its inadjudicability on that basis.

4.2 *Models of Remedies for the Right to an Adequate Standard of Living*

From the perspective of international law, when a country signs and ratifies the International Covenant on Economic, Social and Cultural Rights, it agrees to fulfill a series of obligations under the Covenant and is subject to accountability to the United Nations. This monitoring and accountability constitute a remedy procedure, i.e. external remedies. At the domestic level, citizens can file lawsuits against government violations of the right to an adequate standard of living in the relevant courts, which also constitutes an internal remedy for the right to an adequate standard of living.[61]

4.2.1 External Remedies for the Right to an Adequate Standard of Living

External remedies for the right to an adequate standard of living primarily involve reporting procedures under international organizations. The Committee on Economic, Social and Cultural Rights is primarily responsible for monitoring the implementation of economic, social, and cultural rights, including the right to an adequate standard of living. In accordance with the Charter of the United Nations, the Committee conducts thematic studies, makes recommendations, and drafts international human rights instruments in the field of human rights, submitting them to the General Assembly. It also investigates allegations of human rights violations, deals with communications relating to human rights violations, expresses views on the human rights situation in the country concerned, and adopts resolutions. Moreover, it is responsible for considering the reports periodically submitted to the United Nations by States parties on the steps taken to promote and protect economic, social, and cultural rights and on the progress made in the enjoyment of human rights. The Committee requests the reporting State to provide relevant information on the right to an adequate standard of living, the poverty line and the annual income status of the poor, and whether the standard of living of citizens has improved over a given period based on real living standards. Based on these reports and other reports from United

[60] United Nations. *Committee on Economic, Social and Cultural Rights.* U.N.ESCOR, 22d; Charian [34].

[61] For the discussion of the following part, the author draws on the relevant research of Mr. Xia Lian, See Charian [34].

Nations specialized agencies, the Committee makes general recommendations to the United Nations Economic and Social Council to assist States parties in fulfilling their obligations to implement the Covenant.[62] It also draws attention to deficiencies in their reports and recommends ways to improve the reporting procedure to promote accelerated action by States parties, international organizations, and United Nations specialized agencies to achieve the full enjoyment of economic, social, and cultural rights.[63]

4.2.2 Internal Remedies for the Right to an Adequate Standard of Living

The so-called internal remedies for the right to an adequate standard of living mainly involve bringing violations of the right to health by the government and the State to the relevant constitutional court or specialized court for safeguarding citizens' right to health through constitutional litigation. According to Mr. Charion's research, the attitude of States towards the International Covenant on Economic, Social and Cultural Rights differs, and thus, towards the internal remedies of the right to health. In particular, in the Netherlands, once ratified by the Dutch Government, an international treaty automatically becomes part of its domestic law, and citizens have access to judicial remedies under the international convention. India adopts a dualist approach to the application of international law, i.e. international law must become part of domestic law before it can be applied by domestic jurisdiction. Since the Constitution of India does not provide for the right to health, the Constitutional Court of India can only cite the right to life provisions of Article 21 of the Constitution of India as the basis for judicial decisions in constitutional proceedings concerning the right to health. But as can be seen in the 1992 C.E.S.C. Limited v. Subbash Chandra Bose case, judges clearly interpret the right to life in their constitution on the basis of the right to health in international law.[64]

The right to an adequate standard of living is mostly addressed through internal remedies. Although South Africa signed the International Covenant on Economic, Social and Cultural Rights in 1994, it has yet to ratify it. However, the fundamental concept of the right to an adequate standard of living has been incorporated into South African law. When the government violates the right of individual citizens to an adequate standard of living or fails to fulfill its obligations in this regard, individuals may bring proceedings before the specialized Constitutional Court. Through cases like Subramoni v. Minister of Health and Therapeutic Action Campaign v. Ministry of Health, the Constitutional Court established that the courts should be guided by utilitarian and dynamic principles in internal remedies for the right to health.[65]

---

[62] See Anonymous Simonides, Human Rights: Concept and Standards, Ashgate Publisning Company, 2000, pp. 128–129.

[63] See Charian [34].

[64] See Charian [34].

[65] The author has devoted an article to this issue, See Zheng [35].

4.3 *Basic Principles of the Right to an Adequate Standard of Living Remedies—The Case of the South African Right to Health Remedies*

South Africa adopts the model of domestic remedies with regard to the right to health, i.e. constitutional litigation, and the legally binding judgements rendered by the South African Constitutional Court are one of the important sources of law. Therefore, in the following, I will attempt to reveal the basic principles underlying the remedy of the right to health in South Africa by analyzing two classic cases in constitutional litigation on the right to health.

4.3.1 An Introduction to Two Classic Cases of the Right to Health in South Africa

The first case was the 1996 case of Soobramoney v. Minister of Health in South Africa.[66] The facts of the case are as follows: Mr. Subramoni suffered from diabetes, heart disease, cardiovascular disease, and other illnesses. In 1996, he suffered from permanent kidney failure and requested dialysis from a national hospital. However, his request was refused on the grounds that it would only be given to patients who could be cured or those waiting for a kidney transplant. Mr. Subramoni relied on Article 27(3) of the South African Constitution, which provides that no one may be denied emergency medical treatment, and Article 11, which provides that everyone has the right to life. He filed a constitutional lawsuit with the Constitutional Court, arguing that the hospital's actions violated his constitutional right to health. However, the Constitutional Court ultimately rejected Mr. Subramoni's claim.

The second case was the Treatment Action Campaign v. Minister of Health, heard in the High Court of Pretoria, South Africa, in August 2001.[67] In this case, Nevirapine, a new drug to control AIDS, was not being promoted by the South African Ministry of Health. The Treatment Action Campaign, a South African AIDS NGO, filed a constitutional case in the Pretoria High Court, arguing that the Ministry's refusal to promote Nevirapine violated the relevant provisions of the Constitution. In December of the same year, the Pretoria High Court ordered the Minister of Health of South Africa to provide Nevirapine in all public hospitals and clinics with diagnostic equipment. Additionally, the Minister of Health was instructed to develop a comprehensive plan to prevent and reduce vertical mother-to-child transmission of HIV and to report this plan to the High Court of Limpopo. The South African Ministry of Health subsequently appealed the case to the South African Constitutional Court. In July 2002, the Constitutional Court of South Africa ruled in favour of the Pretoria High Court, finding that the Ministry of Health had an obligation to promote the use of Nevirapine.

---

66 See *Soobramoney v. Minister of Health*, 1997(12)BCLR 1696(HIS).

67 See *Treatment Action Campaign v. Minister of Health*, 2002(4)BCLR356(T).

4.3.2 The Principle of the Right to Health Remedy

A general description of two cases on the right to health in South Africa shows that although in Subramoni v. Minister of Health, the Constitutional Court ultimately rejected Subramoni's claim for the right to health, in the case of Treatment Action Campaign v. Ministry of Health, The Pretoria High Court and the Constitutional Court of South Africa both upheld the claims of the Treatment Action Campaign in relation to the right to health. On the whole, the South African courts recognized the justiciability of the right to health, and the two judgments had legal effect as soon as they entered into force, which also provides a strong basis in practice for future litigation on the right to health. Therefore, an in-depth analysis of these two cases and their judgments provides insight into the basic principles followed by the courts in internal remedies for the right to health, which will facilitate our better understanding of the remedies of the right to health in South Africa. Specifically, South African courts have followed the following two basic principles in relation to the right to health:

First, the utilitarian principle. The utilitarian principle is the principle of satisfying the greatest happiness or interests of the greatest number of people. According to this principle, a policy decision or action is made to satisfy the happiness of the greatest number of people and thus to maximize the benefits of society.[68] In the case of Subramoni v. Minister of Health, Subramoni suffered from an incurable disease, and dialysis on him could not save his life. The hospital's decision to refuse to give Subramoni kidney dialysis was reasonable because dialysis was a subsistence resource, and providing it to Subramoni would mean depriving other people who have hope of continuing to survive of the chance to survive. From the perspective of the interests of society as a whole, providing dialysis to Subramoni does not in itself maximize the benefits of society. Therefore, the court held that citizens must be subject to the priority allocation of government resources in the process of equal realization of the right to healthcare.[69]

The second principle is the principle of agency. In the case of Treatment Action Campaign v. Ministry of Health, the court held that the government's ban on the use of nevirapine in public hospitals was unreasonable for two reasons: first, the policy was inflexible and did not take into account the needs of specific vulnerable groups; secondly, the restrictions on nevirapine seriously affected the overall AIDS prevention plan, and the government's policies were too mechanical. Due to the reality of South Africa's domestic economic development, the court had to take into account the government's financial budget situation and be flexible. In other words, the courts have to find a balance between political and legislative competence and judicial competence. This objectively requires the court to give full play to its initiative and flexibly interpret the Constitution and government policies to determine whether the government's actions are "reasonable". Specifically, the courts must make historical interpretations of the history of development and its significance

[68] Bentham [36].

[69] See *Soobramoney v. Minister of Health*, 1997(12)BCLR 1696(HIS).

through the interpretation of constitutional texts related to the right to health. They must make specific judgments on the manner of protection and the criteria for the reasonableness of government actions through case-by-case analysis.[70] This guarantees the dominant position of the government in economic, social, and cultural development, while effectively defending the individual rights of citizens.

5 Realization of the Right to an Adequate Standard of Living in China: Taking the Low-Cost Housing System as an Example

In recent years, the realization of the right to an adequate standard of living has increasingly become a hot issue in legal circles. Existing research has focused on how to legalize and effectively protect this right through remedies. This line of research reflects the shift from the legitimacy of the right to its actual realization. This undoubtedly advances the de facto development of the right to an adequate standard of living. However, the biggest problem with this reflection in jurisprudence, particularly in constitutional and administrative law and human rights, is the lack of necessary attention to the social effects of the practical operation of the right to an adequate standard of living.

In fact, from the perspective of social effects, China's right to an adequate standard of living plays an important role in ensuring the living conditions of vulnerable groups, and in constructing the underlying social identity of these vulnerable groups. This construction of social identity at the bottom is mainly manifested in the "labeling" effect of the right to an adequate standard of living, the self-identification of vulnerable groups in specific life situations, and the "othering" attitude adopted by society towards vulnerable groups. We will use China's low-cost housing system as an example to illustrate this problem, with a view to raising necessary alarms for the realization of the right to an adequate standard of living in China.

5.1 The Actual Standards and Subjects of the Right to an Adequate Standard of Living in China

Since China has acceded to and ratified the International Covenant on Economic, Social and Cultural Rights, it is required to submit its periodic report to the United Nations Committee on Economic, Social and Cultural Rights within two years of the entry into force of the Covenant, and every five years thereafter, to describe the legislative, judicial, policy, and other measures taken by the country to ensure the

---

[70] See Hu [37].

enjoyment of the rights contained in the Convention.[71] China legally recognizes the right to an adequate standard of living and must do its utmost to guarantee the full enjoyment of this right. The low-cost housing system is an important system for citizens to realize an adequate standard of living. The "Measures for the Administration of Low-rent Housing for Urban Families with the Lowest Income," which were deliberated and adopted at the 22nd executive meeting of the Ministry of Construction on November 15, 2003, and issued on December 2003 as Order No. 120 by the Ministry of Construction, the Ministry of Finance, the Ministry of Civil Affairs, the Ministry of Land and Resources, and the State Administration of Taxation on March 31, 2004, is the basic guiding norm for the construction of low-rent housing in cities and towns nationwide. By analyzing the Measures and relevant local practices, we can grasp the efforts made by China as a whole in striving to realize the right to an adequate standard of living.

5.1.1 Simplification of the Right to an Adequate Standard of Living, an Appropriate Standard

Good housing and a suitable home environment are essential conditions for human life in modern society. The United Nations Committee on Economic, Social and Cultural Rights has defined the content of the right to housing based on a review of numerous national reports.[72] While a state may unilaterally declare the legal effect of denouncing or modifying the application of certain provisions of a treaty under Article 2 of the Vienna Convention on the Law of Treaties, the Convention and internationally accepted norms do not permit reservations.[73] At the legislative level, a country's level of economic development constrains the appropriate standard of the right to an adequate standard of living, and the actual situation of a country must be taken into account when linking international standards with domestic standards. When a state signs and ratifies the United Nations International Covenant on Economic, Social and Cultural Rights, it may make appropriate reservations to specific standards of the right to housing, which is permissible under international law. Therefore, our standards for the protection of low-cost housing may not fully adopt the standards set by the United Nations Committee on Economic, Social and Cultural Rights. However, when formulating corresponding standards for low-cost housing, we should take full account of the standards established by the Committee on Economic, Social and Cultural Rights mentioned above.

As for the guarantee standards of low-rent housing in China, the Measures for the Administration of Low-Rent Housing for Urban Families with the Lowest Income and the Measures for the Administration of Low-rent Housing in Cities and Towns formulated by various localities mainly adopt two regulatory models (Table 1): the

---

[71] See Yang [38].

[72] See Will [39].

[73] See Yang [40].

Table 1 Urban low-rent housing guarantee standards

City	Application criteria	Safeguard standards
Beijing	7.5 m^2/person	10 m^2/person
Nanking	8 m^2/person	Households with less than two people are about 40 m^2, and households with more than three people are about 50 m^2
Shanghai	5 m^2/person	The standards for guaranteeing the per capita area of low-rent housing for the lowest income families in cities and towns shall be periodically published by the municipal people's government
Hangzhou	15 m^2 or less, or 45 m^2 (inclusive) for families with more than 3 people The following	The guaranteed area shall be controlled according to the standard of construction area of not less than 36 m^2 and not higher than 50 m^2
Wuhan	6 m^2/person	Not less than 8 m^2/person
Sian		The standards for guaranteeing the per capita area of low-rent housing for the lowest income families in cities and towns shall be periodically published by the municipal people's government
Ningbo	Less than 36 m^2 per household or 18 m^2 per person	The per capita housing floor area is 18 m^2, and the floor area of each household is not less than 36 m^2

first model specifically stipulates the guaranteed area, while the second model delegates the power to stipulate the guarantee standards for the per capita low-rent housing area of the lowest income families in cities and towns to the municipal people's government, which regularly publishes it. Both the specific guaranteed area model and the authorized provision model place great emphasis on the minimum guaranteed area of low-cost housing. However, they ignore other criteria for housing rights. These specific regulations do not stipulate other supporting facilities of low-cost housing, living environment, cultural factors of housing, etc.

In fact, not only did China ignore appropriate standards for low-cost housing in the legislative process, but also academic and public opinion circles did not fully recognize the appropriate standards for low-cost housing. Recently, Mao Yushi, a well-known economist in China, suggested that "low-cost rental housing does not have toilets to prevent the rich from buying," which caused an uproar on the internet. In response to this, some netizens suggested the development of "poor people's cocoons" to replace low-cost housing, which "can be tailored to the size of the poor, occupying little space, can be placed anywhere, hanging under a tree like an insect egg, adsorbed outside the building, arranged on both sides of the street…" The ironic "toilet theory," extremely spoofing, got popular among netizens.[74]

[74] See "Netizens spoof Mao Yushi's remarks that low-cost rental houses do not have toilets", available at: http://news.sina.com.cn/s/2009-03-25/050517475298.shtml, 2009-04-05.

In fact, both the "toilet theory" and the "poor cocoon" spoofed by netizens simply equate the appropriate standard of low-cost housing with the minimum guaranteed area of low-cost housing. According to a general comment issued by the United Nations in 1991, "We should not interpret housing rights narrowly. For example, the right to housing is regarded as merely a shelter from the wind and rain on the head, protection from the cold and heat... Rather, it should be seen as the right to live somewhere in safety, peace, and dignity..." The Japanese scholar Akira Osuka also clearly pointed out the significance of the relevant articles of the Japanese Constitution: "It is well known that Article 25, paragraph 1, of the Constitution guarantees The 'minimum standard of subsistence' generally refers not to the minimum subsistence allowance necessary for the survival of man, but to a certain cultural standard of living. This means that it is not permissible to maintain a subsistence security based on the right to subsistence only to guarantee the minimum subsistence allowance or close to this level; In other words, in the guarantee of the right to subsistence, the minimum subsistence allowance constitutes only part of its indispensable prerequisites.[75] Therefore, the life support of citizens equivalent to the minimum subsistence can only be an absolute prerequisite for ensuring the 'minimum subsistence'. "Eating, drinking, pulling, scattering, clothing, eating, sheltering, and walking are themselves one, and they constitute the most basic element to measure a person's quality of life. Therefore, the formulation of housing standards cannot only look at the size of the house, but also consider other factors such as hardware facilities and software environment. Regarding low-cost housing in China, there is indeed a problem of the rich buying it. However, the reason why the rich buy it is not because the poor who are in economic hardship do not have the ability to buy, but because of our low-cost housing system. Therefore, we should find solutions from the system itself and absolutely not from lowering the standard of low-cost housing itself. The absence of toilets in low-cost housing may indeed prevent the rich from buying, but the price is the convenience of "toileting" and "convenience" for the disadvantaged poor. The misunderstanding of the standards of low-cost housing in academic circles and public opinion circles has fully exposed the weak awareness of human rights of the Chinese people. From the perspective of human rights strategy, this will leave a pretext for people with ulterior motives to criticize China's human rights situation and is not conducive to enhancing China's human rights image.

5.1.2 Specificity of the Subject of the Right to an Adequate Standard of Living

According to Judge Thatchar, the former United Nations Special Rapporteur on housing rights, in his 1995 report on the promotion of the right to adequate housing, the State, as the subject of housing obligations, must assume the following obligations: First, once States parties have formally recognized their obligations under the right to housing, they should use all possible means to ensure that everyone has

[75] Osuka [40].

access to housing resources that guarantee adequate health, welfare, and security and are compatible with other human rights. Second, if a person is homeless, inadequately housed, or generally unable to acquire a package of rights intrinsically linked to the right to housing, a claim or demand to society to provide or access housing resources may be made. Thirdly, following its direct commitment to legal obligations, States parties should take a series of measures to demonstrate their policy and legal recognition of the various constituent aspects of the right to housing. Zachar's report essentially distinguishes the right to adequate housing between policy claims relating to housing and means of subsistence claims relating to housing.[76]

Based on our analysis of the right to housing, we believe that everyone is entitled to the right to demand access to adequate housing from the government when their housing situation is threatened. However, China's low-cost housing system mainly serves orphans, the elderly, the sick, the disabled, and families facing special difficulties. In practice, disabled soldiers, families of military martyrs, and model workers are the main beneficiaries of low-cost rental housing (as shown in Table 2). Furthermore, many cities have specific requirements for low-rent housing eligibility, such as having a non-agricultural permanent household registration in the city and actually residing there, and at least one family member having obtained the city's non-agricultural permanent household registration for a specified number of years. Such requirements are mainly due to China's economic development level and the need for ease of management. However, the Maastricht Guidelines on Violations of Economic, Social and Cultural Rights, adopted in 1998, state that "lack of resources shall not excuse States parties from fulfilling their minimum obligations to implement economic, social, and cultural rights."[77] Therefore, in essence, the right to housing should apply to everyone whose housing situation is threatened. In other words, most of the low-cost rental housing beneficiaries in China are the objects of state preferential care, and the country's low-cost housing system emphasizes political factors rather than human rights factors. For instance, Article 9 of the Implementation Rules for the Guarantee of Low-Rent Housing for the Lowest Income Families in Nanjing, promulgated in 2005, specifically outlines the conditions for applying for rent-in-kind allotment, such as orphaned persons over the age of 60 or with first-class disability certificates. The conditions for model workers at or above the municipal level are formulated separately by the municipal real estate management department in conjunction with the municipal federation of trade unions. However, there is no legal provision on whether other entities can apply for low-cost housing.

[76] See Eide et al. [41].

[77] The Maastricht Guidelines on Violations of Economic, Social and Cultural Rights. (1998). Human Rights Quarterly, (8).

Table 2 Occupancy of low-cost housing community in Guangqumen Beili, Beijing[a]

	Model workers	Disabled servicemen	Military martyrs	Other
Household	28	162	61	20
Percentage	10.33%	59.78%	22.51%	7.38%

[a] See Wang [42]

5.2 *Survival, Poverty and Our Low-Cost Housing System*

The reason why China's low-cost housing system has problems with simplifying the guarantee standard and the specificity of the subject of rights lies in China's understanding of the right to an adequate standard of living itself. The right to an adequate standard of living in China reflects a human logic of survival, not a logic of life. This logic of survival is based on the concept of poverty resulting from a lack of resources.

5.2.1 The Survival Logic of China's Low-Cost Housing System

Based on the above analysis, the author believes that China's implementation of the low-cost housing system is not only due to its commitment to fulfill its obligations under the International Covenant on Economic, Social and Cultural Rights but also to address the gap between economic growth and social development. Therefore, the low-cost housing system has a strong political dimension. Here's why:

Firstly, China's low-cost housing system focuses on the right to an adequate standard of living as a matter of "survival" rather than "life". According to Mr. Yao Jianzong, the fundamental difference between humans and animals is that people not only "live" but also "truly live". The difference between the two is that "survival" only requires following the natural laws of biological species to continue life without considering the "meaning" of its continuation, while "life" is based on the "meaning" and "value" of this "survival" itself, as well as the "ultimate basis" and "reason" of this "existence", which involves reflecting on and creating meaning and value. Therefore, "life" is unique to humans.[78] In other words, "the life activity of an animal is its existence, and its survival is its life activity." Animals adapt to nature with the life instinct given by nature, so as to maintain their own survival. This vital activity of existence is purely natural. Man not only exists through life activities, but is also aware of his life activities and carries them out according to his own will and consciousness. In this way, the activity of human life becomes an activity to realize the purposive requirements of man, a way to transform one's own purposive requirements into the reality desired by adults, and a way to make the world meet its own needs. Because of this, man's life activity is no longer a way of subsistence that purely adapts to nature to maintain its own existence, but a way of life that changes

[78] See Yao [43].

nature to create a world of man. Furthermore, "man's 'life' activity and animal's 'survival' activity are not only two different activities of man and animal to maintain 'life', but also two different activities of man and animal to continue 'life'." The life activity of animals is to continue the life activity of its kind in a 'copying' way, and is therefore an 'ahistorical' way of continuation; Human life activities are perpetuated by creating 'culture' and 'cultural' inheritance, and are therefore a continuation of 'history'. Man's 'living' activity is a 'historical' activity distinct from all animal 'survival' activities."[79] This "historical" activity, which perpetuates its kind in the form of "culture" and "cultural" inheritance, constitutes the "relational world" of man, which is the "society" of real people.[80]

Based on the analysis above, it is evident that the primary difference between survival and life lies in the existence of cultural and dignity factors. These factors also constitute the substantive content of the right to an adequate standard of living, including the right to housing. In line with this, the United Nations Committee on Economic, Social and Cultural Rights considers that the rights under the International Covenant on Economic, Social and Cultural Rights stem from the "inherent dignity of the human person," which is primarily manifested through adequate housing standards. The Global Strategy for Shelter to the Year 2000 states that "adequate accommodation" means the right to a suitable solitary home, adequate space, security, lighting and ventilation, infrastructure, and the right equipment for employment, all of which should be reasonably priced.[81] However, China's existing laws and regulations regulate the guarantee standards of low-cost housing mainly from the perspective of protection, as mentioned above, and there are few provisions for other supporting facilities and infrastructure of low-cost housing. In particular, the cultural and dignity elements of low-cost housing are not reflected as they should be. Mr. Mao Yushi has repeatedly stressed in his recent articles that low-cost housing should adopt lower standards, and he believes that "the low construction standards of low-cost housing are discriminatory towards the poor, but they also provide helpful and preferential treatment for the poor."[82]However, in accordance with the spirit and thrust of the International Covenant on Economic, Social and Cultural Rights, "every human being is entitled to realize his or her basic needs with the dignity of the human person". In other words, no one may be compelled to meet their basic needs by sacrificing or being forced to give up their fundamental freedoms, such as begging, prostitution, or hard labor.[83] Whether in concrete practice or theoretical circles, the reason why the standard for low-cost housing is set so low in China is mainly because the right to an adequate standard of living, including the right to housing, is positioned at the level of "survival" rather than the level of "life". The right to housing is understood narrowly as shelter from the elements. In this

79 Sun [44].

80 Yao [43].

81 See Yang [38, p. 45].

82 Mao [45], 2009-03-22.

83 Liu [3].

Table 3 Table of changes in China's Gini coefficient (1995–2006)[a]

Year	1995	1996	1997	1998	1999	2000
Gini coefficient	0.389	0.375	0.379	0.386	0.397	0.408 9
Year	2001	2002	2003	2004	2005	2006
Gini coefficient	0.403 1	0.432 6	0.438 6	0.438 7	0.47	0.496

[a] This data comes from http://baike.baidu.com/view/186.htm#3, 2009-04-05

sense, some scholars understand low-cost housing as a means of realizing the right to adequate housing in terms of human biology rather than human culture.

Second, China's low-cost housing system primarily serves to address the excessive wealth gap in society and maintain social stability and harmony.

Since the mid-90 s, there has been a disparity between economic growth and social development in China, with the economy experiencing relatively rapid growth while the majority of people in society have not benefited from it. According to data reflecting China's residents' income gap change in the Gini coefficient from 1995 to 2006, China exceeded the United Nations threshold of 0.4, reaching 0.4089 in 2000. Moreover, from 2000 to 2006, the Gini coefficient value continued to increase, indicating that the wealth gap in the country is gradually widening (see Table 3). From the perspective of economic growth and employment growth, in 1997, China's GDP increased by 8.8%, while the number of employees increased by only 1.1%. In 1998, GDP grew by 1.8%, while employment increased by only 0.5%. In 1999, GDP grew by 7.1%, while employment increased by only 0.89%. In 2000, GDP grew by 8%, and employment increased by only 0.79%. This means that although the economic growth rate has been maintained at 7–8%, this high-speed growth has not led to an increase in employment opportunities.[84] From the perspective of social security standards, vulnerable groups have not benefited from rapid economic growth. For example, in Beijing, unemployment insurance benefits increased from 291 yuan in 1999 to 374 yuan in 2002, while the basic living expenses of laid-off workers increased from 286 yuan in 1999 to 326 yuan. The dibao standard, a form of social assistance for those in poverty, increased from 273 yuan in 1999 to 290 yuan in 2002. As a result, social security standards are growing much slower than the rate of economic growth.[85]

As the gap between the rich and the poor gradually widened, China began the process of "commodification of housing" in 1998, using the housing system as an important means to stimulate domestic demand and promote economic development. Since 2002, the price of commercial housing has shown a rapid upward trend, resulting in a gap between real estate prices and the actual income level of residents that is much larger than the internationally recognized reasonable price-to-income ratio of 6:1.[86] Under the dual background of the Gini coefficient exceeding the

[84] See Sun [46, p. 82].

[85] See Sun [46, p. 84].

[86] See Wang [42, p. 1].

warning line and the housing price-to-income ratio exceeding a reasonable value, by the end of 2007, the country's urban homeless population is estimated to be as high as 240 million people, accounting for 40.4% of the entire urban population. This means that about 40% of the country's urban citizens are now "homeless".[87]

Although China has vigorously promoted the affordable housing system in various cities, there is a major problem with the system: it cannot protect the most vulnerable people, because affordable housing mainly helps middle-income individuals. The neediest simply cannot afford affordable housing.[88]

In the process of the rupture between economic growth and social development, social stratification has become increasingly apparent. The contradiction between the powerful and vulnerable in society has become more pronounced. Hatred of the rich and discriminatory attitudes are becoming more prominent in social life. The housing sector has become a focal point for prominent social contradictions. On the one hand, there are procedural and substantive defects in the demolition process, which leads to the expansion of contradictions between the government and individual citizens, and individual citizens' behavior against the government occurs from time to time. On the other hand, the various power supports behind high housing prices and the various "house speculation groups" that have emerged in society have intensified the contradictions between individuals, especially vulnerable groups, and power groups and the wealthy class. These factors directly affect the stability and harmony of our society. Keeping these vulnerable groups alive is the primary goal of stability and harmony. Therefore, the "Several Opinions of the State Council on Solving the Housing Difficulties of Low-income Urban Families" clearly state that it is necessary to accelerate the establishment and improvement of a policy system that focuses on the low-cost housing system and solves the housing difficulties of low-income urban families through multiple channels.

Third, China's low-cost housing system essentially adopts a model of charitable welfare, rather than a model of entitlement welfare.

The charitable welfare model is a manifestation of humanitarianism. It emphasizes, on the one hand, that it is the responsibility of society and the government to help the poor, and on the other hand, it emphasizes that individuals should take responsibility for their own well-being. It holds that poverty is a personal failure and opposes the idea of the "healthy poor" as the object of social assistance. As a result, social welfare is provided only to a limited extent, as a humanitarian charitable relief measure, to the "disabled person." In contrast, the entitlement welfare model emphasizes that people's demands for welfare come from human rights.[89] As far as the origin of the right is concerned, it "exists in the established rules ... Rights should be seen as a strong demand for justice that is insisted on as legitimate or formally justified, rather than as an expression of humanity and tolerance that exists

---

[87] Shen Xiaojie. The Truth of China's Housing Crisis Covered Up in the Rescue Market. available at: http://qzone.qq.com/blog/62200607112275-37150, 2009-04-05.

[88] See Mao Yushi. It's Wrong to Build Affordable Housing, available at: http://www.tianya.cn/publicforum/content/house/1/125739.shtml, 2009-04-05.

[89] See Qian [47].

in civilized society".[90] In the area of housing rights, these two models correspond to what Bengtsson calls "universal housing policies" and "selective housing policies", respectively. The biggest difference between the two models is the intervention model of the state: in the selective housing policy model, the right to housing implies that the state provides the necessary physical form; in the universal housing policy model, the right to housing does not imply that the state's obligations are fully fulfilled at all times and in all individual cases, but rather implies a general policy of the state to correct the market.[91]

In essence, China's low-cost housing system mainly reflects a model of charitable welfare. Firstly, the low-cost housing system does not cover the entire real estate market and Chinese officials have no intention of adjusting the structure of the market in the short term. On the contrary, the implementation of the low-rent housing system aims to stabilize the price of real estate.[92] Secondly, the supply of low-cost housing in China falls within the scope of administrative payments, and Chinese citizens cannot file a lawsuit against the low-rent housing system or the appropriate standards of low-cost housing. They can only file a limited lawsuit on whether the government should approve low-rent housing. Thirdly, the low-cost housing system only applies to certain groups, such as orphans, the elderly, the sick, the disabled, and families in urgent need of assistance. The law does not provide an enumeration of what constitutes urgent need, which essentially denies the possibility of "healthy poor" applying for low-cost housing. Finally, the development of China's low-cost housing system has been seriously affected by the concept of economic benefits. Human rights and efficiency are fundamentally consistent, but they may also contradict each other in specific social life. The development of human rights is primarily based on equality and fairness, while efficiency places greater emphasis on respective strengths and competition based on them. Such competition can adversely affect equality and fairness and the development of human rights based on them. The charitable welfare model is mainly based on competition, while the rights welfare model emphasizes human equality and justice. Therefore, the charitable welfare model is to provide certain care to the lives of others on the premise of fully realizing efficiency. The rights-based welfare model places more emphasis on the self-esteem of people as human beings, as well as competition and cooperation based on self-respect. Under the charitable welfare model, once the low-cost housing system is no longer beneficial to the local government, they will lack enthusiasm. This is also the main reason for the slow progress in the construction of the low-rent housing system in various parts of China.[93]

---

[90] Freeden [48].

[91] See Will [49].

[92] CIC consultants estimate that the low-cost housing initiative, which is a government project aimed at improving people's living conditions, is worth around 9 trillion yuan. This initiative is unlikely to have a significant impact on the current real estate market, particularly the commercial housing market, and may even help to stabilize house prices to some extent., available at: http://esf.gz.soufun.com/newsecond/news/2477345.htm, 2009-04-07.

[93] See "China's Housing Security "Roadmap" Outlines a New Curve of Policy Change, available at: http://news.xinhuanet.com/house/2007-11/28/content_7157892.htm, 2009-04-05.

5.2.2 The Basic Positioning of China's Low-Cost Housing System to Poverty

The deeper reason why China's low-rent housing security standards adopt a single guarantee area standard, while ignoring the dignity factors and cultural factors of low-cost housing security standards, lies in China's understanding of poverty itself. Poverty can be divided into two basic situations: poverty in the sense of lack of material resources and poverty in the structural sense. The right to an adequate level, including the right to housing, primarily addresses poverty in the structural sense. However, China's low-cost housing system is primarily based on poverty in the sense of a lack of material resources.

The so-called poverty in the sense of lack of material resources mainly refers to "extreme inadequacy" in the means of subsistence, "lack of money, and poor livelihood".[94] The so-called poverty in the structural sense means that the cause of poverty is not only due to the scarcity of the means of subsistence in the natural sense, but also due to the existing structure of society and the inaction of the government in some aspects. From the perspective of structural poverty, the causes of poverty include at least the following two aspects: on the one hand, it is caused by the scarcity of natural resources; on the other hand, it is caused by our view of poverty as a quantifiable lack of natural resources, and governments are only passively reducing it, rather than actively eliminating it. Therefore, if poverty is regarded as a violation of human rights, it will undoubtedly increase the responsibility of the government, thereby changing the government's response to poverty from passive to proactive.[95] In this sense, the structural concept of poverty looks at poverty from a human rights perspective and therefore has a human rights dimension.

China's low-cost housing system is based on attributing the poverty of residents' basic living standards mainly to the lack of material resources. The scarcity of material resources is indeed an important reason for poverty in China, but it is not the only reason. The concept of poverty in the structural sense should also be an important theoretical basis for us to establish a low-cost housing system. The reason why China's low-rent housing system is based on the concept of poverty in the sense of lack of material resources is mainly due to the following aspects: First, the focus of China's low-rent housing system is to materially help the most difficult people to obtain low-rent housing. However, the parties do not have the right to object to the entire low-cost housing system and the entire welfare system itself. China's current low-cost housing system is premised on the dual structure of urban and rural areas and the continued differentiation of urban society. For example, in China, the application conditions for low-cost rental housing often stipulate that family members have non-agricultural permanent household registration in the city and actually reside. This in fact recognizes the dual structure of urban and rural areas in China. Although China has implemented a series of welfare systems, including the low-cost housing system, China's urban Gini coefficient still continues to rise, which means that the

[94] Zhang [50].

[95] See Sané [2].

poverty gap in China's cities continues to expand, and the differentiation of urban society continues. Second, China's low-cost housing system mainly attributes the poverty of individuals to individuals, ignoring the impact of China's current social structure on everyone. As mentioned above, the main applicants for low-cost rental housing in China are mainly orphans, the elderly, the sick, the disabled and other families with special difficulties. Judging from the reasons for the poverty of these special families, they lose part or all of their ability to work mainly due to old age and infirmity. In practice, families whose members are healthy but still have a difficult life find it difficult to obtain low-cost housing. On the one hand, such regulations and operations are based on economic considerations; on the other hand, they are also based on the consideration of preventing the phenomenon of unearned gain in society. This also, in fact, indicates that a person will not or should not fall into poverty as long as he is strong. This perception clearly reflects the concept of poverty in the sense of material deprivation.

In fact, poverty in China increasingly reflects the characteristics of structural poverty. Since the reform and opening up, the most fundamental change in China's social structure has been the transformation from an overall society to a differentiated society, and the fundamental driving force of this change is structural reform. The most typical manifestations of this kind of structural reform in cities and towns are the restructuring and transformation of state-owned enterprises, as well as the displacement of laid-off personnel.[96] In this industrial restructuring with structural reform as the core, elements such as precision, knowledge, standardization, and stratification have come to the fore. Due to the influence of the times, it is difficult for these laid-off and displaced personnel to meet the basic requirements of precision, knowledge, standardization, and section-leveling. For the vast majority of them, it is simply impossible to return to the dominant industry of society, and under the current system, they cannot return to the original stable employment system. Moreover, sunrise industries will not provide them with many jobs. This is also the de facto poverty of this part of the population.[97,98] Moreover, due to China's lack of experience in the process of structural reform, it has placed too much trust in the market. Some elements that should not be subject to market forces have also been pushed to the market. For example, when laid-off workers are displaced, many units advocate a "one-size-fits-all" and "one-time buyout" approach. The number of participants in old-age insurance and unemployment insurance nationwide increased from 112.03 million and 79.61 million in 1998, respectively, to 201.07 million and 116.45 million by the end of 2007. However, this effectively means that social security coverage

[96] Sun [46, p. 6].

[97] Sun [46, p. 111].

[98] In 1990, China's urban poor population was 130 million. By 1995, it had increased to 191 million people. See Sun [51, p. 74].

is shrinking from the original, and some people lose it. The main groups that lose social security are unemployed laid-off workers and "flexible workers".[99]

At the same time, the rise in real estate prices in China far exceeds the growth of residents' income. The price-to-income ratio is one of the basic indicators used to measure the level of housing rights security in a certain place or country. The so-called house-to-income ratio refers to the ratio of the average price of housing in a place to the average annual income of each household. The comprehensive research department of Shanghai E-House Real Estate Research Institute recently provided a research report called "Research on China's House Price to Income Ratio: House Prices Have Fallen, First-tier Cities Are Still High". The report shows that from 1997 to 2003, the national price-to-income ratio maintained a relatively stable operating trend, at about 6.15. From 2003 to 2007, as house prices grew faster than per capita disposable income, the ratio of house prices to income increased significantly. In 2007, the ratio reached an all-time high of 7.44, indicating a serious imbalance. The situation in some large cities is even worse. For example, Beijing's ratio increased from 9.55 to 13.09; Shanghai increased from 6.7 to 11.25; Guangzhou increased from 6.49 to 12.09; Shenzhen increased from 5.85 to 13.15; Xiamen increased from 5.41 to 13.22; Chongqing increased from 3.07 to 5.15; and Tianjin increased from 4.41 to 9.34.[100] This high price-to-income ratio means that China's house price level is much higher than the income level of Chinese residents, and house prices are disproportionate to the increase in residents' income. As a result, residents remain in relative poverty, with the vast majority of residents unable to afford to purchase a home.

5.3 The Realization of the Right to an Adequate Standard of Living in China Constructs the Social Identity of the Underprivileged Groups

China's low-rent housing system is based on the basic need for human survival, and is founded on the concept of resource poverty. In specific legal practice, the system reflects a strong element of charitable welfare. This charitable welfare has a continued impact on the basic lives of people at the bottom of society and, to some extent, creates an underlying identity for these vulnerable groups, exacerbating the emergence of the "other" identity for those at the bottom.

[99] For a discussion of this issue, see Sun [51, p. 76]. The data of the year 1998 comes from Sun [51, p. 76]; The data of the end of the year 2007 comes from http://www.cn12333.com/article_view.asp?id=4864, 2009-04-10.

[100] Liu [52].

5.3.1 The "Labeling" Effect of Low-Cost Rental Housing and the Construction of the Social Identity of the Underprivileged Groups

From the perspective of China's low-cost housing, there are mainly two forms: the first is the original public housing vacated and meets the low-rent housing standards stipulated by the local government, and the second is low-rent housing built centrally by the government. China's "Measures for the Administration of Low-Rent Housing for Urban Families with the Lowest Income" clearly stipulates that "the source of low-rent housing with rent-in-kind allocation should be mainly the purchase of existing old housing." However, China's relevant low-rent housing management measures restrict the centralized construction of low-rent housing, making the government's procedures for building low-rent housing more complicated, and there are more restrictions in the actual operation process. Nevertheless, it is still one of the main sources of low-cost housing in China.

Regarding the existing old housing in China, it is relatively poor in terms of the structure and standards of the house itself, as well as in the external environment and supporting facilities. The low-cost rental housing built by the Chinese government is mainly concentrated in the suburbs of cities. Taking Jinshazhou, a large residential area in the western part of Guangzhou with a population of about 165,000, as an example, "it not only has the largest new community of low-cost rental housing and affordable housing in China but also has a number of hot limited-price housing projects." However, as of April 1, 2008, more than 900 out of 3,148 double-special hardship households with 3,148 low-cost rental houses have not moved into the new community. The reason is that, on the one hand, Jinshazhou lags behind in planning, and the investment subjects of public supporting facilities are not clear. Historically, Guangzhou's emerging urban areas still have no successful local cases to learn from in the construction and operation of public facilities such as schools, hospitals, and commercial centers. On the other hand, this concentration of low-cost housing is far from the city center, and the cost of work and living is high, which brings economic pressure to those who have a difficult life and cannot afford the cost of management, rent, transportation, food, and so on. Therefore, some people choose to give up low-cost housing.[101]

Whether it is the transformation of existing old housing into low-cost rental housing or the government's concentrated construction of low-rent housing, it has a strong "labeling" effect. According to sociological analysis, each object not only has a utilitarian meaning but also a semiotic or symbolic meaning. This semiotic or symbolic meaning often forms a value judgment on the object. Specifically, "every object, according to its purpose and scope of use, often automatically becomes a tool for dividing groups and embodies a social label after entering social use." It implies the user's income, status, pedigree, taste, etc. and is a sign of social class. For example, driving a BMW car is regarded as a sign of wealth or power, and living in a villa

[101] See "Guangzhou low-cost rental housing away from the urban area is inconvenient Abandoned by Special Hardship Households", available at: http://wh.house.sina.com.cn, 2009-04-12.

means belonging to the affluent class. The social label of this object, consciously or unconsciously used in the field of social life, becomes an important feature of the self-identification or identification of the population."[102] The conversion of old houses into low-cost housing generally takes place in the old city or town, which has a strong traditional character, while the new city often reflects a strong modern atmosphere. This creates a sharp contrast between the new and old areas and between commercial and low-cost rental housing. People who live in low-cost housing in the old town are often seen as losers, poor, migrant workers, low-skilled workers, or people with heavy financial burdens. These labels are powerful economic indicators that suggest they belong to a less powerful, less influential, and socially problematic class.[103] At the same time, the majority of residents of low-cost housing are economically disadvantaged, and economic weakness often leads to psychological vulnerability. The old houses renovated in the old city carry a strong psychological implication for these vulnerable people, suggesting that they are losers in market competition. They may feel that their own talents and efforts are insufficient to compete in the market, eventually leading to their elimination from market competition.

Although concentrating on building low-cost housing in the suburbs can reduce construction costs, it can also give the impression that low-cost housing is not an integral part of the city and perpetuate the social status of the poor.[104] In many cases, this approach simply transfers the slum problem to a new location, without fundamentally addressing the underlying issues. For example, in Buffalo, USA, a low-income residential complex called Townte Place was built by the federal government in 1954. However, the area soon became a blight on the community, hindering development in the surrounding area. To address this, the government built another similar residential complex nearby and relocated the residents of Townte Place. However, the new complex soon faced the same problems as the old one, as this approach simply duplicated the problems of slums and did not address the root causes of poverty.[105]

5.3.2 Self-Identification of the Social Identity of the Underprivileged Groups

The homogeneity of the subjects who have the right to obtain low-cost rental housing in China is high.[106] Since the community types of the residents of low-rent housing are mainly traditional communities in the old city, people have gradually developed similar lifestyles and status identities. Additionally, most of them are preferential

[102] "The Grey Social Label of Low-Cost Housing", available at: http://iamzpz.m.oeeee.com/blog/archive/2006/12/12/174667.html, 2009-04-12.

[103] See "The Grey Social Label of Low-Cost Housing", available at: http://iamzpz.m.oeeee.com/blog/archive/2006/12/12/174667.html, 2009-04-12.

[104] See Jacobs [53, p. 440].

[105] See Jacobs [53, pp. 441–442].

[106] In accordance with the Measures for the Administration of Low-Rent Housing for Urban Families with the Lowest Income, low-rent housing with rent-in-kind allocation will mainly come from acquiring existing old housing, while limiting the concentrated construction of low-cost housing.

Table 4 Neighbourhood relationships among low-cost housing households[a]

Household awareness rate (%)	Interaction rate (%)	Neighbor help rate (%)
93.1	42.9	5.3

[a] This data comes from the research group of the Department of Sociology, Tsinghua University:"Research Report on "Building a Harmonious Society and Building a Livable Community" in Chongwen District, Beijing

families, so the homogeneity of community members is high. Community members have high expectations of community identity and community life, and they take positive actions.[107] From the perspective of neighborhood relationships among low-cost housing, the household awareness rate and interaction rate are high (see Table 4). The high homogeneity of rights subjects makes it easy to form an "acquaintance society" as described by Mr. Fei Xiaotong. This can overcome many problems caused by the "stranger society" formed by the heterogeneity of subjects. For example, it is conducive to preventing people from committing crimes. However, this high degree of homogeneity also raises the important problem that these rights subjects are very likely to form a subcultural group. This subcultural group is likely to oppose the dominant culture.

Although China's low-cost housing system stipulates an exit mechanism and adopts the principle of only guaranteeing "one generation" in specific operations, from the perspective of the "generation" that is guaranteed, they are often disabled soldiers or military martyrs. The government guarantees their right to housing by allocating rent in kind. On the one hand, this is done out of consideration for their difficult living conditions, and on the other hand, awarding low-cost housing to them serves as a material reward. Therefore, in this sense, there is a sense of pride in their residence in low-cost housing. This pride is highly likely to influence their entrepreneurial spirit.

For some vulnerable groups living in low-cost housing, they are mainly laid-off workers from state-owned enterprises. "The 'superiority' that they enjoyed for many years, including the 'iron rice bowl', has disappeared, and their economic status has declined significantly. As a result, they can easily feel the vacillation of their status as a 'leading class' and the illusory connotation of 'master'." They are prone to a kind of "nostalgia" in their hearts. At the same time, "their life expectations and consumption desires are very low. They are easily satisfied and content with the status quo." This negative social psychology is essentially an identification of vulnerable groups with their own weak status.[108] In fact, a similar situation has occurred in British history. In 1795, Britain enacted the Speenhamland Act, which reflected the principle of the "right to live" system. It provided wage subsidies at the prevailing price of bread, along with a family allowance. Its purpose was to create employment in rural areas where the law applied and to prevent the poor from wandering. The law stipulated that "as long as a person's income was lower than the subsidy standard, they could

[107] See Wang [42, p. 46].

[108] Wen [53].

receive relief even if they had a job." This system protected the poor for a certain period of time, but in the long run, the consequences were dire. Although it took some time for individuals to reduce their self-esteem to the point that they would rather receive poor relief than wages, wages supplemented by public funds eventually became a bottomless pit that forced people to rely on subsidy rates. The people in the countryside gradually became poor, and the proverb "Once you rely on relief, you must always rely on relief" held true.[109] Moreover, the construction of low-cost rental housing in China adopts a centralized transformation and construction method, which means that people with financial difficulties live together, resulting in a lack of understanding of the social life of other classes and a lack of necessary reference in their daily lives.

From the perspective of their daily lives, they have a higher level of homogeneity and awareness, with not many opportunities for reemployment. For older people, small talk and playing chess are the main activities, while young people tend to be idle, spending their time sleeping and watching TV. Although they express some dissatisfaction with society in interviews, these young people often compare themselves to urbanites and migrant workers who cannot live in low-cost housing, thinking that their cultural level is low and that they lack skills. They are satisfied with their living environment.

5.3.3 The Right to an Adequate Standard of Living and the "Other" Attitude of Society

China's low-cost housing system is based on a "survival" understanding of people rather than a "living" understanding, and the poverty of socially vulnerable groups in China is mainly seen as resource poverty rather than structural poverty. Correspondingly, the low-cost housing system adopts an "othering" attitude towards the rights subjects.

As mentioned earlier, China's low-cost housing system adopts a charitable welfare model, not a rights-based welfare model. In the charitable welfare model, "welfare is given to the poor as relief and charity for the loser, and once a person receives welfare relief, they are labeled as 'incompetent' and rejected by mainstream society as an 'abnormal person'. Receiving welfare means a stigma or loss of dignity for the individual, and security of life comes at the expense of the dignity and self-respect of the individual".[110] The essence of this low-cost housing system as charitable is to treat disadvantaged groups in society as an "other" in life. It looks at the weak in society from the perspective of the subject-object dualistic model and does not, and is unwilling to, look at the weak from the perspective that society has a structural role and directly affects the status of the weak.

In terms of determining the subject of rights in China's low-cost housing system, there are two issues. Firstly, the system distinguishes between the "deserving poor"

[109] Polanyi [54].

[110] Qian [47, p. 221].

and the "undeserving poor," which becomes the moral judgment principle of social welfare. This eligibility check leads to strong social stigma for recipients, and the process of receiving relief becomes humiliating and morally degrading.[111] This morally discriminatory relief deviates from the purpose of its charity. Secondly, existing laws and regulations in China do not clearly stipulate specific rights that administrative agencies should enjoy when exercising their investigative powers in welfare. As a result, welfare investigators often infringe on the privacy rights of the parties, such as inquiring about the source and status of their income, concealed partnerships, and reasons for refusing unreasonable wages. This invades the privacy of some families or individuals, leading them to endure poverty rather than seek help from the government and society and giving up their right to assistance.[112] In the process of applying for low-cost rental housing by vulnerable groups, investigators often violate citizens' privacy rights.

References

1. Eide, A. (2001). The right to an adequate standard of living including the right to food. In A. Eide, C. Krause, & A. Rosas (Eds.), *Economic, social and cultural rights* (pp. 133–148). Brill.
2. Sané, P. (2004). Poverty, the next frontier in the struggle for human rights. *International Social Science Journal, 56*, 271–275.
3. Liu, H. (1998). The right to an adequate standard of living and social development. *Journal of Legal Studies, 1998* (2)
4. Zhang, W. (Ed.). (2003). *Marxist jurisprudence* (p. 323). Higher Education Press.
5. The Institute of Law, Chinese Academy of Social Sciences (Ed.). (1993). *International human rights instruments and institutions* (p. 10). Social Science Literature Publishers.
6. Liu, H. (1998). The right to an adequate standard of living and social development. *Journal of Legal Studies, 1998*(2).
7. Chen, X. (2000). *Study of land systems in south africa* (p. 41). Ph.D. dissertation, Chinese Academy of Social Sciences, Beijing.
8. Friedmann, H., Dreze, J., & Sen, A. (1991). Hunger and public action. *Contemporary Sociology, 21*, 42.
9. Brand, D., & Heyns, J. (2005). *Partner-economic rights in South Africa* (p. 158). Pretoria University Law Press.
10. Brand, D., & Heyns, J. (2005). *Partner-economic rights in South Africa* (pp. 163–164). Pretoria University Law Press.
11. Fitzpatrick, G., & Slye, R. C. (2003). Republic of South Africa v. Grootboom. Case No. CCT 11/00. 2000(11) BCLR 1169 and Minist of Health v. Treatment Action Campaign. Case No. CCT 8/02. *The American Journal of International Law, 2003*(3), 675–676.

[111] Qian [47, p. 44]. On August 10, 2007, the Urban Construction and Environmental Protection Committee of the Beijing Municipal Committee of the Chinese People's Political Consultative Conference held a symposium on affordable housing policies. During the symposium, some members of the Chinese People's Political Consultative Conference suggested that individuals who are able to work do not require government guarantees. These members believed that applying for government security by individuals who can work is essentially an act of seeking something for nothing, which is morally reprehensible. See Promoting the Low-Cost Housing Policy Let low-cost housing fulfill the housing dream of low-income people", available at: http://news.xinhuanet.com/house/2007-08/10/content_6506905, 2009-04-12.

[112] Tang [55], Hu [56].

12. Holmes, S., & Sunstein, C. R. (2004). *The cost of rights: Why liberty depends on taxes* (p. 23, J. Bi, Trans.). Peking University Press.
13. Pieterse, M. (2004). Coming to terms with judicial enforcement of social rights. *South African Journal on Human Rights Conference, 20*(3), 383–417.
14. Zhang, X. (2008). Commentary on the "Reasonableness Review Criteria" of the constitutional court of South Africa. *Hebei Law, 2008*(11), 164.
15. Zeng, Q. (1999). Achievements of the new South African diplomacy. *International Information, 1999*(7), 23.
16. Hu, M., & Song, H. (2004). The welfare rights controversy in the U.S. constitution. *Politics and Law, 2004*(3), 31–32
17. Simonides. (2002). *Human rights: Concept and standards* (p. 132). Ashgate Publishing Company.
18. Deng, Z. (2004). Chinese jurisprudence in a global structure. *Journal of Social Sciences, Jilin University*, (3).
19. Milne, A. J. M. (1994). *Human rights and human diversity: An essay in the philosophy of human rights* (p. 3, Y. Xia et al., Trans.). China Encyclopedia Publishing House.
20. International Human Rights Law Course Project Leader. (2002). *International human rights law course* (Vol. 1, pp. 319–320). China University of Political Science and Law Press.
21. Gao, H. (1998). Human beings are moving towards self-conscious "quasi-existence". *Journal of Social Sciences, Jilin University*, (1).
22. Yao, J. (2003). *The ecological environment of the rule of law* (p. 279). Shandong People's Publishing House.
23. Milne, A. J. M. (1994). *Human rights and human diversity: An essay in the philosophy of human rights* (p. 1, Y. Xia, et al., Trans.). China Encyclopedia Publishing House.
24. Junren, W. (2000). The modern construction of political liberalism. In J. Rawls (Ed.), *Political liberalism* (p. 630). Translin Press.
25. Tylor, E. (1981). *The definition of culture* (p. 98, G. Xiaoming, Trans.). Zhejiang People's Publishing House.
26. Crookhorn, C., et al. (1986). *Culture and the individual* (p. 4, G. Jia et al., Trans.). Zhejiang People's Publishing House.
27. Yuehong, H., & Shuxing, S. (2006). Interpretation of human dignity and the dignity of life. *Philosophical Studies, 3*, 63–64.
28. Yang, F. (2008). Obligations of positive rights to legislators in the context of the Grootboom case in South Africa. *Shandong Social Sciences, 2008*(1), 59.
29. Huang, J. (2006). Possibilities and limits of judicial guarantees of economic and social rights. *Global Law Review, 2006*(1), 67.
30. Ma, J. (1999). South Africa's demographics and employment. *International Economic Cooperation, 1999*(1), 48.
31. Mu, Y. (2006). Tax reform and implications in South Africa. *Tax Research, 2006*(10), 86.
32. Yu, L. (2008). The development of rights and obligations and the construction of a state under the rule of law. *Legal and Social Development, 2008*(3).
33. Wu, S. (2007). Jurisprudence and evidence on the juridability of environmental rights. *Legal Science, 2007*(6).
34. Charian. (2008). Cascadability of economic and social rights. *Legal and Social Development, 2008*(2).
35. Zheng, Z. (2009). On the remedies for the right to health in South Africa. *West Asia and Africa, 2009*(2).
36. Bentham, J. (2005). *An introduction to the principles of morals and legislation* (p. 27, S. Yinhong, Trans.). Commercial Press.
37. Hu, M. (2006). On the cascadability of social rights. *Legal Science, 2006*(5), 30.
38. Yang, Y (Ed.). (2005). *Bodies of the United Nations human rights conventions and the essence of the classics* (p. 6). Chinese Public Security University Press.
39. Yang, Y. (2003). *Human rights act—<International Covenant on Civil and Political Rights> research* (pp. 23–24). Chinese Public Security University Press.

40. Osuka, A. (2001). *The right to survival* (p. 192, Linhao, Trans.). Law Press.
41. Eide, A., Krause, C., & Rosas, A. (Eds.). (2001). *Economic, social and cultural rights* (pp. 152–196). Brill.
42. Wang, J. (2007). *The evolution and practice of low-cost housing system: A case study of Beijing low-rent housing community*. Master's thesis, Tsinghua University.
43. Yao, J. (2007). The philosophy of legal life contemplation: The wisdom of the philosophy of law. *Northern Methodology, 2007*(2).
44. Sun, Z. (2001). *Beyond consciousness* (pp. 2, 4). Jilin Education Press.
45. Mao, Y. (2009). *Why low-cost housing should be of low standard?* Beijing News
46. Sun, L. (2004). *Transformation and rupture: Changes in China's social structure since the reform* (p. 82). Tsinghua University Press.
47. Qian, N. (2007). *Social justice, civil rights and collectivism* (p. 221). Social Science Literature Publishers.
48. Freeden, M. (1998). *Rights* (p. 8, S. Jiaming & Y. Jianhua, Trans.). Laureate Books.
49. Will, B. (2001). Housing as a social rights: Implications for welfare state theory. *Scandinavian Political Studies, 2001*(4).
50. Zhang, Q. (2006). Seeing poverty through the law. *Journal of Shandong University, 2006*(5), 23.
51. Sun, L. (2006). *The game: Conflict of interest and harmony in a fractured society* (p. 74). Social Science Literature Publishers.
52. Liu, X. (2009, 13 April). The report shows the national price-to-income ratio has declined for the first time in years. Oriental Morning Post.
53. Wen, J. (2005). On the negative social psychology of the weak. *Journal of Anqing Normal University (Social Science Edition), 2005*(5), 28–29.
54. Polanyi, K. (1989). The great transformation: The political and economic origins of our time (pp. 14, 160–161, S. Huang, et al., Trans.). Yuanliu Publishing Business Corporation Limited.
55. Tang, J. (2003). *Report on urban poverty and anti-poverty in China* (p. 161). Huaxia Publishing House.
56. Hu, M. (2008). Welfare administrative investigation power and beneficiary rights protection. *Contemporary Jurisprudence, 2008*(2), 84.

Chapter 10
The Right to Clean Drinking Water

Hao Zhang

1 Introduction

Water is the source of life and the blood of human evolution and social development. Clean drinking water is an indispensable and extremely scarce precious resource for human beings.[1] Water is also central to alleviating poverty.[2] However, with the rapid expansion of the global population and severe pollution caused by the process of industrialization, already limited water resources have become scarcer. In the twenty-first century, the already limited water resources must meet the needs of six billion people around the world. With population growth, economic development, and the expansion of large cities, the demand for drinking water is increasing. How to effectively protect and share rare water resources will surely be a major issue facing mankind in the twenty-first century. The Universal Declaration of Human Rights of 1948, International Covenant on Economic, Social and Cultural Rights of 1966, Committee on Economic, Social and Cultural Rights of the United Nations Economic and Social Council in 2002 General comment No. 15: The right to water (economic, Articles 11 and 12 of the International Covenant on Social and Cultural Rights), the Convention on the Rights of the Child, and the Convention on the Elimination of All Forms of Discrimination against Women all contain certain provisions on the right to clean drinking water. China is a party to the International Covenant on Economic, Social and Cultural Rights, and the state respects and protects human rights in its Constitution in the Amendment to the Constitution of the People's Republic of China, adopted at the Second Session of the Tenth National People's Congress in 2004. Therefore, the government has a national obligation to guarantee the realization of the right to clean drinking water. However, due to the limitations of China's actual national conditions (serious lack of water resources, uneven distribution, serious

H. Zhang (✉)
Cadre of Hebei Provincial Public Security Department, Master of Laws, Hubei, China

[1] Shahi and Athar [1].

[2] Ruspekhofer [2].

J. Yao (ed.), *The Legal Issues of the Emerging Rights*,
https://doi.org/10.1007/978-981-97-0499-6_10

pollution, poor sanitation facilities, etc.) and the imperfection of relevant laws and regulations, the realization of our national obligation to clean drinking water is still a long way off compared with the requirements of the Convention.

2 Overview of the Right to Clean Drinking Water

United Nations General Assembly has, through Resolution no. 64/292 dated July 28, 2010, recognized clean drinking water and sanitation as a basic human right.[3] The right to clean drinking water encompasses the inherent, inalienable, and indispensable right to access adequate, safe, acceptable, accessible, and affordable water supply for personal and family life as human beings. It is one of the basic prerequisites for individuals to realize economic, social, and cultural rights, and to seek survival and development. Moreover, it is a necessary guarantee for the realization of political and civil rights.

2.1 Historical Development of the Right to Clean Water

The historical development of the right to clean drinking water can be grasped at both the international and national levels.

2.1.1 International Level

Universal Declaration of Human Rights, 1948

The Universal Declaration of Human Rights, adopted and proclaimed by the United Nations General Assembly on 10 December 1948, was the first wide-ranging human rights statement proclaimed by an international organization. Although it did not contain an explicit provision on the right to clean drinking water, it enumerates economic and social rights in detail, which have special significance for the protection of the right to clean water. Despite not directly stipulating the right to clean water, it serves as the basis on which the right to clean drinking water rests. In its preamble, the first sentence reads: "Whereas recognition of the inherent dignity and equal and inalienable rights of all members of the human family is the foundation of freedom, justice and peace in the world."[4] This shows that human dignity, which is the foundation of the right to clean water, is recognized at the beginning of the Universal Declaration of Human Rights. Article 3 of the Universal Declaration of Human Rights states: "Everyone has the right to life, liberty, and security of person."

---

[3] Shahi [3].

[4] Hu [4], pp. 24–25.

The right to clean drinking water is a prerequisite for life.[5] There is also Article 22: "Everyone, as a member of society, has the right to social security and to the realization of economic, social, and cultural rights necessary for the free development of his personal dignity and personality…"[6] Article 25 states: "… Everyone has the right to a standard of living adequate for the health and well-being of himself and his family, including food, clothing, housing, medical care, and necessary social services; the right to protection in the event of unemployment, sickness, disability, old age, or other lack of livelihood in circumstances beyond his control…".[7]

International Covenant on Economic, Social and Cultural Rights, 1966

The International Covenant on Economic, Social, and Cultural Rights declares that the rights contained in the Covenant are based on the "inherent dignity of the human person" and form "the foundation of freedom, justice, and peace in the world." Part III of the Covenant lists the rights protected by the Covenant, and Articles 11 and 12 provide for the right to an adequate standard of living and the right to health, respectively. Article 11 provides that: "The States Parties to the present Covenant recognize the right of everyone to an adequate standard of living for himself and his family, including adequate food, clothing, and housing, and to the continuous improvement of living conditions… The States Parties to the present Covenant recognize the fundamental right of everyone to be free from hunger…"[8] It follows that "the use of the word 'including' indicates that the rights referred to are not exhaustive". The right to water is clearly one of the necessary guarantees for the realization of the right to an adequate standard of living, especially since it is one of the most fundamental conditions for survival.[9] Article 12 of the International Covenant on Economic, Social, and Cultural Rights provides that "States Parties to the present Covenant recognize the right of everyone to the enjoyment of the highest attainable standard of physical and mental health…", and the right to clean drinking water is closely linked to the attainment of the highest attainable standard of physical fitness and health.[10]

Convention on the Elimination of All Forms of Discrimination Against Women, 1979 and Convention on the Rights of the Child of 1989

Article 14, paragraph 2, of the Convention on the Elimination of All Forms of Discrimination against Women provides that: "States Parties shall take all appropriate measures to eliminate discrimination against rural women and to ensure their

[5] Hu [4], pp. 24–25.
[6] Hu [4], pp. 24–25.
[7] Hu [4], pp. 24–25.
[8] Hu [4], pp. 6–8.
[9] Yang [5], p. 144.
[10] Hu [4], pp. 6–8.

participation in and benefit from rural development on a basis of equality of men and women." In particular, they are guaranteed the right to "enjoy adequate living conditions, particularly in the areas of housing, sanitation, water supply, transport and communications."[11] Article 24, paragraph 2, of the Convention on the Rights of the Child provides that "States Parties shall endeavor to realize this right fully and, in particular, shall take appropriate measures to: 'The eradication of disease and malnutrition, including the use of available technologies and the provision of adequate nutritious food and clean water in the context of primary health care, taking into account the dangers and risks of environmental pollution." Both of these sui generis human rights conventions explicitly refer to issues relating to the right to clean water.[12]

General Comments Adopted by the Committee on Economic, Social and Cultural Rights

The general comment adopted by the Committee on Economic, Social and Cultural Rights aims to "... bring to the benefit of States parties the experience traditionally gained through the examination of these reports, thereby assisting and facilitating their further implementation of the Convention and drawing the attention of States parties to deficiencies in a large number of reports; to recommend that the reporting procedure be improved, and that the activities of States parties, relevant international organizations, and specialized agencies in the progressive and effective realization of the rights recognized in the Covenant are promoted in the full and progressive manner."[13] Thus, the role of the Committee's general comments is to provide a clearer interpretative indication of the intent, meaning, and content of the International Covenant on Economic, Social and Cultural Rights. And: "... The General Comment of the Committee on Economic, Social and Cultural Rights has evolved into a document of a judicial nature independent of the reporting procedure of the International Covenant on Economic, Social and Cultural Rights..."[14] General Comment No. 15 of 2002: The right to water (Articles 11 and 12 of the International Covenant on Economic, Social and Cultural Rights) provides a clearer and more specific explanation of the standard content of the right to clean water, its implementation mechanisms, and the obligations of States to realize the right to clean water.

[11] Hu [4], pp. 10–12.
[12] Hu [4], pp. 17–20.
[13] Yang [5], pp. 32–38.
[14] Yang [5], pp. 22–44.

2.1.2 Domestic Level

Domestic legislation on the right to clean drinking water is essential for its realization. The amount of legislation relating to the right to clean drinking water in modern countries is gradually increasing. The right to clean drinking water can be expressed as a fundamental right in a variety of ways, with some provisions setting out general or more specific state obligations in the field of sanitation or water law, while others define clean drinking water as a right. Other countries enshrine the right to clean drinking water directly in their constitutions, such as Section 27 of the Bill of Rights Act, Chapter I of the 1961 Constitution of South Africa, which states, "(1) Everyone has the right to access... plenty of food and water .... (2) States shall adopt reasonable legislative and other measures to make significant progress in the realization of these rights, within available resources."[15]

2.2 The Nature of the Right to Clean Water

From the perspective of the right to clean drinking water, it is considered a basic human right. The so-called basic human rights, also known as universal human rights, refer to the political, economic, cultural, and other rights that accompany the attributes of "people as human beings" and recognize the inherent value and dignity of all individuals, regardless of their social status, ethnicity, property, and actual abilities (such as education level, intelligence, insight, etc.). These rights are considered universal and fundamental in society and other areas.[16]

First, practicality. The feasibility criterion is a practical standard. Cranston argues that if something is to be regarded as a right, then it must be possible; it must be within human reach. If it is impossible to do something, it is absurd to consider it a right.[17] Therefore, a human right in the sense of a moral right can only be elevated to a human right in the legal sense if it is feasible. However, there is no equivalence between "enforcement" and "human reach," nor does it mean that such rights are out of reach. If the State is obliged to "respect and protect human rights," then this "guarantee" must be premised on the possibility that such human rights can be realized. On the basis of this possibility, "guaranteeing" human rights does not become an empty phrase. In other words, whether the right to clean drinking water can be considered a human right depends on whether it can be transformed into an empirical right through political and legal means, and whether the requirements of actual proof can be realized. If the right to clean drinking water is a practical right, then it has the potential to be a human right. The right to clean drinking water, which guarantees everyone access to sufficient, safe, acceptable, accessible, and affordable water for personal and family life, clearly shows that the content required by this right is a

[15] Hu [6], p. 20.

[16] Guan [7], p. 39.

[17] See Cranston [8], pp. 43–53.

minimum standard with the possibility of security and realization. At the same time, it is also something that States and Governments, as subjects of the main obligation of human rights, can generally achieve.

Second, the standard of universality. Cranston believes that human rights are the moral rights of all people at any time and in any situation. He stresses that human rights do not depend on the identity or circumstances of the individual and that they should be enjoyed simply because the person is a human being.[18] Objectively speaking, as long as individuals are human beings, they must have a universal right to common survival needs. All people in the world objectively need certain things like food, drinking water, clothing, and shelter to maintain basic survival. Therefore, people have an inherent universality in the need to maintain their survival. Furthermore, access to sufficient, safe, acceptable, accessible, and affordable water supplies is necessary for everyone at all times and in all situations as it is a prerequisite for the survival and development of a person.

Third, paramount importance. Cranston believes that a human right must be something extremely sacred that cannot be easily taken away. Therefore, it is difficult to qualify as a human right without being of vital importance.[19] The right to clean drinking water is directly related to the survival or death of human beings and to their living conditions, so its vital importance is unquestionable. The availability of clean air, water, appropriate food, clothing, housing, and a minimum of public health care are prerequisites for human survival. From another perspective, human rights are based on the inherent dignity of the human person. Both the International Covenant on Civil and Political Rights and the International Covenant on Economic, Social and Cultural Rights recognize at the outset that these rights derive from the inherent dignity of the human person. If the right to clean drinking water is denied, it is a serious violation of human dignity.

3 The Content of the Right to Clean Drinking Water

3.1 Content of the Right to Clean Water

First, in general, the right to clean drinking water includes both freedom and entitlement. This interpretation is in accordance with General Comment No. 15: The right to water (Articles 11 and 12 of the International Covenant on Economic, Social and Cultural Rights). "Freedom" means "the right to access the existing water supply necessary for the enjoyment of the right to water, as well as the right not to be interfered with, such as the right not to be arbitrarily cut off or polluted".[20] For the

---

[18] See Cranston [8], pp. 43–53.

[19] See Cranston [8], pp. 43–53.

[20] United Nations [9], p. 108.

holder of rights, this requires the state to fulfill its obligation not to act or interfere with the subject of rights and to avoid infringing on the subject of rights. For example, the state must not arbitrarily cut off or pollute the water supply. Unlike "freedom", "entitlement" refers to the right to access water supply and plumbing systems, which provides equal opportunities for people to enjoy the right to clean drinking water.[21] Objectively speaking, the spatial distribution of water resources is not balanced, which inherently sets up obstacles to the enjoyment of the right to clean drinking water. The use of water supply equipment has become an important way to remove this obstacle.[22] The entitlement content of the right to clean drinking water requires duty-bearers (primarily states) to provide water, water facilities, and equipment as part of their obligation. They must ensure that water, water facilities, and water installations are accessible to all persons within their jurisdiction without discrimination, and that the costs are affordable for all.

Second, the specific content of the right to clean drinking water includes three aspects: availability, quality, and accessibility. Although the resource situation and development status of countries and regions in the world today are different, the three aspects of availability, quality, and accessibility are the minimum standards that should be applied to all situations, and the quantity necessary to enjoy the right to clean drinking water may vary depending on different conditions. Specifically:

a. Possession. Possession is a requirement for the amount of water necessary to fulfill the right to clean water. There must be adequacy and continuity in the quantity of water supply, and the amount of water required by each individual should comply with World Health Organization guidelines. Additionally, special circumstances should be taken into consideration, such as the fact that some individuals and groups may require more water than others due to factors like health, climate, or working conditions.[23]
b. "Qualityworthiness" is a requirement for ensuring the quality of the water supply necessary to fulfill the right to clean drinking water. In short, water supplies for individuals and households must be safe and fit for human consumption. Therefore, the water supply should not contain microorganisms, chemical substances, or radiological hazards that pose a threat to personal health, and it should have an acceptable color and taste.[24]
c. Accessibility. Accessibility is concerned with the possibility and equity of realizing the right to clean drinking water, and emphasizes that water, water facilities, and water supply equipment must be accessible to all individuals within the jurisdiction of States parties without discrimination. Accessibility includes four overlapping aspects: physical accessibility, economic affordability, non-discrimination, and availability of information.[25]

---

[21] See United Nations [9], p. 108.

[22] Xia [10].

[23] See United Nations [9], p. 108.

[24] See United Nations [9], p. 108.

[25] See United Nations [9], pp. 108–109; Hu [6].

3.2 Subjects of Rights to the Right to Clean Drinking Water

Based on existing international legal provisions and legal practices, the subjects of the right to clean drinking water can be divided into two categories: general subjects and special subjects.

3.2.1 The General Subject of the Right to Clean Drinking Water

The term 'everyone' is emphasized in Article 2, Paragraph 1 of the Universal Declaration of Human Rights as 'Everyone is entitled to all the rights and freedoms set forth in the present Declaration', and the term 'everyone' is also emphasized in Articles 25 and 11 of the International Covenant on Economic, Social and Cultural Rights. Therefore, the subject of the right to clean drinking water should be everyone, that is, every 'natural person'. As long as an individual is a 'person' in the natural sense, they enjoy the right to clean drinking water. Regardless of their state of existence, such as statelessness, imprisonment, displacement, and so on, the enjoyment of this fundamental human right cannot be denied in these circumstances.

3.2.2 Special Subjects of the Right to Clean Drinking Water

While the subject of the right to clean drinking water is everyone, in practice, some groups are more vulnerable than others or have historically faced discrimination, which deserves special attention. The UN Committee on Economic, Social and Cultural Rights has described these groups as 'the most vulnerable' or 'particularly disadvantaged groups', including women, children, minorities, indigenous peoples, refugees, asylum-seekers, internally displaced persons, migrant workers, prisoners and detainees, and other persons particularly affected, as outlined in General Comment No. 15: The Right to Water (Articles 11 and 12 of the International Covenant on Economic, Social and Cultural Rights). In line with the principle of non-discrimination, this comment focuses on individuals and groups who have difficulties in enjoying the right to clean drinking water.

3.3 The Burden of Obligations on the Right to Clean Water

Under international human rights law, human rights obligations are primarily borne by states. Therefore, the discussion of the burden of obligations regarding the right to clean drinking water in this section primarily revolves around state obligations.[26]

[26] See Sun [11].

3.3.1 The Nature of State Obligations

The Universal Declaration of Human Rights imposes a moral obligation on all states to strive for the realization of economic, social, and cultural rights. Under Article 2 of the International Covenant on Economic, Social and Cultural Rights, states have legally binding obligations to take steps to exhaust all means to progressively achieve the full realization of the economic, social, and cultural rights set forth in the Covenant. The obligations corresponding to the right to clean drinking water are mainly the obligations of the state. The state bears primary responsibility for the realization of the right to clean drinking water, and the subject of the obligation for the right to clean drinking water is mainly the state.

First, the measures taken by states should be comprehensive. Among these measures, legislation is the basis for taking the necessary steps and an indispensable method. The adoption of legislative measures is one of the three forms of human rights, and a sound legislative basis plays an important role in the effective implementation and enforcement of economic and social rights in domestic jurisdictions. Although the legislative approach is fundamental, it should also be noted that legislative measures alone are not enough. General Comment No. 3: Nature of States Parties' Obligations, adopted by the Committee on Economic, Social and Cultural Rights at its fifth session in 1990 (Article 2 of the Covenant, paragraph 1), emphasizes: "... As the International Covenant on Economic, Social and Cultural Rights specifically states, the adoption of legislative measures is in no way the end of a State Party's obligations ...".[27] Therefore, "using all appropriate means" should not be narrowly understood, but must be fully and precisely. In addition to legislation, General Comment No. 3 also mentions other important methods, including judicial remedies, administrative methods, financial methods, educational methods, etc. Only when these methods are considered together can a correct and comprehensive understanding of "all appropriate means" be achieved. For example, paragraph 5 of the General Comment states that measures that may be considered appropriate also include the provision of judicial remedies under rights that fall within the scope of judicial measures in the national legal system. In paragraph 7, it was stated that some other measures could also be considered 'appropriate', since the purposes of Article 2 included administrative, financial, educational and social measures, etc. In paragraph 8, it is stated that the obligation to take steps by all appropriate means, including, in particular, legislative means, neither requires nor precludes the use of any particular governmental or economic system as a pattern for taking steps, as long as the system is democratic and respects all human rights.[28] It can be seen that the realization of the right to clean drinking water, with the state as the subject of obligations, requires a multi-pronged approach based on a legislative approach.

Second, the State assumes a progressive obligation. Based on the term "progressive realization," the obligation of states with respect to the realization of economic,

---

[27] See United Nations [9], p. 13.

[28] See United Nations [9], p. 15.

social, and cultural rights can be considered a progressive obligation.[29] For the right to clean water, the starting point of the progressive obligation is to maintain a minimum level of human life and health, on the basis of which standards and quality are progressively raised. The understanding of the obligation of progressivity should not be one-sided, and it is important to emphasize the correct understanding of "progressive realization": "progressive realization" is a term that can easily be misinterpreted and has indeed been or is being misinterpreted in reality. The concept of "progressive realization" also implies the recognition of the full realization of all economic, social, and cultural rights, which is generally impossible to achieve in the short term. For example, Article 3 of General Comment No. 9: The nature of States parties' obligations (Article 2, paragraph 1, of the Covenant) states that the concept of progressive realization is equivalent to an acknowledgment that the full realization of all economic, social, and cultural rights is generally not possible in the short term, but that this stage must also be examined in the context of the overall objective.[30] In other words, it is necessary to establish clear obligations for states to realize these rights as soon as possible. The general comment, therefore, emphasizes that "... The long-term or progressive realization of the present Convention should not be misunderstood as a release from obligations with full meaning... It establishes an obligation to pursue its objectives as expeditiously and effectively as possible..."[31] In addition, General Comment No. 15: The right to water (Article 11 of the International Covenant on Economic, Social and Cultural Rights and 12), paragraph 37, also sets out, inter alia, the core obligations that need to be fulfilled immediately for the realization of the right to clean drinking water. It can be seen that the "progressive obligation" for the realization of the right to clean drinking water does not contradict the realization of the right to clean drinking water "expeditiously and effectively." They are not two separate formulations. On the contrary, the "progressive obligation" inherently includes rapid and effective implementation of this element.

Thirdly, the obligations assumed by States are minimal. General Comment No. 3 on the nature of States parties' obligations (Article 2, paragraph 1, of the Covenant) emphasizes that each State party has a responsibility to assume a minimum core obligation to ensure that the realization of each right is at least at a minimum level.[32] Moreover, both the International Covenant on Economic, Social and Cultural Rights and General Comment No. 15 on the Right to Water (Article 11 of the International Covenant on Economic, Social and Cultural Rights and 12) establish the standard content of the right to clean drinking water, and the State's obligations are a minimum standard, not an excessive requirement. The obligation of States to realize the right to clean drinking water is minimal. When States fail to ensure that the most basic needs of individuals for clean drinking water are met, it violates the International Covenant on Economic, Social and Cultural Rights.

---

[29] See Singh [12], p. 10.

[30] See United Nations [9], p. 15.

[31] See United Nations [9], p. 15.

[32] See United Nations [9], p. 15.

3.3.2 State Obligations

(1) Obligation to Respect. The right to clean drinking water is regarded as one of the economic, socio-cultural rights. The enjoyment and realization of human rights require that the State refrain from interference or non-infringement of them. That is, the State has an obligation to respect these human rights. It is worth emphasizing that the State's obligation to respect human rights is not limited to civil and political rights but also to economic, social, and cultural rights.[33] In particular, the obligation to respect requires States to refrain from interfering with the enjoyment of the right to clean drinking water, whether directly or indirectly. General Comment No. 15 on the Right to Water (Articles 11 and 12 of the International Covenant on Economic, Social and Cultural Rights) elaborates on this obligation in paragraph 21. It mainly uses the words "non-participation", "non-arbitrary interference", "non-utilization", "non-restriction use", or "non-destruction", reflecting the nature of its negative obligations.[34] According to the General Comment, such obligations include not engaging in any action or activity that deprives or restricts equal access to adequate water, not arbitrarily interfering with customary or traditional water allocation arrangements, refraining from illegally reducing and polluting water sources through the use of waste from State-owned facilities or through the use and experimentation of weapons, and not restricting the use or destruction of water supply equipment and infrastructure in violation of international humanitarian law during armed conflict. In addition, the General Comment emphasizes that States should also ensure that citizens, detainees, and prisoners have access to adequate water during armed conflict, states of emergency, and natural disasters.

(2) Obligation to protect. The obligation to protect is directed at third parties other than the rights holders, which are regarded as potential infringers, and it requires States parties to adjust the obligations of rights holders and third parties, primarily by providing relief to rights holders in the event of a risk of harm caused by third parties or in the event of harm, since "In a stricter sense, the most important way for States to fulfil this obligation is to provide effective remedies to victims of human rights violations."[35] (General Comment No. 15: The right to water, Articles 11 and 12 of the International Covenant on Economic, Social and Cultural Rights). The third parties mentioned include, but are not limited to: individuals, groups, companies, and third parties who operate or control water supply equipment. The obligations referred to in the Convention include, inter alia, "to take necessary and effective legislative and other measures to prevent third parties from depriving them of equal access to water; pollution and inequitable extraction of water resources, including natural

[33] See Sun [11].

[34] General Comment No. 15: The Right to Water (International Covenant on Economic, Social and Cultural Rights, Articles 11 and 12). In Section 21, the paragraph uses the word "including". The content of the obligation to demonstrate respect is not limited to what it enumerates.

[35] See Sun [11].

water resources, wells, and other water distribution systems."[36] In addition, the general comment specifically mentions that where water supply equipment (e.g. water supply networks, water storage tanks, river and well intakes) is operated or controlled by third parties, States Parties must prevent them from impairing access to adequate, economical, and accessible means of equitable, economical, and convenient means of the right to safe and acceptable water. Effective management mechanisms, including independent oversight, genuine public participation, and penalties for non-compliance, should be put in place to that end.[37]

(3) Obligations to be fulfil. The obligation to fulfil is positive in nature and imposes a claim on the State, as outlined in General Comment No. 15: The right to water (Articles 11 and 12), paragraph 26: "The obligation to fulfil requires States parties to take the necessary measures for the full realization of the right to water."[38] According to the General Comment, such obligations include, but are not limited to, the following: fully recognizing this right within the national political and legal system, preferably through regulations governing the implementation of the law; developing national water strategies and action plans to realize this right; ensuring that water is affordable for all; promoting improved and sustainable means of water withdrawal.[39]

(4) Obligation to provide international cooperation and assistance. First, states parties must respect the enjoyment of this right by other peoples and refrain from actions that directly or indirectly interfere with the enjoyment of the right to water by other peoples. Any action taken within the jurisdiction of a state party should not deprive another state of its ability to realize the right to water for the people under its jurisdiction. Second, the second level of obligations directs third parties, mainly their own citizens and companies, and requires states parties to take measures to prohibit their citizens and companies from infringing on the right to clean drinking water of individuals and groups in other countries. These measures include, but are not limited to, legal and political means. Finally, the third level emphasizes the obligation of states parties to provide assistance to other states in specific circumstances, primarily from economically developed countries to poorer developing countries, which is, of course, a positive obligation.

(5) Core obligations that need to be fulfilled immediately. The core obligations that need to be fulfilled immediately require states to ensure that the right to clean drinking water is realized at least at the minimum necessary level. These obligations include the following: (a) ensuring the right of individuals and families to have access to the minimum necessary quantity of adequate and safe water for disease prevention; (b) ensuring the right of all people, especially poor

[36] United Nations [9], p. 111.

[37] See United Nations [9], pp. 112; Hu [6].

[38] See United Nations [9], pp. 112.

[39] See United Nations [9], pp. 112.

or marginalized groups, to access and use water supply facilities and equipment without discrimination; (c) ensuring the right to access facilities and water equipment that provide adequate, safe, and regular water supply in practice; ensuring that there are a sufficient number of water intake points to avoid excessive waiting times and that the distance from the residence is appropriate; (d) ensuring that there is no danger to personal safety when drawing water; (e) ensuring the equitable distribution of all water facilities and water equipment; (f) adopting and implementing national water strategies and water action plans for all populations; developing and regularly reviewing water strategies and water action plans in a participatory and transparent manner; water strategies and water action plans should pay attention to poor or marginalized groups; (g) monitoring the extent to which the right to water is realized or not realized, etc.[40]

4 Implementation Mechanisms for the Right to Clean Drinking Water

The existing international human rights protection and enforcement mechanism are established through a series of international human rights conventions, mainly including implementation mechanisms at the international level and implementation mechanisms at the domestic level. At the international level, the implementation mechanism mainly refers to "monitoring," the purpose of which is to monitor the implementation of the obligations of states parties under the Convention. At the domestic level, it mainly refers to "fulfillment." Like the implementation mechanism of human rights in general, the implementation mechanism of the right to clean drinking water is mainly composed of two parts: the implementation mechanism at the international level and the implementation mechanism at the domestic level. Of these, the implementation mechanism at the domestic level is the basis and key to the implementation of the right to clean drinking water.

4.1 Implementation Mechanisms at the International Dimension of the Right to Clean Water

Implementation mechanisms at the international level reflect the relationship between states parties, between states parties and international human rights bodies, and between states parties and individuals at the level of international human rights law. The implementation mechanism of the right to clean drinking water at the international level is mainly a monitoring mechanism, and the role of the implementation

[40] See United Nations [9], pp. 114; Hu [6].

mechanism at the international level is to monitor the implementation of the content of all aspects of the right to clean drinking water by states parties.

(1) Reporting procedures. The reporting procedure, which is the process by which states parties provide their national reports to international monitoring bodies, can also be seen as a periodic monitoring system. The reporting procedure has been established in a number of important human rights conventions, including the International Covenant on Economic, Social and Cultural Rights, and has been universally accepted. It takes a constructive dialogue approach by requesting states parties to submit reports on the implementation of the Convention, measures taken, achievements, and existing problems, which are then considered by expert bodies in order to help states design better policies. General comment No. 1: Status of submission by States parties, adopted by the Committee on Economic, Social and Cultural Rights in 1989, sets out seven objectives of the reporting procedure, which can be summarized as follows: (1) Review domestic legislation, administrative provisions, and practices to bring them into line with the Covenant as fully as possible; (2) Monitor the implementation of rights to make states parties aware of the extent to which all individuals within their territory or under their jurisdiction enjoy or do not enjoy rights; (3) Establish policy objectives for states parties, including the identification of priorities, basis, and guidance reflecting the provisions of the Convention; (4) Promote people's monitoring and participation in policies; (5) Evaluate the progress of implementation in states parties and identify problems and shortcomings; (6) Promote the exchange of information and raise awareness of common issues.[41]
For the right to clean water, the report submitted by the State party should include the following: (1) a brief description of the basic national situation, mainly on the total amount of water resources, distribution, pollution, etc.; (2) under the International Covenant on Economic, Social and Cultural Rights and General Comment No. 15: The Right to Water, information on the implementation of Articles 11 and 12 of the Covenant and the status of these rights in the domestic law of the State party; (3) a description of the implementation of the right to clean water, including the legislative status, strategies and policies, indicators and benchmarks of the right to clean water, and remedies and accountability for individuals or groups deprived of the right to clean water; (4) the role of States parties in international cooperation and assistance for the implementation of the right to clean water.
(2) Inter-State Accusation Procedure. The inter-State complaints procedure is quasi-judicial in nature and is intended to address the deteriorating human rights situation in a given State party. Theoretically, the inter-State complaints system could play a role in promoting mutual monitoring between States parties in the protection of human rights. However, since the inter-State complaints procedure is an optional mechanism under international human rights treaties, it only applies to

[41] Yang [5], pp. 33–35.

States parties that have recognized the jurisdiction of the monitoring authority to receive and consider complaints between States parties. Many countries prioritize their own political and economic interests, and as a result, this procedure has never been used in practice. Therefore, this section does not discuss this procedure in detail.

(3) Individual grievance procedures. The individual complaints procedure is a system through which individuals can lodge complaints with relevant international supervisory authorities for violations of their human rights by the State. It serves as a remedy for individuals' right to clean water. The International Covenant on Economic, Social and Cultural Rights does not provide for an international procedure for individual complaints, which is primarily provided for by the International Covenant on Civil and Political Rights. The individual complaints procedure can be divided into two stages. First, at the stage of receiving complaints, the Human Rights Committee, as the monitoring body, receives complaints from individuals or groups of individuals about violations of their right to clean drinking water. Complaints must be examined for eligibility under the individual complaints procedure in light of the provisions of the relevant human rights treaties. These conditions include, among others, that the complaint should be named, domestic remedies must be exhausted, there has been no abuse of the right of individual complaint, and the complaint shall be in accordance with the provisions of the Convention. Secondly, during the fact-finding phase, if the Human Rights Committee decides to entertain a complaint relating to the right to clean drinking water, the respondent State should be informed of the decision on the admissibility of the complaint and the factual review procedure. The respondent State should submit its own interpretation or statement on the complaint, which reflects the principle of "equality of procedural rights." In the final stage, the Human Rights Committee, the monitoring body, issues a concluding observation based on all available written information. It determines whether the State party has violated its treaty obligations and violated the individual's right to clean water, and if so, what measures should be taken. It should be noted that this concluding observation is not legally binding on the State party, and its usefulness is greatly diminished.

4.2 *Implementation Mechanisms at the Domestic Level of the Right to Clean Water*

The domestic dimension of the implementation of the right to clean water refers to measures taken domestically to realize the right to clean drinking water for individuals under a State's jurisdiction. The right to clean drinking water must first be implemented at the national and local levels, and the State has the primary responsibility for its realization for those living under its jurisdiction. Since the implementation mechanism at the international level can only play an important supporting or complementary role and cannot replace the implementation mechanism at the domestic level, the realization of the right to clean drinking water mainly depends on the implementation mechanism at the domestic level.

4.2.1 Legislative Mechanisms for the Realization of the Right to Clean Drinking Water

The implementation and realization of the right to clean drinking water depend on the degree of empirical and institutionalized completeness, and the legislative method is the most basic way to prove and institutionalize the right to clean drinking water. The approach of legislation is particularly emphasized in the International Covenant on Economic, Social and Cultural Rights and other human rights conventions. For example, Article 2, paragraph 2, of the International Covenant on Economic, Social and Cultural Rights requires States parties to use all appropriate means, including the legislative implementation of obligations under the Convention. Legislation in this area is essential if the right to clean drinking water is to be truly realized.[42] In particular, (1) legislation should be guided by the principles of non-discrimination and people's participation, and (2) the right to clean drinking water should be fully recognized in existing laws.

4.2.2 Administrative Mechanisms for the Realization of the Right to Clean Drinking Water

First, the administrative authorities of States Parties should ensure that water is affordable for all by adopting appropriate low-cost skills and technologies, implementing reasonable pricing policies (e.g., free or low water prices), and providing income subsidies. They should also promote improved and sustainable access to water, especially in rural and poor urban areas, and ensure access to adequate sanitation facilities for all, especially women and children, in these areas, which require greater attention. Secondly, States parties should fully consider the possible impact of other administrative acts on the realization of the right to clean drinking water when their governments carry them out. Before any action by the state or any third party that interferes with the right to clean drinking water, the relevant authorities must ensure that such action is legally permissible and conforms with the provisions of the International Covenant on Economic, Social and Cultural Rights. Furthermore, the relevant authorities should engage in genuine consultation with those affected, disclose the measures to be taken in a timely and adequate manner, reasonably inform them of the actions, and allow the affected persons access to justice and seek remedies, providing the legal aid needed to obtain legal remedies. If the above-mentioned action is taken because the water user is unable to pay the water bill, their capacity

[42] China's Collection of International Covenants on Human Rights [13], p. 2.

to pay must be taken into account. Under no circumstances should individuals be deprived of the right to the minimum amount of water necessary.[43]

4.2.3 Judicial Mechanisms to Realize the Right to Clean Drinking Water

The judicial enforcement mechanism of the right to clean water means that States parties allow individuals to bring violations of their right to clean water before domestic courts and to seek judicial remedies. Through domestic judicial remedies, States parties can provide redress and compensation as soon as possible in the event of violations of the right to clean drinking water of individuals within their territory and jurisdiction. It should be noted that the judicial enforcement mechanism is primarily a remedial mechanism. When the right to clean water is violated, any individual or group of persons should be guaranteed judicial solutions at the national level, and those who have violated the right to clean water should be held accountable and provide appropriate reparation, including in the form of restitution, compensation, satisfaction, or guarantees of non-repetition. At the same time, States should encourage legal practitioners (mainly lawyers, judges, and others) to pay greater attention to violations of the right to clean drinking water in the performance of their duties.

5 The Right to Clean Drinking Water in Contemporary China

We are parties to the International Covenant on Economic, Social and Cultural Rights and the International Covenant on Civil and Political Rights, and Article 24 of our Constitution Amendment (2004) clearly states that "the State respects and guarantees human rights." My government, therefore, has an obligation to respect, protect, and fulfill the right to clean drinking water for individuals and groups within its territory and jurisdiction.

5.1 The Problems in China

In contemporary China, there are still a series of problems regarding the right to clean drinking water that need to be urgently solved. For a considerable number of people, the realization of the right to clean drinking water is only preliminary and very insufficient. There is a significant gap between China's realization of the right

[43] See United Nations [9], pp. 118.

to clean drinking water and international requirements. These problems are mainly reflected in the following aspects.

5.1.1 Clean Drinking Water Resources Are Scarce in China

First of all, China is a country with severe water shortages. Wang Shucheng, former minister of water resources, pointed out in an interview with Xinhua News Agency that "China's per capita water resources are only 2,185 cubic meters, less than a quarter of the world average. In the past 20 years, the amount of surface water resources and total water resources in the country have not changed much, but the river runoff and total water resources in the southern region have increased, with an increase of nearly 5%. The amount of water resources in the northern region decreased significantly, among which the Yellow River, Huaihe River, Haihe River, and Liaohe River areas were the most affected, with surface water resources reduced by 17% and total water resources reduced by 12%. Among them, the amount of surface water resources in the Haihe District decreased by 41%, and the total water resources decreased by 25%. Some northern river basins have changed from periodic water shortage to absolute shortage." Wang also warned that "water shortage has become an unavoidable problem threatening China's future water environment security."[44]

Secondly, China's water pollution problem is serious. Water pollution encroaches on a large amount of water resources available for consumption and endangers human health, which results in worse drinking water quality for residents. With the continuous rapid growth and industrialization of China's population, the increasing degree of urbanization, as well as institutional deficiencies and management omissions, the problem of water pollution has become a serious social problem.

Thirdly, China's water resources are uneven in both time and space. On the one hand, the geographical distribution of China's water resources is significantly uneven. There is more water in the north and less in the south, and more in the east and less in the west, leading to a huge disparity. This inequality severely impacts the equal access and enjoyment of the right to clean drinking water. On the other hand, China's water resources are also uneven in terms of their temporal distribution, with precipitation varying greatly from year to year. In some years, there is a lot of rainfall, while in others, there is very little, and there are even consecutive years of drought, especially in the northern part of China. Rivers such as the Yellow River and the Haihe River often experience disruptions in their flow. In North China, where water scarcity is severe, precipitation is only concentrated in the summer, and rainfall in other seasons, particularly in winter, is significantly different.

[44] Wang [14].

5.1.2 The Dual Urban–Rural System Restricts the Realization of the Right to Clean Drinking Water

Fundamentally, the main root cause of the clean drinking water problem is not the lack of drinking water but the lack of access to clean drinking water for certain parts of society due to poverty or other social reasons. Due to historical reasons, China's economy and society have clearly exhibited the characteristics of an urban–rural dual structure, which has long been a hindrance to the implementation of the right to clean drinking water. Since the groups with drinking water difficulties in China are mainly in rural areas (as mentioned earlier, more than 300 million farmers in China do not have access to clean water), the existence of the dual structure of urban and rural areas has resulted in the exclusion of rural areas from the decision-making process on water resources and water rights allocation of public resources, with a clear preference for urban areas. Most of the drinking water facilities and equipment paid for by the state are located in cities (for example, most of the waterworks are located in cities), and capital investment in rural areas is far less than in cities. The guarantee system for clean drinking water has not been extended to rural areas, and the vast rural areas can only rely on digging wells to directly draw groundwater or build water cellars to collect rainwater, or draw water directly from rivers to solve the problem of drinking water. This is particularly true in remote mountainous and arid areas. What is more serious is that the water source of drinking water for rural residents is polluted, and problems such as high fluoride, high arsenic, bitter salt, and microorganisms such as schistosomiasis in the water body are relatively common in rural areas in China and have always plagued rural areas. It can be said that the urban–rural dualism has created a wide gap between urban and rural drinking water facilities, and this tendency is still expanding today. The right to clean drinking water is a basic human right that should be enjoyed by all, and the irrational allocation of such resources has produced implicit discrimination, highlighting the unfairness in the implementation of the right to clean drinking water in China.

5.1.3 There Are Deficiencies in China's Existing Laws and Regulations

The provisions regarding the right to clean drinking water exist in our legal and policy system, but they remain flawed. Article 24 of the Amendment to the Constitution (2004) adopted by the National People's Congress in 2004 made it clear in China's Constitution for the first time that "the State respects and protects human rights." This is a general and abstract statement, but it is clear that the right to clean drinking water should not be excluded. It should be a part of respecting and guaranteeing human rights. In 2002, the new Water Act, which was completely revised, reflected the content of the right to clean drinking water. For example, Article 33 of the Law states, "The State shall establish a system of protection zones for drinking water sources. The people's governments of provinces, autonomous regions, and municipalities directly under the Central Government shall designate drinking water source protection zones and take measures to prevent the depletion of water sources and pollution of water bodies, and ensure the safety of drinking water for urban and rural residents." In addition, the law also clearly stipulates the government's responsibility to actively take measures to improve the drinking water conditions of urban and rural residents, as well as the domestic water system and the production and operation water system. The content of the right to clean drinking water is also reflected in relevant policies and regulations in China, including the "Drinking Water Hygiene Standards" formulated by the Ministry of Health in 1985, and the "Rural Drinking Water Safety and Sanitation Evaluation Index System" formulated by the Ministry of Water Resources and the Ministry of Health. The State Development Planning Commission and the Ministry of Water Resources formulated the "Opinions on Further Doing a Good Job in Solving Difficulties in Drinking Water for Rural People and Livestock" on June 25, 2002, etc.

However, China's existing laws and regulations still have deficiencies. First, the law does not clearly stipulate that the right to water is a human right, which makes it impossible to systematically regulate the content and protection of water human rights. Second, as there are more policy provisions than legal provisions, the practical protection of water human rights is inadequate.[45]

5.2 *The Realization of the Right to Clean Drinking Water in China*

Lack of water resources, serious water pollution, and serious waste of water resources, as well as difficulties in accessing drinking water in rural areas and poor systematization of existing laws and regulations, are some of the challenges that hinder the implementation of the right to clean drinking water in China. Moreover, there are many policy provisions but few legal provisions in place. All these issues together present significant obstacles to achieving the goal of providing clean drinking water to every person and special group in China. In order to truly realize the right to clean drinking water, we must address these problems effectively.

First, in general, a comprehensive approach should be taken to implement a long-term strategy. It is necessary to comprehensively use legal, engineering, economic, administrative, and scientific and technological measures to ensure the realization of the indicators of the right to clean drinking water. Paying particular attention to the use of economic instruments, not only by providing qualified water supply facilities and equipment, but also by providing individuals and groups (especially women, children, people in poor and rural areas) with access to a basic level of sanitation, and providing them with access to clean drinking water. Additionally, developing reasonable water pricing policies that make the direct or indirect costs of drinking water moderate, economically viable, and promote water conservation is important.

Second, equitable implementation of the right to clean water is essential. In China, the institutional constraints of the urban–rural dual structure pose the most

[45] Hu [6], p. 23.

challenging obstacles to realizing the right to clean drinking water. Given that the urban–rural dual system is a long-standing historical issue, it is unrealistic to expect a complete solution in a short period. Nevertheless, it is necessary to take active measures to gradually transform the urban–rural dual structure and allocate public resources fairly. This requires improving the structure of fiscal expenditure, gradually extending public finance to rural areas, and establishing a mechanism to support agricultural growth rapidly. Coordinating the development of urban and rural infrastructure is also important to ensure that appropriate water facilities and equipment are built within safe distances that are accessible to residents in rural areas so they can enjoy good water supply facilities. Furthermore, to ensure that farmers can afford to consume water and access water facilities and equipment, the government should provide appropriate subsidies to individuals and groups facing financial difficulties in this regard. The state should also pay special attention to other individuals and groups facing difficulties accessing clean drinking water in China. At this stage, these groups mainly include women, children, migrant workers, displaced persons (mainly beggars), prisoners, and others. For example, women, children, and migrant workers have specific needs and require special protection and care. Women often bear a disproportionate burden of family responsibilities, which creates problems with water withdrawal, and the government should address this issue. Children are particularly vulnerable, and their access to clean drinking water deserves special attention. Migrant workers are a unique group in China, and their high numbers, poor working conditions, high labor intensity, and lack of guaranteed sanitation create challenges in accessing clean drinking water. Therefore, the government should ensure that they have equal access to water supply facilities as urban residents, and provide them with basic sanitary conditions.

Third, actively solve the problem of capital investment to ensure the safety of drinking water. As an economic, social, and cultural right, the right to clean drinking water requires states and governments to increase their obligations to promote and provide improved and sustainable access to water by establishing universal drinking water facilities and equipment in a proactive and productive manner. For example, the construction of water purification and treatment facilities, the installation of tap water in rural areas, and so on. To solve the problem of drinking water safety in China, the government must invest a lot of money, which is the main channel. However, China is limited by the level of economic and social development, and insufficient funds have become a bottleneck in implementing the right to clean drinking water in China, especially in China's poor and backward areas. Addressing this bottleneck requires the government to invest more in improving drinking water services and increase their budgets in national or regional development strategies. At the same time, the government's financial investment alone cannot solve the huge funding gap for improving water facilities and equipment. It is also necessary to raise funds from multiple parties and leverage the strength of non-governmental organizations, enterprises, and private investors to establish a mechanism for multi-party investment and benefits. To attract more funds for investment in drinking water service facilities, a combination of government financial support and farmers' self-financing could be used to build village water access projects, especially in rural areas. In short, it is only with the efforts of all parties that it will be possible to completely solve the problem of clean drinking water in China.

Finally, the priority of the right to clean drinking water needs to be established. The priority position mentioned here refers to the priority position at the level of laws and regulations and the level of national strategy. It is necessary not only to explicitly recognize the right to clean drinking water and regulate the content of the right to clean drinking water in domestic laws and policies but also to establish the priority of the right to clean drinking water in legal policies and operational strategies to ensure that the right to clean drinking water is not adversely affected by other legal policies or operational measures. For example, in the process of promoting urbanization and industrialization, the government should implement the strategy of building a water-saving society and establish a reasonable water management system. In addition, it is necessary to strategically reduce the development of industries with high water consumption and high pollution because this will inevitably lead to a serious shortage of drinking water, crowd out ecological water, and deteriorate the ecological environment around cities, including drinking water source protection areas.

References

1. Shahi, S. K., & Athar, M. (2021). Impact of Covid-19 on human right to access clean & safe drinking water in India. *Vidyabharati International Interdisciplinary Research Journal, 74*, 0–748. https://zenodo.org/record/5655766
2. Ruspekhofer, S. (2006). The human right to water and food: Insights from the work of the special rapporteur on the right to food. Völker- und Europarecht AKTUELL. http://www.alexandria.unisg.ch/28846/
3. Shahi, S. K. (2021). Discussion on right to clean drinking water- a basic human right. *Sambodhi (UGC Care Journal), 44*(1), 55–66. https://zenodo.org/record/4624447
4. Hu, Z. (Ed.). (2004). *Collection of China's international covenants on human rights* (2nd ed.). China International Translation and Publishing Company.
5. Yang, Y. (Ed.). (2005). *Bodies of the united nations human rights conventions and the essence of the classics*. China Public Security University Press.
6. Hu, D. (2006). The human right to water: The right to water in human rights law. *Hebei Law, 5*.
7. Guan, J. (Ed.). (2003). *Protection of basic human rights and legal practice*. Xiamen University Press.
8. Cranston, M. (1967). Human rights, real and supposed. In D. D. Raphael (Ed.), *Political theory and the rights of man* (pp. 43–53). Indiana University Press.
9. United Nations. (n.d.). International human rights instruments—compilation of general comments and general recommendations adopted by human rights treaty bodies. United Nations Publications.
10. Xia, Y. (2004). Basic problems of the philosophy of rights. *Journal of Legal Studies, 3*, 5.
11. Sun, S. (2001). On the state's obligations under international human rights law. *The Law Review, 2*.
12. Singh, N. (1986). Enforcement of human rights in peace and war and the future of humanity. *Kluwer Law International*, 10.

13. China's Collection of International Covenants on Human Rights. (2004). China International Publishing Group.
14. Wang, S. (2010). *Water scarcity has become a bottleneck for sustainable development in China*. Retrieved April 18, 2010, from http://www.gov.cn/jrzg/2007-03/21/content_556928.htm

Chapter 11
The Right to Food

Yuxia Zhang

1 Introduction

In our world, hunger is a daily reality for many people, particularly children. "Many people around the world are suffering from all kinds of unfreedom,"[1] and famine continues to persist in some areas, depriving thousands of their fundamental right to live. This is not only an immoral issue but also an illegal violation of international human rights law.[2] It violates people's fundamental freedoms, including the right to food, health, and even life. Currently, the right to food is widely recognized and universally acknowledged as an international human right. The Universal Declaration of Human Rights, International Covenant of Economic, Social and Cultural Rights, and the Convention on the Rights of the Child (CRC), as well as other international and regional legal documents, contain relevant provisions on the right to food. Of particular note is the theme of World Food Day 2007, "The right to food." However, theoretical research on this right is still inadequate, particularly in many developing countries where it is not fully guaranteed. Taking China as an example, the right holder's enjoyment of the right to food is not a legal right, and there is little theoretical research on this right. It will take some time for it to be popularized and realized in China. Although China's legislature ratified the International Covenant on Economic, Social and Cultural Rights in 2001, threats and violations of the right to food persist. According to the 2006 National Situation Report on Analysis and Forecasting of China's Social Situation, "The number of poor people in rural China has fallen from 250 million in 1978 to about 25 million at present, and its proportion of the world's poor has also increased from one quarter to one-quarter It has dropped to 1/20, and the

[1] Sen [1, p. 11].

[2] See UN Human Rights: The Right to Food, available at: http://www.un.org/chinese/hr/ssue/food.htm,E/CN.4/2005/47, 2008-03-20.

Y. Zhang (✉)
Judge of Changchun Intermediate People's Court of Jilin Province, Changchun, China

J. Yao (ed.), *The Legal Issues of the Emerging Rights*,
https://doi.org/10.1007/978-981-97-0499-6_11

rural poverty line has also increased from less than 200 yuan per capita net income of farmers to 637 yuan. However, there are still about 75 million poor people in rural China (roughly equivalent to the current rural poor plus low-income people) who live on less than $1 (PPP dollars, according to the United Nations) income or consumption per person per day. Moreover, in recent years, the number of people living in difficulty in urban areas has remained high. Whether in rural areas or cities, the "relative poor population" is lower than 1/2 of the average per capita income line, and due to the widening income gap and the large number of low-income groups, there has been no significant and rapid reduction."[3]

The right to food is a fundamental human right that is relevant to everyone's daily life and deserves more attention. However, it is often overlooked in practice. In 2004, the Chinese Constitution included respect for and protection of human rights, which demonstrates that China has taken a significant step in the protection and construction of human rights. This move has greatly promoted theoretical research in related fields. Through the introduction of the relevant content of the right to food, this study aims to take the issue of the right to food in contemporary China as the starting point. The focus is to shift from the introduction of the general theory of the international dimension of this right to the current reality in China, in order to study the possibility of implementing the right to food in China. The objective is to seek the best possible means of realizing and protecting this right.

2 Food and the Right to Food

2.1 The Meaning of Food

Article 25, paragraph 1, of the Universal Declaration of Human Rights, article 11 of the International Covenant on Economic, Social and Cultural Rights, article 27 of the Convention on the Rights of the Child, and the preamble to the Convention on the Elimination of All Forms of Discrimination against Women, as well as several regional documents, regulate food as a human right.

In light of the above, the inherent characteristics of "food" in the term "right to food" can be interpreted as follows: availability and access to food are adequate and durable. "Suitable" refers to food that is appropriate and can meet the nutritional needs of the human body. This means that the nutrients in the food are beneficial and safe for the human body's dietary requirements (i.e., free from toxic and harmful substances), and the food is culturally acceptable and consumable by the individual who consumes it (i.e., does not violate their dignity and religious beliefs). "Adequacy" means that food provision is sufficient to meet the daily nutritional needs of each person, understood in the sense of nutritional structure, not in the sense that different types of food provide the same types and quantities of nutrients (i.e., conversion and

[3] Ru, X., Lu, X., & Li, P. (Eds.). (2006). Analysis and Countermeasures of China's Social Situation 2006. Available at http://www.showchina.org/gqbg/200701/t105659.htm. Accessed 20 Mar 2008.

replacement between various foods is allowed). On the one hand, "persistent" means that food access is available and obtainable, while on the other hand, "existing" means that food that cannot exist is meaningless, and food that is not available to individuals and that is distributed does not have the attribute of "holding." "Access to food" should be accessible to all, including individuals with physical disabilities. "Persistent" also means that access to food is sustainable, as the human life cycle requires the continuous absorption of new nutrients to meet different needs at different stages.

Based on the above, the essential characteristics of "food" in the "right to food" can be summarized as follows: it is sufficient in quantity and quality to meet the individual's dietary needs, does not contain harmful substances, and is culturally acceptable. Such food should be accessible in a sustainable manner that does not impede the enjoyment of other human rights.[4]

2.2 *General Interpretation of the Right to Food*

Mill explains "rights" quite well, arguing that "When we call something a man's right, we mean that he has a legitimate reason to ask society to protect him from possessing it," whether it is the power of recourse to justice or the power of education and public opinion. If a person has good reasons for society to vouch for something, then we say that he has a right to it.[5] Society must guarantee individuals' rights when they have reasonable grounds for enjoying them. As can be seen from Mill's formulation, rights include both legal and moral rights, but for the purposes of this chapter, we will only emphasize the former. Legal rights refer to "an institutional arrangement in which interests are protected by law, choices are guaranteed by legal effect, and goods and opportunities are provided to individuals on a secure basis."[6] This right requires the individual to enjoy the most basic interests and freedom to make his own choices, which must be protected by law; otherwise, it will harm the individual's rights and interests. Moreover, the law must guarantee that individuals have access to sufficient goods for their personal needs. From the previous explanation of food, it can be seen that "food" is a necessary condition for everyone's survival, and without the guarantee of this necessary condition, no individual can survive. Thus, everyone has a "right to food" that must be protected by the force of law, and society and the law must guarantee that sufficient food can be provided to the individual on a secure basis. To do otherwise would be a significant breach of the fundamental rights of the individual.

The right to food, as a fundamental human right, is protected by international human rights law and international humanitarian law. General Comment No. 12 (1999) of the Committee on Economic, Social and Cultural Rights authoritatively

---

4 See Yang [2, p. 96].

5 Mill [3].

6 Deng [4].

defines the realization of the right to food: "The right to adequate food is realized when the physical and economic conditions or means of obtaining adequate food are available at all times, either alone or in association with others."[7] In the framework of this general comment, the Special Rapporteur further defines the right to food as follows: "The right to food is the right of consumers to regular, permanent, and unrestricted direct access or financial purchase of food of adequate quality and sufficient quantity in accordance with their cultural traditions to ensure that it is possible to live a dignified life in physical and mental terms, individually and collectively, in accordance with needs and free from fear."[8]

In response to the above definition, the right to food is understood as follows:

The right to food in the modern sense originated from Roosevelt's famous "Four Freedoms" speech during World War II, in which freedom from want was widely recognized.[9] After the Second World War, through the efforts of many experts and scholars, the relevant research results were absorbed into the Universal Declaration of Human Rights and then adopted by the International Covenant on Economic, Social and Cultural Rights. The Food and Agriculture Organization of the United Nations convened a special conference on the right of mankind to be free from hunger in 1963 and issued a statement about it. The 1974 World Food Conference declared: "Men and women, young and old, everyone has the right to be free from hunger and undernutrition in order to develop one's physical and mental capacities. These rights may not be arbitrarily deprived."[10] In 1996, at the World Food Summit organized by the Food and Agriculture Organization of the United Nations, political leaders jointly issued the Rome Declaration on World Food Security, which expresses their determination to guarantee the right to food for all and to eradicate hunger in all countries.[11] The Committee on Economic, Social and Cultural Rights, 1999 General Comment No. 12 provides an authoritative definition of the right to food.[12] In 2002, the Anti-Hunger Programme proposed a "twin-track" plan to reduce poverty and hunger.[13] The 2004 Committee on World Food Security report builds on the compilation of recommendations incorporating provisions of the Voluntary Guidelines for the Progressive Realization of the Right to Adequate Food. Recommendations were made to ensure world food security.[14]

---

[7] See Yang [2, p. 95].

[8] United Nations Human Rights: The Right to Food, available at: http://www.un.org/chinese/hr/issue/food.htm,E/CN.4/2005/47, 2008-03-20.

[9] See Eide et al. [5].

[10] Quoted from Zheng [6].

[11] See Zheng [6].

[12] See Twentieth Session of the Committee on Economic, Social and Cultural Rights (1999) General Comment No. 12:The right to adequate food, available at: http://www1.umn.edu/humanrts/chinese/CHgencomm/CHgencomment12.htm, 2010-04-19.

[13] See UN Global Action for the Millennium Goals:Goal I: Contribution of the Food and Agriculture Organization of the United Nations, available at: http://www.un.org/chinese/millenniumgoals/unsystem/goal1fao.htm, 2008-03-21.

[14] See Food and Agriculture Organization of the United Nations:Intergovernmental Working Group to Develop a Set of Voluntary Guidelines to Support the Progressive Realization of the Right to

As is well known, the Universal Declaration of Human Rights, the International Covenant on Civil and Political Rights, and the International Covenant on Economic, Social and Cultural Rights constitute the International Bill of Human Rights (the International Charters of Human Rights). The Universal Declaration of Human Rights clearly states in its preamble: "The advent of a world in which everyone enjoys freedom of expression and belief and freedom from fear and want has been proclaimed the highest aspiration of ordinary people."[15] The protection of economic, social, and cultural rights has been taken into account in the elaboration of the International Bill of Human Rights, of which social rights are primarily embodied in the right to an adequate standard of living. As a specific institutional expression of the right to an adequate standard of living, the right to food, together with the right to health,[16] housing, and adequate care, constitutes the main content of the right to an adequate standard of living. This is as Liu Hainian said: "Because there is no immortal who does not eat human fireworks, eating, clothing, and housing are the most basic conditions for human survival, and therefore the most basic needs and basic human rights of human beings."[17]

In summary, access to adequate food is a basic condition for a minimum standard of living and one of the prerequisites for survival, and the right to food is an extremely important social right and a sine qua non for freedom from hunger and poverty. Therefore, it is necessary to conduct further in-depth research on the right to food on this basis in order to better protect it.

3 The Content of the Right to Food

3.1 Institutional Framework of the Right to Food

3.1.1 Provisions on the Right to Food in International Human Rights Law Instruments

Article 25, paragraph 1, of the Universal Declaration of Human Rights stipulates that: (i) everyone has the right to a standard of living necessary for the maintenance of their health and that of their family, including food, clothing, housing, medical care, and necessary social services; the right to protection in the event of unemployment, sickness, disability, widowhood, old age, or other circumstances beyond their control. Mothers and children have the right to special care and assistance, and

Adequate Food in the Context of National Food Security, available at: http://www.fao.org/righttofood/zh/23416/index.html, 2008-03-21.

[15] Cheng et al. [7, p. 80].

[16] The right to health is recognized as a fundamental right, and it is the duty of the State to achieve its realization. See: Naved [8].

[17] Liu [9].

all children, whether born in or out of wedlock, shall enjoy the same social protection.[18] Article 11 of the International Covenant on Economic, Social and Cultural Rights provides that: (1) States Parties to the present Covenant recognize the right of everyone to an adequate standard of living for themselves and their family, including adequate food, clothing, and housing and capable of continuous improvement of living conditions. States parties will take appropriate steps to ensure the realization of this right, recognizing the importance of international cooperation based on voluntary consent to this end. (2) The States Parties to the present Covenant, recognizing the fundamental right of everyone to be free from hunger, shall take such measures as may be necessary, individually or through international cooperation, for the following purposes, including specific plans: (a) improving methods of food production, conservation, and distribution by making full use of scientific and technological knowledge, disseminating knowledge of business principles, and developing or reforming land systems for the most efficient development and utilization of natural resources; (b) to ensure that world food supplies are equitably distributed in accordance with need, taking into account the problems of food-importing and food-exporting countries.[19] Article 27 of the Convention on the Rights of the Child provides that: (1) States parties recognize the right of every child to a standard of living adequate for their physical, mental, spiritual, moral, and social development. (2) Parents or other persons responsible for the care of the child have the primary responsibility to ensure the living conditions necessary for the child's development, to the extent their means and economic conditions permit. (3) States Parties, in accordance with their national conditions and within their means, shall take appropriate measures to assist parents or other persons responsible for the care of children in realizing this right and, where necessary, provide material assistance and financial programs, especially in terms of nutrition, clothing, and housing. (4) States Parties shall take all appropriate measures to recover maintenance for children from parents or other persons who have financial responsibility for the child within or outside the country. In particular, States parties should promote accession to or conclusion of international agreements and other appropriate arrangements in situations where persons with financial responsibility for children live in countries different from those of children.[20] The preamble to the Convention on the Elimination of All Forms of Discrimination against Women states that it is concerned that, in situations of poverty, women often have the least access to food, health care, education, training, employment, and other needs.[21]

---

[18] Cheng et al. [7, p. 84].

[19] Cheng et al. [7, p. 113].

[20] See Cheng et al. [7, p. 168].

[21] See Cheng [7, p. 120].

3.1.2 Provisions on the Right to Food in Regional Human Rights Law Documents

The preamble to the European Social Charter states that it is determined to make every joint effort to improve the standard of living of urban and rural dwellers and to promote their social welfare through appropriate provisions and actions. In the first part, States parties consider that the purpose of their policies, through all appropriate means, including national and international means, is to achieve conditions that enable the effective realization of the following rights and principles: all workers are entitled to remuneration for work sufficient to guarantee a decent standard of living for themselves and their families. Part II, Article 4, of the right to fair remuneration provides that, in order to ensure the effective implementation of the right to equitable remuneration, States Parties undertake to recognize the right of workers to remuneration sufficient to provide a decent standard of living for themselves and their families.[22] The American Convention on Human Rights (and the Additional Protocol to the Inter-American Convention on Human Rights) contains the ideal of freedom from fear and want.[23] Article 7 of the Additional Protocol to the American Convention on Human Rights provides for fair and satisfactory living conditions, guaranteeing, as a minimum, decent remuneration for all workers and their families, equal pay for work of equal value, without discrimination, and equal working conditions for women as for men. Article 13 clearly enshrines the right to food: everyone has the right to be guaranteed adequate nutrition for the highest possible level of physical, mental, and intellectual development.[24]

3.2 *The Content of the Right to Food*

3.2.1 A General Elaboration of the Content of the Right to Food

In accordance with the authoritative definition of food contained in General Comment No. 12 of the Committee on Economic, Social, and Cultural Rights, the right to food should not be interpreted narrowly or restrictively and should not be simply equated with a minimum calorie, protein, and certain other nutrients. With reference to the Special Rapporteur's definition of the right to food, the author elaborates on the content of the right to food in detail as follows:

First, the cultural acceptability of food in terms of consumption or preparation is key to safeguarding the dignity of those who eat it. Human beings live in different forms of society, forming various customs, habits, and different kinds of religious beliefs, and giving rise to different forms of cultural traditions and ethics, thus developing specific and even greatly disparate food concepts and cultures. This requires

[22] See International Human Rights Law Project Research Group [10, pp. 132–133, 135].

[23] See International Human Rights Law Project Research Group [10, pp. 182, 204].

[24] See International Human Rights Law Project Research Group [10, pp. 205–207].

that we take into account as much as possible the non-food-based values of food and food consumption (e.g. personal preferences, cultural traditions, and religious beliefs), as well as consumer concerns about the accessibility of food. Food should be provided to meet the requirements of a particular culture, and people should not be forced to eat food that is contrary to their religious beliefs or habits, or forcibly forbidden to consume certain foods. Mill made a powerful argument for this in his famous book "On Freedom," arguing that in a country where the majority is Muslim, eating pork will cause disgust and dissatisfaction among the majority, but if these majorities pass a law prohibiting a minority from eating pork, it is unreasonable, because the eating of pork by a small number of people only violates the customs of others and does not cause harm to others, which cannot be a sufficient reason for the public to interfere with the dietary freedom of a minority.[25] Similarly, in our society, no one has absolute freedom in the process of obtaining and consuming food, and no one has the right to interfere with the legitimate rights of others or the interests of the general public.

Respecting eating habits is an endorsement of cultural traditions and religious beliefs, which is especially important in a pluralistic society where differences are celebrated. Every human being must meet their basic requirements for life while maintaining their dignity. In other words, the fundamental premise of obtaining or consuming food is that it should not compromise the basic dignity of the human person. No one should be compelled to engage in activities that undermine their dignity, such as begging, prostitution, or hard labor, to satisfy their basic food needs.[26]

Secondly, the adequacy of food lies at the heart of the right to food. It has two aspects: first, food should meet the dietary needs of individuals in terms of quantity and quality; second, the provision of these foods should be safe. "Dietary needs" refer to whole foods that contain nutrients, including micronutrients such as vitamins and iodine, necessary for physical and mental development, maintenance, and physical activity. These nutrients must be consistent with the physiological needs of people at all stages of life and must be able to meet the needs of different people and occupations. It is therefore necessary to take measures to maintain, adapt, or enhance food diversity and appropriate consumption and feeding patterns, including breastfeeding. This must be done while ensuring that food availability and access do not adversely affect food quality and intake.[27] This means that the quantity of food intake required for adequacy is constantly changing due to obvious individual differences. Additionally, there are many types of food, and there is a certain degree of similarity in nutrient composition between different types of food. Therefore, the quality of food allows for substitution and conversion between different types of food.

On the other hand, ensuring the adequacy of food also requires that the provision of food be safe, which necessitates corresponding requirements for food safety. With the development of modern science and technology, food safety has garnered increasing

[25] Mill [11].

[26] See Liu [9].

[27] See Yang [2, p. 96].

attention from society. Chemical fertilizers are widely used in agricultural products, and a large amount of melamine, pesticides, and various insecticides in milk powder can cause agricultural products to contain many substances harmful to human health. Moreover, many genetically modified products also have the potential to be dangerous to the human body. Therefore, effective measures must be taken to strictly regulate all aspects of food acquisition and consumption to prevent harm to human health caused by food safety violations.

Thirdly, the durability of food is fundamental to guaranteeing the realization of an individual's right to food. Access to food should not only meet the body's daily nutritional needs but also be available for a sustained period of time. The operation of living organisms is a long-term and continuous cycle, rather than a momentary existence. Metabolism requires us to constantly supplement new nutrients to meet the daily needs of the human body. For those struggling with poverty and hunger, ensuring a sustained supply of food to realize their right to food requires effective distribution mechanisms that can ensure long-term, efficient, and rational allocation of food.

3.2.2 Focus on the Content of the Right to Food

Fundamentally, the main cause of hunger and malnutrition is not the lack of food, but the inability of hungry people to access enough food to sustain their lives due to poverty or other social reasons. Amartya Sen has noted that "hunger is not only related to the expansion of food production and agriculture, but also to the functioning of entire economies, and even more broadly, to the functioning of political and social arrangements. The latter can directly or indirectly affect people's ability to access food, maintain their health, and improve their nutritional status. Undernutrition, hunger, and famine are all influenced by the functioning of the economy and society as a whole, not just by food production and agricultural activities."[28] Therefore, the content of the right to food should not be limited to the general understanding described above, but should focus on the intermediate links of access to food, namely "availability" and "accessibility".

First, "availability" refers to the possibility of obtaining food directly from productive land or other natural resources, or the possibility of well-functioning distribution, processing, and marketing systems that transport food from the point of production to the place of need where it is required.[29] Farmers can provide food directly from productive land or other natural resources, and the state needs to promote the rational distribution, processing, and marketing of food so that it can be efficiently allocated according to market supply and demand through exchange prices. This way, all people have access to sufficient, safe, and nutritious food at all times without preventing individuals from obtaining the minimum necessities necessary to maintain their physical fitness due to insufficient income or other natural factors.

---

[28] Sen [1, p. 163].

[29] See Yang [2, p. 97].

Secondly, according to the General Comment, "accessibility" covers both "economic accessibility" and "physical accessibility." The former means that the level of expenditure of individuals or households related to access to adequate food should be limited to the extent that the achievement or satisfaction of other basic needs is not affected or impaired. "Economic accessibility" applies to any means of access or qualification by which people obtain food and is a measure of the appropriateness of such access or qualification for obtaining sufficient food, depending largely on the quid pro quo of the ability to sell and buy food and the relative prices of different foods. The different proportions of personal or household expenditure by which these qualifications are achieved reflect differences in the accessibility of the right to food.

"Physical accessibility" means that everyone must have access to food, including the physically vulnerable. As a human right, the right to food is something that everyone can enjoy and should not be treated differently based on ethnicity, race, sex, skin color, language, religion, property, etc. Among all individuals, children need special protection and care because they are not yet physically and mentally mature, and their physical access to food deserves our attention. The situation of children regarding physical access to food is not entirely satisfactory in both developed and developing countries. Children's issues continue to be of universal concern to the world.[30] According to the website of the British "Daily Telegraph" on February 13, 2008: "One in five children in the UK grows up on government funding. The UK government acknowledges that more than 2.2 million British children, or one-fifth of the total, now live in households dependent on government assistance." Hunger and disease seriously threaten the lives of African children. According to Al Jazeera in 2008, "The United Nations Children's Fund released an annual report yesterday that says as many as 260,000 children under the age of 5 have died from hunger and poverty in the past year."[31]

Based on this elaboration and interpretation of the right to food, and the description of the less optimistic reality, it is evident that the protection of the right to food is crucial. Further study is necessary to explore the obligations of states in protecting the right to food.

3.3 *The Burden of Obligations on the Right to Food*

3.3.1 The Core Obligation of States to Protect the Right to Food

Article 2 of the International Covenant on Economic, Social and Cultural Rights states that: (1) Each State party must take steps to the best of its ability, either individually or through international assistance and cooperation, especially in the areas

[30] "United Kingdom: One in five children lives on government handouts", available at: http://news.xinhuanet.com/world/2008-02/15/content_7609012.htm, 2008-02-15.

[31] Hunger and disease threaten the lives of Africa's children, available at: http://world.people.com.cn/GB/1031/6811058.html, 2008-01-24.

of economic and technical capacity, to utilize all appropriate means, including, in particular, the obligation to progressively achieve by legislative means the full realization of the rights recognized in the present Covenant. (2) The States Parties to the present Covenant have a responsibility to ensure that the rights proclaimed in the present Covenant are exercised universally, without discrimination of any kind, such as race, color, sex, language, religion, political or other opinion, national or social origin, property, birth, or other status. (3) Developing countries, with due consideration to human rights and their national economies, may determine to what extent they guarantee to non-nationals the enjoyment of the economic rights recognized in the present Covenant.[32] As evidenced above, the State has a fundamental obligation to protect its citizens' right to food. This obligation can be understood in the following ways:

Firstly, States should take measures to ensure the full realization of the right to food using all appropriate means, particularly through legislation. Additionally, administrative, judicial, policy regulation, and educational measures can be implemented to ensure that everyone can enjoy this right. At the same time, State parties should specify whether the measures or methods they have adopted are appropriate or not.

Secondly, the right to food should not be misinterpreted by State parties as a gradual obligation to achieve the full realization of this right. The progressive obligation implies that State parties, irrespective of their level of economic development, should make the most of the resources available to them and take immediate action to ensure the realization of the right to food. "Progressive realization" not only recognizes the challenges involved in achieving the right to food as a social right in the short-term, but also clarifies the obligation of State parties to work towards realizing this right.

Thirdly, "to ensure the fulfillment to the maximum of its means" requires State parties to use their available resources prudently and to seek international economic or technical assistance provided by international organizations or benefits derived from international cooperation to enhance the protection of the right to food of their citizens. At the same time, State parties must not neglect their minimum obligations to protect the right to food, even in cases of severe food insecurity caused by economic or other factors, and may not arbitrarily exempt themselves from their minimum obligations. For instance, in times of national famine, the State should take all necessary measures to ensure the provision of food necessary for the basic survival needs of its citizens.

Fourthly, fulfilling the obligations of States parties without discrimination is essential to enable certain groups and individuals to enjoy the right to food in a fair manner.[33] This is also extremely important since, as mentioned earlier, the right to food is severely impacted by social injustice, which is largely the result of food insecurity in today's society, not because of food scarcity but due to the unequal distribution of food. This requires States parties to strive to ensure that social resources

[32] See Cheng et al. [7, p. 110].

[33] See Yang [2, pp. 13–15, 38–43, 97–99]. Eide et al. [5, pp. 15–31, 121–178].

are allocated fairly and justly. Social and economic inequalities should be arranged in such a way that they can meet the ideal conditions that Rawls describes: "(1) consistent with the principle of storage of justice, appropriate to the best interests of the least beneficiaries; and (2) open to all persons in accordance with conditions of fairness and equality of opportunity,"[34] so that everyone has the opportunity and ability to obtain adequate food.

3.3.2 The Obligation of International Organizations Such as the United Nations and Some Regional Organizations to Protect the Right to Food

The United Nations and other international organizations also have certain obligations to promote the realization of the right to food, especially the Food and Agriculture Organization of the United Nations (FAO), which has more obligations in the realization of the right to food. In addition, the European Committee of Social Rights and the Inter-American Commission on Human Rights, regional organizations such as the African Commission on Human and Peoples' Rights, also have corresponding obligations to ensure and promote the realization of the right to food in the region.

In summary, corresponding to the right to food, States parties have three corresponding types of obligations, namely the obligation to respect, protect, and fulfill (or fulfil) the right to food. The obligation to respect existing access to adequate food requires States parties to respect the space and legitimate rights of everyone who can produce or obtain the food they need through barter and to refrain from any measures that may impede such access. The obligation to protect requires States parties to take measures to ensure that individuals or societies do not deny individuals access to adequate food and to protect the right to food and its resource base from third parties. The obligation to fulfill (or fulfill) includes the obligation to help and provide, which means that States parties must actively and effectively facilitate access to livelihoods and to resources and opportunities for food for the full realization of their right to food.

In addition, States parties are under an obligation to provide direct assistance to an individual or group of persons who, for reasons beyond their control, are unable to enjoy adequate food (this obligation also applies to victims of natural or other disasters). International organizations such as the United Nations and some regional organizations have the obligation to promote and urge States parties to fulfil their obligations.[35]

---

[34] Rawls [12].

[35] See Yao [13].

4 Mechanisms for the Implementation of the Right to Food

4.1 The Leading Role of the State in the Implementation Mechanism of the Right to Food

States have a core obligation to promote the realization of the right to food by all appropriate means. In particular, States should enhance and strengthen the implementation mechanisms of the right to food in the following areas.

4.1.1 Legislative Guarantees

In a modern society governed by the rule of law, the concrete realization of universal human rights requires the legislative regulation of these rights through States parties, and the realization of the right to food is no exception. Only by establishing a complete set of legal protection mechanisms can the state transfer the protection of the right to food from the conceptual and value level to the institutional and practical level. Only by amending the Constitution and enacting relevant laws, formulating a series of laws and regulations to protect the right to food, regulating the rights that need to be guaranteed through legislation, and implementing the right to food at the level of domestic law, can the State better protect it. A country's constitution is generally regarded as having the highest legal force, and the provision of provisions on the right to food in the constitution can guarantee that right at the level of fundamental law. In some countries, the right to food is enshrined directly in the Constitution, while in others the courts protect the right to food through constitutional interpretation. For example, the economic and social rights enshrined in the South African Constitution can be broadly divided into three main categories. The second category underpins everyone's right to adequate housing, health care, food, water and social security.[36] In some countries, the right to food is statutory, i.e. enforced by the courts in accordance with the provisions of national authorities. There are also different types of law protecting this right in different countries, as well as various legal mechanisms through which individuals or groups can claim this right. Article 30 of the European Social Charter, as amended in 1996, adds the right to freedom from poverty and social exclusion.[37] In contrast, the protection of the right to food through general legislation is more specific and detailed than constitutional protection, and thus more legally operational. The legislative approach requires the establishment of effective, accessible and viable legal mechanisms for the right to adequate food, which is the most basic and important link in whether the right to food can be protected in a State party. If it is not constitutionally or legally enshrined, the legitimacy of its existence as a legal right in the State party will be called into question and the judicial protection of the right to food will not be sustainable.

---

[36] Eide et al. [5, pp. 50–75].

[37] See Zhu [14, p. 132].

4.1.2 Judicial Guarantees

The protection of the right to food cannot be fully realized by a sound legislative system alone, and judicial safeguards are particularly necessary when remedies are required for damages to the right to food. In the process of guaranteeing the realization of the right to food, effective judicial proceedings based on the right of suit need to be protected. In its general comment No. 3, the Committee on Economic, Social and Cultural Rights stated that measures appropriate for the protection of the right to food include, inter alia, the provision of judicial remedies for rights that fall within the jurisdiction of the national legal system.[38]

In general, judicial proceedings are the last and most effective means for protecting the right to food, as they can provide the greatest remedy for violations of this right. Without the final guarantee of corresponding judicial processes, even the most perfect legislation cannot avoid being abandoned, and the protection of the right to food by law can only remain on paper. The right to food, as guaranteed in the legal system, can only be successfully realized if there are no obstacles to its realization. However, once this right is hindered, interfered with, or otherwise violated, victims must rely on judicial procedures to obtain effective legal remedies for their violated rights. In the case of Mill above, for instance, if the public prohibits a small number of people from eating pork in Islamic countries, it constitutes an infringement of their legitimate right to food. National legislation must prohibit such infringements from occurring, and if they do occur, due processes of justice must be followed.

4.1.3 Other Safeguards

States parties need to use all appropriate means to ensure the realization of the right to food, especially with regard to the security of the right to minimum food, and to exhaust all means to ensure that their nationals are free from hunger, without shirking their obligations to bear the right to food on various grounds. In cases where the right to food cannot be effectively guaranteed by law, and in order to ensure the enjoyment of this right by all, Governments of States parties should actively adopt other administrative, economic, social, and educational measures to protect the right to food. Administrative measures are particularly important here, as the executive has the means to enforce the coercive power of the State, has many important resources at its disposal, and whose decisions play a key role in the realization of the right to food in exceptional times.

If economic hardship or a state of emergency requires derogation from the content of the right to food of its nationals, such derogation shall not preclude the minimum fulfillment of the right to food and shall ensure that, once the economy recovers or the state of emergency is eliminated, such derogation shall not be derogated from. The enjoyment of the right to food should also be restored and not less than the extent before the derogation. For example, during the 2008 Southern Ice and Snow Disaster,

[38] See Zhu [14, p. 132].

the Ministry of Commerce organized transportation on the basis of giving full play to the market allocation of resources. The government organized the transportation of some vegetables to the disaster-stricken areas, and used the national reserves to release central reserve meat, including frozen meat reserves and live reserves, to the main disaster-stricken areas, such as Guizhou, Anhui, Hubei and other places during the Spring Festival to ensure the supply of the main necessities of life in the affected areas. This minimizes the erosion of the right to food in emergency situations.[39]

4.2 The Important Role of International Organizations in the Implementation Mechanism of the Right to Food

There are four main ways in which international organizations can play a role in the implementation of the right to food:

4.2.1 Reporting System

First, Part IV of the International Covenant on Economic, Social and Cultural Rights provides for a reporting system for States parties, which is of great significance for the international monitoring of the realization of human rights. Expert bodies can effectively monitor the realization of the right to food through the reports of States parties. Through the periodic reports submitted by States parties on the realization of specific economic, social and cultural rights, the United Nations can comprehensively review the compatibility of each State party's legislation, judicial, policy, administrative provisions and procedures, and practices with the provisions of the Covenant in order to monitor the realization of their right to food. At the same time, it can provide comprehensive monitoring of States parties, identify problems and shortcomings in the realization of the right to food, evaluate the implementation of this right by States parties, and provide recommendations on common problems faced in the realization of the right to food to supervise the more effective realization of the right to food.[40]

Secondly, some regional organizations have also established reporting systems for States parties on the right to food. For example, under the European Social Charter, each State party is obliged to submit regular and irregular national reports to the Secretary-General of the Council of Europe. The Chairman of the Council of Europe Conference deliberates and makes recommendations for implementation in the countries concerned.[41]

---

[39] See "The Ministry of Commerce Uses National Reserve Meat to Supply the Disaster-stricken Market", available at: http://news.sina.com.cn/c/2008-02-14/120614938178.shtml, 2008-03-21.

[40] See Yang [2, pp. 33–35].

[41] See Zhu [14, p. 137].

4.2.2 International Cooperation

Today, the realization of human rights is not only an internal affair of a country, especially in today's increasingly international community, where international cooperation plays a more important role. Moreover, since human rights are indivisible and interdependent, specific economic, social, and cultural rights are interrelated and interdependent (even with other fundamental civil and political rights). Hunger and poverty are also part of this interrelated whole of rights, so that any State confronted with difficulties in the effective protection of the right to food is, in fact, faced with a more complex challenge linked to a range of other factors. It is difficult for one country alone to address this dilemma better, and extensive international cooperation is, therefore, required. Not only is poverty in developing countries the focus of government work, but there are also many low-income groups in developed countries. In the case of the United States, the United States Human Rights Record 2007, published by the Information Office of the United States Department of State on 13 March 2008, states that "Poverty in the United States is increasing. According to statistics released by the U.S. Census Bureau in August 2007, the rate of poverty in the United States by the end of 2006 was 12.3 per cent, or 36.5 million people and 7.7 million families, living in poverty, equivalent to almost 1 in 8 Americans.[42] UN Secretary-General Ban Ki-moon declared 2008 the Year of the Bottom Billion and called for action to help them. Ban Ki-moon stressed the need to focus on the world's poorest countries and people, who are excluded from the mainstream of the international community, least powerful to combat climate change, and least lacking in basic human rights. He, therefore, proposed that 2008 should be the "Year of the Bottom Billion", a year in which the United Nations would strengthen its work in the area of development. The United Nations had established the Millennium Goals Africa Steering Group in 2007, and the United Nations Conference on Trade and Development in 2008 would focus on how to help poor countries achieve the Millennium Development Goals (Millennium Development Goals) problem.[43] These phenomena illustrate that we have begun to seek cooperation across borders and globally to promote the enjoyment of the right to food by the poor.

4.2.3 International Assistance

Article 22 of the International Covenant on Economic, Social and Cultural Rights clearly provides that the Economic and Social Council may bring to the attention of other United Nations bodies, their subsidiary bodies, and relevant specialized agencies engaged in technical assistance, measures taken within the limits of its competence, and to express this right clearly in general comment No. 2 of the Committee

---

[42] America's Human Rights Record 2007, available at: http://news.xinhuanet.com/newscenter/2008-03/13/content_7779687.htm, 2008-03-21.

[43] See Ban Ki-moon Proposal2008The year should be the "bottom billion people", available at: http://world.people.com.cn/GB/1029/42408/6750081.html, 2008-03-22.

on Economic, Social and Cultural Rights.[44] UN agencies, notably the Food and Agriculture Organization of the United Nations, the Office of the United Nations High Commissioner for Refugees, the United Nations Development Programme (UNDP), World Food Programme, and other institutions, have played a very important role in promoting the realization of the right to food and solving refugee problems (inter-country roles), including through the United Nations Development Assistance Framework. "FAO has set up a fund to help poor countries ensure food security. According to Xinhua: "news from Ouagadougou, the capital and largest city of Burkina Faso: The Food and Agriculture Organization of the United Nations has launched a fund of $17 million to help poor countries that are completely dependent on food imports to develop agricultural production to respond to the food shortage crisis that may be triggered by rising global food prices."[45] Other institutions, such as the World Bank and the International Monetary Fund (IMF), as well as any other specialized agency, should also play a corresponding role in protecting the right to food of the poor and vulnerable."

4.2.4 Grievance System

The complaints system is well established and plays a corresponding role in the First Optional Protocol to the International Covenant on Civil and Political Rights. However, the individual communications complaint procedure is not established in the International Covenant on Economic, Social and Cultural Rights. At present, with the growing interest in the protection of economic, social, and cultural rights, a number of regional organizations have also established complaints procedures. For example, the collective complaints procedure established in the European Social Charter provides an institutional basis for the protection of the right to food. Under this procedure, international and national employers' or workers' organizations (within the framework of certain options), as well as non-governmental organizations working in this field, have the right to submit a written complaint to the Secretary-General of the Council of Europe.[46] In the Inter-American human rights system, the Protocol of San Salvador provides for a limited complaints system.[47] Although there are still many disadvantages in the implementation of the complaint system in the area of economic, social, and cultural rights, regional practice undoubtedly provides an effective guarantee for more comprehensive protection of the right to food.

[44] See Cheng et al. [7, p. 117].

[45] FAO Establishes Fund to Help Poor Countries Ensure Food Security, available at: http://finance.qq.com/a/20080118/002084.htm, 2008-03-22.

[46] See Zhu [14, pp. 138–139].

[47] See Eide et al. [5, pp. 472–506].

4.3 *The Active Role of Non-Governmental Organizations in the Implementation Mechanism of the Right to Food*

In addition to the effective monitoring and facilitating role played by international organizations to fulfill their obligations in good faith, some non-governmental organizations whose purpose is to protect human rights (e.g. Amnesty International, The International League for Human Rights, among others) can also provide more effective oversight of the realization of economic, social and cultural rights. On the one hand, NGOs help international human rights bodies to achieve effective monitoring by reviewing the submission of reports by States parties on the implementation of the Convention. On the other hand, the fact that some non-governmental organizations spontaneously formed by civil society have evaluated and made corresponding recommendations on the implementation of the Convention by States parties is not a malicious attack on the State party's compliance with its obligation to protect the right to food. Rather, it supports and assists States parties in more effective and correct implementation of their obligations under the Covenant on Economic, Social and Cultural Rights relating to the protection of the right to food. In recent years, these non-governmental organizations, active outside the United Nations and regional organizations, have played a very important role in monitoring the fulfillment by States parties of their obligations related to the protection of the right to food.[48]

5 Theoretical Difficulties in the Right to Food

5.1 *Whether the Right to Food as a Human Right Has Universal Standards*

As a specific economic, social and cultural right, the right to food is a right to which everyone is entitled. Can the right to food as a human right be universal?

Xia Yong, a human rights scholar in China, pointed out: "The advocates of natural rights declare the 'nature' that human beings possess as human beings as rights, and natural rights are natural rights. This right comes from 'nature', so it is innate. Even so, natural rights exist beyond positive law and are inalienable. Since nature is common to all human beings and expresses the basic rules of human beings, then the rights of nature are common to human beings. So, natural rights or natural rights are human rights."[49] British human rights scholar A.J.M Milne, in his book The Philosophy of Human Rights, points out that some scholars believe that certain rights belong to all people, at any time, in any place, regardless of whether they are recognized or not. These are the rights that all human beings have simply because they are human beings,

[48] See Mo [15, pp. 75–76].

[49] Xia [16].

regardless of ethnicity, religion, sex, social status, occupation, wealth, property, or any other ethnic, cultural, or social characteristics that are distinct from each other. Human rights are an objective fact of human life and are not subject to the subjective will of any individual or group, organization, or institution.[50] This statement affirms the universality of human rights, indicating that human rights, as a right that human beings are born with, should be enjoyed by everyone. It follows that the same is true of the right to food, which is one of the most fundamental components of fundamental human rights. However, this does not fully infer that the right to food has universally applicable standards. Milne also elaborates on this issue, arguing that a person cannot be socially and culturally neutral, that he is always the product of a certain social and cultural environment, and that different cultural and civilizational traditions represent different ways of life of human beings. Therefore, the rights that belong to all people in all regions of all times will be the rights they enjoy as beings "out of society" and "out of civilization". But they are not and cannot be such beings, and therefore cannot have such rights.[51] Milne's statement shows the specificity of human rights, which cannot exist in isolation from the specific circumstances in which people live, nor the right to food as a human being. Milne goes on to argue that "the existence of human rights, the existence of human rights that universal minimum moral standards require to be respected, is not a question of experience."[52] Rather, it is a question of the meaning of social life itself and whether these meanings include such a standard. "This universal minimum moral standard requires that everyone has the right to be respected, and this should be a universal moral right. Since universal moral rights are minimal and can therefore exist in conditions of diversity, the right to food is a universal moral right." This emphasizes both the fundamental right to food as a human right for all and the fact that the right to food also has a certain degree of specificity.

Universal moral rights are derived from the concept of natural law. However, since the concept of natural law is vague and controversial, it is difficult to sufficiently persuade how human rights (natural rights) are derived from natural law. There is another way to justify human rights, which is to justify and defend human rights from the perspective of human nature or basic human values. "The only reason people have rights is that they are human beings. Humans have rights because they are persons. Therefore, human rights are rights that we should enjoy as human beings. Human rights have arisen historically and are the rights that human beings should enjoy based on their natural attributes and social existence. Every human being who is a member of the human race should have rights based on such a basic fact. Therefore, human rights are universal and common. However, human beings are specific individuals who live in different social and cultural traditions, subject to different levels of economic development and social systems. Therefore, human rights are always relative. Relative human rights require us to pay attention to the

[50] See Milne [17, p. 2].

[51] See Milne [17, p. 7].

[52] See Milne [17, p. 13].

particularity of human rights."[53] As a fundamental human right, the right to food is also a unity of universality and specificity, and the enjoyment of the right to food by everyone should be taken into account in the context of the economic and cultural development of each country.

It follows from this that, in any event, a government should fulfill the minimum obligation to protect its citizens from hunger (at least above the poverty line), which is required of states in the universality of the right to food. At the same time, states and regions should fully realize the right to food with national characteristics of their nationals in accordance with the specific conditions of their countries and regions. This is extremely important in today's context, where the right to food is undermined mainly because of inequality.

5.2 Reasons for Differences in the Standards of the Right to Food

First, in Part II of the Vienna Declaration and Programme of Action adopted by the World Conference on Human Rights in June 1993, Paragraph 3 states: "All human rights are universal, indivisible, interdependent and interrelated, and the international community must view them in a comprehensive and fair manner with equal emphasis."[54] All states should promote the progressive enjoyment by their nationals of different categories of specific human rights in accordance with this criterion (the subdivision of adequate food into several elements by the UN Committee on Economic, Social and Cultural Rights in order to reach consensus in the international community and thus facilitate national practical practice). However, the realization of human rights is ultimately implemented by different countries, and the speed of realization depends on the economic and cultural development of each country. The realization of any right is inseparable from material conditions based on socio-economic development and the cultural traditions that emerge from them. The same is true for the enjoyment and realization of the right to food, which is not only directly related to the level of economic development but also to the cultural traditions of different countries.[55]

In terms of economic conditions, the realization of the right to food is based on a corresponding level of socio-economic development, and its realization requires corresponding protection and assistance from the state. At present, there is still a difference between developed and developing countries in the world, and for developed countries, because they are backed by strong economic strength, the standards set out in the Vienna Declaration and Programme of Action can be said to have been achieved or basically achieved. However, for the vast number of developing countries, it is difficult or even impossible to meet these standards in the short term. However,

[53] Zhang [18]. See Yao [13].

[54] Quoted from Zheng [6, p. 19].

[55] See Liu [9].

a relatively mature and complete institutional system has been formed in the field of international human rights, and the basic order in international human rights relations has been established. Any newly established country must be integrated into the international community and recognize the existing human rights system, the vast majority of which are new accessions and developing countries. With regard to the right to food, the minimum obligation of states to ensure that their citizens are free from hunger is not difficult for developed countries but difficult for some developing countries. Moreover, excessive income disparities, both between and within countries, add new difficulties to the universal enjoyment of the right to food. The figures provided in the UN Development Funds in the Human Development Report 1999 prove that the gap between rich and poor countries has widened since the early nineteenth century. In 1820, the gap between the richest and poorest countries was about 3:1, and it has been widening. In 1992, it had widened to a staggering ratio of 72:1.[56]

Second, although the enjoyment of the right to food is not directly linked to cultural traditions, a country's culture plays a role in accelerating or delaying the realization of the right to food. As a cultural phenomenon, human rights refer to certain ideas, beliefs, and value systems. Human rights concepts, beliefs, and value systems are the fruits and symbols of the development of civilization to a certain stage. Since culture has a national character, this determines the national nature of the concept of human rights, including the right to food as a basic human right. Human rights issues must not be separated from the cultural traditions, customs, and religious beliefs of a country and a nation. We cannot enforce the same standard for the right to food, nor can we compel anyone to eat food that they do not accept, no matter how beneficial and indispensable it may be to the human body.

At the same time, cultures that are more open are generally more receptive to accepting foreign lifestyles, while closed cultures may be more resistant to new values. This cultural openness or resistance can play an important role in the acceptance of new human rights concepts. The role of culture is particularly evident in countries where the concept of human rights is not well-established. This has led these countries to pay closer attention to the specific cultural influences on the realization of the right to food within their borders.

5.3 Problems Encountered in the Realization of the Right to Food

In today's world, poverty affects half of the world's population. We should not accept the poverty created by society, which kills people more than the killing of knives and guns, and is more widespread and worse than the damage caused by floods or earthquakes. Poverty, which is essentially a violation of fundamental human rights, aims to preserve human dignity by pointing out the contradiction between the claim

[56] See Eide et al. [5, pp. 601–660].

to equality of rights and the growing inequality in access to the means of subsistence in reality. Such appeals are not aimed at alleviating or even weakening poverty, but at eradicating it at its roots. Poverty will disappear only when it is seen as a violation of human rights and is eradicated in that sense. This is the crux of the problem and the basic prerequisite for solving it. Fundamentally, poverty is not a standard of living, much less a condition of existence: it is both a cause and a consequence of the total or partial denial of human rights.[57]

Human rights cannot be abolished and are indivisible. Violations of human rights fundamentally violate human dignity as a whole, not just a minor inconvenience for unrelated individuals. Therefore, such behavior must be brought to an end, and a single approach is imperative: poverty must be eradicated. The rights-based approach to food security emphasizes that "meeting people's basic needs is a matter of rights, not a good deed." Under this approach, people hold their governments accountable for protecting the right to food and make themselves participants in the human development process rather than passive recipients. A rights-based approach is relevant not only to the end result of eradicating hunger but also to the ways and means to achieve it. The application of human rights principles is an integral part of this process.

Key human rights principles in policy formulation and implementation include accountability, non-discrimination, transparency, empowerment, and participation. An independent judiciary is also essential for the effective protection of human rights at the national level. A rights-based approach empowers rights holders to acquire the right to adequate food by actively involving them in the process of realizing the right to food. This places responsibility on all actors in the realization of the right to food to promote it. This can be achieved through legal, administrative, or political mechanisms. Rights holders, whether individuals or, in certain circumstances, groups, can demand that governments respect, protect, and promote the realization of their right to food.[58]

Poverty is the greatest violation of human rights, as defined by the UN Committee on Economic, Social and Cultural Rights, which considers it to be "the ongoing or prolonged denial of resources, capacities, choices, security, and rights necessary to enjoy an adequate standard of living and other civil, cultural, economic, political, and social rights," and poverty has always been a prevailing social and economic reality. The poor are not poor because they should not be treated as human beings, or because their physical or mental conditions are worse than those who live in better conditions. On the contrary, their poverty is often directly or indirectly caused by society's failure to establish equal and fair mechanisms in social and economic relations.[59] In his book, "Poverty and Famine," Amartya Sen pointed out that "In a sense, poverty is clearly only a characteristic of the poor rather than of the rich, and poverty should be

[57] See Sané [19].

[58] See FAO report: Implementing the Right to Adequate Food: The Outcome of Six Case Studies. available at: http://www.fao.org/righttofood/zh/index.html, 2008-03-22.

[59] Poverty is a violation of human rights, available at: http://www.hrol.org/hrfile/manual/Cn_ESC_Poverty.html, 2008-03-22.

viewed in conjunction with relative poverty. Deprivation of basic viable capacities due to inadequate income, unemployment and gender inequality can lead to hunger or famine." Poverty eradication is considered to be a fundamental requirement of essential human rights that must be respected, protected, and fulfilled.[60] A human rights approach to poverty requires the recognition of the inherent dignity of human beings, which must be guaranteed and upheld as the primary objective of every right. The right to adequate food, like other human rights, requires respect for the dignity of the eater and not merely as charity.

In response to the above, States Parties shall respect available means of access to adequate food and refrain from any measures that impede access to food. Furthermore, steps should be taken to protect the right of all people to adequate food by preventing societies and individuals from depriving them of effective means of access to food. States parties should implement policies conducive to the progressive realization of the right to adequate food and undertake activities to enhance access to and use of food-related resources and means to safeguard people's livelihoods and food security. Each State Party shall, within the limits of its national resources, establish and maintain food safety nets or provide other assistance to ensure the availability of food for those who are unable to feed themselves.[61]

In a national human rights-based approach to food security, emphasis should be placed not only on the universal, interdependent, indivisible, and interrelated concept of human rights, but also on the obligations of states and the active role of relevant stakeholders. The realization of food safety is an important element in the realization of existing rights, including some of the key rights: the need to enable individuals to realize the right to take part in the conduct of public affairs, the right to freedom of expression and the seeking, access, and imparting of information, including for decision-making for the realization of the right to adequate food. Such an approach should take into account the poor and vulnerable groups who require attention but are often excluded from the process of identifying policies to promote food security, as well as the need for states to treat the interests of all segments of society equally in fulfilling their obligations to promote and respect the right to food. In this approach, the people are both accountable to the government and themselves participants in the human development process, rather than passive recipients. A human rights-based approach requires states and societies to propose not only the ultimate goal of hunger eradication but also the concrete means by which it can be achieved, and the application of human rights principles is an important component of the protection of the right to food. For rights holders who have suffered violations of the right to food, no matter how much attention is given to poverty alleviation and prevention of food and nutrition insecurity in the overall policy environment, effective mechanisms are

[60] Sen [1, p. 17].

[61] See FAO report: Implementing the Right to Adequate Food: The Outcome of Six Case Studies. available at: http://www.fao.org/righttofood/zh/index.html, 2008-03-22.

needed to identify the causes of food insecurity and understand the reasons for the vulnerability of rights holders.[62]

The implementation of the plan is not generally optimistic in terms of identifying target or vulnerable groups with effective and appropriate detailed criteria. This is primarily a fundamental issue of development approaches rather than technological development related to data and analytical capabilities. Strategies and action plans must be based on the results of comprehensive and detailed socio-economic assessments of different groups for national food security plans to identify the causes of food insecurity and the specific scope of vulnerable groups. A detailed survey of vulnerable groups is particularly useful in this regard. A human rights approach is a necessary condition for the protection of the right to food by constantly focusing on and identifying those rights holders who have not realized their rights or have had them violated and why their rights have not been realized or violated.[63]

At the same time, when formulating policies related to the right to food, governments should not neglect to pay attention to other rights that are based on the right to food. They should not only emphasize the right of rights holders to be free from hunger and to food, and use this as an excuse to evade their responsibility to protect other human rights related to the right to food. Freedom from hunger is undoubtedly a fundamental human right, but it cannot be effective if it is isolated because it is inseparable from other fundamental human rights. The realization of all other human rights—civil and political and economic, social and cultural—is based on the fundamental human right to be free from hunger. The indivisibility of human rights should be emphasized so that they are not used as a pretext by autocrats, tyrants, and dictators to make unmet basic needs the primary condition for democratization.[64] "Poverty makes the poor dependent and resigned to their fate,"[65] and poverty itself is a violation of the right to food, but it also leads to violations of other economic and social rights, making it impossible to realize other human rights and fundamental rights of individual human beings.

Common measures aimed at helping the needy not only fail to provide a way out of the crisis but also lead to a situation where the needy settle for poverty. When they receive any benefits, they feel relieved that they are not at risk of extreme poverty. In a sense, "these people live on the minimum benefits of handouts, they have no 'rights'".[66] Therefore, when States take effective measures to protect the right to food, especially the right to be free from hunger, they cannot neglect the protection of other relevant rights such as political, social, and economic rights. This is necessary to ensure that individuals can effectively acquire autonomy in realizing their right to food and that the resolution of their right to food does not undermine

[62] See FAO report: Implementing the Right to Adequate Food: The Outcome of Six Case Studies. available at: http://www.fao.org/righttofood/zh/index.html, 2008-03-22.

[63] See FAO report: Implementing the Right to Adequate Food: The Outcome of Six Case Studies. available at: http://www.fao.org/righttofood/zh/index.html, 2008-03-22.

[64] See Koubi [20].

[65] Koubi [20].

[66] Koubi [20].

their other rights. Additionally, the protection of other rights can, in turn, contribute more effectively to the protection of the right to food.

6 The Right to Food in Contemporary China

6.1 An Overview of the Right to Food Under the Current Legal Situation in Contemporary China

Although the Standing Committee of the National People's Congress ratified Human Rights Convention A on 28 February 2001, which stipulates the fundamental right to be free from hunger (Article 11 of the Convention), there is still a significant gap between China's current system of protecting human rights in domestic law and the Convention's requirements. Regarding the specific right to food, China's ratification of the International Covenant on Economic, Social and Cultural Rights did not contain reservations or declarations of any kind to the provisions of the right to food. Therefore, China must fully comply with its obligations to guarantee the rights set forth in that article. However, from the current legislative status in China, the right to food has not become an explicitly protected right in the Constitution and laws, and only part of this right is reflected in domestic legislation. "Our Constitution stipulates that citizens' lawful private property is inviolable. The Property Law stipulates that the property rights of the State, collectives, private individuals, and other right holders are protected by law and may not be infringed upon by any unit or individual. The Law on the Protection of the Rights and Interests of the Elderly, the Law on Maternal and Infant Health Care, the Law on the Protection of Minors, the Law on the Protection of Persons with Disabilities, and other laws and regulations strengthen the protection of special groups. The Regulations on Minimum Subsistence Guarantees for Urban Residents and the Regulations on the Work of Providing Five Guarantees for Rural Areas stipulate that basic livelihood guarantees are provided to urban poor and rural peasants who have no ability to work, no source of income, and no one to support, raise or support. Regulations such as the Regulations on Preferential Treatment of Pensions for Servicemen and the Regulations on the Resettlement of Retired Conscripts stipulate the State's system of bereavement and preferential treatment for retired and injured servicemen and their families."[67]

However, the aforementioned laws and regulations do not clearly stipulate the right to food. Considering that the right to food and the idea of protecting human rights established in China's Constitution are consistent in their basic connotations, they should be more specifically and clearly reflected in subsequent legislation. The right to food can also only be implemented and protected in the administration of justice if it is explicitly enshrined in legislation. In this regard, Mo Jihong proposed

[67] White Paper on the Construction of the Rule of Law in China, available at: http://www.showchina.org/zfbps/ndhf/2008/200803/t151704.htm, 2008-03-22.

a draft expert proposal on the human rights protection law in the book "International Covenants on Human Rights and China", which stipulated the relevant content of the right to food in Article 85.[68] In practice, judicial protection of the right to food is mainly reflected in civil cases. Civil disputes occur between citizens, legal persons, or other organizations that are equal subjects and involve property relations and personal relations.[69] The International Covenant on Economic, Social and Cultural Rights stipulates that individuals enjoy the right to work, health, social security, marriage and family, an adequate standard of living, the right to education, etc. These rights are more vulnerable to violations in civil disputes. In the absence of clear constitutional and legal provisions, there have been no cases in the judicial field where legal provisions on the right to food are invoked to protect individual rights. This is bound to adversely affect the protection of this right.

In addition, although the right holder has a certain understanding of the content of the right to food, the right to food as a basic human right has not been universally recognized, and the concept of the right to food has not been widely disseminated, let alone a corresponding awareness of rights. A sine qua non for the widespread dissemination of the right to food concept is the explicit provision of the right to food in legislation. Without a clear legal provision on the right to food, it is difficult for the popularization and realization of the right to food to be recognized and valued by the public. Although domestic policies and social measures may reflect the relevant content of the right to food in some respects, they are not protected as a fundamental human right. This is bound to be detrimental to the full enjoyment and realization of the right to food by citizens. Therefore, in the protection and realization of the right to food, in addition to seeking international cooperation and assistance as far as possible to provide for the right to food as soon as possible in domestic legislation, the enjoyment and realization of the content of the right to food should also be promoted in some specific substantive aspects to better fulfill the obligations relating to the right to food under the International Covenant on Economic, Social and Cultural Rights.

6.2 Food Safety in China

The international community has made a series of provisions on the concept of "food security". In November 1974, the Food and Agriculture Organization of the United Nations adopted the International Undertaking on World Food Security at the World Food Conference. It defines food security as "ensuring that everyone, anywhere, has access to enough food for survival and health."[70] In April 1983, the United Nations

---

[68] See Mo [15, pp. 237, 252–254, 362].

[69] See Zhao Zhengqun. Human Rights Protection in China's Administrative Jurisprudence and Its Contribution to Building a Harmonious Society. available at: http://www.china.com.cn/aboutchina/zhuanti/renquan/txt/2006-12/13/content_7501048.htm, 2010-04-19.

[70] Quoted from Mei [21].

FAO World Safety Committee adopted a new concept of food security, which states that "the ultimate goal of food security is to ensure that all people can both buy and afford the basic food they need at all times."[71] The Rome Declaration, adopted by the Second World Food Summit in November 1996, and the Plan of Action, state world food security as follows: "Only when all people at all times have access to sufficient, material, and economic resources, food security is achieved when safe and nutritious food meets their dietary needs and food preferences for an active and healthy life."[72] Among these, food harmlessness is an important part of achieving food security, and food safety is becoming more prominent worldwide.

The issue of food security, including access to sufficient and nutritious food, is particularly prominent in contemporary China, which should focus on realizing the right to food after having achieved basic food and clothing needs.

The adequacy of food is at the heart of the realization of the right to food, which has two aspects. First, food should not only meet the dietary needs of individuals in terms of quantity and quality. Second, the provision of these foods should be harmless, which puts forward clear requirements for food safety. Only harmless food can further ensure that the quantity and quality of food is provided adequately, thus fully meeting the requirements of the right to food adequacy. At present, food safety has attracted more and more attention from the whole society. Xinhuanet reported that in 2007, there were 13,280 food poisonings and 258 deaths nationwide. Among them, 526 people died due to poisonous mushroom poisoning, accounting for 43.80% of the total number of food poisoning deaths.[73] The emergence of these serious situations requires the functional departments of the Chinese government to take effective measures to prevent and manage them and prevent the destruction of food safety and the harm caused to human health.

Due to China's special national conditions, we need to make a more detailed definition and explanation of food safety. Lu Liangshu pointed out that, "From the first proposal of the concept of food safety to the present, after nearly 30 years of development, the meaning of 'food safety' includes the following aspects: From the perspective of quantity, demanding that people be able to both buy and afford the basic food they need, and that the total amount of food can meet the basic needs of all the people of China. From the perspective of quality, food is required to be of high quality, hygiene, health (no pollution), and the nutritional structure of food is reasonable. The food enjoyed by the right holder must not only be safe but also be nutritious and meet people's needs for an active and healthy life. From a development perspective, access to food is required to focus on the good conservation of the ecological environment and the sustainability of resource use. That is, to ensure the sustainability of food sources and to ensure the sustainability of food across generations. That is, the access to food by the present generation in China cannot

[71] Quoted from Mei [21].

[72] Quoted from Mei [21].

[73] Xinhua: Food Poisoning Affected 13, 280 People Across the Nation in 2007, Study Finds, available at: http://www.cq.xinhuanet.com/food/2008-03/06/content_12626471.htm, 2008-03-22.

affect the food security of future generations."[74] From the perspective of the meaning of the right to food, quality, hygiene, and health (no pollution) are important contents to achieve food quality, and there are many shortcomings in this regard in China. This needs to be improved. As far as the catering industry is concerned, Xinhuanet reported that "there are five major health and safety problems in China's catering industry. On the issue of qualifications, the phenomenon of unlicensed operation of catering enterprises is widespread. On the issue of raw materials, the purchase channels of the catering industry are chaotic. On the issue of supervision, the insufficient strength of the regulatory authorities has led to a regulatory vacuum. In terms of production, many catering enterprises have food safety risks. In the problem of packaging and transportation, recycling and recycling are common."[75]

In recent years, although China has accelerated economic development and increased food production, it has made long-term efforts to protect the ecological environment and control pollution, and has listed it as an important part of the national economic and social development plan. However, due to the weak economic foundation and low level of technology, environmental pollution has become a serious problem.[76] Especially under the conditions of modern industrial production, food pollution is increasingly harmful to human health, and we must rethink industrialization. The development and progress of modern large-scale industry and cities, on the one hand, have created a lot of wealth for human society, but on the other hand, they have indeed caused serious environmental pollution, and this increasingly severe environmental pollution is also polluting China's food. If the government and society fail to take effective policy measures to improve the environment in the short term to reduce pollution, food contamination will be further aggravated. Therefore, the Chinese government should find feasible solutions for food and resource pollution, and curb the spread of pollution through effective measures such as education and administrative and legislative regulation.[77]

According to scientists, "although the basic problem of agroecology is that it cannot increase the input of exogenous nutrients, it can still increase food production." However, agroecology's initiatives to promote environmental protection and reduce pollution are noteworthy. "For quite some time, humans will have to pay a high price for food contamination,"[78] especially nitrite, aflatoxin, and pesticides, as well as heavy metals such as lead, mercury, and cadmium. Nitrates in food can be converted into carcinogenic nitrite after entering the body; Aflatoxin is a major culprit in inducing tumors, especially liver cancer. Some people feed small animals with moldy feed (rich in aflatoxin), and they developed liver cancer in just three months. The residual pesticides in food sneak into the human body and accumulate,

[74] Quoted from Mei [21].

[75] Xinhua, "Five major health and safety problems in China's catering industry", available at: http://news.xinhuanet.com/fortune/2006-11/22/content_5363952.htm, 2008-03-22.

[76] Quoted from Mei [21].

[77] See Quoted from Mei [21].

[78] Mei [21].

which can damage the liver, brain, kidney, and other organs in the light case and cause acute poisoning and death in severe cases.[79]

Based on the above analysis, we believe that the gradual realization of pollution prevention and control in industrial and agricultural production and the transformation from end-of-line control to whole-process management is the only way to prevent and control food pollution. Specifically, the following aspects should be addressed: First, relevant policies, laws, and regulations should be formulated for cleaner production, green food production, or non-polluting food production. Second, the government should comprehensively implement the green food production management model in a step-by-step and sub-regional manner to strengthen the country's supervision and management of food production. Third, it is essential to carry out publicity and training on food safety, improve the technical level of food production, and develop clean and pollution-free food.[80]

Food safety requires regulatory authorities to take the following measures to pay close attention to food quality and safety, improve food supervision, and ensure that the right to food harmlessness is realized: First, strengthen the quality and safety of agricultural products. Second, establish and strictly implement the food quality and safety access system. Third, strengthen national supervision and spot checks on food quality. Fourth, strengthen the special rectification of small food workshops. Fifth, implement the regional supervision responsibility system for food safety and establish a system with "three members and four determinations, three advances and four maps, two books, and one report" as the main content. Sixth, strengthen the supervision of food circulation and implement the "Three Green Project" with "advocating green consumption, cultivating green markets, and opening up green channels" as the main content. Seventh, strengthen the supervision of food safety in consumption links such as catering. Eighth, comprehensively carry out a special rectification of food quality and safety. Ninth, strengthen the construction of risk early warning and emergency response mechanisms. Tenth, establish and improve the food recall system and strengthen the establishment of a food safety credit system.[81]

6.3 Poverty in the Right to Food in China

Jean A. Smith, Special Rapporteur on the right to food, stated in Ziegler's report on his 2005 trip to India that "although famine has been overcome, millions of Indians remain chronically undernourished and severely deficient in some basic micronutrients, especially women, children, and people belonging to lower castes and tribes. Deaths from starvation have not been completely eliminated. Discrimination against

[79] See Food contamination is harmful, Pay attention to the prevention is not terrible", available at: http://www.qsepe.com/xinjiang/bencandy.php?id=11136, 2008-03-22.

[80] See Mei [21].

[81] A discussion of the above measures to be seen: 'Food quality and safety in China: White Paper', available at: http://www.showchina.Org/zfbps/ndhf/2007/200801/t142778.htm, 2008-03-22.

women and inferior castes, corruption, impunity, and a range of human rights violations, including forced labor, debt bondage, and forced evictions, remain serious obstacles to the implementation of the right to food. In the current transition to a more open, market-oriented economy, the poorest bear the greatest cost, and undernutrition is rising as government spending on rural development and social programs is cut. Food insecurity, especially in rural areas, is worsening as wages for agricultural workers fall, more and more people lose their land, and food prices rise. Recent economic growth, which has been largely the creation of jobs in the high-tech sector, has not offset the loss of livelihoods from agriculture, on which two-thirds of Indians still depend. Government spending must, therefore, be directed to smallholder farmers to improve household food security while improving and sustaining effective safety net programs, including public food distribution schemes, to avoid the implementation of the right to food going backwards again in the process of economic transition."[82] India and China are both developing countries, and China faces similar challenges in realizing the right to food. Even developed countries cannot completely solve the problem of poverty. When China encounters difficulties in implementing poverty eradication or alleviation policies, many people increasingly believe that this is a task that cannot be accomplished in the short term.

The development of the Western 'welfare state' depends on the desire to guarantee a subsistence minimum for all, especially those temporarily outside the labor market. Citizens look to the state to help prevent disease, unemployment, accidents, and other hardships. As time goes on, their demands increase, and although state intervention has become broader, it is difficult to meet their needs. This creates a 'crisis' of the welfare state. In the richest societies, poverty cannot be eradicated, although it must be acknowledged that it has been greatly reduced. In fact, the modernization of science and technology has greatly improved the scientific and technological level of workers, and many young people have been trained in new technical fields. However, many people have been excluded from the new system. Moreover, even many young people with training find it difficult to find work, and these unemployed individuals face increasing threats to their livelihoods. They may even face permanent precarity, a situation in which underincome can seriously undermine the enjoyment of the right to food.[83]

In the process of China's economic development, due to the continuous improvement of the economic system and the unequal opportunities caused by the dual structure of urban and rural areas, the gap between the rich and the poor is very serious and showing a trend of intensification. While the original poor population has been reduced, new poor people are also generated. Because of this gap, many people do not enjoy the right to food equally. At a press conference, Professor Li Peilin, editor-in-chief of the 2007 Social Blue Book, said that the widening income gap has shown that the real income gap between the top 20% of China's population and the lowest income earners is about 18 times, and the gap is still increasing. The

[82] See FAO report: Implementing the Right to Adequate Food: The Outcome of Six Case Studies. available at: http://www.fao.org/righttofood/zh/index.html, 2008-03-22.

[83] See Mbonda [22].

widening income gap will inevitably lead to increased poverty, creating a greater obstacle to the realization of the right to food. This should prompt the government to improve systems, create equal opportunities for development, address emerging poverty, and ensure the full enjoyment of the right to food for all.[84]

The issue of poverty has always been the focus of our government's work, and the poor people in China mainly include: urban laid-off unemployed, traditional widows and lonely urban poor people, and rural poor people. In addition, the unemployment of college students and the shock to China's job market brought about by WTO accession have also led to many job losses. Accordingly, since the mid-1980s, the Chinese government has implemented planned, organized, and large-scale poverty alleviation and development throughout the country. After more than 20 years of hard work, China has made remarkable achievements in poverty alleviation and development.[85] The number of poor people has been greatly reduced from 250 million in the early days of reform and opening up in 1978 to 125 million in 1986. China's first comprehensive moderately prosperous development report (2006), published at the end of 2006, revealed that according to China's national poverty line, there are currently more than 48 million poor people in the country, accounting for about 3.7% of the total population. However, according to the international poverty line, the country currently has about 1.35% of the population living below the poverty line, which is still equivalent to hundreds of millions of people.[86] According to the World Bank, since 1980, China's poverty alleviation accounts for more than 70% of the number of poverty alleviated in developing countries in the world.[87] As early as 2005, the United Nations Development Programme (UNDP) assessment report concluded that China had achieved the Millennium Development Goal of reducing poverty ahead of schedule, that is, the number of poor people fell by half, and living conditions in poor areas improved. Social insurance coverage has been continuously expanded, ensuring the livelihood of the urban poor has been basically guaranteed.[88]

Despite the remarkable results in poverty reduction, China's poverty alleviation efforts still face severe challenges. On one hand, China has the world's largest population, and a significant number of poor people who require assistance are widely distributed, meaning that many individuals still need to be lifted out of poverty. On the other hand, there is a serious imbalance in the development of the east and west,

[84] See Wang Linxia. Eradication of Poverty and Hunger: The Inherent Needs of the Right to Subsistence and the Right to Development, available at: http://www.humanrights-china.org/cn/rqlt/yjj gxzls/xsyd/t20070629_264236.htm, 2008-03-22.

[85] See Tiankui [23].

[86] See Wang Linxia. Eradication of Poverty and Hunger: The Inherent Needs of the Right to Subsistence and the Right to Development, available at: http://www.humanrights-china.org/cn/rqlt/yjj gxzls/xsyd/t20070629_264236.htm, 2008-03-22.

[87] See Wang Linxia. Eradication of Poverty and Hunger: The Inherent Needs of the Right to Subsistence and the Right to Development, available at: http://www.humanrights-china.org/cn/rqlt/yjj gxzls/xsyd/t20070629_264236.htm, 2008-03-22.

[88] See Wang Linxia. Eradication of Poverty and Hunger: The Inherent Needs of the Right to Subsistence and the Right to Development, available at: http://www.humanrights-china.org/cn/rqlt/yjj gxzls/xsyd/t20070629_264236.htm, 2008-03-22.

coastal and inland areas, and between urban and rural regions. Economic development in poor areas is slow, making it a long-term and arduous task to eliminate the wealth gap between regions and to provide adequate assistance to impoverished areas.

At the same time, as China's poverty alleviation efforts have deepened, the task of eradicating poverty has become more challenging. The remaining poor are concentrated in areas with poor living conditions, low-quality labor, and inadequate social security. Even if they are temporarily lifted out of poverty with external assistance, unexpected events such as natural disasters or family accidents can easily cause them to fall back into poverty. Returning to poverty after poverty alleviation is an even more difficult issue, highlighting the long journey ahead for China's poverty reduction efforts. Furthermore, poverty reduction is not the end goal but rather a path towards comprehensive development. China's development-oriented poverty alleviation approach emphasizes "government-led, social participation, self-reliance, and all-round development".[89] The poor should not only be lifted out of poverty but should also achieve comprehensive and equitable economic, cultural, and educational development, enabling them to fully enjoy the rights outlined in the International Covenant on Economic, Social and Cultural Rights (of which the right to food is just one of the most critical aspects). The realization of these rights is a long and challenging process.

While carrying out large-scale poverty alleviation and development, the Chinese government should further strengthen and improve the construction of the social security system. After the establishment of the social security system, the unemployed can receive unemployment benefits, the elderly can receive pensions, and the poor can receive a certain amount of minimum living security. Social security systems affect the realization of everyone's rights, especially in times of famine. While promoting social redistribution and achieving equity, social security can strengthen the cultivation of human rights awareness of right holders and promote the realization of economic, social, and cultural rights. In particular, more needs to be done by the government in the area of the right to food.[90]

7 Conclusion

Many specific rights do not exist around us, but the existence of these rights is not currently attracting enough attention and discussion. With the continuous development and deepening of China's human rights cause, the pursuit of rights themselves will inevitably require us to study more and more new specific rights. The right to food has only emerged as a fundamental right in the past few decades, but it is

---

[89] See Wang Linxia. Eradication of Poverty and Hunger: The Inherent Needs of the Right to Subsistence and the Right to Development, available at: http://www.humanrights-china.org/cn/rqlt/yjjgxzls/xsyd/t20070629_264236.htm, 2008-03-22.

[90] See Sen [24].

unquestionable as a fundamental human right. Although research and reflection on this right are still in their infancy, the foundation and importance of this right have gradually been generally accepted and recognized.

The ongoing issue of hunger and various other food-related violations of fundamental rights by the international community have made us more aware of the importance of the right to food. The basic survival needs faced by everyone have led to a gradual recognition of the right to food and the fundamental place it should have. Whether it is the theme of World Food Day 2007, the human rights challenges in twenty-first century China, or the "bottom billion" initiative proposed by the United Nations Secretary-General, it shows the growing importance that countries attach to the right to food. Therefore, it must be studied in depth to better protect the right to food.

References

1. Sen, A. (2002). *Development as freedom*. (R. Zhao & Y. Zhen, Trans.). Chinese Minmin University Press.
2. Yang, Y. (Ed.). (2005). *Bodies of the United Nations human rights conventions and the essence of the classics*. Chinese Public Security University Press.
3. Mill, J. S. (2007). *Utilitarianism* (p. 122, J. Ye, Trans.). Kyushu Publishing Company.
4. Deng, Z. (Ed.). (1992). *Blackville encyclopedia of political science* (p. 661). China University of Political Science and Law Press.
5. Eide, A., Krause, C., & Rosas, A. (Eds.). (2001). *Economic, social and cultural rights* (pp. 10–20). Brill.
6. Zheng, Z. (2007). *Determination of adequate standards for the right to an adequate standard of living*. Master's thesis, Jilin University.
7. Cheng, W., Yang, C., & Yang, Y. (Eds.). (2000). *United Nations human rights conventions and criminal justice literature*. China Legal Publishing House.
8. Naved, Z. Z. (2021). Right to health as a human right in times of Covid-19. *Indian Journal of Law and Legal Research, 3*(01), 1–16.
9. Liu, H. (1998). Adequate standards of living and socio-economic development. *Journal of Legal Studies, 1998*(2), 36–37.
10. International Human Rights Law Project Research Group. (2002). *International human rights law course* (Vol. 2). China University of Political Science and Law Press.
11. Mill, J. S. (1959). *On liberty* (pp. 101–102, X. Baokui, Trans.). Commercial Press.
12. Rawls, J. (1988). *Theory of justice* (p. 302, H. Huaihong, et al., Trans.). China Social Science Publishing House.
13. Yao, J. (2006). *Jurisprudence—general legal science* (p. 167). China University of Political Science and Law Press.
14. Zhu, X. (2003). *Study on European human rights legal protection mechanisms*. Law Press.
15. Mo, J. (2005). *International covenants on human rights and China*. World Knowledge Press.
16. Xia, Y. (2001). *Origins of the concept of human rights: The historical philosophy of rights* (pp. 137–141). China University of Political Science and Law Press.
17. Milne, A. J. M. (1991). *Human rights and human diversity: An essay in the philosophy of human rights* (X. Wang & Q. Shi, Trans.). Oriental Press.
18. Zhang, W. (2006). *A study of western philosophical thought in the twentieth century* (pp. 428–439). Law Press.
19. Sané, P. (2004). Poverty, the next frontier in the struggle for human rights. *International Social Science Journal, 56*, 271–275.

20. Koubi, G. (2004). Poverty as a human rights violation. *International Social Science Journal, 56*(180), 327–337.
21. Mei, F. (2005). Analysis of the development of the concept of food security. *Food and Nutrition in China, 5*, 5.
22. Mbonda, E.-M. (2004). Poverty as a violation of human rights: Towards a right to non-poverty. *International Social Science Journal, 56*(180), 277–288.
23. Tiankui, J. (2004). Minimum subsistence guarantee system: Features and significance. *Journal of the Graduate School of the Chinese Academy of Social Sciences, 2004*(4), 4.
24. Sen, A. (2001). *Poverty and famines: An essay on entitlement and deprivation* (p. 12, Y. Wang & W. Wang, Trans.). Commercial Press.

Chapter 12
Protection of the Rights of Socially Vulnerable Groups

Ning Wu

1 Introduction

The existence of socially vulnerable groups is a universal social phenomenon, present in any period of human history and in any country in the world. As long as there are differences between people, the opposition between the strong and the weak is inevitable. Therefore, treating and coordinating the relationship between the strong and the weak, and between the strong and the vulnerable, has become a major issue that cannot be avoided in any society.

Since the reform and opening up of China, the structural adjustment of social stratification triggered by the development of the market economy has made the problem of vulnerable groups in society increasingly prominent. In 2001, the term "socially vulnerable" first appeared in China's government work report. In 2002, the report of the 16th National Congress of the Communist Party of China more clearly stated the idea of protecting vulnerable groups in society and proposed a guiding plan for system building. In the current ideal of establishing a harmonious society based on "democracy and rule of law, fairness and justice, honesty and fraternity, full of vitality, stability and order, and harmonious coexistence between man and nature", the issue of vulnerable groups in society has been raised to a new level.

2 The Rights of Vulnerable Groups in Contemporary China

The existence of vulnerable groups in contemporary Chinese society has its own uniqueness, which comes from China's unique historical situation and its current social structure. A large number of socially vulnerable groups in China have emerged during the transformation of the economic system, and the turbulent economic

N. Wu (✉)
Tongji University Law School, Shanghai, China

J. Yao (ed.), *The Legal Issues of the Emerging Rights*,
https://doi.org/10.1007/978-981-97-0499-6_12

reforms have had a strong impact on the original social and economic operating mode and the social behavior mode that was determined by it. However, the reform of the social superstructure such as the law lags far behind the reform of the economic system itself. Therefore, after the original pattern of rights and benefits distribution has been disrupted, a new stable and effective institutional form for adjusting rights and interests has not yet been formed. In addition, Chinese society has had a long-standing dual structure of urban and rural areas, and the household registration system has significantly strengthened the separation between urban and rural areas, which has created a hidden risk of unequal rights between urban and rural citizens.

When examining the situation of vulnerable groups in contemporary Chinese society, it becomes clear that their weak position in society is not due to any inherent weakness of the disadvantaged groups themselves, but rather to their lack of institutional resources. The reason why vulnerable groups in contemporary China are weak is that they face significant obstacles at all levels of rights enjoyment, realization, and relief.

First, there is an imbalance in the enjoyment of legal rights between the socially disadvantaged and the powerful. Chinese society has long developed a unique urban–rural dual social structure, and this situation will continue to exist for a long time to come. This social structure has led to serious imbalances in the distribution of benefits and the possession of rights. At present, the peasants, who make up the vast majority of China's population, are increasingly disadvantaged in the distribution of benefits and rights, and some scholars have summarized this phenomenon as the "weakening of major groups" in society. The targets and issues addressed by a series of basic laws in China are mainly focused on urban residents, and the vast number of peasants are simply not included in the adjustment of these laws, resulting in a serious lack of rights for Chinese farmers. From the perspective of peasants' political rights, China's peasants are very different from urban residents in terms of the mechanism of possession of political rights and the expression of interests, and what is particularly serious is that this difference is directly reflected in legislation. The Election Law stipulates that the number of representatives represented by each rural and urban representative in the election of people's deputies at all levels shall be 4:1; In municipalities, cities, and districts directly under the Central Government, it is stipulated that the number of people represented by each representative in rural areas shall be greater than the number of people represented by each representative in urban areas. From the perspective of the composition of previous NPCs, there were 63 peasant deputies in the first session, accounting for 5.41%; 67 people in the second session, accounting for 5.46%; 209 people in the third session, accounting for 6.87%; 662 people in the fourth session, accounting for 22.9%; 720 people in the fifth session, accounting for 20.59%; 348 people in the sixth session, accounting for 11.7%; The seventh session together with workers' representatives accounted for 23%; 280 people in the eighth session, accounting for 9.4%; The ninth session had 240 people, accounting for 8%.[1]

[1] See Zhou [1].

It is evident that the representation of peasant representatives is extremely disproportionate to their population in the country. Due to the lack of political participation and representatives, it is difficult for the interests of the farmers to be fully reflected in practice. The distribution of economic and institutional resources is limited and unequal, which further exacerbates the vulnerability of farmers. For example, the Labor Law of the People's Republic of China excludes most agricultural laborers in the countryside from the basic labor-related rights that are protected by law. This includes the right to equal employment and choice of occupation, the right to rest and vacation, the right to occupational safety and health protection, the right to receive vocational skills training, and the right to enjoy social insurance and welfare. The same problem exists with regard to the right to social security, where rural residents lack basic social security. The current social security legislation in China lacks a unified basic law on social security, with only urban residents' social security guaranteed. The establishment of the rural social security system lags behind, and Chinese farmers lack an effective social safety net to cope with various risks in their lives and the market economy. Another group that faces unequal rights is urban migrant workers. Their marginal status leads to their marginalized status in society, and the social security system does not include them. "Citizenship is a potentially unique resource, especially for those who lack other kinds of resources.[2] Originally, citizenship, as an institutional resource, was the most important way for vulnerable groups in society to alleviate and change their vulnerable status, but, at present, the lack of civil rights is at the root of the vulnerable groups in Chinese society, not only failing to play this function of citizenship but also becoming a link in a vicious circle that leads to the weaker of the weak.

Second, vulnerable groups in society face many obstacles to the realization of equal rights. In the era of the universalization of human rights, the equal enjoyment of human rights by vulnerable groups in society has become a self-evident axiom and a universal institutional practice. However, if this is the case, the rights of the vulnerable groups in society cannot be substantially improved, and the obstacles faced by the vulnerable groups in the realization of equal rights make true equality of rights only a utopian ideal and an unattainable mirage.

Civil rights equality has two main aspects that must be considered: equality in the content of the law, and equality in the application of the law. Any inequality in either of these aspects constitutes an infringement on the rights and interests of vulnerable groups in society. Legislative inequality occurs when socially vulnerable groups are ignored and neglected in legislation, resulting in inequality in the enjoyment of rights. Inequality in legal realization occurs when vulnerable groups in society are entitled to equal rights but cannot enjoy them due to various obstacles. In reality, having rights on paper does not always translate into having actual rights. To achieve equality in the realization of rights, a series of conditions must be met. Members of society must have the necessary means to realize their rights, and the external environment should respect and treat them equally. Unfortunately, vulnerable groups in Chinese society face both internal and external challenges when it comes to their rights. Internally,

[2] Lenski [2].

these groups often lack the means necessary to achieve equal rights, and legal provisions are meaningless for them. Externally, due to their marginalized status, they are often not treated equally by society and other members of society. Discrimination is the biggest obstacle to the realization of equal rights for vulnerable groups in Chinese society. Using the right to employment in China as an example, the Constitution states that "citizens of the People's Republic of China have the right and duty to work," and the State should create conditions for employment and strengthen labor protection. The Labor Law also clearly states that "workers shall not be discriminated against in employment on the basis of ethnicity, race, gender, or religious belief." Women are entitled to equal employment rights with men, and may not be refused employment on the basis of sex or face recruitment criteria that are discriminatory. However, the reality is that socially disadvantaged groups struggle to exercise their employment rights, and discrimination is rampant. Discrimination takes many forms, such as household registration, gender, age, education and experience, physical condition, marriage, and childbearing status discrimination. One example of discrimination in employment is health discrimination, where an individual's health status is used to deprive them of re-employment or equal opportunities for employment, even when they meet the physical and work requirements specified by law. Currently, health discrimination in the field of employment is a serious issue that lacks specific legislation to regulate it. Overall, achieving equality in civil rights is a complex issue that requires addressing both legislative and societal obstacles.[3] By recognizing and addressing these challenges, we can work towards a more just and equitable society for all.[4]

The goal of the law is not merely to declare equal rights, but to ensure their equal realization. The ultimate objective is for vulnerable groups in society to achieve equal realization of their rights and overcome their vulnerable status.

Thirdly, there is a lack of mechanisms in place to provide relief for vulnerable groups in society when their rights are violated or when obstacles prevent them from realizing their rights. Proclaiming and conferring rights is not enough; a system of rights remedies must also be established. As the saying goes, "without remedies, there are no rights." This is especially true for the most vulnerable members of society. If there is no recourse for redress when their rights are violated, then legal declarations are as futile as a moon in the water or a flower in a mirror. Unfortunately, vulnerable

[3] Ye and Wei [3].

[4] In 2003, the Chinese media dubbed it the "anti-discrimination year" for hepatitis B virus carriers in China. This was due to a series of events that drew attention to the issue of employment discrimination against hepatitis B virus carriers. On April 3, 2003, a homicide case occurred in Zhejiang which highlighted the issue. Later, on November 20, 1611 citizens jointly signed a proposal called "Request to the Nation's 31 Provincial Governments," which was submitted to the Standing Committee of the National People's Congress, the Ministry of Health, and the Legislative Affairs Office of the State Council. The proposal aimed to limit legislative protection of hepatitis B virus carriers in the recruitment of civil servants. Additionally, in Wuhu City, Anhui Province, the District People's Court accepted the country's first case of a hepatitis B virus carrier suing the Wuhu Municipal Personnel Bureau for health discrimination in the recruitment and hiring of state civil servants. This case represented the fight of the country's 10% population infected with hepatitis B for their rights to equality and work. See Ye and Wei [3].

groups in our society not only lack access to their rights but also face many obstacles to realizing them. There is no perfect system for rights remedies to rely on, which means that there are no straightforward avenues for these groups to seek redress. This situation has exacerbated an already bleak outlook for the rights of vulnerable groups in society, pushing them deeper into an abyss of inequality and injustice.

First of all, China lacks an unconstitutional review system, leaving vulnerable groups in society with no way to complain about the numerous violations of their rights by normative documents. The infringement of the rights of socially vulnerable groups first appears as a violation of their equal rights, which is often based on the existence of discriminatory normative documents. If vulnerable groups have no means to seek redress, violations of their rights will intensify, and there will be no protection for them.

Secondly, China's administrative litigation system remains imperfect. Abstract administrative acts are not covered by the scope of cases under the Administrative Procedure Law. Although the Legislation Law provides provisions for reviewing the legality of these acts, the lack of relevant supporting systems poses significant practical difficulties. In protecting the rights of vulnerable groups in society, administrative organs have multiple obligations, including the protection of vulnerable group rights through administrative legislation. When administrative organs fail to enact adequate legislation, vulnerable groups may be left without a legal avenue for seeking redress, thus greatly weakening their protections.

Thirdly, the traditional theory states that the primary purpose of constitutional fundamental rights provisions is to guarantee individual freedom from state power infringement. These rights are negative in nature, serving as a defence against the state. Therefore, fundamental rights do not apply in civil relations between private individuals, and thus are not justiciable. However, in recent years, due to changes in social structure, individuals and groups with significant economic power in industrial societies have infringed upon the basic constitutional rights of other disadvantaged individuals. This has seriously threatened the human dignity of vulnerable groups in society. Clinging solely to traditional theories will inevitably lead to blind spots in addressing situations that infringe on the rights of vulnerable groups. In China's current judicial practice, attention is being given to the direct application of constitutional fundamental rights in specific cases. This practice has brought about a trend that allows for the direct application of constitutional rights when there is no legal basis for the infringement of the rights of vulnerable groups in society. This trend will inevitably strengthen the protection of the rights of vulnerable groups in society.

In short, the vulnerability of disadvantaged groups lies in their limited access to and enjoyment of their rights, as well as their lack of access to effective remedies when their rights are violated. To address this, it is crucial to incorporate the protection of vulnerable groups into our perspective on rights. The "short board theory" illustrates this point: just as a barrel's capacity is limited by its shortest plank and a chain's strength by its weakest link, a country's level of human rights development is determined by the status of rights for socially vulnerable groups. As we promote the concept of rights, seek to build harmonious societies, and pursue all-round social progress, it is essential to pay attention to and protect the rights of vulnerable groups. Doing so is an inevitable requirement of our times.

3 The Meaning of Protecting the Rights of Socially Vulnerable Groups

Protecting the rights of socially vulnerable groups is necessary to address the dilemma they face. However, this protection is not a one-dimensional issue; it contains multiple levels of meaning. To truly understand what "protection of the rights of vulnerable groups in society" means and to lay a sufficient foundation for the development of related issues, we must comprehensively explore these different levels of meaning.

3.1 Protection of Rights as a Means of Protection

The first level of meaning behind protecting the rights of socially vulnerable groups is to protect them through their rights. This implies that there are various methods of protecting vulnerable groups in society, such as through policies or charities. However, the focus here is on protecting their rights specifically.

3.1.1 The Historical Presentation of Rights as a Means of Protection

Upon examining the history of the development of rights, it becomes clear that the process of strengthening the protection of vulnerable groups in society takes shape in the form of rights. In other words, the evolution of rights is closely linked to the protection of marginalized populations.

(1) From the perspective of the development of three generations of human rights, the protection of the rights of vulnerable groups in society

Human rights are a constantly evolving system that adapts to changes in social and historical conditions. According to Karel Smith, former UNESCO Legal Adviser to the United Nations, the historical trajectory of human rights can be summarized by the "three generations of human rights" theory. This theory suggests that the first generation of human rights was formed during the American and French Revolutions and mainly focused on civil and political rights. The second generation of human rights, which emerged during the Russian Revolution, focused on economic, social, and cultural rights. The third generation of human rights is a response to the phenomenon of global interdependence and includes rights such as the right to peace, the right to a clean environment, and the right to development.[5] While there

[5] See Shen and Huang [4].

is ongoing debate about this classification, the theory of human rights in the three generations provides a relatively objective and accurate description of the historical development of human rights.

The victory of the modern bourgeois revolution marked the end of the feudal society characterized by hierarchical identity and set in motion the process of building a modern, free, and democratic society guided by the spirit of reason. This process began with the creation of modern constitutional documents and codes that adhered to the idea of natural law and promoted values such as freedom, equality, and fraternity. The United States Declaration of Independence states that "We hold these truths to be self-evident, that all men are created equal, that they are endowed by their Creator with certain unalienable Rights, that among these are Life, Liberty and the pursuit of Happiness." The French Declaration of the Rights of Man and of the Citizen of 1789 similarly declares that "men are born and remain free and equal in rights" and that "the aim of all political association is the preservation of the natural and imprescriptible rights of man," including freedom, property, security, and resistance to oppression. The establishment of the right to individual freedom is not only the primary objective of modern constitutions, but also permeates and embodies various specific legal fields. The French Civil Code of 1804, for instance, established the three modern civil law principles of absolute ownership, freedom of contract, and fault liability. These principles became the foundation of modern private law and the entire legal system. Absolute ownership and freedom of contract are the most direct embodiment of the realization of freedom rights under the concept of autonomy of private law. Meanwhile, the principle of fault liability excludes faults that are beyond the control of individuals from the scope of attribution, which is essentially a guarantee of individual freedom.

The first generation of human rights placed the right to freedom at its core, advocated for the "night watchman state" as the function of the government, and emphasized the state's immunity and inaction. This is why the first generation of human rights is also known as negative human rights. By prioritizing the right to freedom, the first generation of human rights achieved "equality before the law" and established a framework for the equal realization of rights. However, this first generation of human rights, which was based on the philosophical concept of formal equality, ignored the "weakness" of socially vulnerable groups. The first generation of human rights, with its emphasis on negative rights, aimed to limit the power of the state and protect the individual from state intervention. This approach was important in the context of the American and French revolutions, which sought to establish liberal democracies that protected individual rights. However, the focus on negative rights also meant that the first generation of human rights was limited in its ability to address social and economic inequalities. This led to the emergence of the second and third generations of human rights, which expanded the scope of human rights beyond individual liberties to include economic, social, and cultural rights, as well as collective rights.

Granting rights is one thing, but realizing them is another. Although socially vulnerable groups may enjoy some formal freedoms, these freedoms are often difficult to realize in practice. A fairy tale illustrates this point: the fox invited the long-billed stork to drink milk together, but served it in a flat plate. While the fox enjoyed the milk with relish, the long-billed stork could only look at the milk and sigh. This tale teaches us that giving someone the right to enjoy something without giving them the means to actually enjoy it renders that right meaningless. The enjoyment and realization of rights are intrinsic and inseparable components of rights, and unrealizable rights are void and have no real meaning. It is not enough to simply grant rights on paper; we must also ensure that they can be fully realized by providing the necessary means and resources. For example, the right to education is meaningless if children do not have access to schools, teachers, and educational materials. Similarly, the right to healthcare is meaningless if people cannot afford medical treatment or do not have access to healthcare facilities. Therefore, we must not only recognize and respect human rights, but also work to eliminate the social, economic, and political barriers that prevent vulnerable groups from realizing their rights.

Secondly, while granting rights is one thing, realizing them is another. Although socially vulnerable groups may have formal freedoms, they often struggle to exercise those freedoms. A fable illustrates this point: a fox invited a stork to share milk but served it on a flat plate, which allowed the fox to drink with ease while the stork could only gaze longingly at the milk. The moral of the story is that simply granting the stork the right to drink milk is not enough; without the means to actually exercise that right, the stork is still unable to drink the milk. The enjoyment and realization of rights are integral components of rights, and unrealizable rights are meaningless. Furthermore, formal equality can lead to widespread inequality due to real differences among individuals. Formal equality ignores the unique circumstances of individuals when granting rights, instead emphasizing abstract equality. It only requires that institutions providing fundamental freedoms apply equally to everyone, without considering how each person can actually exercise those rights. "It has long been recognized that the wealthy have an advantage in law: in various countries, the law tends to favor the strong over the weak, and it helps those who own property against those who do not." The emphasis on the right to freedom as a right to equality of opportunity disregards the specific outcomes of individuals in exercising their freedom, which can lead to economic poverty and polarization.

In the early twentieth century, some developed capitalist countries moved towards monopoly capitalism, further intensifying inherent contradictions in capitalist societies. The conflicts between economically disadvantaged and powerful groups continued to escalate. To overcome these issues and promote social stability, the concept of social rights emerged, demanding active State intervention in areas that were previously considered private to secure human rights genuinely. Social rights are a general term used for all rights guaranteed to all persons, enabling them to live with dignity and human rights based on the welfare state or social state.[6] The formation of social rights aims to address several social contradictions, such as labor-capital antagonism, disparity between rich and poor under developed capitalism, prevent the traditional guarantee of freedom from being empty, and seek substantive freedom

[6] Kiyonomiya [5].

and equality of all citizens, particularly those who are socially and economically weak. This approach aims to establish a new form of human rights.[7]

Social rights are a distinct type of human right that differs from the right to freedom. The difference between social rights and freedom rights lies in the subject of rights. The right to freedom applies to all citizens, while social rights, as a human right, are primarily focused on vulnerable groups in society. Social rights aim to provide these groups with a decent and dignified life, enabling them to live like normal people. Vulnerable groups may include the elderly, children, orphans, and disabled individuals. The content of rights also differs between social rights and freedom rights. The right to freedom ensures the broadest autonomy and freedom of all citizens in the field of private law, making the state power passive and inactive, which is a negative right. In contrast, social rights demand the action of the state in protecting and assisting economically weak individuals in society, requiring the active intervention of the state, which is a positive right. In terms of the value base and value goal, the right to freedom corresponds to the national view of the night watchman state and the free country. Freedom is the value goal pursued. On the other hand, social rights correspond to the welfare state and the active state view, where the safety and harmony of society as a whole are the value goal. The right to freedom developed from its ideological source on the basis of natural law. Social rights, on the other hand, are closely related to modern classical human rights and rooted in natural law, but primarily based on the idea of social welfare, compensating for the shortcomings of the high development of the right to freedom.[8] Regarding the realization of the protection of rights, the right to freedom has no boundaries in principle and no conditions. However, social rights have limits and conditions, and their realization depends on the cooperation of legislation and the executive, as well as the state of the country's finances.[9]

The Weimar Constitution is considered a landmark in modern social rights legislation. It established the general principle that "the organization of economic life is compatible with the principles of citizenship and the purpose of human survival and maintenance". The Constitution also included provisions for labor social rights, which served as a blueprint and model for the legislation of social rights in countries like Italy and Japan.

The second generation of human rights, with social rights as the core, can be considered the era of the rights of vulnerable groups in society. The concern and protection of vulnerable groups in society are embodied in several ways. Firstly, social rights can essentially be said to prioritize vulnerable groups in society in the enjoyment and realization of rights. Although social rights are also universal human rights owned by all citizens, they are latent for people who are not vulnerable since these citizens do not have the necessary conditions for the exercise of social rights. For vulnerable groups in society, they not only have the conditions stipulated by social rights but also the urgency of realizing them. Failure to exercise and realize social

[7] Tagami [6].

[8] Hui [7].

[9] Hui [7].

rights endangers their survival, making social rights a priority for socially vulnerable groups both in substance and in time. Secondly, the concept of formal equality has been replaced by the concept of substantive equality, providing stronger theoretical support and philosophical argument for the protection of vulnerable groups in society. Thirdly, social rights place greater emphasis on state obligations, ensuring that the realization of the rights of vulnerable groups in society has a strong institutional support and practical guarantee. The shift in the focus of law and rights from the right to freedom to the right to society is a significant historical leap forward in the protection of the rights of vulnerable groups in society.

It is important to note that the shift towards social rights does not mean the rejection of freedom rights. In fact, freedom rights remain the most fundamental and basic rights in modern democratic society, and their importance cannot be undermined. While social rights are a distinct type of rights from freedom rights, their ultimate goal is to ensure better realization of civil liberties. "Social rights exist to supplement freedom rights within a welfare state that modifies the idea of a free state to a certain extent. This does not change the historical nature of the state, but rather addresses its shortcomings and improves its posture towards politics."[10] "The right to equality within social rights is attached to the principle of formal equality and becomes a fundamental right that supplements the guarantee of equality within freedom rights. Formal equality takes precedence, and substantive equality is subordinate. Therefore, the right to equality within social rights, whether quantitative or qualitative, is limited to a narrow scope."[11]

The third generation of human rights is represented by the right to development, which extends the subject of human rights to countries and nations, thus forming collective human rights. It is based on social solidarity and is valued through fraternity. The right to development was the demand of developing countries in the 1950s and 1960s to break the old international economic order and get rid of the "neo-colonial" rule. It was developed during a national democratic movement that actively strives for political, economic, cultural, and social development. The Declaration on the Right to Development defines the right to development as "the right of every person and all peoples to participate in, promote, and enjoy economic, social, cultural, and political development in which all human rights and fundamental freedoms can be fully realized". Chinese scholars express the right to development as "a basic human right for individual human beings and their collective participation, promotion, and enjoyment of their coordinated, balanced, and sustainable development within different time and space limits." By extension, the right to development is a fundamental human right for all individuals and their groups to freely claim to the domestic and international community the benefits of participation, promotion, and enjoyment of development in all its aspects, political, cultural, and social. The most important breakthrough of third-generation human rights over traditional human rights is that the collective has become the subject of human rights.[12] The equality

[10] Akira [8].

[11] Akira [8].

[12] Xigen [9].

of opportunity for development is a unique right of the state and the individuals that make it up. The subject of the right to development includes both individuals and collectives composed of individuals, but the value of the right to development should still be the individual. "Compared with individual human rights, collective human rights are only a means right, and the collective is not the ultimate target and real beneficiary of the benefits contained in collective human rights." The subject of human rights that exists as a goal is always and can only be an individual. Emphasizing that collective human rights are intended to guarantee individual human rights and that collective human rights are only justified in the sense that they are guaranteed.[13] Without the individual, human society is nothing more than abstract empty and empty concepts. The first premise of human history can only be the existence of living individuals, and all the activities of the human collective are conditioned by the actual activities of individuals. Therefore, the history of human development is always the history of individual development.

The formation of the right to development marks a new stage in the development of human rights. It has expanded and improved upon the right to freedom and the reasonable content and value orientation of social rights. This development also indicates that the protection of the rights of vulnerable groups has entered a higher level.

The right to development has taken the protection of vulnerable groups in society to a new level.

First of all, it has expanded the focus of protection from the internal factors of the subject to the external "ecological environment" of vulnerable groups, moving from "corrective protection" to "preventive protection". Previously, the protection of the right to freedom and social rights for socially vulnerable groups focused mainly on the intrinsic factors of these groups. The right to development, however, considers both the internal factors of the subject and the external environment, aiming to eliminate the factors that cause the weak status of members of society by addressing the root causes of vulnerability.[14] The confirmation of the right to development also extends the protection of constitutional human rights to collective subjects, including the independent choice of national political development models and paths, as well as the rational construction of economic, social, and cultural evolution paths and mechanisms. By improving the external "ecological environment" in which vulnerable groups live, the right to development addresses the deeper issues underlying the protection of vulnerable groups. The formation of vulnerable groups is not unrelated to the country's political, economic, and cultural development model. The right to development fundamentally improves this external environment, which is essential to eliminating disadvantage.

Secondly, the right to development offers broader and deeper protection to vulnerable groups. "While freedom laws focus on people's political liberation, and social rights laws focus on achieving people's economic value, the right to development

---

[13] Xiangfei [10].

[14] Xigen [9].

encompasses both the realization of people's political and economic value, emphasizing both human free development and the equal development of individuals. It not only protects individual rights but also acknowledges social interests, and has valuable advantages, comprehensiveness, and functional dominance."[15] The right to development implies the primary obligation of the State to promote the development of its people, including by formulating appropriate national development policies to continuously improve the well-being of the people, and ensuring equal access to basic resources, food, housing, health care, education, employment, and the distribution of goods. The right also protects the integrated development of people in the political, economic, cultural, and social spheres by eliminating uneven development and social injustice. At the level of subsistence, while the right to subsistence guarantees the most basic survival of socially vulnerable groups, the right to development deepens their protection to include their development. The right to subsistence only determines the minimum standard of survival. To fully develop and realize the sociality of human beings, it should evolve from the survival instinct of human beings to the pursuit of quality of life. This enables people to have the right to develop their own survival ability and improve their quality of life within their own survival time and space.

Thirdly, the right to development harmoniously integrates the protection of vulnerable groups' rights into society as a whole. The overall development of society requires attention to vulnerable groups and their development, which is also an essential component of society's development. According to the Declaration on the Right to Development, development is a comprehensive process that includes economic, social, cultural, and political aspects, aimed at improving the well-being of all individuals through active, free, and meaningful participation and the equitable distribution of benefits. Implicit in this concept of development is the idea that development is pluralistic and not limited to economic growth alone. Economy, culture, education, science, and technology are all interconnected and complementary, converging to ensure people-centered development.[16] In 1991, the World Bank introduced a measure of overall annual development, which included eight aspects, including growth, infant mortality, changes in education, changes in women's education, changes in the education gap between men and women, level of education, level of education of women, and political and civil liberties. The right to development encompasses a pluralistic and comprehensive concept of development, which inevitably involves the realization of vulnerable groups' rights in society. Individual and society are inseparable entities in the chain of social relations. While the theory of social rights and its legalization emphasize society's effective intervention in protecting individual interests, it mainly focuses on balancing individual interests from the perspective of the state. Therefore, social rights remain individualistic, whereas the right to development adopts a holistic concept, recognizing socially vulnerable groups as an integral part of society.

[15] Xigen [9].

[16] Xigen [9].

Finally, the right to development deeply enshrines the protection of vulnerable groups in society as a core value, in pursuit of the ideal of human freedom, equality, and all-round development. According to the United Nations Declaration on the Right to Development, "the right to development…aims at the constant improvement of the well-being of the entire population and of all individuals, on the basis of their active, free and meaningful participation in development and in the fair distribution of benefits resulting therefrom." The right to development is a human right based on universal respect for human dignity, the promotion of equitable development among human beings, and the elimination of obstacles to human development. It embodies the ultimate concern for people by eliminating the differences among the weak and pursuing fair distribution of benefits. The right to development is the fullest expression of human potential, maximizing opportunities for people to participate equally in the development process and share the fruits of development. The protection of vulnerable groups in society is a central aspect of the ideals of fraternity and solidarity embodied in the right to development. It seeks to eliminate barriers that prevent marginalized groups from fully participating in the development process and accessing the benefits of development. This reflects a commitment to ensuring that all members of society are able to enjoy their human rights and achieve their full potential.

Hegel once said, "When a flower blooms, the bud disappears, and people might say that the flower negates the bud. Similarly, when the plant bears fruit, the flower is seen as a false form of existence, and the fruit becomes the true form of the plant, replacing the flower. Although these forms are distinct and incompatible, their fluidity makes them integral parts of the organism. They not only don't contradict each other in the continuum of the organism but are equally necessary for each other. It's this same necessity that constitutes the entirety of life."[17]

The development of human rights can be seen as a progression from the right to freedom to social rights and finally to the right to development. The latter form of human rights is built upon and transcends the former, rather than renouncing them. This relationship can be likened to the stages of buds, flowers, and fruits. Over time, the protection of vulnerable groups in society has progressed from a lower stage to a higher one. A historical investigation of the right to freedom, social rights, and the right to development can reveal the trajectory of rights development. When studying the protection of vulnerable groups in society, it is important to consider all three of these rights simultaneously.

(2) From the perspective of changes in human rights subjects, the protection of the rights of vulnerable groups in society

a. Atomic individual-group-collective-individual in the community

The modern constitutional codes and documents of industrial countries after the bourgeois revolution uphold the idea of natural law and promote the spirit of equality and natural rights for all. However, in practice, the universality of human rights has not been fully realized. The 1776 U.S. Declaration of Independence used the word

---

[17] Hegel [11].

"men" instead of "human" or "all," excluding women from human rights, and Indians were not considered "people" because they did not pay taxes. The French Declaration of Human and Citizens' Rights also limited human rights subjectivity, using the word "person" in article 1 of the Declaration, "All men are and always will be, free and equal," which excludes women.[18] Section 1 of the 14th Amendment, known as the Magna Carta for Human Rights in the United States, declares that equal protection of the law is the constitutional right of any person, but Section 2 denies women the right to vote. Section 2 of the 14th Amendment requires that citizens of the United States who vote for federal and state officials must be men over the age of 21. The equal rights proclaimed in the bourgeois constitution have been transformed into male privileges, and disadvantaged groups in society either do not have these rights at all or have no possibility of realizing them. The historical development of human rights subjects has transformed from a limited human rights subject to a universal human rights subject, accompanied by the rise in the pursuit of the ideal of freedom and equality and the surging struggle of socially vulnerable groups. Under the historical conditions of the universalization of human rights subjects, socially vulnerable groups have also become the subjects of human rights in the sense of non-discriminatory people.

Despite formal equal freedoms being granted to socially vulnerable groups, their situation has not substantially improved. These groups merely enjoy the shell of rights without the means to realize them, resulting in a lack of actual enjoyment of rights. The rise of social rights has changed the subject of human rights, expanding it beyond the general population. To protect the rights of certain categories of people, legislation now directly uses these groups as the subject of legislation, such as women and the disabled. This approach aims to protect the actual enjoyment of their rights and indicates that the protection of vulnerable groups' rights is more direct and powerful. The rights of socially vulnerable groups are sometimes called "quasi-human rights," which differ from collective human rights. The subjects of these rights are not organized collectives but specific categories of people. The emergence of these special categories of human rights subjects is intended to protect individuals who face obstacles to realizing their rights due to their weak position in society. This distinction based on "class" aims to achieve equal treatment in a deeper sense. Marx also observed that "rights, by their very nature, consist only in the use of the same scale, but unequal individuals must be measured by the same scale, only by looking at them from the same perspective, to treat them from a specific aspect."[19] To avoid these issues, rights should not be equal but unequal. The human rights of such subjects are still essentially individual rights.[20] Group rights refer to the rights enjoyed by individuals with common interests and the same status or situation within a particular group in a particular society. Group rights are not the sum of individual

---

[18] See Harro von Senger. From the limited to the universal concept of human rights: two periods of human rights. Wang Changbin (trans.). Shen and Huang [4].

[19] Selected Works of Marx and Engels (2nd Edition), Beijing, People's Publishing House, 1995, Volume 3, p.305.

[20] Qu [12].

rights, nor are they collective rights distinct from individual rights. They can only be said to be individual rights expressed in the common form of group rights.[21] The relationship between quasi-human rights and the human rights of each individual of their class is the same, and quasi-human rights can be directly implemented into the human rights of each individual. The two are the same without enlargement, reduction, or transformation.[22]

Individual human rights enable the realization of human freedom and equality, but the context of the era of globalization has challenged this purely individualized perspective, resulting in the emergence of collective human rights. The reason why the collective can become the subject of human rights is that human beings are not just isolated individuals, but also members of a community. The community is essential to an individual's human existence, as without it, their existence becomes rootless and drifts aimlessly, akin to "skin without a body." The purpose of collective human rights is to seek a more optimal structure and space for the realization of individual human rights. The collective is a group of human beings with close bonds, who are regarded as people with equal dignity and the same potential. Within the collective, the strong and the weak are inseparable, and the concern for the survival and development of vulnerable groups is itself the proper meaning of collective survival and development. The emergence of collective human rights subjects dissolves the confrontation between the strong and the weak in society, uniting them into a cohesive whole. The individuals who make up the collective can be restored, and at this time, the individuals who are restored after forming the collective are no longer individuals in the original abstract equal sense, but rather individuals who carry richer community connotations and shoulder the heavy responsibility of community values. This is a higher stage in the development of things after the "negation of negation".[23] It should be emphasized that human rights have developed to the stage of collective human rights subjects, but individual people are still part of the community, and the real existence of individuals is still the rights of individuals in the collective. This is because "any group or 'collective', whether big or small, is just a combination of countless individuals. Groups have no rights other than those of individual members. In a free society, the 'rights' of any group derive from the rights of its members, through the voluntary choice and contractual consent of the individual, and the exercise of the individual's right in the performance of special activities." In other words, there can be no rights other than the rights of every citizen.[24]

The development of human rights subjects has progressed from limited human rights subjects to universal human rights subjects, and then to group human rights subjects and collective human rights subjects. Each stage of development represents a historical progress in protecting vulnerable groups in society.

---

[21] Sun [13].

[22] Qu [12].

[23] Rand [14].

[24] Rand [14].

b. Identity—Contract—"Identity"

The British historian Maine famously asserted that "the movement of all progressive societies, up to this point, is a movement 'from identity to contract'."[25] In pre-capitalist societies, the relationship between individuals was based on their specific identities, which determined their rights and obligations. Legislators did not assign rights and obligations directly to individuals, but instead established social statuses and combined certain rights and obligations with those statuses.[26] In the context of the hierarchical identity system, different identities represented different rights and obligations. Maine's concept of "contract" essentially means equal identity and autonomy. The capitalist system rejects hierarchical identity and establishes the idea of equality for all, embodied in equality before the law, ensuring that all citizens enjoy equal rights. Additionally, individuals are free to dispose of their private rights on the basis of equal status. Modern citizenship maximizes legal rights equality as it is held by the broadest number of nationals and is linked to the widest range of rights. However, formal equality does not guarantee that socially vulnerable groups will enjoy their rights in practice. Therefore, legislation must consider the "identity" factor to ensure greater social justice. This "identity" is distinct from the hierarchical identity of pre-capitalist societies and is a generalization of vulnerable characteristics. Special legal guarantees are granted to individuals with such "status" to promote the realization of human rights. The process of "negation of negation" from identity to contract and back to "identity" implies progress in the protection of vulnerable groups in society.

3.1.2 The Historical Necessity of Rights as a Means of Protection

(1) The feasibility of rights as a means of protection

Firstly, legal rights serve as an institutionalized mechanism for allocating resources. In sociological terms, resources provide the opportunity to generate benefits and gain freedom. "Resources are the primary source of freedom, and although not the only source, the more resources we possess, the more freedom we have. Talent provides us with more resources, while disabilities limit them." Social resources can be divided into factual and institutional resources, with legal rights being the most significant institutional resource.[27] Having rights grants individuals the power to assert claims that are often more important than utilitarian, social, or moral foundations.[28] The possession of rights determines key parameters, including individuals' economic and political status, and their opportunities for development in society. Thus, legal rights

[25] Maine [15].

[26] Zheng [16].

[27] Quoted from Li and Feng [17].

[28] Donnelly [18].

have become the most critical institutional social resource. While the distribution of factual social resources may be unequal in society, we can adjust the possession of factual resources through the rational allocation of rights. By legalizing and realizing the legitimate demands of vulnerable groups, legal rights provide them with crucial support and protection. Therefore, the recognition of the legitimate interests and needs of vulnerable groups through legal rights is a systematic approach to compensating for differences in natural conditions.

Secondly, rights serve as a crucial mechanism for adjusting interests. Essentially, rights are interests that are protected by the law. "To recognize people's interests, we must recognize their rights because the legal expression of interests is rights. Only when interests are legalized into rights can they be deemed legal, secure, and predictable."[29] In the process of adjusting interests, rights perform diverse functions, including identifying, defining, and distributing interests while reconciling conflicting interests. In real society, resource scarcity often leads to competitive access to resources. In this competition, socially disadvantaged groups often face disadvantages, and their benefits are difficult to realize. As a result, the distribution of resources creates social imbalances, where "the strong are stronger, and the weak are weaker." Therefore, we can only resolve the conflict of interests and confrontations between the strong and the weak by giving full play to the tilted protection of rights and balancing interests.

(2) Advantages of rights as a means of protection

Protecting vulnerable groups in society through a rights-based approach is an effective means of protection. There are several reasons for this. Firstly, the protection of legal rights is institutionalized. Rights are established through rules, possess stability, and are backed by the coercive power of the state. Protecting vulnerable groups through rights means that this protection "is not a gift or charity, nor does it appeal to ordinary brotherhood, love, or friendship." Rather, they are a 'right' or 'entitlement' and not merely a wish or request. 'Rights', as the name suggests, encompass both 'power' and 'benefit'."[30] Secondly, the protection of legal rights is morally significant. As Dworkin has analyzed, "Rights make the law itself more moral because it prevents governments and officials from making, implementing, and using laws for selfish or improper purposes." Rights give us confidence that the law is 'legitimate', meaning that it will treat everyone justly and fairly or compel people to uphold their promises. We are inclined to be fully committed to the law because we know that if a particular rule of law or its enforcement is 'illegitimate', our legal rights will prevent that rule from being enacted. This is why the law is authoritative and holds a unique effect, unlike other forms of coercive orders. Rights are granted to individuals, and their laws are guided by moral principles rather than the selfish interests of those with sufficient political rights.[31] "The recognition and special protection of the rights of vulnerable groups in society by legal rights is merely an expression of the notion of

[29] Zhang [19].

[30] Dong and Liu [20].

[31] Dworkin [21].

human rights; therefore, the rights of vulnerable groups in society are not a gift or a charity, but they should be possessed by the vulnerable groups themselves."

3.2 Protection of the Human Rights of Socially Vulnerable Groups

The above discussion highlights two levels of protection for the rights of socially vulnerable groups. The first level refers to the relative protection of their rights compared to other groups, while the second level, within the framework of human rights, pertains to the specific protection of the human rights of vulnerable groups.

In the age of universal human rights, the legal entitlement to equal rights for all citizens has become an undeniable institutional norm. However, this seemingly universal application of human rights creates a logical paradox when discussing the protection of the human rights of vulnerable groups in society. To resolve this, it is important to recognize that socially vulnerable groups are those whose rights are frequently violated, and merely granting equal enjoyment of human rights does not offer them adequate protection. They require special measures to effectively safeguard their human rights and allow them to enjoy their rights equally. Thus, the special protection of the human rights of vulnerable groups is not just about their enjoyment of human rights, but also about their protection.

Socially vulnerable groups are entitled to the same rights of freedom, society, and development as any other member of society. However, the nature of these rights differs, and therefore, the special protection of these rights for vulnerable groups also varies.

3.2.1 Protection of the Right to Freedom of Socially Vulnerable Groups

The right to freedom is the cornerstone of the rights system and the essence of the law. It embodies the fundamental interests and needs of people in their daily lives, such as civil and political rights and property rights, which are closely related to citizens' fundamental existence. The right to freedom is a negative right, which means that the state's role is to provide negative guarantees by refraining from intervening or interfering. For socially vulnerable groups, the right to freedom is safeguarded through a series of preferential policies that create better conditions and opportunities for their realization. To enhance the ability of vulnerable groups to participate and compete fairly in society, preferential policies should first be established to promote their effective participation in public life. This can be achieved through appropriate skills training and improving their capacity for social participation. Such policies will enable vulnerable groups to enjoy equal opportunities for development and the ability to participate in society on an equal footing.[32] In other words, we cannot

[32] Zhou [22].

solely rely on external assistance to support vulnerable groups in society. Instead, we should also focus on enhancing their ability to "hematopoiesis" to achieve long-term development. One direct way to guarantee the right to liberty for vulnerable groups in society is through the "quota system." This involves giving special protection measures to vulnerable groups based on their status, such as reserving certain places for ethnic minority students in institutions of higher learning, and reserving quotas for members of certain disadvantaged groups in recruitment, employment, promotion, and other areas. These measures will help vulnerable groups to enjoy equal opportunities for development and participation in society. For example, the Law of the People's Republic of China on the Protection of Women's Rights and Interests stipulates that women enjoy equal rights with men to vote and stand for election. It also requires an appropriate number of women deputies in the National People's Congress and local people's congresses at all levels, with a gradual increase in the proportion of women deputies. This provision provides women with further legal guarantees for their enjoyment of political rights. In summary, the right to freedom is a negative right, and state power cannot directly intervene. Therefore, the special protection of the right to freedom for vulnerable groups in society can only increase their chances of realizing their rights. Preferential policies that improve their ability to realize their rights are "favorable." This preferential special guarantee is only indirect for the realization of the right to freedom of vulnerable groups in society.

3.2.2 Protection of Social Rights for Socially Vulnerable Groups

Unlike the right to freedom, social rights are positive rights, and the state must take affirmative measures to ensure their realization. "These rights are not meant to protect individuals against the government or other people in power, but to draw the attention of public authorities to the realization of freedoms that individuals themselves possess through other freedoms..."[33] Fundamental human rights include not only freedom from infringement by the government but also the satisfaction of basic needs and the improvement of living standards, which the government must actively provide and guarantee.[34] The realization of social rights is a special guarantee granted by the state to vulnerable groups in society through the fulfillment of positive obligations. This special guarantee is direct and necessary for the realization of social rights. Moreover, the unique feature of social rights is that they offer protection to vulnerable groups in society, and this protection is not only preferable but necessary.

Social rights, such as the right to subsistence, are among the most prominent rights represented in the law. The "right to life" was first introduced as a clear legal concept in the Austrian utopian socialist tendencies of jurist Ann Ah Menger's 1886 book "The History of All Labor Rights." Menger believed that the right to work, the right to fair wages, and the right to life are the foundation for creating a new generation

[33] Friedrich [23].

[34] Henkin [24].

of human rights, which she called the right to economic foundation. The right to subsistence reflects the fact that, among all human desires, the desire to survive takes precedence, and that the distribution of social wealth should be based on a general objective criterion that ensures everyone can acquire a basic share commensurate with the conditions of their existence. According to this criterion, members of society have the right to demand from the state the goods and labor necessary for their own survival, prioritizing their own survival over other people's desire to survive.[35]

The French Constitution of 1791 guarantees in its Basic Provisions that "a general institution of public relief shall be established or organized for the purpose of raising abandoned children, rescuing poor disabled persons, and providing work for the able-bodied poor who have not been able to obtain work." In 1793, this provision was further developed in the Declaration of the Rights of Man, which states that "Public relief is a sacred obligation." Society has a duty to maintain the livelihood of its less fortunate citizens by either providing them with work or with the means of subsistence for those who are unable to work. Accordingly, socially vulnerable groups have the right to receive assistance from society. Article 151, paragraph 1 of the French Constitution states that "the organization of economic life shall be commensurate with the principle of fairness and the purpose of human existence." Similarly, the Weimar Constitution includes provisions on the social right to work, and the state establishes an insurance system to ensure workers are not adversely affected by illness, old age, or infirmity.

The main purpose of the right to subsistence is to enable vulnerable groups in society to acquire basic dignity and lead normal lives as human beings. As a superior concept, the right to subsistence encompasses many aspects of fundamental rights related to people's basic survival, particularly for socially vulnerable groups. Japanese scholars refer to it as a fundamental right in the aspect of the right to life. These different basic rights to life safeguard and guarantee the basic survival of vulnerable groups in different fields and aspects, providing comprehensive protection to vulnerable groups in society.

3.2.3 Guarantee the Right to Development of Socially Vulnerable Groups

Survival and development are the two major themes of the current era, and the right to development is an inevitable requirement of the right to subsistence and an inevitable result of the right to subsistence. The right to development of socially vulnerable groups is the right to development as individual subjects in the field of domestic law. Socially vulnerable groups are an integral part of the social organism, and ensuring their right to development is crucial for ensuring the overall development of society.

The right to development has its own uniqueness, which is reflected in the fact that it is neither simply a civil and political right constituted by the right to freedom, nor is it simply equivalent to economic, social, and cultural rights with the right

---

[35] For a related discussion, see Xu [25].

to subsistence as the core. It is a kind of benign interaction between members of society, which fully reflects the integrity of human rights and the joint rights of integration. The comprehensiveness of the right to development is embodied in the following three aspects: First, the right to development includes both material and spiritual rights. For a person's survival and development, material is the foundation, so the right to development is also first manifested as a right in material form. The realization of the right to development is not only premised on certain prerequisite material rights, but also aims to obtain a higher level of economic development and realize a higher level of material rights. "It is only through development that people's rights to food, clothing, shelter, health, employment, and education can be fully realized."[36] At the same time, the right to development is not only an economic right but also carries a certain spiritual meaning, that is, the recognition and promotion of the subject's freedom and spiritual values. Article 2 of the Declaration on Social Progress and Development declares: "Social progress and development shall be based on respect for the dignity and worth of the human person and shall ensure the promotion of human rights and social equity." Secondly, the right to development has the attributes of both negative and positive rights. On the one hand, the right to development requires that public power passively refrain from encroaching on and eliminate harm, and on the other hand, that public power take positive measures to promote and guarantee its realization. Finally, the right to development combines freedom and equality in one right by guaranteeing both citizens' free participation in the development process and their equal share in the fruits of development. "The right to development is not a simple addition of existing political and civil rights and economic, social, and cultural rights, nor is it a hodgepodge of existing human rights, but its unique meaning is that it is a universal right to equal development opportunities and freedom of all-round development enjoyed by mankind based on existing rights."[37]

The right to development is a universal human right, but it holds greater meaning for vulnerable groups in society, just like the right to survival as a social right. With the widening gap in social development, it becomes an inevitable requirement to strengthen the guarantees for the right to development of vulnerable groups. Unequal development opportunities and widening development gaps can result in social injustice. The comprehensive nature of the right to development poses a challenge in protecting the rights of vulnerable groups in society. "Traditional legal protection that focuses solely on individual or societal rights needs to be integrated and improved to protect the right to development."[38] The state's obligation to ensure the realization of the right to development of socially vulnerable groups can be summarized into four aspects: First, protection. The government must prevent itself and others from infringing on the right to development of socially vulnerable groups. The state's protection obligation is typically implemented through legislation. Second, the direct

---

[36] Li [26].

[37] Wang [27].

[38] Wang [27].

provision of resources. The state must directly provide resources to support the development of vulnerable groups in society. Third, promoting participation. The state should create equal opportunities for vulnerable groups in society to participate in development and guarantee the full realization of their right to freedom. Finally, promoting the sharing of development results. The sharing of development results is not evenly distributed, but the state should adopt various measures to enable vulnerable groups in society to share a portion of the distribution of development results to avoid excessive disparities between the rich and the poor.

The differences in the nature of the right to freedom, social rights, and the right to development determine the differences in the protection of different types of human rights for vulnerable groups in society. To sum up, the guarantee of the right to freedom of vulnerable groups in society is preferential in nature, the guarantee of social rights is a priority, and the guarantee of the right to development is comprehensive. Among them, the guarantee of the right to subsistence and the right to development is of crucial significance to the vulnerable groups in society, and only when the problems of the vulnerable groups in society are included in the perspective of the right to survival and the right to development can they obtain sustained and effective protection.

In short, the protection of rights and the protection of human rights are the two meanings of the proposition of protecting the rights of vulnerable groups in society. The former is addressed to outsiders and is distinguished from other forms of protection. The protection of the rights of socially vulnerable groups is internal to ensure the realization of the human rights of socially vulnerable groups.

4 Institutional Mechanisms for the Protection of the Rights of Socially Vulnerable Groups

Mechanism is a very general concept that includes concepts, norms, organizations, procedures and other elements. The exploration of the protection mechanism of the rights of socially vulnerable groups is the final destination of the study of the theoretical problems of socially vulnerable groups. In fact, it answers the question of "how to protect the rights of vulnerable groups in society".

4.1 Due Process for the Expression of the Interests of Socially Vulnerable Groups

In modern society, legislation is the primary means of distributing benefits and burdens among members. However, this process is not inherently just and often involves fierce struggles and compromises. The dominant group tends to enjoy more rights, leaving socially disadvantaged groups at a disadvantage due to the lack of channels to express their interests. Therefore, it is essential to explore mechanisms that enable vulnerable groups to express their interests and protect their rights.

4.1.1 A Democratic Way of Expressing Interests

Since the time of the ancient Greeks, democracy has been favored as a relatively good form of governance. Democracy is essentially an institutional choice made by people in pursuit of good government. The most basic requirement of good government is to involve all people under its jurisdiction in the decision-making process so that the will and freedom of each person can be fully expressed and incorporated into the life of the community. Democratic governance provides a platform for equal participation of members of society, making the realization of this ideal value possible. The democratic governance method is a majority decision-making mechanism with the equal participation of members of society, and the implementation of the democratic system is based on the assumption that individual rationality is limited, and one's understanding is always incomplete. The knowledge of the majority has a higher probability of being correct than the knowledge of an individual, so most decisions are better than individual decisions. Under conditions of direct democracy, all citizens are allowed to participate in decision-making in public affairs. In conditions of indirect democracy, representatives of all citizens are elected through an electoral procedure, and political power is exercised by them. The superiority of democracy has been enthusiastically celebrated. Aristotle believed that the advantages of direct democracy lie in the fact that a large number of participants can concentrate the opinions, wisdom, strength, virtues, and even wealth of members of society more fully. It is easy to shake the feelings of one person, but it is difficult to shake the feelings of the whole people, so democracy can make a society more stable. Direct democracy makes decisions that reflect the will of the majority, and the participation of the majority in politics reduces strife and civil unrest. Dahl outlined ten advantages of democracy: a. Democracy helps avoid the tyrannical and evil rule of dictators; b. Democracy guarantees its citizens many basic rights that non-democratic systems will not and cannot do; c. Democracy can guarantee citizens a wider range of freedoms than other viable options; d. Democracy helps people safeguard their fundamental interests; e. Only democratic governments can provide individuals with the greatest opportunity to exercise the freedom of self-determination, that is, the freedom to live under the rules of their own choosing; f. Only democratic governments offer the greatest opportunity to fulfill moral responsibilities; g. Democracy can enable the fuller development of human nature than other possible options; h. Only a democratic government can create a relatively high level of political equality; i. Modern representative democracies are not at war with each other; j. Countries with democratic governments are always more prosperous than countries with non-democratic governments.[39]

Just as there are two sides to a coin, where there is light, there is shadow, and while the majority rule embodies the superiority of democracy, behind it lies infinite

[39] See Dahl [28].

danger. It is impossible for all members of the community to agree on issues, and if the principle of the minority obeying the majority means that the views of the minority are sacrificed and not respected as they deserve, they might even be trampled upon. Sartori once pointed out that "by forming a majority, it is possible to take into account the different views of the minority, and there is no doubt that this approach has obvious authoritarian overtones."[40] In this case, the situation of a few is no different, or even worse than that under an absolute monarchy. Tocqueville once vividly described the disadvantage of the few, "You are free and do not have to follow my thoughts; your life, your possessions, everything you have, belong to you. But henceforth, you will be an outsider among us. You can keep your privileges in society, but these privileges will be of no use to you because if you want your fellow citizens to elect you, they will not vote for you; and if you want them to respect you, they will pretend to respect you. You will remain among us, but you will lose your right to be human."[41]

Modern society distributes and affirms the meaning of various benefits through democratic legislation. In the process of democratic legislative decision-making, individuals do not represent themselves in isolation, but usually in the form of groups. However, the power balance between these groups is not always equal, leading to a process of group interest struggles. Democracy itself contains inherent paradoxes and often fails to fully consider the opinions and voices of minority groups in decision-making, which further exacerbates the vulnerability of these groups in society. This creates a vicious circle that goes against a minimum sense of justice, and measures must be taken to overcome the negative effects of democracy.

"One of the basic principles followed by modern society in reconciling the conflict between minority groups and majority groups, and between individual interests and the interests of society as a whole, is that when considering the interests of society as a whole, we cannot ignore the existence and value of individual interests and their significance in promoting or hindering social progress. When the interests of the majority are the main value orientation, the voices of the minority should not be ignored, but their interests should be accommodated as much as possible, in accordance with the basic principles of the modern rule of law. When people sacrifice the interests of the minority in order to safeguard the interests of the majority, it is necessary not only to justify the superiority of the former over the latter in value but also to compensate the interests of the minority who made the sacrifice, either through institutional or assistance to vulnerable groups who are the most vulnerable."[42]

4.1.2 Due Process Guarantees for the Expression of the Interests of Vulnerable Groups

In practice, overcoming the limitations of democracy is primarily achieved through the institutionalization of due process. As an institutional arrangement, the operation

[40] Sartori [29].

[41] de Tocqueville [30].

[42] Lin [31].

and realization of democracy must be embedded in a certain program design. Due process is an inherent and inevitable requirement of a democratic system. The superiority of democracy is realized and manifested within the time and space provided by due process, and the limitations of democracy can only be effectively controlled and overcome under the guidance and restrictions of due process. The harm that may be caused to vulnerable groups in society in the legislative process due to the inherent limitations of democracy can be minimized in due process. The reason why due process has such a function is determined by the intrinsic value of due process. Democratic due process takes a series of criteria as its evaluation scale, and in this series of evaluation standards, the core can be summarized into two points: equal participation and openness of the procedure. First, due process must ensure that all members of society participate in the decision-making process and are treated equally. Equal participation carries the value of justice and respect for human dignity through the full and equal opportunity to participate in the process by those whose rights and interests may have a stake in or influence on the outcome, to express their views in the legal process, and to influence the outcome. Second, due process requires openness and transparency. The rules and standards used in the democratic process must be open, the decision-making process transparent, and the adoption of some views and the sacrifice of others must be fully justified and acceptable to a rational population. This ensures that even if some people's interests and rights are sacrificed, they are duly respected in doing so, and can be convinced.

The basic requirements of due process are based on the protection of the rights and interests of vulnerable groups in society. The essence of due process lies in restricting unbridled arbitrary decision-making by powerful groups and giving vulnerable groups the ability to confront such decisions. This capacity for confrontation is embedded in a range of procedural rights, including the right of citizens to equal participation. Legislation is the process of distributing social benefits and confirming rights, so it is crucial for vulnerable groups to participate in the legislative process and effectively influence decision-making. Without the equal participation rights of vulnerable groups in society, all their other rights will become meaningless. Moreover, vulnerable groups should also have equal decision-making power. It is not enough for them to enjoy equal rights to participate; they should also have equal decision-making power. Only in this way can vulnerable groups gradually change their status by striving for more legitimate rights. Additionally, citizens' right to know is essential for vulnerable groups. Without the right to know, they cannot effectively exercise the right to vote, and they cannot give opinions and suggestions on the handling of public affairs related to their own interests.

These rights guarantee due process, but procedural rights cannot be entirely separated from substantive rights. Therefore, these rights are the prerequisite basis for the protection of substantive rights for vulnerable groups in society.

4.2 Mechanisms for Realizing the Protection of Human Rights of Socially Vulnerable Groups

The principle of due process provides a procedural prerequisite for protecting the rights of vulnerable groups in society, while the realization of the protection of the rights of vulnerable groups in society depends on the observance of the principle of safeguarding human rights in substance. The inherent mechanism of the democratic system implies the danger and possibility of eroding individual freedom, which may come from the authority of the majority based on majority decision-making and governance. Its direct consequence is that it is easy to lead to the tyranny of the majority. For example, in ancient Greece, in the name of a beautiful democracy, serious violations of individual freedom occurred. Gunsdown writes, "You hardly see them enjoying any of the freedoms we call modern man. All private operations are heavily monitored. The independence of the individual from public opinion, labor and, above all, religion is not given the slightest attention. The freedom of individuals to choose their own religious beliefs, which we today regard as so precious, was considered a crime and blasphemy to the ancients. The authority of society intervenes in those areas that we consider most beneficial, namely, the will of the individual. Moreover, public authority interferes in the internal relations of most families."[43] The principle of guaranteeing the fundamental human rights of the individual is precisely the substantive limitation of this majority authority. That is, even the opinion of the majority cannot be allowed to violate and trample on the most basic human rights of mankind. The most essential content of human rights is human freedom, dignity, and worth. 'Freedom is a unique, original birthright of every human being because of his humanity.[44] Freedom requires granting an individual an 'autonomous space' that is independent of the outside world, a territory of self-discipline that no one else, including the state, can interfere with. Man is not a means or object of the state or society; on the contrary, the individual, who exists prior to the state, is the purpose and foundation for the state's existence. Moreover, the autonomy of the individual is of greater value than that of the state, as everyone should retain an independent sphere of life that is not subject to state power.[45] Therefore, in a democratic system, any decision-making must be measured against human rights, and the unconditional violation of individual freedom, trampling of personal dignity, and disregard for individual values cannot be allowed. The principle of human rights ensures that even vulnerable groups in society have their rights protected, and that a minimum standard of rights is upheld for all.

---

[43] Constant [32].

[44] Kant [33].

[45] Li [34].

4.2.1 Adoption of Special Safeguard Measures

The state plays a crucial role in guaranteeing the realization of human rights. First and foremost, the idea of limited government and sovereignty belonging to the people needs to be established, which serves two purposes—limiting the arbitrary exercise of government power and establishing the state's obligation to act. The realization of the rights of socially vulnerable groups is premised on the active exercise of the state's obligations, which require positive measures from the state. In the human rights system of socially vulnerable groups, social rights are the most typical. To understand the human rights realization mechanism of vulnerable groups in society supported by state obligations, we can take the realization of the right to education, labor, and social security in social rights as a window.

(1) The right to education is guaranteed for socially vulnerable groups

The right to education is a special right that combines the nature of both a civil and a social right. The right to education for socially vulnerable groups is guaranteed through:

First, the law guarantees the equal right to education of socially disadvantaged groups. The equal right to education is a concrete embodiment of the right to equality, and the lowest level of protection of the right to education for socially vulnerable groups is the exclusion of any form of discrimination.

Secondly, the adoption of compulsory education provisions removes obstacles to the realization of the right to education for economically disadvantaged groups in society. Article 26 of the Universal Declaration of Human Rights states: "Everyone has the right to education, which shall be free, at least in the elementary and fundamental stages. Elementary education shall be compulsory. Technical and professional education shall be made generally available, and higher education shall be equally accessible to all on the basis of merit."

Third, the law guarantees the realization of the rights of vulnerable groups in society through special protective measures. The Convention on the Elimination of All Forms of Discrimination against Women specifies specific measures to be taken by States parties to develop the realization of women's right to education, notably vocational and vocational counseling in educational institutions, whether rural or urban, equal opportunity to study and acquire a diploma, equal choice of courses, examinations, and quality of school premises, encouragement of co-education and other forms of education that contribute to this end, and revising textbook curricula and teaching methods. The opportunity to award scholarships and other research grants should also be equal, reducing female dropout rates, and providing programs for adolescent girls and women leaving school prematurely.

Fourth, reserving certain places for education for socially disadvantaged groups, which is usually for ethnic minority students or students with disabilities.

The goal of education is the improvement of the comprehensive quality of human beings and the free and comprehensive development of human beings. Therefore, the realization of the right to education can enhance the self-ability and social competitiveness of the vulnerable groups in society, lay the foundation for the realization of other rights, and eliminate the vulnerable position of the vulnerable groups in society.

(2) Protection of the labor rights of socially vulnerable groups

Before social rights were recognized by law as a right of a distinct nature, many elements of social rights were covered by the right to freedom, including the right to work. In the early stages of capitalist development, the state did not intervene in employment, labor remuneration, and other fields, allowing for free competition. However, this free competition caused the living conditions of the weak to deteriorate, prompting the state to take active measures to ensure the realization of the right to work. This social right pays more attention to protecting the interests of vulnerable groups in society.

The protection of labor rights for socially vulnerable groups is achieved through the following means:

First, equal labor and employment rights are stipulated in legislation, and any form of discrimination against socially vulnerable groups in labor and employment is excluded. For example, the Labor Law of the People's Republic of China stipulates: "Workers shall not be discriminated against on the basis of ethnicity, race, gender, or religious belief." Relevant United Nations documents require States parties to take all appropriate measures to eliminate discrimination against women in employment to guarantee them equal labor rights on the basis of equality between men and women. This includes the right to equal employment opportunities, freedom of choice of profession and occupation, promotion and job security, social security, and the right to health and safety at work.

Second, special protective protection should be given to the labor rights and interests of vulnerable groups in society. For instance, the Labor Law stipulates that employers shall not arrange minors to engage in underground mining, toxic and harmful work, state-prescribed fourth-level manual labor intensity labor, and other prohibited labor. Furthermore, employers shall conduct regular health examinations for juvenile workers. The Labour Code also stipulates that women receive special care during menstruation, pregnancy, childbirth, and breastfeeding. Women who give birth to employees are entitled to three months of paid maternity leave, and during pregnancy, childbirth, or breastfeeding, the employer shall not terminate the contract.

Third, the realization of the right to work and employment is guaranteed by reserving a certain number of employment places for vulnerable groups in society. In 1987, the 7th United Nations Conference on the Decade of Persons with Disabilities emphasized the need for states to consider the employment of persons with disabilities as a priority issue and to promote the proportional employment of persons with disabilities in national legislation. Japan's Law on the Promotion of Employment of Persons with Disabilities stipulates that 1.5% of persons with disabilities must be employed in private companies, 1.9% in public enterprises, and national and local government offices and public institutions. China's Law on the Protection of Persons with Disabilities also stipulates that organs, groups, enterprises and institutions, and urban and rural collective economic organizations shall arrange employment for disabled persons in accordance with a certain proportion and select appropriate jobs and positions for them. When the relevant government departments issue targets for the recruitment and employment of employees, they shall determine a certain amount for persons with disabilities.

Labor is the most direct source of human living conditions, therefore, protecting the right to work of socially vulnerable groups is the most direct means to ensure their survival, and it creates conditions and possibilities for the further development of socially vulnerable groups on the basis of survival.

(3) The right to social security for socially vulnerable groups is guaranteed

The social security system is a product of the development of modern large-scale industry and market economy, and the first legislative reflection of social security was the British Poor Law. At that time, the act of poverty was a "correction" technique practiced by the ruling class, and for the poor who received relief, it was premised on the loss of personal dignity, personal freedom, and political rights. As industrialization progressed and socioeconomic, political, and ethical attitudes changed, it became increasingly recognized that labor bailouts might increase rather than decrease productivity. Industrialization imposes on workers the dangers arising from its own development, and the existential risks of such workers should be borne by society as a whole. In this context, survival insurance systems have emerged in some countries to provide assistance to workers in the event of illness, disability, old age, etc. This system was created to guarantee the basic survival of vulnerable people in order to preserve their freedom and dignity.

According to the ILO literature, social security refers to the protection that society provides to its members through a series of public measures to combat economic and social deprivation caused by the suspension or drastic reduction of wages due to illness, maternity, work injury, unemployment, disability, old age, and death, and to provide medical care and supplies to families with children.

The right to social security has been recognized as a citizen's entitlement. The right to social security is the right of citizens to enjoy material guarantees provided by the state and society in the event of incapacity for work or temporary difficulties due to old age and infirmity, illness, disability, unemployment, etc., to meet their basic living needs and improve their living standards. The right to social security has been enshrined as a fundamental human right by a number of international instruments. For example, Article 22 of the Universal Declaration of Human Rights stipulates that "as a member of society, human beings are entitled to social security and to the realization of economic, social and cultural rights necessary for the dignity of the individual and the free development of the individual." Such achievement depends on national measures and international cooperation and should be carried out within the capacity of national institutions and resources. Article 25 stipulates: "Everyone has the right to a standard of living necessary for the well-being of himself and his family, including clothing, food, housing, medicine, and social services necessary for them; and the right to protection in case of unemployment, illness, disability, widowhood, old age, accidents due to force majeure, and other circumstances of incapacity for life." Article 9 of the International Covenant on Economic, Social and Cultural Rights provides that: "States Parties to the present Covenant recognize the right of everyone to social security, including social insurance." Article 11 states: "The States Parties to the present Covenant recognize the right of everyone to an adequate standard of living for himself and his family, including adequate food, clothing, shelter, and an ever-improving living environment. The state party will take appropriate steps to ensure the realization of such rights, while recognizing the importance of international cooperation based on free consent in this regard."

The basic idea of the right to social security is that when the working capacity of members of society decreases, temporarily or permanently loses their ability to work, and thus becomes a vulnerable group in society, society provides an assistance measure to ensure their basic human life with dignity and dignity. "The basic concept of modern social security is not only to guarantee the right to life but also to maintain a 'decent' living condition for people so that people can maintain a standard of living that does not feel low when they talk to other members of society on an equal footing and maintain their dignity as members of 'society' and as human beings."[46]

The right to social security is a universal human right enjoyed by all citizens, but the degree of realization of this right varies between different groups. The right to social security should realistically be enjoyed by persons who are socially vulnerable. The goal of modern social security is not only to protect the income and maintain the survival of members of society when they fall into economic and social poverty due to lack of pay or drastic reduction of wages due to illness, maternity, work injury, unemployment, disability, old age and death, but also to maintain and preserve their working capacity, or restore the working capacity of these members of society to the same level as the working capacity of normal members of society. This is to ensure their ability to take care of themselves, stand on their own feet in society, and promote their return to social production and life. It can be seen that another fundamental purpose of the right to social security is to eliminate the "weakness" of socially vulnerable groups and completely change their vulnerable situation by enhancing their own "hematopoietic" function. This departs from the old-fashioned concept of aid, transforming it from a branded "charity" designation into a right, while prohibiting social and political discrimination against recipients.

Social security consists of both social insurance and social assistance. There is a distinction between social security benefits "earned" by workers and their families, and need-based assistance received by any individual or group from public funds. Social security in a broad sense includes these two aspects. The International Labour Organization's Social Security (Minimum Standards) Convention, 1952, sets out the specific elements of social security in a menu-style manner. These include health care, sickness benefits, unemployment benefits, old-age benefits, employment injury benefits, family benefits, maternity benefits, incapacity benefits due to illness and disability, and survivor benefits.

The right to social security itself is a strong guarantee for vulnerable groups in society, and the above nine aspects have basically covered various unfavorable situations that may occur in the industrial era. They can provide basic protection for socially vulnerable groups caused by various reasons. The right to social security

[46] Li [35].

for socially vulnerable groups provides the most basic guarantee for their right to subsistence.

4.2.2 Grant of Special Legal Rights

At the level of legal norms, the human rights of socially vulnerable groups and the special legal rights of socially vulnerable groups are two components of the rights system for socially vulnerable groups, and the complementary relationship between the two seems to form "equal protection" and "special protection." However, "equal protection" and "special protection" are relative, and the key here is how to understand equality. If the concept of substantive equality is adopted, "special protection" should be the proper meaning of "equal protection" itself. This is because only by granting special legal rights to vulnerable groups in society can the equal realization of the human rights of vulnerable groups in society be guaranteed. The reason why vulnerable groups in society enjoy special rights under the law is derived from the protection of human rights. In other words, the special legal rights of socially vulnerable groups are only a means to realize the human rights of socially vulnerable groups.

Human rights are first institutionalized in a country's constitution through the fundamental rights of citizens. In order to give practical effect to the ideas and principles of the Constitution, a series of legal rights arise in sectoral laws. Is there a qualitative difference between the legal rights arising from the Constitution and the fundamental rights stipulated in the Constitution? What is the logical relationship between human rights, constitutional rights, and legal rights? The answers to these questions directly determine the status of special legal rights other than the human rights of vulnerable groups in society in the rights system of vulnerable groups in society. The relationship between human rights, constitutional rights, and legal rights can be understood in this way: human rights have two meanings. First, human rights are a value that serves as the criterion for evaluating the legitimacy of constitutional rights and legal rights in the current legal system. In this sense, human rights are both the starting point and the ultimate destination of constitutional and legal rights. Second, human rights are manifested as realistic human rights, which are embodied through constitutional rights. Constitutional rights occupy a unique position in a country's legal system. "Constitutional rights are legally the product of the contract between the people, and its rationality comes from the people's declaration of the basic rights that the people should enjoy when formulating the Constitution; The people still have the right to retain rights not proclaimed in the Constitution as residual rights."[47] Of all legal norms, only one norm has the highest effect, and that is the human rights norm in the Constitution. The entire power of the State exists for human rights, and all the norms in the law revolve around human rights. All legislation, tested for its effectiveness, is ultimately measured by human rights norms.[48] Taking a look

[47] Mo [36].

[48] Zhang [37].

at legal rights again, it can be said that "legal rights are created by the legislature, and these rights revolve around the realization of constitutional rights. The legislature formulates these rights as conditions to fulfill its duty of protecting the civil rights that are protected by the constitution in accordance with the constitution." Therefore, in this sense, the rights stipulated in the laws enacted by the legislature essentially serve as a means to realize the rights of citizens stipulated in the "Constitution and serve as auxiliary conditions for transforming constitutional rights from a state of subjective rights to objectively enjoyed rights by citizens."[49] What is the relationship between legal rights and human rights? "The legislature is free to create legal rights, but such legal rights must serve the purpose of effectively guaranteeing the realization of the basic human rights established in the Constitution."[50] In sum, human rights are institutionalized through constitutional rights, legal rights are the development of constitutional rights, and legal rights must be consistent with the purpose of human rights.

Analyzing the relationship between human rights, constitutional rights, and special legal rights of socially vulnerable groups, we can understand that protecting the human rights of socially vulnerable groups is realized through the basic rights of freedom and social rights of socially vulnerable groups in the Constitution, and the legal rights of socially vulnerable groups further develop the basic rights of the Constitution. Because of the special situation of vulnerable groups in society, special legal rights can be created to transform equal human rights recognized by legal norms into equal human rights that can be actually enjoyed. Therefore, the basic constitutional rights, as institutionalized human rights, are the mother rights and source rights, and the special legal rights of vulnerable groups in society are derivative and auxiliary rights created to protect the basic constitutional rights. It can be concluded that the special legal rights of socially vulnerable groups are based on a more basic premise of human rights, and these rights are used as a means to ensure the realization of these human rights. These rights are therefore based on the individual characteristics of different categories of socially vulnerable groups.

For example, China's "Law on the Protection of the Disabled" stipulates that "the state and society take rehabilitation measures to help disabled persons restore or compensate for their functions and enhance their ability to participate in social activities." This gives vulnerable groups in society a special right to rehabilitation, which is intended to ensure the realization of the right to life of the disabled. With regard to minors, China's "Law on the Prevention of Juvenile Delinquency" stipulates that in cases of juvenile delinquency, news reports, film and television programs, and public publications must not disclose the name, address, photograph, or information that can be inferred from the minor. Moreover, minors have the right to request a closed hearing during a court hearing. These provisions are aimed at protecting the physical and mental condition of minors and give them special rights for their healthy growth. These special rights are intended to ensure the realization of minors' right to healthy growth and privacy. For women, China's Marriage Law stipulates that "a

---

[49] Mo [36].

[50] Mo [36].

woman may not file for divorce during pregnancy, within one year after childbirth, or within six months after termination of pregnancy." Giving women the right to refuse to consent to divorce for a specified period of time is essentially intended to better protect women's personal rights. Singh once pointed out: "There is no moral status of rights without the so-called 'rights' given to all."[51] "I think that even if it is necessary to take measures to remedy previous inequalities, it is not necessary to take privileges into account. The very nature of rights contradicts the concept of 'differential treatment of rights'."[52] These special legal rights of socially vulnerable groups are not privileges. Whether a special legal right is a privilege or not, the purpose of granting it should be considered. The purpose of granting special legal rights to vulnerable groups in society is to ensure the complete realization of the equal human rights of vulnerable groups in society. The special legal rights of socially vulnerable groups are justified in the pursuit of this purpose.

4.3 Mechanisms for Remedy for the Rights of Socially Vulnerable Groups

It is generally accepted that 'no remedy is no right', meaning that the right remedy is decisive for the existence of a right. The granting and special protection of the rights of vulnerable groups in society are not only static proclamations in the Constitution or other laws but also fragments and links in the dynamic operation system of the law. For vulnerable groups in society, whose rights are easily violated, the ability to effectively initiate rights remedy procedures and obtain substantial rights compensation is an important indicator of the quality of the rights of socially vulnerable groups in a society.

The infringement of the rights of vulnerable groups in society can be understood in both a broad and narrow sense. In the broad sense, it includes any form of infringement of the rights of vulnerable groups in society, such as infringement based on their social status or identity, for example, the denial of equal labor rights to women in the workplace, or the infringement of the right to personal freedom of a female citizen. In the narrow sense, the infringement of the rights of vulnerable groups only refers to the former type of infringement. This article focuses on the narrow sense of infringement of the rights of vulnerable groups in society and discusses remedies for such infringement.

---

[51] Singer [38].

[52] Singer [38].

4.3.1 Constitutional Remedies for the Equal Rights of Socially Vulnerable Groups

The author believes that the infringement of socially vulnerable groups based on their "weak" status or "weak" characteristics is essentially an infringement of the equal rights of socially vulnerable groups. The right to equality is a basic right of citizens stipulated in our Constitution, so this infringement is also a violation of the constitutional rights of socially vulnerable groups. This also highlights the need to explore constitutional remedies for the infringement of the rights of socially vulnerable groups.

The protection of the rights of vulnerable groups in society is achieved through two levels: First, it is necessary to eliminate discrimination against vulnerable groups so that they are not disadvantaged in the enjoyment of their rights due to their ethnicity, race, gender, family origin, or other vulnerabilities. This goal and ideal aim to give socially disadvantaged groups a formal right to equality. Second, it is necessary to grant substantive equal rights to vulnerable groups in society according to their specific circumstances. As Mr. Lin Laifan concluded, "Formal equality aims to oppose unreasonable differences, while substantive equality necessarily recognizes reasonable differences."[53] These two aspects are interrelated and complementary. In the rights system of socially vulnerable groups, the primary right is the right to equality, which can be considered the "right of rights" of socially vulnerable groups. Without the legal concept and legal system foundation established by the right to equality, all other rights of vulnerable groups in society will be empty promises. The uniqueness of the right to equality in the system of constitutional rights of citizens and in the system of rights of vulnerable groups is reflected in its transcendent position in the entire system of basic constitutional rights. It embodies principles such as racial equality, gender equality, political equality, economic equality, educational equality, and more, serving as the foundation for the realization of civil and political rights, economic rights, education rights, and other rights.[54] "The right to equality has its own unique features; it does not have a clear and specific content like other rights, and its essence is mainly reflected in the process of exercising or realizing other rights. For instance, equality is reflected in the value of exercising other rights, such as political, economic, cultural, social, and family rights."[55] Therefore, the degree of equality in the realization of each specific right becomes the measure of the realization of the right to equality. In other words, the right to equality is a fundamental, formal, and permeable constitutional right. The right to equality is of paramount importance to vulnerable groups in society because the first goal of protecting vulnerable groups in society is to achieve equality between vulnerable groups and other members of society. The right to equality can be combined with the freedom and social rights of vulnerable groups in society to achieve the dual protection of the rights of vulnerable groups in society. Only under the umbrella of the right to equality can the rights of

---

[53] Lin [39].

[54] Xu [40].

[55] Mo [41].

vulnerable groups in society to freedom and social rights gain practical significance. The combination of the right to equality and the right to freedom can fully realize formal equality, and the combination of the right to equality and social rights can achieve substantive equality. In fact, in the constitutional sense, the protection of the rights of socially vulnerable groups is to realize equal rights to freedom and social rights. In social reality, discrimination against socially vulnerable groups on the basis of gender, health, and other reasons in the right to work and education is a violation of the right to equality as a basic constitutional right of socially vulnerable groups.

Based on the understanding above, the next question is how effective the equal right of vulnerable groups is as a basic constitutional right. Can socially vulnerable groups file lawsuits for violations of the right to equality? Can the right to equality, enshrined in the Constitution, be the basis for adjudication? This series of problems relates to constitutional remedies for the equal rights of vulnerable groups in society.

"Constitutional fundamental rights" and why they have become a constitutional practice in the world today.[56] In other words, the Constitution stipulates the basic rights of citizens, and when such rights are violated, a constitutional case is formed, and citizens have the right to file a lawsuit based on constitutional rights, and the courts can directly hear cases in accordance with citizens' basic constitutional rights. A distinctive feature of modern constitutional rule of law is the remedy of rights through constitutional judicial means, and "any legal right can only effectively enter the real operation process through the mechanism of constitutional remedies."[57] "Ordinary litigation can generally only solve the problem of specific administrative acts of the government not complying with the Constitution's requirements to guarantee human rights. However, abstract acts of the government, especially laws passed by the legislature, that violate the basic human rights enshrined in the Constitution must also meet the requirements of human rights protection. Only then can the legal system truly exhaust all legal measures for the legal protection of human rights. If citizens cannot guarantee their human rights under the Constitution, this means that the legislative power or other powers of government have privileges vis-à-vis human rights before the Constitution. Thus, the absence of a constitutional procedural system of de jure human rights protection can only motivate the government to fulfill its responsibility to guarantee human rights partially, but not fully. Therefore, in the absence of a constitutional litigation system, because the right to sue is restricted by the system, the legal reality of human rights in law is seriously flawed, and the legal protection of human rights is ineffective."[58] It can be seen that the establishment of the constitutional remedy system has ultimate significance in guaranteeing the realization of citizens' basic rights. "The entry of the constitution into litigation is the bottleneck and the final difficulty for the ultimate realization of the rule of law, and the touchstone of whether the rule of law can be realized. If the Constitution does not enter litigation, it means that we still have these fundamental issues that are vital

[56] Zhou [42].

[57] Cheng and Wang [43].

[58] Mo [36].

to China to be solved by 'illegal' means in a disorderly state."[59] Incorporating the equal rights of vulnerable groups into the track of constitutional remedies is the only way to effectively guarantee their rights and ensure real protection for these groups at the constitutional level.

The violation of the right to equality as a fundamental constitutional right to socially vulnerable groups has the following characteristics: the violation of the right to equality of socially vulnerable groups is based on a normative document that violates the constitutional principle of equality. In other words, the concrete infringement of the right to equality against the socially vulnerable groups is premised on abstract infringement. Therefore, the constitutionality of normative documents must be examined in the process of examining specific cases. This is what distinguishes constitutional litigation from ordinary litigation. Constitutional litigation cases are "the unconstitutionality of abstract administrative acts prosecuting the government", and "constitutional litigation is usually not a matter between two citizens, it generally refers to the relationship between state organs and citizens". At present, there are three most typical constitutional litigation cases in which the rights of vulnerable groups in society have been violated: first, the "Qingdao Three Examination Students Sued the Ministry of Education for Infringement of Their Equal Right to Education".[60]The essence of the case is a lawsuit by plaintiffs Wang Yulun and Li Erxian against the village committee of Vegetable Village in Wujin Town for violating their right to equality in the distribution of collective economic benefits, which should also be considered as a constitutional litigation case; The second is "the case of plaintiffs Li Xianbin and Chen Xiaofang v. Zhejiang Provincial Health and Family

---

[59] Wang [44].

[60] On August 22, 2001, three fresh high school graduates from Shandong Qingdao named Jiang Yan, Luan Qian, and Zhang Tianzhuyin filed an administrative complaint with the Supreme People's Court in Beijing. Accompanied by a lawyer, they argued that the Ministry of Education violated citizens' equal right to education through its administrative act of the National General College Education Enrollment Plan for the year 2001. The admission score line in Qingdao was much higher than the score line in Beijing and other regions, which led to unequal opportunities for students in different geographical scopes. In their cause of action, they stated that according to the Constitution of the People's Republic of China, citizens have an equal right to education. The Ministry of National Education's formulation of the enrollment plan resulted in unequal treatment of candidates in different regions of the country, violating citizens' equal right to education. In summary, the Ministry of Education's action violated the equal right to education of the majority of candidates. See Complaints against the Ministry of Education for Violations of the Right to Equal Education Qingdao Candidates Enter Beijing to Submit Complaint. Hebei Daily, 2001-08-23; Qingdao Graduates Plan to Sue Ministry of Education Over Alleged Score Line Discrimination, Qilu Evening News, 2001-08-22.

As China lacks a constitutional litigation system, this case was filed as an administrative lawsuit. However, China's Administrative Procedure Law currently does not include abstract administrative acts of administrative organs within its scope, even though provisions for reviewing such acts exist in the Legislation Act. As there is no supporting system, China's practice in this area remains weak and confusing.

Planning Commission".[61] The essence of the case was a lawsuit against unconstitutional village rules and people's covenants, and the court ultimately supported the plaintiff's claim based on the constitutional principle of equality between men and women, namely the right to equality[62]; The third case is "Jiang Tao v. People's Bank of China Chengdu Branch," filed by a student from Sichuan University Law School. The essence of the case is a lawsuit against bank job postings that discriminate against highly disadvantaged groups, in order to fight for equal labor and employment rights.

Since there is no constitutional remedy system in China, these cases have been brought in the form of administrative or civil litigation. Currently, in China, the main obstacles to constitutional litigation come from two aspects. The first is the understanding of the nature of constitutional fundamental rights. Traditionally, the primary purpose of the provisions of the basic rights of the Constitution is to ensure that the scope of the right to individual liberty is not violated by the power of the state. Fundamental rights are negative rights, rights of defense against the State, and therefore do not apply in civil relations between private individuals. In other words, the fundamental rights enshrined in the Constitution are not justiciable in civil relations. However, in recent years, due to changes in the social structure, groups and individuals with strong economic power in industrial society have overwhelmingly violated the basic rights of the Constitution over other disadvantaged private individuals. This seriously threatens the human dignity of vulnerable groups in society. Holding on to traditional theories will inevitably lead to blind spots in the relief of some situations that infringe on vulnerable groups in society.

The second obstacle is that there are some inherent drawbacks in China's litigation system. In cases of infringement of the right to equality, most of the infringing subjects are administrative subjects. The modern government no longer plays the role of a passive night watchman, but has an active obligation to promote economic development and social welfare. The activities of administrative subjects involve

[61] In the case in question, the village committee of Wujin Town, Xinjin County, Sichuan Province had formulated rules and regulations stipulating that any woman who married someone from outside the village had to move out of her hukou. Failure to do so meant that she would not be entitled to all the benefits enjoyed by the villagers. After the plaintiff got married, she did not move her hukou to her husband's place of residence. When land transfer fees were allocated, other villagers in the village received equal shares of the fee as per the village's rules and regulations. However, the village refused to pay the plaintiff compensation for the land transfer. Not satisfied with the decision, the plaintiff filed a lawsuit in the people's court. In the absence of relevant legal provisions, the court relied on the constitutional provisions relating to the equal right of men and women to equality as the basis for adjudicating the legal effect of unconstitutional acts involved in litigation. The court observed that village agreements are civil agreements and therefore should be constitutional. The clause in question requiring women to remove their hukou after marriage was discriminatory and contrary to the constitutional principle of equality between men and women, and hence invalid.

[62] The People's Bank of China Chengdu Branch has a job posting that states "Male height must be 1.68 m or taller, and female height must be 1.55 m or taller." As a result, Jiang Tao, a law student at Sichuan University, who is only 1.65 m tall, was excluded from the application process. Jiang Tao believes that the bank's specific administrative act of height requirements for national civil servant recruitment constitutes "height discrimination" and violates his equal rights and political rights to serve as an employee of a state organ in accordance with the law. On January 7, 2001, he filed a petition and took the People's Bank of China Chengdu Branch to court.

every corner of society and are related to the realization of everyone's economic and social rights. China has not established a constitutional litigation system, and in the current litigation system, only administrative litigation is the only way to accept disputes between administrative subjects and citizens. Therefore, filing an administrative lawsuit has become a helpless option for people to protect their right to equality. However, at present, China's administrative litigation has great limitations and cannot effectively protect the basic rights of citizens. The scope of review of China's current Administrative Procedure Law is very limited. The court's review is limited to the specific administrative acts of administrative subjects and a very small number of abstract administrative acts. In fact, what is closely related to the basic rights of citizens, except for a few specific administrative acts made against specific people or specific facts, are more generally binding normative documents formulated by administrative subjects. Moreover, the abstract administrative acts of administrative subjects violate the Constitution, and the damage caused to citizens' right to equality is often institutional, and the consequences are more serious. Therefore, the establishment of a constitutional remedy system is imperative.

Currently, there are three different forms of constitutional remedies for rights worldwide, namely judicial review, constitutional court review, and constitutional council review. Among them, judicial review has the most extensive impact, as it involves the examination of the right to constitutional remedies by ordinary courts through constitutional litigation in specific cases. Constitutional court review, on the other hand, can only be carried out through the litigation of specific cases and cannot be used to review the law on its own initiative in isolation from specific cases. Only the parties concerned can bring constitutional proceedings. The peculiarity of the Constitutional Court is that its rights and remedies sometimes go beyond the rights and obligations disputed by the litigants to conduct abstract reviews of the constitutionality of the law. The judge has the power to review the relevant legal provisions that the complainant did not object to in the proceedings. The Constitutional Council review exists mainly in France, which has a well-developed administrative court system, and it itself has the color of judicial review. A large number of constitutional remedies in France have been integrated into the remedies system of the ordinary and administrative courts, so the scope of the Constitutional Council's review is quite limited.[63]

The various styles of constitutional remedies used around the world can provide valuable experience for us to reference. However, given the current situation in China, the most important thing is to establish the prerequisites for a constitutional remedy system based on our actual circumstances. Firstly, it is necessary to readjust and improve China's current power distribution and restraint mechanisms. This includes granting the judicial organs greater authority to supervise legislation and administrative power, and especially giving courts the power to review laws, regulations, and rules for unconstitutionality. Secondly, the citizens' right to sue should be elevated to a constitutional right. By elevating the citizen's right to sue from a general right

[63] For a more detailed discussion, see Cheng and Wang [43].

to a constitutional right of appeal, the openness of citizens' right to sue can be guaranteed.[64] Because 'if there is a field that cannot be the object of litigation, then the law lacks authority in the ultimate sense,' modern justice requires that the right of action be open, allowing all legal problems that cannot be solved by ordinary judicial systems to find the ultimate legal path in the constitutional judicial system.[65]

In short, the right to equality occupies the status of a fundamental right in the constitution because of its own generality and formality, and the right to equality of socially vulnerable groups is the mother of the rights of such groups. The right to equality can only be guaranteed if it is finally implemented in the judiciary. The establishment of China's constitutional remedy system will be a major milestone in the protection of equal rights for vulnerable groups in society.

4.3.2 The Justiciability of the Social Rights of Socially Vulnerable Groups

As mentioned above, the right to equality can be combined with the right to freedom and social rights, providing protection for citizens' rights through equality, freedom, and society. In this process, the State's obligation is to ensure citizens' equal rights to freedom and social rights, and a violation of this obligation breaks or violates the equal relationship between citizens. It is often the rights of socially vulnerable groups that are sacrificed in these violations, making the right to equality a talisman for these groups. The implementation of constitutional remedies for the right to equality of vulnerable groups in society ultimately guarantees their right to equality. While paying attention to the equal social rights of the socially vulnerable groups, the significance of the social rights of the socially disadvantaged groups themselves to the socially vulnerable groups cannot be ignored. Social rights differ from freedom rights in that they mainly require the State to ensure the realization of citizens' rights through positive obligations. When the State violates this obligation through omission, it is a significant infringement on the interests of vulnerable groups in society. If the State's violation of the obligation to guarantee equal social rights leads to an imbalance in the relationship between the powerful and the weak, then the violation of social rights and obligations directly infringes on the interests of vulnerable groups. Therefore, can vulnerable groups in society seek redress through judicial channels for violations of their rights resulting from the State's inaction? There has always been considerable controversy over the nature of social rights and the justiciability of social rights. We believe that any right can only be guaranteed ultimately if it can enter the judicial process, and that the social rights of socially vulnerable groups should be justiciable.

---

[64] See Zhu [45].

[65] Mo [36].

(1) The theory of the effectiveness of social rights for socially vulnerable groups

The effectiveness of the social rights of socially vulnerable groups determines the nature of state obligations. The nature of state obligations, in turn, determines the form of state obligations, which naturally leads to the form of violation of state obligations. The violation of state obligations also causes infringement of the social rights of socially vulnerable groups, and as a result, vulnerable groups in society seek remedies for their rights. It is along these lines that the following discussion will advance layer by layer.

We know that citizens have four positions within the state, which, in turn, form four relationships with the state. They are: a. passive status, that is, citizens are in a position of obedience to the power of the state, and the relationship between citizens and the state is the relationship of obedience of citizens to the state; b. negative status, that is, individuals enjoy freedom from the interference or encroachment of the public power of the state, and the relationship between citizens and the state is the relationship of citizen resistance to the state. In this relationship, citizens are in a negative position, gaining the right to various forms of freedom; c. active status, that is, citizens actively participate in the exercise of state power, the formation of state opinions, and the formation of citizens' decision-making relationship with the state between citizens and the state; d. positive status, that is, citizens demand that the state should do certain things, obtain specific benefits through the fulfillment of state obligations, and form a relationship between citizens and the state to request the state.[66]

This analysis of the relationship between the state and citizens paves the way for determining the nature of rights. The social rights of socially vulnerable groups place citizens in an active position, and the realization of these social rights depends on the fulfillment of positive obligations by the state. With regard to social rights, all countries have made principled provisions in their constitutions, forming complex theories on the nature of social rights. German scholars have put forward four theories: First, it is regarded as a "policy clause," which means that the social rights stipulated in the constitution are only guidelines for future legislation, and the process of legalizing social rights is left to future legislation. The political and moral significance of social rights in the constitution is greater than the legal significance. Second, it is regarded as "constitutional delegation," which means that the constitution is only a principled provision in its provisions and entrusts the specific and detailed acts of other state organs to implement it. The legislator obtains a legislative mandate through the social rights clause of the Constitution. The constitutional mandate is different from the policy clause, the former having the binding force of law, and if the legislator legislates against the social rights clause, it will have unconstitutional consequences. Third, it is regarded as an "institutional guarantee," which regards social rights as an institutional guarantee of the Constitution, and if the legislator

[66] See Xu [25], p. 575.

violates the basic content and purpose of these systems in the future, these laws will constitute unconstitutionality. Fourth, it is regarded as a "public law right." This is the most radical theory. According to this theory, social rights are public law rights granted to the people by the constitution, and citizens can request redress from the court when they are infringed, just like fundamental rights such as freedom, which have direct and coercive effect.[67] The theory of the effectiveness of social rights in Japanese academic circles was deeply influenced by German theory and formed the theory of programmatic, abstract rights, concrete rights, and legal rights. The Programmatic theory denies the justiciability of social rights, arguing that social rights are not specific rights under private law but merely proclaim the political and moral obligations of the State. "It is not conferred a specific right of claim, nor is the State conferred on a specific obligation corresponding to it, so that a national cannot obtain a remedy by litigation when the practical measures do not in substance confer such a right on the individual national." "Even if the legislation and facilities are not sufficient from the perspective of the realization of the right to life, it cannot be claimed through the courts that this is unconstitutional but can only be improved by means of a political nature as a matter of legislative policy."[68] The "abstract rights theory" proposes that social rights are legal rights, at least in the constitutional sense, and the government has an obligation to protect this right. Citizens can request the legislature to implement legislation to protect this right or request the executive to take relevant administrative measures to protect this right, making the State obliged to legislate and adopt administrative measures to protect the social rights of its citizens. Nationals have the right vis-à-vis the State to require it to take legislative and other measures. However, this right cannot be directly used as the basis for a trial. "In the absence of such legislation, citizens cannot use this provision as a basis for litigation to assert specific rights."[69] The "theory of concrete rights" holds that social rights are specific claims of citizens to the state. Citizens can request the active operation of public powers, such as legislative and judicial powers of the state, to fully guarantee the realization of this right. The state has direct constitutional obligations to protect social rights. If the legislature fails to enact legislation to protect social rights and the executive does not take necessary measures to protect these rights, it quickly constitutes a violation of constitutional obligations. In such cases, an aggrieved citizen can claim tortious legal liability for the state's omission. At this point, the judiciary has an obligation to exercise judicial remedies to protect constitutional rights provisions. Through judicial review and other means, the judiciary can eliminate the infringement of the state's omission or insufficient legislation in protecting citizens' rights.[70]

From the perspective of the practice of various countries, with the "constitutional mandate" and "abstract rights theory" as the mainstream, it cannot be said that the content of the constitution is empty, nor can it be considered that all rights are

[67] For a related discussion, see Gong [46].

[68] Ito [47]. Quote from: Ito [27].

[69] Kiminori [48]. Quote from: Wang [27].

[70] For a related discussion, see Wang [27]. Gong [46].

embodied in the law. On the contrary, it should be said that everything is laid down in the Constitution, and the law only reflects the contents of the Constitution in greater detail.[71] Since national legislation now recognizes the positive obligations of states to guarantee the realization of social rights, we will further explore the specific content of states' obligations and the forms of breach of obligations.

(2) State obligations corresponding to the social rights of socially vulnerable groups

The obligations of the State are primarily legislative and administrative. The legislative obligation of the legislature is a behavioral obligation, and the legislator respects and protects the realization of civil society's rights by enacting laws. Legislation is an indispensable element in many areas, such as anti-discrimination, education, and so on. Many human rights conventions stipulate that legislation is the most important measure to protect the rights of vulnerable groups in society.

For example, Article 2, paragraph 1, of the International Covenant on Economic, Social and Cultural Rights sets out the nature of the legal obligations assumed by States parties, which include obligations of conduct as well as obligations of result. One of the most important of the obligations to conduct is the obligation to "take steps" under the article, the means used to fulfill the obligation to take steps, i.e. "by all appropriate means, including, in particular, by legislative means" provided for in the article. "Legislation is a prerequisite means to protect the rights of vulnerable groups in society, and only through legislation can the obligations of the state be clarified and stereotyped, and the normative prerequisites for the implementation of the specific positive obligations of the state can be established."

Unlike the right to freedom, which delineates areas in which state power cannot intervene, the rights groups of socially vulnerable groups with social rights as the main body require a clear delineation of the scope of obligations that the state must fulfill, which can only be clarified through legislation. At the same time, only through legislation can the objective rights of subjects be transformed into subjective rights. "Objective rights are the sum of all legal norms, the basis for legal obligations and their corresponding subjective rights."[72] Objective rights are guaranteed by the constitutional state but do not give the holders of basic rights the right to claim guarantees. Citizens must have subjective rights in order to make claims to the State for the protection of their fundamental rights. "Subjective rights are a concept in general jurisprudence that refers to the power conferred on individuals by legal norms, namely, the right to demand that others do or refrain from doing certain acts, to tolerate or refrain from certain actions in order to realize personal rights and interests."[73] That is, "a right of the individual in society". Through legislation, the vulnerable groups in society can obtain subjective rights, so that the realization of the rights of the vulnerable groups in society has truly gained backing and guarantees.

The rights of socially vulnerable groups need to be actively promoted by the state to be realized, which is consistent with the initiative and initiative of the exercise of

---

[71] Quoted from Gong [46].

[72] Quoted from Gong [46].

[73] Quoted from Gong [46].

administrative power, and determines that the most important path for realizing the rights of vulnerable groups in society is the active exercise of state administrative power, without the law enforcement guarantee of state administrative power The realization of the rights of socially vulnerable groups is impossible. Administrative measures to ensure the realization of the rights of vulnerable groups in society take a variety of forms, which can be summarized into two categories: one is administrative legislative measures that formulate and issue generally binding rules for the implementation of laws; The other category is administrative law enforcement measures that take specific actions for the implementation of laws and administrative regulations and rules. Among them, the adoption of administrative law enforcement measures is the core link in the protection and operation of the rights of vulnerable groups in society, and is the most direct guarantee for the realization of the rights of vulnerable groups in society. The most powerful and effective safeguard measures for the protection of social rights include measures for the management of state funds, measures for the allocation of resources, and measures for the planning and management of economic, social and cultural undertakings.

(3) Exploration of the forms of violations of state obligations and remedies

The obligation of the state, which corresponds to social rights, is a positive duty. Therefore, the passive omission of the state constitutes a breach of its obligation. Most of the basic rights guaranteed by the constitution are norms that establish the freedom of the state to demand certain inactions. Therefore, human rights violations caused by the active actions of the state have actually become the majority of human rights violations. In fact, this has become the mainstream of human rights theory.[74] The most fundamental breakthrough in modern human rights law theory, as compared with modern human rights law, lies in the development of a system of "human rights that can be violated by inaction." "Inaction" does not mean "doing nothing," but rather "not doing what is required," that is, failing to carry out the desired action.[75] The term "omission" here mainly refers to the violation of the law by the obligee, i.e., the public power of the state, who refuses to perform certain acts, resulting in the violation of basic human rights. The infringement of omissions can often only be another type of human right corresponding to the traditional system of freedom rights, namely economic, social, and cultural rights. This is mainly manifested in social rights such as the right to subsistence.

The violation of state obligations can be manifested in two aspects. First, in the legislative aspect, which is characterized by negative or insufficient legislation by the legislature. Second, in the administrative aspect, which is manifested in the passive administration of administrative organs. The so-called negative legislation, or legislative inaction, means that the legislature has the obligation to enact laws and implement the Constitution in accordance with the constitutional entrustment clause. If the legislature does not actively enact laws, or does not completely enact laws, it constitutes legislative inaction. Scholars in Taiwan call it "legislative laziness."

[74] Osuka [49].

[75] Quote from Wang [27].

In short, legislative inaction means that the legislator has not carried out the act of further concretizing the provisions of fundamental rights through law. Inadequate legislation means that although there is a legislative act, it is insufficient, which also constitutes a breach of the state's obligations. Positive infringement by administrative organs is often manifested in discrimination against vulnerable groups in society, and passive administration refers to the failure of administrative organs to fulfill their positive obligations to take necessary administrative measures as stipulated by the Constitution or laws. Effective remedies should be sought for violations of state obligations in these two areas, i.e., in both forms of violations of the rights of vulnerable groups.

Negative legislation and inadequate legislation should be remedied through an unconstitutional review system. Although this type of judicial initiative is still extremely limited in the legal practice of various countries, there are already precedents and practices in this regard.[76] For the negative administration of administrative organs, it is natural to solve it through administrative litigation.

5 The Limits of the Protection of the Rights of Vulnerable Groups in Society

Discrimination against socially vulnerable groups has been rejected in practice because it is contrary to constitutional equal treatment provisions and the concept of social justice. However, can the protection of the rights of socially vulnerable groups be unlimited? In fact, the protection of the rights of vulnerable groups in society has already faced the challenge of "reverse discrimination." Therefore, the protection of the rights of vulnerable groups in society should be limited to reasonable bounds.

---

[76] The Basic Law of the Federal Republic of Germany, Article 12, stipulates that "everyone has the right to develop his or her personality freely." Article 3 further states "equality before the law." One of the embodiments of this entity content is found in the first section, Article 6, which clearly states that "legislation shall provide children born out of wedlock with the same opportunities for physical and mental development and the same social status as children born in wedlock." Thus, the Constitution provides for the right to free physical and mental development in two ways: On the one hand, the right to free physical and mental development is recognized in substance for everyone on an equal basis. No one shall be "discriminated against or favored" in relation to this right. The equal enjoyment of the right to free development of children born out of wedlock is a compulsory and guaranteed right by law. On the other hand, procedurally establishing legislation with constitutional obligations on the equal development of children born out of wedlock is necessary. The legislative process must provide sufficient norms of equal protection so that the right has a legal basis and legal safeguards. This is clearly an obligation of the legislature to carry out the relevant legislative acts. Failure to comply with this legislative obligation constitutes a constitutional violation of legislative omission. At this time, the use of constitutional proceedings is the most effective way to hold accountable for legislative inaction to ensure that violated rights are restored. See Xige [9].

5.1 Appropriateness of Protection of the Rights of Socially Vulnerable Groups

In 1945, a man named Sweet applied to the University of Texas Law School but was not admitted because state law stipulated that only whites could enter law school. The Supreme Court declared that the law violated Sweet's rights under the 14th Amendment to the U.S. Constitution, which stated that states could not deny equal legal protection to anyone.[77] By continuing to move forward on the basis of opposing discrimination and treating vulnerable groups equally, we have developed to give special treatment to vulnerable groups beyond equal treatment under the guidance of certain social goals. However, this raises the issue of reverse discrimination in practice. In 1971, a Jew named DeFunis applied to the University of Washington School of Law. His test scores and college entrance scores were enough to get him admitted, but he was rejected. DeFunis asked the Supreme Court to declare that the University of Washington's lowering of standards for minority students violated his rights under the 14th Amendment.[78] Coincidentally, in 1978, the Barker v. University of California Board of Regents case once again took aim at reverse discrimination. Barker applied to join the University of California School of Medicine, which reserved six places for students from minority backgrounds. Barker did not meet the generally prescribed admission threshold, but he found that some minority students admitted with the reserved places did not perform as well as him. He then sued the school's admissions policy for violating rights protected by the principle of equal legal protection under the 14th Amendment to the Constitution and constituting reverse discrimination against whites.[79] The end result of the DeFonnis case was that he was admitted to law school after a lower court ruled in his favor, and the case ended up being treated as moot. Judge Douglas, however, disagreed with the decision, holding that the Supreme Court should have ruled on DeFonnis' claim on the merits. Many foresaw that in the future, the Supreme Court would be dominated by Justice Douglas's opinion, thus changing the practice.[80] Sure enough, in Barker, the Supreme Court ruled 5:4 in favor of the school. Judge Powell held that the practice of reserving seats for minority candidates "should directly be judged invalid." The mere fact of favoring any racial or ethnic group, without more, cannot justify a racial classification.[81]

Can the arguments in favor of the first case be equally applied to the second and third cases? Does the special protection of the rights of socially vulnerable groups constitute reverse discrimination against others? We need to justify the special protection of the rights of vulnerable groups in society. At the same time, special protection

---

[77] See Dworkin [21].

[78] See Dworkin [21].

[79] See Wang [50].

[80] See Dworkin [21].

[81] Quoted from Qiu [51].

for the rights of vulnerable groups in society cannot be unlimited, otherwise it may lead to reverse discrimination against others and have a negative impact on society.

Special protection of the rights of socially vulnerable groups is preferential and prioritized, which presupposes a special status. In practice, the implementation of this policy poses two main difficulties: First, the policy may "place other 'innocent' individuals at a disadvantage, violating the principles of merit and fault" and these 'innocent' individuals may demand equal treatment. The second difficulty is examining the criteria for preferential policies, that is, whether such policies meet the principle of appropriateness between the objectives they wish to achieve and the means used.[82] Thus, "the justification of special protection measures depends objectively on revealing institutionalized discrimination and its effects in the history or reality of human society, while at the micro level examines the appropriateness of the objectives and methods of the specific measures themselves".[83] Therefore, the review of the legitimacy of special protection measures for vulnerable groups in society is mainly carried out from two aspects: first, it examines the application of the principle of performance and fault; The second is the appropriate balance between the goals and means of preferential policies.

5.1.1 Restrictive Application of the Principles of Performance and Fault

"The adverse effects on 'innocent' victims as a result of preferential policies is a complex issue. Based on an individualistic philosophy, the principle of performance requires that each person should be treated and rewarded only for their personal abilities, and the principle of fault requires that everyone should be held accountable only for their own actions and not for the actions of others. Therefore, individuals should not pay the price or be liable for social and historical acts that harm others."[84] The principle of performance and fault is one-sided because it rejects social and historical considerations based on a thoroughly individualistic philosophy. The principle of performance is not as objective as it might seem, as discrimination is not just the result of individual fault. The standards of individual performance and behavior are deeply rooted in the fabric of society and the continuity of history.[85] Important studies on social discrimination now show that discrimination is not only the attitudes and behavior of individuals, but also a social phenomenon embedded in the fabric of society. Knowles and Prewitt made a classic analysis of racism as institutionalized discrimination. Their research found that when an individual appears as racist, he or she is usually not required to make choices about his or her possible ways of behaving, and that the rules and procedures of social organization already structure the individual's choices. The individual only needs to obey the rules of operation of this social organization, and the system itself will practice this discrimination

[82] Zhou [22].

[83] Zhou [22].

[84] Zhou [22].

[85] Zhou [22].

on their behalf.[86] The perspective of institutionalized discrimination has led to a reflection on the objectivity of performance standards and the fairness of the principle of individual fault. Everyone in society lives in the three-dimensional world of the past, present, and future, and each generation enters this existing society as a continuation of the past at some point in time, with the identity of their group and a specific social status. The vulnerable groups of every society and their members are exploited, discriminated against, and marginalized in certain aspects of social life, and are denied opportunities for full development. Since the life opportunities of individuals are distorted by institutionalized discrimination, the principle of pure performance operates on the basis of the institutionalized exclusion of vulnerable groups in society.[87]

The formation of socially vulnerable groups and social discrimination against them are structural and historical. Special protection measures for vulnerable groups can also be seen as redress for injustice. Even Nozick admits that 'although the introduction of socialism as punishment for our sins has gone too far, the injustices of the past may have been so severe that a more functional state aimed at correcting them was necessary in the short term.'[88] Therefore, the principle of performance and fault has its own temporal and spatial conditions for application, and cannot be universally explained as an absolute standard. Special protection measures for vulnerable groups in society are justified wherever there is structural and institutionalized discrimination in society. All kinds of discrimination have historical and cultural continuity, and a reasonable degree of special protection measures are only the correction of previous inequalities and do not constitute 'reverse discrimination.' Although the pursuit of greater equality in society as a whole disadvantages the rights of certain members of society, as Dworkin points out in his commentary on the De Fonnis case, 'In some cases, a policy that disadvantages many people because it makes society as a whole better off is reasonable.' Dworkin objected to treating 'discrimination' in the first, second, and third cases as equal.[89] The arguments in favor of an admissions policy that discriminates against Blacks are all utilitarian views. This violates the constitutional right of Blacks to be treated as equal individuals. The idea of supporting an admissions policy that positively discriminates against Blacks is both utilitarian and idealistic.[90] The situation is better in the utilitarian sense, that is, although the welfare of some people has declined, the level of welfare of the whole society has improved, either on an average or collective basis.[91] Ideal things get better, that is, because society is fairer, or in some other way closer to an ideal society, regardless of whether the average welfare of society has improved.[92] Although the citizens of a society tend to

[86] Knowles and Prewitt [52]. Quoted in Zhou [22].
[87] Zhou [22].
[88] Quoted from Yao [53].
[89] See Dworkin [21].
[90] See Dworkin [21].
[91] See Dworkin [21].
[92] See Dworkin [21].

be unequal, a more egalitarian society is a better society. Such a view does not deny the right of any person to be treated as an equal individual.[93]

5.1.2 Trade-Offs of the Appropriateness of Ends and Means

In order to achieve substantive equality, special protection for socially vulnerable groups can be achieved either by enhancing the capacity of their target groups or individuals to participate in fair competition and ensuring equality of opportunity, or by directly pursuing equality of outcome. But whatever measures are taken must have a legitimate purpose, as discussed above, and the means chosen to achieve that end must be appropriate. The justification of special measures to protect the rights of vulnerable groups in society lies in the consideration of the appropriateness of ends and means when implementing such policies. In general, it can be divided into two steps. First, consider the controversial objective and decide whether it is so important that the constitutionally protected right should be limited to ensure its achievement. Secondly, consider whether the choice of means to achieve this end is necessary and appropriate in a free and democratic society.[94]

The necessity and appropriateness of means are also essential aspects to consider when determining the legitimacy of special protection measures. Sometimes the purpose may be legitimate, but the means may not be appropriate, leading to the violation of the rights of others and contradicting the original purpose of special protection. In the Barker case, Judge Powell held that the vital interest of the nation lay in having a multiracial student body. While he agreed that university admissions policies could take into account the ethnic background of applicants, he found the additional reservation of places to achieve that goal to be inappropriate. He suggested that the race factor should be considered as an "additional" factor in conjunction with other qualification characteristics. Similarly, in recent years, the welfare system has been a growing concern. The more welfare that is provided, the greater the possibility of moral hazards and fraud. The level at which welfare is maintained has always been the subject of welfare economics research. Economist Arthur Lindbeck, who conducts research in the context of the Swedish welfare system, points out that from a humanitarian standpoint, the state has an obligation to provide generous assistance to people affected by unemployment, illness, disability, or other risks covered by the welfare system. However, a dilemma arises: the more welfare relief the state provides, the greater the likelihood of moral hazards and fraud. He believes that moral hazards will be worse in the long run than in the short term. This is because social habits are formed over time, and people define what is considered 'normal.' Heavy reliance on welfare benefits is no longer viewed as dependence but becomes 'expected' behavior. The consequences of this situation include an increasing number of people applying

---

93 See Dworkin [21].

94 Zhou [22].

for social assistance, a growing number of people not going to work under the pretext of health reasons, and fewer and fewer people actively seeking work opportunities.[95]

5.2 *Guidelines for the Protection of the Rights of Vulnerable Groups in Society*

According to the analysis above, the legitimacy of special protection for the rights of vulnerable groups in society has become a strong voice. However, the special protection of the rights of vulnerable groups in society must have certain boundaries, otherwise it will cause endless harm. Special protection of the rights of socially vulnerable groups should be limited to the following general principles: First, the principle of rational delineation of the scope of socially vulnerable groups. The objects of explicit protection should be limited to specific groups that have been chronically disadvantaged in society as a result of prejudice, discrimination, and denial of rights, and should not be expanded or narrowed. At present, the main problem is the narrowing of the object of protection. Many people who should be protected cannot be protected, such as AIDS patients, children born out of wedlock, homosexuals, dwarfs, and other vulnerable groups. Second, the principle of compatibility of means with ends. Special protection should be treated differently according to the characteristics of different groups. Each type of vulnerable group has unique characteristics of vulnerability that are different from other vulnerable groups. Therefore, special protection of the rights of vulnerable groups should be targeted towards the unique characteristics of each group. For example, children's right to healthy growth is emphasized, disabled persons' right to education and employment, women's right to political participation and education, and ethnic minorities' freedom of religious belief is emphasized. The principle of "same treatment in the same situation" is not complete in itself, and until it is supplemented, it does not guide behavior with certainty. "'Same as in the same situation' must retain a space. In order to fill this space, we must know when the situation in question should be considered homogeneous for the purposes of the present what difference makes sense." It is an indisputable fact that there are both similarities and differences between people.[96] Equal treatment under the law must first determine the purpose of the granted right, and then compare similarities and differences based on that purpose. If similarities prevail over differences, then equal treatment should be given. If differences prevail over similarities, then differences should be used as the standard to treat rights differently. Discrimination in rights based on purpose and difference is reasonable. Thirdly, the principle of "proportionality" in the degree of protection should be applied. The special protection of the rights of vulnerable groups in society should be based on fairness, reasonableness, and objectivity. The positive protection received should be commensurate with their circumstances. The theory of the British scholar Milne provides us with useful references. Milne summarized

[95] Giddens [54].

[96] Hart [55].

the principle of "proportional equality" based on Aristotle's theory of "fairness." This means that (a) if treatment is appropriate in a particular context, then all cases that are equal in the particular aspect to which the treatment relates must be treated equally; (b) all cases in which the particular aspect to which the treatment is not equal must be treated unequally; and (c) the relative inequality of treatment must be proportional to the relative difference in the situation.[97] Milne also pointed out that "proportional equality allows for the giving of disadvantage to the superior and preferential treatment to the inferior, so that competitors of unequal ability are given equal opportunities, but this disadvantage must be given fairly." In other words, "it must be proportional to the unequal capabilities of competitors."[98]

6 Conclusion

China's vulnerable groups not only face the common problems of vulnerable groups around the world but also have unique problems that stem from the current historical situation in China. To analyze the plight of vulnerable groups' rights situation in China, we must identify the deep social causes that have led to this situation. Based on this, we must reflect on cultural, institutional, and other aspects. Improving the rights of vulnerable groups in contemporary China is a systematic project and requires an all-round transformation of the whole society, from concept to system, from legislation to law enforcement and justice.

At the conceptual level, we should establish the idea that human beings are ends, and all human beings' rights are equally respected. In the reform of the economic system, we should learn the principle of "Pareto optimality," which means that some people's situation can be better without making the situation of others worse. At the institutional level, we should improve the current human rights protection mechanism, ensure the smooth expression of the rights of vulnerable groups in society through due process, and ensure the realization of the rights of vulnerable groups in society by actively implementing state obligations. Through the establishment of a constitutional litigation system, we can open the door to remedies for the rights of vulnerable groups in society, among other measures.

Gradually dissolving the weak status of socially vulnerable groups and eventually reducing or even eliminating them is the value ideal of any modern civilized society. Although we have not yet achieved this ideal, we have enough reason and confidence to aspire to it. This reason and confidence come from our faith in rights, our faith in human reason, and our faith in our human nature for good.

Protecting the rights of vulnerable groups in society is the result of advocating rights, pursuing a good social system, and building a harmonious and beautiful society under the guidance of the human "kind" complex. Protecting the rights of vulnerable

---

97 Milne [56].

98 Milne [56].

groups in society means equal respect for everyone's dignity as an independent individual, allowing everyone in society to share the sunshine of justice.

References

1. Zhou, Q. (2000). Legal guarantee of farmers' right to equality. *Law and Business Studies, 2.*
2. Lenski, G. E. (1988). *Power and privilege: A theory of social stratification* (G. Xinping, Trans., pp. 103–104). Zhejiang People's Publishing House.
3. Ye, J., & Wei, Q. (2004). Research on several legal issues of discrimination in health employment. *Human Rights, 3*, 43.
4. Shen, Z., & Huang, F. (Eds.). (1994). *Western doctrine of human rights (Part II)* (p. 282). Sichuan People's Publishing House.
5. Kiyonomiya, H. (1986). *Constitution I* (p. 22). Yuhikaku Publishing.
6. Tagami, J. (1984). *Constitutional matters* (p. 105). Qinglin Academy News Agency.
7. Hui, W. (2003). *Study on the inclusion of the right to education in the constitution* (p. 102). Peking University Press.
8. Akira, O. (2001). *The right to survival.* Hao, L. (trans.) (p. 36). Law Press.
9. Xigen, W. (2002). *Basic human rights in a society under the rule of law: A study on the legal system of the right to development* (p. 60). Chinese Public Security University Press.
10. Xiangfei, Q. (2001). Human rights subjectivity. In X. Xianming (Ed.), *Human rights studies (vol. 1)* (pp. 36–37). Shandong People's Publishing House.
11. Hegel, G. W. F. (1983). *Phenomenology of spirit* (p. 2). Commercial Press.
12. Qu, X. (2001). Human rights subjectivity. In X. Xianming (Ed.), *Human rights studies* (Vol. 1, p. 51). Shandong People's Publishing House.
13. Sun, G. (Ed.). (1993). *Human rights: The ruler towards freedom* (p. 60). Shandong People's Publishing House.
14. Rand, A. (1993). *The moral basis of individualism* (Q. Yu, Trans., pp. 100–101). Shanghai Sanlian Bookstore.
15. Maine, H. (1959). *Ancient law: Its connection with the early history of society, and its relation to modern ideas* (Shen Jingyi, Trans., p. 97). Commercial Press.
16. Zheng, C. (1991). Rights-based theory. *Chinese Law, 1*, 32.
17. Li, C., & Feng, X. (2001). Equality of minority rights and their protection. *Modern Jurisprudence, 10*, 18.
18. Donnelly, J. (2001). *Universal human rights in theory and practice.* Wang P. (trans.) (p. 4). China Social Science Publishing House.
19. Zhang, W. (2001). *Studies in the scope of philosophy of law (revised version)* (p. 366). China University of Political Science and Law Press.
20. Dong, Y., & Liu, W. (Eds.). (1991). Overview of the universal covenants on human rights (p. 75). Sichuan People's Publishing House.
21. Dworkin, R. (1998). Take rights seriously (pp. 3–4). Xin C. & Wu Y. (trans.). China Encyclopedia Publishing House.
22. Zhou, Y. (2002). *Jurisprudence of minority rights: International judicial protection of the rights of national, religious and linguistic minorities and their members* (p. 29). Social Science Literature Publishers.
23. Friedrich, C.J. (1997). *Transcendent justice: The religious dimension of constitutionalism* (Y. Zhou, Trans.) (pp. 94–95). Life·Study·New Knowledge Triple Bookstore.
24. Henkin, L. (1997). The age of rights (p. 189). (X. Chunying, Y. Wu, & L. Lin, Trans.). Knowledge Press.
25. Xu, X. (1999). The right to survival. In W. Zhang & B. Li (Eds.), *Jurisprudence series (vol. I)* (p. 560). Law Press.

26. Li, L. (Ed.). (1996). Contemporary human rights theory and practice (p. 318). Jilin People's Publishing House.
27. Wang, X. (2002). *Basic human rights in a society under the rule of law: A study on the legal system of the right to development* (p. 243). Chinese Public Security University Press.
28. Dahl, R. A. (1999). *On democracy*. Li, B. & Lin, M. (trans.) (pp. 51–68). Commercial Press.
29. Sartori, G. (1993). *The theory of democracy revisited* (p. 343). Feng, K. & Yan, K. (trans.). Beijing: Oriental Press.
30. de Tocqueville, A. (1996). *Democracy in America* (p. 294). Dong, G. (trans.). Commercial Press.
31. Lin, Z. (2003). Protecting the human rights of AIDS persons. *China Party and Government Cadres Forum, 2003*(3), 40.
32. Constant, B. (1999). *The liberty of ancients compared with that of moderns*. Yan, K., & Liu, M. (Trans.) (pp. 26–27). Commercial Press.
33. Kant, I. (1991). *Metaphysics of morals*. Shen, S. (Trans.) (p. 50). Commercial Press.
34. Li, Z. (2002). *Human dignity and human rights protection* (pp. 10–12). Taiwan Yuanzhao Publishing Company.
35. Li, C. (2003). Basic concepts of modern social security. In X. Xu (Ed.), *Human rights studies (vol. III)* (p. 451). Shandong People's Publishing House.
36. Mo, J. (2001). *The logical basis of a modern constitution* (p. 438). Law Press.
37. Zhang, W. (Ed.). (1999). *Jurisprudence* (p. 193). Higher Education Press, Peking University Press.
38. Singer, B. J. (2001). *Pragmatism, rights, and democracy* (Wang, S. et al., Trans.) (p. 121). Shanghai Translation Press.
39. Lin, L. (2001). *From constitutional norms to normative constitutions: A preface to jurisprudence* (p. 116). Law Press.
40. Xu, C. (Ed.). (1999). *The constitution* (pp. 153–154). Chinese Minmin University Press.
41. Mo, J. (2002). The right to equality of our citizens and its misunderstandings. *Guangxi Social Sciences, 2002*(3), 168.
42. Zhou, Y. (1997). On the direct effect of fundamental rights of the constitution. *Chinese Law, 1997*(1), 20.
43. Cheng, L., & Wang, R. (1998). *Rights and remedies* (p. 377). Shandong People's Publishing House.
44. Wang, Z. (1999). Can our constitution enter the litigation. *Law and Business Studies, 1999*(5), 35.
45. Zhu, Y. (2002). Judicial protection of the right to equality in education. *Politics and Law, 3*, 39.
46. Gong, X. (2004). *The right to education* (pp. 123–126). Chinese Public Security University Press.
47. Ito, M. (1979). *Introduction to the constitution* (New Edition) (pp. 128–129). Yuhikaku Publishing.
48. Kiminori, H. (1970). *The complete works of modern jurisprudence* (p. 347). Seirin Shoin Publishing.
49. Osuka, A. (2001). The right to survival (Lin Hao, Trans., p. 69). Law Press.
50. Wang, X. (2000). *Principles and compromises: The spirit and practice of the U.S. constitution* (p. 560). Peking University Press.
51. Qiu, X. (2005). *Equal protection of the law: A study of the fourteenth amendment to the U.S. constitution* (p. 349). Peking University Press.
52. Knowles, L. L., & Prewitt, K. (1970). *Institutional racism in America* (1st edn, p. 143). Prentice-Hall.

53. Yao, D. (2000). *After modern times* (p. 84). Oriental Press.
54. Giddens, A. (2000). *The third way: The renewal of social democracy* (Z. Ge, Trans., p. 119). Peking University Press.
55. Hart, H. (1996). *The concept of law* (Z. Wenxian et al., Trans., p. 157). China Encyclopedia Publishing House.
56. Milne, A. J. M. (1995). *Human rights and human diversity: An essay in the philosophy of human rights* (Y. Xia & Z. Zhiming, Trans., p. 59). China Encyclopedia Publishing House.

SPRINGER NATURE

GPSR Compliance

The European Union's (EU) General Product Safety Regulation (GPSR) is a set of rules that requires consumer products to be safe and our obligations to ensure this.

If you have any concerns about our products, you can contact us on ProductSafety@springernature.com

In case Publisher is established outside the EU, the EU authorized representative is:

Springer Nature Customer Service Center GmbH
Europaplatz 3
69115 Heidelberg, Germany

The manufacturer's authorised representative in the EU is Springer Nature Customer Service Centre GmbH, Europaplatz 3, 69115 Heidelberg, Germany. If you have any concerns regarding our products, please contact ProductSafety@springernature.com

Printed and bound by CPI Group (UK) Ltd, Croydon, CR0 4YY
30/09/2026
02225314-0016